CANADA'S

FOUNDING DEBATES

Canada's Founding Debates is about Confederation – about the process that brought together six out of the seven territories of British North America in the years 1864–73 to form a country called Canada. It presents excerpts from the debates on Confederation in all of the colonial parliaments from Newfoundland to British Columbia and in the constituent assembly of the Red River Colony. The voices of the powerful and those of lesser note mingle in impassioned debate on the pros and cons of creating or joining the new country, and in defining its nature.

In short explanatory essays and provocative annotations, the editors sketch the historical context of the debates and draw out the significance of what was said. By organizing the debates thematically, they bring out the depth of the founders' concern for issues that are as vital today as they were then: the meaning of liberty, the merits of democracy, the best form of self-government, the tension between collective and individual rights, the rule of law, the requirements of political leadership, and, of course, the nature of Canadian nationality. *Canada's Founding Debates* offers a fresh and often surprising perspective on Canada's origins, history, and political character.

JANET AJZENSTAT is Professor Emeritus of Political Science at McMaster University.
PAUL ROMNEY has been writing on Canadian history for thirty years.
IAN GENTLES is Professor of History at Glendon College, York University.
WILLIAM D. GAIRDNER is an author and independent scholar interested in Canadian history and politics.

CANADA'S FOUNDING DEBATES

EDITED BY JANET AJZENSTAT,
PAUL ROMNEY, IAN GENTLES,
AND WILLIAM D. GAIRDNER

UNIVERSITY OF TORONTO PRESS
Toronto Buffalo London

First edition published as
Canada's Founding Debates
© William D. Gairdner 1999
Published by Stoddart Publishing Co. Limited

Paperback edition © William D. Gairdner 2003

University of Toronto Press
Toronto Buffalo London

Printed in Canada

ISBN 0-8020-8607-1 (paper)

Printed on acid-free paper

National Library of Canada Cataloguing in Publication

Canada's founding debates / edited by Janet Ajzenstat ... [et al.]

Includes index.
ISBN 0-8020-8607-1

1. Canada – History – Confederation, 1867 – Sources.
2. Canada – Politics and government – 1841–1867 – Sources.
3. Canada – Politics and government – 1867–1873 – Sources.
4. Canada – History – 1841–1867 – Sources.
5. Constitutional history – Canada – Sources.
I. Ajzenstat, Janet, 1936–

FC472.C354 2003   971.04'9   C2003-900684-0
F1032.C266 2003

University of Toronto Press acknowledges the financial assistance to its
publishing program of the Canada Council for the Arts
and the Ontario Arts Council.

University of Toronto Press acknowledges the financial support
for its publishing activities of the Government of Canada through the
Book Publishing Industry Development Program (BPIDP).

CONTENTS

Maps   vi
Acknowledgements   ix
Introduction   1

PART ONE WHAT THEY SAID ABOUT LIBERTY

1 Constitutional Liberty   13
2 Responsible Government   22
3 Parliamentary Government and the Upper House   77
4 Equality of Representation   103

PART TWO WHAT THEY SAID ABOUT OPPORTUNITY

5 Economic Prosperity and Individual Ambition   123

PART THREE WHAT THEY SAID ABOUT IDENTITY

6 British or American?   167
7 British or Canadian?   200
8 What Is a Canadian?   229

PART FOUR WHAT THEY SAID ABOUT THE
          NEW NATIONALITY

9 Federal Union   261
10 Minorities and Minority Rights   327

PART FIVE HOW TO MAKE A CONSTITUTION

11 Consulting the People in Constitution Making   357
12 Direct Democracy: Pro and Con   420

Appendixes
  A The Quebec Resolutions   465
  B The Legislators   473
  C Afterword on Books   477
Picture Credits   483
Index   485

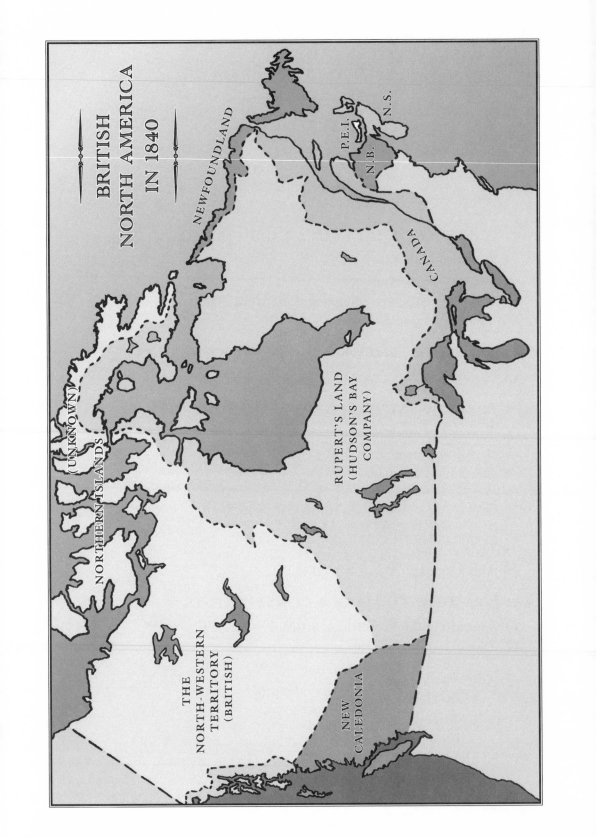

BRITISH NORTH AMERICA IN 1840

NEWFOUNDLAND

P.E.I.

N.B.

N.S.

CANADA

RUPERT'S LAND
(HUDSON'S BAY
COMPANY)

(UNKNOWN)

NORTHERN ISLANDS

THE
NORTH-WESTERN
TERRITORY
(BRITISH)

NEW
CALEDONIA

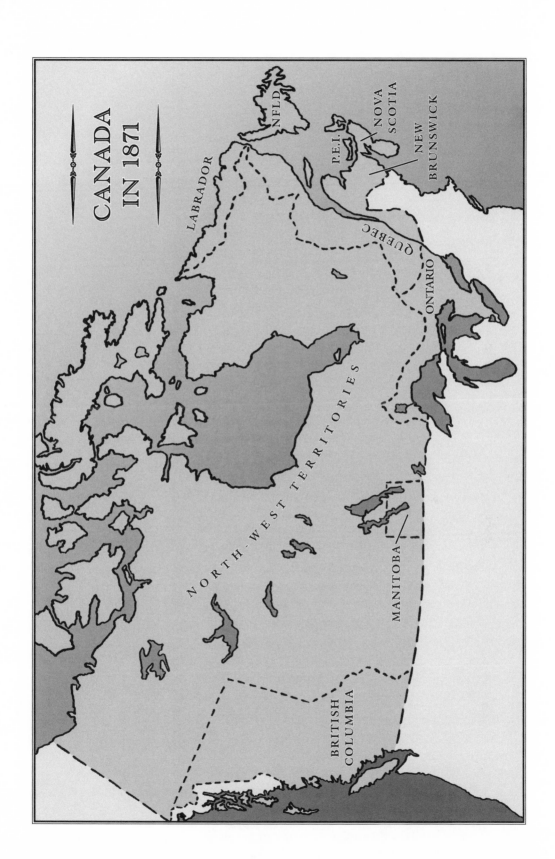

CANADA IN 1871

LABRADOR

NFLD

P.E.I.

NOVA SCOTIA

NEW BRUNSWICK

QUÉBEC

ONTARIO

NORTH-WEST TERRITORIES

MANITOBA

BRITISH COLUMBIA

ACKNOWLEDGEMENTS

T HE EDITORS GRATEFULLY ACKNOWLEDGE the generous assistance of the Donner Canadian Foundation in support of their research and in the preparation of the manuscript for publication.

We thank Jeffrey L. McNairn for his invaluable help in assembling the Confederation documents of the Atlantic and western provinces and for his advice on crucial aspects of the project. Mistakes are ours alone. We gratefully acknowledge the help of archivists and librarians in Ottawa, Toronto, Hamilton, and the provincial archives of the Maritime provinces and British Columbia. And we thank the students, spouses, and colleagues who traced historical references on the Internet and in libraries and searched the picture archives.

To Don Bastian and to Rosemary Shipton we owe a special debt for the tact and skill they brought to the task of editing and designing this book.

Canada's Founding Debates is a William D. Gairdner production. The conception, choice of researchers, and the energy behind the project are entirely his. In the winter of 1996–97 he read excerpts from the debates of 1865 in the legislature of the Province of Canada, and the idea blossomed. He wrote the Donner Canadian Foundation: "There is a book of passionate, interesting material to be assembled by scholars who know how to tease out the spirits of Montesquieu, Rousseau, Burke, Locke, and others who haunt these pages and point to the fascinating conflicts of political, constitutional, economic, and social opinion that were common fare in our founders' day and that echo still." From the beginning he envisaged the commentary as a "conversation with

the founders." The pages of manuscript quickly multiplied, and the conversations among ourselves about our conversation with the founders were soon burning along the e-mail lines. Some decisions were easy to make: to include the legislative debates of all colonies. Some were difficult: to organize the material thematically. Throughout, our objective has been the one Bill expressed originally: "to bring the debates alive," to recapture the "vital vision that shaped our beginning." "We live at a time when Canada has perhaps never been quite so threatened by its lack of unity and purpose," he wrote in that first letter. "I suggest one of the reasons is that we have forgotten our founding arguments."

JANET AJZENSTAT

INTRODUCTION

⟨⟩

THIS BOOK IS ABOUT CONFEDERATION — about the process that brought six of the seven territories of British North America together in the years 1864–73 to form a country called Canada. It presents excerpts from the debates on Confederation in all the colonial parliaments from Newfoundland to British Columbia and in the constituent assembly of the Red River Colony. All parties and political persuasions are represented: conservatives and liberals, confederates and anti-confederates. Their arguments have never before been published in a single volume. Many of the speeches have not been published since Confederation.

Our aim is to present the Fathers of Canadian Confederation, their supporters, and their opponents not merely as thinkers about their country but as thinkers about politics — men consciously acting within a tradition of political thought. It is trite to say that the founders were pragmatists. Of course they were, in the sense that they were practical men with practical goals. Too often the label "pragmatist" is taken to mean that they had no strong commitment to political values, no interest in political ideas. That is nonsense, and pernicious nonsense, because it purges political values from Canada's founding. It suggests that Canada was created as a mere framework — an empty shell, waiting to be filled with whatever political content Canadians chose.

Canada belongs to Canadians, and the country is theirs to alter as they choose from generation to generation. It would be wrong to suggest that the Canada of today and tomorrow should be subservient to the founders' values, good or bad. But it is sensible to listen to the founders — and to their opponents — and

consider what they have to say to us, not least because we are still for the most part living under the constitution they made.

The immediate question before the legislators in these years is whether and on what terms to join the union. Should British Columbia join a country 2,000 miles away? Should the proud province of Nova Scotia give up its independence? How can the Red River settlement protect its unique character against the impending invasion of "foreigners"? But these concerns lead rapidly to deliberations of a deeper character. What is the best form of government? Are parliamentary institutions the only choice? What is the purpose of government? Liberty? Prosperity? Democracy? Is parliamentary government democratic? What gives a constitution legitimacy in the eyes of the people? What makes a nation great? Much of the fascination of the debates for readers today lies in what the speakers say on these perennial topics.

They bring to the enterprise broad knowledge of law, history, political science, and modern political thought. They cite British, American, and French authorities; they study European constitutions and compare federal systems. They readily refer to the founding of the United States, and to American constitutions and constitutional practice, both of the United States and of individual states. They draw on British political thinkers of their day, especially John Stuart Mill. Although they seldom quote directly from the seventeenth- and eighteenth-century political philosophers, they are clearly steeped in the thought of Thomas Hobbes, John Locke, Montesquieu, and Rousseau. They illustrate their arguments with references to European history through the centuries, the great poets, and the Bible.

One thing especially strikes today's reader. The debates represent political deliberation at a high level. It is true that speakers sometimes fall back on very human and not always admirable emotions. They boast of their own accomplishments; they mock their opponents; they quibble and equivocate. Some of them are very angry; some are confused. But over and over they assert their confidence in the capacity of reasoned debate, grounded in broad knowledge of principles, history, and current facts, to move participants towards a better understanding of the issues. With John Stuart Mill they proclaim their belief that good arguments lead to good resolutions.

The debates take place in two stages. Rome wasn't built in a day, and Confederation doesn't happen in a year! The first stage begins with the Charlottetown and Quebec conferences in

The Canadian Confederation Medal, 1867. Struck in Britain at the request of John A. Macdonald, and with the permission of Queen Victoria, it bears a portrait of the queen on the obverse side, surmounted by the motto "Victoria, by the Grace of God Queen of Great Britain, Defender of the Faith." The reverse side shows Britannia, with a trident in her right hand and her left hand resting on a lion, presenting the charter of Confederation to the four sister provinces of the new dominion. Ontario holds a sickle and sheaf of corn; Quebec, a canoe paddle; Nova Scotia, a miner's spade; and New Brunswick, a lumberman's axe. The motto reads: "Canada Reorganized 1867, Youth and Ancestral Vigour."

September and October 1864. Charlottetown is planned to consider the union of the Maritime provinces alone, but the Province of Canada has recently acquired a government committed to federalizing its current constitution and to the pursuit of transcontinental union. Frustrated by the instability of Canadian politics, old enemies — the Conservative John A. Macdonald and the Reformer George Brown — have come together with Macdonald's French-Canadian ally, George-Étienne Cartier, in a scheme designed to further the aspirations of the three men and the interests they represent. All three men and a company of their colleagues descend on the capital of Prince Edward Island to make their pitch to the assembled maritimers.

Charlottetown generates enthusiasm for the project of broader union. The subsequent Quebec Conference produces concrete proposals — the famous Quebec Resolutions — which are then debated in the legislatures of Nova Scotia, New Brunswick, Canada, Prince Edward Island, and Newfoundland. By 1866 the Province of Canada has approved the Quebec Resolutions *in toto*, and Nova Scotia and New Brunswick (the latter after *two* general elections) have passed resolutions approving union, though not the "Quebec scheme" in all its details. After last-minute modifications at a conference in London, England, in December 1866, the union resolutions are cast in legal language and enacted by the British parliament as the British North America Act, 1867. The act unites the provinces of Canada, New Brunswick, and Nova Scotia, dividing the old Province of Canada into two: Ontario and Quebec. The Dominion of Canada is born. The first stage is over.

The second begins almost at once. Newfoundland and Prince Edward Island continue their deliberations, only now the British North America Act defines the debate. Two new debates begin in the west: in the province of British Columbia and the settlement of Red River. In 1869 Newfoundland decides against Confederation. Red River is annexed in 1870, along with the rest of the North-West Territory (the domain formerly governed by the Hudson's Bay Company under a royal charter), and is incorporated in the new province of Manitoba. British Columbia enters in 1871, and in 1873 Prince Edward Island commits itself at last. The second stage is over.

There were still provinces to come, of course. Saskatchewan and Alberta took shape as the northwest was populated, joining the federation in 1905. In 1949 Newfoundland reversed its orig-

inal decision, becoming Canada's tenth province, and in our own time we are seeing the formation of provinces in the far north. The significant date remains 1873; all the colonies in existence at the time of the Quebec Conference had made their decisions, and all but one had been brought into the fold. The dominion stretched from sea to sea, and the creation of new provinces as the land was settled appeared inevitable.

Writers on Confederation have fleshed out this string of dates with vivid accounts of the scramble to forestall an American takeover of the prairies and British Columbia, and of the provinces' soul-searching over the price of admission. They have gloried in the audacity of the founders' vision and have minutely analyzed the struggle to invent a federation more cohesive than the United States, then racked by civil war. But those accounts have concentrated too much on what was said in central Canada (what was then the Province of Canada) and on the words of a few leading politicians. In emphasizing the theme of nation-building, they have neglected what was just as important to the founders: the political principles that were to govern the new union and the legitimacy of its founding.

This book is designed to avoid those shortcomings. It presents excerpts from every colony, arranged in five topical parts, which treat the themes of liberty, prosperity, identity, federalism and provincial rights, and how to make a constitution.

Liberty is the theme of Part One. What form of government is most compatible with individual freedom? For most of the legislators the answer is clear: the best form is the parliamentary system. The constitutional principle defining parliamentary politics is "responsible government": it requires the political executive (the cabinet) to maintain the support of the majority of elected representatives in the legislature. The eastern provinces are well acquainted with responsible government, which Britain had conceded more than a decade before. They are proud of the independence it confers. Although still subordinate to Britain in their external affairs, Canada, Nova Scotia, New Brunswick, and even Newfoundland and tiny Prince Edward Island resemble small independent nations in their domestic politics. Almost all speakers in these provinces, liberals and conservatives alike, argue that responsible government guarantees political liberty, political equality, and individual rights. But some ask whether parliamentary institutions are compatible with federalism, and others whether responsible government can be reconciled with an elec-

tive Legislative Council (Senate). Still others quarrel about definitions of representation and democracy.

In the west the debate on parliamentary institutions is especially heated. Neither British Columbia nor Red River enjoys responsible government. Although British Columbians elect representatives to a Legislative Council, neither people nor representatives have much influence on political affairs; the government is responsible to the British government, not to the colonists. British Columbia's liberals make the most ardent case for responsible government of the entire debate, but the conservatives have some interesting responses. They sometimes argue that it is too early for responsible government; it will come in good time. But they also make the far more challenging claim at times that parliamentary institutions are a deficient prescription for liberty. In Red River, where parliamentary institutions are least developed, we find speakers who dream of direct democracy; in their speeches we see at least the sketch of a profoundly egalitarian criticism of parliamentary government. Where other debates reflect the values and prescriptions of John Locke, here Jean-Jacques Rousseau is the presiding philosopher.

Part Two addresses the issues of economic prosperity and individual ambition. There is general agreement that good political institutions promote prosperity. But whose prosperity? Some welcome Confederation as good for business; others foresee ruin for the little man. Some look forward to an expanded field for political ambition. Following John Locke and Adam Smith, they argue that parliamentary government does at least as good a job as teachings of virtue and moderation in curbing the excesses of ambition, since it forces party élites to compete with each other for the favour of the electorate; the ambitious "few," the politicians, find themselves encouraged by their very ambition to work for the "many." Other speakers are not convinced. Is the ambition of politicians so easily reconciled with the rights of the people? Won't the sheer size of the government at Ottawa allow it to dominate the people in outlying regions? Won't central Canada grow rich at the expense of the east and the west?

Part Three takes up the themes of identity and nationality. Pride in British parliamentary institutions and British traditions of liberty breeds loyalty to the empire. John A. Macdonald is famous for saying "A British subject I was born, and a British subject I will die," and here a Prince Edward Islander says the same a quarter-century earlier. Yet those who boast of their British iden-

tity are at odds over Confederation. To some it is a way of remaining British by preventing absorption into the United States; to others it is a short-cut to either annexation or independence, and thus a threat to the British connection. (One or two less loyal voices argue that if liberty and prosperity are the ends of government, it might be best to join the United States.) And what of the "new nationality" that Confederation-boosters so proudly proclaim? Even if it does not threaten the British tie, what does it mean for cherished colonial and ethnic identities?

Part Four takes up the issues of federalism and minority rights. While some supporters of Confederation present the Quebec scheme as a way of reconciling the "new nationality" with the preservation of provincial identities, others — both confederates and anti-confederates — see it as a false federation, fated to turn into a legislative union with but a single central government at no distant date. A particular concern for the Canadians is the safety the scheme offers to cultural groups and nationalities that will become minorities in the new federation: anglophones in Lower Canada and francophones in the country at large. In Newfoundland and Prince Edward Island the question of ethnic and cultural differences arises in a different form. Here it is hoped that federation will alleviate long-standing tensions between Catholics and Protestants. Will petty local quarrels be forgotten in the excitement of building a nation from coast to coast?

Part Five addresses the question that all parties regard as fundamental: How are constitutions made? What process of constitution making serves the people best? Who should have the last word: the people or the people's representatives? Many speakers propose consulting the people directly. They contend that the federal union will curtail (some say destroy) the sovereign powers of the local parliamentary institutions on which the rights of the people rest. It follows that the people should be consulted, either in a single-issue general election or in a binding referendum — a "yea or nay" vote, as it is called. No change that could be interpreted as a threat to the people's constitutional rights should go forward without their approval.

The other side stands on the traditions of constitutional government. There are no precedents in British law for an election or referendum on constitution making. (In British Columbia in 1870 the government will hold a general election to consult the people on union with Canada, but that is because British Columbia does not have a representative legislature.) What those

opposing direct appeal to the people chiefly fear is this conundrum: to send members into parliament with instructions to vote for a particular position limits the free exchange of views and the free appreciation of opposing arguments. If there is no give and take of argument, some views, especially less popular ones, may go unheard. Minority voices may be stifled. In short, those opposing the direct appeal to the people see it as a threat to the people's rights. The very measure (direct popular reference) that the one side believes essential to the people's rights, the other side regards as a danger, suitable perhaps for mustering support in a despotism, but out of place in a free parliamentary regime.

The Confederation period is the first era of constitution making on a grand scale in this country, and the last until our own day. No one who reads the speeches in Part Five can miss the parallels with current Canadian preoccupations.

DEBATES AND PROCEEDINGS

OF THE

HOUSE OF ASSEMBLY,

DURING THE

THIRD SESSION OF THE TWENTY-THIRD PARLIAMENT

OF THE

PROVINCE OF NOVA SCOTIA.

1866.

JOHN GEORGE BOURINOT.
Reporter to House of Assembly.

HALIFAX, N. S.

1866.

Most of the excerpts are from official reports of the debates in the different colonies. These sources are of varying quality. The Canadian one is especially full and clear, since the legislature had this exceptionally important debate reported verbatim and referred back to the individual speakers for correction. That of 1866 from the Nova Scotia House of Assembly is comparably full. It was prepared by two distinguished Canadians-to-be: the future Sir John George Bourinot, authority on parliamentary procedure, was aided by the future Sir John Sparrow Thompson, premier of Nova Scotia and prime minister of Canada. The report of the British Columbia debate of 1870 is also admirably full in parts. Other reports are not verbatim accounts but synopses, more or less thorough, as was typical of colonial parliamentary reporting at the time. We catch a glimpse of the parliamentary reporter at work when he records a speaker's words in the third person, or, disconcertingly, switches from third person to first in the course of a single speech. The New Brunswick debates of 1864, and those of 1865 in Newfoundland, were not officially reported, and newspaper accounts have been used. The Red River material also comes from a newspaper: Louis Riel's *New Nation*.

The reader should bear these differences in mind for several reasons. First, it has influenced the choice of excerpts. We have tended to favour clear, full, and elaborate statements over those that are garbled or unclear. Second, a report of the latter sort

must not be taken as evidence of the speaker's intelligence. It does not follow from the more polished aspect of the Canadian reports that Canadian legislators were any smarter or more learned than those in New Brunswick or Prince Edward Island. In a synoptic report, the speaker's thought is refracted by the reporter's intelligence, and the latter is unlikely to have accurately reported what he imperfectly understood. A synoptic report may also reflect political bias — especially those in newspapers, for nineteenth-century papers were unabashedly partisan. *The Newfoundlander* favoured Confederation and may have devoted disproportionate space and care to reporting the views of like-minded legislators. The *New Nation*'s report was produced as much for an Ottawa as for a local audience, and was meant to project the most favourable impression of the quality and freedom of the debate at Fort Garry.

The Newfoundlander.

3,643. St. John's, Thursday, March 2, 1865.

MR. A. SHEA'S SPEECH ON CONFEDERATION IN THE HOUSE OF ASSEMBLY ON TUESDAY, 21ST FEBRUARY.

MR. A. SHEA said he did not intend to offer any practical objection to the resolution embodying as it did the views of the public generally on this important subject; but he felt, nevertheless, that in the interest of the public it was in its present shape open to some objection. His opinion was that the resolution the House should adopt was one affirming the principles contained in the Report of the Quebec Conference, but at the same time providing that their decision should be subject to the expression of public opinion at the next general election. He felt this was the course the House should adopt, because on such a resolution there would be a division, and every member of the House would then stand before the constituencies in an intelligible light, while the present Resolution being one on which no division can take place, the public are without that security at the next elections which a clear avowal of the opinions of members would afford and which may now be avoided by any who desire to return to the House under false pretences. He thought therefore for the protection of the public that it would have been desirable to submit a more definite proposition than was contained in the Resolution before them. Before proceeding farther he would refer to a discussion that had been had in another place on this subject in which some very extraordinary assumptions were made the groundwork of the argument. The question had been dealt with as one by which it was designed to set up the Markets of Canada against those of the United States and to impose disabilities on our trade with the latter. He (Mr. Shea) was at a loss to know where the warrant had been found for such a conclusion, which only serves to show how little the subject was comprehended by those who can so express themselves. There was nothing in the proposed Confederations by which the ports of the United States would be rendered less open than at present to our commerce, and no one would deprecate more than he (Mr. Shea) any attempt by fiscal regulations to

equal rights and privileges, the concession of which he hoped to extort from the fears of the British Government which that agitation was more likely than any other to call up. The whole tenor of his speeches shows that a Union with England based on terms of equality and general equity would have found him a willing supporter. What analogy then, said Mr. Shea, can be drawn between a Union such as I have correctly described, and the proposed combination of these British North American Provinces where the just rights of all are alike respected, and the conditions of honorable partnership upheld. And even as respects the Irish Union, repeal has now no advocates, for the policy of the British Government has of late years become less anti-social, and the efforts of the leading Irishmen is now being directed to the attainment of those practical reforms which would promote the social and material advancement of the country which there is a growing disposition in England to advance. In the history of France we have another example of the power of Confederation to further the greatness and prosperity of a country. The vast Empire which existed in the days of Charlemagne fell to pieces under the rule of his feeble successors who divided the Empire, and granted provinces to the high nobility, completing the feudal system under which the country became so dismembered, that in one hundred years after the death of that great monarch the crown had but two provinces and some small districts remaining under its control. France ceased to be a real European Power until partly by marriages and treaties, and by the accession of the great Henry IV., these fiefs were again united to the central state, and under the policy of Richlieu and Mazarin was brought to be the leading Power of Europe during the reign of Louis XIV. Spain owed her greatness to the union of the several petty kingdoms and countries under the crowns of Arragon and Castile, which became themselves united by the marriage of Ferdinand and Isabella. From the time of this union Spain increased her power and wealth until she became the Empire of Philip II., which was the greatest and most powerful in the world. It was the dreams of Universal Empire on the part of Charles, followed by the mad ambition of his son Philip, to dominate the seas, that involved the exhausting consequences which ultimately led to the decline of

should each form distinct and separate communities apart from those whose pursuits were different. To his mind the variety of pursuits formed the strongest reason why communities should confederate, because this caused the exchange of productions and supplying their mutual necessities, the interests of all were conserved by the association. But when we look to other Confederations do we find no difference in their pursuits? what can be more diverse than the trades and avocations of the people in different parts of the United States? Have we not the manufacturing and the agricultural and various other interests in England, and even the fisheries of Scotland are combined with these under one Government and we have not found that the difference in the pursuits of the people have militated against their common property. John Stuart Mill, one of the profoundest thinkers of the day, in speaking of the conditions necessary for the beneficial Confederation of States says "the strongest of all is identity of political antecedents; the possession of a national history, and consequent community of recollections; collective pride and humiliation, pleasure and regret, connected with the same incidents in the past." Have we not these essentials in strict accord with those Provinces with whom we propose to confederate, and when we consider the experience on which such views are founded, how small is the weight that should attach to objections that are thus so strikingly rebutted. From a fair and careful consideration of the case presented in the Quebec Resolutions it would he thought be difficult to dispute their beneficial application to this Colony, more especially in the circumstances in which it now stands, when almost any change must be an improvement to the labouring population. But a pregnant question now presents itself, have we the unqualified power to decide our own destiny in this respect. It would be idle to suppose that the meeting at Quebec was not inspired by the Imperial Government. No one who has paid any degree of attention to the tone of British opinion regarding these Colonies for some years past, can have failed to see that a change in the relations they held to the Mother Country was surely coming about. It became a mere question of time when we obtained Responsible Government, and with it virtual independence in the Government of these Colonies. We ...

would be insisted on. He hoped he had shown that the principle itself was desirable and tended to progress; that even if less desirable, it was in view of all fair reasoning, the inevitable destiny of the Provinces, and that it was the evident design of the Imperial Government that this colony should form part of the proposed Confederation. He would now go into the consideration of the leading objections urged against the scheme, and most prominent amongst these is the question of Taxation. There is no word more vague in its signification than that of taxation. In the sense in which it is used by those who employ it to get up a hostile cry in the present case, it is an abstraction from the means of the people for which they receive no return. Against taxation of this character people naturally rebelled, and the Legislature should also set its face with equal resolution. But there was another kind of taxation which signified not oppression, but progress and public advantage, and which nurtured and promoted the prosperity of the people. We see high rates of taxation in many prosperous countries, as in England for example, and in Canada, whose taxes had been so much spoken of, there was to his mind no part of the administration of affairs in that country which spoke more highly of the statesmanlike sagacity of her public men than the system of taxation by which the resources of the country have been brought into life, and their vales enhanced, giving to the people ten-fold means for paying the taxes imposed upon them. As compared with our wretched system, under which but a fractional part is devoted to purposes of public usefulness, the taxation of Canada stands out in remarkable contrast. He would be but too glad to see the way clear for a very large increase of our present taxation. He regretted that there was no public undertaking similar to those on which public money had been expended in Canada —undertakings which opened up their resources and permanently enlarged the means for the employment of their industry. This fruitful expenditure was what we stood so much in need of and taxation for such a purpose instead of being the hated thing as it is often popularly and ignorantly regarded, would be beneficial and invigorating in its results. If the nature of our resources were such as would justify the application of fifty thousand pounds in this manner in the present

Another thing to remember is the distorting effects of translation. The Canadian debates took place in two languages. We have used the English version, with its sometimes stilted or inaccurate translation of the French speeches.

In addition to the quality of the reports, the nature of the debates themselves has influenced our choice of excerpts. In

every province but Canada, the debate is essentially one about "joining Canada." This is as true of the colonies that took part in the first stage of the debates, the Confederation process, as it is of British Columbia. (The inhabitants of Red River hardly had a choice.) To Canadians, by contrast, the details of the federal scheme are at least as important as its extension to the other colonies. And one aspect is uniquely interesting to them: its provision for minority rights. For these reasons Part Four, which deals with guarantees for minorities, gives pride of place to the Canadian debate.

But other colonies have their own special concerns that inspire their legislators to flights of eloquence and profundity. The British Columbian debate on responsible government is one example. Others are the New Brunswick and Nova Scotian debates on identity, and the Nova Scotian argument over referring the question to the people. We have tried to do justice to the special character and concerns of the debate in the other colonies too: Red River's anxiety to protect its distinct society; the island colonies' preoccupation with the problem of sectarian animosity; the widespread concern with the preservation of local autonomy, and the perception of conflict between that ideal and the prospect — tempting to some, ominous to others — of participation in a transcontinental polity. To reflect these concerns, we have presented the arguments colony by colony within each chapter, beginning with the colony that has the liveliest debate, or the one that sets out the issues most clearly.

Spelling varied widely in the Confederation period, from province to province and year to year. We have imposed uniform spelling, punctuation, and capitalization. We call the constitution of 1867 by its old name: the British North America Act. That was its official title from 1867 until 1982, and it was what people usually called it (often shortening it to BNA Act), although nineteenth-century Canadians sometimes termed it the Confederation Act or the Constitutional Act. It was not called the "Constitution Act, 1867" until official usage was changed by a provision of the Constitution Act, 1982, the legislation that introduced the Canadian Charter of Rights and Freedoms and the current amending formula. One unfortunate consequence of this name change is that some Canadians have been left with the confused impression that Canada discarded the BNA Act in favour of the Constitution Act, 1982. Students coming into political science classes are sometimes surprised to be told that Canada is still gov-

erned by the old BNA Act, under its new name, in addition to the Constitution Act, 1982.

The editors' footnotes have two functions. The unsigned notes are meant merely to provide historical background about persons, places, and events. Notes signed with the editor's initials reflect his or her engagement with themes, topics, and arguments; they are notes with an "attitude." They should not be taken as the last word in interpretation, and readers may well disagree with them. Indeed, the editors quite often disagree with each other. Throughout the process of collecting and commenting on these debates we have thought of ourselves as being engaged in a sympathetic conversation with the founders, and our notes are best seen as an invitation to readers to join the discussion.

PART ONE

———⟫•◦•⟪———

WHAT THEY

SAID ABOUT

LIBERTY

———⟫•◦•⟪———

Chapter One

CONSTITUTIONAL
LIBERTY

THESE SPEECHES TOUCH ON MAJOR THEMES of the debates in the chapters to come: constitutional liberty and the rights of minorities; pride in the tradition of the British Constitution; ethnic diversity and nation-building. They reveal the speakers' high sense of the seriousness of the occasion as well as their confidence in parliamentary institutions and in parliamentary deliberation. They invite a free and full examination of Confederation from every point of view.

The British North America Act, 1867.

BRITISH COLUMBIA

Henry Crease: I am deeply impressed with the momentous character of the discussion into which we are about to enter, the grave importance of a decision by which the fate of this our adopted country of British Columbia must be influenced, for better, for worse, for all time to come. And I earnestly hope that our minds and best energies may be bent to a task which will tax all our patriotism, all our forbearance, all our abnegation of self, and selfish aims, to combine all our individual powers into one great, united effort for the common good.

Now, therefore, is the time for those honourable members who, notwithstanding the previous resolutions of this house so frequently affirming the principle . . . still conscientiously object to the principles of Confederation, to come forward and explain to this honourable body, and to the country at large, their views — why they still refuse to aid in the consolidation of British interests on the North American continent, by the Confederation

of this colony with the dominion, and the creation of one homogeneous nationality from sea to sea.

— *Legislative Council, March 9, 1870*

CANADA

George Brown: Here is a people of two distinct races, speaking different languages, with religious and social and municipal and educational institutions totally different; with sectional hostilities of such a character as to render government for many years well-nigh impossible; with a constitution so unjust in the view of one section as to justify any resort to enforce a remedy. And yet, sir, here we sit, patiently and temperately discussing how these great evils and hostilities may justly and amicably be swept away forever. (Hear, hear.) We are endeavouring to adjust harmoniously greater difficulties than have plunged other countries into all the horrors of civil war. We are striving to do peacefully* and satisfactorily what Holland and Belgium, after years of strife, were unable to accomplish. We are seeking by calm discussion to settle questions that Austria and Hungary, that Denmark and Germany, that Russia and Poland, could only crush by the iron heel or armed force. We are seeking to do without foreign intervention that which deluged in blood the sunny plains of Italy. We are striving to settle forever issues hardly less momentous than those that have rent the neighbouring republic and are now exposing it to all the horrors of civil war. (Hear, hear.) Have we not then, Mr. Speaker, great cause of thankfulness that we have found a better way for the solution of our troubles than that which entailed on other countries such deplorable results? And should not every one of us endeavour to rise to the magnitude of the occasion, and earnestly seek to deal with this question to the end in the same candid and conciliatory spirit in which, so far, it has been discussed? (Loud cries of hear, hear.)

Brown refers to the Belgian overthrow of Dutch rule in 1830, the Hungarian rising against Hapsburg rule in 1848, the rising of 1863 in Russian Poland, the Danish-German war of 1864 over the provinces of Schleswig and Holstein, the continuing struggle for Italian unity and independence, and the civil war in the United States. He congratulates Canadians on finding a better way of resolving "national" disputes — a tribute both to their own civility and to the enlightenment of British colonial governance and parliamentary institutions. — PR

The scene presented by this chamber at this moment, I venture to affirm, has few parallels in history. One hundred years have passed away since these provinces became by conquest part of the British Empire. I speak in no boastful spirit — I desire not for a moment to excite a painful thought — what was then the fortune of war of the brave French nation might have been ours on that well-fought field. I recall those olden times merely to mark the fact that here sit today the descendants of the victors and the vanquished in the fight of 1759, with all the differences of language, religion, civil law, and social habits nearly as distinctly marked as they were a century ago. (Hear, hear.) Here we sit today seeking amicably to find a remedy for constitutional evils and injustice complained of — by the vanquished? No, sir — but complained of by the conquerors!* (Cheers by the French Canadians.)

Here sit the representatives of the British population claiming justice — only justice; and here sit the representatives of the French population, discussing in the French tongue whether we shall have it. One hundred years have passed away since the conquest of Quebec, but here sit the children of the victor and of the vanquished, all avowing hearty attachment to the British crown — all earnestly deliberating how we shall best extend the blessings of British institutions† — how a great people may be established on this continent in close and hearty connection with Great Britain. (Cheers.)

Where, sir, in the page of history, shall we find a parallel to this? Will it not stand as an imperishable monument to the generosity of British rule? And it is not in Canada alone that this scene is being witnessed. Four other colonies are at this moment

---

*As far as Brown is concerned, what needs fixing is Upper Canada's grievance at the lack of representation by population in the Province of Canada, and the undue influence that the predominantly French-speaking Lower Canada consequently exercises over the government of the united province. — PR

† In the past, a common belief in responsible government was one of the things that helped to unite French and English Canadians. Our modern difficulties stem in part from the waning of this and other shared convictions. The last fifty years, and still more the last twenty, have witnessed a largely unreflecting rejection of the values that inform these founding debates — in particular, the faith in parliamentary institutions and the clarifying effects of parliamentary debate. — JA

occupied as we are — declaring their hearty love for the parent state, and deliberating with us how they may best discharge the great duty entrusted to their hands, and give their aid in developing the teeming resources of these vast possessions.

— *Legislative Assembly, February 8, 1865*

*"The two great
things that all men
aim at in any free
government
are liberty and
permanency."*

Thomas D'Arcy McGee: The two great things that all men aim at in any free government are liberty and permanency. We have had liberty enough — too much perhaps in some respects — but at all events, liberty to our hearts' content. There is not on the face of the earth a freer people than the inhabitants of these colonies. But it is necessary that there should be respect for the law, a high central authority, the virtue of civil obedience, obeying the law for the law's sake; even when a man's private conscience may convince him sufficiently that the law in some cases may be wrong,* he is not to set up his individual will against the will of the country expressed through its recognized constitutional organs. We need in these provinces, we can bear, a large infusion of authority. I am not at all afraid this constitution errs on the side of too great conservatism. If it be found too conservative now, the down tendency in political ideas which characterizes this democratic age is a sufficient guarantee for amendment. That is the principle on which this instrument is strong and

---

* This sentence warns Canadians that they are not to lean towards the philosopher John Locke's idea, or the same idea as laid out in the American Declaration of Independence, that there is in certain circumstances a right of revolution. — WDG

A man may not, as an individual, set himself up against lawfully constituted authority. But an oppressed community may follow its collective conscience and oppose an unjust ruler, as the English, acting through their parliament, did in 1688 and the Americans in 1776. No speaker in these pages condemns the Glorious Revolution of 1688, which contemporaries saw as the foundation of parliamentary government and ranked with Magna Carta as a milestone in the progress of British liberty. Some speakers are very understanding of the American Revolution, too. — PR

In a parliamentary democracy, laws must be obeyed, but complaints about laws are permitted — indeed, encouraged. A person is always free to organize to demand that parliament amend or repeal its enactments. McGee may be arguing against a right to revolution; he is certainly arguing against civil disobedience. He also praises freedom of civil opposition and dissent. "We have liberty enough." — JA

Sir Antoine-Aimé Dorion (1818–1891), a lawyer and practising Catholic who favoured the separation of church and state. Dorion led the Lower Canadian liberals from his election to the Legislative Assembly in 1854. He was the first, in 1856, to propose a federal solution to the growing tensions between Upper and Lower Canada, but he opposed a broader colonial union and attacked the Quebec scheme as a legislative union in disguise. In 1873–74 he was a federal cabinet minister, before becoming chief justice of the Court of Queen's Bench of Quebec.

worthy of the support of every colonist, and through which it will secure the warm approbation of the imperial authorities.

We have here no traditions and ancient venerable institutions; here, there are no aristocratic elements hallowed by time or bright deeds; here, every man is the first settler of the land, or removed from the first settler one or two generations at the furthest; here, we have no architectural monuments calling up old associations; here, we have none of those old popular legends and stories which, in other countries, have exercised a powerful share in the government; here every man is the son of his own works. (Hear, hear.) We have none of those influences about us which, elsewhere, have their effect upon government just as much as the invisible atmosphere itself tends to influence life, and animal and vegetable existence. This is a new land — a land of pretension because it is new; because classes and systems have not had that time to grow here naturally. We have no aristocracy but of virtue and talent,* which is the only true aristocracy, and is the old and true meaning of the term. (Hear, hear.)

— Legislative Assembly, February 9, 1865

A.-A. Dorion: It is but natural that . . . [the] honourable gentlemen opposite want to keep as much power as possible in the hands of the government — that is the doctrine of the Conservative Party everywhere — that is the line which distinguishes the Tories from the Whigs — the Tories always side with the crown, and the Liberals always want to give more power and influence to the people. The instincts of honourable gentlemen opposite, whether you take the Honourable Attorney General East [George-Étienne Cartier] or the Honourable Attorney General West [John A. Macdonald], lead them to this — they think the hands of the crown should be strengthened and the

---

* The lack of aristocracy was considered a special political problem in North America because of the belief that a balanced mixture of the three principles of monarchy, aristocracy, and democracy would produce the best government of all, on the British model, as reflected in a king or queen, a senate or house of lords, and a house of commons. This balanced system had been made widely desirable to the reading public by Montesquieu in his Spirit of the Laws (1748). But absence of a traditional aristocracy in North America meant that a defence of a "natural aristocracy" composed of good and wise people was required. The contrast is between inherited, unearned, aristocratic privilege and earned privilege. — WDG

influence of the people, if possible, diminished — and this constitution is a specimen of their handiwork, with a governor general
appointed by the crown; with local governors also appointed by
the crown; with legislative councils, in the general legislature,
and in all the provinces, nominated by the crown; we shall have
the most illiberal constitution ever heard of in any country where
constitutional government prevails. (Hear.)

— *Legislative Assembly, February 16, 1865*

Richard Cartwright:* All I hope is that in adjusting our new
constitutions, local and general, we shall not allow our minds to
be warped by antiquated notions of the dangers which threaten
our liberty. No fear here, Mr. Speaker, for many a day to come at
least, of perils which await us from the tyranny of hereditary
rulers,† or the ambition of aristocratic oligarchies. No, sir, no; and
while it is true that here, as elsewhere, there are always dangers

---

** Cartwright was the grandson of a prominent Upper Canadian Loyalist of
the same name. His words epitomize the sentimental Loyalism that burgeoned
in the 1860s as English Canadians sought to define the differences between
their own country and the increasingly similar society of the United States.
The juxtaposition of British liberty to American equality and of reform to
revolution, the allusion to lynching, and the emphasis on protecting the
rights of individuals and minorities against the tyranny of the majority are
all typical of this thought. Cartwright later quit the Conservative Party and
joined the Liberals, and in later years his opposition to the National Policy
made him a target for Conservative accusations of disloyalty. — PR*

*† A parliamentary democrat like Cartwright sees two great threats to lib-
erty: on the one hand is the threat from the hereditary tyrant (such as the
seventeenth-century European autocrats) or from aristocrats and oligarchs.
On the other is the threat posed by rulers who profess to represent the people,
but in fact exploit them and seek to perpetuate rule in defiance of their
wishes. Cartwright argues that in British North America the second threat
is more serious. His contention is a standard one in the nineteenth century;
we will see it argued at length in chapters to come. When speakers oppose
"democracy," it is very seldom liberal democracy they have in mind; it is this
"democratic" — "republican" — tyranny. Note how confident Cartwright is
that "British liberty" will steer a safe course between the two great threats. Is
his fear of "democracy" farfetched? In the twentieth century we became all
too familiar with forms of government akin to the democratic tyranny he
describes, in countries such as the People's Republic of China and the German
Democratic Republic. — JA*

enough to retard our progress, I think that every true reformer, every real friend of liberty, will agree with me in saying that if we must erect safeguards, they should be rather for the security of the individual than of the mass, and that our chiefest care must be to train the majority to respect the rights of the minority, to prevent the claims of the few from being trampled under foot by the caprice or passion of the many. For myself, sir, I own frankly I prefer British liberty to American equality. I had rather uphold the majesty of the law than the majesty of Judge Lynch. I had rather be the subject of an hereditary monarch, who dare not enter the hut of the poorest peasant without leave . . . than be the free and sovereign elector of an autocratic president, whose very minister can boast the power of imprisoning one man in New York and another in St. Louis by the touching of a bell-wire! . . .

I am glad to find [that] one lesson at least, which the British Constitution ought to teach us, is beginning to be impressed upon our people. That constitution . . . while it does not require the possession of those lofty, impracticable virtues which most republican institutions demand from their votaries, does nevertheless presuppose a reasonable amount of discretion at the hands of those who are intrusted with the carrying out of its details. And, sir, though it is true that it does recognize the calm, deliberate, just decision of the majority — and the calm, deliberate decision is almost always just — as final in the last resort, it does still so abound with safeguards — with latent checks of all kinds — checks established, many of them, more by custom and usage than by positive law — as to make it all but impossible for any majority, however strong, to perpetrate any gross act of injustice on a minority, so long as that minority could command but one or two resolute representatives on the floor of parliament. Sir, it is impossible not to feel that it is in a very great degree to this fact, to the instinctive sense of the inherent powers of self-defence which our customs give to the weak against the strong — to the conviction that to drive any party to despair would create an inevitable deadlock — that England owes it that she has contrived to administer her affairs for near two hundred years without any overt acts of tyranny or one direct collision or irregular interference with the ordinary course of law. Sir, I rejoice to see that we will continue to adhere to a system which has borne such good fruit, as a whole, in the parent land; and I think the reflection how difficult, if not how dangerous, it is to oppress a determined minority under such a system may serve to calm the

"[The British Constitution,] while it does not require the possession of those lofty, impracticable virtues which most republican institutions demand from their votaries, does nevertheless presuppose a reasonable amount of discretion at the hands of those who are intrusted with the carrying out of its details."

fears of those honourable gentlemen who dread the loss of local rights and privileges at the hands of the stronger race.

For the rest, Mr. Speaker . . . I trust I may be pardoned for expressing my conviction that the loyalty and fidelity of the early settlers of this country — and I speak here without regard to any special nationality — is destined to be rewarded in the way in which they would most have desired to see it rewarded if they had lived to see this day, by the establishment of a kingdom on the banks of the St. Lawrence which, without binding itself down to a slavish adherence to the customs of the Old World, would yet cherish and preserve those time-honoured associations our American neighbours have seen fit so recklessly to cast away. Sir, our forefathers may have had their faults; but still, in spite of all, I dare affirm that the brave, self-sacrificing spirit they displayed — their manful struggle against heavy odds — and last, but not least, the patient, law-abiding spirit which has ever induced them to prefer reform to revolution, even when engaged in sweeping away the last vestiges of worn-out feudal systems in church and state from their midst — I say, sir, that these afford us ample proof that the men to whom, I hope, we shall soon look back as the founders of a new nation were ancestors of whom any people might be proud . . .

— *Legislative Assembly, March 9, 1865*

NEW BRUNSWICK

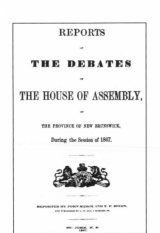

Amos Botsford: Is it not apparent . . . that united in one common bond of alliance under one general government, with free institutions guaranteed by the protection and prestige of Britain, we must assume a position of importance among the nations of the world, of which we could not dream . . . ?

— *Legislative Council, April 4, 1866*

James Gray Stevens: It is the glory of the British Constitution that it was raised stone by stone with the wisdom that was gained by experience. This Confederation is a new thing, and it has to undergo the test of trial before it can become perfect. We believe we have attained the best scheme that can be given to us . . .

— *House of Assembly, May 13, 1867*

RED RIVER

Louis Riel: There is ample ground . . . for the belief that Canada is disposed to do us justice. She has shown a disposition, a willingness, a readiness to do us justice. (Cheers.) It would seem that at the first the Canadian government forgot to speak to us of certain of our rights. But later events refreshed their memory and caused them to recollect what they were willing to do for us.

[W]e must not allow the rights of the people to be jeopardized by our mode of treating them at this meeting. We are to be firm. (Cheers.) We are to stand as a rock in defence of the rights and liberties of the country. Canada at the outset ought to have known our wishes and respected the people of this country; but she had not done so in a satisfactory manner. Now that she begins to respect us, we are not unwilling to meet these advances and consider them fairly and justly. (Cheers.)

Donald Smith:* I need hardly say now that Canada is not only disposed to respect the people of this country, but is most desirous of according to them every privilege enjoyed by any province of the dominion — all the rights of British subjects, in fact, which are enjoyed in any portion of the dominion. (Cheers.)

— Convention at Fort Garry, English and French
Delegates in Council, January 27, 1870

---

* Later 1st Baron Strathcona (1820–1914). A Hudson's Bay Company executive, he had been sent to Fort Garry by the Canadian government as an intermediary. — PR

Chapter Two

RESPONSIBLE GOVERNMENT

N O ONE DOUBTS THAT THE GENERAL GOVERNMENT of the new federation will be parliamentary in form, with political institutions and practices like those of Britain (home to the "mother of parliaments"). Most, but not all, of the colonies already enjoy parliamentary government, and speakers praise this system as a guarantee of liberty and democracy. It is not empty praise. In these debates there is a more searching analysis of the parliamentary system, especially its central feature, the constitutional principle we call responsible government, than historians and political scientists have supposed. Speakers compare parliamentary government to American congressional government and to forms of republican democracy.

Responsible government, then and now, has two aspects: first, the requirement that the governor of a colony or province (today, the lieutenant governor, or in the case of Canada the governor general) exercise the powers of the state only on the advice of an executive council or cabinet. With the introduction of responsible government, governors no longer govern! The second and complementary feature is that the members of the executive council or cabinet must be drawn from the elected representatives of the people in the House of Commons, or from the Senate, and — here is the heart of the matter — the cabinet must maintain the support of the majority in the House of Commons on taxing and spending legislation. We are all familiar with the results. The governor general (or lieutenant governor) invites the leader of the party winning the most seats in a general election to form the government — that is, to select members for appointment to the cabinet. The party then governs as long as it maintains that crucial support in the Commons.

Before responsible government, the British North American colonies had representative institutions, usually two legislative houses (a House of Commons, called the Legislative Assembly or House of Assembly, and a Senate, called the Legislative Council). Yet Britain withheld the vital principle, responsible government. Why? Until the mid-nineteenth century Britain insisted that its imperial sovereignty required colonial governments to be responsible to British officials, not to the people of the colony. Once Britain conceded responsible government, the breadth of the colonial franchise made them, to all intents and purposes, parliamentary democracies.

Responsible government was established in the provinces of Nova Scotia, New Brunswick, and the united Province of Canada in 1848, in Prince Edward Island three years later, and in Newfoundland in 1855, after valiant struggles by members of the colonial Liberal and Reform parties. Conservatives in these provinces were slower to support it, but by the time of the Confederation debates the Conservatives have had a complete change of heart and argue for responsible government with as much enthusiasm as if it had been their own invention.

How gallingly undemocratic politics is without responsible government emerges clearly from the complaints of speakers in British Columbia and Red River. These two colonies are the only ones without responsible government at the time of the Confederation debates.

BRITISH COLUMBIA

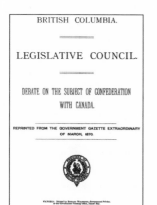

BRITISH COLUMBIA.

LEGISLATIVE COUNCIL.

DEBATE ON THE SUBJECT OF CONFEDERATION WITH CANADA.

REPRINTED FROM THE GOVERNMENT GAZETTE EXTRAORDINARY OF MARCH, 1870.

John Robson: [British Columbia's] form of government has rendered progress impossible. I believe that the illiberal form of government has had much to do with keeping away population — with *driving* away population — and with destroying the spirit of manly enterprise of those who are here . . . [I]f we persist in remaining alone we shall be told by the imperial government that we are not fit for liberal institutions,* and not prepared for self-government. We should get no amelioration. Downing Street

---

An organized colony for less than twenty years, British Columbia had not attained responsible government. There was only one legislative house, called the Legislative Council, which consisted of nine elected and fifteen appointed members, the latter including the governor's Executive Council. Official appointments were in the gift of the British government. Robson blames the

officials would say that we are not fit for responsible government, and that we ought to confederate.

I believe that there are terms [for joining the Canadian federation] of the greatest importance which ought to be added. But anything that can be added will not meet the wishes of the people of this colony, unless the fundamental principle of self-government accompanies them. I believe that the Canadians are a great, a wise, and a conservative people; but I conceive we should be doing a great wrong to ourselves, to our children, and to those who are to come after us if we left out responsible government.

— *Legislative Council, March 9, 1870*

Joseph Trutch: Confederation does not, to my mind, mean responsible government, as some honourable members hold. British Columbia will assuredly get responsible government as soon as the proper time arrives, as soon, that is to say, as the community is sufficiently advanced in population, and in other respects, to render such a form of government practically workable; sooner probably through Confederation than by any other means, and the sooner the better, I say. But I do not think it desirable to fetter or cumber the proposed terms of union with anything about responsible government, and specially for the reason that we should find it very difficult to arrive at any conclusion in favour of it.

Under the Organic Act* this colony could get responsible government. In fact it is the special prerogative under this act of each province to regulate the constitution of its own executive government and legislature; and whence this desire to act so prematurely now in this respect?

T.L. Wood: If we come into Confederation, we come in, as I understand it, under this Organic Act; and it is on account of the overwhelming influence of Canada in the joint legislature of the

---

colony's depressed economy and loss of population on this "illiberal" system, but a more immediate cause may have been the transition from surface to underground mining in the goldfields. — PR

* Robson wants to make British Columbia's annexation to Canada conditional on the introduction of responsible government. Trutch remarks that, as a province of Canada, British Columbia will be able to acquire responsible government whenever she likes; under the British North America Act, provinces could amend their own constitutions at will. — PR

dominion, as given by that act, that I object to the general principle of Confederation of the North American provinces of Great Britain. I am told I am in error, that profound statesmen in Great Britain and in Canada have determined otherwise, and that Confederation, on the basis of the Organic Act of 1867, is the policy of Great Britain. I regret, sir, that I cannot be silenced by the weight of such authority. No statesmanship, no conclusion, is of any value except for the reasoning on which it is founded; and I am ready to rest the whole matter on simple argument and reason. All states large enough and populous enough to warrant such a privilege, eagerly and passionately desire the power of self-government. It is the common passion of our race. Formerly, even now, in other places, it is British policy to give these powers; and as New South Wales has thrown off Victoria and Queensland, so would it appear to be reasonable to extend the principle to the British provinces of North America, rather than to adopt a different policy, for the simple reason that it is in accordance with the instincts of the Anglo-Saxon race and the just rights of man.

"We want self-government, which means the protection of our own interests and the establishment of our own welfare in our own way; the passing of our own estimates in our own way; the selection of those who rule, and the subsequent meeting of our rulers face to face, in open council, that they may show us the results of their ruling."

We want self-government, which means the protection of our own interests and the establishment of our own welfare in our own way; the passing of our own estimates in our own way; the selection of those who rule, and the subsequent meeting of our rulers face to face, in open council, that they may show us the results of their ruling. It means the imposition and collection of our own taxes, fostering our own industries, and the power of the purse. These are the elements of self-government, and they are reserved to the dominion government* and taken from the provinces; hence my objection to the Organic Act. For these reasons I say that Confederation — or rather union — with Canada cannot be fair and equal on account of the overwhelming influence of Canada in the dominion parliament, now and in the future, for it always must be so . . .

I do not profess to be a statesman or a politician, but as a lawyer of mature age, pretending to a fair share of common sense and a knowledge of human nature, I will venture to say that

---

* *Wood argues that British Columbia can't hope for self-government within Confederation, since the BNA Act assigns to the dominion government all the powers that he identifies as attributes of self-government. Oddly enough, in view of his vaunted contempt for British policy, Wood was a colonial official. Like others of his class, he feared that responsible government and annexation to Canada would jeopardize his job. — PR*

if there is one passion more powerful in the minds of colonists of Anglo-Saxon origin than another, it is the passion of self-government; in all English communities there is an ardent passion for self-government. Colonists here, as everywhere else, are animated by an intense desire to govern themselves in the way they think best, and to delegate that power to others is destructive of every feeling of self-respect and of social and political liberty. It is not necessary for me to prove that this is the case; it is too notorious for comment, and as long as the spirit of liberty exists in the British nation we shall find that no one province will submit to legislation at the hands of a legislature in which its interests and welfare are overwhelmed and over-borne. To secure submission to a legislature such as that of the Dominion of Canada, where the majority of the Canadian members make the law, uniformity of interest and feeling is necessary; and not only will the feeling of any separate province be wounded by the consciousness that self-government is withheld from it, but on finding that its interests, or its feelings, are overwhelmed and subjected to the interests and feelings of a dominant portion, the sense of discontent and dissatisfaction will become universal and national, hence will ensue a condition of things most perilous to British interests generally.

When Lord Granville* spoke of "comprehensiveness" and "impartiality" in a legislature, surely he must have lost sight of the constituent elements of a house of commons. For let us consider, without any reflection upon the House of Commons at Ottawa, what is the nature of the House of Commons of England, or of any other assembly of the same nature. Every house of commons is but an assemblage of the members of parliament pledged to support the material interests of their constituents, whenever these interests are affected. I never can anticipate anything but the representation of the views and the material interests of constituents in any house of commons. I believe that members would always vote according to the interests of men whose votes they would have again to solicit, and of whose interests public opinion holds them to be the acknowledged advocates.

— *Legislative Council, March 10, 1870*

---

* *Granville George Leveson-Gower, 2nd Earl Granville (1815–1891), colonial secretary from 1868 to 1870. In 1869 he named Anthony Musgrave to the governorship of British Columbia with instructions to expedite the colony's union with Canada.*

Robert Carrall: I do not believe, sir, that, with our present population, with our people scattered over a vast extent of thinly populated country, and having regard to the various conflicting interests consequent on remoteness from the centre, the principle of responsible government can be satisfactorily applied to this community at present. I believe entirely in the ability and fitness of the Anglo-Saxon race to govern themselves, but I say that the time has not yet arrived under which that particular form of government, generally known as responsible, can be satisfactorily worked in this colony.

I believe that the scheme foreshadowed by the governor* for representative government will be the best that, under present circumstances, the colony can have. The popular members under that system will have a clear majority, and, consequently, the people will have the control of the purse-strings. I do not speak these words as a member of the Executive Council, but as the expression of my own deliberate opinion. Sir, I was not sent here pledged to any particular platform.† My constituents had confidence in me, and were content that I should act on my own judgement.

The British government wanted British Columbia's annexation to Canada to be authorized in advance by the voters in a general election. In order that the members thus elected should be in a majority, Musgrave proposed to reduce the number of appointed members in the Legislative Council from fifteen to six. Needless to say, the proposal was a long way short of satisfying men like John Robson. — PR

† Carrall echoes the view expounded by Edmund Burke in his Speech to the Electors of Bristol *(1774), when he declared that, as a member of parliament, he did not feel obliged to act as a cipher for the views of his constituents, but would vote on issues as his judgement and conscience dictated. — IG*

In Carrall's words we hear an inkling of the as-yet-unresolved conflict between the pure democratic idea — that a representative is to take specific instructions from local voters — and the alternative and more common idea found in the parliaments of liberal democracies — that the representative once elected must represent the whole people and, as Burke put it, that he must not sacrifice his judgement to their opinion. A certain tension continues in modern Canadian politics on this very issue. The Reform Party of Canada (which though considered radically conservative in its policies supports radical democratic ideas) specifically supports the taking of instructions by representatives. The other parties are silent on the matter, leaving them room to adopt either viewpoint. — WDG

Speaking officially, I say that responsible government is not a question of union. The act of union gives us the exclusive right to alter our own laws with respect to everything connected with the internal and local government of the province, so long as the federal prerogative, if I may so call it, is not infringed. If the majority of the people want responsible government after Confederation, neither Governor Musgrave nor any other power on earth can prevent their having it. It is unfounded, unfair, and unjust, on the part of those who are opposed to the government on the question of Confederation, to endeavour to put any other complexion upon the matter.

Henry Crease: Now I earnestly deprecate, on the part of the government, the unfair allegation which one honourable member [John Robson] has so improperly insinuated that the government or government officials considered the *people* of British Columbia unfit for self-government. Why, sir, neither the governor nor any member of the government, or any other official, ever said or thought that the people of this colony were individually or collectively unfit for responsible government. The utmost that has ever been said on this side of the house has been that, under the present *circumstances of the colony*, it would be unwise, excessively costly — nay, impracticable. As I have said before, and again repeat, the governor has no power of himself to alter the constitution. He can only refer it where it has already gone, to the decision of the Queen in Council [that is, the British cabinet], which we ought in common justice to await before bringing forward any resolution for responsible government. Now, how would the country, if a unit on this point, get responsible government after Confederation? After Confederation the people can have responsible government, if they desire it, under clause 92 of the British North America Act, 1867,* by which power is given for the provinces to change their own constitution.

— *Legislative Council, March 11, 1870*

---

* Here Crease is advising the legislature as attorney general. But is his opinion correct? The clause to which he refers bars the legislature from making laws concerning the office of lieutenant governor, and the appointment of executive officers is a crucial function of that office. In the early years of Confederation, the right of the legislature to limit the lieutenant governor's discretion in this respect might well have been questioned. — PR

"All liberty and improvement have been infused into communities by the shock of revolution, or violent agitation. There is no hope of political improvement in time of tranquility and without agitation."

Thomas Humphreys: Mr. Chairman, I do not think it necessary to take up the time of the house. I am perfectly satisfied in my own mind that the official members are convinced that the people are in favour of responsible government. As a student of history, young as I am, I begin to realize this truth; that all liberty and improvement have been infused into communities by the shock of revolution, or violent agitation. There is no hope of political improvement in time of tranquility and without agitation. The official members of this council are remarkable for their profound indifference to right and wrong. It is in their interest to postpone the settlement of this question of responsible government.

I hold that . . . the question ought to be settled now and forever. Why should we be compelled, year after year, to fight these battles for reform over and over again?: let this question be settled so that we may have leisure for other things. Honourable gentlemen say the people are not in favour of responsible government; time will show. I say that they will almost as a unit insist upon it, and I lay down this proposition — no responsible government, no Confederation; no Confederation, no pensions. Instead of tightening the governmental reins, they should be slackened. If responsible government is not granted, these officials will still lose their power; for then in all probability a mightier nation than Canada will take charge of us.

I am in favour of Confederation if it gives us permanent advantages, not otherwise. We must have a free constitution. My conscience tells me that my vote on these resolutions is not prompted by selfish motives; if the people get responsible government, I am satisfied. His Excellency [Governor Musgrave] admits that he would not like to extend the liberal form of government to this colony. My opinion is that there is no community not fit to govern themselves; government is not a complicated machine, there is very little difference between carrying on a government and carrying on a business. One half of the depression in this colony is in my opinion attributable to the despotic form of government. Just fancy the head of a mercantile house allowing his clerks to carry on the whole business of the firm as they pleased. (Hear, hear from Mr. De Cosmos.) Without responsible government you will lose Confederation; it is not necessary to say any more; let us have something like the government of Ontario. Those whom I have the honour to represent sent me here to advance responsible government.

JOHN ROBSON
(1824–1892), a busi-
nessman, journalist, and
Upper Canadian who
moved to British
Columbia in 1859. As a
newspaper editor from
1861 on, Robson cam-
paigned for responsible
government. Having
predicted transconti-
nental federation as
early as 1862, he became
a strong advocate of
annexation to Canada
after 1867. A provincial
cabinet minister from
1883, and premier from
1889–92, he favoured
votes for women,
because they supported
morality, but not for
Indians and Asians.

*"All true governments
derive their power
from the people."*

Robson: Mr. Chairman, I will address myself to the question
before the house, which I feel to be the most important clause in
these terms; a question, in fact, which underlines the peace, prosperity, and happiness of British Columbia; a question which, if
carelessly or improperly treated now, may eventuate in the most
serious consequences to the colony; for I believe the people are as
ready now as in earlier days to fight for freedom, and to shed
their blood in defence of their political rights. It becomes us,
then, to be candid with ourselves and with each other, very
serious, firm, and dispassionate in discussing this clause, as it
might result in most disastrous consequences.

What is responsible government? I have been led to believe
that considerable confusion of ideas exists upon this point: and I
was the more impressed with this upon listening to the remarks
of the honourable member for Cariboo (R.W.W. Carrall) a few
days ago. That honourable gentleman compared the introduction
of responsible government into this colony to applying the
machinery of the *Great Eastern* to a dairy churn. Now, sir, responsible government is not a quantity; it is a principle; and as such it
is applicable to the *Great Eastern** or to a dairy churn, capable of
being applied to a tiny lady's watch. It is a principle admirably
adapted to the largest communities in the Old World. It is a principle admirably adapted to the smallest communities in the New
World. It is a principle that may be worked out in a cabinet of a
hundred. It is a principle which may be successfully worked out
in a cabinet of three. Without it no government can, in the true
sense, be called a people's government.

All true governments derive their power from the people. All
true governments must be responsible to the people. Responsible
government is, then, a principle which may be adapted to, and
successfully worked out in, this community. If this proposition is
incontrovertible, which I maintain it is, who can say that British
Columbia is not large enough for responsible government?
There are men here of ability to form a cabinet. The cabinet of
the day is, under the responsible system, the government, just so
long as it has the confidence of a majority of the representatives of
the people in the house. In the event of that confidence being lost,
one of two courses is open. The ministers place their resignation in
the hands of the governor, who commonly calls upon a prominent

---

*A British liner built in 1858. By far the largest vessel of its day, it was
unsurpassed in size for forty years.*

member of the opposition to form a ministry: or if they believe that the house does not truly represent the people upon the question at issue, they advise a dissolution and an appeal to the country.

What would responsible government have to do here? In dealing with this question, I, of course, assume British Columbia to be a province of the dominion, and, I confess, that were it otherwise, were it proposed to remain a separate colony, the case would be different. I do not say that even then I would not advocate the introduction of responsible government, but that advocacy might be less hearty and less firm. Regarding British Columbia as a province of the dominion, the chief objections are removed by the removal to Ottawa of all those larger and more complex questions of legislation which might threaten to crack the brain of our embryo statesmen. The local government would alone have to discharge [them], scarcely more difficult, in fact, than [discharging] those falling within the functions of a large municipality in Canada. Are the people of British Columbia fit for it? And here I would express my sincere regret that the representative of Her Majesty in this colony [Governor Musgrave] has felt it to be his duty to pronounce an adverse opinion. I will yield to no one, either in this house, or out of it, in entertaining a high respect for His Excellency, for his talent, experience, and honesty of purpose. But I do say, and I say with respect, more in sorrow than in anger, that I cannot think his knowledge of the people of this colony was such as to justify him in so early pronouncing upon their fitness for self-government.

Crease: The honourable member for New Westminster [John Robson] will, I am sure, pardon the interruption, but I feel it my duty to deny that the governor ever said, or that any member of the government has said or thought, that the people of British Columbia are unfit for self-government.

Robson: I thank the honourable and learned attorney general and I appreciate his motives. Yet I cannot conceal from myself the fact that a mere play upon words* will not mend matters. Whether it is the colony or its inhabitants that has been pronounced unfit for self-government, the practical results remain the same, and it is with these we alone are concerned. From my

---

* Carrall's speech below makes it clear that official reservations extended to the character of the population, not merely to the conditions of colonial society. — PR

WHAT THEY SAID ABOUT LIBERTY

own knowledge of the people, and it is the result of eleven years' contact with them, I have no hesitation in saying they are pre-eminently fitted for self-government. There are scores of men in the country with callused palms and patched garments well fitted by natural endowments, education, and practical experience in the working of responsible government in other colonies to occupy seats either in the Legislative Assembly or in the cabinet of British Columbia. He who would judge of the intelligence and mental acquirements of men in this colony by outward appearance and by present occupation certainly would not judge righteous judgement.

The opinion of His Excellency the Governor to the contrary, notwithstanding, I boldly assert that the people of British Columbia are fit for responsible government. Do they want it? Doubtless there are those in this house, possibly even in the unofficial ranks, who will deny that the people of British Columbia really desire to have responsible government under consideration. It is sometimes difficult to account for divergence of opinion; but I venture to think that I have the weight of both argument and evidence on my side when I assert, as I do, that the great body of the people, certainly the overwhelming majority, do earnestly and intelligibly desire that form of government.

It is difficult to believe that any man who has given due thought to the subject can possibly hesitate. Look at the position this colony would occupy* under Confederation, without the full control of its own local affairs — a condition alone attainable by means of responsible government. While the other provinces with which it is proposed to confederate upon equal and equitable terms retain the fullest power to manage all provincial matters, British Columbia would surrender that power — her local as well as her national affairs would be managed at Ottawa. Could a union so unequal be a happy and enduring one? The compact we are about to form is *for life*. Shall we take into it the germ of discord and disruption? The people desire change; but they have no desire to exchange the imperial heel for the Canadian heel. They desire political manumission.

I stand here and, in the name of my ancestors, protest before heaven against the surrender of constitutional rights purchased

"I stand here and, in the name of my ancestors, protest before heaven against the surrender of constitutional rights purchased by the best blood of our race — a priceless legacy we have no right to barter away, even if we would."

---

* If British Columbia joins Canada without first attaining responsible gov-ernment, says Robson, it will be a colony of Canada, and the federal principle of the Canadian Constitution will not apply to it. — PR

by the best blood of our race — a priceless legacy we have no right to barter away, even if we would. We owe it to our ancestors to preserve entire those rights which they have delivered to our care. We owe it to posterity* not to suffer their dearest inheritance to be destroyed.

But, if it were possible for us to be insensible of these sacred claims, there is yet an obligation binding upon ourselves from which nothing can acquit us; a personal interest which we cannot surrender. To alienate even our own rights would be a crime as much more enormous than suicide, as a life of civil security and political freedom is superior to a condition of serfdom; and if life be the bounty of heaven, we scornfully reject the noblest part of the gift if we consent to surrender that certain rule of living and those constitutional rights without which the condition of human nature is not only miserable, but contemptible.

I know but too well that the people of this colony have, during these years past, been unjustly and unconstitutionally deprived of their rights; but the perpetration of a wrong in the past can constitute no argument for perpetuating that wrong in the future; and it would appear a most fitting moment, when a new constitution is about to be offered, to demand the full restoration of political rights of which we have been for some time so unjustly deprived.

"All governments are naturally conservative."

I am constantly told that this is not the proper time to ask for responsible government — that if the people want it they will possess, under the new constitution, the ready means of obtaining it. Sir, I do not see the matter in that light. I see in the proposed constitution a condition of things which promises a five years', possibly a ten years' agitation for what the people are prepared for now, desire now, are entitled to now. All governments are naturally conservative. All persons holding positions of honour, power of emolument are conservative. Think you those holding office by appointment will favour or promote a change which would make them responsible to the people — exchange their commission from the crown for the most brittle tenure of public opinion? On the contrary, we should find those in power opposed to the people in their struggle for responsible government; and how long the struggle might last it would be idle to predict.

---

* Robson echoes Burke's doctrine, enunciated in his Reflections on the Revolution in France (1790), that society is a partnership between the living, the dead, and those yet to be born. — IG

Besides, the people of Canada do not desire to see British Columbia occupying any such false position. They know too well the value of free institutions, and their adoption to new countries, to think of withholding them from us. These constitutions were not won without a long and bloody struggle, even in Canada; and the prosperity and contentment of that people date from the inauguration of responsible government. The failure of representative institutions formerly enjoyed* upon this island is frequently cited as an argument against responsible government being introduced here. I admit the partial failure of those institutions. That failure was not, however, on account of the institutions being "representative," but because they were not "responsible." The essential principle was wanting. There was no constitutional connecting link — no bond of sympathy between those who sat by the will of the people and those who sat contrary to, and in defiance of, that will. The system, painted though it was, in popular dress, was rotten at the core — proved a delusion and a sham. The people, sometimes in indifference and contempt, permitted unsuitable men to be elected, and the whole thing came to rack and ruin. It is to avoid a repetition of that unseemly farce that the people demand that any new constitution which may be conferred upon the colony shall be based upon the only true principle of responsibility. This question should be finally settled. The colony desires political rest. To inaugurate a fresh political agitation with union is most undesirable and might lead to disastrous results. The possible consequences of a refusal to grant responsible government coincident with Confederation is a part of the subject I almost hesitate to touch. I would neither prophesy, predict, nor threaten; but I would ask the government to read well and carefully the lessons written in blood in other countries.

Human nature is much the same on both sides of this great continent. Has the Anglo-Saxon race become so utterly degenerate here that it is prepared to barter away for mere money subsidies those rights which were purchased with so much blood elsewhere? I utterly refuse to think so meanly of this people. We have seen that even the half-breeds of Red River have too much

---

From 1856 until its union with British Columbia ten years later, the colony of Vancouver Island had a representative legislature, but not responsible government. Robson refers to the legislature's irresponsible conduct during the fiscal crisis of 1865–66. — PR

of the old blood in their veins to permit a fancied political wrong. I am not going to predict a rebellion here. Heaven grant there may be none. But I do feel it my duty to warn the government against unnecessarily provoking such a possible contingency. Why should there be such an unaccountable antipathy to investing the people of British Columbia with those political powers enjoyed under the British Constitution? Why is the present form of government so unpopular with the people? I will tell you why. It is just because it is not a people's government. They had no hand in making it. They have none in working it. They can have none in unmaking it.

Only let the people have a hand in forming the government, in selecting men of their own choice to rule over them, and we would find a popular government, a strong government, strong in the heart and confidence of the people. The very same gentlemen who are unpopular now, because ruling without the consent of the people, would be popular then, because ruling by the act and with the consent of the people. The people of British Columbia are naturally a conservative people. Restore to them their political rights, and no government would need to fear an undue desire for change. The people know best* how to manage their own local affairs. Depend upon it, sir, the people are seldom wrong in their opinions; in their sentiments they are never mistaken.

"The people know best how to manage their own local affairs. Depend upon it, sir, the people are seldom wrong in their opinions; in their sentiments they are never mistaken."

---

* At the end of his speech, Robson moved in amendment that: "Whereas no union can be either acceptable or satisfactory which does not confer upon the people of British Columbia as full control over their own local affairs as is enjoyed in the other provinces with which it is proposed to confederate, therefore be it RESOLVED. That an humble address be presented to His Excellency the Governor, earnestly recommending that a constitution based upon the principle of responsible government as existing in the Province of Ontario, may be conferred upon this colony, coincident with its admission into the Dominion of Canada." — PR

Robson, as a radical, is referring to the classical notion that the people collectively are never wrong — their voice is as the voice of God (vox populi vox dei). The assertion that the people are naturally conservative can be traced to John Locke in his Second Treatise of Government (1690). Justifying the popular right to revolution, Locke states that the people are normally patient and conservative, and will rebel against their government only as a last resort. — IG

Amor De Cosmos:* I look upon British Columbia as a municipality under the British crown. Under Canada it will be a municipality with less power. Anyone who knows anything of municipal law knows that it is based upon three principles: territory, authority, and responsibility. This colony has the first two, and we are now asking for the third, and the terms sent down to the council do not contain the elements of responsibility of the executive to the people. Everything is tending to this point. Without responsibility, no matter how elective the new council is, it will be a failure. The people want responsible government and representative institutions under any circumstances. I think the people would be traitors to themselves if they accepted any form of government which had not the element of responsibility. I would rebel if there were enough like me in the colony, and arrest every member of government that I thought was robbing me of my rights. I would go to a further extreme.

Carrall: Mr. Chairman. I should like to ask what all this breeze is about? It is perfectly clear to all that as soon as we enter the confederacy, the people of this country can have any form of government they desire. I refuse to take up the issue without Confederation, in a state of isolation. We are dealing with Confederation. I am, equally with the honourable member for New Westminster [John Robson], aware of the priceless boon of responsibility, which exists in England, which may fairly be called the standard-bearer of nations, and I am equally aware that the same responsibility does not exist in the United States. During the late war I was in the United States' army. [Edwin McMasters] Stanton, the then secretary of war, was a most unpopular man. They wanted to get rid of him, but he could not be removed.

---

*De Cosmos (born William Alexander Smith) and John Robson were the two most ardent campaigners for responsible government in British Columbia. De Cosmos does not show much fire in these debates, but listen to him speaking at a convention of the nineteenth-century Reform Party in Toronto in 1867: "I know what it is to struggle, in that remote country, with governors and governments; contending for these inalienable rights and privileges which Englishmen inherit, and which as British Americans we ought to enjoy. Having for nine long years battled against combinations, against incorporated companies, such as have held in chains a vast portion of British America, and against governments, often standing almost alone, with few to sympathize, I know what these things are . . . " — JA

When I took the ground that responsible government was not expedient, it was not because I did not approve of the system. It is, I say, the wisest and best form of government, but it is too cumbrous for this colony. I will repeat my objections: the council contains no men of influence,* the constituencies are too remote, and the inhabitants are all engaged in bread-seeking; there are few men of independent means who would take part in responsible government and, consequently, the direction of public affairs would fall into the hands of men who are not fitted or qualified to govern the country, or otherwise into the hands of Victorians; neither of which I, for one, wish to see.

The Executive Council do not care one fig what sort of government the people take. The executive say the question is one for the people to decide. The governor has left you to choose any government you deem best. Do you think it would be better to have as permanent heads of departments two or three gentlemen who are familiar with the wants of the colony, or a moveable ministry going out on a question of repairs to Cowichan road, or something of that kind. These are amongst the things that you have to consider, and if after due consideration the people desire responsible government they will have it. I am here to state that His Excellency the Governor has no wish or desire to keep back responsible government; if he had any such desire, is it likely that he would have reconstituted his Executive Council so as to make it elected? I apprehend that people do not consider what they are talking about when they ask for responsible government; they have not probably considered the failures that have been made in respect of responsible government; there have been some failures, as, for instance, in Jamaica and in Victoria. A class of people get into power under responsible government whom no person would like to have as rulers. There are petty interests mixed up

---

* *In classical times it was objected that a democratic system was not feasible if people had to work all day for a living, and was especially compromised if they were dependent on others for their livelihood. Such a people would not have the time to study or direct political life. Rousseau even wondered if direct democracy of the ancient type is possible without a class of slaves to free the citizenry for political life! The discussion touches on the idea that a nation is "ready" for representative government, including some element of democracy, only when the people are sufficiently leisured to carry out such duties independently and responsibly. "No time; no citizen" sums up this idea from Aristotle on. — WDG*

with politics in small communities which prevent the system working as well in them as in large countries like Great Britain, where there is a healthy tone, and a vast population and consequently great questions of national importance. I maintain that after Confederation, the questions connected with local affairs will be so small and so entirely connected with particular localities that a staff of permanent heads of departments will be far better for the colony than responsible government.

Trutch: I say, then, that responsible government is not desirable, and is not applicable to this colony at present, is practicably unworkable, and here I would deprecate the interpretation which is being so assiduously instilled in the people of this colony concerning what has been said of the unfitness of the colony for responsible government. His Excellency the Governor has never said, nor has any member of the government ever said, that the people are unfit, individually, to govern themselves. I say that, man for man, this community will compare favourably with any people on this continent. (Hear, hear, from Attorney General Crease.)

Nor is it even the smallness of the population that I consider to be [a] great objection, although I admit that this is a drawback; but it is the scattered character of that population. It would be practically impossible to organize electoral districts so that they should properly represent the interest of the separate parts, and of the whole colony, as Victoria is the centre of wealth, and intelligence also if you will; under present circumstances the government would be centralized in the hands of Victorians who would thus rule the colony, and this would be objectionable (hear, hear, from Mr. Henry Holbrook), and I say also that there would be a great difficulty in getting proper representatives to represent the respective districts. I do not agree with the honourable member who has stated that only the chaff of the people is blown into this house, for I say, sir, that this council, constituted as it is, has proved that men fit to represent the people do come here.

Responsible government will come as a matter of course when the community is fit for it, but that form of government is not fitted for communities in their infancy. It has never been so considered. I look abroad into the world and you will find large populations without responsible government. There is no necessity to look far off to see whether the Anglo-Saxon race must necessarily have responsible government. I look across the Strait where there is a population of, I suppose, 30,000 people, and

there they have neither responsible government nor representative institutions. Look at Oregon, also with no representation until the population exceeds 45,000. Look at the Red River settlement, also with a population larger than ours; they do not apply for responsible government. It does not follow according to the rule of Anglo-Saxon minds that this form of government must prevail. I do not think the sort of responsibility which is advocated would be suitable to this colony at present, or would promote its true interests.

But I think, sir, that our present form of government is practically a more real responsibility to the people than that proposed by the honourable member for New Westminster [Robson], this form which the honourable member for Lillooet [Humphreys] finds it so easy to animadvert upon. For we are in reality, if not directly, responsible to the people. We, as servants of the crown,* are directly and immediately responsible to the governor, and the governor is responsible to the queen, who is the guardian of the people's rights. This is no mere idea, for the fact of responsibility has been, over and over again, proved. If you have any good grounds of complaint, you know where to lay them and get redress. This responsibility which we know is more real, less fluctuating, less open to doubtful influences, and under it the rights of the whole country are secured and protected, and not those of the majority to the prejudice of the minority, as under the so-called responsible government, which really means party government, advocated so warmly by the honourable member for New Westminster.

But the honourable members for New Westminster [Robson], for Victoria District [De Cosmos], and for Lillooet [Humphreys] tell you that the people desire responsible government, that they must have it and will have it. I say, sir, that if they do say so, which I very much doubt, it is because the population have been educated up to it by those who have agitated the subject through the press and through speeches; some no doubt press for it from conviction and some with a view to serving their own ends, but I believe, sir, that what the people really want is such an administration of the government as will tend to bring back prosperity to the colony. You are told that the present officials have no sym-

---

The underlying idea is that the monarch represents and unites everyone, whereas winning parties and their leaders unite only those who vote for them — often less than half the country. — WDG

pathy with the people, that they are not of the people, that they move in a different sphere, and constitute a class by themselves. Is this true — or is it not rather the fact that persons who have ends to serve have put us in a class by ourselves? The honourable member says that the hands of the benefactors of the people must be callused with labour. Who, I ask, are those throughout the world who have laboured most for the people by speech and pen? I say that the real statesmen who have done most to advance the truest interests of the people have not sprung from the ranks of those whom the honourable member classes as the people.

The honourable member for New Westminster says that the present government officials are well enough able and honest, but that they cannot enjoy the confidence of the people because they are not *their* officials, they are not elected by them. And, be as able as we might, and as honest and work as we might, and do what we might for the people's good, we could not claim their confidence because we are not directly responsible to them. And the honourable member sympathized with us for the position! Now, sir, I say, sir, if it be true, as he says, that the government have not the confidence of the community when, he says, they deserve it, whose is the fault? I say, sir, it is the fault of those who, by voice and pen, have for years sedulously prejudiced the public mind of this community against that government not by pointing out faults to be remedied but by general and indiscriminate faultfinding, descending to personal abuse, and even to the verge of scurrility.

I have always asserted that we must take our steps to responsible government gradually. Having representative institutions, we can go on to the other. No one ever stated that the people were unfit to govern themselves; all acknowledge that they have talent enough. But this I do assert, that thus far the people have shown an unwillingness to govern themselves — have taken but little interest in the matter. It is not because they are unfit, but unwilling; they prefer looking after their own business; it pays them better. I do not refer to the difficulty of getting members, and doubtless some of us sit here from that cause; and it is no doubt true, as has been said, that better could have been found outside. If you have responsible government it will fall into the hands of those who wish to make a living by it. No one has said that it would be economical — it would not be so. It would require at least thirty members.

The truth is there would be a great difficulty in getting members, and without a large body of members it could not be carried

---

"Now, sir . . . if it be true . . . that the government have not the confidence of the community . . . whose is the fault? I say, sir, it is the fault of those who, by voice and pen, have for years sedulously prejudiced the public mind of this community against that government not by pointing out faults to be remedied but by general and indiscriminate faultfinding, descending to personal abuse, and even to the verge of scurrility."

on.* You would find that the best men would avoid politics, and soon there would be very great corruption.

G.A. Walkem: The honourable member (for New Westminster) [John Robson] says that responsible government is a principle which may be applied either to the *Great Eastern* or to a dairy churn, or to a lady's watch; that it is a principle capable of being carried out by three, or three hundred. This is utterly incorrect; it is not a principle but a form,[†] one element of which is responsibility to the people. It is a form adopted by the people, but it does not follow as a matter of induction that it can be used or carried out in every place or by every community.

In 1837 the rebellions in Canada for the purpose of acquiring responsible government took place. The rebellion was raised and the question agitated simply for changing the form of government. What was the population? It was in the neighbourhood of 2,000,000[‡] in 1837, and of 2,500,000 in 1861.

Look at the difference of the population of this colony after deducting the aliens and females; there is scarcely a voting population through the whole colony of 3,000.

We have nine members, and out of these nine, under responsible government, we should have to elect a colonial secretary, an

---

* Opponents of responsible government base their objection on the size, character, and dispersion of the population. In 1871 the European population in British Columbia numbered fewer than 10,000 and the entire population about 35,000, divided between Vancouver Island and the mainland. The Europeans were mostly transient miners or farmers. In a tradition of thought deriving from Aristotle's Politics, *Carrall and Trutch stress the importance to a self-governing community of an aristocracy: a leisured class of secure wealth, whose members have the time and independence to consider public affairs fully and dispassionately. Where such a class is lacking, popular representative government must mean corrupt government by professional politicians, and minority rights will be vulnerable to the tyranny of the majority. — PR*

† When Robson called responsible government a principle, he was treating the term as synonymous with self-government. *(He was a Canadian, that is, from the Province of Canada, and Canadians often did so.) Walkem correctly points out that responsible government is a particular form of representative government. — PR*

‡ One million would be more accurate for 1837, and is probably what Walkem said.

attorney general, a chief commissioner of lands and works, and probably two other cabinet ministers, altogether five in office and four struggling for power. Make the whole number eighteen and you then have a constant struggle for power, a struggle such as we have not had in this colony before, and such as I hope we shall not see.

The honourable member for New Westminster [Robson] says if we go in without responsible government, we shall go in with agitation. Does anyone believe that if we had responsible government tomorrow, politicians will have no subject on which to agitate? Political agitation will never cease. Let us go further. As the honourable chief commissioner [Trutch] says, we have the United States advocating responsible government, and that form of it which is said to be the best in theory, a form in reality democratic, but the people are not educated to the extent of the principle itself. Americans are averse to granting [to] not only small but large territories the freedom which we now ask. They say, "You shall be a territory until you are properly educated."

"I believe there are men with tattered garments in the upper country quite capable of giving a sensible vote upon all questions likely to come before a council in this colony, but we find that they have too much to do, they have no time for politics, they have to earn their own bread. "

I believe there are men with tattered garments in the upper country quite capable of giving a sensible vote upon all questions likely to come before a council in this colony, but we find that they have too much to do, they have no time for politics, they have to earn their own bread.

— *Legislative Council, March 18, 1870*

W.T. Drake: If we go into Confederation bound head and foot with the same form of government as now, we shall have no power to change the form. We shall then have Canada as a Queen Regent: we shall then have an executive who will, if so directed, vote against responsible government. This colony would be a preserve for Canadian statesmen and Canadian patronage: we shall be no more advanced than now. Without going into argument, I may be pardoned, I trust, if I quote three propositions of John Stuart Mill* on responsible government. First, "Do the people require it; or are they unwilling to accept it?" We are told that this has not been made a question. I deny

* *Mill was the founding father of modern liberal thought. In* On Liberty *(1859) he penned an eloquent defence of individual freedom, based on utilitarian ethics. In* Considerations on Representative Government *(1861) he defended democratic participation, but only under strict conditions designed to protect the position of the virtuous élite. Finally, in* The

this statement. It has been made a question, more or less, in Victoria at every election; every election depends, more or less, on this point. Second, "Are the people willing to take the burdens which are imposed on them by such a form?" I say that we have the answer to this proposition in the fact of there being people willing to come here where they are practically useless. Do not persons come forward to represent the people? A very large majority of the people take part in every election. Third, "Are the people willing and able to do that which will enable the government to perform its functions properly?" This I contend is the condition of the colony.

The main argument of the chief commissioner [Trutch] in his very able speech, a broad argument and very well put, is that the population is scattered. I say this argument cannot be used with effect. We are told that the government would fall into the hands of Victoria as the centre of population and wealth; no great harm if it did. Victoria is dependent upon all parts of the colony and they on her; the interests are identical. Another objection that has been raised is that we cannot get more of proper intelligence and qualifications for positions of honour and trust. Looking round this council board we see men who have come out to this colony to make their own fortunes and homes: out of them the present members of the government have been chosen, and out of our present population there can be found an equal number of men who can properly fulfil the duties of the government. I cannot see that it is impossible to find proper men. If we find men willing to sit in this council now, we shall find plenty ready and anxious to share in the burdens of responsible government. The sufficiency or insufficiency of the population is not an element in the question.

The United States has been pointed out to us as an example. I say there is no responsible government in the United States; it is an absolute despotic democracy, absolutely irresponsible to the

---

Subjection of Women *(1869) he defended women's right to political equality with men. His influence was at its peak in the mid- to late-nineteenth century. Reflecting this influence, he is the most often-cited political thinker in the Confederation debates. — IG*

The reference is to Mill's Considerations on Representative Government. *Drake quotes Mill's account in chapter 7 of three conditions for representative government; but Drake uses responsible government as a synonym for representative government much as Robson used it as a synonym for self-government. See also E.G. Alston's speech in this section. — PR*

people except once in four years. There is no such thing as responsibility in the form of government of the United States; the only means of getting rid of a minister is by impeachment.

"All the civil wars and troubles have not arisen from the uneducated, but from the ambitions of the so-called educated classes."

Humphreys: One honourable member says that it rests on numbers. I say that intelligence is the only qualification* for responsible government; numbers have nothing to do with it. If I err, I am proud in erring with some of the greatest sons that England ever produced. The honourable chief commissioner [Trutch] has admitted that the population, taken man for man, is equal to that of any country. Then I say we have the proper qualification; let us have practical and not theoretical means of governing. What is really the case? Under the present form of government the people have to pay for the privilege and benefit of a few gentlemen sitting round this board. Take away the form of government and make it more liberal, and what is the danger?

All the civil wars and troubles have not arisen from the uneducated, but from the ambitions of the so-called educated classes. The people have been the conservatives who come forward to keep the country going; take away the so-called intelligent and educated classes and it will be no great loss, the labouring classes can always supply men to fill their places; but take away the working classes and you kill the world, the educated classes cannot fill their places. In my opinion, sir, the people want prac-

---

* *The discussion is revolving around the matter of suitability to lead, some arguing that innate ability is sufficient, some that qualification is required. All were aware of the general critique of government "by the people," which is that it opens the system to government by the mediocre. Plato had ridiculed societies that use democracy with the example of a ship lost at sea with passengers who, though knowing there was a highly qualified seaman aboard certain to lead them to safety, instead drew random lots to select a leader. In the eighteenth century, Britain was the most liberal nation on earth, but far from democratic in that before the Reform Act of 1832, only about 5 per cent of the adult population voted in elections. By the time of these debates, that figure had risen to about 15 per cent. Hence, intelligent people still worried greatly about the opening of the sluice-gates to unqualified people. They preferred to weigh votes rather than merely count them, and did so by insisting on qualifications — usually some combination of citizenship, property owned, income or rents earned, sex, age, education, literacy, and so on. The historical trend in Western democracies has been to eliminate all qualification. In Canada today most prisoners of age may vote. — WDG*

tical reality. They have endured too long the law's delay, and the insolence of those in office.* Why should we come here, year after year, to ask for a change in the form of government?

J.S. Helmcken: Great heavens! What terrible things are said and done in the name of the people. To hear honourable members talk, one would think that they were the people, but the people are quiet while honourable members are very loud. I intend to support the government; I do not mean to say much for or against. I take the position that the people can have responsible government when they want it, and their representatives ought to be satisfied to take it when the people really and seriously ask for it. Responsible government has been one of the watchwords of a certain set of politicians who want to bring on Confederation. A government of, from, for, and by the people, without regard to the material interests of the colony — this means government by politicians. These gentlemen will sacrifice every benefit to the colony for responsible government. Confederation to me means terms; to them it means pickings, office, place, and power. This will be represented, I am well aware, as being the result of being in the Executive Council; it is said that there is a great difference between the atmosphere of the two councils. I acknowledge it. There with closed doors people speak the truth without any *ad captandum* arguments [arguments to flatter the people] addressed to the galleries; there people can state what their opinions really are; here popularity has to be sought.

We are told that the people will fight for responsible government. That is mere nothing — words only. The honourable member for New Westminster [Robson] in his able speech erected a very handsome structure, but like most fancy structures it will be a very expensive one. He wants a government like Ontario, that is a government of one house, with eighty members. For a government of that kind not less than forty or fifty would be absolutely necessary.

Francis Barnard: It is beyond question that the intelligent portion of the community are in favour of responsible government, but there is a grave question in regard to its adaptation to the colony. The words coming from His Excellency are worthy of careful consideration. They contain strong reasons against the

---

* *From Hamlet's famous soliloquy in Act 3, Scene 1.*

introduction of responsible government. Public opinion is not settled on the island. The principal men of Victoria are averse to taking upon themselves the duties and labours of legislating for the country. Men of standing and wealth stand aloof. The merchants, manufacturers, and professional men take no interest in the matter of legislation. There is a great difficulty in getting good representative men.

There are, I admit, many good reasons which might be urged against the measure, and I have no doubt that dissatisfaction, to some extent, may ensure. I agree with the commissioner of lands and works [Trutch] in his remarks about the press influencing the public unfavourably to the government, but the blame is not in the press but in that system of government which keeps the rulers silent. The members of the government ought to be in a position to defend themselves both by pen and speech. I have glanced at a few reasons against the admission of responsible government, but I will now look at the other side. Look at the fact of all the larger subjects, under union, being dealt with by the federal power. This fact of itself is as strong an argument as we need. What honourable member can go to his constituents and tell them that he thinks the local business of the colony could be managed better at Ottawa than it can be by ourselves? The official members of this government will no doubt avail themselves of the retiring pension, and appointees from Ottawa will take their places. Will these latter officials have to be pensioned off by this colony when we adopt responsible government?

How long are we to wait? Canada was told the same story when she had a population of 600,000. All the other provinces were told the same thing. Must we wait for such an increase, or must we fight* as did Canada? Throw us on our own resources as a colony and we will soon learn valuable lessons in the science of government. There were gentlemen of good families and of good education who came here in the early days, who had never suffered any privations of any sort before they came here; sent out to make fortunes, or, at all events, homes for themselves; their roughing it was rough indeed; bad news had come from the mines, the avenues of trade were closed, there were no agricultural pursuits for them to turn to. The consequence was that they had to lie round hotels; after failing to get government employ-

---

*An allusion to the rebellions of 1837–38, which were widely supposed to have been instrumental in Canada's attaining responsible government. — PR

"Self-reliance is the best means of education in politics as in anything else. If our rulers are sent us from England or Ottawa we will always lack self-reliance."

ment, for which, as a matter of course, they applied, some kept bars whilst waiting for remittances. The reason was that they never had been taught self-reliance; we shall be in the same position if we are constantly to have rulers from England, or Canada, but throw us on our own resources and we shall succeed. Self-reliance is the best means of education in politics as in anything else. If our rulers are sent us from England or Ottawa we will always lack self-reliance. Self-reliance is written on every line of the British North America Act. "Rely upon yourselves" is the cry of the people of England. It is better to grapple with the difficulties now when the issues are small and comparatively unimportant, and should we make blunders they will not be so serious when our interests are small; and for what errors we do commit, the consequences will fall upon ourselves. We will, no doubt, blunder at first and there may be chaff blown here. If responsible government will bring the scum to the top, dross will go to the bottom. The scum will be ladled off — the chaff will be blown away by the breath of public opinion.

Wood: I am in favour of the extension of representative institutions little by little, to the utmost verge of safety. But I am opposed, in this community at least, to the establishment of what is called responsible government. These are my views shortly. I will start, sir, at once from an historical point of view. The honourable member for New Westminster [Robson] has, as I understand him, asserted that responsible government is the immemorial birthright of Englishmen,* and that the principle of cabinet ministers going in and out, with votes of a majority in the House of Commons, is a principle of ancient days. My understanding of the history of my country leads to a different conclusion, and however much it may be clear and obvious that representative institutions are our natural and inalienable

---

In the clash between parliament and the monarchy which culminated in the English Revolution of 1641, parliamentarians condemned the constitutional bastions of royal power as feudal corruptions of an ancient constitution of immemorial, meaning pre-Norman, origin. This notion of the immemorial liberties of Englishmen became the common currency of radical discourse, available as a justification for any libertarian project. Wood challenges Robson's attempt to identify responsible government with the immemorial liberties of Englishmen by arguing that the principle was not asserted until the overthrow of Lord Bute's ministry in 1763. John Stewart

birthright — however much it may be established that the power of self-taxation resides and has always resided in the representatives of the country, in the Commons of England, carrying with it the overwhelming power of the purse — it is, I believe, clearly admitted that the principle of responsible government, as now understood, has existed for little more than 100 years, say from the accession of George III and the termination of Lord Bute's administration, so that I admit the honourable gentleman's proposition only so far as this. Responsible institutions are the birthright of the British nations, representative institutions and the privilege of taxing ourselves.

Now, sir, I believe the whole scope of representative institutions to be greatly misrepresented. It is the fashion for honourable members to say that the government of this or any other community are bound to govern according to the well-understood wishes of the people; that *vox populi* is the *vox dei*; that ministries and governments are responsible to the people. But the true principle, as we all very well know, is that government and ministries are responsible, not to the people as a populace, but to the representatives of the people,* properly and reasonably chosen. Governments and ministries are responsible not to numerical majorities, but to the country. Now, sir, representative institutions are liable to this obvious and well-known danger. I will quote the words of a well-known political writer, Herbert

---

(also known by the English form Stuart), 3rd Earl of Bute (1713–1792), had become prime minister in 1762 as the favourite of King George III, but the Whig political élite forced him from office and insisted that tenure of ministerial office must depend on the support of a majority of the House of Commons. The principle was not firmly established for many years thereafter, but Wood's history is a good deal more exact than the prevailing idea among British North American politicians that responsible government had somehow come into being in Britain as a consequence of the Glorious Revolution of 1688–89. — PR/IG

* When Wood remarks jovially that representative government is itself being misrepresented, he is correct. Europe at the time was alive with discussion of the relative merits of the various forms of government. Rousseau had earlier set the world afire for pure democracy, and the French Revolution was still a fresh and frightening spectre of how an abstract democracy can become totalitarian. Despite lofty declarations and constitutions, the American experiment had just barely survived the death rattle of the bloodiest civil war in history, much of it focused on disagreement over the democratic rights of

Spencer.* "Whenever the profit according to the Representative individually, from the passage of a mischievous measure largely exceeds his loss as a unit in the community from the operation of the injurious law, his interest becomes antagonistic to that of his constituents, and sooner or later will sway his vote." How true and how obvious this is. I might go further when the private and personal, the direct and immediate interest of the representative or of the constituents, whose advocates and delegates they are, is opposed to any matter of legislative action. The direct and material interest will, of a certainty, prevail over the distant and more remote welfare of the community in all but very few instances. This is the danger that threatens all representative institutions, and the only safeguard against it is the qualification — the pecuniary and material qualifications of the elector, and accordingly we see representative institutions flourishing and successful only when this safeguard practically exists.

Let us turn to the example of England. In England, representative institutions and responsible government work smoothly. And why? Because of the notoriously aristocratic and plutocratic character of the legislature of Great Britain. Political life is a sealed book to any but the wealthy classes. Every member of parliament is a man of property, no other can afford the luxury of legislative life, and society is secure in the hands of representatives whose property would suffer from the results of vicious or reckless legislation. The cream of all legislation is taxation, and my solid conviction is that representative institutions and responsible government will fail whenever the working majority is in the hands of an unsubstantial class of representatives or of electors.[†]

"Political life is a sealed book to any but the wealthy classes. Every member of parliament is a man of property, no other can afford the luxury of legislative life, and society is secure in the hands of representatives whose property would suffer from the results of vicious or reckless legislation."

states against *their central government. And so our founders' arguments about the best system for Canada were charged with historical poignancy. Wood makes light of the "fashion" for* vox populi vox dei *(the voice of the people is the voice of God), seeing in it a recipe for majoritarian oppression of minorities. Because the cream of all legislation is taxation, he fears a democratic class war of the poor in the guise of the voice of the people that is driven by envy of the established classes. His alternative is a moving plea for a leadership by the wise and established who have no need of financial gain. — WDG*

* A more extreme libertarian than J.S. Mill, the nineteenth century English philosopher Herbert Spencer argued that the state should exercise only the minimum of defence and police functions. It was his conviction that the struggles of individuals would strengthen the nation along Darwinian lines. — IG

† Wood is presenting the familiar conservative argument that democracy can

I have thus, sir, treated of representative institutions and responsible government somewhat in the abstract. I will now refer more particularly to its application to this colony, and this apart from any question of Confederation, and I will repeat that I am in favour of the extension to the utmost possible limits of the representative elements of this council, but averse to responsible government. With respect to the constitution of the Legislative Council of British Columbia, it might, I think, hardly be necessary in the present condition of the colony to advocate a second chamber — a council as distinct from an assembly. However advisable this may be in an advanced condition of the colony, advanced in numbers and wealth, few, if any, would advocate such an institution as a second chamber. The elements for forming such a chamber are sadly wanting in the present state of affairs, and the matter may be dismissed without further comment — without discussing the advisability in a general way of such a body. But with regard to the legislature on the supposition of its consisting of one single house, it will be necessary to speak at somewhat greater length. Of what elements ought such a legislative body to consist? At present it consists of official members, heads of departments; official members not heads of departments but representing for the most part different magisterial districts; a few nominated members — nominated, I think it is reasonable to presume, from an impression of their being tolerably intelligent and moderate — and a few representative members.

It is asked whether the constitution of this council should be altered so as to establish direct responsible government, or what may be looked upon as its equivalent, a large working majority of responsible members. At present it is obvious, and must be felt by all of us, by official members no less than by independent members, that our position as a crown colony is what is commonly called a *false position*. We are individually as well fitted for self-government as our brothers or our cousins in the Old Country or in Canada. I will go further; I will say that the community taken individually in this colony is *better* qualified to demand and have representative institutions. I say taken *individually*, and I mean it in its strict sense. Man for man, I believe the colonist a better politician than his English cousin. The aristocracy hardly exists,

only work if the levers of power remain in the hands of the minority who own most of the property. Should the unpropertied wield power, property would be in jeopardy and the very future of society in doubt. — IG

"The colonist is more enterprising and more pushing than the stay-at-home Englishman. He has better knowledge of the world and of human nature, he graduates in a school in which politics is prominent, and he is free from an immense amount of ignorance and prejudice which is thought and written and acted in the Old World."

it is true. It is an injustice to presume for a moment that the colonist in this or any other colony of Anglo-Saxon origin is in any way unfit for the enjoyment of the freest political liberty. Higher classes we have none, but the middle and lower classes are, I do not hesitate to say it, superior to the middle and lower classes at home. The colonist is more enterprising and more pushing than the stay-at-home Englishman. He has better knowledge of the world and of human nature, he graduates in a school in which politics is prominent, and he is free from an immense amount of ignorance and prejudice which is thought and written and acted in the Old World.

But then comes the consideration, What elements are indispensable in the community to form the representative body, if as is contended that element is to be supreme, or what is the same thing in point of actual power when that element constitutes the working majority? I will answer, 1. Localized and permanent population. 2. Established diversified interest; wealth, whether capital or regular income, the well-doing of professions, business and industries, agriculture, substantial industries, staples. Population herein we are deficient — 6,500 adult white men — sporadic, scattered, and temporary. How many care to vote, how many are aliens? Established interests here also are deficient; isolation is our drawback; staples we have, but they are undeveloped or unlucky; gold mining is depressed; agriculture under a disadvantage and no good market; coal not much sought after and minerals a speculation; lumber unfortunate; fisheries unestablished and commerce in the way of export killed by the abolition of the free port, or inferior from the absence of a large home demand. These are all our material elements of wealth and we have them in no great abundance. Now without them what have we? A sparse community in which the only thriving interest is agriculture, and that only because supply is not equal to demand; or in other words small in numbers and importance and no wealthy class at all. Can self-government be trusted to such a population? I say emphatically no! Now I am not greatly in favour of a high qualification for representatives for members of the council; it is sufficient for me that they represent substantial interests: but when we have unsubstantial representatives representing unsubstantial and small constituencies, I can hardly understand anything more dangerous, and, I might add, more ridiculous or more extravagant.

That representatives should be substantial people is desirable,

but that they should represent substantial interests is indispensable. If representatives are unfaithful to their trust, the remedy is possible; but where the class of electors is needy and unsubstantial, it seems impossible to conceive anything more disastrous. Taxation, as before has been observed, is the cream of legislation; and taxation at the hands of unsubstantial men, or men forced to advocate the interests of unsubstantial constituencies, will be nothing but tyranny. Opinions may be divided in many other matters, the votes of a party may be split on many points, but in the hands of the masses the substantial class will be heavily and unmeasurably taxed to suit the views of those who have nothing to lose and all to gain by any contemplated movement.

And, sir, having treated on representative and responsible government as applied to this colony, let us see its bearing on the subject of Confederation, and here I follow in the footsteps of the honourable member for New Westminster [John Robson]. His reasoning is mine, but not his conclusion. Without responsible government, or its equivalent, or its approximate government by a representative majority, we have no safeguard against a government of Canadian officials. British Columbia will be a colony of Canada, a dependency of a dependency, and Canadian interests will prevail. Dependence on England is bearable; they have no interests apart from ours, but dependence on Canada would be unbearable; their interests are different from ours. That is the conclusion that is inevitable; it is but a logical conclusion. Confederation without responsible government, or government by a working majority of representative members, is out of the question. Such a government cannot be had; therefore Confederation is out of the question. I have thus, sir, given my opinion on a point which is sure to meet with popular disfavour.

— *Legislative Council, March 21, 1870*

E.G. Alston: Sir, I am in favour of responsible government, but not the form that has been discussed in this house at so great a length. I believe all representative governments are responsible. The honourable and learned member for Victoria city has quoted John Stuart Mill. I believe, sir, that the word responsible government does not occur in his book;* he shows that the form

---

Alston is right: although Mill discusses executive responsibility, the phrase "responsible government" does not occur in Considerations on Representative Government. W.T. Drake may have misremembered "representative govern-

applicable to one country will not do for another. We have heard enough in this council to make me believe that the people do not want responsible government; I believe that a representative form of government is the only form that will suit this colony.

The American form of government is in a certain sense responsible, executive officers being elected for a term of four years. England possesses a different form, and Canada differs again from England. The smallest colony possessing responsible government is Prince Edward Island, and we who do not possess a population one-twelfth the size of Newfoundland are asking for responsible government. The honourable and learned member for Victoria city (Mr. Drake), who seems to uphold responsible government against his own convictions, admits that all power would be held in Victoria, and, he says, that there would be no harm in such centralization. I think, sir, that he has read John Stuart Mill to little purpose if such be his convictions.

"The ruler hugs power as the miser does his gold."

Robson: Sir, a certain proportion of chaff may be blown into this house under responsible government, as is the case now; but depend upon it, under the form of government we seek, the chaff would quickly be blown out at the back door before the breath of public opinion. The people can always discriminate between wheat and chaff, and responsible government supplies the most effective winnowing fan with which to separate the two . . . That honourable gentleman [Joseph Trutch] was content to give the same answer to the main object as that given all round the government end of the table, viz., that the Organic Act provides the necessary and ready means of obtaining what we seek; and he further tells us that, inasmuch as responsible government relieves the governors of responsibility, a governor would naturally be ready to make the concession. Such, however, is not the accustomed working of human nature. Such is not the lesson of history. The ruler hugs power as the miser does his gold, nor parts with it only as it is extorted piecemeal by the people.

The honourable gentleman [Trutch] tells us that it is impossible to work responsible government with a population so scattered; and in the same breath he tells us that we have responsible government now, that the officials are responsible to the governor, and he to the queen. Well, certainly, this is a sort of

ment" as "responsible government." Mill also believed that too much centralization was both ineffective and a threat to freedom. — IG

"The honourable gentleman tells us that if the present government is unpopular with the people, that responsibility rests with the press . . . The honourable gentleman has confounded cause and effect. The press has opposed the government because it is unpopular; and the government is unpopular because it is not a people's government."

responsibility; but it is not precisely the kind we want. The responsibility now existing takes the wrong direction.* It is not responsibility to the people, but to the supreme power. In this sense the most despotic form of government in the world may be termed responsible government. The members of the government of the czar of Russia are responsible to him, and he is responsible to the Great Ruler of all; ergo, Russia has responsible government! He next tells us that if the people desire responsible government, it is because they have been educated up to it by the press. There is more truth than argument in this. Doubtless the press is, in this, as in other civilized countries, the great educator of the people, especially in matters political. Have not the people of England been similarly educated up to every great political reform? Such constitutes a legitimate and important function of the press.

But the honourable gentleman goes further and tells us that if the present government is unpopular with the people, that responsibility rests with the press which has, by misrepresentation, created prejudice in the public mind. This proposition I beg most unqualifiedly to deny. The honourable gentleman has confounded cause and effect. The press has opposed the government because it is unpopular; and the government is unpopular because it is not a people's government — because it does not possess the principle of responsibility to the people. It must be remembered

---

In this single line Robson sums up the most common and widespread complaint as to the provenance of power. For the duration of Christendom, the common belief was that monarchs were above the positive law of the people, but below the natural law of God. They were ministers of God on earth, and power rightly flowed downward to the people. The influence of the eighteenth-century "Age of Reason," combined with declining religious faith in general and increasing commercialization, led to a natural demand for the inversion of power. Power must be legitimized to be accepted, and when faith in one source is lost, another will be found. So Robson argues a qualified vox populi vox dei position: power should come from the bottom, but only as filtered by chosen representatives. The Canadian system was a compromise. Rousseau, for example, would have dismissed our entire system of representation as an alienation of the people's true will. And this debate is far from over. Modern Canadians (and their representatives) are still confused over the meaning of democratic representation. Recent calls for referendums, recall, and people's initiatives — all methods for circumventing the institutions of representation — are vivid expressions of this ongoing struggle between the conflicting ideas of power from the top and from the bottom. — WDG

that the press subsists on popular favour; and in order to subsist it must oppose an unpopular form of government. The press of this colony has acted rather as the exponent than the moulder and leader of public opinion in its opposition to the present form of government. As I have repeatedly said, it is not the officials that are unpopular so much as the system under which they administer. No officials can be popular under such a system. It places them in a false position. The press is, therefore, not to blame; it is the faithful exponent of public opinion.

The colony is about to become a province of the Dominion of Canada. No union can be equitable and just which does not give this colony equal political power — equal control over their own local affairs with that possessed by the people of the provinces with which it is proposed to unite. I care not how good the other terms may be, if the people of British Columbia are placed in a false political position they will not be content, and the inauguration of such a union will only prove the beginning of new political discontent and agitation. Mistakes will doubtless result from the first workings of responsible government, but these mistakes were better made now than years hence, when the consequences might be more serious. The period of lisping, stammering infancy must be passed. Surely it is better to pass it now, while the political questions are few and simple and the interests comparatively small, than to wait for great development.*

— *Legislative Council, March 22, 1870*

NEWFOUNDLAND

John Casey: He considered that if we joined the Confederation, we would be doing this country a great wrong. We had already free institutions; and there was no colony in which the principles of governmental responsibility had worked better than in this. There was nothing to prevent our young men from attaining elected positions here and now; and the rewards to be obtained should satisfy their ambition. He felt that there would be a great deal of ability brought to bear upon this question, and that matters would be put before the public in a plausible light. It was idle to suppose that if we joined this Confederation, we should be

---

* Robson's motion was rejected, but British Columbia joined Confederation on the understanding that she should have responsible government whenever provincial public opinion clearly favoured it.

exempt from an increase of taxes. How were an army and navy for the Confederation to be supported? In four or five years hence we would have as much increased taxation as we received from Canada.

Daniel Prowse: No, honourable gentlemen did not want progress; no Confederation for them, and one honourable gentleman, Mr. Casey, used as an argument against the Confederation scheme, as a proof, said he, how brilliantly responsible government has worked with us, and that we want no change. One party remained in office during the whole of one parliament, and when the next party came in, they did the same. No wind of popular opinion was ever found strong enough to blow them out of office, certainly a most extraordinary proof of our fitness for representative institutions.

Now, sir, this is not the proper time to go into the merits of this great question of Confederation, but I will take the opportunity of expressing my opinion on the question. The honourable member, Mr. [Henry] Renouf, tells us that we ought not to express our opinion upon this question; he most grievously misapprehends the position of a representative here when he says so. What are we here for but to express our opinions on all questions coming before this house? And the man is a coward and a miserable driveller, unfit for his position as a representative, who shrinks from expressing his conscientious opinion on any question, who is frightened by the clamour of noisy politicians outside, or who is crushed under the weight of the mercantile influence which is arrayed against this question, and dares not express his opinion.

Every man who has anything to lose by the curtailed expenditure of our local government and our local legislature, all the host of official vampires and small fry of newspapers and reporters are dead against it, and so are all those whose interests as merchants will, as they fear, be affected, or whose trade will be turned into new channels, or whose hatchets will be better ground now. But on the other hand, will anyone believe that the six dollars a day for our delegates and other leading gentlemen is sufficient inducement or bribe for them to sell their country?

— *House of Assembly, January 27, 1865*

Ambrose Shea: We are here rival parties, one having possession of the government whose chief aim was to keep themselves in office, and who made every public question subordinate to this

"The man is a coward and a miserable driveller, unfit for his position as a representative, who shrinks from expressing his conscientious opinion on any question."

object. On the other hand is an opposition intent on displacing the government, and equally with their opponents discarding all measures that come into conflict with the main design. Some will tell you that better things and sounder legislation may be looked for when better men obtain seats in the assembly. But it is idle to suppose that any possible change of personnel will lead to any marked difference in result where the other conditions and circumstances remain unaltered.

We have here a signal illustration of the value of our "independent" legislation; nor are we very different in this respect from some of our neighbouring provinces. And it is, therefore, no wonder that the conviction should be forcing itself on the minds of prominent public men in these colonies, that for the higher purposes of legislation the present constitutions are not equal to the task.

— House of Assembly, February 2, 1865

"Self-government was the best system we could have, but it would not make up for short fisheries and a starving population."

E.D. Shea: Self-government was the best system we could have, but it would not make up for short fisheries and a starving population. We would still have self-government on a larger scale, for we were to have a voice in the general government and legislature of the union in proportion to our population, while our local government for merely local affairs was to be as much our own as now.

— House of Assembly, February 6, 1865

John Kavanagh: The British government had, in their wisdom, conferred upon us a free constitution, fully satisfied that we were able to manage our own affairs. Were we, then, going to give up that great boon? He (Mr. Kavanagh) said no. Let our hearts' blood flow to preserve our free constitution under the British flag.

— House of Assembly, February 28, 1865

George Hogsett: They had fought for responsible government, which meant self-government, and is it because they found a little difficulty in working it out and looked more after their own interests than after those of the country [that] that institution, which was the boast of every British subject, and which made the British people what they are, was to be given up and handed over to the Canadians? It may be that the country had not derived such great advantage from responsible government as was expected, but would any intelligent man be content to give it up and go back to the days of that government which was responsible only to impe-

rial authorities? There was no nation nor no race of men without its difficulties, but were they on that account to take their hats in their hands and go and beg of any other country to take them under their protection?

He was not afraid to say that his mind had undergone various changes on this subject. He as well as others might have been caught with the glare and glitter of the statement that they were about to become part of a great nation. But were they to form part of a great nation? He (Mr. Hogsett) was inclined to think so once, but when he found that the imperial government interfered with the action of the parliament of the dominion he concluded that the imperial government had its paw on them as well as on the smallest of its colonies.

Though we were told that the dominion would be ruled over by a prince of the blood,* and that it would have the control of its own affairs, it is today as much in leading strings as it was twenty years ago. If Newfoundland, then, were to become a part of the dominion, it would be doubly subservient, not only to the imperial interests but also to the veto of the dominion itself.

Robert Pinsent: We had been told that the Canadians would have complete control over our properties, our liberties, and our lives. Now honourable members must recollect that Confederation once accomplished, we shall all become Canadians, and Canada cannot injure us without an equal, nay a larger amount of injury to herself. What have we to dread with regard to our property? A law to affect us must necessarily affect the other provinces, and was it to be supposed that they would enterprise any suicidal policy, that they would legislate to the injury of their property, which is so infinitely superior to ours? How were our liberties, then, to be affected?

Let us see first what we understand by the expression. The culmination of our liberties appeared to be the power of returning a certain number of representatives to this assembly. This consummation of liberty was certainly not a subject for any great congratulation; and when honourable gentlemen opposite considered that the people had returned to office men so unworthy as the present ministry, they surely must consider the liberty as of very small amount. How, then, were our liberties to be affected? We should still continue to return representatives,

---

* *A member of the British royal family.*

and though they would be fewer in number, if they had within them any sentiments of pride, they would rejoice in having a voice in the large and extensive affairs of the dominion. Our liberties would, in fact, be vastly extended, and we should move in a grander, wider, and nobler sphere.

But how were our lives to be affected? Were the honourable gentlemen going to resurrect the bugbear of the bleaching bones? We should live under equal laws, and no man would be decapitated in Newfoundland for a crime which was not so punishable in other parts of the dominion. But we were threatened that if war with America should arise, our people would be carried away to fight. The prospect of such a war was very remote. He believed it would never be. But if it should take place, or any similar catastrophe, were we not in as much peril as if we were part of the dominion, while less capable of defence? The day has gone by when the public placed faith in such spurious alarms, or were to be frightened by them, and when they hear this and such like arguments addressed to them, and when they hear questions of the highest gravity made the opportunity for attack and recrimination, he believed they suspected the lot of them, and regarded the executive and the opposition as engaged in nothing but a fight for office.

— *House of Assembly, February 11, 1869*

F.B.T. Carter: The constitution was composed of those three estates to which they were already so well accustomed – the monarch, the Senate, and the House of Commons, elected by the people; with that principle there was no disposition to interfere. Here we have responsible government — in fact we have tried almost all sorts of government. We had a governor and council, [an] irresponsible government, and now a responsible government. Responsible government was considered by some as an essential principle to all states having a representative system, whilst others considered it as beneficial only to those states whose population and interests were large. He (the Honourable Attorney General [Carter]) thought it was difficult to conceive the idea of representation without responsibility. That was preserved in this constitution. He had stated four years ago that he believed the conferring of these constitutions to be like the establishment of normal schools to educate those colonies for an enlarged sphere of political action, and now here were his anticipations realized in this union.

"Every possible precaution for the preservation of their lives, their properties, and their liberties had been taken. Every principle of the British Constitution, which tends towards the preservation of these [principles], was to be found in their new constitution."

Every possible precaution for the preservation of their lives, their properties, and their liberties had been taken. Every principle of the British Constitution, which tends towards the preservation of these [principles], was to be found in their new constitution. If it be intended to form a semi-nationality, it will be necessary to have a central authority with all the attributes of power free of conflict with local authority. That had been a matter of very grave consideration, and was attained by the resolutions adopted in Quebec and [in] the British North America Act.

It was proposed that there should be a Senate which would in the union take the place of the House of Lords — the senators would be nominated by the crown and appointed for life — and would be composed of seventy-two members. There had been much debate as to whether the body should be elective or nominative, but the majority was in favour of nomination, and that course appeared to have met with approval in England, as tending better to prevent the happening of a deadlock than would two representative bodies.

— *House of Assembly, February 23, 1869*

Henry Renouf: We are not able to legislate for ourselves, and thus we are wanted to enter the union and send eight men to the dominion to do there what thirty cannot here accomplish. Palpable absurdity! Was it because the present government failed that other governments would fail also, and that there was no recourse for us but union? He (Mr. Renouf) was for giving our own constitution another trial and applying the principles of reduction to our civil expenditure.

— *House of Assembly, February 24, 1869*

Stephen Rendell: Honourable members on each side of the house had expressed their ideas on the matter from the particular points at which they viewed it. The legal gentlemen, as was natural, had regarded it in a somewhat legal point of view. For instance, they had taken up the constitution of the new dominion and compared it with that of the United States and with our own system of responsible government. That was of course very proper, and he (Mr. Rendell) had no doubt that it was very interesting to the public to have the constitution fully explained.

The men of the Old Country, and especially of the old school, fancied that no form of government was as good as the monarchical form. And though that was an idea which had not the same

hold on men's minds on this side of the Atlantic, yet it was certain that all English-speaking people, whatever the nature of the constitution under which they lived, loved law and order, so that he did not think the mere form of the constitution made very much difference. Whatever the form, all will enjoy equal rights and privileges, and that civil and religious liberty which all so highly prize, so that the constitutional view of the matter, though highly interesting and well worthy of inquiry, he did not think very material or one that was much thought of by the general public.

He looked at the matter in a commercial point of view, and the influence which it would have on the general prosperity of the country, and he believed that the time would come when the public generally would consider such a change necessary, even admitting that some were not hesitating to give it their adhesion.

As regarded the present system of responsible government, he considered it to be too expensive for this colony. Expenses went on increasing until the load had become too heavy, and he saw no chance of change except in the radical change of connection with the new dominion. After that is accomplished it will then behoove all to look well for the best and most economical system of government for the management of our local affairs.

"Responsible government worn out? No. Self-government never wore itself out in any country. It required only that the men who conducted the machinery should be earnest, active, energetic working men."

Hogsett: Who wore out responsible government? Did it wear out in the other colonies? Those who [argue that it is worn out] are incapable of conducting the government, and because such is the case, therefore Newfoundland must join the dominion. Responsible government worn out? No. Self-government never wore itself out in any country. It required only that the men who conducted the machinery should be earnest, active, energetic working men. Self-government requires active and energetic men. Are the government so constituted? [No.]

Renouf: He did not believe the conclusion of the honourable member for Trinity [Stephen Rendell] that responsible government had worn itself out in this colony. It was in full blast in all the neighbouring colonies, and its principles were no more worn out here than they were there. He agreed with the honourable and learned member, Mr. Hogsett, who said that it was not because the present government was incompetent to work it [that] none others could. Did not the honourable and learned Attorney General [Frederick Carter] say that the leading principle of the union would be responsible government? He (Mr.

Renouf) was not surprised to hear such views expressed by some who were always opposed to anything that would give to the people independence and their rights, and could we recollect how, in the struggle for responsible government, they endeavoured to raise a feeling against it. The country had made rapid progress under responsible government . . . responsible government had not worn itself out. It was not the principle, not the measures, but the men, that were incompetent.

— House of Assembly, February 25, 1869

PRINCE EDWARD ISLAND

Edward Palmer: We know that as long as we have a separate government we can have the remedy for all our grievances in our own hands, and perhaps it can be much more easily and effectually applied. I do not think it follows that because we are small we would be better to be united to the neighbouring colonies. The Isle of Man is a very small dependency, and though it is close to Great Britain, yet it maintains a separate government to this day, and I do not think it is any worse for remaining so.

— Legislative Council, April 30, 1864

Francis Kelly: We have, sir, sovereign legislative powers, whereby we can make our own laws and direct the application of our own monies among our own people at our own pleasure, and I hope the day is far distant when this, our parliament, shall be converted into a barracks or a bank or ourselves deprived of the constitutional privileges which we have so long enjoyed under the guarantee of the imperial government.

— House of Assembly, March 30, 1865

Alexander Anderson: As far as I can see, there is no chance of gaining anything, but there are many chances to lose. I think the offer is something like this: if we will give up one-half of our revenue to the Canadians, and allow them to tax us as much as they please, they would then take charge of us. We fought hard and contended long for responsible government, and are we now going to give up our constitution and say we are not able to govern ourselves? I do not think that any man or any body of men in Canada can know the wishes or wants of the people of this island as well as we do ourselves.

— Legislative Council, April 1, 1865

George Coles: We were told that, as it was the positive desire of the home government that we should agree to confederate, we would be looked upon as rebels if we did not. No fear of that. So long . . . as Great Britain shall allow us to remain in our present independent position, there will be no fear of our assuming towards her anything like a disloyal or rebellious attitude; and a manifestation of our sacred regard for the priceless boon of self-government, which she has conferred upon us, and our determination to retain it unimpaired, as long as we shall be able to do so, will never be looked upon by her as a proof of disaffection, but rather as an undeniable evidence of our most just and grateful appreciation of that inestimable blessing.

What drove Canada into rebellion was the home government's refusal to grant her responsible or self-government; and what had brought her back to loyalty and affection was the conferring upon her, under a free representative constitution, the full control and management of her own revenue and affairs. Great Britain well knew that the boon of responsible or self-government was the greatest which she could confer upon any of her dependent colonies, and that which bound them most strongly in loyalty and affection to her; and, as respected any colony or dependency upon which she had conferred that privilege, as long as it continued true in its allegiance to her and obedient to the laws and desired to retain that form of government in all its independent integrity, so long, he firmly believed, would she consider it to be beyond the constitutional stretch, even of her imperial power, either to suspend or withdraw that form of government from such colony or dependency or even to impair it.

We had not obtained that form of government by rebellion, but by an exercise of constitutional means; and, both on account of the mode by which we had obtained it, and the happy manner in which . . . we had carried its privileges into practice, we were entitled to the especial consideration of the home government; and, he doubted not, we would receive it. If we went into the proposed union, we would be at the mercy of those who do not think as we do on the subject of parliamentary representation. We have universal manhood suffrage and an elective legislative council; but they have neither.

— House of Assembly, May 8, 1866

Frederick Brecken: It was said by some that were we to enter Confederation we would lose the glorious privilege of self-

"It was said by some that were we to enter Confederation we would lose the glorious privilege of self-government. Well, that was a very taking argument . . . Here also we could worship God as we pleased; but if we became a part of the dominion, would our freedom in this respect be tampered with? The liberty of the press was another of those glorious privileges of which we boasted in this colony, but was the press less free in Canada? Would the right of trial by jury be taken from us were we in the dominion?"

government. Well, that was a very taking argument. Self-government was a great blessing, and we were undoubtedly about as free as any part of the world. Greater freedom existed here than even in the United States, as was evidenced by the difficulty there a short time ago between President Johnson and Congress.* Here there could be no deadlock of that kind, for as soon as this house passed a vote of want of confidence in the government, the administration was overthrown.

Here also we could worship God as we pleased; but if we became a part of the dominion, would our freedom in this respect be tampered with? The liberty of the press was another of those glorious privileges of which we boasted in this colony, but was the press less free in Canada? Would the right of trial by jury be taken from us were we in the dominion? Had the people there not the same sun to shine upon them, the same dews to moisten them, and the same showers to water their fields as we had on this island?

Then why all this outcry about losing our self-government, when the whole question between us and Canada resolved itself into one of money? In considering the subject of Confederation, there was no occasion to soar to the regions of political fancy; just look at our various public officers, what a miserable pittance they received. Yes, it was money we needed, so let the government go to work and make up their bill, and tell Canada what they wanted. At a recent public meeting in this city, he had heard gentlemen in high-sounding strains ask their auditors whether they would sell their rights for money. Such language could only be addressed to the passions of the people, for it must be evident to every unprejudiced mind that not one feather would be plucked from the eagle of our liberty by uniting with the dominion.

— *House of Assembly, March 8, 1870*

Andrew McDonald: We have a system of responsible government by which the voice of the people is expressed through their representatives, and we can legislate, not only upon all subjects which would be considered local after the change would be made, but upon those which would be legislated upon by the general government. And while the people have a direct influence through their representatives, and can consult them almost daily, legislation is more likely to be such as will meet the wishes of the people, than when their representatives would be sent to a distant

---

* *A reference to the impeachment of President Andrew Johnson in 1868.*

parliament, of which they would form but a very small part, and where their influence would be very small to carry into effect any measure that they might consider would be a benefit to their constituents, for the views of their constituents might be opposed to the views of the people of the other provinces of the dominion.

— *Legislative Council, April 12, 1870*

William Lord: We enjoy the privileges of responsible government which we fought hard for. Many of the leading men of the day were opposed to it. They thought it would be granting too much power to the people, but I am glad that they are disappointed, and that now when there is an opportunity afforded of changing the constitution of the colony they are opposed to any change.

— *Legislative Council, April 13, 1870*

RED RIVER

Louis Riel: It would be unjust to allow the governor* . . . to override the wishes of the people; and, as he [Riel] attached great importance to the majority of the people triumphing in this country, we should be careful to do nothing which would endanger this. It was true that hitherto we had been governed by English law. But England had chosen to neglect us for one or two

---

* Red River's discussion of the role of colonial governor is confusing at first reading. The delegates to the Fort Garry constitutional convention are not thinking of the governor as the kind of honorific figurehead that governors had become elsewhere in British North America after the introduction of responsible government. They describe a powerful individual, appointed by Ottawa, who will lead and direct the political business of the colony. In short, they are not asking for responsible government. The question is: Why not? James Ross explains: The delegates assume that Red River will enter Confederation as a territory rather than as a province. Red River will have to serve a political apprenticeship. Thus they first prescribe the kind of powerful governor they believe appropriate for a territory, and then they find themselves worrying about how they are going to rein him in, and how they are going to assert the power of the people over government. Their best suggestion at this stage of their deliberations is that a two-thirds vote in the popular legislature should override the governor's veto. But by the end of the constitutional debates they have given up the idea of territorial status. The last version of the "bill of rights" demands that Manitoba enter Confederation as a province, with all the rights and privileges of responsible parliamentary government. — JA

centuries back, and he did not suppose we were under any very great obligation to respect her laws. He argued very strongly for the right to curb the governor by the two-thirds vote.*

W.B. O'Donoghue: I do not believe that the constituents of any member here would be opposed to this article. The voice of the people, I believe, will find it absolutely necessary to have a bill like this passed. No matter who may come as governor, he will not be so likely to know and respect the wishes of the people as those representatives.

Judge John Black: No doubt the principle involved in this article is one inconsistent with the principles of the British Constitution — or rather with what we have to look to more immediately, the principles of the Confederation into which we propose to be admitted. We profess a desire — and I believe you have a sincere desire — to be admitted into the Confederation on just and equitable principles. Having that desire, it seems reasonable that we should endeavour to induce nothing in the list [Red River's list of terms for admission] likely to be so objectionable in the eyes of Canada as to endanger our chance of being admitted into Confederation.

With regard to the veto of the governor, it does look rather a formidable power. But we must not forget that this power is very seldom exercised by the governor alone. (Hear, hear.) Again, the legitimate object, as I understand it, of this veto power is not to enable the governor to carry out, arbitrarily, any caprice of his own. Its object is twofold: in the first place, to prevent precipitate legislation; and in the next place, in order that the lieutenant governor — who is supposed to take a more comprehensive view of the relations of the colony at the head of which he stands than the colonists themselves, and is expected to see things which may not appear immediately to the local legislature — imperial interests, for instance — may check us if he sees that we are doing anything likely to give us trouble, or likely to give trouble to our brother colonists. Now, is it not of some consequence — great consequence indeed — that he should be in such a position as to enable him to come forward and say, stop, stop and think!†

This proposal would have been the more controversial because it was taken from the constitution of the United States. — PR

† Black is alluding to the constitutional theory then current, which held that

If we propose to introduce into the constitution of our legislature a principle plainly inconsistent with the constitution of the Confederation, this is, let me tell you, the danger that will arise; the danger will be that Canada will come to the conclusion that our minds are set upon having principles applied to the government of this country which are inconsistent with those applied to any other member of the Confederation, principles of so vital a character that, if we insist upon them, Canada may be obliged to say that she cannot enter into the compact.

This is, I believe, a great era in the history of this country; and if we can get incorporated into the dominion, on conditions which we believe Canada is willing to agree to, this country will be greatly the gainer; for what is the position in which we now stand? That of deriving at once the benefits of responsible government for the country — a boon obtained in other countries only after years — I may say generations — of toil and trouble, and the benefits also of Confederation. This we have offered to us now . . .

Not only is there held up before us the prospect of responsible government, but responsible government under conditions more favourable than have been given to any colony which I can remember. (Cheers.) We are offered responsible government, with the benefit of all the strength, all the influence, all the power and dignity of that great Confederation which, even now, looms large in the eyes of the world. We are not to be left, as most other colonies have been left, to work out our destiny under responsible government. We are not to be left without a helping hand. We are not to be left single-handed to encounter all these difficulties and dangers which belong to the time of youth, whether we regard communities or individuals. But we are to be started upon this splendid career with the shield of this great Confederation over us, with the hand of the dominion stretched above our heads, and practically signifying to all the world: "That people is under the protection of the dominion; the dominion is

---

the governor, as representative of the sovereign, had the power not to take any positive action but merely — by his veto — to prevent wrong being done. (See William Blackstone, Commentaries on the Laws of England (1st ed., 1765), vol. 1, 150). By the late nineteenth century the veto power had practically withered away. As Walter Bagehot phrased it, the powers of the sovereign boiled down to three things: "the right to be consulted, the right to encourage, the right to warn." (The English Constitution [1st published 1867]; Brighton and Portland: Sussex Academic Press, 1997, 43). — IG

under the protection of the queen of England. You cannot rough them with impunity. *They* stand as long as *we* stand, and never, till *we* fall, shall *they* be allowed to fall." (Cheers.)

Are these considerations not grave and important? Are these considerations not valuable? And ought we not to be careful lest we put forward anything so unreasonable as to deter Canada from entering into a compact which would place us in possession of such great advantages — advantages which would open up to us such prospects — which would give us such prosperity — and elevate this country, as it were with one lift, to a point of importance which, unless we enter into this Confederation, we must struggle long before we can reach? (Cheers.)

"The English constitution . . . is, as I understand it, one which can be set aside or modified according to circumstances. It is not a written constitution, which requires a special act to do away with or amend any part of it. "

O'Donoghue: The English constitution, in the colonies at least, is, as I understand it, one which can be set aside or modified according to circumstances. It is not a written constitution, which requires a special act to do away with or amend any part of it. The English constitution is not such as to suit every one of her colonies. It is modified to suit circumstances. And are we to be debarred from doing as other colonies have done? Again, it has been urged that the governor will have imperial interests at heart in an especial manner, and therefore ought to have more power than is given to him by this article. To that I answer: imperial interests are looked after by the general government. The action of the local legislature is confined to local affairs.

James Ross: This is a question on which two sides might very fairly be taken. A good deal might be said for and against it. The principle on which the British law is based is that there should be three branches of the legislature,* and the consent of all three is necessary in order that a law pass. Of course, when any one of the three branches withholds concurrence, it proves fatal. I would say that while I admit at the outset that it is unconstitutional that a two-thirds vote should override the veto of the governor, because it is unrecognized by the constitution of England or the

---

* The three branches were the monarch (or in this case the governor), the Lords (or upper house or Senate), and the Commons. Ross was strictly correct that the two houses did not possess the right to override the monarch's veto. What he did not say was that by the 1860s this veto was hardly ever used. In the United States, by contrast, the president's veto was real, but could be overridden by a two-thirds vote of both houses of Congress. — IG

colonies, I think on consideration we can find sufficient reasons for taking the position of asking for it.

I think it possible that though unprecedented in England or the other colonies, this principle is admissible here; and for my part I think that in itself it is desirable. I like the principle of having a check on the governor. Whenever the time comes that two-thirds of the people vote against the governor, there is a fair presumption that the views of the majority of the people are against the views of the executive of the country. (Cheers.) It is fair to presume that the views of a majority of the representatives would be favourable to the benefit of the country. (Cheers.) There is just this objection to the principle, that it is without precedent in England or the colonies. But it is not a vital principle; and, under our peculiar circumstances, I do not think Canada would be opposed to conceding it. Then we only ask this, mark you, while we are a territory. Perhaps when we become a province, reasons might come up why it should be otherwise.

Another thing to be considered is that the dominion has a right to review the acts of the local legislature, and they can veto any inconsistent measure. I am not at all of the opinion that we are going to lose our union with Confederation in this question, and for that reason I would not press the opposition to it. (Cheers.)

— *Convention at Fort Garry, English and French*
Delegates in Council, January 31, 1870

Riel: Gentlemen, we have been assembled in this chamber on several occasions, having been sent here by the people to deliberate on the political state of the country and to adopt such measures as would secure the prosperity of the present and future generations . . . We have worked here in the past in anxiety and fear. But we have worked conscientiously . . . One result of our labours is that the people generally now have, for the first time in the history of this land, a voice in the direction of public affairs. They have here a full representation. Herein, we may congratulate ourselves that our work has been a good one . . .

At present, we are now, perhaps, in a position to proceed to business. But at the same time we have arrived at that stage when there is some public security. (Cheers.) Let us, then, see to it that the public are no more allowed to rush together, on one side or the other,* in such a manner as they have gathered of late. Let us

---

* *Riel is uneasy about political dissent. The kind of consensus he is recom-*

be friends — let our friendship be hearty and sincere. (Cheers.) On many occasions, since last fall, I have heard professions of friendship in this chamber; and I must say I was sorry to hear those professions, for I knew they were — as they afterwards proved to be — insincere. There was too much of fear and estrangement to allow of that friendship being hearty. But now that we have come together once more, I believe we are actuated by such feelings as will lead to a thorough union. (Cheers.)

— *Rupert's Land, Legislative Assembly*
[of the provisional government], March 9, 1870

CANADA

"When I speak of representation by population, the house will of course understand that universal suffrage is not in any way sanctioned, or admitted by these resolutions, as the basis on which the constitution of the popular branch should rest."

John A. Macdonald: The legislature of British North America will be composed of King, Lords, and Commons. The legislative council will stand in the same relation to the lower house as the House of Lords to the House of Commons in England, having the same power of initiating all matters of legislation, except the granting of money. As regards the lower house, it may not appear to matter much whether it is called the house of commons or house of assembly. It will bear whatever name the parliament of England may choose to give it, but the "House of Commons" is that name we should prefer, as showing that it represents the commons of Canada, in the same way that the English House of Commons represents the commons of England, with the same privileges, the same parliamentary usage, and the same parliamentary authority. In settling the constitution of the lower house, that which peculiarly represents the people, it was agreed that the principle of representation based on population should be adopted, and the mode of applying that principle is fully developed in these resolutions. When I speak of representation by population, the house will of course understand that universal suffrage is not in any way sanctioned,* or admitted by these reso-

---

mending does not fit well with the freedom to oppose the governing party that is traditionally one of the glories of parliamentary responsible government. — JA

* Macdonald is giving his assurance that the house need not fear the spectre of mob rule, which is what many informed people at the time would have expected from universal suffrage in a democratic system. We tend now to believe that democracy and liberalism go together, but his comment reminds us that an important strand of thought in the nineteenth century thought of

John A. Macdonald

lutions, as the basis on which the constitution of the popular branch should rest . . .

We have introduced all those provisions which are necessary in order to [allow] the full working out of the British Constitution in these provinces. We provide that there shall be no money votes,* unless those votes are introduced in the popular branch of the legislature on the authority of the responsible advisers of the crown — those with whom the responsibility rests of equalizing revenue and expenditure — that there can be no expenditure or authorization of expenditure by address or in any other way unless initiated by the crown on the advice of its responsible advisers. (Hear, Hear.)

— Legislative Assembly, February 6, 1865

George-Étienne Cartier: He was opposed, he might as well state most distinctly, to the democratic system which obtained in the United States. In this country of British North America we should have a distinct form of government, the characteristic of which would be to possess the monarchical element. When we had Confederation secured, there was not the least doubt but that our government would be more respectable — that it would have more prestige, and command more respect from our neighbours. (Hear, hear.)

The great want under the American form† — the point they all admitted formed the great defect — was the absence of some

---

them as separate things, and understood that although at the time Canada did not have universal suffrage, it was a very liberal country among nations of the world. In this writer's opinion it was in many respects more liberal than today. — WDG

* Executive control of expenditure in the manner described here is a crucial incident of responsible government. Its purpose is to subject budgetary appropriations to an overall plan and limit anarchic competition among elected legislators for expenditures to benefit their own districts, a blight that had plagued the budgetary process in the colonies before responsible government and still does in the United States. Of course, executive control of expenditure strengthens the government politically. — PR

† Cartier is wrestling with the then accepted fact — somewhat forgotten today — that in its majoritarian aspect, democracy is a theory of power distribution, and not a theory of freedom or unity. Many likely saw it as a solemn celebration of divisiveness every four or five years. A president under the American system will be lucky to speak for half the electorate, and then

SIR GEORGE-ÉTIENNE
CARTIER
(1814–1873), lawyer,
businessman, railway
promoter, and
modernizer of the
Lower Canadian legal
system. Cartier fought
bravely in 1837 at Saint-
Denis, the sole Patriote
victory. In the 1840s he
became the right-hand
man of Louis-Hippolyte
LaFontaine in the
struggle for responsible
government. He served
as co-premier with
John A. Macdonald
from 1857 to 1862 and
set Confederation in
motion in 1864 by
accepting George
Brown's proposal to
federalize the province.
In 1870 he played a
leading role in securing
the Red River Colony's
accession to Canada on
equitable terms.

respectable executive element. How was the head of the United States government chosen? Candidates came forward, and of course each one was abused and vilified as corrupt, ignorant, incapable, and unworthy by the opposite party. One of them attained the presidential chair; but even while in that position he was not respected by those who had opposed his election, and who tried to make him appear the most corrupt and contemptible being in creation. Such a system could not produce an executive head who would command respect. Under the British system, ministers might be abused and assailed; but that abuse never reaches the sovereign.*

— *Legislative Assembly, February 7, 1865*

Joseph Perrault: During the past twenty-five years we have progressed politically in a manner unprecedented in colonial history; and Canada has furnished a magnificent instance of the good result of responsible government in an English colony, notwithstanding diversity of races and religions. In 1840 we had just terminated a glorious struggle, during which, unfortunately, many lives had been lost — a struggle undertaken in order to secure responsible government, which had, up to that time, been refused, and which was then accorded us as the reward of the struggle. At that period Lower Canada was united as one man; she had forwarded to England petitions, bearing 60,000 signatures, asking for responsible government.

---

only the half who actually bother to go to the polls. The rest are unrepresented and may vividly sense a political vacuum at the top. In contrast, in Canada, although the prime minister represents only the government, the monarch represents the people as a whole. Cartier was certainly aware that in the absence of a monarchical system or principle, democracy can turn demagogic, and in a search for the missing unity may wallow in mystical theories of "the people" that make the whole system vulnerable to tyranny, as had occurred under the Jacobins in France who manipulated Rousseau's theory of the General Will for their own radical purposes. — WDG

* Cartier echoes the ancient constitutional principle that "the king can do no wrong." When there is wrongdoing, it must be the fault of the king's "evil" counsellors. — IG

Colonial discussions of responsible government tend to stress its significance in facilitating local self-government, but as first developed in Britain its chief importance was to divert criticism of public policy from the sovereign himself towards his responsible ministers. — PR

> *"In 1840 we had just terminated a glorious struggle, during which, unfortunately, many lives had been lost — a struggle undertaken in order to secure responsible government, which had, up to that time, been refused, and which was then accorded us as the reward of the struggle."*

We then had in our ranks men who did not shrink from the struggle, men accustomed to resist oppression, men who had grown up in the midst of a strife with an arrogant minority, which sought to overrule the majority; and these were the great men who secured the triumph of our nationality,* and upheld the rights of Lower Canada, by securing responsible government at the same time that the union was forced upon us. Let us now see the results of their labours. Is it true that we have progressed both socially and materially since that period? Anyone who reflects on what Canada was in 1840, and what it is in 1865, cannot but admit that we have progressed in a degree almost unprecedented in the history of the prosperity of nations; that we have immensely extended our territory, by clearing away the forest; that our population has increased in a wonderful manner, that the population is prosperous and contented.

— *Legislative Assembly, March 3, 1865*

> *"The tone of feeling among the prominent men of the country has rather deteriorated than improved, since the introduction of responsible government."*

Arthur Rankin: Though the country has become more important, though our population has increased, and our prosperity advanced, in perhaps as rapid a degree as any reasonable person could have expected, there are still some respects in which we have not advanced, but rather retrograded than otherwise. I mean that the tone of feeling among the prominent men of the country has rather deteriorated than improved, since the introduction of responsible government. I, sir, am old-fashioned enough to believe that although there may have been some objections to the mode of government which existed prior to the union, there was a higher tone among our public men in those days than has prevailed for some years past. Still, no doubt there was much cause of complaint on the part of those who originated the agitation, which resulted in the rebellion of 1837. And speaking now in the light of the experience, many of us would probably be prepared to admit those gentlemen who took a prominent part in bringing about that rebellion, and whom we then considered it a duty to put down, were in reality true benefactors of the country. (Hear, hear.)

The result has proved that they differed only from those who thought it their duty to oppose them in that they were in advance of the men and the sentiment of that day. They foresaw, indeed, earlier than their neighbours, that the state of things which then

---

* *Speaking in French, Perrault praises responsible government for its efficacy in securing French-Canadian political power within United Canada. — PR*

existed could not long continue — they appreciated grievances sooner than others. (Hear, hear.)

— *Legislative Assembly, March 10, 1865*

NEW BRUNSWICK

John Robinson: Call it by what name you will, the conclusion is evident that Canada would be the preponderating power, and her influence would rule the rest, and the cabinet would really be no more responsible to us than the colonial secretary. I never could consent to put this province under the foot of Canada, which would be the result of Confederation, no matter what the form of the executive might be, whether regency or a governor general. Nor am I disposed to subject the province to the governorship of such men as we have lately had travelling through this country from Canada, and endeavouring to induce people to go in for Confederation.

— *Legislative Council, May 27, 1865*

Amos Botsford: Admitting that we have all those constitutional privileges under the existence of British institutions which a free people ought to possess, the question presents itself to the thinking mind from our local position, from the extent of our population, and our area of country, surrounded as we are and circumscribed in narrow limits by other colonies: Are we in as favourable a position to derive all the legitimate advantages of those institutions which we would enjoy was there a larger field of operation? I think a little candid thought must bring the conviction home to every mind that, admitting the advantages and beauty of our form of government, past experience has proved that, in a province of such limited population as ours, there is not room properly to develop and work out the system of responsible departmental government.

Then look at the anomalous position of other colonies. Prince Edward Island, with a population of only 75,000, not as much as that of a second-class city of the United States, or of Montreal, in Canada; with a revenue of $65,000, she has all the paraphernalia and machinery of government calculated and adapted for millions of people, and how can responsible government be carried on in that small colony, or even in New Brunswick with 250,000 inhabitants, only equal to the population of a third-class city in the Old World? Here, some little paltry influences have frequently inter-

fered to prevent the proper working of institutions eminently calculated to benefit the whole people, and we have sufficiently
proved that it is impossible for a small representative branch to
work out effectively those principles of self-government which
have been conceded to us. Does it not often occur that a small
number of men, in opposition, of no decided political views, may
influence and thwart the desires of those in power, so as to defeat
the object of good government, the general benefit of the whole
people — a few individuals, where parties are so evenly balanced
as they must be in small legislatures, knowing that they are thus
masters of the position, will and must have all they want, or their
constituents want, or they will desert their party. We know such a
state of things often exists, and are forced to the conclusion that
our institutions, however desirable they are in principle, are not
adapted for a small colony.

This brings us, then, to a point from which we perceive the
necessity for some change, and from the documents before us I
am satisfied that the government of the day believe a change necessary, and the paragraph in the speech just read by His Honour,
the chairman, is an acknowledgement that we are not now in a
position to take advantage of passing opportunities to improve
our position, and that the government is forced to the conclusion
that the provinces cannot remain as they are. How indeed, I may
ask, can anyone duly considering our position, and being influenced by any ambition for the future prosperity of this country,
fail to arrive at the same conclusion?

— Legislative Council, April 4, 1866

John Mercer Johnson: It is provided in our institutions that
those who take office have both executive and legislative duties to
perform. The legislature of the country must be under their
direction, and they must have such a majority in both branches as
to be able to carry forward those measures they think will be for
the interest of the country, and to resist those measures which
they think will be prejudicial to it. They take the responsibility
and they must control the legislature of the country, and if placed
in a position in which they cannot control it they must resign
their seats. It is not necessary that they should resign if defeated
upon a question of minor importance, because it frequently happens that a government is defeated and still has a majority. If they
then resign the minority has to rule.

— House of Assembly, July 2, 1866

*J.S. Helmcken and Robert Carrall of the British Columbia Legislative Council at
Niagara Falls in 1870. Helmcken and Carrall, along with Joseph Trutch, were in
Ontario to negotiate the terms of British Columbia's admission to the dominion.*

Chapter Three

PARLIAMENTARY
GOVERNMENT
AND THE
UPPER HOUSE

———————

S HOULD THE SENATE (in the pre-Confederation period usually called the Legislative Council) be appointive or elective? Surprisingly, the Conservatives are often willing to accept an elective one while the Liberals are divided. Some Liberals object to the very idea of appointed legislators, just as one would expect; but others insist that exactly because an elective Legislative Council would have more legitimacy with the people than an appointive one, it would detract from the powers of the people's true legislative house, the House of Commons (House of Assembly). An elective Senate would jeopardize that prized principle of the parliamentary system, responsible government. To favour an appointed Senate was not necessarily proof of political backwardness in the pre-Confederation period!

Some of the provinces had begun to experiment with elective upper chambers. Speakers in Prince Edward Island are clearly proud of their elective Legislative Council. The Province of Canada at this time has also introduced an elective Legislative Council, but the surviving appointed members retain their seats.

The Canadian Senate has always had two quite distinct functions. As the upper house in a parliamentary democracy, it is expected to act as a check on the House of Commons. It is this function that the speakers below address. But the Senate also represents the provinces, or rather, the regions, in the federal government. In the Quebec Resolutions the new nation is divided

into three regions: Upper Canada (later Ontario), Lower Canada (Quebec), and the Atlantic region (Nova Scotia, New Brunswick, Prince Edward Island, and Newfoundland). The first two are each allotted twenty-four seats in the federal upper house. The Atlantic region is given twenty-eight; ten each for New Brunswick and Nova Scotia, and four each for Prince Edward Island and Newfoundland. Speakers take up this function of the Senate in Part Four.

CANADA

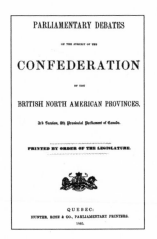

PARLIAMENTARY DEBATES

ON THE SUBJECT OF THE

CONFEDERATION

OF THE

BRITISH NORTH AMERICAN PROVINCES,

3rd Session, 8th Provincial Parliament of Canada.

PRINTED BY ORDER OF THE LEGISLATURE.

QUEBEC:
HUNTER, ROSE & CO., PARLIAMENTARY PRINTERS.
1865.

John A. Macdonald: As may be well conceived, great difference of opinion at first existed as to the constitution of the Legislative Council. In Canada the elective principle prevailed; in the lower provinces, with the exception of Prince Edward Island, the nominative principle was the rule. We found a general disinclination on the part of the lower provinces to adopt the elective principle; indeed, I do not think there was a dissenting voice in the conference against the adoption of the nominative principle, except from Prince Edward Island. The delegates from New Brunswick, Nova Scotia, and Newfoundland, as one man, were in favour of nomination by the crown. And nomination by the crown is of course the system which is most in accordance with the British Constitution. We resolved then that the constitution of the upper house should be in accordance with the British system as nearly as circumstances would allow. An hereditary upper house is impracticable in this young country. Here we have none of the elements for the formation of a landlord aristocracy — no men of large territorial positions — no class separated from the mass of the people. An hereditary body is altogether unsuited to our state of society and would soon dwindle into nothing. The only mode of adapting the English system to the upper house is by conferring the power of appointment on the crown (as the English peers are appointed), but that the appointments should be for life.

The arguments for an elective council are numerous and strong; and I ought to say so, as one of the administration responsible for introducing the elective principle* into Canada. (Hear, hear.) I hold that this principle has not been a failure in Canada;

By a provincial act of 1856, all future appointments to the Legislative Council were made elective. Upper and Lower Canada were each divided into twenty-four constituencies, each constituency electing one member every

but there were causes — which we did not take into consideration at the time — why it did not so fully succeed in Canada as we had expected. One great cause was the enormous extent of the constituencies and the immense labour which consequently devolved on those who sought the suffrages of the people for election to the council. For the same reason the expense — (laughter) — the legitimate expense was so enormous that men of standing in the country, eminently fitted for such a position, were prevented from coming forward. At first, I admit, men of the first standing did come forward, but we have seen that in every succeeding election in both Canadas there has been an increasing disinclination, on the part of men of standing and political experience and weight in the country, to become candidates; while, on the other hand, all the young men, the active politicians, those who have resolved to embrace the life of a statesman, have sought entrance to the House of Assembly. The nominative system in this country was to a great extent successful, before the introduction of responsible government. Then the Canadas were to a great extent crown colonies, and the upper branch of the legislature consisted of gentlemen chosen from among the chief judicial and ecclesiastical dignitaries, the heads of departments, and other men of the first position in the country. Those bodies commanded great respect from the character, standing, and weight of the individuals composing them, but they had little sympathy with the people or their representatives, and collisions with the lower house frequently occurred, especially in Lower Canada.

When responsible government was introduced, it became necessary for the governor of the day to have a body of advisers who had the confidence of the House of Assembly which could make or unmake ministers as it chose. The lower house in effect pointed out who should be nominated to the upper house; for the ministry, being dependent altogether on the lower branch of the legislature for support, selected members for the upper house from among their political friends at the dictation of the House of Assembly. The council was becoming less and less a substantial check on the legislation of the assembly; but under the system now proposed, such will not be the case. No ministry in Canada in future can do what they have done in Canada before — they cannot, with the view of carrying any measure or of strength-

---

eight years and elections occurring in a quarter of the constituencies every two years. The existing life members retained their seats. — PR

ening the party, attempt to overrule the independent opinion of the upper house by filling it with a number of its partisans and political supporters. The provision in the constitution, that the Legislative Council shall consist of a limited number of members — that each of the great sections shall appoint twenty-four members and no more — will prevent the upper house from being swamped from time to time by the ministry of the day, for the purpose of carrying out their own schemes or pleasing their partisans. The fact of the government being prevented from exceeding a limited number will preserve the independence of the upper house and make it, in reality, a separate and distinct chamber, having a legitimate and controlling influence in the legislation of the country.

The objection has been taken that in consequence of the crown being deprived of the right of unlimited appointment, there is a chance of a deadlock arising between the two branches of the legislature; a chance that the upper house, being altogether independent of the sovereign, of the lower house, and of the advisers of the crown, may act independently, and so independently as to produce a deadlock. I do not anticipate any such result. In the first place we know that in England it does not arise. There would be no use of an upper house if it did not exercise, when it thought proper, the right of opposing or amending or postponing the legislation of the lower house. It would be of no value whatever were it a mere chamber for registering the decrees of the lower house. It must be an independent house, having a free action of its own, for it is only valuable as being a regulating body, calmly considering the legislation initiated by the popular branch and preventing any hasty or ill-considered legislation which may come from that body, but it will never set itself in opposition against the deliberate and understood wishes of the people. Even the House of Lords, which as an hereditary body, is far more independent than one appointed for life in Canada can be, whenever it ascertains which is the calm, deliberate will of the people of England, it yields, and never in modern times has there been, in fact or act, any attempt to overrule the decisions of that house by the appointment of new peers, excepting, perhaps, once in the reign of Queen Anne.* It was true that in 1832 such an increase was threatened in consequence of the reiterated refusal

---

*In 1712 the Tory ministry prevailed on the queen to create a dozen peers with the intention that they should support the ministry in the peace negoti-

of the house of peers to pass the Reform Bill.* I have no doubt the threat would have been carried into effect, if necessary; but everyone, even the ministry who advised that step, admitted that it would be a revolutionary act, a breach of the constitution to do so, and it was because of the necessity of preventing the bloody revolution which hung over the land, if the Reform Bill had been longer refused to the people of England, that they consented to the bloodless revolution of overriding the independent opinion of the House of Lords on that question. (Hear, hear.)

Since that time it has never been attempted, and I am satisfied it will never be attempted again. Only a year or two ago the House of Lords rejected the Paper Duties Bill, and they acted quite constitutionally, according to the letter and, as many think, according to the spirit of the constitution in doing so. Yet when they found they had interfered with a subject which the people's house claimed as belonging of right to themselves, the very next session they abandoned their position, not because they were convinced they had done wrong, but because they had ascertained what was the deliberate voice of the representatives of the people on the subject.

In this country, we must remember that the gentlemen who will be selected for the Legislative Council stand on a very different footing from the peers of England. They have not like them any ancestral associations or position derived from history. They have not that direct influence on the people themselves, or on the popular branch of the legislature, which the peers of England exercise, from their great wealth, their vast territorial possessions, their numerous tenantry, and that prestige with which the exalted position of their class for centuries has invested them. (Hear, hear.) The members of our upper house will be like those of the lower, men of the people, and from the people. The

> "The members of our upper house will be like those of the lower, men of the people, and from the people."

---

ations at Utrecht, and in the rapidly approaching problem of the succession to the throne. — IG

* A long-debated measure of parliamentary reform that altered the franchise and the distribution of seats in order to make the system of parliamentary representation more uniform and more truly reflective of public opinion. Its enactment symbolized the final defeat of the political reaction that had dominated Britain since the outbreak of the French Revolution. In 1911 the government again coerced the House of Lords by threatening to create new members when the house persisted in rejecting legislation limiting its powers after the government had won two general elections on the issue. — PR

man put into the upper house is as much a man of the people the day after as the day before his elevation. Springing from the people, and one of them, he takes his seat in the council with all the sympathies and feelings of a man of the people, and when he returns home,* at the end of the session, he mingles with them on equal terms and is influenced by the same feelings and associations, and events, as those which affect the mass around him.

And is it then to be supposed that the members of the upper branch of the legislature will set themselves deliberately at work to oppose what they know to be the settled opinions and wishes of the people of the country? They will not do it. There is no fear of a deadlock between the two houses. There is an infinitely greater chance of a deadlock between the two branches of the legislature, should the elective principle be adopted, than with a nominated chamber — chosen by the crown, and having no mission from the people. The members of the upper chamber would then come from the people as well as those of the lower house, and should any difference ever arise between both branches, the former could say to the members of the popular branch — "We as much represent the feelings of the people as you do, and even more so; we are not elected from small localities and for a short period; you as a body were elected at a particular time, when the public mind was running in a particular channel; you were returned to parliament, not so much representing the general views of the country, on general questions, as upon the particular subjects which hap-

---

* Compare John Locke on the "legislative power" in The Second Treatise on Government (1690): "Representatives . . . chosen for that time by the people . . . afterwards return into the ordinary state of subjects." Locke's point is that in a liberal democracy, law-makers do not remain permanently in office. There is no permanent class of professional law-makers (as there is typically in a monarchy or authoritarian regime). He regards this impermanence as a great boon. Because legislators must "go home" from time to time, they must always keep in mind that they will have to live as ordinary citizens with the laws that they are making. This feature of parliamentary democracy is one of the guarantees of citizen equality, and a guarantee especially that representatives do not depart too far from the wishes of "the ordinary state of subjects." Macdonald's point is similar. Although the senators he describes will not be chosen directly by the people, they are, nevertheless, representatives of the people; they are not an extraordinary, permanent class of law-makers, and they must periodically "return home," to live under the laws they promulgate. — JA

pened to engage the minds of the people when they went to the polls. We have as much right, or a better right, than you to be considered as representing the general will of the people on general questions,* and therefore we will not give way." (Hear, hear.) There is, I repeat, a greater danger of an irreconcilable difference of opinion between the two branches of the legislature, if the upper be elective, than if it holds its commission from the crown.

— *Legislative Assembly, February 6, 1865*

George Brown: I have always been opposed to a second elective chamber, and I am so still, from the conviction that two elective houses are inconsistent with the right working of the British parliamentary system. I voted, almost alone, against the change when the council [in the Province of Canada] was made elective, but I have lived to see a vast majority of those who did the deed wish it had not been done. It is quite true, and I am glad to acknowledge it, that many evils anticipated from the change, when the measure was adopted, have not been realized. (Hear, hear.) I readily admit that men of the highest character and position have been brought into the council by the elective system, but it is equally true that the system of appointment brought into it men of the highest character and position. Whether appointed by the crown, or elected by the people, since the introduction of parliamentary government, the men who have composed the upper house of this legislature have been men who would have done honour to any legislature in the world.

---

* Macdonald states more succinctly than we are prone to hear today the republican defence of the traditional Senate. Namely, a Senate is free to properly restrain the impulsivity of an elected commons only if it is appointed, for it is then not subject to popular opinion or political parties. In the traditional view, the triplicate form of mixed government corresponded to the classical and deeply Christian image of the human being. This was an image comprised of Spirit (monarch), Mind (Senate), and Body (the Commons). It was considered the function of the bodily passions to move, the mind to direct, and the spirit to unite. To elect a Senate was therefore to spoil this balance — in effect to dismember the corporate body politic and enslave the whole system to the passions. The increasingly secular views that have become predominant with universal suffrage and democratization take the opposite view: that as our emotions are the most authentic element, control on them is an imposition on freedom by unwanted authority, and therefore a good political system requires only elected bodies. This approach stands the Christian political body on its head. — WDG

But what was most feared was that the legislative councillors would be elected under party responsibilities; that a partisan spirit would show itself in the chamber; and that the right would soon be asserted to an equal control with this house over money bills. That fear has not been realized to any dangerous extent. But is it not possible that such a claim might ere long be asserted? Do we not hear, even now, mutterings of a coming demand for it? Nor can we forget that the elected members came into that chamber gradually; that the large number of old appointed members exercised much influence in maintaining the old forms of the house, the old style of debate, and the old barriers against encroachment on the privileges of the Commons. But the appointed members of the council are gradually passing away, and when the elective element becomes supreme, who will venture to affirm that the council would not claim that power over money bills which this house claims of right belong to itself? Could they not just say that they represent the people as well as we do,* and that the control of the purse strings ought, therefore, to belong to them as much as to us? (Hear, hear.) It is said they have the power. But what is to prevent them from enforcing it? Suppose we had a Conservative majority here, and a Reform majority above — or a Conservative majority above and a Reform majority here — all elected under party obligations — what is to prevent a deadlock between the chambers? It may be called unconstitutional — but what is to prevent the councillors (especially if they feel that in the dispute of the hour they have the

---

* Brown focuses on the illegitimacy of competitive representation, and the power of an elected Senate to halt government entirely on the grounds that it is also a legitimate voice of the people. In fact, floating through many of the speeches in this section is the frequent hint that, because historically Senates are filled with people more established, experienced, and independent ("the best men of the country") than those sent to a Commons, they might, if elected, be able to lay claim to a higher legitimacy than that of the lower house, thus reversing the source of the "initiative" of legislation and throwing into turmoil the whole question of political sovereignty. This is not an idle fear. Senatorial institutions holding the initiative have descended from groups of aristocratic advisers to monarchs. Modern democrats are surprised to learn that even in the vaunted ideal of ancient Athenian democracy, almost all the laws were formulated by the upper house (the boule) and then handed down to the people for discussion and a positive or negative vote. The people could consent to or refuse a law, but the upper house held the initiative. — WDG

country at their back) from practically exercising all the powers that belong to us? They might amend our money bills, they might throw out all our bills if they liked, and bring to a stop the whole machinery of government. And what could be done to prevent them?

But, even supposing this were not the case, and that the elective upper house continued to be guided by that discretion which has heretofore actuated its proceedings — still, I think, we must all feel that the election of members for such enormous districts as form the constituencies of the upper house has become a great practical inconvenience. I say this from personal experience, having long taken an active interest in the electoral contests in Upper Canada. We have found greater difficulty in inducing candidates to offer for seats in the upper house than in getting ten times the number for the lower house. The constituencies are so vast that it is difficult to find gentlemen who have the will to incur the labour of such a contest, who are sufficiently known and popular enough throughout districts so wide, and who have money enough — (hear) — to pay the enormous bills, not incurred in any corrupt way — do not fancy that I mean that for a moment — but the bills that are sent in after the contest is over, and which the candidates are compelled to pay if they ever hope to present themselves for re-election. (Hear, hear.)

But honourable gentlemen say — "This is all very well, but you are taking an important power out of the hands of the people, which they now possess." Now this is a mistake. We do not propose to do anything of the sort. What we propose is that the upper house shall be appointed from the best men of the country by those holding the confidence of the representatives of the people in this chamber [the Legislative Assembly].* It is proposed that the government of the day, which only lives by the

Queen Victoria's proclamation declaring the unification of the four provinces, and fixing July 1, 1867, as the date on which the Dominion of Canada would come into legal existence. The proclamation names the individuals summoned from each province to the Senate of Canada.

---

* Brown answers the charge that to appoint senators takes power "from the hands of the people" by proposing that those who have already been filtered by election as the best representatives of the people will then filter once more by appointing the best men of the country as senators. He argues that this double filtration protects the people better than a simple election. He is also voicing the classical defence of democracy which says that political wisdom is found in people of accomplishment with "a stake" in the country and sufficient leisure for political responsibilities. The American system began with the election of senators by state legislatures, but subsequently succumbed to the democratic impulse. In 1919, less than half a century after this speech, the seventeenth

approval of this chamber, shall make the appointments and be responsible to the people for the selections they shall make. (Hear, hear.) Not a single appointment could be made with regard to which the government would not be open to censure, and which the representatives of the people, in this house, would not have an opportunity of condemning. For myself, I have maintained the appointed principle [for the Legislative Council], as in opposition to the elective, ever since I came into public life, and have never hesitated, when before the people, to state my opinions in the broadest manner; and yet not in a single instance have I ever found a constituency in Upper Canada, or a public meeting, declaring its disapproval of appointment by the crown and its desire for election by the people at large.

When the change was made in 1855, there was not a single petition from the people asking for it . . . The real reason for the change was that before responsible government was introduced into this country, while the old oligarchical system existed, the upper house continuously and systematically was at war with the popular branch and threw out every measure of a liberal tendency. The result was that in the famous ninety-two resolutions,* the introduction of the elective principle into the upper house was declared to be indispensable. So long as Mr. Robert Baldwin† remained in public life, the thing could not be done; but when he left, the deed was consummated.

But it is said that if the members are to be appointed for life,

---

amendment changed a system of indirect election of senators by state legislatures to direct election by the people. Canadians remain torn between appointment, election, and abolition of their Senate, each a move closer to the common people and away from what is ever at issue but rarely mentioned outright in discussions of senates: they inevitably rely on some hierarchical ranking of human qualities that is increasingly felt to be anti-egalitarian and therefore anti-democratic. — WDG

* A series of resolutions passed by the House of Assembly of Lower Canada in 1834, making a full statement of the ideology and program of the Patriot Party led by Louis-Joseph Papineau.

† Robert Baldwin (1804–1858), Reform Party leader; attorney general, Canada West; and co-premier of Canada, 1842–43 and 1848–51. He and his father, William, had led the campaign for responsible government in the province since the 1820s. He objected to an elective Legislative Council both because it offended his aristocratic values and because he thought it inconsistent with the system of responsible government. — PR

the number should be unlimited — that in the event of a dead-lock arising between that chamber and this, there should be power to overcome the difficulty by the appointment of more members. Well, under the British system, in the case of a legisla-tive union, that might be a legitimate provision. But honourable gentlemen must see that the limitation of the numbers in the upper house lies at the base of the whole compact on which this scheme rests.* (Hear, hear.) It is perfectly clear, as was contended by those who represented Lower Canada in the [Quebec] confer-ence, that if the number of the legislative councillors was made capable of increase, you would thereby sweep the whole protec-tion they had from the upper chamber.†

But it has been said that, though you may not give the power to the executive to increase the numbers of the upper house, in the event of a deadlock you might limit the term for which the

---

*An allusion to the federal aspect of the proposed council. French Canadians were willing to concede representation by population in the lower house only if the upper were constituted on the basis of representation by region. This scheme entailed a fixed number of members from each region of the dominion. In the British North America Act (section 26), a limited flexi-bility was provided by empowering the governor general to appoint three or six new members, representing equally the three regions (Ontario, Quebec, and the Maritime provinces) according to which representation in the Senate was originally distributed. — PR

† The Quebec Resolutions had no provision to allow the appointment of addi-tional senators. But at the 1866 London Conference, before the Canada bill was presented to the British parliament, the British government argued that such a provision was needed to prevent deadlock between the House of Commons and the Senate, and was not out of keeping with British parliamen-tary tradition. Macdonald devised a formula that ensured that the additional appointments would not disrupt the regional balance in the Senate. The result was section 26 of the British North America Act. There were no successful uses of section 26 from 1867 to 1982. Originally the power to appoint addi-tional senators was vested in the monarch personally, but since 1982 it has rested solely with the governor general, and is thus effectively the prime min-ister's. In 1988 Prime Minister Mulroney, using section 26, appointed eight additional senators following a deadlock between the House of Commons (dominated by Conservatives) and the Senate (dominated by Liberals) over the Goods and Services Tax (the GST). The strategy successfully tipped the senatorial balance of power in the Senate to the Conservatives, and the bill passed. The Senate has since reverted to its normal size of 104. — JA

members are appointed. I was myself in favour of that proposition. I thought it would be well to provide for a more frequent change in the composition of the upper house and lessen the danger of the chamber being largely composed of gentlemen whose advanced years might forbid the punctual and vigorous discharge of their public duties. Still, the objection made to this was very strong. It was said: "Suppose you appoint them for nine years, what will be the effect? For the last three or four years of their term they would be anticipating its expiry, and anxiously looking to the administration of the day for reappointment; and the consequence would be that a third of the members would be under the influence of the executive." The desire was to render the upper house a thoroughly independent body — one that would be in the best position to canvass dispassionately the measures of this house and stand up for the public interests in opposition to hasty or partisan legislation. It was contended that there is no fear of a deadlock. We were reminded how the system of appointing for life had worked in past years, since responsible government was introduced; we were told that the upper chamber had been too obstructive a body — not that it had sought to restrain the popular will, but that it had too faithfully reflected the popular will. Undoubtedly that was the complaint formerly pressed upon us — (hear, hear) — and I readily admit that if ever there was a body to whom we could safely entrust the power which by this measure we propose to confer on the members of the upper chamber, it is the body of gentlemen who at this moment compose the Legislative Council of Canada.

— *Legislative Assembly, February 8, 1865*

Alexander Campbell: Does the honourable gentleman [Mr. Reesor] suppose that the members of this house [the Legislative Council] will owe their nomination to the political services they can render in this house?

David Reesor: Not solely, but rather to their political services at elections and otherwise before their nomination. The honourable gentleman will remember a certain little domestic arrangement he made on the other side of the house, while in opposition, in which he had many warm friends. Does he expect to forget those?

Campbell: I hope not. (Hear, hear.)

"The desire was to render the upper house a thoroughly independent body — one that would be in the best position to canvass dispassionately the measures of this house and stand up for the public interests in opposition to hasty or partisan legislation."

Reesor: Well, there it is. The honourable gentleman acknowledges his determination to reward his political supporters. Is this the way to obtain an independent branch of the legislature, one that will operate as a wholesome check on hasty legislation? Those who receive favours from a political party are not likely to turn their backs upon that party. I think we are not likely, under any circumstances, to have a more independent house under the proposed system [an appointive upper house] than we now have, or one which will better advance the interests of the country. If you wish to raise the elective franchise for elections to the upper house — if you would confine their election to voters on real estate of $400 assessed value, and tenants hold a leasehold of $1,000 annual value, and thus place these elections out of the reach of a mere money influence that may sometimes operate upon the masses — if you think this body is not sufficiently conservative, let them be elected by a more conservative portion of the community — that portion which has the greatest stake in the community — but do not strike out the elective principle altogether.

Walter McCrae: I am among those of the Reform Party who think that making the members of this house elective was a step in the wrong direction; and though I am free to admit that, but for the elective principle having been applied to this house [the Legislative Council], I should never have had the honour of a seat within its walls, yet I am prepared to . . . sanction a return to the nomination of members for life by the crown, under the advice of ministers responsible to the people through the Legislative Assembly.

I deny that the extension of the elective principle to this house was ever sought for, or petitioned for, by the people . . . It is quite true, honourable gentlemen, that before the union of Upper and Lower Canada, and during the palmy days of the Family Compact* and the irresponsibility of the government, when the assembly had no control over the executive, except by stopping the supplies, the Legislative Council was chosen for the mere purpose of opposing the public will, and they did it most effectually. Every

---

*A name applied to the administrative oligarchy that had dominated the government of Upper Canada before the colony's union with Lower Canada. Derived from the name given to three eighteenth-century treaties between the Bourbon monarchs of France and Spain, the term imputed a despotic character to the government. — PR

measure calculated to elevate the people and promote their best interests was sure to be tomahawked, as the phrase went, by that very obstructive body. Short-sighted politicians of those days, who did not very well understand the working of the British Constitution, fancied the only remedy was by making this house elective. But the memorable resolutions of September 3, 1841,* at Kingston, established the true British principle of responsible government, and I maintain that since that time the people never demanded that this house should be made elective.

I apprehend that my conservative friends and I, who agree with each other on this point — the nomination of members to this house — come to the same conclusion by a very different process of reasoning. They hold that the elective principle applied to this branch of parliament gives too much power to the people, while I, on the other hand, argue that they have not by it as quick and as sharp a remedy against a stubborn [legislative] council as they had under the system of nomination. The great beauty of the old system [nomination] was the promptness with which at the critical moment it could be brought to bear, and the history of its operations, both in this country and in England, clearly shows its superiority.

"I have always held as a political principle that as much political liberty as possible should be conceded to the masses, combined always with a government strong enough to maintain order and administer the laws."

L.-A. Olivier: The spirit of modern society is to give to the people as much political liberty as possible; and it is my belief that by this plan of Confederation we shall sacrifice whatever liberty is already possessed by the people of this country. When I expressed this idea, a short time since, the honourable premier [Etienne-Paschal Taché] seemed to give an ironical assent to it, as if he considered my notions exaggerated. I am bound to tell him that I neither love nor approve of mob rule any more than he does, but I have always held as a political principle that as much political liberty as possible should be conceded to the masses, combined always with a government strong enough to maintain order and administer the laws; and herein I consider that I con-

---

* A set of resolutions moved on behalf of the provincial government in the Legislative Assembly of the Province of Canada. The Reform Party took them as a formal admission that responsible government prevailed in the province, and therefore as a surrender of the crown's discretion in making executive appointments. This understanding formed the basis for the nineteenth-century view that Canada had attained responsible government in 1841 rather than later in the decade. — PR

form to the principles of modern society, without giving in to the dictates of demagogy.

I am favourable to democracy, but not to demagogy . . . I say, then, that in taking from the people for all time the right which they acquired after long struggles of electing members to this house, we are retrograding, making a step backward, and I am sure the people will not look upon this project with a favourable eye.

— *Legislative Council, February 13, 1865*

"There are persons who wish that all the offices under the state should be submitted to universal suffrage, because they know that in such circumstances they could impose upon the sympathy and the judgement of the people."

Joseph Armand: I know that many persons, I will not say urged by an inordinate liberalism degenerating into demagogy — for I do not believe we have in our young country any of those fierce demagogues — but I will say, that there are persons who wish that all the offices under the state should be submitted to universal suffrage, because they know that in such circumstances they could impose upon the sympathy and the judgement of the people. But I would say to such persons — gentlemen, do not suppose yourselves wiser statesmen than those of the mother country, who have established their constitution after centuries of efforts and contests, and who work it after the experience of centuries.

I would further tell them "do not suppose yourselves better able to appreciate the British Constitution than Monsieur Montalembert,* one of the great *literati* of the day, the historian and eminent statesman; or than M. Berryer, the prince of the French bar, both of whom proclaimed but recently that constitution was one of the most beautiful and free that could possibly be desired." I congratulate the government upon desiring to preserve so much of this law as may appear rational and good. I refer to the territorial divisions and the propriety of causing them to be represented by persons who have vested interests therein; and indeed how could anyone represent with equal devotion and advantage a division as the man who had sacred rights therein, whether by personal residence or the ownership of the property upon which his qualification rests, and who clings to it because it has descended to him from his ancestor,† or because he has

---

* Charles-Forbes-René, comte de Montalembert (1810–1870), French historian and liberal Catholic politician. His works include De L'avenir Politique de L'Angleterre *(1856). "M. Berryer": Pierre-Antoine Berryer (1790–1868), French royalist lawyer and politician.*

† Charles Montalembert had deep connections with English political life and constitutional matters. His father was an emigré French nobleman serving

acquired it by the sweat of his brow, his vigils, and his toils.*
— *Legislative Council, February 15, 1865*

Thomas Ryan: If the constituents of both houses are merely the same, you lose the power of check, or at least you will not have it effectual, because you will have the same sentiments and feelings represented in this house [the Legislative Council] as in the other. I am not singular in this opinion, but were I to cite the opinions of men who are of a conservative turn of mind, and who have always

---

in the British army who left him to be raised by his English grandfather, James Forbes, a Protestant who nevertheless educated Charles in the Catholic faith of his father. To Montalembert this was a personal lesson in English liberalism. In 1830 he joined the editorial board of L'Avenir, a fledgling journal known as the organ of liberal Catholicism in France. However, in 1832 it was condemned by Pope Gregory XVI for its free-thinking doctrines. Throughout his life Montalembert championed the freedom of citizens and in particular the freedom of religious belief and association. His love of intellectual and spiritual independence brought him increasing isolation, however, both from the Church and from the regime of Napoleon III, which had previously, and unsuccessfully, tried to win him over. His steadfast credo was "God and liberty: these are the two principal motive powers of my existence. To reconcile these two perfections shall be the aim of my life." — WDG

It is possible that Armand quotes Montalembert and Berryer rather than Montesquieu because they have commented "recently" on the modern British Constitution. In the Canadian debates, certainly, the speakers tend to cite authorities of their own generation, or the generation immediately preceding, men like Lord Durham. Of course, there are some references to earlier authors such as Blackstone, Burke, and the American founders. — PR

* Ownership of land, buildings, rents, or income was deemed to fuse the common good with self-interest, thus resulting in political prudence. The word "sacred" in relation to property rights was laden with import owing to God's command in Genesis (1:28) to be fruitful, multiply, and subdue the earth. Armand is careful also to include hereditary property rights as sacred — a standard part of the defence against levellers and egalitarians everywhere — along with property in general. — WDG

This labour justification surely refers to John Locke's famous defence of private property, where he argues that ownership of a man's person extends to the work of his hands, and so by mixing his labour with anything in the state of nature he "thereby makes it his property" Locke, Second Treatise of Government, chapter 5 (emphasis in original). — WDG

upheld the privileges of the aristocracy and the prerogative of the crown, I should, perhaps, give you opinions which would carry less weight . . . than will that of a gentleman whose views I will cite, who has written a great deal, and very ably, and who belongs to the ranks of the advanced Liberal Party in England — I mean Mr. John Stuart Mill. In his chapter on the second chamber (*Considerations on Representative Government*, page 242), he says:

> That there should be in every polity a centre of resistance to the predominant power in the constitution — and in a democratic constitution, therefore, a nucleus of resistance to the democracy — I have already maintained and I regard it as a fundamental maxim of government. If any people who possess a democratic representation are, from their historical antecedents, more willing to tolerate such a centre of resistance in the form of a Second Chamber or House of Lords than in any other shape, this constitutes a strong reason for having it in that shape.*

Now, honourable gentlemen, I think a second chamber, constituted nearly in the same way as the lower chamber, would be wholly ineffectual to stop the current of legislation coming from that chamber; the point, indeed, admits of very little question. (Hear, hear.)

— *Legislative Council, February 20, 1865.*

Alexander Mackenzie: The most important question that arises relates to the constitution of the upper house. It is said that in this particular the scheme is singularly defective — that there has been a retrograde movement in going back from the elective to the nominative system. I admit that this statement is a fair one from those who contended long for the application of the elective principle to the upper house; but it can have no weight with another large class who, like myself, never believed in the wisdom of electing the members of two houses of parliament with coordinate powers. I have always believed that a change from the present system [the elective Legislative Council] was inevitable, even with our present political organization. (Hear, hear.)

---

* *The above quotation may be found in the standard modern edition of Mill's* Collected Works, *ed. J.M. Robson, vol. 19 (Toronto: University of Toronto Press, 1977), 515.* — IG

The constitution of an upper house or Senate seems to have originated in the state of society which prevailed in feudal times; and from being the sole legislative body — or at least the most powerful — in the state, it has imperceptibly become less powerful, or secondary in importance to the lower chamber, as the mass of the people became more intelligent, and popular right became more fully understood.

Where there is an upper house, it manifestly implies on the part of its members peculiar duties or peculiar rights. In Great Britain, for instance, there is a large class of landed proprietors who have long held almost all the landed property of the country in their hands, and who have to pay an immense amount of taxes. The fiscal legislation of Britain for many years has tended to the reduction of impost and excise duties on articles of prime necessity, and to the imposition of heavy taxes on landed property and incomes. Under such a financial system, there are immense interests at stake . . . We have no such interests, and we impose no such duties, and hence the upper house becomes a mere court of revision, or one of coordinate jurisdiction; as the latter, it is not required; to become the former, it should be constituted differently from the House of Assembly. The United States present the example of a community socially similar to ourselves establishing an upper house. They have — reasoning doubtless from the same premises — not only given the legislatures of the respective states the power of nominating the members of the Senate, but have also given that body powers entirely different from those possessed by the elective branch.

While it is my opinion that we would be better without an upper house, I know the question is not, at the present moment, what is the best possible form of government, according to our particular opinions, but what is the best that can be framed for a community holding different views on the subject.

— *Legislative Assembly, February 23, 1865*

"The question is not, at the present moment, what is the best possible form of government, according to our particular opinions, but what is the best that can be framed for a community holding different views."

Joseph Blanchet: Long ago the privileges of *caste* disappeared in this country. Most of our ancient nobility left the country at the Conquest, and the greater number of those who remained have sunk out of sight by inaction. Accordingly, whom do we see in the high offices of state? The sons of the poor who have felt the necessity of study, and who have risen by the aid of their intellect and hard work. (Hear, hear.) Everything is democratic with us, because everyone can attain to everything by the efforts of a

"There are some men who have enough patriotism to approve of everything done elsewhere, but to find fault with everything done at home — it is a pitiful crotchet in the human mind. "

noble ambition. The legislative councillors appointed by the crown will not be, therefore, socially speaking, persons superior to the members of the House of Commons; they will owe their elevation only to their own merit. They will live as being of the people and among the people as we do. How can it happen, then, that having no advantage over us greater than that of not being elected, they will not be subject in a legitimate degree to the influence of public opinion?

There are some men who have enough patriotism to approve of everything done elsewhere, but to find fault with everything done at home — it is a pitiful crotchet in the human mind.

— *Legislative Assembly, March 2, 1865*

NOVA SCOTIA

William Annand: Look at the clause of the bill which refers to the appointment of senators: seventy-two of them are to be created in one batch for life — and what more likely than a deadlock between them and the House of Commons? And if so, how is it to be overcome? I never was in favour of the upper house being elective, as regards Nova Scotia, while our institutions are monarchical; but under Confederation, I should say, by all means let them go out in rotation, so that branch may be influenced by public opinion. Is it not evident that when the embryo republic is fairly in operation, if the local legislatures pressed by various constituencies should, for instance, propose that the lieutenant governor, instead of being nominated by the governor general, be elected by the people — and I can fancy that such a proposal might be made — at its first meeting here, the conflict that would in such a case ensue between the various legislative bodies would result in serious collision — perhaps smash the whole confederacy into pieces.

Suppose a resolution were adopted declaring that the senators should be elected — and I may here say that such a change would be a misfortune to some persons who have stood for a day on the hustings and only secured a handful of votes — you will then be creating not a monarchy, but a republic — a poor imitation to that of Mexico, to be crumpled up whenever the American eagle chooses to grasp it in its talons.

— *House of Assembly, March 19, 1867*

NEW BRUNSWICK

Arthur Gillmor: We have heard that [at the Quebec Conference] in the constitution of the federal council there was a difference, and that part of the scheme was carried by the casting vote of the chairman, who was Mr. [Leonard] Tilley. I think that body should at first at least have been elected, so that the people in the first instance could have chosen that branch of the legislature, a branch powerful enough if they chose, to stop all legislation. Canada did some seven years ago adopt the elective principle for their Legislative Council, and the British government evidently thinks it should be so in this scheme and suggests it.

— *House of Assembly, June 5, 1865*

"Without the check, which the upper branch has been, to hasty and reckless legislation in the lower house, our statute book would have been filled with injudicious and unwise statutes."

Peter Mitchell: Instances of the proper exercise of the legislative functions of the middle branch might be multiplied indefinitely were it necessary; and I would recommend those gentlemen who condemn our conduct, undervalue our influence, decry our position, or desire to restrain our powers to refer to the history of constitutional countries and study them before they assert that there is no parallel to the powers here assumed.

We are told we must be swept away; that the majority are "effete, antiquated politicians," representing no one but ourselves, and having no regard for the people's interests, desirous only to gratify our ambition, our selfishness, and our interests . . . Does Mr. [Albert] Smith not know, and has he not often repeated the fact, that without the check, which the upper branch has been, to hasty and reckless legislation in the lower house, our statute book would have been filled with injudicious and unwise statutes?

— *Legislative Council, April 16, 1866*

James Gray Stevens: [He] was glad to embrace the opportunity of raising his voice against the assertion made against the Legislative Council that they represented nobody but themselves. The constitution of Great Britain had received the plaudits of all writers of history. The reason of this is because of the admirable checks which one branch has upon another. We should, therefore, endeavour to prevent the usefulness of the upper branch being done away with by any remarks calculated to bring them, as an independent branch, into contempt.

It has been urged by one honourable gentleman that the Legislative Council was endeavouring to force upon the people a

scheme which they had previously rejected,* and because the scheme had been once rejected the people never ought to have another opportunity of expressing an opinion upon it. They were prepared to meet this constitution question in all its bearings. The action of the lieutenant governor was strictly constitutional in all its details. There was no endeavour to subvert the constitution or to force upon the people a scheme that they did not wish. The Legislative Council cannot carry anything into effect without the concurrence of the other branches. They did as they were asked to do by the imperial government, and in consequence of doing that they brought matters to an issue, which caused the resignation of a government that had been in power long enough, and this was proved by the result of the elections.

— *House of Assembly, June 23, 1866*

NEWFOUNDLAND

Robert Pinsent: He presumed it would not be denied that this house has an independent right to declare its opinions upon public questions, irrespective of outside influences of any kind, and it was not bound to await the result of action in any quarter. We have no constituencies to consult, no country to appeal to, to regulate the course of action we should pursue, and are consequently in a position to give an untrammelled opinion on questions of a public character. Honourable members of this house possess considerable stake in the country and are deeply interested in its present and future welfare; and being unswayed by personal or party motives in their legislative action, it was only just to expect from them a dispassionate consideration of such important subjects as this.

— *Legislative Council, February 13, 1865*

George Hogsett: [The Dominion of Canada] had a Senate to which Newfoundland would send four members, who could be outvoted upon every question affecting the policy of Newfoundland.

A general election early in 1865 had resulted in the defeat of Leonard Tilley's government, which favoured Confederation. In the course of 1865, however, public opinion shifted rapidly in favour of Tilley's policy. In April 1866, in an effort to force the anti-Confederation government of Albert Smith to open the question, the Legislative Council adopted an address to the queen expressing its support for Confederation. — PR

"We have here a constitution for which the people nobly fought, and which was reluctantly wrung from the British government. We had the right of taxing ourselves, or legislating for ourselves, and were we then to satisfy the paltry ambition of our Newfoundland aspirants, to give up all the rights we possess, rights which, if properly worked and administered, would secure us all the advantages and prosperity a people can want or require."

These senators would be elected for life, and would become, not the servants of the colony, but of the dominion. On their appointment they would become independent of the colony, and we knew what the tone of the aristocratic circles of this and most other colonies was. They were not like the aristocracy of Great Britain and Ireland, gentlemen by birth and gentlemen by blood, but they were generally men raised from an insignificant sphere, and in most cases the higher they climbed the more you could see the monkey.

It was one of the secrets of the success of the republic of America that no man or body of men could have a life interest in any political office, and in this respect the Senate of the dominion differs from that of the United States. These states had their troubles, their anxieties, their revolution; so had every European country; but nevertheless, America has been and now is the refuge of every man who felt himself oppressed or who wished to earn an honest livelihood . . . We have here a constitution for which the people nobly fought, and which was reluctantly wrung from the British government. We had the right of taxing ourselves, or legislating for ourselves, and were we then to satisfy the paltry ambition of our Newfoundland aspirants, to give up all the rights we possess, rights which, if properly worked and administered, would secure us all the advantages and prosperity a people can want or require. We were a colony today, and if we entered the dominion we would be a colony still. Aye, worse than a colony, because our very laws will be subject to the veto of the dominion, as well as to that of the imperial government. Therefore we would be doubly a colony.

— *House of Assembly, February 23, 1869*

Joseph Little: It appears by the constitution that we may be represented in the Senate of the new dominion by eight members or peers. The gentlemen are to be and remain senators for life. Distant from the land they are to legislate for, and irresponsible to those who first placed them in power, they would necessarily be subject to the influences of the central government and forgetful of those of this colony. He regarded this body as a mere attempt to perpetuate, on this side of the water, institutions which were gradually decaying in the mother country. No attempt to create a domineering aristocratic body will be acceptable to the American mind.

Honourable gentlemen wish us to believe that in the forma-

tion of this constitution, that of the United States was followed as nearly as possible. Is it so in this particular? No! It is only a flimsy attempt to ape the institutions of the Old World and the New. He regarded our representation in the Senate and House [of Commons] of the dominion as powerless for good, our numbers there would be contemptible.

— *House of Assembly, March 2, 1869*

PRINCE EDWARD ISLAND

George Coles: I made strong objections [to the limited number of representatives from Prince Edward Island] at the [Quebec] conference, and fortunately for me I also referred to the matter in the public prints before the colonial minister's dispatch was received. My reason for opposing such a provision was that as the members of the Legislative Council were to be nominated from the existing councils in the different provinces, a number of them would be old men who had been obstructive, and might remain so all their lives; consequently a deadlock would probably soon occur between the two branches of the legislature, in which case an appeal would have to be made to the imperial government to settle the dispute.

They have had quite enough of disputes in Canada already. In that province, sir, the Parliament Buildings have been burned,* and the Stars and Stripes thrown out to the winds.† Such proceedings, sir, have never been seen in the lower provinces. (Cheers.) And are we now to be told that we must enter a union with them, and submit to such taxes as they may choose to impose?

It has been said by some of the advocates of the Quebec scheme that we should not blame the Canadians if it contains objectionable provisions, for, at the conference, votes were taken by provinces. They were not at fault in all cases; in a few instances the delegates from the lower provinces were most to blame. Several of the Canadians were in favour of the elective principle for the Legislative Council; but nearly all the delegates from the lower provinces declared against it. They seemed to be carried away with the idea of the members of the upper house

---

An allusion to the destruction of the Parliament Building in Montreal by a mob in 1849.

† *Possibly an allusion to the Montreal-centred movement of 1849 for annexation to the United States. — PR*

GEORGE COLES
(1810–1875),
businessman and Prince
Edward Island's first
premier under
responsible government.
Cole was the island's
leading Liberal for more
than twenty years and
premier in 1851–59
(except a few months
in 1854) and 1867–68.
He introduced public
education, enfranchised
virtually all adult males,
and carried legislation
enabling the government
to purchase estates from
absentee landlords for
resale to their tenants.
He attended the
Charlottetown and
Quebec conferences,
but failing to gain
satisfactory financial
terms, rejected
Confederation.

being taken from the existing Legislative Councils in the several colonies and voted that they should be appointed for life. On this question the delegates from the other lower provinces acted in a most selfish manner. They even agreed to the Canadian proposition that the number of councillors should be fixed. This, as I have already stated, I consider a very objectionable feature in the new constitution.

We know that in Nova Scotia they had to break through the warrant of Her Majesty and appoint additional councillors to carry responsible government. And we also know that in Britain it is sometimes found necessary to create new peers* in order to carry certain measures.

I considered it advisable that the men who should represent each province in the Legislative Council, as they would be few in number, ought to be appointed by and possess the confidence of both branches of the local legislature. This provision I deemed especially necessary as regarded the interests of this island, for it is extremely doubtful, should the union take place, whether we shall ever have a single representative in the general government; and if otherwise, we at least cannot expect more than one. My motion, however, was lost. I will not accuse my brother delegates from this island, who voted against it, of being actuated by the same motives as the majority from the other provinces evidently were. These saw the difficulty of the Confederation scheme receiving the sanction of the present legislative councils of the several provinces unless their leading members felt secure of a seat in the upper house of the general legislature; therefore they provided that the legislative councillors of the federal parliament should be nominated from the existing councils. To ensure as much unanimity, also, as possible at the conference, a clause was thrown in to the effect that due regard should be had to the claims of the members of the Legislative Council of the opposition in each province. But this provision will be of little account, for after the divisions which the discussion of the Confederation question has caused, I think it will be difficult to tell how individuals stand with respect to parties. When I saw the drift of the whole section in regard to the constitution of the Legislative Council as it now stands in the report, I strongly expressed the

---

*New peers were created in 1712 to guarantee passage of the Treaty of Utrecht. Their creation was threatened in 1832 to win passage of the Great Reform Bill.

hope that the delegates would except this island from such a piece of corruption.

— *House of Assembly, March 31, 1865*

James McLean: [He] said that no people could be called free and independent unless they had power to make their own laws, and on looking at the position we would occupy in the dominion, were we to join it, he concluded we would be virtually deprived of that privilege. In the Senate we would certainly have no representation because whoever might represent us there would be appointed by the governor general, and not by us. This, he considered, would be bordering on despotism.

It might be argued by honourable members of the opposition that Her Majesty the Queen had the power of appointing the British peers. This he admitted to be true, but she might be said to hold her position by divine right, or inheritance from King William III,* who was placed on the throne by the unanimous voice of the people. But no such right existed in, or should be conferred upon the governor general of the dominion. He was nothing more than a loyal British subject who received his appointment from the crown and not from the people.

T. H. Haviland: He agreed with the remark of the honourable member from East Point (Mr. McLean) that no people were independent unless they had a right to make their own laws, but he took exception to the application of that principle to the union of this island with Canada, for, in case such a union should take place, our local government would still make our local laws and we should have representatives in the parliament at Ottawa, who would assist in making the general laws of the dominion.

The honourable member (Mr. McLean) had been very indignant that the senators should be appointed by the governor general and not elected by the people; but the former great leaders of the Liberal Party in this island, Messrs. [George] Coles

---

* *In the "Glorious Revolution" of 1688–89, James II was driven off the throne and replaced by William of Orange and Mary II, who reigned as joint monarchs. The constitutional significance of this change was precisely that divine right monarchy was repudiated and replaced by the principle of elective monarchy. Though it is hardly true that William and Mary were placed on the throne "by the unanimous voice of the people," their accession was ratified by both houses of parliament. — IG*

and [Edward] Whelan, had always argued in favour of leaving the Legislative Council nominative and not elective.

He (Mr. Haviland) had given it as his opinion four years ago that Confederation was only a work of time. Then there were only three or four confederates on the island, but now there were more than the honourable member for Belfast (Mr. James Duncan) would like to see. The young men of the country, who were being liberally educated, would understand this subject and would be strong advocates of Confederation. In the middle of the nineteenth century, to say that isolation was preferable to Confederation was contrary to the spirit of the age. If states were better apart than joined, why had the United States not permitted the southerners to have their independence instead of expending so much to force them back to their allegiance? The petty German states were being absorbed by the larger countries around them. Scotland had prospered* since her union with England, and was now ahead of almost any other country in pro-portion to her size. If we joined the dominion we would be of some importance, and not the miserable wretched sandbank in the Gulf of the St. Lawrence that we now were.

— House of Assembly, March 8, 1870

---

* Scotland and England negotiated a political and economic union in 1707. Although the Scottish parliament was eliminated, the country was permitted to retain her own legal system and established church. For the next two centuries, Scotland flourished economically and intellectually as never before. — IG

Chapter Four

EQUALITY OF
REPRESENTATION

—————➤➣◗◖◄———————

THE QUEBEC RESOLUTIONS allowed the individual provinces representation in the new federal House of Commons on the basis of each province's population. "Rep by pop" in the elective house, regional equality in the upper house: that's the deal. Thus Nova Scotia would have 19 elected representatives in a house of 194; New Brunswick, 15, and so on. The smaller provinces are torn between respect for the principle of representation by population and a very understandable desire to beef up representation from the Atlantic region. They don't want to be swamped by Upper Canada and her 82 members.

Rep by pop expresses liberalism's commitment to the principle of human equality. It commands respect even in this period, when the franchise is restricted to male property owners. It is first cousin to the principle of "one person, one vote," the rule that in time will wipe out property qualifications and justify votes for women and for aboriginals. Everyone understands the consequences of rep by pop: the smaller provinces are not entitled to enhanced representation: a vote cast in Nova Scotia should not count for more than a vote in Upper Canada. A vote's a vote.

Ah, but there is a precedent. When Upper Canada and Lower Canada were united in 1840, each was allotted the same number of representatives in the shared legislature: a clear violation of rep by pop, since Lower Canada at the time had a larger population. By 1865 Upper Canada has the larger population and thus too few representatives, as George Brown never ceases to point out; rep by pop is still being flouted.

Given this precedent, why can't principles be shaved again, and the smaller provinces be allowed just a few more members than

population warrants, to give them a little more clout in Ottawa? As they work their way through this dilemma, we see the speakers coming to grips with key features of Canadian federalism.

In Red River the question of representation takes another form. Here the speakers are not discussing representation as an aspect of federalism; they focus directly on the franchise — who gets to vote. There are three main questions. Should all males vote, or only householders? What sort of residential qualification should be required of newcomers? And should a lesser qualification be required of British subjects than of aliens?

NOVA SCOTIA

Charles Tupper: I must glance now at one or two points that were arranged at that conference for the government of British North America [the Quebec Conference]. The principle of representation by population was adopted, and there have been found people in this province to question its soundness and judiciousness. It has been said that it is a false principle and that therefore it should have been repudiated and rejected — that it was not one which Conservatives ought to support. It will not be necessary to go into any elaborate defence of representation by population as applied to British America. That principle was approved twenty-five years ago, by a statesman as distinguished as Lord Durham.* It was stated by him, in a report which will make his name ever famous in the annals of British America, and I may

---

*John George Lambton, 1st earl of Durham (1792–1840), liberal politician, was sent to Canada as governor general after the rebellions of 1837. His report on the causes of the rebellions recommended union of the North American colonies, or, failing that, of Upper and Lower Canada, under a single legislature based on representation by population. He endeared himself to Canadian reformers by recommending the introduction of responsible government in the united province.

The British bill to unite the Canadas originally provided for representation by population, but was altered to provide equal representation for the two sections in order to placate Canadian Conservatives, who feared that English-Canadian reformers would combine with French Canadians in the legislature to impose liberal institutions on the province. Lower Canada then (1840) had the larger population, and sectional equality was a means of reducing the proportion of French-Canadian members in the legislature. — PR

say Great Britain, that it was the only true and safe principle on which the legislatures and the governments could be constructed in British America. That eminent statesman predicted, twenty-five years ago, in reference to Canada, that, if they undertook to ignore the principle of representation by population, the day would come when the country would be rent in twain.

Who does not know the difficulties that arose from the false principle that was applied at the time of the union of the Canadas, in order to give the ascendancy to Upper Canada, whose population at the time was less than that of Lower Canada? Who does not know that the prediction of Earl Durham has been verified? And the time has come when that country has been convulsed, in order to rid themselves of a principle so unsound as that a certain number of people in a certain locality shall have an amount of representation arranged not according to their numbers, but exhibiting a disparity with some other section. But were we to put ourselves in the position of saying that the intelligence of our people was such — that the want of intellect and ability amongst us was so marked, that in order to have sufficient influence in a legislative assembly in British North America, we should demand that the principle of representation by population should be ignored?

When it is said that the principle should be discountenanced by Conservatives, I call the attention of the house to the fact that the Quebec scheme has been submitted to the most severe ordeal that any scheme of constitutional government could be subjected to, and to a tribunal perhaps as competent to pass upon it as any in the world — I mean the government and people of England, as represented by a press which for standing, character, and intelligence is not equalled in any part of the civilized world. I ask any public man to show me, although the scheme has been rigidly examined, a single statement in the press of England, or of any other country, calling into question the soundness of the principle of representation by population, as applied to British North America.

It has been said that, assuming the principle to be right, it would nevertheless place these provinces in a position that would jeopardize the interests of the people in connection with this scheme of government. I would ask this house to consider that, in the first place, under that principle Nova Scotia would be entitled to 19 representatives in all in a parliament of 194 members. I would ask this house, when any man ventures to question

whether the nineteen members, or the forty-seven,* would not have a fair share of influence in the united parliament, to look at the only criterion by which it is possible to come to any conclusion on the subject.

Look across the Atlantic at the parliament of England — at the House of Commons of 600 members — where the parties into which the country are divided, the Liberals and Conservatives, are separated by lines less strong than those which divide Upper and Lower Canada, and must divide them for a century to come. There you will see a dozen independent men controlling parties and influencing the destinies of the country. Is not this evidence that in a British American parliament of 194 members the representatives of the Maritime provinces would render it impossible for their interests to be ignored or set aside? It may be said they would not be united — personal antagonism would arise to keep them divided. I grant it. But the moment that parliament would attempt to touch the interests of any part of these Maritime provinces, would you not see them forced into such a combination as would enable them to dictate to any party that would attempt to override them? Go to Canada and take your illustration there. Not nineteen, but three or four members only, for years, have dictated which party should control the government of the country.

Therefore I feel that this principle is not only just in itself but is one that gave to the Maritime provinces all the control and influence to which they were entitled. Look again at the parliament of England and you would see, although Ireland has an insignificant number of members† — insignificant in a numerical point of view in comparison to what Nova Scotia would send into a British American parliament — yet for years they have occupied that position that they can dictate to the parliament which party shall govern the country.

— *House of Assembly, April 10, 1865*

"Look . . . at the parliament of England and you would see, although Ireland has an insignificant number of members . . . yet for years they have occupied that position that they can dictate to the parliament which party shall govern the country."

William Annand: The honourable provincial secretary (Tupper) has alluded to representation by population, and defended it as a sound principle, and quoted Lord Durham as a high authority on

---

* The total number of members of parliament allotted to the maritime colonies (including Newfoundland) under the Quebec scheme.

† Not so. At that time Ireland sent 100 members of parliament to Westminster, over 15 per cent of the total. Nova Scotia would have 19 members out of 194 in the new general legislature, that is, less than 10 per cent. — IG

the subject. If this system is right as applied to a colony, why is it not equally so in respect to the mother country? Is it in operation in Nova Scotia at the present moment, or in any of the colonies? I ask the honourable member for Cape Breton opposite how it is, if this principle is right, that he sits here with only one colleague, when the small county of Queen's, small in extent, as well as population, has three representatives? Is it right?

John Bourinot: No.

Annand: Cape Breton has a right to additional representation by other considerations than those of population; look at her coal fields, and the vast amount of capital that is now developing the resources of that fine county. It is a sound principle that property and classes should be represented as well as numbers. That principle was recognized as long ago as the union of England with Scotland. Mr. Seton, one of the commissioners for arranging that union, on the very point that property and classes should be represented as well as numbers,* and that the smaller number of representatives was given to Scotland in proportion to her num-

---

* *"It is a sound principle that property and classes should be represented as well as numbers." This simple-seeming statement evokes the deep historical clash between two irreconcilable theories of political representation. The merit theory, on the one hand, is aristocratic in nature and rooted in an assumption of natural — and obvious — human inequality. Its supporters therefore seek to restrict the franchise to those of quality, property, social rank, and education. It generally also promotes the idea of "virtual representation," meaning that even though the franchise is necessarily restricted, all citizens and regions are nevertheless represented by wise members of parliament constrained to consider the whole people. The opposite theory, an egalitarian democratic one, is not surprisingly based on the counter-assumption that all humans are equally meritorious. Its supporters therefore generally propose a system of one man, one vote, whereby the people will express their own real, and not virtual, interests by representing themselves. One method formerly used in Britain to ensure the preference for quality over quantity was a system of "plural" voting, whereby certain individuals were allowed more than one vote (an idea justified even by liberals such as John Stuart Mill). In England by 1911, about 7 per cent of the adult male population, or 500,000 men, had plural votes, some as many as six. It was not until 1948 that plural voting for certain distinguished citizens and university graduates was abolished in England. — WDG*

bers, was justified on the ground that England was a wealthier and more heavily taxed country, whilst the former had to bear smaller burdens of taxation. Lord Durham, it would be remembered, highly respectable an authority as he may be, was considered a radical reformer, as the radical nobleman, and holding opinions opposed both to the Whigs and Conservatives of England. Is Earl Russell, the author of the Reform Bill,* in favour of the principle? On the contrary, he has over and over again declared against it, as inconsistent with the rights and privileges of large classes and interests in contradistinction to mere numbers.

But representation by population, says the provincial secretary [Tupper], is a sound principle as applied to the Confederation of the British American provinces. He has said — and he argued the question at considerable length — that 19 members were as many as Nova Scotia, and 47 as many as all the Maritime provinces were entitled to, in a house of 194. It must be recollected, however, that under the Confederation you have separate interests if you retain separate provinces, and whilst this is the case you must expect difficulties to arise.

— House of Assembly, April 12, 1865

Archibald McLelan: I come now to the nature of the representation. We are to have local governments, and a general government over all. In that general government, Nova Scotia is to have a representation of 19 out of 194. Now the provincial secretary [Tupper] tells us that this is as much as we have any right to expect according to our population, and he stated that if these terms were not just, we had only the delegates to blame. I contend, in view of the geographical position of Nova Scotia — 800 miles from the capital, and almost an island — that the principle of representation by population was not at all sufficient to do her

---

John, 1st Earl Russell, liberal politician (but less liberal than Durham); twice prime minister of Britain. As colonial secretary from 1838 to 1841, Russell was responsible for the union of Upper and Lower Canada; as prime minister from 1846 to 1852, he led the government that conceded responsible government to the North American colonies. His government of 1865–66 promoted Confederation. Russell had originally envisaged the British parliamentary reform of 1832 a final settlement of the question, but later had decided that further reform was necessary. In 1865 he introduced a moderate measure that did not accommodate the radical demand for equal electoral districts. — PR

*"As you recede
from the place of the
meeting of parliament,
representation should
increase in order to
give a balance of
influence."*

justice. You don't give to the city of Halifax a representation pro-portioned to the population because you feel that by the parliament meeting here, influences can be brought to bear upon it that compensate for less representation. As you recede from the place of the meeting of parliament, representation should increase in order to give a balance of influence . . . The influences of the interests of a country like ours (almost an island) are neces-sarily confined within her lines, and when the legislation for our interests is placed in a parliament beyond our borders we should have an increase of numbers in representation to compensate for the entire want of local influence.

But the provincial secretary tells us that we have a large repre-sentation in the legislative council which fully compensates us for the want of representation in the assembly. Mr. George Brown, arguing that question, said that the complaint had been made that they had given us too large a representation in the upper house; but he says "In the Lower House, Canada shall hold the purse strings."* You will further remember that all the lower provinces combined have only twenty-four members in the legislative council, whilst united Canada has forty-eight. But whatever dif-ferences of opinion may have hitherto existed between Upper and Lower Canada, there is no doubt you will find them as one when their interests come into collision with those of the lower provinces. When a man and a wife quarrel, and a third party steps in, they both unite against him. Upper and Lower Canada may have disputes at times too, but whenever the lower provinces come in, they will unite as one province against us. The provincial sec-retary tells us that if our representatives band together, they can exercise an influence which will make them sufficiently felt in the Canadian parliament, and referred in illustration of his argument to the influence that the members for Cape Breton exercise here; but he did not tell us that these form a much larger proportion to the whole number in this house than would the representatives from Nova Scotia exhibit in a parliament of 194 at Ottawa.

But suppose they did band together to make their influence felt in that parliament. Now, I ask the honourable provincial sec-retary to consider the position in which he places this province

---

* *George Brown said this in the Canadian legislature on February 8, 1865 (see chapter 9). The remarks refer to the constitutional primacy of the repre-sentative chamber in dealing with money bills and the fact that Upper Canada was to elect eighty-two members to that chamber. — PR*

and her representatives. I cannot conceive a more degraded, a more humiliating position than the representatives of a spirited people compelled to forgo their political opinions* — their conscientious convictions on all public questions — in order to obtain for their people a consideration in the distribution of the funds. But even supposing our nineteen representatives could so far forget themselves as to turn political hucksters and offer to sell themselves, body and soul, they will never obtain more than a few pickings from the public chest, which we shall do more than our share in filling. Under any circumstances, however humiliating, we shall be powerless to enforce a just consideration of interests.

There is a beautiful work of art representing two hounds chained together by the neck — one is large and powerful, looking down with contempt and indifference upon his lesser companion, who is as beautiful in the formation of limb, apparently as swift to follow the game, and as keen of scent as the other, yet crouches, overawed and helpless. Often as I have looked upon that work, I have felt an impulse rising within me to strike the chain from the little fellow's neck and let him free. And ever since this Confederation scheme has been published — every time I have looked upon a miniature copy of that work, I have thought of Confederation. I have seen Nova Scotia, bound and chained by the neck to Canada, and thinking of my country thus helpless, powerless, and prostrate at Ottawa, with a representation of only 19 in a parliament of 194, the exclamation rises from my heart — "God help the little fellow."

Around me sit the men to whom the constituencies of Nova Scotia entrusted her constitutional rights — her interests and welfare — to whom she, for four years, bared her neck — is there — can there be one among us who will help to fasten upon that neck this chain, prepared by the delegates? No, let us rather keep sacred that trust — let us rather go back to the people and learn of them at the polls their wishes on this great question, lest in after years they have just reason to execrate our memories — lest they pray heaven to strike palsied every hand that touched to fasten a rivet of that chain.

— *House of Assembly, April 17, 1865*

It is probable that McLelan is referring to a picture by Edwin Landseer (1802–1873) like the one shown here. Landseer was famous for paintings and engravings of sporting subjects, some depicting dogs chained in tandem.

---

* McLelan cannot square the idea of politics as a clash of parties and interests with the notion of federal MPs as representatives of their particular province or region. Nowadays, of course, party discipline regularly requires MPs to sacrifice both their local loyalties and their conscientious convictions. — PR

Charles Hamilton: My own opinion is that there is no other true principle than representation by population. It has been said that wealth should be the basis. When discussing this question with a gentleman who has since passed away, I asked him: as Halifax has an amount of wealth equal to Lunenburg, Queen's, Shelburne, Yarmouth, and Digby combined, would you give her the same representation that all these counties have? Certainly you would not. Take production again. I might bring statistics to show that there is more production in Antigonish than in any other county in the province, according to her population. Guysborough is another county which produces very heavily in fish, etc. Therefore I cannot see that it is possible to base representation upon any other principle than population.

If you form a union with the other provinces, on what other principle can you base it? You could not base it on wealth, or production, or territory. Population is the only true and safe principle. Therefore, as far as that principle in the Quebec scheme is concerned, it has my hearty co-operation.

— *House of Assembly, April 17, 1866*

NEW BRUNSWICK

John Costigan: We were three distinct peoples, but were to be governed by one general government, and that was to be carried on by a majority vote; that majority was to rule the country and tax the people as they saw fit. According to the construction of government we would be represented by 15 representatives, and these would have to fight against 145. Although I might have much respect for the ability of our representatives, yet I would not have much reason to expect that they would have much success in anything they undertook for the benefit of the province.

There is one section of the [Quebec] scheme which provides for the readjustment of the representation by population every ten years. According to that, in a few years, taking the increase of population according to the past as the nearest criterion to judge by, the representatives of Upper Canada in seventeen years would outvote the whole of the other provinces. It has been argued that if we had Confederation it would make a great change, and we would become a great country for capitalists, and emigrants would be induced to come here. Would it change the course of our rivers and give more facilities to manufactures? The only change it would make would be to place at the disposal of the general

government in Canada the whole resources of the colonies, and emigration would tend to that part of the Confederation, for we would be removed from any benefit arising from the construction of public works. I believe there is reason for making the assertion that influences are brought to bear abroad to place the people of this province and the government of the day in a wrong position.

— *House of Assembly, May 30, 1865*

James Boyd: When I read [the Quebec scheme] I was somewhat favourably impressed by it, but as I read on and came to the section which provided that the governor general should have the appointment of the governors of the lower provinces, I said at once, then the last link that binds us to England will be broken. I went on further and found that New Brunswick was to be represented in the general parliament by only fifteen members and I then felt that we should be swamped by Upper Canada. The fact was Canada found herself overwhelmed with debt and wanted to get the support of these provinces to relieve her, and so we were to be bought and sold for eighty cents a head. Our people had been content with their position, and if they ever desired a change it was that we might enter into a union of the lower provinces.

John McMillan: The honourable member (Mr. Boyd) says we were "going to be swamped, only fifteen members from New Brunswick and so many from Canada." He seems to forget what matters were to come before the general government to be discussed. What is it that makes dissension and discussion; is it not the matters that are of a local character? But there the question of tariffs and general trade could have caused no such dissension. And then supposing difficulties did arise, what would affect us would in a like manner affect Nova Scotia, and Prince Edward Island, and Lower Canada, and these together would wield a greater influence than could be brought to bear against them. See how it is in Canada, although divisions have taken place there, the parties were so equal that a few members were always able to sustain or overthrow a government. And how shall it be said that Upper Canada, with her 82 members will swamp us, when we are backed by 112 on all discussions of a general character which alone can be brought up . . . In a question of this kind, we should rise above such petty, narrow views, and look at the advantages that would accrue from our being a large, united, and free people.

— *House of Assembly, May 31, 1865*

Edward Chandler: I am not aware how any gentleman forming a government on representative principles could claim for or give to any one locality more than its fair share of representative power. It is not at all uncommon to hear complaints from communities that they have not their fair share of representatives in the legislative body of their particular state, but I am not aware of ever having heard or read of any people or community who enjoyed representation in proportion to their population, complaining. No, because they have their fair share, and no reasonable men can ask more.

Your Honours are very well aware that the great difficulties in Canada have all arisen out of the fact that the respective provinces were not represented according to population. In fact, it is a truism founded upon general and well-established constitutional principles, and underlying the whole policy of representative institutions, and how, then, I ask, could any gentleman having a regard for character as a statesman have got up in the conference and claimed that one man in New Brunswick was equal to two in Canada, or say that when the lower province was awarded her share of representatives, being based upon her population, it was not a fair share. It is an absurdity.

— *Legislative Council, April 4, 1866*

CANADA

George-Étienne Cartier: Everyone who knew anything of his past public course was aware that he was opposed to the principle of representation by population while Upper and Lower Canada were under one government. He did not regret his opposition. If such a measure had been passed, what would have been the consequence? There would have been constant political warfare between Upper and Lower Canada. True it was that the members from Upper Canada, being in the majority, it might have been imagined they would have carried everything before them; but as far as justice to Lower Canada was concerned, such might not have been the case. The consequence of representation by population would have been that one territory would have governed another, and this fact would have presented itself session after session in the house, and day after day in the public prints. (Hear, hear.) . . .

He was accused of being opposed to Upper Canada's rights, because during fifteen or twenty years he had to oppose his hon-

GEORGE BROWN
(1818–1880), born in
Scotland and emigrated
to Canada in 1843 after
six years in New York
City. With financial
backing from leading
Reformers, he founded
the Toronto *Globe*
(forerunner of today's
Globe and Mail) in 1844
to campaign for
responsible government.
Later he attacked the
party leadership for its
indifference to the
separation of church and
state, and sympathy for
Montreal-based big
business. When the
party split in 1854, he
rallied its remnants
behind the policy of
representation by
population, to which he
later added that of
federalizing United
Canada. Cartier's
acceptance of that idea
in June 1864 led to the
formation of the
coalition government
that initiated
Confederation.

ourable friend the president of the council (Mr. Brown). His honourable colleague took the ground that representation should be arranged according to population in each section of the province. He (Mr. Cartier) had resisted that position, believing that the moment such a principle was applied, his honourable friend, who, no doubt, wanted to maintain the peaceful government of the country, would have been disappointed in his wish. It would have given rise to one of the bitterest struggles between the two provinces that ever took place between two nations. He did not mean to say that the majority from Upper Canada would have tyrannized over Lower Canada; but the idea that Upper Canada as a territory had the preponderance in the government by a large number of representatives would have been sufficient to generate that sectional strife to which he had alluded.

He did not oppose the principle of representation by population from an unwillingness to do justice to Upper Canada. He took this ground, however, that when justice was done to Upper Canada, it was his duty to see that no injustice was done to Lower Canada. He did not entertain the slightest apprehension that Lower Canada's rights were in the least jeopardized by the provision that in the general legislature the French Canadians of Lower Canada would have a smaller number of representatives than all the other origins combined. It would be seen by the resolutions that in the questions which would be submitted to the general parliament there could be no danger to the rights and privileges of either French Canadians, Scotchmen, Englishmen, or Irishmen. Questions of commerce, of international communication, and all matters of general interest would be discussed and determined in the general legislature; but in the exercise of the functions of the general government, no one could apprehend that anything could be enacted which would harm or do injustice to persons of any nationality.

— *Legislative Assembly, February 7, 1865*

George Brown: No constitution ever framed was without defect; no act of human wisdom was ever free from imperfection;* no amount of talent and wisdom and integrity combined in preparing

---

* Note Brown's anti-utopianism. He is a reformer; he would never suppose we should give up the search for better political institutions, and he knows our prejudices can get in the way of necessary reforms. But he also knows that politics sometimes requires compromise, and more than this, that attempts to

such a scheme could have placed it beyond the reach of criticism. And the framers of this scheme had immense special difficulties to overcome. We had the prejudices of race and language and religion to deal with; and we had to encounter all the rivalries of trade and commerce, and all the jealousies of diversified local interests. To assert, then, that our scheme is without fault would be folly. It was necessarily the work of concession; not one of the thirty-three framers but had, on some points, to yield his opinions; and for myself, I freely admit that I struggled earnestly, for days together, to have portions of the scheme amended.

But, Mr. Speaker, admitting all this — admitting all the difficulties that beset us — admitting frankly that defects in the measure exist — I say that, taking the scheme as a whole, it has my cordial enthusiastic support, without hesitation or reservation. (Hear, hear.) The people of Upper Canada have bitterly complained that though they numbered four hundred thousand souls more than the population of Lower Canada, and though they have contributed three or four pounds to the general revenue for every pound contributed by the sister province, yet the Lower Canadians send to parliament as many representatives as they do. Now, sir, the measure in your hands brings this injustice to an end — it sweeps away the line of demarcation between the two sections on all matters common to the whole province; it gives representation according to numbers wherever found in the house of assembly; and it provides a simple and convenient system for readjusting the representation after each decennial census. (Cheers.)

— *Legislative Assembly, February 8, 1865*

RED RIVER

"We cannot look on property as the best test of title to vote."

Louis Riel: [The convention is considering a small property qualification for the vote; every British householder will be qualified.] We cannot look on property as the best test of title to

---

get desired reforms sometimes make it harder to get others, perhaps equally good and equally desired. The general discussion of representation illustrates this point perfectly. The principle of "one person, one vote" expresses our commitment to human equality. But "one person, one vote" may make it more difficult to represent minority populations adequately. One can't have all the political "goods" together. And people will always have different ideas about how to order these goods. "No constitution [is] without defect." — JA

vote.* In this country, in fact, the poorer we are, the more honest we are; and to say that only the rich are to be entitled to exercise this right is a slander on our people. My own opinion is that the system prevailing in the States is better than that in Canada . . . Liberty to vote is what would be best for us. There should be no discrimination against foreigners.† Let us do justice to them . . .

I think it is unjust that a man should be required to be a householder before he can vote. Suppose a man's house were burned down, is he to be deprived of his vote? Does he lose his intelligence, because his house happens to be burned down? To advocate a property qualification is to speak in the interests of the rich as against the poor. Are there more honest men among the rich than among the poor? Are we not honest, though poor?

James Ross: [He agrees that many poor are honest and many rich are not.] But that is aside of the question we are discussing. I cannot regard our natives and half-breeds as poor in the sense alluded to. I think our population is extremely well off, and will compare favourably with the rural population of any foreign country. (Cheers.) I am proud and thankful for it. For poor people we must go to those foreign countries. I do not think that our people will ever be classed among that miserable class of paupers who have to be clothed and fed from day to day, and nurtured like children. We are well off‡ — hardly a poor person within our whole limits. Almost every man has a house and land, horses and

---

In Britain, the Second Reform Act of 1867 had extended the vote to all urban (but not rural) male householders. For centuries the argument against extending the franchise to the unpropertied was that, being in the majority, they would use the power of the franchise to attack the rights of property. Such was the position of Henry Ireton in the debate on the Leveller Agreement of the People in 1647, for example. In the New World, however, social realities were different. The majority of adult males did own property; therefore giving all of them the vote did not entail the same risk that they would use it to attack property. — IG

† Earlier (see his speech in chapter 8), Riel had recommended treating all outsiders, be they American or British, as foreigners. There is no contradiction between that argument and this one. Now he is opposing a proposal to restrict the franchise to British subjects, and foreigners means "non-British." In short, he is saying that there should be no discrimination among "foreigners." — PR

‡ Ross associates poverty with dependency. Is he also suggesting it is caused by

cattle. Thanks to our industry and intelligence, we have a settlement composed of men not in the rank of paupers. (Cheers.)

"It is important, in giving a man the right to vote in any country, that that man should have some interest in the country."

This question of the voting power is one of great importance: for the voters, after all, will have to decide all the questions which come up in the legislature — they have the source of power in their hands. If we put this source of power in the hands of parties not working for the good of the country, we are practically doing this: while on the one hand we secure certain benefits, on the other we provide machinery to cheat us out of them . . . It is important, in giving a man the right to vote in any country, that that man should have some interest in the country. In this country we have a mixed population. Take the population at present here, and I would be quite willing to look upon them as having an interest in the country, even though they had not a shilling or a house. But in view of emigration,* we ought to provide that a man shall have some material interest in the country before he be allowed to vote. The original resolution proposed that a man having had a three years' residence in the country, without any household qualification, should have a vote. The amendment proposed one year's residence and household qualification. My opinion is that it ought to be three years' residence and household qualification for all except the present inhabitants. We should fence ourselves in such a way as to prevent us from being swamped by outsiders having no stake in the country.

Alfred Scott: [He approves of the three-year qualification, but not the property qualification.] It is well known that the poor people more than any other class in the country need a representative. For the poor more than the rich is the protection of good laws needed. If the rich only are represented among the lawmakers of the country, what follows? The laws are made for the rich and are of such a character as will make the rich man richer and the poor poorer. What cared the rich man[†] for placing an efficient school system within the reach of all? He can educate

---

dependency? His statement is heart-stopping. "Our people" (the Métis; Ross describes himself as a half-breed) will never be poor. — JA

* Ross refers to immigration. The word was often used in this sense in British North America. It reflects an imperial perspective, in that many immigrants to British North America were emigrants from the United Kingdom. — PR

† It is remarkable that this modern problem was a matter of concern in 1870

his children at a private seminary. Look again at the priests across the river, who are sworn to poverty. Are they to have no voice in the making of the laws, because they are not rich? It is preposterous. Why, on the same principle, if the twelve apostles came to this country, they would not have any vote either. (Laughter.) Is it, I would ask, the house or the man who is to vote?

William Cummings: Almost no one is so poor as [to be] unable to meet household qualification.

Judge John Black: [The three-year requirement supported by Ross and Riel] seems to imply a very great distrust, on our part, of British subjects who may come to this country from any other colony. (Hear, hear.)

Scott: Is it the intention of the convention to allow women to vote?* No doubt many such will come in and be householders. (Laughter.)

— *Convention at Fort Garry, English and French Delegates in Council, February 3, 1870*

NEWFOUNDLAND

Henry Renouf: Newfoundland, the key of the St. Lawrence and the Confederation by the sea, with her valuable fisheries, rich minerals, extensive trade and commerce, splendid harbours, and great natural advantages, would have only the same representation as a town with the same population in the backwoods of Canada. It was not so much on the basis of population as by position and resources that she was entitled to a larger representation.

— *House of Assembly, April 3, 1865*

---

in a small, isolated community in the midst of the North American wilderness. — PR

* It is not surprising that the idea of allowing women to vote should provoke laughter, since almost no one at the time — male or female — supported it. The notable exception was John Stuart Mill in his Thoughts on Parliamentary Reform (1859). — IG

*The original Parliament Buildings, Ottawa, in a watercolour of 1866 by
Otto Jacobi. Modelled on the Gothic Revival style of the British Houses of
Parliament, the structure was begun in 1859, following Queen Victoria's
designation of Ottawa as the new capital of the united Province of Canada.
It was destroyed by fire in 1917.*

PART TWO

WHAT THEY

SAID ABOUT

OPPORTUNITY

Chapter Five

ECONOMIC
PROSPERITY AND
INDIVIDUAL AMBITION

———◆◎◆———

T HE MEN WHO DRAFTED THE QUEBEC RESOLUTIONS
in 1864 were confident that colonial union would improve
prospects for economic prosperity in every colony. It is a central
tenet of nineteenth-century political science that a constitution
guaranteeing liberty and protecting minorities promotes the
people's material well-being. The Confederation leaders were
satisfied that they had designed a good constitution. Wealth
should follow.

But in the provincial parliaments and assemblies where the
Quebec Resolutions are being debated, the speakers don't always
agree. A number argue forcibly that union would enrich the central provinces at the expense of those on the periphery: the
Atlantic colonies, Red River, and British Columbia. How familiar
such statements sound even today!

Threaded through the debate on regional economic conditions are observations on the ambition of public men. Few
speakers believe that men are naturally modest in their ambitions;
it is assumed that in public men especially, whatever their party
affiliation, the desire for status and for the financial rewards associated with political office bring powerful temptations to betray
the public interest. Several remedies are suggested, among them
simple disapproval of ambition and the appeal to standards of
public virtue. Though some endorse this approach, more think it
better to rely on the traditional checks and balances of the parliamentary system and the competition of political parties; these are,
presumably, institutions that reward politicians with office only

when they have demonstrated their ability to win the public's favour. Thus ambition is not diminished; rather, it is harnessed for the public good. But are such checks on ambition really effective? And will their effectiveness hold up in a federal union where the most ambitious men can choose between local politics and the new, promising arena of dominion politics?

NOVA SCOTIA

Adams Archibald: He was of the opinion that a union would open up a wider field for public men.* He looked upon it as likely to soften, to a large extent, the asperities of political life. Every person knew that in proportion to the size of the country is the acrimony and asperity. By giving breadth to the sphere of operations, we would necessarily liberalize the feelings and elevate the character of our public men.

— House of Assembly, March 18, 1864

"[Confederation] would tend to decrease the personal element in our political discussions, and to rest the claims of our public men more upon the advocacy of public question than is possible at the present moment whilst these colonies are so limited in extent."

Charles Tupper: I am satisfied that looking at emigration, to the elevation of public credit, to the elevation of public sentiment which must arise from enlarging the sphere of action, the interests of these provinces require that they should be united under one government and legislature. It would tend to decrease the personal element in our political discussions, and to rest the claims of our public men more upon the advocacy of public question than is possible at the present moment whilst these colonies are so limited in extent. We have only to look to Prince Edward Island to find that political differences are expanded, political acrimony engendered, and the difficulty of government increased, just in an inverse ratio to the size of the country, and that when you increase the area of the country you decrease the political acrimony and difference of opinion that are calculated

---

* *The idea that enlarging the political arena would soften the asperities of political life was one that inspired such prominent founders of the United States as Alexander Hamilton and James Madison. It was supposed to achieve that effect by increasing the supply of desirable government jobs and by widening the distance between citizens and the government. — PR*
In his Report on the Affairs of British North America *(1839), Lord Durham makes an argument very much like Madison's on the benefits of enlarging the political arena. Durham's source was Adam Smith,* The Wealth of Nations *(1776). — JA*

to place one section in such antagonism to the other as to render it impossible to advance measures of public improvement.

> "He did not accede to the doctrine that the union would abate sectional jealousies and personal animosities. He need only point to Canada . . ."

Avard Longley: A great deal of importance had been attached to the argument that the union would afford a wider sphere of political action for our politicians and thereby soften the asperities that arise in a contracted sphere of political action. He had little doubt that there were several leading gentlemen in these provinces whose ambition sought a wider range, and it was certainly a great pity that their desires could not be gratified. He looked upon the geographical position, resources, and financial condition of this province as far superior to those of any other of the provinces, and felt that it would be unwise to jeopardize a condition of things that was so eminently satisfactory.

He did not accede to the doctrine that the union would abate sectional jealousies and personal animosities. He need only point to Canada to show that there was more corruption among its public men, and more violent political rancour, at the present hour, than there was before the union [of Upper Canada and Lower Canada]. He was very far from believing that a union of these lower provinces was going to mitigate any existing evil, but was rather inclined to the opinion that it would bring into play various influences and interests that we should rather seek to avoid.

— *House of Assembly, March 28, 1864*

William Annand: The honourable provincial secretary [Charles Tupper] has referred to the local governments and declared that they will not be insignificant in character — that the houses will still be in place, where men of as great ability will aspire as those who sat here in former times. At that time there was only one place of political preferment that those gentlemen could aspire to, that was this house. Now there will be two — one at Ottawa, where the salaries will be large and the government liberal to a degree unknown* in this country. I would like to hear the provincial secretary tell us what kind of local government we are to have — Is there to be one house or two? — and if only one chamber, how many members are to sit there? Are we to have responsible government as now with heads of departments? These are matters of great importance to the people of this country in connection with

---

* *The word* liberal *refers to the scale and expense of the government, not to its political character.* — PR

this subject — they are interesting to those gentlemen who do not expect to go to Ottawa but aspire to come here again. They wish to learn whether this body is to be only a little more important than a court of sessions or a city council. I pause for a reply from the provincial secretary, but I know in vain.

— *House of Assembly, April 12, 1865*

William Ross: The whole history of Confederation is based on the ambition of some of our public men and on the necessities of Canada. Ambition is the sin of angels, and even politicians, finding that they were losing power, must go to Ottawa. They are like the evil one, as described by Milton,* who would rather rule in hell than fill a subordinate place in heaven.

I have no ambition to gratify, no self-interest to advance — but as I was early taught that responsible government was government according to the well-understood wishes of the people I will not agree to sell their birthrights without asking their consent, but will on the contrary stand by what I consider the dearest rights of Nova Scotia and the express views of those whom I represent.

"In a free government there must always be divisions and parties; and there should be, because eternal vigilance is the price of liberty."

William Lawrence: In a free government there must always be divisions and parties; and there should be, because eternal vigilance is the price of liberty,† and nothing so stimulates vigilance as the conflicting opinions of parties. But we should ever remember that the claims of our country stand far above the claims of party. Why does a patriot await the result with suspended animation and peaceable cheek? Because upon the issue hangs the fate of his country. If victory light upon his standard, his altar and his fireside are safe. Now, sir, with our fertile soil, our noble streams, our mineral wealth, large seaboard for navigation and shipbuilding — our population intelligent, enterprising, and religious — these will enable us to advance with steady and sure march in civilization. And I am for that sort of industry which spreads wealth among the labouring classes and elevates them gradually in the scale. I believe in a firm protection of the rights of the weak, whensoever they are in danger by the power

---

* *In Milton's epic poem* Paradise Lost, *Satan, originally one of the chief angels, falls from heaven on account of his ambition to overthrow God.* — IG

† *A common corruption of a remark by John Philpot Curran (1750–1817), Irish lawyer and politician: "The condition upon which God hath given liberty to man is eternal vigilance."* — PR

of the strong; and wherever you find Englishmen, Irishmen, and Scotchmen, you will find that they carry with them the high qualities of their race* which have led the way in civilization by spreading the great principle of freedom — freedom in religion and freedom in government — over the world. Their prosperity has been brought about by an overruling Providence.

— House of Assembly, April 17, 1866

John Bourinot: In looking at the prospects of the Confederation which is to be, I feel that we have all the elements of greatness within us. We have a territory larger than that of the United States, we have a supply of those minerals upon which the might and prosperity of England have so long rested, we have gold, we have our fisheries and our timber and the agricultural capacities of Canada, which is only second among grain-producing countries of this continent, and is one of the granaries of the world. Then there is our mercantile marine, the third or fourth in the world, and I feel that the time will come when we will stand among the very first on the list.

— House of Assembly, March 16, 1867

NEW BRUNSWICK

John McMillan: [There] are objects that should animate us with a spirit of progress. What is the cry of England? "Free trade, free trade with the world": and this should be our motto, not as I said, the other day, to build a China wall around us and crop us up in our little eggshell, and call all outside of us barbarians. This is not the principle of the day; this should not be our policy, but to enter into an alliance that will enable us to have free trade with our neighbours;† and this union of the provinces, I maintain, would be commercially the best step we could take.

— House of Assembly, May 31, 1865

---

* It must not be supposed that because Lawrence believes "the great principle of freedom" originated in Britain, he necessarily thinks only the British are entitled to enjoy it. At its best the kind of liberal constitutionalism Lawrence is advocating argues that all peoples, whatever their origin, prefer liberty to dependency. There are no naturally slavish peoples; there are no people anywhere in the world on whom political institutions of dependency and slavery can be justly imposed. — JA

†While Confederation increased New Brunswick's freedom of trade with the

Robert Thomson: I thought it was my duty as a British subject, with British feelings, to strive to retain our privileges from the grasp of parties who tried to sweep away the rights of our province. At one time we were united with Nova Scotia, but were separated by the consent and direction of the British government because it was thought it would be conducive to our welfare. This proposed union is not for the purpose of having one legislature, but is a federal union where the dominant party will have power to tyrannize over us if they think proper.

It is an old saying that we should "Give glory to God, honour to the king, and live honestly with all men."* The Liberals have not done this, for they have taken all the glory themselves, and have honoured neither king, country, nor anything else. This country was not big enough for them, and they wanted to extend it, like the fable of the frog and the horse. The frog enlarged himself until he burst, and so it was with these delegates; they would not act in such a way as was commensurate with their means. This country was too small for them, and they must get up this big scheme; but the "handwriting was upon the wall," and their place knew them no more. If there are any influences at work in England in regard to legislating for this province, we should send a delegation home to counteract it; we must protect ourselves, for "self-preservation is the first law of nature."

"We must protect ourselves, for 'self-preservation is the first law of nature.'"

The expenses of this scheme would have been enormous, inasmuch as we would have had to have kept up our own legislature and a union of all the legislatures in Canada, and we give them the power to tax us as much as they please; if there was any necessity for this union it would be better to have one parliament for all; by this means we would save a great deal of expense.

— *House of Assembly, June 1, 1865*

Abner McClellan: I may here advert to a remark of Lord Durham to show that a colonial union was necessary, in the opinion of that eminent constitutionist, in order to rid the separate colonies of the disorders arising from the influence of designing and ambitious individuals, as by affording a large scope for the desires of such men as shall direct their ambition into

---

other provinces of Canada, it increased barriers to her trade outside Canada. The dominion tariff was higher than New Brunswick's from the start, and it rose considerably with the adoption of the National Policy in 1879. — PR

* *I Peter 2:17.*

the legitimate character of furthering, and not of thwarting, their government . . . I am anxious to give my friend, the president of the council [Albert J. Smith], a wider scope for his powers and ability . . .

— *House of Assembly, June 2, 1865*

Andrew Wetmore: It is our duty to legislate for those who come after us; and it is our duty as statesmen not to give up our country to gratify a few vain individuals. When we find men who, instead of looking after the interests of the people who have elevated them to a high position, attempt to fly still higher, their flight is generally downwards, like that of a man who went to the top of a house with paper wings to make a bird of himself. This has been the case with statesmen before, and will be so again.

George Hill: It appears that the mantle of prophecy has fallen upon these gentlemen. They are like Miller* prophesying the destruction of the world; when the time comes for the prophecy to be fulfilled, they prophesy anew. These gentlemen imitated the rallying cry of Mahomet, "Great is Allah and Mahomet is his Prophet," and substitute "Great is Confederation and many are its profits." But the profits would be to Canada, and the expense to New Brunswick and the other Maritime provinces.

— *House of Assembly, June 3, 1865*

Albert J. Smith: No man denied that [the Confederation scheme] originated in the necessities of Canada. The people of this country have no right to be made subservient to the political necessities of Canada. If we could get a scheme of union upon such terms as are fair and equitable, such terms as would be promotive of the welfare and prosperity of this country, I would be in favour of it, but

---

This is likely a reference to William Miller (d. 1849), an American Baptist lay preacher and New York State farmer who was the founder of what become known as the "Millerite" movement, a northeastern American religious phenomenon of about 40,000 members which spread into the Middle West and to Canada. Miller was a Doomsday millenarian who predicted that, according to biblical prophecy, the world would end on October 22, 1844. For a decade before this date, he travelled widely and preached his message to large audiences. When the Great Disappointment, as it was later called, became apparent the next morning, his most ardent followers reacted by organizing themselves as Seventh-day Adventists. — WDG

I will not consent to ignore the prosperity of my country for the sake of relieving the political necessities of Canada.

— *House of Assembly, March 14, 1866*

Thomson: This Confederation scheme cannot benefit our trade. We have not a single article we can send to Canada . . . We would soon have all our offices filled with the employees of the Canadian government, while we would have to pay three times the taxes in proportion to our numbers, for the French scarcely consume any dutiable articles, the very sugar they use they produce from the maple . . . We would be worse than the slaves, for they have a hope of getting something done for them, while we would have none. If they could enter into some fair principle of union, such as was entered into between England, Scotland, and Ireland,* which was not the question of a day or a year, but here we had a scheme brought forward of which we knew nothing, and we were expected to pass it at once.

— *House of Assembly, March 21, 1866*

John Lewis: He believed that the union of the provinces would be of a great benefit to New Brunswick. It would lead to the construction of the Inter-Colonial Railway,† to the opening up of the country and its advancement in wealth and progress. Notwithstanding all that had been said against the Quebec scheme, it was better than no scheme at all. If the government were not prepared with a better measure, better let them accept the Quebec scheme at once.

— *House of Assembly, March 24, 1866*

Benjamin Beveridge: Had they ever, he would ask, heard of a poor man being unwilling to unite in business with a man who was a great deal wealthier than himself — the benefits must be greatly on the side of the poor man.

---

* England and Scotland negotiated a mutually satisfactory union in 1707. In 1800 the English government, led by William Pitt the Younger, coerced and bribed the Irish parliament, in which only Protestants were represented, into consenting to its own abolition, and the union of Ireland with Britain. — IG
† The Quebec Resolutions stipulated that the general government would secure the completion of a railway link between Nova Scotia and central Canada. The task was made incumbent on the dominion government by section 145 of the British North America Act.

William Needham: He would take up the remark of the honourable member for Victoria, Mr. Beveridge, who said that they had never heard of a poor man who was not willing to go into partnership with a rich man, applying this to the union of New Brunswick with Canada. No doubt there were great advantages to a poor man in a union of that kind; but the benefits of such a partnership were not so evident when the riches of the reputed wealthy man — and he applied this to Canada — were reported to be of a very doubtful character, and especially when entering into such a partnership, the poor man had to give up the control of his own effects and the general management of his own affairs.

— *House of Assembly, March 31, 1866*

"Bring us near to the darling of our souls, the far-away Ottawa, with its miles of cornice and its acres of plaster, and let us revel there . . ."

Needham: I know there are men who would soar away beyond us, who are not satiated with all that little New Brunswick can give them, and they reach forward to the celebrated towers and palaces of far-off Ottawa; for this they would let New Brunswick go to the winds and be lost for ever. Bring us near to the darling of our souls, the far-away Ottawa, with its miles of cornice and its acres of plaster, and let us revel there in vice-regal glory. But there are loyal sons of New Brunswick who will not be carried away by all this splendour, and when the time comes it will be seen that its splendour has been like a dissolving view to their eyes, become "the baseless fabric of a vision which leaves not a wreck behind."*

— *House of Assembly, April 3, 1866*

Edward Chandler: Your honours, there is a large class of persons in the province who never inquire into financial matters at all, who do not investigate the public accounts, who don't know and don't care, so long as the ordinary appropriations are made, where the money comes from; and these persons careless of consequences, looking neither at causes nor results, will meet us with "Let well alone." There are farmers who, so long as seed-time and harvest come and crops grow, without regarding the general interest, say, "Let well alone." The bankers who grow wealthy, even on the exigencies of trade, say, "Let well alone." Rich merchants who have and do control the business of the country to a large extent say, "Let well alone."

Obstructives generally, who only look at one side of the ques-

---

* *Shakespeare*, The Tempest, *Act 4, scene 1.*

tion and fail to comprehend how they must reap an abundant share in the general harvest of rich results from whatever advances the prosperity of the whole country, say, "Let well alone," because it seems well with their own personal interests. But the statesman, the patriot, who desires to see the individual provinces of British North America advance, who desires for them a future compatible with their position as members of the great empire of Britain; as territories possessing resources abundant and rich in all that is calculated, properly developed, to make a country great; possessing hardy, industrious intelligent populations; I say the true statesman, and true patriot, influenced by such desires, and seeing these provinces as they are, under the present proscriptive regulations, working out each its own narrowed career of selfishness; in debt, and running still deeper in debt; without satisfaction in the present or hope for the future, must hail the opportunity now offered for uniting these fragmentary territories, giving them at once unity, position, influence, wealth, and power.

— Legislative Council, April 4, 1866

Peter Mitchell: Isolation [is] dangerous to our liberty and destructive to our progress. Our people are industrious — our resources abundant — but union is necessary to our success. Association by national union with three or four millions of people, attached to the institutions of our parent state, would give us a strength and importance which we do not possess. We would have extended markets for our ships and other manufacturers, and by increased trade, an increased home market for the farmer. Situated as we are as the great outpost sentinels towards Europe on the stormy Atlantic, we in these Maritime provinces would become from our favourable position the outlet and shipping post for the great trade of the far west.

Railroads ere long would connect our principal cities and towns with the world outside of us, and in course of time we might look forward to their extension across the continent. Those outlying portions of the empire stretching from the Great Lakes across the Rocky Mountains to the Pacific would conduce to our greatness. Their wealth and their exports must increase our commerce, and our ships must find employment in the prosecution of their trade. The water and bed of the Great Lakes and the mighty St. Lawrence are capable of sustaining twenty millions of people alone.

We are now as colonists comparatively a free people, but history indicates that a small province cannot long remain independent beside a powerful and rapacious neighbour. In union there is strength, security, and continued freedom. Out of it there is before us annexation and extinction of national existence, with the doubtful advantage of having to pay a share of the enormous war debt of our neighbours.

— *Legislative Council, April 16, 1866*

"Under union we would advance more rapidly in science and literature, in railroads and telegraphs, in civilization and religion, than we do at present."

Francis Hibbard: Under union we would advance more rapidly in science and literature, in railroads and telegraphs, in civilization and religion, than we do at present. I believe that when the general assembly meets at Ottawa they will not infringe the rights of New Brunswick, for we will form one people, and our interest will be their interest. We will start in the race of national greatness, and go out to the world as competitors with those who will compete with us.

— *House of Assembly, June 18, 1866*

CANADA

George Brown: Our scheme is to establish a government that will seek to turn the tide of European emigration into this northern half of the American continent — that will strive to develop its great natural resources — and that will endeavour to maintain liberty, and justice, and Christianity throughout the land.

T.C. Wallbridge: When?

George-Étienne Cartier: Very soon.

Brown: Sir, the whole great ends of this Confederation may not be realized in the lifetime of many who now hear me. We imagine not that such a structure can be built in a month or in a year. What we propose now is but to lay the foundations of the structure — to set in motion the governmental machinery that will one day, we trust, extend from the Atlantic to the Pacific. And we take especial credit to ourselves that the system we have devised, while admirably adapted to our present situation, is capable of gradual and efficient expansion in future years to meet all the great purposes contemplated by our scheme.

If the honourable gentleman [T.C. Wallbridge] will only recall to mind that when the United States seceded from the mother country, and for many years afterwards their population was not nearly equal to ours at this moment; that their internal improvements did not then approach to what we have already attained; and that their trade and commerce was not then a third of what ours has already reached; I think he will see that the fulfilment of our hopes may not be so very remote as at first sight might be imagined. (Hear, hear.) And said I not rightly that such a scheme is well fitted to fire the ambition and rouse the energies of every member of this house? Does it not lift us above the petty politics of the past, and present to us high purposes and great interests that may well call forth all the intellectual ability and all the energy and enterprise to be found among us? (Cheers.) . . .

The crusading campaigner George Brown; from cartoonist J.W. Bengough's Caricature History of Canadian Politics.

I go heartily for the union, because it will throw down the barriers of trade and give us control of a market of four millions of people. (Hear, hear.) What one thing has contributed so much to the wondrous material progress of the United States as the free passage of their products from one state to another? What has tended so much to the rapid advance of all branches of their industry as the vast extent of their home market, creating an unlimited demand for all the commodities of daily use and stimulating the energy and ingenuity of producers? Sir, I confess to you that in my mind this one view of the union — the addition of nearly a million of people to our home consumers — sweeps aside all the petty objections that are averred against the scheme. What, in comparison with this great gain to our farmers and manufacturers, are even the fallacious money objections which the imaginations of honourable gentlemen opposite have summoned up? All over the world we find nations eagerly longing to extend their domains, spending large sums and waging protracted wars to possess themselves of more territory, untilled and uninhabited. (Hear, hear.) Other countries offer large inducements to foreigners to emigrate to their shores — free passages, free lands, and free food and implements to start them in the world. We ourselves support costly establishments to attract immigrants to our country and are satisfied when our annual outlay brings us fifteen or twenty thousand souls. But here, sir, is a proposal which is to add, in one day, near a million of souls to our population — to add valuable territories to our domain, and secure to us all the advantages of a large and profitable commerce, now existing. And because some of us would have liked certain of the little details

otherwise arranged, we are to hesitate in accepting this alliance? (Hear, hear.)

Have honourable gentlemen forgotten that the United States gladly paid twenty millions in hard cash to have Louisiana incorporated in the republic? But what was Louisiana then to the Americans, in comparison with what the Maritime provinces are at this moment to Canada? I put it to honourable gentlemen opposite — if the United States were now to offer us the state of Maine, what possible sum could be named within the compass of our ability that we would not be prepared to pay for that addition to our country? (Hear, hear.) If we were offered Michigan, Iowa, or Minnesota, I would like to know what sum, within the compass of Canada, we would not be prepared to pay? These are portions of a foreign country, but here is a people owning the same allegiance as ourselves, loving the same old sod, enjoying the same laws and institutions, actuated by the same impulses and social customs — and yet when it is proposed that they shall unite with us for purposes of commerce, for the defence of our common country, and to develop the vast natural resources of our united domains, we hesitate to adopt it!

If a Canadian goes now to Nova Scotia or New Brunswick, or if a citizen of these provinces comes here, it is like going to a foreign country. The customs officer meets you at the frontier, arrests your progress, and levies his imposts on your effects. But the proposal now before us is to throw down all barriers between the provinces — to make a citizen of one, citizen of the whole; the proposal is that our farmers and manufacturers and mechanics shall carry their wares unquestioned into every village of the Maritime provinces; and that they shall with equal freedom bring their fish, and their coals, and their West India produce to our three million of inhabitants. The proposal is that the law courts, and the schools, and the professional and industrial walks of life, throughout all the provinces, shall be thrown equally open to us all. (Hear, hear.) But [moreover], Mr. Speaker, I am in favour of a union of the provinces because — and I call the attention of honourable gentlemen opposite to it — because it will make us the third Maritime state of the world. (Hear, hear.) When this union is accomplished, but two countries in the world will be superior in maritime influence to British America — and those are Great Britain and the United States . . .

Mr. Speaker, I go for a union of the provinces because it will give a new start to immigration into our country. It will bring us

out anew prominently before the world — it will turn earnest attention to our resources and bring to our shores a stream of immigration greater, and of a better class, than we ever had before. I hesitate not to say that it should be accompanied with a vigorous effort to give a new impetus to our industrial enterprises, to open up fresh lands for settlement, and to cheapen the transport of our produce to the seaboard. With the consummation of this union, I trust we will have a new immigration and a new land settlement policy — that we will ascertain every lot of land we actually own, so that a printed list may be placed in the hands of every immigrant — that the petty price we have been heretofore exacting will no longer be exacted, but that to the actual settlers, who come among us to hew out for themselves and their children homes in the forest, no burden or condition will be demanded beyond resident occupation for a certain number of years and a fixed amount of improvement on the land.

Luther Holton: Unfortunately for your argument, the lands will be in the hands of the local governments.

"The gentlemen who formed the conference at Quebec did not enter upon their work with the miserable idea of getting the advantage of each other, but with a due sense of the greatness of the work they had on hand and with an earnest desire to do justice to all, and keeping always in mind that what would benefit one section in such a union must necessarily benefit the whole."

Brown: So much the better. My honourable friend can manage his public lands in Lower Canada as he likes, and we will manage ours . . . On this question of immigration turns, in my opinion, the whole future success of this great scheme which we are now discussing . . . And this question of immigration naturally brings me to the great subject of the North-West Territories. (Hear, hear.) . . . Sir, the gentlemen who formed the conference at Quebec did not enter upon their work with the miserable idea of getting the advantage of each other, but with a due sense of the greatness of the work they had on hand and with an earnest desire to do justice to all, and keeping always in mind that what would benefit one section in such a union must necessarily benefit the whole. (Cheers.) It has always appeared to me that the opening up of the north-west ought to be one of the most cherished projects of my honourable friends from Lower Canada . . .

Mr. Speaker, I am in favour of a union of these provinces because it will enable us to meet, without alarm, the abrogation of the American Reciprocity Treaty,* in case the United States should insist on its abolition. (Hear, hear.) I do not believe that

---

American Reciprocity Treaty. A treaty establishing tariff reciprocity between the United States and United Canada had taken effect in 1854.

the American government is so insane as to repeal that treaty. But it is always well to be prepared for contingencies — and I have no hesitation in saying that if they do repeal it, should this union of British America go on, a fresh outlet for our commerce will be opened up to us quite as advantageous as the American trade has ever been. I have never heretofore ventured to make this assertion, for I know well what a serious task it is to change, in one day, the commercial relations of such a country as this. When the traffic of a country has passed for a lengthened period through a particular channel, any serious change of that channel tends, for a time, to the embarrassment of businessmen and causes serious injury to individuals, if not to the whole community. Such a change we in Canada had in 1847.* But as it was in 1847, so it will be in 1866, if the Reciprocity Treaty is abolished. Our agricultural interest had been built up on the protective legislation of Great Britain, and in 1847 it was suddenly brought to an end. We suffered severely in consequence for some years; but, by degrees, new channels for our trade opened up — the Reciprocity Treaty was negotiated — and we have been more prosperous since 1847 than we ever were before. And so, I have not a doubt, will it be in the event of the Reciprocity Treaty being abolished.

— *Legislative Assembly, February 8, 1865*

L.-A. Olivier: [P]ublic opinion is composed especially of that of the industrial and commercial classes, and it is the interest of those classes to favour Confederation. But let us consider whether the interests of those classes is ours also.† I consider that our present political course should be to see to the interests of the agriculture, the trade, and the industry of our country before labouring to build up that of English traders and artisans. If by Confederation we unite provinces, the inhabitants of which find it their interest to have a very low tariff adopted, it might very well

---

Knowledge of the U.S. government's decision not to renew it on its expiration in 1866 provided a stimulus to Confederation. Despite Brown's protestations here, the United States did not renew the treaty.

* Brown refers to the British government's shift from imperial tariff preference to free trade about that time. — PR

† Olivier is speaking in French and addressing himself to his fellow francophones. His argument exemplifies an identification with the land and hostility towards commerce which was predominant among French Canadians in the nineteenth and early twentieth centuries. — PR

happen the agricultural interest of Canada might not find itself so well off, and in such a case what would be the result? The result would be that we should very soon have an enormous debt, and that, should the customs revenue not suffice to meet it and provide for the expenditure, the deficit would have to be made up by means of direct taxation, which would weigh upon the agriculture and industry of the country. If we have a tariff of 20 per cent, it protects the industry of our native land and is a source of revenue wherewith to provide for the public expenditure; but if we make it too low, real property will suffer, for on it will be laid the burthen imposed to meet the deficit. Confederation would appear to me to be very costly, for money is scattered on all sides in handfuls.

— *Legislative Council, February 13, 1865*

Henri Joly: The honourable minister of finance [Alexander Galt], faithful to the doctrine that the greatness of a state is proportioned to the greatness of its debt, announces to us that our credit will be considerably increased and that we shall be enabled to borrow much more extensively than we have hitherto done, a prospect at which he seems greatly to rejoice. This facility of borrowing is not always an unmixed good, but it must be remembered that our credit will depend entirely on the success of our Confederation. If it should not succeed, if any serious difficulty should arise within it — a thing which is possible — public opinion will be more prompt to take alarm, in that our federal form of government does not afford strong guarantees for the maintenance of order and peace, and our credit will soon be worth less than the credit of a single province is worth today.

[If] in order to meet the extravagant expenditure the Confederation must bring with it, the people find themselves taxed beyond their resources, the government need not be surprised, if they should ever appeal to the courage of the people and call upon them to meet the enemy, to receive the answer the old man got from his donkey in Lafontaine's fable.* When at the approach of the enemy the old man wished to mount and fly, the donkey refused to bear him, and commenced the following dialogue with his master:

"On me double burthen do you think they will lay?"

Jean de La Fontaine (1621–1695), French poet; author of two collections of Fables. — PR

"Not so," said the old man, ere he toddled away.
"Then what odds," cried the donkey, "to whom I belong?
You may take to your heels and leave me to feed.
The donkey's real enemy is his own master's greed,
And I trust you'll admit that the argument's strong."

Lafontaine, it will be seen, found means, 200 years ago, of saying serious things in a laughing way. If the government treat the people as a beast of burthen, to be pitilessly overladen, the people will one day make them the same answer that the donkey made to his master, in Lafontaine's fable. Lord Bacon,* in his essays, expresses the same thought in more serious terms. But apart from purely material interests, which are nevertheless highly important, for happiness and poverty rarely go hand in hand, there are other interests of a higher order which rouse the courage of a people and sometimes render it capable of sustaining the most unequal struggles. Deprive the French Canadians of their nationality, and you deprive them of the enthusiasm which would have doubled their strength . . .

— *Legislative Assembly, February 20, 1865*

W. McGiverin: If the north-west contains land, as I believe it does, equal to almost any on this continent, it should be placed in precisely the same position as regards Canada that the western states occupy in relation to the eastern. I believe we should endeavour to develop a great grain-producing district; for whatever may be said, there is not any appreciable quantity of grain-producing land in the hands of the government not now under cultivation in Canada for the benefit of our increasing population. It is a melancholy fact that for the want of such a country our youth seek homes in a foreign land, who would remain under the British flag if homes were open to them there. (Hear, hear.) If we had that country open to them,† to say nothing of the foreign immigration it would attract, it would afford homes for a large population from amongst ourselves now absorbed in the western states.

— *Legislative Assembly, February 24, 1865*

---

* Francis Bacon treats of the oppression of the people by the rich and powerful in his essay "Of Seditions and Troubles."
† McGiverin's vision is imperial. He regards the north-west — at this time still largely the property of the Hudson's Bay Company, but today Manitoba, Saskatchewan, and Alberta — as a territory to be colonized by central

Christopher Dunkin: We are . . . assured of our own immense resources, are told that we are so wonderfully great and wonderfully rich that we are something like — I don't know whether we are or not — the third or fourth power, or maritime power, one or other, in the world. Really, I would not undertake to say how great we are, or are not, according to honourable gentlemen. They startle one. I had no idea how great we were! (Hear, hear.)

Many honourable gentlemen appear to think they have done all that need be done when they have answered to their own satisfaction the one question, What is the amount of our resources? Starting with the vastness of our territory, they go into all kinds of statements as to our trade and so forth, multiplying tonnage impossibly, adding together exports and imports — those of the intercolonial trade and all. I only wonder they do not, on the same principle, calculate our inter-county and our inter-township tradings, or our dealings between cities and country, adding exports and imports of course all round, and so proving that we have done more trade than all the rest of the world put together.

The question is not simply, What are our own resources? We must supplement it with a second — What are they . . . as compared with those of the United States? And while we are asking this question we may as well not take it for granted as a fact that the larger our country, the stronger we must be. Suppose we are to be four millions of people in a country as large as Europe or larger. I wish to heaven we were four millions of people — with all the adjacent unexposed territory you will — but in a country smaller than England . . . Too much of territory, and above all too much of exposed frontier, does not increase our strength but lessens it. Ours is the "long thin line of red," which is not so well able to receive a charge as the solid square.

Colonel Frederick Haultain was understood to signify dissent to some of the propositions here advanced.

Dunkin: If the honourable member for Peterborough [Haultain] thinks that in a military point of view, the length and narrowness of our territory adds to our strength — if he thinks we are the stronger for our length of frontier, I would respectfully recom-

---

Canada. Just as Britain, the imperial centre, sent its excess population to British North America, so Canada, the British American centre, would send its excess population to the west. — JA

mend him to attend one of our military schools. (Laughter.) But seriously, sir, if we are to compare our resources with those of the United States, we shall find, as I have said, that theirs are unmistakably, and beyond count, greater.

Haultain: Than the British Empire?

Dunkin: That is not the comparison. We are continually hearing of what Confederation is to do for ourselves, how it is going to make us a great power in the world. It is going to do nothing of the kind.

— Legislative Assembly, February 28, 1865

BRITISH COLUMBIA

J.S. Helmcken: It would be absurd for us to sacrifice our interests in order that laws may be made for us by a people who know little of our condition and wants, and who in fact must necessarily legislate for the great number — the people of the Atlantic provinces. It is dangerous to place ourselves at the disposal of superior numbers.

If we are confederated with Canada we become its tributary,* and in all that concerns us chiefly Canada has to act for us. In all our chief concerns — commerce, shipping, and mercantile laws, agriculture, trade, navigation, fisheries, currency, banking — Canada rules. She may tax us to any extent and in any manner she pleases, so that it is quite possible we may have export duties on gold and coal. All such things as require money for their performance are left for the colony to provide; those that require intellect are supplied by Canada. Is it necessary that we should pay for the intellect of Canada? Is our own not as good? Cannot we do all as well as they? Cannot we pay our colonial intellect to do our business well, instead of theirs to do it badly?

John Robson: I believe that much of the present opposition arises out of ancient prejudices. Why do we find an honourable gentleman [John S. Helmcken] who has grown grey in the service of his country, and for whom we have respect amounting to veneration, talking of centralization of every interest under

---

* *Helmcken's forebodings prefigure later complaints about the west's quasi-colonial subordination to central Canada. — PR*

Confederation at Ottawa? Does the union of Washington Territory and Oregon, with other states of the great republic, mean centralization at Washington?

Helmcken: Yes.

Robson: The nature of the union will be such as to make the interest of this part of the dominion identical with other parts. We cannot suppose that the dominion parliament would seek to injure this province. A man would not wantonly injure the smallest member of his body. He could not do so without feeling it . . . Community of interest is the best guarantee for fair play to every section. The dominion is made up of provinces, and the prosperity of the dominion means the prosperity of the provinces of which it is composed.

"We cannot suppose that the dominion parliament would seek to injure this province. A man would not wantonly injure the smallest member of his body."

If we could believe that the government of the dominion were composed of men of so little wisdom as the opponents of Confederation seem to think, I would say do not let us join them. But I believe, sir, and the imperial government believes, and British Columbia believes, that the government of the dominion is composed of statesmen. And I say, sir, that since these statesmen have grasped the great idea of Confederation, they have proved themselves fit to govern an empire.

— *Legislative Council, March 9, 1870*

Henry Holbrook: As we shall, from our position on the Pacific coast, be the keystone of Confederation, I hope we may become the most glorious in the whole structure, and tend to our own and England's future greatness.

— *Legislative Council, March 10, 1870*

Francis Barnard: Open those millions of acres [the prairies] to the settler and you will see such a rush of immigration — not only from the older countries of Europe but from the United States — as will astonish the world and stand unparalleled in the history of immigration. Canada's hardy sons who have left their homes for the western states — allured by the advantages of prairie over wooded lands — will join in swelling numbers and once more plant their feet on British soil.

Amongst the statesmen of Canada we may safely look for men fully competent to control the affairs of a young nation. They are men of as much ambition and grasp of thought as are the rulers

in the adjoining states; and, depend upon it, nothing will be left undone to advance the prosperity and well-being of every portion of their vast dominion. They can steer the good ship "Dominion" and hold her on her way.

— *Legislative Council, March 11, 1870*

Robson: Did I believe that the overland railway would not be made, I should hesitate very much about Confederation because I should be apprehensive that the whole scheme would fall to pieces. I think that great haste must be used to build up an English-speaking nation alongside of another existing English-speaking country. To accomplish this end, I think that the overland railway is necessary, and must be pushed through to speedy completion to be an immediate success. In ten years' time, without an overland railway, I do not believe that we should have any English territory here at all.

The great work must be undertaken with the assistance of both the Canadian and imperial governments, and pushed through to a speedy success. It is true that a sort of union might exist without a railway, such as the union between British Columbia and Great Britain. But we proposed to establish a union that will endure, and that will render an overland railway* just as necessary as the veins in the human body are necessary to circulate the blood and to keep up life.

— *Legislative Council, March 16, 1870*

NEWFOUNDLAND

"No doubt the lawyers took a warm interest in the matter [of Confederation], having before their eyes judgeships, governorships, and other lucrative appointments."

John Casey: No doubt the lawyers took a warm interest in the matter [of Confederation], having before their eyes judgeships, governorships, and other lucrative appointments. It would, no doubt, be a fortunate thing for them, when they were pocketing their salaries; but what substantial benefit was to be conferred on Newfoundland was to him (Mr. Casey) a mystery. He felt convinced few men would support such a spoliation of the rights of the people of this colony.

---

* Like the Maritimers, British Columbians believed that the success of Confederation depended on a rail link to central Canada. The Canadian Pacific Railway was completed in 1885, fourteen years after British Columbia joined Confederation. — PR

John Kent: There was an expansive benevolence and an enlargement of views generated by amalgamating with large and
populous communities. Our isolation and contracted sphere of
action was apt to operate injuriously in many respects, whereas
union with the neighbouring provinces would produce increased
intercourse, and an interchange of sentiments and hospitalities
must result beneficially in many respects.

Thomas Talbot: He had given it a great deal of consideration . . .
and after all he could not make up his mind upon it. There might
be something in the advantages pointed out by its supporters. He
had regarded it in the light of history and experience, and it
struck him to be a measure calculated to prove fatal to the liberties of the country. He would like to see in it a measure calculated
for relieving the country from pauperism, which at present
pressed it down. But he did declare he could not see in it any
practical benefit calculated to lift the people from that state of
poverty into which so many of them were plunged.

   He could see some advantage in extended territory and a population of so many millions under one government; but the
question of our liberty was involved; and for liberty people have
been ready to sacrifice everything. People regarded liberty as
dearer than life itself. The proposed Confederation appeared to
him like people bartering away their liberty for a certain price.

— House of Assembly, January 27, 1865

Ambrose Shea: [It] was said we were destroying the liberties of
the people.* He was surprised to hear such a statement put forward. Would any person have his liberty curtailed by taking up
his residence in Great Britain, in Nova Scotia, New Brunswick,
or Canada? These countries all had responsible government
before we had it. And it was the very first decision come to at the

---

** Is it merely my enjoyment of civil rights and liberties that makes me free?
Can I be free if the community with which I identify is not autonomous?
Shea's opponents see Confederation as a threat to Newfoundlanders' liberties
because they think it will put an end to the province's autonomous existence.
They see the freedom of the individual as a matter of community rights as
well as personal rights. Shea flouts their concern, just as Pierre Trudeau was
to flout Québécois sensibilities in supposing that a charter of individual rights
could make up for his refusal to accede to demands for a special status for the
province of Quebec. — PR*

SIR AMBROSE SHEA
(1815–1905), a
newspaperman,
businessman, and
Roman Catholic who
favoured the separation
of church and state.
Born in Newfoundland
of Irish parents, Shea
disliked the intolerance
of the Catholic Irish
immigrants who
dominated the Liberal
Party. This attitude
limited his political
prospects at home and
stimulated his enthusiasm
for Confederation.
Later he joined the
Conservatives, but his
religion precluded his
succeeding Carter as
leader and, in 1886,
thwarted the British
intention to make
him governor of
Newfoundland.
Embittered, he left
home forever, serving
as governor of the
Bahamas, 1887–94, and
then retiring to Britain.

[Quebec] conference that with a view to the perpetuation of our connection with the mother country, and the promotion of the best interests of the people, the model of the British government should be followed, so far as circumstances would permit, the government being vested in Her Most Gracious Majesty and administered by her representative in accordance with the well-understood principles of the British Constitution.

With responsible government, the ministry of the day responsible to the people not merely of Canada, but also of New Brunswick, Nova Scotia, Newfoundland, and Prince Edward Island, would not our liberties be as well secured as at present and our British connection perpetuated for ages to come? But it was said, "You are going to bind us to Canada." Now we had heard that said by persons who had never seen Canada, who had never been out of this colony; and perhaps it would be as well for some of them to travel a little and visit that magnificent province, as well as Nova Scotia and New Brunswick, which were advancing so rapidly in material prosperity and in all that tended to make a people great and respected. How many had emigrated from this colony to Canada and found there a home where their industry was rewarded with competence for themselves and their families? But we were to be united, not merely to Canada, but to Nova Scotia and New Brunswick, and in the legislature of the union we would all be represented according to our population. It was a treaty, which, if carried out, would give us all one great country, extending from the Atlantic to the Pacific, in whose onward course and prosperity we would participate, and whose glory and renown would be the inheritance of your children.

Our alliance was not to be with Canada alone, but also with Nova Scotia and New Brunswick. These countries were all more prosperous than we are . . . What future was there for any young man brought up in this country? If his object was to engage in commercial pursuits, where was he to get his training? How were we to get a mercantile education for many of our sons, with the importations which were annually made from Britain? Some must go to another country, and where were they to go to, with the British provinces broken up into fragments? To the United States? Every feeling of patriotism dictated that they should remain under the British flag. Supposing they now went to Canada, who were they to apply to? But if we formed part of the same country, they would find our members there, and if we were careful in their selection, they would be such as would make

themselves felt, limited as was the number to which our population entitled us. Our young men could apply to these members whose interest would be made available to forward their views. Look at Scotland, for instance. How many went from Scotland, and on application to their members in the imperial parliament, got appointments which enabled them by the proper exercise of their talents to rise to eminence?

If Confederation was carried out it would be the means of depriving some of our local politicians of the positions they have occupied for some years past; and we all know how difficult it was for small politicians to give up that from which they derived a certain local importance. They knew how difficult it was for those who traded on the passions and prejudices of the people to submit to an arrangement by which their occupations would be gone. They did not like the prospect of it, and therefore they pretended great zeal for the interests of the people, our fisheries, the militia that is to be, and increased taxation, while all the time they regard their own private interests, for which they are ready to sacrifice the best interests of the country.

Talbot: When I think how we are shut up here in our isolation, sharing so little in the great enterprise and civilizing strides that are being made east and west of us, apparently content with our own littleness, and occupied almost entirely with our petty party squabbles and our contemptible sectarian contentions — I say when I think of these things, I feel that our alliance with the more powerful neighbouring colonies would be greatly beneficial. If these evils could be swept away by Confederation, I would welcome it at any price.

I feel, too, that the Speaker [Ambrose Shea] does not overrate the inconvenience to which our young men are subjected here from want of employment, though I doubt the effectiveness of the remedy he sets up. We educate our young men, and for what? Merely that they may walk about the streets, eating out their hearts and brains, and their energies, for lack of occupation. They lose ambition, they lose moral standing, they become a burden to themselves. Our native young men, Mr. Chairman, are not second in industry, in energy, and in ability to any of those of the neighbouring nations. All that they lack to secure to them honourable positions in life is opportunity. Some who have gone from us have raised themselves to most respectable conditions in life, and there are others yet with us who would do so if the

"We educate our young men, and for what? Merely that they may walk about the streets, eating out their hearts and brains, and their energies, for lack of occupation. They lose ambition, they lose moral standing, they become a burden to themselves."

opportunity were given them. Is not that a strong argument, then, why we should endeavour to get out of the crawling and creeping isolation which wraps us about as a garment? But, sir, I am not satisfied that Confederation will change this for us.

— House of Assembly, February 2, 1865

Thomas Glen: There had been a great deal said about the distress and misery of the people; but there was not a single argument put forward to show us how Confederation would ameliorate our condition or in any way confer any substantial benefit upon us. It was well known that we lived entirely by our fisheries and how Confederation was going to benefit them he (Mr. Glen) was utterly at a loss to conceive.

E.D. Shea: Again, it was said that while the supporters of Confederation spoke of the openings in Canada for their children, they had no regard to the interests of the fishermen's children. If we regarded the present state of our operative population, they would appear to have the deepest interest in that question. What had our legislation been for several years past but unsuccessful efforts to raise the labouring classes from their depressed condition? And what had we accomplished but to join with the receiver general [Thomas Glen] in jeremiads over the distressed state of the country, without being able to strike out anything to relieve the general distress? We have now come to such a state of depression that we can proceed no further, and it was our solemn duty to consider whether this proposed Confederation offered any means of relieving the people.

— House of Assembly, February 6, 1865

James Clift: It is said that we have a surplus population, more people than the circumstances of the colony can support, and that the new nation would present an extensive and profitable field for their employment. Was this the remedy for our chronic pauperism? Were we to send away the productive men of the country and leave behind the lame, and halt, and the blind? If this be the anticipated mode of decreasing the poverty of the country, he must for his part say he considered it was more calculated to have the contrary effect.

Edward Morris: He felt how impossible it was to give a satisfactory idea of the probable future results of the proposed

Confederation by any facts or figures we can bring to bear upon it. It may perhaps be shown that so far as pecuniary results are concerned, there is nothing to induce our participation in the union, that no appreciable consequences would attend it in the present day. But he insisted that in legislating on so vast a question as this, the pecuniary view should be made subordinate to the great fact that we would be legislating for generations yet unborn.

He would admit that comparatively little advantage was probable from a Confederation of the provinces for those now living. Nations are not built up in a day, nor in a year, nor can we imagine the great future that is in store for those colonies when, united together under a salutary and powerful government and progressive institutions, the now disjointed territories extending from the Atlantic on the east to the Pacific on the west shall form a nation inferior to few of the great countries of the earth. The provinces now proposed to be united extended over a vast region of space. They contain within themselves all the elements of national prosperity, but waiting for development.

Confederation with our more wealthy and prosperous neighbours would attract a proportionate share of that wealth upon us. He had faith in it. He believed that all the provinces would benefit largely by a combination of means and interests, that from their union would hereafter emerge a mighty nation, peopled by the descendants of the old lands, of the energetic Celt and the industrious Saxon, whose influence has pervaded all the countries of the earth. That its power would increase in proportion with its territory and its undoubted capabilities, and that it would be able to extend the arm of protection and defence to all outlying portions of the British possessions on this side of the Atlantic.

Robert Pinsent: The honourable gentleman opposite (Mr. Morris) has deemed it sufficient to discuss so important a subject in general terms, and nothing could afford a more suitable opportunity for the exercise of that honourable gentleman's fine bass voice and florid oratory and powerful imagination than this grand question of Confederation! He thought, however, that [that] advocate who had to discover the advantages to be derived from the present scheme of Confederation, in the benefits that would be felt by generations yet unborn, and who could point to no material blessing for those immediately concerned, must be sensible to the weakness of his cause, and it was a course certainly calculated to leave that impression in the minds of others . . .

We were equally entitled to a guarantee of intercolonial communication as the North-West Territory, and should not trust to promises or to the condescension of the general government. He anticipated great advantage from extending the channels of communication and those means of intercourse which as readily overcame the difficulties of time and space. This, the chief blessing to be derived from closer political connection with our neighbours, was left unprovided for. We know, as in the human, so in the national body, circulation must be less active and vigorous at the extremities than at and near the centre.

— *Legislative Council, February 14, 1865*

Hugh Hoyles: We were invited to join a Confederation which, in half a century, would be second to no power on the face of the earth, with a population, at present numbering four millions, stretching from the Atlantic to the Pacific, and which would number fifty millions within the lifetime of some of our children; with a country abounding with resources such as could not fail, in the hands of an energetic people, to place us in the first rank amongst the nations of the earth — a Confederation whose commerce would cover every sea, whose flag would be respected in every quarter of the globe, and which should take place in the great family of nations, second to none, in influence, in wealth, in power, in resources, in all that tended to illustrate and magnify the position and standing of a people . . .

True, these considerations were not such matters as could be measured by pounds, shillings, and pence. Nevertheless they were such as powerfully influenced nations as well as individuals in their ordinary conduct. There were other things of value in this life for both, besides dollars and cents; and as in private life were found individuals ready to pay for rank, station, and influence, so among nations, the last shilling in the exchequer would be expended, and the last man sent to fight, with the object of maintaining the national honour and preserving the character and position of the commonwealth. When, therefore, we turned to the consideration of great national questions, such as this was, surely there were other matters to be regarded besides the mere pecuniary aspect of the manner.

With regard to our public men, it opened up a field worthy of their ambition. Let the honourable member for Ferryland, Mr. Glen, consider the enlarged sphere of advancement which Confederation opened up to him if sent up as a member to the

House of Commons, where talent must take the lead whether it came from Newfoundland or Vancouver; and where he would have an opportunity, one day, of discussing some important question affecting the interests of Columbia, and on another, one involving those of New Brunswick, while on a third those of the great Saskatchewan valley would be taken up; and the compensation, when his talents and experience placed his services in demand as a minister of the crown, would be in proportion to the importance of his position; while the height of his ambition in Newfoundland was to be receiver general, at £500 a year.

Surely it should stimulate the youth of the country to have the prospect before them of attaining to a position in public life, such as none of the colonies could offer while they continued in their present fragmentary condition. Surely there was something more elevating and ennobling in such prospects than the narrow party struggles of our present colonial politics could offer. But it was not merely to politicians that Confederation offered a field worthy of their ambition. It must benefit young men in all the professions. They had before them an enlarged field for their exertions, and proportionally larger prizes to stimulate these exertions in the professions of law and medicine. And it must be supposed that, in the course of time, there would be an army and a navy, in which our youth would have an opportunity of rising to eminence . . . It would give a stimulus to the exertions of our young men in all the professions; taking *excelsior* as their motto, they would press forward in every art and science, and ultimately many would attain an eminence to which few in the colonies at present aspired.

— House of Assembly, February 14, 1865

John Haywood: The honourable member, Mr. Shea, had endeavoured to prove that we would derive great benefit from the proposed connection with the confederate provinces; and the supporters of the proposition, who appear to be in ecstasies with what they call a grand idea, would induce us to believe that, by its adoption, this country would be largely benefited. One would suppose, from the picture painted by them, that a howling wilderness would be turned into a garden of Eden — a paradise, but he thought it would be a paradise lost — that we would have a little heaven here below; and be, in all times to come, in a perfect state of beatification.

The privilege of governing ourselves would be transferred into

"This house was looked to to maintain the rights of the people of Newfoundland. If we entered into the proposed Confederation, they would be gone. We would have no independent legislature."

other hands and gone from us. He believed this discussion about Confederation had inspired the people with more confidence in the House of Assembly, as the guardian of their rights. This house was looked to to maintain the rights of the people of Newfoundland. If we entered into the proposed Confederation, they would be gone. We would have no independent legislature; and what could eight men* sent to Canada do to protect our interests?

At present we are legislating in the face of our constituents, having an election every four years; and if we oppress them or overtax them they can supply our places with those men worthy of their confidence. But if we united with Canada we would have no redress, for Canada would make our laws and do with us as she pleased. What influence would eight men have to prevent our taxation being doubled?

"It makes no difference how fallacious the arguments of those opposed to Confederation may be shown to be, the ready answer to all reasoning is — 'Oh, all you show us in favour of Confederation is purely speculative, wholly theoretical.' These gentlemen are not satisfied unless they can clutch futurity in their fists and put it into their breeches pockets."

Daniel Prowse: But it makes no difference how fallacious the arguments of those opposed to Confederation may be shown to be, the ready answer to all reasoning is — "Oh, all you show us in favour of Confederation is purely speculative, wholly theoretical." These gentlemen are not satisfied unless they can clutch futurity in their fists and put it into their breeches pockets. No political philosophy has any reference to us. We have nothing to do with the arguments and political economy of John Stuart Mill.

The experience we derived from the study of history does not teach us, and he (Mr. Prowse) would ask them — where are we to go then for a parallel? Are we to be guided by the political experience of the king of Dahomey, or to follow the king of the Cannibal Islands?

What is the present situation of this country as regards education and enlightenment? We are like a lot of little boys in the lowest class of a country school. We have been using our well-thumbed horn books† so long that we have got to think of nothing beyond them. But let us come in contact with people who have a splendid system of education, who are enjoying all the advantages of railways and steamers, and who are in a higher state of civilization than we are. Does anyone suppose that if we

---

* The Quebec scheme allotted Newfoundland eight seats in the federal House of Commons.

† A paper containing the alphabet and the Lord's Prayer, or other wholesome elementary reading-matter, mounted on a wooden tablet with a handle and protected by a thin layer of horn.

formed part of the Confederation, we would have been so long trembling on the brink of a great public work like Toad's Cove Breakwater or Flower Hill Firebreak? Do you think we should have remained so long satisfied with that wretched tub the *Ellen Gisborne*, or with the imperfect manner in which local steam is at present carried out, or our present miserable postal system? No, we cannot remain as we are. Increased intercourse with our fellow colonists, especially Canada, will have the same effect on us that it has everywhere else. We must improve. We never can go back in the path of progress.

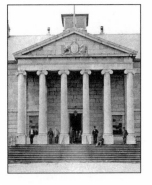

The Colonial Building, Newfoundland. Opened in 1850, it remained the seat of the Newfoundland legislature until 1960.

Henry Renouf: It, therefore, becomes our solemn duty, as the custodians of the rights, liberties, and privileges of a free people, to clearly understand how far those elements of success and future prosperity for this country are contained in the terms proposed by the Quebec report, and which can only be fairly arrived at by the calmest inquiry, the most mature consideration, and the deepest investigation.

He (Mr. Renouf) did not believe this Confederation scheme would be such a potent remedy for our ills, but would be somewhat like a celebrated quack medicine which promised to cure everything, even earthquakes, but after being tried was found to be only an imposition for getting money.

Another great inducement held out was the large field the Confederation would give to our youth seeking that honourable and lucrative employment which was debarred them at home, owing to the limited field of operations. From that it would be inferred that our sons are all to get situations in Canada, and more particularly having eight members as their friends to apply to. It might so happen that our members would be so absorbed in their own interests as hardly to bestow a thought upon the wants of others; and we know to a certainty that no influence those members could possibly bring to bear on the general government would prevent the Canadians enjoying, as they do at present, the patronage of their offices to make place for ours. Here the government and every officer under it, the legislature, etc., are with a few exceptions filled by our sons; but could this state of things continue under Confederation? We transfer our customs, post office, and lighthouses to the general government, and in the event of a vacancy taking place in either of these institutions, would not the appointment be made at headquarters and not in favour of natives? The curtailment of our legislature alone would

destroy more patronage than we should enjoy at the hands of the general government.

Our political history since 1832, with our elections every four years, is further evidenced by the Honourable Attorney General [Hugh Hoyles] as a potent reason why we should be in this confederacy, as if every country with representative institutions is not subject to the same ordeal of excitement. Was there any exception to this rule out of Newfoundland? Would the acerbity of feeling be less with a reduced House of Assembly, and with eight members to be returned for the House of Commons in Canada? Was it less so even in Canada or the other provinces? This is a specimen of the humbug and claptrap used by honourable members who favour that scheme; but the delusion was too transparent to merit even serious consideration. Now it was evident that certain honourable members, after selfishly monopolizing for years the emoluments of office amongst themselves and their friends, were anxious to destroy our legislature and sacrifice the liberties and privileges of the people which it protects, that they might on its ruins take splendid positions under the new government.

— *House of Assembly, February 22, 1865*

Pinsent: Many intelligent persons placed great faith, and were willing to accept Confederation in view of the general benefits and blessings which history and experience and the laws of progress and political economy taught that equitable unions produced. But we were not confined to such reflections; our faith must be further strengthened by our own exceptional position. Isolation and solitude were our bane, and yet some would hug and foster this characteristic of barbarism. How were we to remove or mitigate it? Would any intelligent man believe that improved means of intercourse between ourselves and the outside world was not an important step in that direction; that assimilation with a more advanced, more prosperous, wealthy, and progressive people, with its consequent sympathy and example, that mutual freedom of trade and industry would not be attended with those advantages which in all parts of the civilized world had followed from such conditions?

There were some who would cite Ireland* as an example of an unfortunate union, and raise prejudices from such an argument

---

* Ireland was forced to unite with Great Britain in 1800, as a consequence of the rebellion of 1798. Although Ireland was granted 100 seats in the par-

against Confederation. It was not an apt or fair comparison. Here
we associated with equal rights. Here we should enjoy the privileges of the British Constitution in its full perfection, without
blot or blemish; education established on a basis which offended
none; the fullest measure of civil liberty; and perfect freedom and
equality in religion. In another view he regarded this measure of
Confederation as a step in the logic of events that would be
worked out. The history of this colony, so remote as to make it
the most ancient dependency of the crown, was marked with several eras. At the commencement of this century, it was just
allowed to emerge from the condition of a temporary fishing
resort. Then we had an absolute governor and council, next a legislature, then the system of responsibility. So we had been
educated and fitted for a broader, grander, and more national
position and sphere of action. Having enjoyed the questionable
blessing and been taught by the experience of local government,
the parent state having guided and controlled our infant steps to
a degree of maturity, points us to a field of action where the exercise of constitutional government can be better and more
effectively applied.

The machinery and paraphernalia of our present system are
too much for this country, and they will be reduced in their scope
and shorn of their costliness, while we shall still have a local government and a voice in the concerns of a great people and a
united and progressive dominion.

— *House of Assembly, February 3, 1869*

*"[Pauperism] is
better than parting
with your liberty."*

Talbot: [Pauperism] is better than parting with your liberty, your
property, and possibly with your lives.* It was not because people
were surrounded by poverty that they should part with their lib-

---

*liament at Westminster, the franchise was initially limited to Protestants,
who constituted little more than one-tenth of the population. Catholics were
admitted to the franchise after 1829. — IG*

*The union required and received the assent of the Irish parliament. What
made it "unfortunate" was the repressive nature of British colonial rule both
before and after the event. The enfranchisement of Roman Catholics made
little difference. Not until the British parliamentary reform of 1884–85 did
the chief victims of British rule in Ireland — the Catholic peasantry — gain
a voice in politics. — PR*

* The phrase describes the person's basic human rights. In the Second
Treatise on Government *(1690), John Locke argues that men would not*

erties and rights, and link themselves to another country which had no sympathy with them. No country was so discordant as Canada, which was made up of so many antagonistic elements and races. He (Mr. Talbot) said it would be wise to pause and try all feasible things before surrendering themselves in that way.

— *House of Assembly, February 9, 1869*

Hoyles: [Mr. Talbot] says "will you give up your liberty, your lives, and property to Canada?" Why, one would fancy from such expressions that Nova Scotia, New Brunswick, and Canada had no liberty, no property, and no lives. The honourable member must recollect that long before we had responsible government, that boon had been conferred upon Canada, that Nova Scotia and New Brunswick had also received it before us, and yet one would fancy from the argument of the honourable member that they had given up everything that Britons valued, and when these colonies had confederated and were impressed that it was for their interest and good, could we have any doubt upon our minds that we would enjoy with them the same benefits and advantages which they at present possess?

Why, what was the object of Confederation? Was it not the consolidation and strengthening of British interests? Was it not the consolidation of liberty itself? Here when disunited, each separate parliament was making laws adverse to the interests of each other. We had different tariffs, and different currency, different laws, yet all expressing to be governed by the constitution of Great Britain. This then was seen, and with one desire we met together in full liberty and freedom to prepare a measure which had been commended by British statesmen on all sides and as having emanated from enlightened men and statesmen.

Newfoundland has hitherto been isolated from the outer

---

subject themselves to government "were it not to preserve their lives, liberties and fortunes." The American Declaration of Independence of 1776 declares "life, liberty and the pursuit of happiness" to be all men's rights. Article XIV of the American Constitution forbids the states to deprive "any person of life, liberty, or property, without due process of law." Section 7 of the Canadian Charter of Rights and Freedoms (1982) reads: "Everyone has the right to life, liberty, and security of the person and the right not to be deprived thereof except in accordance with the principles of fundamental justice." Canadian common law and statute law can be interpreted to support property rights, but there is no explicit guarantee in the Charter. — JA

world, and according to the honourable member it was to remain so. Were we to be cut off from all civilized countries? Were we to stand still or retrograde that we should never enjoy the advantages and progress of civilization?

— *House of Assembly, February 11, 1869*

Ambrose Shea: [The Quebec] plan had met with the approval of the leading men of England of all politics, and were they blind and incapable of forming an opinion? Not one of them but spoke in praise of the constitution as framed at Quebec, and was not that a significant fact, which might well influence the minds of some who ought to feel that they were incapable of forming an opinion on such a subject? A test like that, the opinions of men well versed in the science of government, whose integrity and impartiality cannot be doubted, who look calmly on from a distance and say that this system of government calculated to advance the interests and secure the prosperity of these colonies, should have due and great weight with me, whose experience and knowledge of such matters is by no means so large.

He did not mean to say the honourable gentlemen should not exercise their own reason on the subject. The duty and the responsibility lay with them, and they were bound to see and examine into the matter, for themselves. After all, what was Confederation? It simply meant that four or five provinces, having similar institutions and laws, and owing allegiance to a common sovereign, should unite for their common benefit. Enlightened by the example of the United States, they believed that such a union would promote general prosperity and give stability to all, and that in co-operation each would find benefits which individually they could not obtain.

— *House of Assembly, February 12, 1869*

"Every day America was becoming less European in ideas and less dependent on European associations, and day by day the desire of every man to look to the westward is becoming more and more apparent."

Kent: Every day America was becoming less European in ideas and less dependent on European associations, and day by day the desire of every man to look to the westward is becoming more and more apparent. Was it common sense to oppose entering into union with a country in a high state of civilization, which would be a large consumer of all our products and which was willing to make and carry into effect arrangements which would be advantageous to all? He would ask honourable gentlemen who profess to be alarmed about giving up our privileges to consider well what would be our position if we remained outside of Confederation.

Our rights are perfectly secure. All the people require is roads and public improvements. What do the people of the outports care for the form of government?

Ambrose Shea: Honourable gentlemen opposite spoke of it as an extraordinary fact that the dominion was to be entrusted with an unqualified right of taxation, as if any power could sustain itself without that right. The argument was just as strong against the United States, as against the dominion. The states, each of them gave up a certain portion of their individual liberty for the sake of common security, and other collateral benefits of union. And yet, the constitution of the states was the acme of political science, and the object of the idolatry of honourable members opposite.

Were the states unwise in giving up their individual liberty, and vesting it in a central authority for the benefit of all? It was the wisest measure which they have ever adopted, and one without which they could never have attained to that position which they at present maintain in the councils and government of the world . . . But again our rights and liberties were to be given away! By the union of the states were the rights and liberties of the people of America given away? Were they not on the other hand stabilized and promoted, and did we ever hear the smallest state of the union allege as matter of complaint that it was deprived of its rights and liberties?* And yet this was the claptrap and rubbish addressed to reasoning men at a time when this subject should engross our soberest consideration. Here we have our population starving and the honourable member Mr. Glen asks us to stereotype that state of things and remain as we are. They would go to their constituencies and tell the people that from the present state of things there was no hope. Our system of government had been tried by men of all parties under the most favourable circumstances and what had been its results? Though we professed those much vaunted rights and liberties, the people of the island from one end of it to the other were starving. They had not the right to live and the sum total of their rights was the right to beg or starve, and these were the rights which honourable members opposite were so anxious to preserve intact.

— *House of Assembly, March 2, 1869*

"Our system of government had been tried by men of all parties under the most favourable circumstances and what had been its results? Though we professed those much vaunted rights and liberties, the people of the island from one end of it to the other were starving. They had not the right to live and the sum total of their rights was the right to beg or starve, and these were the rights which honourable members opposite were so anxious to preserve intact."

---

* *One would hardly guess that the U.S. Civil War had ended less than four years previously. Shea again shows his lack of sympathy with other members' concerns for Newfoundland's autonomy. — PR*

PRINCE EDWARD ISLAND

Roderick McAulay: Sir, I believe that this scheme has been devised more in the interests of the ruling parties in the neighbouring colonies than in regard for those of the people. The Tilleys and Tuppers would fain have a wider field for the exercise of their talents and the extension of their sway, but it is our duty to protect the rights of those whose representatives we are, and what public man will not hesitate, ere he votes that our institutions shall become nonentities?

Edward Whelan: These colonies are as old as, some older than, the thirteen which, in 1775, revolted from Great Britain; but are we as prosperous as they? Is this island in wealth equal to the little state of Rhode Island? Are these maritime colonies as advanced as any of the states to which I have referred? The answer is obvious, and equally so is the reason — it is to be found in our dependent position. It is simply a solemn mockery for us to go through the farce of passing through the legislative acts,* the fate of which may be announced to us by the colonial minister after the lapse of some eight or nine months.

If our legislative and constitutional privileges were as free and unrestrained in operation as those of Rhode Island, we would not be wasting months in discussing matters which are more appropriate subjects for the deliberations of a Court of Quarter Sessions[†] or a Vestry.[‡] If the proposed union would give us so much influence as to leave our legislative action unfettered by the underhand intrigues and influence of the proprietors[§] at the Colonial Office, I would support it . . .

— *House of Assembly, April 18, 1864*

Apparently a reference to the British government's legal power to disallow colonial legislation. — PR

[†]The assembly of magistrates, which was responsible for county government in Britain itself, and also in various British colonies, until county councils were established.

[‡] The board that administered parish affairs.

[§] In 1767 the British government divided almost all of Prince Edward Island among a group of proprietors, who were supposed to take up residence and settle tenant farmers on their land. Few lived up to either of these obligations, but the land remained in their and their successors' hands for generations owing to their influence at the Colonial Office, the British department responsible for governing the colonies. — PR

"It is true greatness to produce great men."

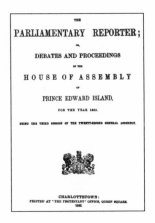

George Sinclair: The advocates of union can easily occupy time in speaking on this question. Extensive railways, large canals, and cities springing rapidly into existence make such a beautiful and glowing picture that it forms a theme on which they can expatiate at pleasure. But, Mr. Speaker, when we seek to examine the picture it is found to be nothing but dreams and vanishes away. I think it would be most detrimental to the interests of Prince Edward Island to enter the proposed union. But still I am open to conviction. I have, however, listened to the able speeches of the advocates of Confederation without my opinion being changed — without being able to think otherwise than that union with Canada would ruin the island politically and financially.

One great argument of the friends of union is the "glory argument." It would, say they, open up a wide field for our young men. This colony, however, small as it is, might send forth talented individuals from among her sons. It is true greatness to produce great men. We might belong to Russia with her vast territories, but would that make us great? What is it that leads Englishmen, Scotchmen, and Irishmen to be proud of their respective countries? It is because they have been distinguished by many great men. And this island might be the same. I am proud of [being] descended from British ancestors, but I am proud also of being an islander. (Hear, hear.) I believe that the people of Prince Edward Island can take their position beside the people of any country on the globe. There is nothing in her present situation to prevent her sons from rising in the world.

But then, again, by this scheme we will be required to give up our political independence. What is dearer to a man than his country and its institutions? By accepting Confederation we would be surrendering everything which we can politically hold dear. While we have a system of self-government, we can sometimes get into difficulties, yet affairs will soon rectify themselves; but if we cast in our lot with others more numerous than ourselves we will be driven wherever their fancy leads.

— *House of Assembly, March 29, 1865*

James Duncan: I have a few words to say on this great scheme which is to make this a wonderful country, give us a market of three millions of people, and cheap tea all the way from China. All those who have been in this colony heretofore, it appears, are but children in trade; let them, however, only go up to Canada a

"We are to become a great nation, but how this is to be effected the promoters of the scheme scarcely understand themselves. One of the advantages of it is that our members of parliament will go to live at Ottawa, and we will be left here to pay them!"

few weeks and they will come down perfectly prepared to argue out any question on trade and finance.

We are to become a great nation, but how this is to be effected the promoters of the scheme scarcely understand themselves. One of the advantages of it is that our members of parliament will go to live at Ottawa, and we will be left here to pay them! We are told also that our young men will rise to be chief justice in Canada. They need not deceive themselves, for none but those belonging to Canada will have much chance of attaining to such distinction. The local legislature, which the Quebec report contemplates to leave us, would be little better than a town council;* we would have this building here merely to look at. As to the general legislature, I consider the representation in it allowed to this island unfair and unjust. I think the four lower provinces, at least, should have as many members in the upper branch as Canada. The five representatives allotted to us in the lower house would not give this colony much influence there; but as our population will not increase so rapidly as that of Canada, there is a prospect, through the operation of one clause in the report, that our five representatives would dwindle down to three.†

— *House of Assembly, March 30, 1865*

George Coles: Talk of our young men rising to judgeships, and to premiers in Canada; why, sir, they have far too many hangers-on of their own, for our youth ever to expect any favours at their hands. The politicians in that province are sometimes put to their wits' end‡ how to provide snug berths for persons they wish to shelve out of their way. A little transaction of this kind occurred when the delegates were there. A member of the legislature was appointed to a judgeship under the Stamp Act, in order to make room for the provincial secretary, who had lost his election in the district in which he formerly represented. Under Confederation

---

* This disparagement of the powers allotted to the provincial governments under the Quebec Resolutions is typical of opponents of Confederation. — PR
† Under the 1911 census, Prince Edward Island's representation in the House of Commons did indeed dwindle to three, but the BNA Act was amended in 1915 to assure the province a minimum of four seats. — PR
‡ In order to vacate Lanark North for William McDougall, Robert Bell (1808–1894) was appointed not to a judgeship, but to the newly created post of inspector of canal revenues. — PR

such work would, no doubt, be carried on to a much greater extent, and amid the intriguing of Canadian office seekers on the spot the young aspirants of the lower provinces would stand very little chance of success.

— House of Assembly, March 31, 1865

Kenneth Henderson: The "glory argument," as it is termed, is largely dwelt upon by our unionists to a man, in pressing the claims of their hobby.

— Legislative Council, April 1, 1865

George Beer: For a number of years we have been striving to free the country from the influence of absentee proprietors, and have partially succeeded. Our prospects have become brighter — prosperity appears to have set in — and we hope soon to get the estate of the last proprietor purchased. The evils of absentee proprietorship are acknowledged everywhere. Wherever it prevails, the country is drained of its natural resources, and the inhabitants, feeling their dependent position, become disheartened and retrograde rather than improve.

Let the proposed Confederation be consummated and the now beautiful and flourishing Island of Prince Edward will be virtually sold to a large, extravagant, and absentee proprietor named Canada, who will graciously allow us to expend about one half of our earnings, but will exact from us the other half, to be expended a thousand miles away. The natural result would be that the island in a few years would be in the same condition as a farm let out on the halves,* and consequently had become exhausted and beggared.

Now, your honours, is it not surprising that there should be found among the representatives of Prince Edward Island those who advocate, and endeavour to bring about, a state of things so much to be dreaded — who advocate in reality the abrogation of our independent constitution, and the surrender of ourselves into the power of the most extravagant set of politicians to be found on British soil — men who have already broken faith with their sister provinces — men who are continually charging each other with pocketing immense sums of money by virtue of their polit-

---

* This phrase refers to a sharecropping tenancy, with landlord and tenant each taking half the crop. The tenant had no interest in preserving the fecundity of the soil.

ical positions? When I contemplate the state of this question, and observe the shameful manner in which it is attempted to be brought about in the other colonies, entirely ignoring responsible government, and the voice of the people . . . When I see and hear of several who have most prominently condemned the Confederation scheme, but who are now prepared to surrender our rights, liberties, privileges, and revenue, together with our constitution, and are willing that we should become a mere outlying dependency of Canada, it is almost impossible to believe that no inducement is held out to obtain such advocates.

I presume that it will not be unparliamentary to state the belief that prevails throughout the colony on this subject, which is to the effect that some three or four of the most prominent advocates of that measure have reason to believe that if it is carried they will be selected — not elected — as legislative councillors for life, with a salary of not less then £1,000 a year, and that one gentleman is to receive the appointment of lieutenant governor . . . But when I find an attempt made to sell our birthrights, and hand us over to the tender mercies of men in whom we have no confidence whatever, I most solemnly enter my protest against it. It is sought to entrap us into this Confederation scheme by getting an acknowledgement from the legislature of the principle or desirability of union in the abstract; and then, I presume, there would be some apparently tangible reason for another delegation to Downing Street,* the result of which would be the sealing of our doom for all time to come. This clever dodge is no doubt of Canadian origin, and is about as wily and cunning as the means adopted to catch the leading men on each side of politics throughout the Maritime provinces. I trust we shall avoid committing ourselves in any such way . . . Why we have men among us who advocate Confederation in view of these results [taxation, tariffs, etc.], I cannot understand, unless there are some "fat offices" or something of that kind in prospect. For my part I most solemnly protest against it.

James McLaren: It has been said that we are an insignificant colony, and if we would unite we would be part of a strong nation, able to defend ourselves; but the greatest nations are not

---

In London's Whitehall district. The complex contains the town houses of the prime minister and the chancellor of the Exchequer. The Colonial Office was at number 14.

always the happiest. Most of the great nations of antiquity were based on slavery, while a few of the masters were rich and powerful; and I do not consider that true greatness consists in that, but in a contented and happy people.

We have either ourselves or our fathers left our native countries and emigrated to this island — we have made comfortable homes for ourselves out of the forest — and, notwithstanding all the disadvantages of the rent-paying system, and the severities of the climate, we are progressing in material prosperity. Why throw ourselves out of freedom into bondage from which we would never be able to extricate ourselves? We have heard much said against the proprietary system, but Confederation would be ten times worse. We have now a fair prospect of getting the people free from proprietorism, but let us enter Confederation and we will be worse off than when the proprietary system was in the zenith of its power.

— *Legislative Council, May 5, 1866*

Alexander Laird: [It is said that] isolation was played out. If it was played out, how came it that we were so well off on this island, with a trifling public debt, and free newspapers, books, and no stamp duties,* with a people, too, as happy and contented as those of any other country in the world.

— *House of Assembly, March 8, 1868*

Edward Palmer: I acknowledge that I have been agreeably surprised at the advancement and prosperity in Canada since Confederation was first established. Her manufactories have vastly increased and her prospects are good. She has maintained her public credit with great ease; and I am of [the] opinion that upon our going into the union now we will not have the disadvantages we would have had six or seven years ago.

— *Legislative Council, May 2, 1870*

William McNeill: The people, to a certain extent, had prepared themselves for going into Confederation and the terms were fully as good as, or perhaps better than, they expected. As they now see that it is a necessity, they accept the situation quietly, but

---

* Note the early discussion about Canadian taxes on knowledge. Laird means free from the stamp duties that were then levied on newspapers and books, as well as legal documents, in Britain and other countries.

solemnly. As regarded himself and his constituents, they regretted being placed in such a position that it was necessary to give up the constitution of the colony as a separate province. He, himself, felt sorry to think that we were about to give up self-government, after maintaining our position as a colony with an independent legislature for one hundred years.

One circumstance gave him much to hope for. We belong to the great continent of America, and it was probable that before long a union would take place between the Dominion of Canada and the United States of America; if so, we should yet form a part of one of the greatest nations in the world.

— House of Assembly, May 26, 1873

From a Toronto newspaper announcing reduced fares on the Great Western Railway to mark "Confederation Day."

NEW ADVERTISEMENTS.

CONFEDERATION DAY.

Issue of Return Tickets

FOR

Fare and a Quarter,

GOOD FROM

29th June to 2nd July.

THOMAS SWINYARD,

General Manager.

Hamilton, June 26, 1867   4371

Great Western Railway.

PART THREE

WHAT THEY SAID ABOUT IDENTITY

Chapter Six

BRITISH
OR AMERICAN?

WOULD CONFEDERATION CHANGE the colonists' identity? Would it result in a new way of life, new loyalties, new
outlooks? It is an old question in political science whether political institutions shape identity, or identity shapes the institutions.

In the debates below the worry is that Confederation will
destroy the sturdy independence of the individual colonies,
leaving them vulnerable to assimilation to the American way of
life. Some speakers believe America's military power is the great
danger; they fear British identity will be obliterated by a U.S.
invasion. But others find a greater threat in American prosperity.
The desire to emulate the economic policies of the United States,
the mere proximity to American wealth and power, will wear
away British influence.

British or American? Although most speakers cherish their
British identity and the constitutional liberties that it validates,
others are not averse to becoming American. Some even recommend outright union with the United States. Here, as in other
chapters, speakers show that although they are close observers of
the United States, they hold different views about the benefits of
the U.S. system. In the Canadian debates, George-Étienne
Cartier and Thomas D'Arcy McGee regard America as a hotbed
of populist democracy and a threat to liberty, while David
Christie soberly describes similarities between the British and the
U.S. constitutions.

NOVA SCOTIA

James Johnston: I have always felt that one of the most solemn inquiries that can engage a reflective mind who takes an interest in the welfare of his country is the future of British North America. What is it to be? — how is it to be moulded? This is a question which we should regard, not as Nova Scotians merely, but as British subjects.

At the present moment it is impossible to imagine any political communities placed in circumstances more favourable for immediate happiness and comfort than, in a limited view and under certain restrictions, the provinces of British North America. We have perfect freedom almost in every aspect, civil and religious — the privileges, without the perils or responsibilities of nationalities to bear; but that cannot be the case always. The time must come when we must assume a different attitude and be able to fill a broader and larger sphere. There has been always before us the republic of America in all its colossal proportions, and it would seem by the law of attraction the lesser must be drawn to the greater; but that has not met the views and desires of those who really love the British Constitution and glory in her past history, and would, if possible, send down to posterity the name, the honour, the privileges, and institutions of Britain in the New World. But what is it now that gives such a colour to all our sentiments? What is it that separates us in form of speech, or habit, or desire, from our neighbours in the republic? Every person knows that there is a difference — we feel it ourselves. We are almost as republican, I might say, in all our institutions. Our self-government is almost as complete as theirs, and the fact that our governor is appointed for us instead of by us is only a small element of distinction when we reflect that the lieutenant governor has less personal power than the elective head of a republican state.

What is it, then, that creates this marked distinction between ourselves and the neighbouring states? It is the sentiment we breathe — the influence that we have derived from our connection with the parent state. The influences of monarchical institutions have permeated through us and given a marked colour to all our sentiments. It is, however, a distinction that exists in sentiment, and not one that exists in any material or real form. But is this sentiment to be perpetuated?* Can it be

---

Johnston lucidly states what has become an abiding concern for

expected to last in the presence of strong material influences that are continually operating? Are we at last to be absorbed into a pure and, I would like to say, unmitigated, republicanism, or are we to remain animated by all the feelings that republicans enjoy, with the distinctions that are created by those sentiments that exist in older countries where monarchical and aristocratic institutions obtain?

In the early years I held strong democratic sentiments — for strange to say, though I have been a leading Tory in Nova Scotia, I was in my youth actuated by the Whig principles of English statesmen. I was early perhaps captivated, as many young men are, with the illusions of a republic — of a republic that was working out the great problem they had taken in hand; but reflection and observation have gradually sobered down this sentiment, and I feel that, however valuable a republic may be for giving energy to individual action, it is wanting in that power of elevation, of refinement, and responsibility of action which can alone raise nations to that high-toned condition which we desire to see, and our minds figure before us, as the object of our aspirations. I trust that that portion of this continent over which the British flag is waving will continue to possess perfect freedom of action with all the elevation and refinement which proceed from connection with monarchical and aristocratic institutions.

Now I have diverged from the subject under consideration in expressing these opinions and have obviously touched a point to which no answer can be given, for I take it for granted that the future of the British American provinces is at this moment, and must be, shrouded in mystery.

S.L. Shannon: He (Mr. Shannon) regretted that while we were thinking about this great subject of a union of the colonies, and while we were wasting our time in negotiations, the insidious policy of the United States was gradually absorbing within its territories the greater portion of this American continent. Take for example that great inland country which was of so much importance to the prosperity of Canada, and which might be called Inland America. It was now about passing into the hands of the United States . . .

— *House of Assembly, March 28, 1864*

"I feel that, however valuable a republic may be for giving energy to individual action, it is wanting in that power of elevation, of refinement, and responsibility of action which can alone raise nations to that high-toned condition which we desire to see, and our minds figure before us, as the object of our aspirations. I trust that that portion of this continent over which the British flag is waving will continue to possess perfect freedom of action with all the elevation and refinement which proceed from connection with monarchical and aristocratic institutions."

English-Canadian intellectuals: the vulnerability of their people's cultural identity to American influences. — PR

"It is necessary that our institutions should be placed on a stable basis, if we are to have that security for life and property, and personal liberty, which is so desirable in every country."

Charles Tupper: It is necessary that our institutions should be placed on a stable basis, if we are to have that security for life and property, and personal liberty, which is so desirable in every country. It is quite impossible to place any country upon a stable and respectable footing where security has not the guarantee of permanency — a guarantee that will inspire confidence in the world. I do not intend on an occasion like this to make any invidious allusions to the great neighbouring power near us, but I see events transpiring around us that would make it criminal for any public man to ignore facts which are of the most vital importance to British North America.

Yesterday, British America bordered upon a country great in its trade and peaceful pursuits — having a commerce second to none on the globe; but you have seen all that changed as it were in a day. Now you see alongside of us one of the most gigantic military and naval powers that the world has ever seen. Therefore it behooves us to consider whether any public man, in view of the changed attitude of that country, would not be wanting in his duty to the province if he attempted for a single moment to ignore these circumstances . . . Slavery is doomed. The great slave power, which so long exercised control over the destinies of the states, I have ever looked upon as the best safeguard for British North America,* since it was antagonistic to the acquisition of any anti-slavery territory and consequent increase of influence by the North.

I am not wrong in assuming that the desire of every British American is to remain in connection with the people of Great Britain. If there is any sentiment that was ever strong in the breast of our people, it is a disinclination to be separated in any way whatever from the British Empire, or to be connected in any manner with the United States of America. But what is our present position? Isolated and separated as we are now, I ask the house whether all the protection we have is not that which the crawling worm enjoys — and that is, its insignificance is such as to prevent the foot being placed upon it? Does it comport with the position and dignity of freemen, that we should have our only guarantee of security and protection in our insignificance?

Every man who wishes to keep the liberties and rights he now

---

* *Before the Civil War the slave states had resisted the annexation of territory unsuited to slavery for fear that it would diminish their own power within the Union. — PR*

possesses as a subject to the crown of England — who values the institutions he now enjoys, must see the necessity of our taking such a course as would guarantee us security in the case of conflict with any power in the world.

— *House of Assembly, April 10, 1865*

Adams Archibald: [Let] me contrast for a moment the changed aspect of affairs, and it will be readily seen why it is that . . . a revulsion of feeling has taken place in the public mind — across the water — upon this question. Four years ago, when British statesmen looked to America, they saw thirty millions of people engaged in the arts of peace — the cultivation of the soil, the construction of railroads and canals, the building of cities, the creation of manufactories and development of every branch of art and industry. In fact, the reign of materialism appeared to be firmly established, and the rule of the "almighty dollar" supreme. British statesmen then, in view of these circumstances, had a right to assume that in the absence of any great and unexpected convulsion among these people, they had no reason to anticipate difficulties or complications with them.

But now how changed was the scene — that great nation once devoted to the arts of peace had suddenly been turned from a nation of farmers, artisans, and merchants into a nation of soldiers. That nation now had in the field the largest armies the world ever saw, and had increased [its] naval strength more rapidly than any other nation in the world. And instead of the spirit of peace, the war spirit pervaded the whole country. In view of this changed aspect of affairs, then, was it much to be wondered at that British statesmen should regard these colonies with very different feelings from those which animated them at the period I referred to?

Is it to be wondered at, then, that in view of the altered circumstances of the times, Englishmen should begin to think that the time had arrived when it was the duty of the colonies to assume some responsibility and to relieve the mother country of, at all events, some portion of the burden of their defence? This feeling would be found to pervade every debate that had taken place on the subject in the British parliament . . . Not only is this the case, but for several years dispatch after dispatch has been sent from the Colonial Office to Canada, informing her that the time has arrived for the colonies to wake up to the necessity of relieving the mother country from at least a part of the burden of

their defence. That while exercising the rights and privileges of freemen, they must also assume the responsibilities and duties which that position involved. I think, therefore, that no one can question the fact that the time has arrived when a change is about to take place in the attitude of England towards her colonies; and that, whatever we may think of the matter, her statesmen have arrived at the conclusion that it is necessary we should share, to some extent, the military expenditure which our connection with her entails.

Now I would ask, are we in the face of all this prepared to tell the people of England that we despise their advice and reject their counsel? That although it is the opinion of British statesmen and the British press, and the British people, that union is our only safety, we think differently? We will be loyal only in our own way. We will accept the protection of the British forces and fleets, but this must be given on our terms, not on theirs. Is this the course we should adopt? It is clear that the moment the colonies manifest a disposition to separate from the parent state, that moment will the connection be severed. There will be no disposition on the part of England to force us to remain, while on the other hand, the greatest statesmen of the parent country have affirmed in unmistakable terms that if the colonies wish to be loyal, the power of old England will be used to protect them from aggression; all they ask is to put ourselves in a position to make our defence more easy. Whether united with Canada by Confederation or not, we are bound together by a common fate and a common interest, and we must stand or fall together.

— *House of Assembly, April 12, 1865*

Archibald McLelan: The provincial secretary [Charles Tupper] says we are as unprotected and as helpless as the crawling worm. I was amazed beyond measure to hear such an expression fall from an honourable gentleman occupying a position which gives to his declarations an official character. Had I occupied his position, rather than have stood at the table of this house declaring that a portion of the British Empire "are as unprotected as the crawling worm," I'd have crawled down under the table.

A crawling worm are we? Well, what does he make of us under Confederation? I waited in anxiety, expecting to see the "worm" swell and "develop its proportions" and eventually become a terrible dragon that would "gobble up" the American

eagle and still hunger for more. But, alas! He only made the worm longer. He only lengthened it out until it became a tapeworm. Our main protection lies in the power of Britain, but the evident tendency of this Ottawa arrangement is separation from England.* Our minds naturally follow the channels of authority up to the source, and when we have reached that source our ideas centre about it, and it becomes the embodiment of our nationality.

We have hitherto looked to England and have run up through the various channels to the crown, and there affections have centred; but this Confederation comes in and proposes a new order of things. It proposes that we shall have local governments and that the source of our authority shall be at Ottawa. And when our thoughts and affections are turned towards that — provided the various and divers interests of the several provinces will enable us to live in harmony — the effect will be that our affections will cling round that government and shall be withdrawn from the crown of England. Suppose that five or six American states imagined that separately they were too small and accordingly proposed to form a special Confederation under the general government, just as these gentlemen propose with us to form a government at Ottawa. Does not every man see that, before ten years had expired, the feelings of the people would be around that smaller Confederation and in antagonism to the larger? And so would it be in the event of Confederation with the other British American provinces.

Therefore, I believe, instead of diminishing, it would only increase our danger, and render us an easy prey to an invader. Suppose we should become an independent nationality, we would then, indeed, be helpless as the crawling worms, and the American eagle would soon make a "Diet of Worms"† in European history.

— House of Assembly, April 17, 1865

Tupper: The information coming to us from hour to hour shows the existence and widespread ramification of the Fenian organiza-

---

* A lucid prediction of the process whereby English Canadians in particular would eventually develop a sense of Canadian nationality which diminished their identification with Britain. — PR

† Diet of Worms. A jocular reference to the assembly (diet) of the Holy Roman Empire at Worms in 1521, at which Martin Luther, having refused to recant his Protestant doctrines, was declared a heretic and outlaw.

"GREAT FENIAN SCARE," 9th October, 1869.

Review Extra.

Fenians are coming

(BY TELEGRAPH.)

PORT COLBORNE,
JUNE 1, 1866.—3.30 p. m.

Refugees from Fort Erie report the burning of a Bridge 4 miles back of Fort Erie by the Fenians.

They have possession of Taylor's Heights, one mile and a half below Fort Erie, near a place called Waterloo, and the highest land in the vicinity. They have commenced throwing up earthworks there, and have struck towards Brantford road. This you can rely on.

There were reports this morning about the capturing of Port Sarnia and Welland Canal.

FROM COBOURG.

The following telegram was received by Capt. Poole from Brigade-Major Patterson at Cobourg this afternoon :—

"All the Companies in my District are to assemble at Cobourg at once. Tell Captains Kennedy and Rogers, and send word to Capt. Leigh, Lakefield.

ALEX. PATTERSON,
Brigade-Major."

Cobourg, June 1, 1866.

tion.* What ought to be the conduct of a patriot and a statesman in the face of a danger like that? The men who will be held responsible for all [the] horrors [of an invasion of British North America] will be the men who are resisting intercolonial union and indoctrinating our people with sentiments that may shake their allegiance to the crown.

In the presence of a common danger like that the duty of a patriot and statesman would be to sink all differences and combine for the purpose of protection the rights and liberties of British North America. Let the aegis of British protection be withdrawn and what can Nova Scotia do in the face of such danger? Simply nothing.

I will now ask the house if I were corrupted by American gold, enamoured of American institutions, believing that the best thing that I could do would be to transfer this country to the United States of America, what are the most effective measures that I could take? Would it not be to keep the provinces disunited and repel the protection of the mother country, and then button-hole every man whom I could influence, and undermine his confidence in our institutions by whispering into his ear the insidious statement that Great Britain could not protect us — that the power of the United States was too gigantic — that Great Britain herself would fail to protect even the city of Halifax against such ships as were now possessed by the American government? And when I had indoctrinated the minds of my countrymen with that idea, I would tell them that the best plan is to reject the policy of the imperial government.

We all know that the feeling of loyalty to one's country, the pride in its institutions, lies to the fact that [its] institutions are able to afford protection to life and property.† Therefore, the moment you have carried conviction to the minds of the people

---

The Fenians were an Irish-American movement committed to the use of violence to win independence from Britain. By the end of 1865 the organization had several thousand veterans of the American Civil War under arms. Different groups launched futile incursions into New Brunswick in April 1866 and Canada in June. A member of the movement assassinated D'Arcy McGee in 1868. — IG/PR

†*The chief purpose of government is to keep the civil peace and ward off external attack. This hard-headed teaching is familiar from the work of the seventeenth-century British philosophers Thomas Hobbes and John Locke. Undoubtedly, with the growth of the welfare state, people have come to expect*

that Great Britain is unable to protect us, and that they stand in the presence of so gigantic a power that it has only to will to take them, then you undermine their loyalty. Now we have Mr. [Joseph] Howe* in that attitude; since his return, in the streets, and in the clubs, and in the presence of the highest authorities in the land, you find him constantly holding forth the doctrine that Great Britain is impotent to defend this province — that though British America might unite, yet with even Great Britain at her back, all she could do would not prevent [our] being swept away when the American government wished it. If I stood in a position like that, the honourable member for Halifax [Annand] might be justified in making us an object of suspicion and throwing out his taunts and innuendoes about base bribes having influenced public men.

Holding the sentiments I do — believing that the crisis has come when we must decide whether we shall be annexed to the United States or remain connected with the parent state, I would be the blackest traitor that ever disgraced a country if I did not by every means in my power urge upon this legislature to prove equal to the emergency and take that course which, in a few months, will secure that consolidation of British North America and the connection with the crown of Great Britain which I believe, which I know, it is the sincere wish of the people to secure, and which can alone place these provinces in a position that will at once give them dignity of position and ensure their safety.

— House of Assembly, April 10, 1866

Joseph Howe; detail from J.W. Bengough's Caricature History of Canadian Politics.

———◦◦———

"The question that we have to decide is, whether we shall belong to the United States or to Great Britain."

———◦◦———

Henry Kaulbach: The question that we have to decide is, whether we shall belong to the United States or to Great Britain.

John Locke: In adopting this scheme we are giving our country to Canada to be swallowed up with grand schemes and projects of aggrandizement, to a colony notably disloyal. Coming as I do from a county whose inhabitants have come from Loyalist stock, a county settled by men who have sacri-

more from government than this basic protection. But as we are reminded almost daily on the evening news, where governments lose the power to protect life and property, existence becomes impossibly cruel and hopeless. — *JA*

* *Howe (1804–1873), liberal politician, premier of Nova Scotia, 1860–63, was an outspoken opponent of Confederation. In 1867–68 he tried to secure the province's secession.*

ficed their best interests for the sake of [the] British connection, I feel at liberty to express my opinion freely and without fear of the charge of disloyalty . . . I may say that I believe that this scheme of annexation to Canada will drive us into annexation to the United States . . . What are the antecedents of Canada?

One of the gentlemen taking a leading part in the [Confederation] movement, one who has lectured in various places on the subject of union, is well known to have been an Irish rebel.* Many of the leading men of Canada have stood in the same position, in their conduct during the Canadian rebellion. These are the people with whom we are asked to confederate. If we yield, their Orange and Ribbon societies and other such principles will circulate amongst us, and we would become equally disloyal.† If, then, annexation is to be brought about, would it not be better to go in at once to the American union? Because we would thus obtain all the advantages of a separate state, while if Confederation goes on probably in a few years more we will have to go in as a mere county of Canada.

— House of Assembly, April 16, 1866

Shannon: I see no grounds for the assertion that we are to lose our liberties — our laws will be as well administered as ever — the local legislatures will have sufficient funds to meet the local exigencies, and we will enjoy every privilege which we had before. I am convinced that in this respect our people will hardly know the difference.

---

* *D'Arcy McGee, who was involved in an Irish nationalist uprising in 1848.*

† *Most conspicuous among "the leading men" was George-Étienne Cartier, who had fought as a patriot at Saint-Denis in 1837. The Orange order was an Irish secret society founded in 1795 to resist demands for Catholic emancipation. It was named after the Dutch prince, William of Orange (King William III of Britain), who had preserved the Protestant ascendancy in Ireland by ousting Catholic King James II from the British throne and defeating his forces in Ireland. In Canada as in Ireland, the order made much of its loyalty; but it tended to be loyal on its own terms rather than conform to the canons of loyal conduct laid down by the establishment. Locke's perception of this independence as disloyalty reflects the ambivalence of British-American élites towards the order. — PR*

One of my constituents said to me the other day, "What about this Confederation?" I said to him, "You live in the country: you will get up in the morning and attend to your work; the same money will be expended on the roads and bridges, your children will be educated, and you will never know the difference, except when you bring your wares to market you will get a double price for them."

The honourable member for Londonderry [Archibald McLelan] said he wished that we should remain as we are. I think we cannot do so, neither politically nor socially. Does he not know that, notwithstanding our progress, there is a constant depletion of our population owing to our young men leaving us — that they are abandoning their country and going to the United States, and that we cannot retain them until Confederation is accomplished?

— House of Assembly, March 19, 1867

NEW BRUNSWICK

George Hatheway: I am not going to say that our safety consists in our helplessness; but I believe that there is no more danger of the United States declaring war against New Brunswick than there is of our declaring war among ourselves.

— House of Assembly, June 1, 1865

William Gilbert: I think these colonies have a mark to make in history, when they become able to fly their own flag, but that time has not yet arrived. We even now can compare with almost any country save England, France, the United States, and perhaps Russia in our commercial importance as owners of tonnage, and if we had it all within the borders of our own province it would be all right; but with a line to defend from the farther Cape of Newfoundland to the headwaters of Lake Superior, and a population sparse and scattered along the whole of this line, numbering only some four millions, it would be folly to think of hoisting our own flag and striving to guide the ship of state.

Does anyone suppose that a house of 194 members at Ottawa would put up with dictation from Downing Street?* Look at our own house with only forty-one members; we will not submit

---

* *From Britain, 10 Downing Street being the residence of the British prime minister.*

> "I am not prepared as
> a descendant of the old
> refugees, with the blood
> of Loyalists in my veins,
> to be annexed to the
> United States."

to their dictation in anything that we think is injurious to our interests; and would the united colonies long remain attached to the mother country? They would not; we should soon all be "gobbled up" by the neighbouring republic, and I am not prepared as a descendant of the old refugees, with the blood of Loyalists in my veins, to be annexed to the United States. And when the time comes for us to go off by ourselves, will this one-sided scheme be the one to be adopted? No, it will be one that is fair in every respect.

— House of Assembly, June 2, 1865

Arthur Gillmor: [Some honourable members say] parties would be so evenly divided that our men by going to either side could effect their object. That would not be a very moral way to get what we thought belonged to us, to ask our representatives to join any party, right or wrong. [It is] said the [Quebec] conference had tried to copy after both the constitution of Britain and the United States.* They have succeeded in getting a good deal of what is not perfect in both, and not a great deal of the good qualities of either. The truth is, Mr. Chairman, that so long as we remain colonies of England, we do not want any such expensive establishment: we want no such power between the colonial legislatures and the crown. If we are to become separate, then we may copy after the federal union, and perhaps improve some upon their system; but until we are separate we do not want this fifth wheel to our coach.

— House of Assembly, June 5, 1865

Peter Mitchell: History will repeat itself — our destiny is clear — Confederation or annexation! I forewarn your honours what the result will be if we do not now take steps to direct and guide the ships of state. The times are ominous of danger. There are traitors in our midst, and I am much mistaken if the councils of

---

* It is still an important question in political science whether parliamentary government is appropriate in a federation. A parliamentary system has a clear-cut chain of responsibility: the cabinet answers to the House of Commons, which in turn is accountable to the electorate. But in a federation, governments must sometimes put into effect political decisions made at another level, or in another province; accountability is blurred. Perhaps when we adopted federalism we should also have opted for an American-style congressional form of government, at the federal and provincial levels. — JA

our country have not been tainted by some of them. I find in a Halifax paper which I now hold in my hands the statement of a leading anti, formerly a member of the government, in which he declares that he would rather see the Stars and Stripes float over Citadel Hill than see Confederation of British America. I will not repeat what I have heard of some of our own prominent men, and I hope for their sake that the treasonable utterances ascribed to them are untrue, and I would fain hope that they would not prove traitors even if they should persist in their anti policy.

— *Legislative Council, April 16, 1866*

John Mercer Johnson: One great reason of [American] difficulties, and one of the great reasons of their war, was that there was not sufficient power in the general government.* Each state claimed an independent sovereignty. If you read the constitution of the United States as a lawyer, and I think a large portion of the lawyers would come to the conclusion that they had that right — that it was a simple co-partnership entered into by these separate states, and they had a right upon the face of the constitution to declare themselves out of that constitution. It was fortunate for the United States that while that would be the construction put upon it by a lawyer, it was not the construction put upon it by the United States themselves,† and they had sufficient power to maintain what they considered their right.

If there be one way more sure than another to drive us or lead us into the neighbouring republic, it will be by forgetting the good old time-honoured constitution of our country, and becoming familiar with and practising the constitution of the United States. The moment we found our Confederation upon the American principle, we will gradually settle into the United

---

A common British North American judgement on the U.S. constitution in the 1860s, often tied to the fact that the constitution assigned only specified powers to Congress, reserving the residue of legislative power to the individual states. — PR

†*British North Americans tended to see the United States as the creation of the individual states, and to perceive the Union as a compact from which a state could withdraw at will. This understanding was also the ground for the Southern secession in 1861. The alternative view, which the Union imposed by force during the Civil War, was that the United States was created by the American people. For a lucid statement of this view of the U.S. constitution, see the words of Charles Fisher (New Brunswick) in chapter 9. — PR*

"We want nothing better than British institutions, for under them we have as much liberty, and a little more, than they have in the United States."

States. If we become American in practice, we will very soon become American in fact. I do not wish to have American institutions under the British flag. We want nothing better than British institutions, for under them we have as much liberty, and a little more, than they have in the United States.

Our institutions are more republican than the institutions of the United States.* Our people have more power over their government than the people of the United States have over theirs. If the veto power be exercised by the sovereign, the ministry must go out and another party come in. The ministry cannot retain their power and refuse a bill that has passed through the legislature. In the United States, if the veto power is exercised, it requires a two-thirds vote before the bill passed can become law. If there be one man less than two-thirds, the minority must rule the majority and prevent them from having a measure for the public interest.

"In the formation of society we have to give up some of our natural rights, and if they were not given up, society could not be formed. The provinces going into Confederation must give up some of their local interests."

In the formation of society we have to give up some of our natural rights, and if they were not given up, society could not be formed. The provinces going into Confederation must give up some of their local interests. It is not we who are giving up more than others, but we yield one point and they yield another.

— *House of Assembly, July 2, 1866*

CANADA

E.-P. Taché: If we were anxious to continue our connection with the British Empire, and to preserve intact our institutions, our laws, and even our remembrances of the past, we must sustain the measure [in favour of the Quebec Resolutions]. If the opportunity which now presented itself were allowed to pass by unimproved, whether we would or would not, we would be forced into the American union by violence, and if not by vio-

---

* This seems to allude to the lack of constitutional checks and balances under responsible government as compared with the United States, where the president has an effective, though not absolute, veto over legislation and his tenure as head of government does not depend on his enjoying the confidence of the elective legislature. But since the presidency is an elective office, it seems odd to cast this distinction, as Johnson does, in terms of "the people's power over the government." The force of the checks and balances in the U.S. system lies in the different bases on which the president, Senate, and House of Representatives are elected, and in the character of the constitution as a written charter of rights. — PR

lence, would be placed upon an inclined plane which would carry us there insensibly. In either case the result would be the same. In our present condition we would not long continue to exist as a British colony. To sustain this position he thought it was only necessary to look at the present state of Canada, its extent, its agricultural and mineral resources, its internal means of communication — natural and artificial . . .

Yet with all these advantages, natural and acquired, he was bound to say we could not become a great nation. We laboured under a drawback or disadvantage which would effectually prevent that, and he would defy anyone to take a map of the world and point to any great nation which had not seaports of its own open at all times of the year. Canada did not possess those advantages, but was shut up in a prison, as it were, for five months of the year in fields of ice, which all the steam engineering apparatus of human ingenuity could not overcome, and so long as this state of things continued, we must consent to be a small people who could, at any moment, be assailed and invaded by a people better situated in that respect than we were . . .

[During the U.S. Civil War] the people of the northern states believed that Canadians sympathized with the South much more than they really did, and the consequences of this misapprehension were, first, that we had been threatened with the abolition of the transit system;* then the Reciprocity Treaty was to be discontinued; then a passport system was inaugurated, which was almost equivalent to a prohibition of intercourse, and the only thing which really remained to be done was to shut down the gate altogether and prevent passage through their territory. Would anyone say that such a state of things was one desirable for Canada to be placed in? Will a great people in embryo, as he believed we were, coolly and tranquilly cross their arms and wait for what might come next? For his part he held that the time had now arrived when we should establish a union with the great Gulf provinces.

— *Legislative Council, February 3, 1865*

James Currie: That honourable gentleman [E.-P. Taché] stated that if the scheme were rejected . . . Canada would be forced by violence into the American union, or placed upon an inclined plane which would carry us there. Now when men occupying

---

* *The arrangement whereby freight originating in or bound for Canada passed in bond through U.S. territory.*

high positions like the honourable member assumed the responsibility of giving utterance to such startling opinions, they ought to be prepared to support them with very cogent reasons.

Taché: I am quite ready to give them.

Currie: If the case were as represented, it must be because we are quite defenceless, and that except in union with the lower provinces we were at the mercy of the United States. But what did the honourable member mean by the inclined plane? For his part he had not heard of any desire on the part of the people of this province to change their political institutions and turn from the glorious flag under which many of them had fought and bled. Had anything been heard from abroad, to the effect that unless we accepted this scheme, England would cast us off or let us slide down the inclined plane? (Laughter.) Yet these were the sole, or at least the chief, reasons alleged by that honourable member.

Let us ask ourselves whether the scheme provided a remedy for the threatened evils. Would Canada indeed be so physically strengthened seaward and landward by this alliance that, in the event of aggression on the part of the United States, we would be rendered quite safe? It was easy to say that union gave strength, but would this union really give us strength? He could understand that union with a people contiguous would do so, but union with provinces 1,500 miles apart at the extreme points was a very different thing, and more likely to be a source of weakness. In his mind it was like tying a small twine at the end of a large rope and saying it strengthened the whole line.

— Legislative Council, February 7, 1865

George-Étienne Cartier: Confederation was . . . at this moment almost forced upon us. We could not shut our eyes to what was going on beyond the lines, where a great struggle was going on between two confederacies, at one time forming but one confederacy. We saw that a government, established not more than eighty years ago, had not been able to keep together the family of states which had broke up four or five years since. We could not deny that the struggle now in progress must necessarily influence our political existence. We did not know what would be the result of that great war — whether it would end in the establishment of two confederacies or in one as before. However, we had to do with five colonies, inhabited by men of the same sympathies and

interests, and in order to become a great nation they required only to be brought together under one general government. The matter resolved itself into this: either we must obtain British North American Confederation or be absorbed in an American confederation. (Hear, hear, and dissent.)

"Uncle Sam Kicked Out,"
from J.W. Bengough's
Caricature History of
Canadian Politics.
"Young Canada" is saying:
"We don't want you here,"
to which John Bull adds:
"That's right, my son.
No matter what comes, an
empty house is better than
such a tenant as that."

Some entertained the opinion that it was unnecessary to have British North American Confederation to prevent absorption into the vortex of American confederation. Such parties were mistaken. We knew the policy of England towards us — that she was determined to help and support us in any struggle with our neighbours. The British provinces, separated as at present, could not defend themselves alone, and the question resolved itself into this: shall the whole strength of the empire be concentrated into Prince Edward Island, or Canada, as the case may be, in case of a war with the United States — or shall the provinces be left to fight single-handed, disunited? We were not sufficiently united. We had our duties with regard to England to perform. In order to secure the exercise of her power in our defence, we must help her ourselves. We could not do this satisfactorily or efficiently unless we had a Confederation. When all united, the enemy would know that if he attacked any part of those provinces — Prince Edward Island or Canada — he would have to encounter the combined strength of the empire. Canada separate would be, although comparatively strong in population and wealth, in a dangerous position should a war ensue. When we had organized our good defensive force, and united for mutual protection, England would send freely here both men and treasure for our defence. (Cheers.)

He had stated before audiences in the lower provinces that, as far as territory, population, and wealth were concerned, Canada was stronger than any of the other provinces, but at the same time was wanting in one element necessary to national greatness — the maritime one: and that, owing to the large trade and commerce of Canada, extensive communication with Great Britain at all seasons was absolutely necessary. At present, however, this system was insufficient, and for winter communication with the seaboard we were left to the caprice of our American neighbours, through whose territory we must pass . . . Canada, having two or three elements of national greatness — territory and population — wanted the maritime element; and as he had said — the lower provinces had this element and a seaboard, but not a back country or large population, which Canada possessed — and for

the mutual benefit and prosperity of all the provinces, all these elements ought to be united together . . .

We were in the habit of seeing in some public journals, and hearing from some public men, that it was a great misfortune indeed there should be a difference of races in this colony — that there should be the distinction of French Canadian from British Canadian. Now, he desired on this point to vindicate the rights, the merits, the usefulness, so to speak, of the French-Canadian race . . . We were all conversant with the history of the circumstances which had brought about the difficulties between England and her former American colonies in 1775 . . . The province of Quebec contained the most dense population of any British colony in North America at that time. [Its] accession was of course an object of envy to the other American colonies, and strenuous efforts were made by those who had resolved to overthrow British power on this continent to induce Canada to ally herself to their cause . . .

But what was the conduct of the French-Canadian people under these circumstances? What was the attitude of the clergy and the seigneurs? It was right, in treating this chapter of our history, to render justice to whom justice was due, and it was truth to say that the seigneurs, forming as they did the educated class of our population at that early epoch, had fully understood that the object and aim of those who appealed to them was the downfall of the monarchical system in America. (Hear, hear.) . . . The people, as well as the clergy and aristocracy, had understood that it was better for them to remain under the English and Protestant crown of England rather than to become republicans. (Hear, hear.) They were proof against the insidious offers of George Washington; and not only so, but when the Americans came as invaders,* they fought against the armed forces of Arnold, Montgomery, and others. (Cheers.) . . .

Attempts were made to excite hostility to federation on the ground that under the regime of a local legislature, the English Protestant minority would not be fairly dealt with. He thought the way in which the French Canadians had stood by the British connection when there were but few British in the province was a

---

*In the winter of 1775–76 an army of the Continental Congress commanded by Philip Montgomery and Benedict Arnold besieged Quebec City. Another force occupied St-Jean, just south of Montreal. Some Canadiens joined the invader, but more defended the government. — PR

proof that they would not attempt to deal unjustly now by the British minority when their numbers were so much greater . . .

[T]he French Canadians understood their position too well. If they had their institutions, their language, and their religion intact today, it was precisely because of their adherence to the British crown . . . [I]f today Canada was a portion of the British Empire, it was due to the conservatism of the French-Canadian clergy. (Cheers.) . . .

We found ourselves at the present day discussing the question of the federation of the British North American provinces, while the great federation of the United States of America was broken up and divided against itself. There was, however, this important difference to be observed in considering the action of the two peoples. They [the Americans] had founded a federation for the purpose of carrying out and perpetuating democracy on this continent; but we, who had the benefit of being able to contemplate republicanism in action during a period of eighty years, saw its defects, and felt convinced that purely democratic institutions could not be conducive to the peace and prosperity of nations.

We were not now discussing the great problem presented to our consideration in order to propagate democratic principles. Our attempt was for the purpose of forming a federation with a view of perpetuating the monarchical element. The distinction therefore between ourselves and our neighbours was just this: in our federation the monarchical principle would form the leading feature, while on the other side of the lines, judging by the past history and present condition of the country, the ruling power was the will of the mob, the rule of the populace. Every person who had conversed with the most intelligent American statesmen and writers must have learned that they all admitted that the governmental powers had become too extended, owing to the introduction of universal suffrage, and mob rule had consequently supplanted legitimate authority; and we now saw the sad spectacle of a country torn by civil war, and brethren fighting against brethren.

— *Legislative Assembly, February 7, 1865*

Thomas D'Arcy McGee: We may grumble or not at the necessity of preparation England imposes upon us, but whether we like it or not, we have at all events been told that we have entered upon a new era in our military relations to the rest of the empire. (Hear, hear.) Then, sir, in the second place there came what I

"[The Americans] had founded a federation for the purpose of carrying out and perpetuating democracy on this continent; but we, who had the benefit of being able to contemplate republicanism in action during a period of eighty years, saw its defects, and felt convinced that purely democratic institutions could not be conducive to the peace and prosperity of nations."

---

may call the other warning from without — the American warning. (Hear.) Republican America gave us her notices in times past through the press, and her demagogues and her statesmen, but of late days she has given us much more intelligible notices — such as the notice to abrogate the Reciprocity Treaty, and to arm the [Great] Lakes, contrary to the provisions of the addenda to the treaty of 1818. She has given us another notice in imposing a vexatious passport system; another in her avowed purpose to construct a ship canal around the Falls of Niagara, so as "to pass war vessels from Lake Ontario to Lake Erie"; and yet another, the most striking one of all, has been given to us, if we will only understand it, by the enormous expansion of the American army and navy.

I will take leave to read to the house a few figures which show the amazing, the unprecedented growth which has not perhaps a parallel in the annals of the past, of the military power of our neighbours within the past three or four years . . . From January 1861 to January 1863 the army of 10,000 was increased to 800,000 . . . In January 1861 the ships of war belonging to the United States were 83; in December 1864 they numbered 671 . . . These are frightful figures for the capacity of destruction they represent, for the heaps of carnage that they represent, for the quantity of human blood spilt that they represent, for the lust of conquest that they represent, for the evil passions that they represent, and for the arrest of the onward progress of civilization that they represent.

But it is not the figures which give the worst view of the fact — for England still carries more guns afloat even than our war-making neighbours. (Cheers.) It is the change which has taken place in the spirit of the people of the northern states themselves which is the worst view of the fact . . . that terrible change which has made war familiar and even attractive to them.

When the first battle was fought — when, in the language of the Duke of Wellington,* the first "butcher's bill was sent in" — a shudder of horror ran through the length and breadth of the country; but by and by, as the carnage increased, no newspaper was considered worth laying on the breakfast table unless it contained the story of the butchery of thousands of men . . . Have

---

*Arthur Wellesley, 1st Duke of Wellington (1769–1852), British general during the Napoleonic War; prime minister, 1828–30. He commanded the British forces at the Battle of Waterloo.

these sights and sounds no warning addressed to us? Are we as those who have eyes and see not; ears and hear not; reason, neither do they understand?*

If we are true to Canada, if we do not desire to become part and parcel of this people, we cannot overlook this the greatest revolution of our times. Let us remember this, that when the three cries among our next neighbours are money, taxation, blood, it is time for us to provide for our own security . . .

The attorney general east [Cartier] told us in his speech the other night that one of the features of the original program of the American revolutionists was the acquisition of Canada to the United States. They pretend to underrate the importance of this country, now that they are fully occupied elsewhere; but I remember well that the late Mr. Webster,[†] who was not a demagogue, at the opening of the Worcester and Albany Railway some years since expressed the hope that the railways of the New England states would all point towards Canada because their influence and the demands of commerce would in time bring Canada into the union and increase the New England element in that union. (Hear.) . . .

Some honourable gentlemen, while admitting that we have entered, within the present decade, on a period of political transition, have contended that we might have bridged the abyss with that Prussian pontoon, called a Zollverein.[‡] But if anyone for a moment will remember that the trade of the whole front of New Brunswick and Nova Scotia gravitates at present along-shore to Portland and Boston, while the trade of Upper Canada, west of Kingston, has long gravitated across the lakes to New York, he will see, I think, that a mere Zollverein treaty without a strong political end to serve, and some political power at its back, would be, in our new circumstances, merely waste paper. (Hear, hear.)

The charge that we have not gone far enough — that we have not struck out boldly for a consolidated union, instead of a union with reserved local jurisdictions, is another charge which deserves

---

*Mark 8:18.

[†] *Daniel Webster (1782–1852), nationalist lawyer and politician. As U.S. Secretary of State he negotiated the Webster-Ashburton Treaty (1842), which defined the boundary between Maine and New Brunswick.*

[‡] *A "customs union," established in 1834 under Prussian leadership, it played an important part in the establishment of a Prussian hegemony over Germany.*

some notice. To this I answer that, if we had had, as was proposed, an intercolonial railway twenty years ago, we might by this time have been perhaps, and only perhaps, in a condition to unite into one consolidated government. But certain politicians and capitalists having defeated that project twenty years ago, special interests took the place [which] great general interests might by this time have occupied. Vested rights and local ambitions arose and were recognized, and all these had to be admitted as existing in a pretty advanced stage of development, when our conferences were called together. (Hear, hear.) The lesson to be learned from this squandering of quarter centuries by British Americans is this, that if we lose the present propitious opportunity, we may find it as hard a few years hence to get an audience, even for any kind of union (except American union) as we should have found it to get a hearing last year for a legislative union, from the long period of estrangement and non-intercourse which had existed between those provinces, and the special interests which had grown up in the meantime in each of them. (Cheers.)

What risks do we run if we reject this measure? We run the risk of being swallowed up by the spirit of universal democracy that prevails in the United States. Their usual and favourite motto is:

No pent-up Utica* contracts our powers,
But the whole boundless continent is ours.

---

*The couplet in this form — "No pent-up Utica contracts your powers / But the whole boundless continent is yours" — was added in 1778 to Joseph Addison's play Cato (first published 1713) by Jonathan Mitchell Sewall, for a performance in Portsmouth, New Hampshire. Sewall was drawing attention to parallels between the events of the American Revolution and those of the play. In later years, as "No pent-up Utica contracts our powers," it becomes, in McGee's words, "a favourite motto," expressing American ambition to occupy the entire North American continent. William S. Young uses it in a broadsheet of 1861 (advertising the printing services of Franklin Book and Job of Philadelphia) to assert his fervent patriotism and support for the northern states in the Civil War. Both McGee and Benjamin Davies of Prince Edward Island (below) interpret it as a declaration of American ambition to take over British America. The ancient city of Utica, located on the north African coast not far from Carthage, was the key to domination of the surrounding territory. Cato the Younger took command at Utica in 48 BC. — JA

*"Now, I suppose a
universal democracy
is no more acceptable
to us than a universal
monarchy."*

That is the paraphrase of the Monroe Doctrine.* And the popular
voice has favoured — aye, and the greatest statesmen among
them have looked upon it as inevitable — an extension of the
principles of democracy over this continent. Now, I suppose a
universal democracy is no more acceptable to us than a universal
monarchy in Europe, and yet for three centuries — from Charles
V to Napoleon† — our fathers combatted to the death against the
subjection of all Europe to a single system or a single master, and
heaped up a debt which has since burdened the producing classes
of the empire with an enormous load of taxation, which, perhaps,
none other except the hardy and ever-growing industry of those
little islands could have borne up under. (Hear, hear.)

The idea of a universal democracy in America is no more welcome to the minds of thoughtful men among us than was that of
a universal monarchy to the mind of the thoughtful men who followed the standard of the third William‡ in Europe, or who
afterwards, under the great Marlborough, opposed the armies of
the particular dynasty§ that sought to place Europe under a
single dominion. (Hear, hear.) But if we are to have a universal
democracy on this continent, the lower provinces — the smaller
fragments — will be "gobbled up" first, and we will come in
afterwards by way of dessert. (Laughter.)

The proposed Confederation will enable us to bear up

---

* *Enunciated by U.S. president James Monroe in 1823, it recognized
existing European colonies in the Western hemisphere, but forbade further
European colonization there. After its invocation in the 1840s in support of
American claims to the Oregon Territory, British Americans tended to con-
flate it with the expansionist doctrine of Manifest Destiny, first enunciated
then, which declared it to be providential design that the United States
should occupy the entire continent. — PR*

† *Charles V ruled as Holy Roman emperor from 1520 to 1556; Napoleon
Bonaparte ruled France first as dictator, then as emperor, from 1799 to 1814.*

‡ *William III, also known as William of Orange, fought the armies of the
Bourbon king of France, Louis XIV, from 1690 to 1697. War was resumed
in 1702 under the generalship of John Churchill, later Duke of
Marlborough, who vanquished the armies of Louis XIV in several battles
between 1702 and 1711, most notably at Blenheim in 1704.*

§ *McGee ingeniously relates British resistance to U.S. hegemony in North
America to Britain's traditional resistance to the establishment of hegemony
in Europe. Under William III the target of that policy was the Bourbon
dynasty, which occupied the thrones of both France and Spain. — PR*

shoulder to shoulder, to resist the spread of this universal democracy doctrine.* It will make it more desirable to maintain on both sides the connection that binds us to the parent state. It will raise us from the position of mere dependent colonies to a new and more important position; it will give us a new lease of existence under other and more favourable conditions; and resistance to this project, which is pregnant with so many advantages to us and to our children, means simply this, ultimate union with the United States. (Cheers.)

— *Legislative Assembly, February 9, 1865*

Walter McCrae: My honourable friend from Niagara [Currie] says that the union of these provinces would not tend to strengthen our means of defence if, unfortunately, we should be invaded by the United States forces because our frontier would be extended more than in proportion to the increase of our num-

---

* McGee rejects both "universal democracy," which he associates with the United States, and "universal monarchy," the rule of autocrats like the seventeenth-century Bourbons. Both are imperialistic forms of government, antithetical to the liberty of the people. He is drawing on the standard teaching that the British parliamentary system was preferable because it was a mixed form of government; it was neither purely democratic nor purely monarchical, but combined monarchic elements (such as the strong political executive that results from responsible government and continuing allegiance to the queen) with aristocratic elements (such as the Canadian Senate or the British House of Lords), and democratic elements (like the House of Commons). The argument was that the monarchic and aristocratic elements would hold in check potential popular tyrants, while the democratic element (especially if coupled with a comparatively broad franchise) would prevent the rise of would-be Bourbons. Like so many others in these debates, McGee uses "democracy" or "republicanism" to refer to populist tyranny. His language is old-fashioned; it remains that what he and his colleagues are recommending is parliamentary government, not very different from the form of government we enjoy today and call liberal democracy.

The difficulty with McGee's argument in this speech is his picture of the United States as a "universal" democracy, and thus a threat to liberty. Elsewhere in these debates Cartier and others make the same claim. The fact is that although there were advocates of radical populism, or "universal democracy," in the United States in these years, they were in the minority. David Christie, below, gives the more standard picture of the American form of government. — JA

bers. Does not everyone know that it is the settled conviction of the military authorities of the States that their mistake in the last war was invading these provinces in different places at the same time, and that in the event of a second war their policy will be to concentrate all their strength on some one given point — Montreal, for instance? And will my honourable friend contend that the union and the railway will not enable us to concentrate a greater force, and more rapidly, on whatever point danger may be threatened, and also that they will not enable us to obtain aid from the British troops more quickly at any season of the year?

— Legislative Council, February 13, 1865

"Their institutions have the same features with our own. There are some points of variance, but the same great principle is the basis of both — that life, liberty, and the pursuit of happiness are the unalienable rights of man, and that to secure these rights, governments are instituted among men, deriving their just powers from the consent of the governed. This is the secret of the strength of the British Constitution, and without a free and full recognition of it no government can be strong or permanent."

David Christie: All those who have preceded us in the work of constitution making have left, on the structures which they have erected, the impress of that attribute which pervades humanity — imperfection. We have a very lamentable instance of this in the case of our neighbours on the southern side of the line. As was well said by a prominent member of the government* in another place, the constitution of the United States "was one of the most marvellous efforts of skill and organization that ever governed a free people. But to say that it was perfect would be wrong." The wonder is that men with the limited amount of experience which its authors possessed should have framed such an instrument. It has stood many rude tests, and but for the existence in the social compact of our American friends of an element in direct antagonism to the whole genius of their system — negro slavery — the constitution of the United States would have continued to withstand — yes, and after the extinction of that element, will continue to withstand — all the artillery which their own or foreign despotism can array against it.

Their institutions have the same features with our own. There are some points of variance, but the same great principle is the basis of both — that life, liberty, and the pursuit of happiness are the unalienable rights of man, and that to secure these rights, governments are instituted among men, deriving their just powers from the consent of the governed. This is the secret of the strength of the British Constitution, and without a free and full recognition of it no government can be strong or permanent.

— Legislative Council, February 15, 1865

---

* The quotation is probably from a newspaper paraphrase of John A. Macdonald's speech of February 6.

Uncle Sam; detail from J.W. Bengough's Caricature History of Canadian Politics.

J.-B.-E. Dorion: An unseen but very extensive influence is at work in all the country south of the St. Lawrence, above Nicolet and as far as the frontier.* I shall explain it to you. In all that part of the country, a great many young men go to the United States to look for employment. These children of the people find there a wider field for their enterprising minds; in fact, they are forced to leave Canada in order to earn money. When once they are established in the United States, they correspond with their relatives whom they have left behind them. In all their letters they describe the treatment they receive, and boast of their position, the footing they are on in their social relations with Americans, the good wages which they receive, and the state of prosperity at which they soon arrive . . . These communications, these intimacies between Canadians established in the States and their home friends, have greater effect to produce favourable feelings towards the Americans in our country than all the newspapers in the world. It is a portion of the heart of the country removed into a strange land by the force of circumstances. The accounts they hear from their friends prove to them that the Americans are not such horrible monsters as they are said to be in certain quarters, and that their political institutions are far superior to ours; that every man is on a footing of equality with his neighbour, and that he possesses political rights of which he cannot be deprived. This influence of which I am speaking is very great, and certainly it is not to be counteracted, nor the feeling of sympathy for the people and the institutions of the United States to be repressed in the minds of those who confess it, by such changes as those now proposed to be made. (Hear, hear.) . . .

"But," it will be said, "annexation is national suicide, and the people will never consent to it! Look at Louisiana, which has lost itself in the American union!" The people of Lower Canada will reply that Louisiana contained but 30,000 whites when it was sold to the United States for $14,000,000, and that Lower Canada counts for more than 1,000,000 of inhabitants; that there is, therefore, no comparison between the position of Louisiana at

---

* *Dorion's speech is the most pro-American statement in the entire debate on identity. It projects the outlook of the Patriots of the 1830s under the leadership of Louis-Joseph Papineau. As such, it presents a striking contrast to the dominant conservative French-Canadianism of the post-rebellion era, which feared the United States as the chief threat to national survival and valued the British connection as a shield against it.* — PR

that time and that we now occupy. Besides, those 30,000 whites in Louisiana were not all French; for thirty years previous to 1800, Louisiana had belonged to the Spaniards. No one can deny that. It was in 1803 that it was ceded by France to the United States, and yet its French population has not been absorbed and has not disappeared. (Hear, hear.) Since it was ceded to the United States, Louisiana has always governed itself as it liked, and in its own way.

It is true that the official use of the French language has been abolished in its legislature, but why and by whom? It was abolished by the people of the country themselves, to mark their dissatisfaction at having been sold by France. But notwithstanding that fact, and the great influx of foreign population, the original population have remained French, their laws are published in French, the judges speak French, pleading French, numerous journals are published in French; in a word, the country has remained as thoroughly French as it was under the domination of France. (Hear, hear.) To those who tell our people that annexation would annihilate them as a people, and destroy their nationality and their religion, they will reply that there is no danger of their being transported like the inhabitants of Acadia, and that Lower Canada would be as independent as any other of the states of the union; that they would, therefore, manage their own affairs and protect their interests as they thought proper, without fear of intervention on the part of the general government or of the other states; for they would possess, like all the other states, full and entire sovereignty in all matters specially relating to their own interests . . .

I do not ask for the annexation of Canada to the United States, nor do the people desire it; but I assert that changes such as those proposed in our social and political condition are the surest means of bringing it about, because they are of a nature to create serious discontent and a constant conflict between us and our neighbours; and the people, far from being satisfied with that, will be but ill-inclined to defend such a state of things.

— *Legislative Assembly, March 9, 1865*

BRITISH COLUMBIA

Henry Crease: Our only option is between remaining a petty, isolated community 15,000 miles from home, eking out a miserable existence on the crumbs of prosperity our powerful and active republican neighbours choose to allow us, or, by taking our

SIR JOSEPH WILLIAM
TRUTCH
(1826–1904), an
engineer, surveyor,
colonial official, and
entrepreneur who
was born and died in
England. As chief
commissioner of lands
and works and an
executive councillor,
1864–71, he feathered
his own and his cronies'
nests and demolished
the humane Indian
policy of former
governor Sir James
Douglas.
    After leading to
Ottawa the delegation
that negotiated
annexation to Canada,
he became British
Columbia's first
lieutenant governor,
1871–76. Later he
supervised construction
of the Canadian Pacific
Railway in the province.

place among the comity of nations, become the prosperous
western outlet on the North Pacific of a young and vigorous
people, the eastern boundary of whose possessions is washed by
the Atlantic. This is the only option left to faithful subjects of the
British crown.

J.S. Helmcken: The honourable gentleman [Crease] laid great
stress upon the consolidation of British interests on this coast,
but I say, sir, that however much we are in favour of consolidating
British interests, our own interests must come first. Imperial
interests can well afford to wait . . . It cannot be regarded as
improbable that, ultimately, not only this colony, but the whole
Dominion of Canada, will be absorbed by the United States. The
honourable attorney general [Crease] has not attempted to prove
the advantages which will result from Confederation, he has contented himself with vague assertions of advantages.

    Confederation, so far as it has at present gone, is but a mere
experiment. And I believe that considerable dissatisfaction has
resulted from it. If we wait a little longer before seeking to enter
within its pale ourselves, we shall know better about the faults of
its machinery, and perhaps be able to learn what are its draw-
backs, and how we can best avoid them . . . The effect of a large
body and a small body being brought into contact is that the
larger will attract the smaller, and ultimately absorb it. There can
be no permanent or lasting union with Canada, unless terms be
made to promote and foster the material and pecuniary interests
of this colony. The only link which binds this colony to Canada is
imperial.

— *Legislative Council, March 9, 1870*

Joseph Trutch: I will now, sir, come to the consideration of what
Confederation is in the abstract, as I understand it. It is the union
and consolidation of British interests in British territory on this
continent, for the security and advancement of each province
individually, and of the whole collectively, under the continued
support of the British flag. A great idea of great minds, which
have thus given a poetical refutation to that doctrine of "America
for the United States" known as the "Monroe Doctrine" . . . and
on this, if on no other grounds, the principle of Confederation
deserves the support of every British heart in the colony.

    Mr. President, I should do violence to my best feelings were I
to refrain from availing myself of this opportunity of paying my

humble tribute of respect and esteem for the people of that great republic. ("Hear, hear," from all sides.) No one can better appreciate than I do the high and eminent qualities which characterize that great nation, and especially that national feeling — that love of country, so worthy of our imitation — for which they have made such sacrifices . . . led me to form a most appreciative estimate of their social and domestic relations, of which I cannot speak in terms of too much praise. But my experience of the political institutions of that country only led me to prize our own more highly and made me more than ever an Englishman; and I rejoice at the opportunity now afforded me of raising my voice against any movement tending in the direction of incorporating this country with the United States. And so we come to Confederation as our manifest destiny . . .

Henry Holbrook: [Of the annexation petition from Victoria], we may say that liberty had run wild, people have actually become dissatisfied because they have had too much of it. I remember a similar discontent with excess of liberty in Paris, after the revolution of 1848; the people revelled in excess of freedom, and from so much liberty they fell into another revolution.* It is only in a country with such free institutions as England that such a petition† could have been signed with impunity, for if it means anything at all, it did not stop short of treason.

— *Legislative Council, March 10, 1870*

Robert Carrall: I feel a great respect for our neighbours of the great republic; I honour the country and its institutions; particularly I esteem the people of America in the exercise of national and domestic relations; they are true Anglo-Saxons. But, whilst professing great respect for the people and for the government of the United States, I confess that I do not like their political institutions. I have many friends in America, and I have spent some time there myself, in their military service, but I left America a greater Canadian than ever.

And I say, sir, that I deem the action taken by certain for-

---

* *The overthrow of the July Monarchy in February 1848 was followed by a period of political instability, including another popular uprising in Paris in June.*

† *Some residents of Victoria had petitioned for annexation to the United States.*

eigners here, in getting up a petition, which has perhaps been brought into more prominent notice than it was entitled to, exceedingly unhappy, and I know that I speak the sentiments of my constituents when I say so. These foreigners have received every hospitality, and have been treated with respect and liberality in this colony; they enjoyed all the rights and privileges to which they would have been entitled in their own country, and perhaps more; they have acted foolishly towards the flag that sheltered them, and have abused the hospitality which has been extended to them in getting up this petition. If any British subjects signed it, I consider them unworthy of the name; they would be better in the chain-gang.

— *Legislative Council, March 11, 1870*

"I . . . should consider myself unworthy of the confidence reposed on me, as a representative of the people, were I to shrink from the full expression of my opinion upon so great a subject deeply affecting the interests of the colony, simply because my constituents or the people of this colony are supposed to entertain different views."

PRINCE EDWARD ISLAND

W.H. Pope: It is to my mind very evident that we must choose between consolidation of the different provinces and colonies and absorption into the American republic. Consolidation — the placing [of] the revenue and the men of the several provinces under the control of the central power — would, in the event of a war, be absolutely necessary in order to [effect] the efficient organization of our colonial resources. In Britain as well as in the colonies, the opinion is widely entertained that our absorption into the great republic is inevitable. It has therefore been contended by some that in order to avert so great a calamity, the connection between the provinces and the mother country should be severed by mutual consent and that we should become an independent nation. Others, sir, consider that it would be more to our interest to retain our connection with England and to endure, if necessary, the horrors of war — that we should remain a portion of the great empire of Britain, continue to live under the glorious old flag, and our monarchical institutions. The latter is the prevailing opinion . . .

I have been told, sir, that by advocating the adoption of the principle of the Quebec report, I am placing myself in antagonism to the people of this island, and especially to my own constituents. I, sir, should consider myself unworthy of the confidence reposed on me, as a representative of the people, were I to shrink from the full expression of my opinion upon so great a subject deeply affecting the interests of the colony, simply because my constituents or the people of this colony are sup-

posed to entertain different views. The views or wishes of my constituents upon this question can, in themselves, have no influence upon my opinion. In the present instance, I believe Confederation would promote the best interests of the island. Popular opinion is proverbially changeable, and I expect ere long to hear many of those who now denounce the report of the Quebec Conference admit that, after mature deliberation, they have come to the conclusion that its principles are just.

Confederation would prove our best security against foreign invasion and preserve to us our monarchical institutions. I feel, sir, that I am approaching what my eloquent friend, the member for Charlottetown, Mr. [Frederick] Brecken, is pleased facetiously to designate the "glory argument." I attach great importance to this glory argument. I desire to live under monarchical institutions and the glorious flag of old England. Sir, there are in this house honourable members who smile when the glory argument is mentioned. Their fathers made great sacrifices in order that they might enjoy those privileges which are the inheritance of British subjects. In the Maritime provinces are now to be found the descendants of men who left the United States upon the declaration of independence, abandoning their property and the homes in which their children had been born, impelled to do so by the "glory argument." The American Loyalists were attached to monarchical institutions. They valued their privileges as British subjects; and rather than become republicans they made the greatest sacrifices and sought new homes on British soil, in the wilderness in Nova Scotia, New Brunswick, and Prince Edward Island.

— House of Assembly, March 24, 1865

Benjamin Davies: This question, Mr. Speaker, is, in my opinion, forced upon us. If the [United] States were now in the same position as they were before the outbreak of the Civil War, I would oppose any measure of the sort, but they have now become a great military country whose boast it has long been to carry out the Monroe Doctrine, and to spread the principles of republicanism over the whole continent. The imperial government has expressed its willingness to aid us. It has said, "[Contribute] what you can towards your own defence, and we will supplement your efforts." We are too small a people for separate and independent action . . . and we are all aware of the state of feeling which exists in the northern states and Great Britain, which will most likely

find expression in an attempt to realize their oft-repeated chant, "No pent-up Utica confines [*sic*] our powers. But the whole boundless continent is ours."

— *House of Assembly, March 27, 1865*

T.H. Haviland: The [Quebec] report, in my opinion, embraces the best features of the constitutions of Great Britain and the United States applicable to our circumstances, and it is not small satisfaction to those who support the measure of a union that though it may meet opposition in the colonies, it has received approval from the statesmen and press of Great Britain. One great benefit which would accrue from union would be the diversion of the tide of immigration from the United States to these colonies, where his civil and religious liberties would be secured to the stranger the moment he landed on our shores.

Mr. Speaker, I may say that the report of the delegates embodies principles greater in some respects than those of which the constitution of the United States is blessed. The chief ruler of that country is himself, during his term of office, irresponsible to the people, and is surrounded by a ministry equally unfettered. The constitution of the proposed union acknowledges our gracious queen and her successors as the chief authority, and the administration of the confederate colonies will be conducted by her representative to be appointed by herself; but he will be advised by ministers responsible for the acts of the government, and whom an adverse vote in the lower branch of the legislature would at once dismiss from power. In the States, one result of their institutions is the extinction, or perhaps more properly the total ignoring, [of] the rights of the minority. Where, however, British principles obtain, the rights and privileges of a minority are maintained to them inviolate.*

— *House of Assembly, March 28, 1865*

Frederick Brecken: We were bound to return to the people the trust which we received from their hands; but every honourable member ought to express his convictions on the subject under discussion, and not merely the sentiments which he thought would catch the popular breeze. The statesmen and the press of

---

* *This ideal has not always been honoured; witness the recent use of the 1982 amending formula to extinguish religious schools in Newfoundland and Quebec. — IG*

"A person taken blindfolded from these colonies and set down in the United States would scarcely distinguish that he had passed into a foreign country."

England seem disposed to allow the colonists to take the course which they consider most conducive to their interests, whether to retain their connection with the mother country, choose independence, or form an alliance with the great republic. The latter did not involve very great changes. We were really the same people, for we had the same origin, language, and literature. A person taken blindfolded from these colonies and set down in the United States would scarcely distinguish that he had passed into a foreign country. But when we discussed the question of consolidation with the neighbouring states, we should not make ourselves contemptible by talking of it as a step which this colony could take alone. We would go into annexation, if it ever came, just as soon as the rest of British America, and not one day sooner.

He was not in favour of annexation, but he looked upon isolation as played out. Either Confederation or annexation must come, and he believed that Confederation would carry the day. British institutions were being put on their trial on this continent, and if they failed of success he would admit he was wrong in advocating Confederation. He, however, looked upon our entering the dominion as a necessity.

— *House of Assembly, March 7, 1870*

Chapter Seven

BRITISH OR
CANADIAN?

B RITISH IDENTITY, BRITISH LIBERTIES, and the British
Empire: though the colonies that enjoyed responsible government were securely tied to the "mother country" as constituent
parts of the empire, they were also remarkably independent in
government and politics. They had the best of both worlds: the
glory and security of the British connection and the satisfactions
of internal self-government. Could this pleasant situation be kept
up after Confederation?

Confederation's most ardent supporters are confident that the
new nation coming into being will continue as part of the empire.
But just what kind of tie with Britain are they envisaging? A
nation within an empire? Today we make considerable trouble
over ideas like this. We ask how England as a nation can also be
part of the European Union, and how Quebec as a nation can
also be part of Canada. There may be lessons for us here.

A deeper note sounds when speakers raise questions about the
nature of political loyalty. Some philosophers today believe the
great defect of modern liberalism (including British parliamentary government) is that, in contrast to feudalism and
republicanism, it emphasizes the individual at the expense of the
common good. The citizens and subjects of liberal regimes are
said to be too attached to their individual "life, liberty, and property" to be capable of true loyalty; they lack the sense of
community. Yet there is no lack of communal feeling in these
debates. There seems to be no opposition between individualism
and community. Speakers express passionate attachment to the
local community and the empire, and are prepared to defend
community and the empire in war. They describe themselves as

loyal to free governments, and grateful for a political community that gives them the opportunity to be self-reliant individuals.

British Columbia's Joseph Trutch contends that life is "nothing" without loyalty. Loyalty is a natural feeling, necessary to identity; people cannot live well without it. The question for speakers like T.L. Wood is whether the new nation can ever command the kind of loyalty that colonists so freely give Britain and the empire.

NEW BRUNSWICK

Robert Thomson: I would go into Confederation in five minutes if they would only show a reason for it. We have got the most noble confederation now; we are confederated with the United Kingdom of Great Britain. It is a better confederation than they have at Washington.

William Needham: I am willing to go the whole hog to show the British government that we are sincere and that we do not want to sever the connection existing between us or annex ourselves to the States (for I do not believe this feeling resides in the breast of one man). I want them to know that the reason we rejected the scheme was because we love the connection with our mother country, and that the very men who voted against are willing, if necessary, to shed every drop of their blood in defence of her cause and institutions.

— *House of Assembly, April 29, 1865*

Needham: What would we have been had Confederation taken place under this scheme? Would we have been a province? Certainly not. Oh, it is said we can have a local legislature; so we could, and its powers would be confined to making laws to prevent cows from running on the commons, providing that sheep shall wear bells, and to issue tavern licences . . .

We have now a direct communication with the home government, as they appoint our governor; but if we go into Confederation our governor would be appointed by the governor general; that would raise our dignity very much, to have a local governor appointed by the governor general; would not that be derogatory to our political standing, both at home and abroad? I heard a judge, in addressing a grand jury, in the County of York, strive to impress upon their minds the necessity for this "Great British Nationality" as he termed it. Great British Humbug! I

should like to know where there is any nationality in this Confederation scheme that we have not got now. We are "par excellence" Bluenoses; those born in Ireland are Irishmen, in [England] Englishmen, in Wales Welshmen, but we are all British subjects as much as if we were born "Cockneys." We have the real British nationality, and because we did not want any other we rejected the great botheration* or Confederation scheme, for it all amounts to the same thing; thus it is that so far as politics are concerned we are not going to gain anything.

— House of Assembly, May 30, 1865

Thomson: I believe, instead of this union, we should try to get a union with Britain, by getting a few members in the British parliament† for every colony that is of British descent. If there is any change to be made in our constitution we should have a two-thirds vote before we adopt it, and that vote should be given fairly; every man above twenty-one years of age should have a fair vote, let it be for annexation or whatever it may be.

— House of Assembly, June 1, 1865

George Hill: [Union would not stop a U.S. invasion.] If it is loyalty to bury one's head like the ostrich and refuse to see what is clear to all others, then am I open to the charge of disloyalty. But if it is loyalty to have a strong love and admiration for England, for her history, her institutions, and her literature, and to hope that her flag may always float over these provinces, and that I may always live under her sway, then I am loyal.

— House of Assembly, June 2, 1865

Amos Botsford: Never will I forget my feelings when I trod for the first time the soil of old England, and my mind thrilled as all the historical recollections of her greatness and glory came up

---

* A satirical term for Confederation coined by Joseph Howe. — PR
† Thomson anticipates the "imperial federalists" of the early twentieth century, who argued that the great affairs of the empire should be taken care of by a parliament (with taxing powers), probably located in England, elected by all the subjects of the empire in whatever country or colony they lived. The internal affairs of each nation, including Britain, would fall to local legislatures. Other allusions to the idea in these debates include those of George Coles (Prince Edward Island) in this chapter and Christopher Dunkin (Canada) in Chapter 8. — JA/PR

before me, and I felt a portion of that glory reflected upon me as a humble colonist belonging to the great empire. I thought of the fact that the colonies had been so long protected by the fostering arm of that power. I thought how, possessing a proper policy under that fostering influence, the colonies might speedily arrive at a position when, under the full play of British institutions, a strong and healthy manhood should be developed, and when the British North American colonies and those young giants in the Pacific would be able, as willing, should the old fatherland be threatened, to spring to the rescue and make some return for the long years of maternal care Great Britain had bestowed upon them. With their resources and now latent power developed, Britain would stand surrounded by these colonies a spectacle that would eclipse the glory of Rome in her palmiest days of splendour.

I wish now to direct attention to the United States as an example in point, while discussing the principles of union. Read her history and mark the progress she has made since the declaration of independence; as contrasted with the time previous thereto when the country was divided into minor petty provinces, each having a distinctive tariff, and without a central governing power. Union became strength there, and today, as the result of the confederate principle, the United States stands a prodigy — a wonder among the nations.

— *Legislative Council, April 4, 1866*

Charles Fisher: The reason the people of England take such an interest in this question is this: They see by our constitution that we admire the institutions of the mother country and that we are going to form a nation which is to be part of themselves, and they further say, if we wish to separate from them, they do not wish to retain us; but if we wish to remain, all the power of the nation will be put forth to sustain us . . . Let us then form one great country, and depend upon it they will respect us. Let us unite, and we will become a powerful nation, our resources will be developed, our condition improved, our railroads built, and our prosperity increased beyond anything we at present anticipate.

— *House of Assembly, June 30, 1866*

CANADA

John A. Macdonald: I think it is well that, in framing our constitution . . . our first act should have been to recognize the

> *"[At the Quebec Conference] the desire to remain connected with Great Britain and to retain our allegiance to Her Majesty was unanimous."*

"Britannica," a detail from J.W. Bengough's Caricature History of Canadian Politics. *The classical garb and (very small) lion identify the figure representing Great Britain.*

sovereignty of Her Majesty . . . [At the Quebec Conference] the desire to remain connected with Great Britain and to retain our allegiance to Her Majesty was unanimous.

Although we knew it to be possible that Canada, from her position, might be exposed to all the horrors of war, by reason of causes of hostility arising between Great Britain and the United States — causes over which we had no control, and which we had no hand in bringing about — yet there was a unanimous feeling of willingness to run all the hazards of war, if war must come, rather than lose the connection between the mother country and these colonies. (Cheers.) We provide that "the executive authority shall be administered by the sovereign personally, or by the representative of the sovereign duly authorized." It is too much to expect that the queen should vouchsafe us her personal governance or presence, except to pay us, as the heir apparent of the throne, our future sovereign has already paid us, the graceful compliment of a visit. The executive authority must therefore be administered by Her Majesty's representative. We place no restriction on Her Majesty's prerogative in the selection of her representative. As it is now, so it will be if this constitution is adopted. The sovereign has unrestricted freedom of choice.* Whether in making her selection she may send us one of her own family, a royal prince, as a viceroy to rule over us, or one of the great statesmen of England to represent her, we know not. We leave that to Her Majesty in all confidence. But we may be permitted to hope that when the union takes place and we become the great country which British North America is certain to be, it will be an object worthy the ambition of the statesmen of England to be charged with presiding over our destinies. (Hear, hear.) . . .

One argument, but not a strong one, has been used against this Confederation, that it is an advance towards independence. Some are apprehensive that the very fact of our forming this union will hasten the time when we shall be severed from the mother country. I have no apprehension of that kind . . . I am strongly of the opinion that year by year, as we grow in population and strength, England will more see the advantages of maintaining the alliance between British North America and herself. Does anyone imagine that, when our population, instead of

---

* *In actual fact, the governor general was chosen by the British prime minister. Since Canada achieved independence in 1931, the governor general has been chosen by the prime minister of Canada.*

three and a half, will be seven millions,* as it will be ere many years pass, we would be one whit more willing than now to sever the connection with England? Would not those seven millions be just as anxious to maintain their allegiance to the queen and their connection with the mother country as we are now? . . . I believe the people of Canada East and West to be truly loyal. But, if they can by [any] possibility be exceeded in loyalty, it is by the inhabitants of the Maritime provinces. Loyalty with them is an overruling passion. (Hear, hear.) . . .

When this union takes place we will be at the outset no inconsiderable people. We find ourselves with a population approaching four millions of souls . . . And with a rapidly increasing population . . . our future progress, during the next quarter of a century, will be vastly greater. (Cheers.) And when, by means of this rapid increase, we become a nation of eight or nine millions of inhabitants, our alliance will be worthy of being sought by the great nations of the earth. (Hear, hear.)

I am proud to believe that our desire for a permanent alliance will be reciprocated in England. I know that there is a party in England — but it is inconsiderable in numbers, though strong in intellect and power — which speaks of the desirability of getting rid of the colonies; but I believe such is not the feeling of the statesmen and the people of England. I believe it will never be the deliberately expressed determination of the government of Great Britain. (Hear, hear.) . . .

Instead of looking upon us as a merely dependent colony, England will have in us a friendly nation — a subordinate but still a powerful people to stand by her in North America in peace or in war. (Cheers.) The people of Australia will be such another subordinate nation. And England will have this advantage, if her colonies progress under the new colonial system, as I believe they will, that, though at war with all the rest of the world, she will be able to look to the subordinate nations in alliance with her, and owning allegiance to the same sovereign, who will assist her again to meet the whole world in arms, as she has done before. (Cheers.)

It is true that we stand in danger, as we have stood in danger again and again in Canada, of being plunged into war and suffering all its dreadful consequences, as the result of causes over which we have no control, by reason of their connection. This,

---

* *The population of Canada at independence (1931) was a little under 10.5 million.*

however, did not intimidate us. At the very mention of the prospect of a war some time ago, how were the feelings of the people aroused from one extremity of British America to the other, and preparations made for meeting its worst consequences? Although the people of this country are fully aware of the horrors of war — should a war arise, unfortunately, between the United States and England, and we all pray it never may — they are still ready to encounter all perils of that kind for the sake of the connection with England.

So long as that alliance is maintained, we enjoy, under her protection, the privileges of constitutional liberty according to the British system.* We will enjoy here that which is the great test of constitutional freedom — we will have the rights of the minority respected. (Hear, hear.) In all countries the rights of the majority take care of themselves, but it is only in countries like England, enjoying constitutional liberty, and safe from the tyranny of a single despot or of an unbridled democracy,† that the rights of minorities are regarded. So long, too, as we form a portion of the British Empire, we shall have the example of her free institutions, of the high standard of the character of her statesmen and public men, of the purity of her legislation, and the upright administration of her laws. In this younger country, one great advantage of our connection with Great Britain will be that, under her auspices, inspired by her example, a portion of her empire, our public men will be actuated by principles similar to those which actuate the statesmen at home. These, although not material, physical benefits, for which you can make an arithmetical calculation, are of such overwhelming advantage to our future interests and standing as a nation that to obtain them is well worthy of any sacrifices we may be called upon to make, and the people of this country are ready to make them. (Cheers.)

In all countries the rights of the majority take care of themselves, but it is only in countries like England, enjoying constitutional liberty, and safe from the tyranny of a single despot or of an unbridled democracy, that the rights of minorities are regarded.

Macdonald makes two notable claims in this short passage. Parliamentary government (1) protects the people from populist tyranny, respecting the rights of minorities, and (2) protects the people from the "single despot." — JA

† *Macdonald's juxtaposition of constitutional liberty and unbridled democracy epitomizes the English-Canadian conservative's sense of superiority to the United States. Note his conception of the British connection as a bulwark against the penetration of American values in public life. Compare the remarks of Richard Cartwright (chapter 1) and James Johnston of Nova Scotia (chapter 6). Reformers must have scoffed to hear Macdonald extol purity in government: to them he personified corruption in Canadian public life. — PR*

"We should feel also sincerely grateful to beneficent providence that we have had the opportunity vouchsafed us of calmly considering this great constitutional change, this peaceful revolution — that we have not been hurried into it like the United States, by the exigencies of war — that we have not had a violent revolutionary period forced on us, as in other nations, by hostile action from without, or by domestic dissensions within."

We should feel also sincerely grateful to beneficent providence that we have had the opportunity vouchsafed us of calmly considering this great constitutional change, this peaceful revolution — that we have not been hurried into it like the United States, by the exigencies of war — that we have not had a violent revolutionary period forced on us, as in other nations, by hostile action from without, or by domestic dissensions within. Here we are in peace and prosperity, under the fostering government of Great Britain — a dependent people, with a government having only a limited and delegated authority, and yet allowed without restriction, and without jealousy on the part of the mother country, to legislate for ourselves, and peacefully and deliberately to consider and determine the future of Canada and of British North America . . .

[Great Britain] promises to sanction whatever conclusion after full deliberation we may arrive at as to the best mode of securing the well-being — the present and future prosperity of British America. (Cheers.)

— Legislative Assembly, February 6, 1865

Thomas D'Arcy McGee: The next motive for union to which I shall refer is that it will strengthen rather than weaken the connection with the empire, so essential to these rising provinces. Those who may be called, if there are any such, the anti-unionists allege that this scheme here submitted will bring separation in its train. How, pray? By making these countries more important, will you make them less desirable as connections to England? By making their trade more valuable, will you make her more anxious to get rid of it? By reducing their federal tariff, will you lessen their interest for England? By making them stronger for each other's aid, will you make her less willing to discharge a lesser than a greater responsibility? But if the thing did not answer itself, England has answered that she "cordially approves" of our plan of union, and she has always been accounted a pretty good judge of her own imperial interest. (Hear, hear.) She does not consider our union inimical to those interests. Instead of looking upon it with a dark and discouraging frown, she cheers us on by her most cordial approval and bids us a hearty "God speed" in the new path we have chosen to enter . . . (Hear, hear.)

I will content myself, Mr. Speaker, with those principal motives to union; first, that we are in the rapids and must go on; next that our neighbours will not, on their side, let us rest

supinely, even if we could do so from other causes; and thirdly, that by making the united colonies more valuable as an ally to Great Britain, we shall strengthen rather than weaken the imperial connection. (Cheers.)

— *Legislative Assembly, February 9, 1865*

Alexander Campbell: I would merely ask myself this: "Is this Confederation desirable? Do I wish for it as a lover of monarchical institutions? Do I desire it as a subject of the British Empire? Do I wish for the perpetuation of the connection between this country and Great Britain?" If I do I shall waive my objections on this point and the other, in my desire for the success of the principle. This Confederation has been sought after for years, but never until now has it approached so near a consummation — never was it a possibility as it is now a possibility. After years of anxiety, after years of difficulty, after troubles here and divisions there, the scheme is found possible, and I will not put it away from me because I object to this point or that.

— *Legislative Council, February 17, 1865*

NOVA SCOTIA

Charles Tupper: The fact is, if we are known at all across the Atlantic, notwithstanding the immense resources of these Maritime provinces, it is because we happen to be contiguous to Canada. Everything connected with our interests tells us of the insignificance of our position. Therefore it is not a matter of surprise, in view of these facts, and of the position we occupy, that the intelligent men of these provinces have long since come to the conclusion that, if these comparatively small countries are to have any future whatever in connection with the crown of England, it must be found in a consolidation of all British North America. I regret that this harmony does not exist down to the present moment, but I am dealing with the position the question occupied at the time these negotiations were going on.

— *House of Assembly, April 10, 1865*

John Bourinot: A great stress has been laid upon the nationality that these provinces would acquire; instead of being insignificant dependencies, they would form a nation that would be respected abroad. I believe that the formation of such a nation would lead to independence of England. Isolated as we are now, we could

not form an independent state. Perhaps, however, some gentlemen have longings to see such a result obtained.

— *House of Assembly, April 17, 1865*

"I apprehend seriously that Confederation, pure and simple, is another name for independence. I wish to guard against that; my desire is that British America should remain British America."

William Annand: What is there in the Quebec scheme to prevent a separation? I may be mistaken, but I thought I could see in England, during my recent visit there, a desire to get rid of these colonies, and an impression that, by Confederation, England would be relieved of a portion of the expense which we cause at present . . . I apprehend seriously that Confederation, pure and simple, is another name for independence. I wish to guard against that; my desire is that British America should remain British America.

— *House of Assembly, April 5, 1866*

Tupper: [I]f the promoters of union are influenced by motives that are dishonourable to themselves and the legislature, in what position is Her Majesty the Queen?* When he sees the queen, session after session, at the close and opening of parliament, coming down and urging in the most emphatic terms that the royal lips can use this question of Confederation upon the people of British North America, does he mean to say that she . . . is corrupted by base bribes?

— *House of Assembly, April 10, 1866*

William Townsend: I feel a great deal of reluctance in rising to address the house on the present occasion, when I see all the legal talent arranged against me on this important question. I feel, however, that I stand here with the great mass of the people at my back. I contend that we have no right to deal with the question; the people did not send us here to deal with it; they do not yet know its merits. I cannot believe that such immense advantages will spring from union as some gentlemen profess to see ahead. You cannot force trade out of its natural channels. The state of Maine, and not Nova Scotia, is the natural frontage of Canada.†

---

* Of all the advocates of Confederation, none was more unscrupulous than Tupper. It's not clear here whether he's referring to the queen herself speaking at Westminster or to the lieutenant governor speaking as her representative in Halifax; but in either case, as Tupper well knew, the speeches would have expressed the views of the British government, not those of the queen herself. — PR

† The St. Lawrence and Atlantic Railway between Montreal and Portland,

The interests of the people do not lie in the direction of connection with Canada. As far as my own people are concerned, I know if you were to ask them if they would prefer annexation to Confederation, they would answer yes. Their commercial interests are intimately bound up with those of the United States, and it is not therefore surprising that such a sentiment should prevail. They say, give us connection with a country that will protect us. Canada cannot take care of us. I do not feel this way myself, but still I know what I state is perfectly correct. I know that, simple man as I am, I cannot change your sentiments on this question. All the leading talent of the house is against it.

I have yet to hear the arguments to satisfy men of the necessity for this Confederation. Is it advisable to unite with a country [Canada] with such large debts and duties?* To have to pay for the enlargement of her canals, and extension of her railways? What I fear is that if you pass this measure in the mode proposed, you will convulse the country from one end to the other. All we require is to be allowed to manage our own affairs in our own way. I do not think that we can be better off than we are now under any circumstances. Why not let well enough alone and cease disturbing the country at what gentlemen say is a critical period of its history? The Quebec scheme is as good a scheme as any you can devise, but I do not want any at all. I know that my constituents are to a man opposed to the proposed Confederation, and I am determined to stand by them. I feel that they will look upon the present action with horror and alarm. My people, I say, would prefer annexation to Confederation, but only let a thousand Fenians come among them and the fellows would not be heard of. Let England or Canada be assailed, and two-thirds of our young men will volunteer to take care of the country. But still we do not wish to be hurried into Confederation. We want the people to have a voice in the matter.

William Henry: We have been accustomed from our childhood to take an interest in the great country from which we have sprung. We have drawn from that country the principles that lie

---

Maine, completed in 1853, afforded Canada much closer ice-free access to the Atlantic Ocean than Halifax could.

* Canada's per capita public debt, incurred largely in the funding of transportation improvements, was much larger than Nova Scotia's, and her import duties much higher. — PR

at the foundation of all our institutions. We should look at the present question, not merely in the capacity of provincial representatives, but as subjects of the great empire of Great Britain. I hold this doctrine, and I believe it is a patriotic one, that we should consider in our deliberations that we are acting not only for the advantage of Nova Scotia but also in the interests of the great empire on which the sun is said never to set. I have listened with some interest to the speech just delivered by the honourable member for Yarmouth (Mr. Townsend), and although I must condemn his disloyal sentiments, yet I feel he is at all events entitled to some credit for the candour with which he stated them. I can understand that honourable member coming forward and proclaiming to the house and country that the people of Yarmouth have no loyalty except what puts money into their pockets. We can understand that argument against the union of the provinces, and need not therefore be surprised that nine-tenths of the people of that section* are opposed to Confederation.

We therefore see plainly why the honourable gentleman is opposed to a union of British North America. We can understand gentlemen who come forward and say that they are actuated by very different motives — that they wish to keep up the connection with the British crown; they say they are loyal, but that if we confederate we must be eventually annexed to the United States. That is an argument which requires some explanation before it can satisfy those who have studied the question of union and have come to the conclusion that a union of the provinces is necessary to the continuance of their connection with Great Britain, and their only safety against annexation . . .

I have given some of the reasons that influence my judgement in favour of the resolution before the house and now say most emphatically that if there are any persons who prefer annexation to the United States, let them, in heaven's name, follow the example of the honourable member for Yarmouth, but do not let them attempt by false representations to thwart the efforts of those who would bring about a union of the provinces. I say, however, to gentlemen around these benches, who value the flag

---

* *Situated at the western tip of the province, Yarmouth was an early site of Yankee settlement and had strong trading ties with New England. Henry uses Townsend's commercial arguments to discredit those whose objections to Confederation rest on the fear that it will endanger Nova Scotia's ties with Britain. — PR*

that "for a thousand years has braved the battle and the breeze," and that has planted liberty and freedom in every quarter of the globe — to all those who are inspired by a desire to perpetuate the connection with the British Empire, come forward and support the measure which will at once achieve this result, and at the same time give dignity of position and security to the provinces that in their present isolated position they can never hope to obtain. (Cheers.)

— House of Assembly, April 16, 1866

Thomas Killam: I rise to deliver to you a message, not from the lieutenant governor, not from the Legislative Council, not from the colonial secretary, but from the 16,000 of the loyal inhabitants of this province whom I have the honour of representing in this assembly. They are closely identified in interest and feeling with the inhabitants of the other portions of the province, are known far and wide . . . for their industry and enterprise, [and] were the first pioneers in one of our great industrial pursuits — one that has done more to elevate our position and make Nova Scotia known far and wide than any other. This message is sent to me by these, to protest on their behalf against a union of this province with Canada, believing as they do, that such a measure will demoralize the people, alienate their affections from Great Britain, and endanger British institutions — transfer our revenues into the hands of strangers, disarrange financial affairs, and jeopardize our local improvements.

We, as the oldest colony of British North America, have enjoyed a Legislative Assembly for over one hundred, and responsible government for twenty, years, with full liberty to levy and appropriate taxes; and to deprive us of these privileges, as proposed by the resolution, they [my constituents] believe to be most unjustifiable. In making these statements they do not arrogate to themselves any superiority over other counties. They acknowledge the claims of all other sections to consideration, and are proud that this is our common country. It is with pride they remember that they can claim as their own one of the ablest statesmen that ever stood on the floor of this house, to watch over the interests of the people of Nova Scotia. He did not come here, like our leading men of the present day, prepared to destroy, but to improve the constitution we now possess, and not to hand over this province to another country, irrespective of the wishes of the people.

The arguments that have been advanced in support of this

"Miss Canada" detail from J.W. Bengough's Caricature History of Canadian Politics.

resolution show that the scheme is more one of theory than of practice. The argument which they have most laboured is this: that it is necessary to unite with Canada in order to ensure our common safety. Everybody admits that numbers are strength; but those numbers must be in a position to assist each other. If you have a large territory, exposed at all points to danger — just as Canada — separated from you by a great tract of country, you cannot expect assistance from it. Its union with you does not bring strength, but weakness. If you are to have trade, it must be in a position to afford it. If we look at the map and see the configuration of British North America, you can recognize how absurd are the arguments of the advocates of union. Nova Scotia has no natural relation whatever to Canada.

We have thirty millions of people directly before us, in every way more convenient to us than Canada; they are of the same stock, same feelings, as ourselves; they have everything that can make a people great and glorious. If you have to make any political arrangements, let them be consistent and natural. I do not think that the people of Nova Scotia want annexation to the United States, but why should you drive them against their interests and inclinations into a union with Canada — with which they have no natural means of communication and no sympathy? Why, if our young women were to attempt tomorrow to go to Canada by way of the States, they would be courted and married before they got halfway there . . . I do not trust that if any words of mine can have any effect on this house, that a majority will not be found ready to sell their country to the Canadians. If the day should come when Nova Scotia will be wrested from us and given to Canada, it will be one of mourning and lamentation among the people. Of course we shall have to submit to it — for I am not going to counsel rebellion.

— House of Assembly, April 17, 1866

Stewart Campbell: This province until a recent period was a loyal and happy colony, having every reason to be loyal, every reason to be happy until this unfortunate and unhappy measure was brought in and cast among us. Shall I be told that loyalty exists now in the same richness among us as it once and recently did? Mr. Speaker, I strenuously opposed the measure last session on the ground that the course about to be taken would endanger the allegiance and undermine the loyalty of the people, and since that time I have seen that that result is but too probable.

We are told by members of the imperial parliament that it is desirable we should be separated from the British Empire, and further we are told that it is not alone for the interests of Nova Scotia that the scheme has been projected — that there are reasons making it desirable that we should be connected with a large country. To secure Canada from foreign invasion, the rights of Nova Scotians are to be interfered with and trampled upon. I conceive that Nova Scotia has at least as just a claim to the protection of England as Canada. Nova Scotia has been truly loyal, and in every hour of danger she has exhibited a disposition to the uttermost extent of her resources to stand by and maintain the honour and integrity of the empire. I conceive that the transactions of the past few months are exhibiting a poor return for that loyalty and that allegiance. The loyalty which I desire to see is the loyalty of the heart, not the loyalty pampered and fed and fattened by the contents of the treasury. The loyalty of the heart springing from just and honourable motives — that is the loyalty which is desirable, and anything else is unworthy of the name . . .

Pass the act without reference to the people whose rights are to be affected, and do you make them its friends? Do you not rather create in them feelings precisely the reverse? Do you not make them enemies and disloyal?

Adams Archibald: My honourable friend [Campbell] seems to have a great horror of a future national existence. I should like to ask him what he looks forward to in the future. Does he imagine that for all time to come these provinces, which in twenty years hence will count eight millions of people, and which, within the lifetime of many now born, will comprise a population larger than that of the British Isles; does he suppose that this enormous population* is for all time to come to be governed from Downing Street? . . . There is an infancy and a youth and a maturity in nations as there is in men, and while I yield to no man in my desire to retain the connection which we have with the parent state, while I trust and hope that the day may be far distant when the ties that unite us may be severed, I cannot shut my eyes to the fact that in the future — however distant that future may be — we shall have to assume the responsibilities of a separate national existence.

— House of Assembly, March 18, 1867

---

* *Canada's population today is about that of the British Isles in 1867, and about half of their population today.*

BRITISH COLUMBIA

Henry Crease: But the chief reason [for joining the union] is that policy of isolation which has kept us aloof from the assistance and sympathy of a kindred race, and left us in the infant state of one of England's youngest colonies, to support the burdens and responsibilities of a thickly peopled and long-settled land . . . [Confederation] would cement and strengthen, instead of weaken, our connection with the motherland, and ensure the protection of her fleet and army . . . It would enlarge, not contract, our political horizon, and it would infuse new hope and life blood into the whole system of the colony, and not leave us a mere detached municipality, as some suppose, any more than Scotland is separate from the rest of Great Britain, or the County of Kent from England.

— *Legislative Council, March 9, 1870*

"I regard loyalty as one of the most deep-rooted and highly prized treasures of the human breast."

Joseph Trutch: What do these foreign petitioners* propose to transfer? Themselves? Their own property? No; not themselves, nor that which belongs to them, but the whole colony, the soil of this vast domain which belongs to the crown and the people of England; this I regard as treasonable. In supporting Confederation I support the flag I serve. I say that loyalty is no exploded idea, call it a sentiment if you will; life is nothing without sentiment; everyone whose soul is not dead must cling to love of country and attachment to her flag, as one of the most cherished sentiments of the heart, and I regard loyalty as one of the most deep-rooted and highly prized treasures of the human breast. ("Hear, hear," from all sides.)

T. L. Wood: The bond of union† between Canada and the other

---

* *The Victoria petitioners for annexation to the United States, whom Trutch identifies as Americans themselves.*

† *Wood argues that you can't create national sentiment by legislation, and that the provinces won't submit to the suzerainty of the dominion with the same patience as to that of the British government. Note his remark that, even in a crown colony, the government is constrained by the force of public opinion. In the 1830s Robert Baldwin had recommended to British statesmen, including Lord Durham, the introduction of responsible government in Upper Canada as the least disruptive mode in which public opinion could exert its inevitable influence on the government.* — PR

provinces bears no resemblance to the union between England and her colonial possessions. There is not natural love and original feeling of loyalty. The feeling of loyalty towards England is a feeling blind, instinctive, strong, born with us and impossible to be shaken off; and I believe it is impossible to transfer a feeling of loyalty and fealty at will . . .

The crown pretends to no dictation, nor has it any interest at variance with the interests of the colonists. Although a crown colony, the official element is supreme; it is well understood that it is to govern — and public opinion forces it to govern — according to the well understood and well-established wishes of the colony at large. The government cannot and dare not interfere except to prevent crude, irrational, or vicious legislation. There is no direct conflict between the mother country and a colony in these days; but it cannot be supposed that any British province will submit patiently to injustice at the hands of a Canadian ministry or a Canadian House of Commons. If any scheme has been devised more likely than another to raise and keep above local irritation, it is, in my judgement, the scheme of Confederation on the basis of the organic law of 1867.

The question has always appeared to me to be this: confederation with England which we have; confederation in its truest sense; confederation with all the security of protection, and all the pride of self-government, now or hereafter to be, when the colony shall have population and wealth sufficient; or Confederation — or as it should be termed, "incorporation" — with Canada. Incorporation with a country to which we are bound by no natural tie of affection or duty, and remote in geographical position, and opposed to us in material interests. Incorporation with all the humiliation of dependence, and to my mind the certainty of reaction, agitation, and discontent.

I am opposed to the political extinction of this colony,* and its subservience to the will of a majority of the House of Commons at Ottawa, and the administration of its affairs by the political adherents of Canadian statesmen. And all this for what? For "material benefits," for a money consideration, in which the ring of the dollar only faintly conceals the clink of the fetter. I am grieved at the mode in which the change is sought to be effected,

---

* *Like other opponents of Confederation, Wood does not see the federal aspect of the scheme as an effective safeguard of the provinces' political individuality.* — PR

and view the bargain and sale of political independence for ourselves and our descendants for a few dollars in hand, and a few dollars in the future, as equally shameful and void.

Amor De Cosmos: When sitting in the Vancouver Island House of Assembly, in the place now occupied by the honourable chief commissioner [J.W. Trutch], I defined British colonists to be politically nothing but subordinate Englishmen and I contend, sir, that Confederation will give us equal political rights with the people of Great Britain. In labouring for this cause, sir, my idea has been and is to assist in creating a nationality — a sovereign and independent nationality.

— *Legislative Council, March 10, 1870*

"Everyone would welcome that comprehensive brotherhood which embraces all civilized nations. Why should not the English-speaking race live in peace and form one nation?"

David Ring: Everyone would welcome that comprehensive brotherhood which embraces all civilized nations. Why should not the English-speaking race live in peace and form one nation? The people of the United States spring from one common stock with ourselves. I long to see the time when all national sectarianism shall be swept away.

— *Legislative Council, March 11, 1870*

J.S. Helmcken: We are a colony of England, and I don't know that many people object to being a colony of England; but I say that very many would object to becoming a colony of Canada. As a colony of England we have the right to legislate for ourselves; if we become a colony of Canada, that power is taken away.

De Cosmos: No, no.

John Robson: It will give us more power.

Helmcken: I say that the power of regulating our own commerce is taken away and the only power left to us is that of raising taxes for municipal purposes. That is the difference between being a colony of Canada and a colony of England. The distance is so great between this colony and Ottawa, without any railway and without any telegraphic communication, that laws might be passed there which would ruin British Columbia, without our having any notice of them.

— *Legislative Council, March 16, 1870*

NEWFOUNDLAND

*"Wit, indignation,
eloquence, the most
forcible logic sustained
by a long train of
unanswerable
arguments are wholly
unavailing to penetrate
the wooden-headed
obstinacy of the local
mind."*

Daniel Prowse: One of the leading principles of the scheme of Confederation is to bind the colonies more closely to Great Britain; and I believe this was one of the primary objects which animated every delegate at the conference. We shall certainly be joined to England in a different way, if their great idea is carried out. We shall no longer be so many straggling helpless dependencies. We shall be joined as one strong united country, as enlightened British statesmen wish us to be. Like all other great political questions, this is one which in its very nature is theoretical and to a certain extent problematical in its effects. You cannot, by any means at your disposal, reduce it to a matter of pounds, shillings, and pence. You cannot gauge and assay all its advantages and disadvantages, by any array of figures or the most elaborate statement of hard facts. You must reason on it from the established rules of political philosophy. You must bring to bear upon it the light of that experience which history teaches us in the annals of other countries; or are we so peculiarly situated, so singular in our character as a civilized country, that the political principles which have produced certain results in other lands will not do so here?

Local prejudice, local obstinacy, and local stupidity have always been the greatest obstacles in the way of progress. It has always been so. Wit, indignation, eloquence, the most forcible logic sustained by a long train of unanswerable arguments are wholly unavailing to penetrate the wooden-headed obstinacy of the local mind. Logic and arguments all fall back like blunted arrows from the impenetrable walls of obstinate ignorance.

— *House of Assembly, February 6, 1865*

Peter Tessier: Here was a wholesale extinction of the rights and privileges we have enjoyed since the settlement of the colony! Was it not strange there should be found in the colony men who are anxious to destroy the privilege it has enjoyed for centuries, of the fostering care and protection of the imperial government, and of direct communication with and appeal to it in all its difficulties, and entrust it to the keeping of strangers? This would be the inevitable result of the union in the natural course of time and events. Would not every individual in the community rather strengthen the bonds which bind us to the motherland, who has protected us in our weakness and encouraged us in the more

mature periods of our existence, than rashly rush into a course of action that would tend to sever that connection?

— Legislative Council, February 14, 1865

Ambrose Shea: It would be idle to suppose that the meeting at Quebec was not inspired by the imperial government. No one who has paid any degree of attention to the tone of British opinion regarding these colonies for some years past can have failed to see that a change in the relations they held to the mother country was surely coming about. It became a mere question of time when we obtained responsible government, and with it virtual independence in the government of these colonies. We acquired the right to legislate, so that our tariffs became hostile to the commercial interests of England, and with this exercise of independence was it not natural that the question should be asked, Why should they be called on to sustain those whose legislation for their own selfish ends was marked by this unfriendly spirit? This feeling has been gaining strength for some time, but the events taking place in America for the past four years seem to have brought it to the mind of the British government, not only as a question of right and justice, but in regard to the sterner considerations of the practicability of existing means for the defence of the British North American provinces. They evidently see that so many disjointed states, with each its separate organization and right of independent action, could not offer the necessary effective resistance to attack from the American states, which in the course of events might probably arise, and they have concluded that . . . these provinces should combine and be one for the purpose of defence, moved by one central authority . . . [and that backed] by the influence of England, [they] would present an imposing front, and induce the invader to pause in his aggressive designs.

"We are now part of the glorious British Empire; we lived under the sway of our beloved sovereign Queen Victoria, upon whose dominions the sun never sets. Were we to leave the flag that had braved a thousand years the battle and the breeze; be separated from the glorious empire of Britain, and placed on a sandy, muddy, rickety foundation? He (Mr. March) indignantly protested against any such spoliation of our liberties."

Stephen March: They [the people] were bound to this country by the strongest of ties. Their fathers had died to establish its liberty . . . We are now part of the glorious British Empire; we lived under the sway of our beloved sovereign Queen Victoria, upon whose dominions the sun never sets. Were we to leave the flag that had braved a thousand years the battle and the breeze; be separated from the glorious empire of Britain, and placed on a sandy, muddy, rickety foundation? He (Mr. March) indignantly protested against any such spoliation of our liberties.

— House of Assembly, February 21, 1865

SIR FREDRICK B.T.
CARTER
(1819–1900), lawyer.
After attending the
Quebec Conference,
Carter did his best to
take Newfoundland into
Confederation. Through
a Conservative, on
becoming prime minister
in 1865 he nominated
two confederate Liberals
to his cabinet, thereby
forming his country's
first government to
combine Protestants
and Roman Catholics.
He made Confederation
his party platform in the
1869 general election,
but was badly defeated
and did not raise the
issue during the second
administration,
1874–78. In 1878 he
was appointed to the
Newfoundland Supreme
Court, becoming chief
justice in 1880.

F.B.T. Carter: It was not unnatural that great diversity of opinion should prevail respecting a matter which involved so many different interests. They had only to remember the case of the United States to see that they too had these difficulties to contend with. There also were large states and small states, and the small ones were unwilling to give control to the large ones; after considerable deliberation they at least saw that they could consolidate their liberties and power only by mutual concessions. Those who framed the dominion constitution had the advantage of the constitution of the United States to guide them — a constitution which, though admitted by some of their ablest men to be defective, was yet so ably framed as to shed lustre on the names of all concerned in its inception — they were enabled to avoid these defects especially as regards the sovereignty of the states, which so largely contributed to the late civil war.

The United States also tried two or three different constitutions, but finding them all defective they at last adopted that under which they live at present. They commenced when they had just emancipated themselves from the control of England and the throes of a revolution, and yet they took as their groundwork the common law of England, her character, and those statutory provisions which secured the liberties of their ancestors. We also have the advantage of these, and in entering upon this union do not do so out of rebellion, but with the sanctions and approbation of our common sovereign. It is not therefore to be wondered at that we cling to monarchy, or that the chief executive authority should be made to reside in Her Majesty, while at the same time the three estates* are preserved. The leading principle of this union is perpetual connection with the British crown.

The monarch, the Lords, and the Commons: the three estates of the realm, which together constitute the legislature in Britain. It was normal for other legislatures in the empire to have a nominated upper house as a counterpart to the British House of Lords. Led by Ontario in 1867, the Canadian provinces have since departed from this model by dispensing with or abolishing the upper house. The federal government, of course, still retains it. Indeed, Canada's constitution today keeps the formal language of the three estates, describing the parliament of Canada in terms of the queen, an upper house (the Senate), and the House of Commons. The queen acts through the governor general of Canada, who acts on the advice of the governing political party. Thus, in practical terms, parliament now consists of the cabinet and the two legislative houses. — PR/JA

There was no desire to establish a republic or for a separate independent existence. The time might come when the people of this dominion would be strong and powerful and able to stand by themselves, and then they might without any objection on her part separate from the mother country, but in the meantime they were under the aegis of that great power.

George Hogsett: He (Mr. Hogsett) was a British subject, and so long as the rights and privileges of the country in which be lived were conserved, he owed his allegiance to the British crown. The same inherent rights which were claimed by the British people, colonists should also claim, and amongst these the very first was the right of controlling their own affairs. But the dominion government had no control over itself. Look at the act of union. Scan its every clause and you will find that the imperial interests pervade the whole. Why should the dominion government have the appointment of a deputy governor in this colony, while from the mother country we were likely to obtain a gentleman not mixed up with our local politics?

— *House of Assembly, February 23, 1869*

PRINCE EDWARD ISLAND

W.H. Pope: I hold my own opinions respecting a union of the colonies. I have long thought that these provinces ought to have more influence at the Colonial Office. This island, as also the other colonies, have laboured under great disadvantage in this respect — a disadvantage which a union of the whole would probably have removed. Still, it does not appear to me that great benefit would result from a union of the three Maritime provinces. We have been making progress, small as our colony is. I hold in my hand an order of the date of 1790, for one shilling, which is a fair specimen of our currency at that time. Now we have two or three banks and an extensive trade, so I think we [had] better work along with our separate government until it is thought that "the time has arrived" to consummate a federal union of the whole of British America, allowing each colony to retain its own legislature. If this could be effected with the goodwill of the home government — Britain acting towards us in a friendly and paternal manner, just as a father does with a son setting up for himself — it might be well. The new government might be either a monarchy or a republic, but I, for my part,

would prefer a monarchy. All the colonies united from Newfoundland to Columbia would be one of the most powerful governments on the face of the earth; but with only Nova Scotia, New Brunswick, and this island united, we would still be looked down upon by our neighbours. I do not think the people of this island would agree to such a union as is proposed. If they would consent to a change at all, I believe they would desire a union that would place the colonies in a position that would give them some weight among the powers that be.

Edward Whelan: [W]ith an assembly of thirty and a legislative council of seventeen members, any of our proceedings can be set at naught for the time being by the colonial minister,* who knows nothing of the colony. The present position of our legislative,† representing but some 80,000 people, is powerless against the secret influence of the proprietors at the Colonial Office . . . Without subjecting myself to the charge of disloyalty (for I wish to continue the connection with the brightest crown which ever graced the brow of monarchy), I repeat that while the right of irresponsible interference in our affairs is continued, annexation to any foreign power would be preferable to the insulting mockery by which the people of this island, slaves to Sir Samuel Cunard‡ and others of the proprietors, are told that they have the right of self-government.

— *House of Assembly, April 18, 1864*

"[The] object of all others to be desired by every freeman should be the having [of] a strong government at his back to maintain his rights and secure him justice whenever demanded, and certainly, if ever there were a people needing this, it is ourselves."

J.H. Gray: [The] object of all others to be desired by every freeman should be the having [of] a strong government at his back to maintain his rights and secure him justice whenever demanded, and certainly, if ever there were a people needing this, it is ourselves. What a pitiful position we have ever occupied, when knocking at the doors of Downing Street! It is needless for

---

* *Apparently an allusion to the British government's power to nullify colonial legislature.*

† *"Legislative," as a short form of "legislative power," is found in older authors such as John Locke. Whelan is referring to the PEI legislature.*

‡ *Cunard (1787–1865), Nova Scotian entrepreneur and founder of the Cunard Steamship Line, was by 1860 the largest landowner in Prince Edward Island. As such, he influenced the British government to disallow provincial legislation to terminate the absentee proprietorships. J.H. Gray also alludes to his role. — PR*

me to particularize instances too well known to us all; and I can
now truly say after a considerable experience as a member of this
government for six years that I sincerely believe that the acts of
this legislature weigh no more than a feather in the scale, compared with the influence possessed by a few private individuals of
whose second-hand intermeddling we have lately had a pretty fair
specimen. I believe, also, that so long as we occupy our present
isolated position, we must bear patiently and submit with resignation to whatever befalls us; but I would ask, does any honourable
member in this house suppose that the legislative enactments of
the representatives of four millions of people would ever be
imperilled or set at naught any more than those of the imperial
parliament of Great Britain?

— House of Assembly, March 25, 1865

Joseph Hensley: No doubt the idea of forming part of a great
country is very captivating, if we really were a separate and soli-
tary people; but I cannot recognize its force in our case when I
call to mind that we are part and parcel of the great British
Empire.

— House of Assembly, March 27, 1865

Frederick Brecken: Never in the history of this island, since it
became a British colony, has a subject of such consequence been
submitted for the consideration of its legislature. If we are to view
the proposition for a union of the British North American
colonies as an [option], which we may reject without imperilling
our position as a dependency of the British crown, I confess I
cannot see in the terms offered to us in the report of the Quebec
Conference anything to induce us to close with the offer. If, on
the other hand, the choice is between a union with the sister
provinces and a severance of our allegiance to the mother
country, I would say, let us be united, even at a sacrifice of our
local interests. But I do not think that the latter is our position,
although the advocates of the scheme profess to believe that it is.
Why should we be in such a hurry to assume that it is? Previous
to the Quebec Conference, this question had not been pressed
upon our attention by the home government, although we are
now aware, from Mr. Cardwell's* dispatch, written after the receipt

---

* *Edward Cardwell (1813–1886), secretary of state for the colonies,
1864–66.*

of the Quebec report, that the measure is very favourably received by the imperial government. Nor is it at all to be wondered at that they should wish to see our present political position changed. Separate provinces grouped close together with governments independent of each other; separate laws, different currencies, and hostile tariffs; and yet all paying allegiance to the same sovereign is a state of things that will not, in all probability, continue very much longer. I am not opposed to a union, provided just and equitable terms are secured to us; but it does appear to me that the urgent manner in which this question at this time is pressed upon us is entirely owing to the action of politicians on this side of the Atlantic.

— *House of Assembly, March 28, 1865*

George Coles: Here we may see the pitiable condition to which this island would be reduced under Confederation — our revenues taken away, scarcely enough allowed us to work the machinery of the local government, and should more money be required when our population increased it would have to be raised by direct taxation. The people of this colony were battling for years to gain responsible government, and since obtained I believe it has given general satisfaction. But, sir, were we to adopt this report, it would deprive us of our constitution and leave us no corresponding benefit in return. It is urged that, as a compensation for our loss, we would become part of a great union that, in time, would form a mighty nation. But I ask what greater nationality can we enjoy than that with which it is our pride and privileges at present to be connected? What greater flag can wave over us than the time-honoured banner of Old England? . . .

The union which I advocated was one that would give us intercolonial free trade and a uniformity of currency. But here in this report we have a constitution under which we may be taxed at any rate the Canadians think proper. At present we hold the power of taxation* in our own hands; under Confederation, it would be placed almost entirely beyond our control, as well as the power to say what portion of these taxes imposed upon the

---

* *The Quebec scheme gave the federal government exclusive power to impose indirect taxes, while allowing both it and the provincial governments to impose direct taxes. Of the two main sources of taxation in British North America at the time — customs duties and land taxes — only the latter counted as direct taxation, and farmers tended to dislike them. — PR*

people of the colony should be expended for objects in which they are immediately interested.

Taking all these points into consideration, I think it is clear that the report before us is not such as should be adopted by this house. To enter such a Confederation as is here proposed would evidently prove ruinous to the colony. If a change is thought desirable, I consider it would be more for our advantage to have a representation in the British parliament and to pay a percentage to the imperial government out of our revenue for any purpose they may think proper. I believe that one representative there would secure for us a greater share of justice than we are ever likely to receive from a federal legislature in Canada. Should Confederation take place, I believe that in a very few years the people under it will be as heavily taxed as the people of the United States are now at the termination of a civil war.

— *House of Assembly, March 31, 1865*

John Bull "The Ideal" by cartoonist Max Beerbohm.

Brecken: John Bull* had always claimed, as one of his greatest privileges, the right to grumble and to stand out to the last moment for whatever he thought himself fairly entitled to; and that privilege the people of this colony had never been backward to claim and assert. The Quebec Confederation scheme was, it was well known, favourably viewed by the imperial government, and equally so, it was said, by Her Majesty the Queen; yet admitting all that — and he was not disposed to dispute it, for he could see no impropriety in its being so regarded at home — he did not think, as some did, that we could fairly be subjected to the imputation of disloyalty because, so far as that scheme was meant to apply to Prince Edward Island, we were averse to it, and should express our aversion to it in the strongest language. He certainly did not, for one moment, imagine that the imperial government would ever consent to sanction any scheme of Confederation, but which it was obvious to them that the interests of even the smallest and most feeble of the colonies would be sacrificed for the promotion of those of the largest and most powerful.

John McEachen: He was glad to hear the honourable and learned member for Charlottetown (Mr. Brecken) allude to the right

---

* *John Bull, a nickname for Britain, was a cartoon figure invented in the eighteenth century. A slightly curmudgeonly figure, he was also thought to represent the so-called British virtue of sturdy honesty.*

claimed by John Bull to grumble and to be stubborn when called upon to resign anything he believed himself entitled to hold; and to hear the honourable member then base thereon an argument for the people of this island being, like John Bull, stubborn in the retention of their free constitution. Such stubbornness was certainly becoming in a free people; but although he would not deny that the sons of John Bull had an hereditary right to assert that privilege, yet he would say it became them not (the descendants of the men who were conquered by the Normans and lost their liberty at the battle of Hastings) as well as it did the descendant of those men whose ancestors (the Caledonians of old*) beat back from their mountain fastnesses of liberty the conquering eagles of imperial Rome. He was a descendant of those unconquered heroes of the north, and he would never consent that, in asserting our right to preserve our free constitution, with all its rights, privileges, and immunities, we should adopt the cowardly, cringing tone in which it suited venality and corruption to plead for the attainment of the objects of their selfish designs.

There was no reason to fear that we should be driven into the projected Confederation. The people of Prince Edward Island had a constitution as well as Canada; and, if they did their duty, they would never lose it. Mr. Cardwell would, no doubt, be glad if he found us willing to agree to go into the union on the terms of the Quebec scheme; but, if he found we were not willing, be would not dare to force us into it. If once, like the Hungarians and the Poles,† we should be deprived of our constitution, we would never be able to regain it. He would, therefore, support the resolutions, both in the spirit and the letter. They were certainly strong, but they were not too strong for him. We know, said the honourable gentleman in conclusion, what we enjoy under our present free constitution; but we know not what we should have to endure were we, by a union with Canada, on the terms of the Quebec scheme of Confederation, to be deprived of it.

— *House of Assembly, May 7, 1866*

Coles: Confederation, instead of being a means of binding us more closely and indissolubly to the British crown, would, eventually, be the cause of our separation from it. The moment the

---

* The inhabitants of Scotland at the time of the Roman invasion of Britain in the first century AD.

†A reference to the Hungarian rising of 1848 and the Polish rising of 1863.

upper house should come into collision with the lower house, some extreme measure would be had recourse to. Should we, however, remain as we were, we would be safe. If we entered into Confederation, we would be much more in danger of quarrelling with the United States than we are now . . . The glory argument was, that, by confederating with Canada and the other provinces, we should become part and parcel of a great nation; but the people of Prince Edward Island knew themselves to be already part and parcel of a great nation, and they had no desire to belong to any other.

George Sinclair: I would be willing that the views of the British government should be urged upon the colonies with all just authority. While I believe we are willing to allow that — for I consider it to be our duty to give all due consideration to the opinion of the British government in things of that kind — yet, sir, I am of the opinion that we owe a higher duty to our country and to our children — the duty to preserve the inalienable right of self-government. Self-preservation is the first law of nature,* and it will hold good with regard to nations and colonies, as well as individuals. We are willing to contribute of our means, but not to give up our liberties, which our fathers have obtained for us. Though we are a small colony and unable to offer any formidable resistance, that is no reason that we should voluntarily surrender a constitution with which we are satisfied.

We are prepared to do everything in our power, within the bounds of reason, to maintain our connection with the British Empire. We have liberty to tax ourselves, and we are prepared to do our part; therefore, I do not think the British government will ever attempt to coerce us into a union against the wishes of the people, and which we believe would be prejudicial to our inter-ests. It is useless for us to go into the details of the scheme or to point out all the disadvantages to the island of a union with Canada. It is admitted by nearly all, even those in favour of union,

"I consider it to be our duty to give all due consideration to the opinion of the British government — yet, sir, I am of the opinion that we owe a higher duty to our country and to our children — the duty to preserve the inalienable right of self-government. Self-preservation is the first law of nature, and it will hold good with regard to nations and colonies, as well as individuals."

---

* Like so many others in these debates, Sinclair is using the language of the seventeenth-century British philosophers. See Thomas Hobbes, Leviathan [1651], chapter 14): the first "law of nature" is "by all means we can, to defend ourselves." It is this urgent natural desire for self-preservation, says Hobbes, that convinces us of the necessity of founding governments. Sinclair also takes from Hobbes the idea that the first law of nature holds good with regard to nations as well as individuals. — JA

that it would not be an advantage to the island to enter the union on the basis of the Quebec scheme; and, for my part, I do not expect to get better terms, though, even if we could, we are an exception to the other colonies, and a basis of union which would be suitable and advantageous to them would not be so to us.

T.H. Haviland: Some of our island anti-confederates had exercised their wit and talents in disparagement and ridicule of "the glory argument," as it was called; but for his own part, he did not think that any man, either, could truly be said to have a country or to deserve to have one, who could not rejoice and glory in the patriotic and enabling recollections of ancestral virtues . . . Under the glorious rule of Britain he was born, and under it he would die.

— *House of Assembly, May 8, 1866*

Chapter Eight

WHAT IS
A CANADIAN?

WHAT DO OUR SPEAKERS SAY on this now-familiar topic? At first reading they may seem hopelessly old-fashioned. Most believe the British connection, with its guarantee of constitutional rights and freedoms, is the core of the new nation's identity. When they refer to society's diverse groupings they speak in terms of English, Irish, Scots, and French. But nowadays Canada's attachment to Britain is very thin, and the country is home to people from everywhere on the globe. Can the Confederation debate on Canadian identity still have meaning?

Readers must decide for themselves. But surely George-Étienne Cartier's vision — of a "political nationality" of diverse "races" (ethnic groups) and religions united to promote the general welfare — still has the power to move us.

Since speakers repeatedly sing the praises of liberty in this and other sections, it is worth stopping to think what exactly it means to them. It means self-government and representative institutions, security of property, and the rule of law. To many it also means freedom of conscience, including the separation of church and state. Few, if any, however, would have denied the right of the community to impose consensual standards of right conduct on its members, standards that extend to the private conduct of consenting adults.

CANADA

George-Étienne Cartier: Objection had been taken to the scheme now under consideration because of the words "new nationality." Now, when we were united together, if union were

> *"The idea of unity of races was utopian — it was impossible. Distinctions of this kind would always exist. Dissimilarity in fact appeared to be the order of the physical world and of the moral world, as well as in the political world."*

George-Étienne Cartier; detail from J.W. Bengough's Caricature History of Canadian Politics.

attained, we would form a political nationality* with which neither the national origin, nor the religion of any individual, would interfere. It was lamented by some that we had this diversity of races, and hopes were expressed that this distinctive feature would cease.

The idea of unity of races was utopian — it was impossible. Distinctions of this kind would always exist. Dissimilarity in fact appeared to be the order of the physical world and of the moral world, as well as in the political world. But with regard to the objection based on this fact, to the effect that a great nation could not be formed because Lower Canada was in great part French and Catholic, and Upper Canada was British and Protestant, and the lower provinces were mixed, it was futile and worthless in the extreme. Look for instance at the United Kingdom, inhabited as it was by three great races. (Hear, hear.) Had the diversity of race impeded the glory, the progress, the wealth of England? Had they not rather each contributed their share to the greatness of the empire? . . . In our own federation we should have Catholic and Protestant, English, French, Irish, and Scotch,† and each by

---

* The term nationality *is commonly used to denote a people whose feeling of common identity, rooted in a sense of shared history, language, territory, and so on, finds expression in a desire for self-determination. For that reason, in discussing British North American union, the word is sometimes used as a synonym for sovereign independence as opposed to colonial dependence (see the remarks of Philip Moore and Christopher Dunkin in this section, and C.N. Skinner of New Brunswick in chapter 9.) In chapter 7 John Bourinot fears that the creation of such a nationality will lead to independence, while Amor De Cosmos counts on its doing so.*

In this statement Cartier tries to reconcile the project of British North American nationality with the evident diversity of nationalities within the colonies contemplating union. He does so by using the term political nationality *to signify that the proposed union is to form a single society organized for self-government, though comprising divers* races. *Oddly enough, no one in the Canadian debates cites J.S. Mill's highly applicable distinction, in* Considerations on Representative Government, *between "nationality" and "federal representative governments," in which he sees federal institutions of the American kind as something like a halfway house between the nation-state and a federation that binds governments, but does not act directly on their subjects. — PR*

†Cartier's enumeration of so many "races" has been cited as evidence that he did not conceive of Confederation as establishing a political relationship

his efforts and his success would increase the prosperity and glory of the new confederacy. (Hear, hear.) He viewed the diversity of races in British North America in this way: we were of different races, not for the purpose of warring against each other, but in order to compete and emulate for the general welfare. (Cheers.)

— *Legislative Assembly, February 7, 1865*

"If we desired to have a constitution that would afford good hope of permanency, it must be planted deep in the affections of the people — for until their intellects were convinced of its excellence, they would not be prepared to uphold it and resist innovations. But they must feel and comprehend the obligation."

John Sanborn: If we desired to have a constitution that would afford good hope of permanency, it must be planted deep in the affections of the people — (hear, hear) — for until their intellects were convinced of its excellence, they would not be prepared to uphold it and resist innovations. But they must feel and comprehend the obligation. (Hear.) To render it secure, it must be in the hearts of the people. Why was it that the English had always resisted attempts upon their constitution? Because every link of the great chain had been conquered by resistance to oppression, and by sacrifices of blood* — (hear, hear) — by resistance to royal exactions and assumptions — (hear, hear) — and these achievements were preserved, held dear, understood, valued, and clung to with all the tenacity of that great people's nature. (Hear, hear.) This was the reason why it rested upon such a solid foundation, why it had endured so long and was likely to endure for ever. (Hear, hear.)

The constitution asked for was to be built on a flimsy foundation, consisting of certain ideas in the minds of a few men who no doubt wished well to their country; but that constitution was new after all, and they could not, in the small space of time they had given to the project, view the whole subject in all its bearings and aspects, as it was desirable they should . . . [A]n appeal on the subject was due to the people whose voice had not been heard upon it.

— *Legislative Council, February 9, 1865*

---

between two founding nations — "English" and "French" Canadians. But the enumeration comes immediately after his allusion to the "three great races" that together constitute "England" itself. Elsewhere in his speech (see chapter 6) he discusses the difference of races in Canada as one between "French" and "British" Canadians. See also H.-L. Langevin's words in this section. — PR

* Among the examples of resistance familiar to his hearers would have been the Peasants' Revolt against the poll tax and unfree status in 1381; the civil war and revolution of 1642–49 against arbitrary taxation and imprisonment; and the "Glorious Revolution" of 1688–89 against James II's absolutist pretensions and his attempt to return England to the Catholic fold. — IG

Thomas D'Arcy McGee: I wish to say a few words in reference to what I call the social relations which I think ought to exist and will spring up between the people of the lower provinces and ourselves if there is a closer communication established between us . . . And first, I will make a remark to some of the Canadian gentlemen who are said to be opposed to our project, on French-Canadian grounds only. I will remind them . . . that every one of the colonies we now propose to re-unite under one rule — in which they shall have a potential voice — were once before united, as New France. (Cheers.) Newfoundland, the uttermost, was theirs, and one large section of its coast is still known as "the French shore"; Cape Breton was theirs till the final fall of Louisbourg; Prince Edward Island was their Island of St. Jean, and Charlottetown was their Port Joli [Port la Joie]; in the heart of Nova Scotia was that fair Acadian land, where the roll of Longfellow's* noble hexameters may any day be heard in every wave that breaks upon the base of Cape Blomedon. (Cheers.) . . . In New Brunswick there is more than one county, especially in the north, where business, and law, and politics require a knowledge of both English and French . . . Well, gentlemen of French origin, we propose to restore these long-lost compatriots to your protection: in the federal union, which will recognize equally both languages, they will naturally look to you; their petitions will come to you, and their representatives will naturally be allied with you.

— Legislative Assembly, February 9, 1865

Philip Moore: It is . . . said that we are to have a new nationality. I do not understand this term, honourable gentlemen. If we were going to have an independent sovereignty in this country, then I could understand it. I believe honourable gentlemen will agree with me that, after this scheme is fully carried into operation, we shall still be colonies.†

---

* Henry Wadsworth Longfellow (1807–1882). The reference is to his poem Evangeline, *which treats the British deportation of the Acadians from Nova Scotia in 1755.*

*† In constitutional law there was no midpoint between sovereign independence and colonial dependence. Confederation could not of itself raise the provinces concerned to a higher legal status. In an important provincial rights case of 1881 (*Citizens' Insurance Co. v. Parsons), *Oliver Mowat used this argument to rebut the claim that the Dominion of Canada possessed a "supreme*

E.P. Taché: Of course.

Moore: Now, that being the case, I think our local government will be placed in a lower position than in the government we have now.

— *Legislative Council, February 16, 1865*

"What then are the aspirations of the French-Canadians? I have always imagined, indeed I still imagine, that they centre in one point, the maintenance of their nationality as a shield destined for the protection of the institutions they hold most dear."

Henri Joly: What then are the aspirations of the French Canadians? I have always imagined, indeed I still imagine, that they centre in one point, the maintenance of their nationality* as a shield destined for the protection of the institutions they hold most dear. For a whole century this has ever been the aim of the French Canadians; in the long years of adversity they have never for a moment lost sight of it; surmounting all obstacles, they have advanced step by step towards its attainment, and what progress have they not made?

What is their position today? They number nearly a million; they have no longer, if they are true to themselves, to fear the fate of Louisiana, which had not as many inhabitants, when it was sold by Napoleon to the United States, as Canada had in 1761. A people numbering a million does not vanish easily, especially when they are the owners of the soil. Their numbers are rapidly increasing. New townships are being opened in every direction and peopled with industrious settlers. In the Eastern Townships, which it was thought were destined to be peopled entirely by English settlers, these latter are slowly giving way to French Canadians. There is a friendly rivalry between the two races, a struggle of labour and energy; contact with our fellow-countrymen of English origin has at last opened our eyes; we have at last comprehended that in order to succeed, not only labour is needed, but well-directed and skilled labour, and we profit by their example and by the experience they have acquired in the old countries of Europe.

Agriculture is now becoming with us an honourable pursuit; the man of education is no longer ashamed to devote himself to it. Our farmers feel the necessity and desire of attaining perfec-

---

national authority," which required that its legislative powers as enumerated in section 91 of the BNA Act be given a broad construction. — PR

* Here Joly uses the word nationality *in the sense of a group of people whose feeling of common identity, rooted in a sense of shared history, language, territory, and the like, finds expression in a desire for self-determination.* — PR

tion in the art. We possess magnificent model farms, in which we can learn the science of agriculture. We are entering a new era of prosperity. The French Canadians hold a distinguished position in the commerce of the country; they have founded banks and savings banks; on the St. Lawrence between Quebec and Montreal, they own one of the finest lines of steamboats in America; there is not a parish on the great river which has not its steamboat; the communications with the great towns are easy; we have railways, and we now measure by hours the duration of a journey which formerly we measured by days; we have foundries and manufactories, and our shipbuilders have obtained a European renown.

We have a literature peculiarly our own; we have authors, of whom we are justly proud; to them we entrust our language and our history; they are the pillars of our nationality. Nothing denotes our existence as a people so much as our literature; education has penetrated everywhere; we have several excellent colleges, and an university in which all the sciences may be studied under excellent professors. Our young men learn in military schools how to defend their country. We possess all the elements of a nationality. But a few months ago, we were steadily advancing towards prosperity, satisfied with the present and confident in the future of the French-Canadian people. Suddenly discouragement, which had never overcome us in our adversity, takes possession of us; our aspirations are now only empty dreams; the labours of a century must be wasted; we must give up our nationality, adopt a new one, greater and nobler, we are told, than our own, but then it will no longer be our own. And why? Because it is our inevitable fate, against which it is of no use to struggle. But have we not already struggled against destiny when we were more feeble than we are now, and have we not triumphed? Let us not give to the world the sad spectacle of a people voluntarily resigning its nationality . . .

I object to the proposed Confederation, first, as a Canadian, without reference to origin, and secondly, as a French Canadian. From either point of view, I look upon the measure as a fatal error; and, as a French Canadian, I once more appeal to my fellow-countrymen, reminding them of the precious inheritance confided to their keeping — an inheritance sanctified by the blood of their fathers, and which it is their duty to hand down to their children as unimpaired as they received it. (Cheers.)

— *Legislative Assembly, February 20, 1865*

"Under the new system there will be no more reason than at present to lose our character as French or English, under the pretext that we should all have the same general interests; and our interests in relation to race, religion, and nationality will remain as they are at the present time. But they will be better protected under the proposed system, and that again is one of the strongest reasons in favour of Confederation."

H.-L. Langevin: We are told: "You wish to form a new nationality." Let us come to an understanding on this word, Mr. Speaker. What we desire and wish is to defend the general interests of a great country and of a powerful nation, by means of a central power. On the other hand, we do not wish to do away with our different customs, manner, and laws; on the contrary, those are precisely what we are desirous of protecting in the most complete manner by means of Confederation. Under the new system there will be no more reason than at present to lose our character as French or English, under the pretext that we should all have the same general interests; and our interests in relation to race, religion, and nationality will remain as they are at the present time. But they will be better protected under the proposed system, and that again is one of the strongest reasons in favour of Confederation.

— *Legislative Assembly, February 21, 1865*

Christopher Dunkin: The people of the United States, when they adopted their constitution, were one of the nations of the earth. They formed their whole system with a view to national existence. They had fought for their independence and had triumphed; and still in the flush of their triumph, they were laying the foundations of a system absolutely national. Their federal government was to have its relations with other nations, and was sure to have plenty to do upon entering the great family of nations.

But we — what are we doing? Creating a new nationality, according to the advocates of this scheme. I hardly know whether we are to take the phrase as ironical or not. Is it a reminder that, in fact, we have no sort of nationality about us, but are unpleasantly cut up into a lot of struggling nationalities, as between ourselves? Unlike the people of the United States, we are to have no foreign relations to look after or national affairs of any kind; and therefore our new nationality, if we could create it, could be nothing but a name. I must say that according to my view of the change we ought to aim at, any idea of federation that we may entertain had need take an imperial direction. Whenever changing our institutions, we had need develop and strengthen . . . the tie, not yet federal as it ought to be, between us and the parent state. (Hear, hear.)

It is the entire empire that should be federalized and cemented together as one, and not any mere limited number of its dependencies here or there. A general, or so-called general, government,

such as we are here proposing to create, will most certainly be in a false position. As I said just now, the federal government of the United States was to take its place in the great family of the nations of the earth; but what place in that family are we to occupy? Simply, none. The imperial government will be the head of the empire as much as ever, and will alone have to attend to all foreign relations and national matters; while we shall be nothing more than we are now. Half-a-dozen colonies federated are but a federated colony after all . . .

The real difficulty in our position is one that is not met by the machinery here proposed. What is that difficulty? In the larger provinces of the empire we have the system of responsible government thoroughly accorded by the imperial government and thoroughly worked out; and the difficulty of the system that is now pressing, or ought to be, upon the attention of our statesmen is just this — that the tie connecting us with the empire, and which ought to be a federal tie of the strongest kind, is too slight, is not, properly speaking, so much as a federal tie at all. These provinces, with local responsible government, are too nearly in the position of independent communities; there is not enough of connection between them and the parent state to make the relations between the two work well, or give promise of lasting long . . . What is wanting, if one is to look to the interest of the empire, which is really that of all its parts — what is wanting, as I have said, is an effective federalization of the empire as a whole, not a subordinate federalization here or there, made up out of parts of it.

— *Legislative Assembly, February 28, 1865*

> *"These provinces, with local responsible government, are too nearly in the position of independent communities; there is not enough of connection between them and the parent state to make the relations between the two work well, or give promise of lasting long."*

NOVA SCOTIA

Adams Archibald: What attitude, then, ought we to assume in reference to the new duties devolving on us? Is it not natural for British statesmen to look upon the union of the colonies as a means of defence? Do they not feel, have they not a right to feel, that the effect of union would be largely to improve the possibilities of defence? It is a favourite argument against it to say that, by union, we will obtain no more money, no more men, and how is it possible then for union to improve our position? It is true we have no more means, no more men, but what we have is concentrated; there would be one heart, one soul, one purpose, one controlling power, extending over the whole Confederation, from Sarnia to Sydney.

Suppose this argument had been used at the time of the American rebellion, that instead of concentrating their forces, and their means, each state had acted upon its own responsibility; does not everybody know that, instead of being able to maintain a war for seven years against the greatest naval and military power in the world and then to establish their independence, the result would have been very different?

— *House of Assembly, April 12, 1865*

Isaac LeVesconte: There are one or two matters to which I shall briefly refer — one is in connection with the loss of privileges which will be entailed upon the people of this country by the adoption of the scheme of union. The right of being taxed only through the action of their representatives, has always been considered one of the dearest privileges a free people can possess, and it is one that comes home to every man's mind. At present not a single penny of taxes can be imposed upon the country except with the consent of the representatives of the people.* But what will be the result after we are annexed to Canada?† What chance would 300,000 people have against three millions — or what stand could the representatives of Nova Scotia make against the overpowering influence of the government of Canada? We would be in the position that we would have to submit, no matter how iniquitous the tax, or else be taunted as rebels. Now we have the glorious privilege of electing our own representatives and

---

* *No taxation without representation, the constitutional principle for which Americans went to war in 1776, is guaranteed in parliamentary systems by responsible government. Section 53 of the British North America Act, 1867, reads: "Bills for . . . imposing any tax or impost, shall originate in the House of Commons." There's no grand flourish of trumpets in the wording but the meaning is clear: governments may not impose taxes without the approval of the majority in the Commons. LeVesconte is proud of the principle as it operates in Nova Scotia; his complaint is that Confederation will mean that Nova Scotians are taxed by a legislature representing central Canada as well as Nova Scotia. — JA*

† *LeVesconte hits on the reality of the proposed union — a reality duly expressed in the transfer of the name* Canada *from the old province to the new dominion. The prospect haunted opponents of Confederation in all the smaller provinces; subsequently it would find expression in animosity towards "central Canada." Like other opponents of union, LeVesconte dismisses the federal aspect of the scheme. — PR*

arranging our own tariff, and I am happy to say that so far we have done so in a manner that has redounded to the credit of the province and has doubled the resources of the country in the last few years. But what would be the consequence if this attempt to barter away our rights and privileges were carried out? Instead of as now — enacting our own laws, subject to the exercise of the royal prerogative — we would, by our own act, surrender to the supreme government at Ottawa the right of passing any laws, no matter how obnoxious they might be to our people, and we would be compelled to submit, or else be branded as rebels.

"Sorry am I that Nova Scotia's most gifted sons should be found to have entered into this unholy compact to destroy our political existence . . . "

Under the present system, if an act was passed which was not suited to the wants of the people, it could be repealed at the next session — but adopt this union, and we surrender to the Ottawa government all control over our legislature and leave ourselves entirely at their mercy. Mr. Speaker, I regret very much that no abler man than myself should be found to raise his voice against this attempt to barter away our dearest rights and privileges. Sorry am I that Nova Scotia's most gifted sons should be found to have entered into this unholy compact to destroy our political existence but, sir, humble as I am, I should consider myself recreant to my principles, and unworthy of the confidence of those who sent me here, if I failed to denounce, feebly it may be, but to the best of my ability, this scheme, which I consider so detrimental to the best interests of the people of Nova Scotia. Sir, we all remember the old story of Esau selling his birthright for a mess of pottage,* and how he afterwards regretted it with an exceeding bitter cry — but there was this to be said in excuse for his conduct, that he sold it when he was hungry, and at all events he received some return — whereas the province of Nova Scotia was not hungry, and the only return she would receive for the surrender of her rights would be a mess of bitter herbs, to be eaten in sorrow and digested in tears. We have been told that we would not be left without a parliament — that the representatives of the people would be in the same position as when such men as Archibald and Uniacke and Halliburton† adorned these halls by their presence.

Genesis 25:29–34. The point of the Bible story is that Esau gave up his inheritance as leader of Israel merely in order to satisfy his immediate physical appetite.

† Samuel Archibald (1777–1846), Richard John Uniacke (1753–1830), and Sir Brenton Halliburton (1774–1860) were leading lawyers and politicians of the era before responsible government.

But it does not require much argument to prove that such will not be the case. They were the representatives of a province having its own laws, its own tariff, the control of its own resources, while we will represent a dependency of Canada, with powers about as great as the grand jury and sessions of a county. I do hope, if this scheme is carried out, for the credit of old time and old associations, that the title of the representatives will be changed and that instead of the time-honoured name of MPP,* they will substitute that of MCP, or Member of the Council of Puppets . . .

The provincial secretary [Charles Tupper] told us that this union will give us a character and a nationality we do not now possess — that we have now no *locus standi* and have no weight amongst the nations of the world. I ask how is it going to improve our position in that respect to annex us to Canada? Is it going to add to our importance of position to deprive us of our lieutenant governor, and our character as a province, and reduce us to the condition of a mere dependency of a larger province? If it does, I certainly am at a loss to understand it.

S.L. Shannon: In the first place, I may remark that ever since the commencement of the American union, or rather ever since the adoption of the present constitution,† the leading minds connected with the colonies have turned their attention to the subject of a colonial union. It was not to be wondered at that when they saw the great prosperity resulting from that union under the American constitution, they should deem similar benefits might flow from the adoption of a similar course in British North America. Among the earliest who approached this subject was Chief Justice Sewell,‡ who was one of the prominent men of Canada and who wrote upon the question. Again and again the

---

Member of the Provincial Parliament: the term that has been used in Upper Canada/Ontario at least since the 1820s to denote a member of the provincial Legislative Assembly. The terms M(ember of the) L(egislative) A(ssembly) or M(ember of the) H(ouse of) A(ssembly) are neologisms and have no historical warrant. — PR

† Consciousness of this tradition informs several speeches in the Canadian debate too. From one standpoint it constitutes a false genealogy for Confederation, since it obscures the crucial difference between the events of 1864–67 and the earlier unfulfilled dreams: the fact that the successful scheme originated in a decision to federalize the Canadian union of 1841. — PR

‡ Sir Jonathan Sewell (1766–1839), chief justice of Lower Canada, 1808–38.

subject was brought forward, but it was left to Lord Durham to give it greater prominence in his celebrated report. That nobleman came to this continent clothed with the highest powers and on a mission of the greatest importance, that of quieting, if possible, the disturbances of Canada. He saw the isolated condition of these colonies and contrasted them with the strength and power of the United States, and he felt and expressed the necessity of a union.

I have often regretted that advantage had not been taken of that opportunity to have consolidated the whole of British America, not merely to unite Upper and Lower Canada. At that time the colonies were in a different position from what they are now. Then we were subject to the fiat of the colonial secretary,* and an act of parliament could easily have been obtained at the time Lord Durham returned to England, and would have been received as law by all. His Lordship, however, was too much imbued with republican ideas, and I am not sure that he would have arranged his plan upon the monarchical principles, which, I am happy to say, pervades the scheme which was adopted at Quebec.

From the time of Lord Durham down to the present, we have had in every colony, from time to time, statesmen who have brought the subject of union before the public, who have talked of and dreamed about it, who have desired it as one of the greatest boons, but who felt that such were the difficulties in the way, no plan could be possibly agreed upon that would approach to a satisfactory adjustment. All thought it would sometime or other be accomplished, but none that the time for its discussion was at hand or that a solution of its difficulties was practicable. We hoped that a period would arrive when the leading minds of

---

*Shannon seems to think that, before the advent of responsible government, the British North American colonies were subject to a degree of imperial control which would have allowed the British government to impose union upon them (and Durham's proposal was for legislative, not federal, union). This view was far from accepted in Canada, and perhaps not even in Britain. When Montreal commercial interests persuaded the British government in 1822 to introduce a bill to unite Upper and Lower Canada, the attempt was opposed in both colonies as illegal and unconstitutional, and the protests prompted the government to drop the bill. Even in 1839–40 the imperial authorities felt obliged to gain the assent of the Upper Canadian legislature to union. In Lower Canada, parliamentary government had been suspended after the rebellion of 1837. — PR

the different provinces might agree upon some feasible plan, but we hardly dared to expect that it would be in our time. And yet now, strange to say, when the difficulties have been removed, when the leaders of the different parties in all the different colonies have united upon common ground, and the time has come for us to obtain that which we have so long desired, there are found those among us who are unwilling to accept it!

[If] we had union, we should possess more of a national position than we do at present. Let any Nova Scotian cross the Atlantic and he will soon learn the estimation in which he is held as a provincial. I recollect an instance which occurred to me when travelling on the continent, and how keenly I felt the different position a colonist held from that of an American citizen . . . I am persuaded that our leading men, under the union, will have their minds enlarged and take a higher position as statesmen than they can possibly do in the small and degrading discussions which occupy too much of the time of each provincial legislature.

Before the American Revolution, there was not a single man in the old colonies who at that time had acquired an European reputation but Franklin. Washington was only known as a colonel of militia, Adams was but a village attorney, and the same may be said of Jefferson, Madison,* and other eminent men of the day. They occupied positions such as colonists occupy today. When, however, the war was over, and the United States assumed a national character, these men rose to their position and took high rank in the estimation of the world. Though we do not wish independence, but consolidation, in British America, I am convinced that the effects produced will not be less elevating in our case than in that of the neighbouring republic.

[Opponents] say we have not a fair representation in the united parliament. I ask, what has been conceded to us in the Legislative Council? We shall have in that body, which I am happy to see is to be purely of a monarchical character and whose functions will be high and important, greater weight than we were really entitled to. But it is said that the real power of the parliament will be in the House of Assembly, and that there we

---

*Benjamin Franklin (1706–1790), George Washington (1732–1799), John Adams (1735–1826), Thomas Jefferson (1743–1826), and James Madison (1753–1836), leading architects of American independence and the founding of the United States of America. Washington, Adams, Jefferson, and Madison were the first four presidents of the United States.

will not be adequately represented. We shall be represented upon the true principle, that is, according to our population, and I cannot see how such an arrangement can be objected to, or what could be considered more equitable.

— House of Assembly, April 17, 1865

Ferryboat carrying the Maritime delegates to the Charlottetown Conference of 1864.

William Miller: [S]ir, do not let me be supposed to underrate the present position of this province. Far from it. Even as she is, I am proud of my country, and grateful for the happy homes she affords her sons. Yet proud, sir, as I am of the little sea-girt province I call my native land; proud as I am of her free institutions — her moral status — her material wealth; the name of Nova Scotia — a name which the genius and valour of my countrymen have inscribed high on the scroll of fame; proud I say as I am, and may well be permitted to be these things, I have never ceased to entertain the hope, expressed in this legislature in 1864, that the day was not far distant when you, with the inhabitants of these noble provinces, united under one government, might stand before the world in the prouder national character of British Americans.

— House of Assembly, April 3, 1866

John Locke: By a political union we must be absorbed and swallowed up. We will lose our identity and be subject to their will. It is well known that Nova Scotia stood by the crown during the American rebellion. Nova Scotia was loyal then and is now, and by uniting herself to such a country as Canada she will gain nothing. We have enjoyed a parliament of our own for a hundred years, with all the privileges that a free people could ask. We have gone on progressing, and after obtaining responsible government we have become so free that we require nothing more in the way of independence. What will the people say to this parliament being taken from them? We may be told that the local legislatures will remain, but who can tell us anything of their formation? I presume that nothing that we can urge will prevent the adoption of the scheme, but I contend that it would be unfair for the British government to adopt such a measure without the sanction of our people.

William Henry: At present each of the provinces looks to its own safety and does not trouble itself much about its neighbour . . . If we were all united in one, if the Canadian felt that the soil of

> *"At present each of the provinces looks to its own safety and does not trouble itself much about its neighbour . . . If we were all united in one, if the Canadian felt that the soil of Nova Scotia is as dear to him as that of Canada — if Nova Scotia felt that Canada is a part of itself — we would all have a greater guarantee of security."*

Nova Scotia is as dear to him as that of Canada — if Nova Scotia felt that Canada is a part of itself — we would all have a greater guarantee of security. We are told that disunited we can as effectually defend ourselves. I would call attention to the position of Wellington in Spain.* Whilst trammelled by the orders of the British government, Spanish junta, etc., he was powerless, but the moment he determined to act on his own responsibility, success crowned his arms. Everybody must see the great advantage that is derived from the concentration of authority in one hand. The most powerful government for speedy action is that which is despotic. If we have one concentrated authority in the country — one general command — our strength will be vastly increased by the ability to concentrate force when necessary at any important point.

Henry Kaulbach: When we feel we are one people — when we have a national sentiment — when we can present a united population of four millions of people animated by the same interests and affections, we shall have a guarantee of security and prosperity that we cannot have now.

— *House of Assembly, April 16, 1866*

> *"Why, as we know, there is a wilderness between the lower provinces and Canada; we have no sympathies or interests in common with the people of that country."*

Stewart Campbell: What is the condition of these Maritime provinces? Their people are situated in connection with each other, are possessed of the same interests, have the same common sympathies, residing on each others' borders, and having daily intercourse with each other. Is that the character of the people with whom this scheme is to force us to unite? Why, as we know, there is a wilderness between the lower provinces and Canada; we have no sympathies or interests in common with the people of that country. They are as much strangers to us as the people of the West Indies.

Archibald McLelan: Turn to the map of the world and you will find every country, occupying a first-class position, compact in shape, and just as the country departs from that it descends in the scale of nations. England has been styled "the tight little isle of the sea." There is in her a compact territory, which affords that blending of interests which heads to a harmonious co-operation for the good of the whole. We have been frequently reminded

---

* *Wellington commanded the British, Portuguese, and Spanish forces in the Peninsular War against Napoleon between 1808 and 1813.*

since this question arose of the heptarchy in England* and the great results of her union. Union for her was a natural act, and so may it be said of England and Scotland. The boundary line is wiped out by the dense population which flows back and forth, that the influence of the interest of each extends into and operates upon the other, forming a strong and enduring union. Ireland has not this territorial connection. The influence of her interests is bounded by the sea-shore, and naturally seeks a centre within her own territory. There is not the same interweaving of interests, and consequently the bond of union is acknowledged to be weaker than between England and Scotland.

England grew in greatness and power by every union which combined territory and people and interests, having for each a natural affinity, but when she went beyond that she gained only elements of weakness. She crossed the channel[†] into France and attempted to draw that people and country to her, but the more territory she acquired the weaker she became, and eventually yielded to the inflexible law of nature that the drawings of all people are to their natural centre of interest. Look at France upon the map. No straggling arms or long jutting headlands, but all compact, and forming a country which claims and holds a first position among empires. Go over the map of Europe, and just as you find countries departing from that compact shape you find them descending in the scale of nations.

But I may be referred to England's colonies scattered all over the globe and having no territorial connection with England, and be asked how she has held them without their being a source of weakness? Simply by permitting them to manage all matters of internal policy as suited themselves; attempting no action affecting the internal interests of a colony further than was compensated for by a protection of her external interests. By this wise

---

*This term refers to the historical notion (not strictly true) that in the seventh century, Anglo-Saxon England was divided into seven kingdoms: Northumbria, Mercia, East Anglia, Essex, Kent, Sussex, and Wessex. In the ninth century these more or less autonomous kingdoms were united under Alfred the Great. — IG

† After the Norman conquest of 1066, English monarchs had extensive domains in France and from time to time tried to enforce claims to the French throne, especially during the period of the so-called Hundred Years' War (1337–1453). Their claims were eventually nullified by military defeat. — PR

and liberal policy she has seen her colonies grow and prosper in a remarkable degree. She departed from this policy when she proposed to tax the thirteen New England states,* but the people regarded it as a violation of their chartered rights and they severed the connection with the parent state. England saw the mistake Lord North† committed and compelled him to repeal the act imposing a tax on colonists, and from that time to the present the policy pursued by England towards her colonies has been growing more enlightened and liberal . . .

The honourable member for Richmond, Mr. [William] Miller, in calling for this resolution, told us how proud he is of Nova Scotia. It is not he alone who is proud of her. We are proud of being British subjects, of being British Americans, but not less so of being called Nova Scotians. That gentleman, however, seeks to blot out this name. Whilst he addressed the house I thought of that anecdote told . . . of the cod-fishing captain on a voyage to Newfoundland who, on going down to the cabin to consult his chart and finding it in shreds and tatters, told his men they might as well turn about, for the rats had eaten Newfoundland. I do not mean to say that Nova Scotia will be literally devoured, but rats are striving to eat out the name from the map of North America.

Sir, if this proposition be carried into effect without consulting the people, I anticipate the most serious results. There is in the breast of every man claiming British allegiance a principle — a feeling — implanted by God himself that he should be consulted in all changes affecting his rights and privileges and the constitution under which he lives. In no part of the British Empire is that feeling more strong and irrepressible than in this country, and if the provincial secretary carries out his proposition without consulting the people, this province will rebel against the act. I have no hesitation in telling the honourable gentleman that he is tampering with the loyalty and allegiance of the people. He knows our attachment to the mother country is strong, but he must not count too much on it.

— *House of Assembly, April 17, 1866*

> *"There is in the breast of every man claiming British allegiance a principle — a feeling — implanted by God himself that he should be consulted in all changes affecting his rights and privileges and the constitution under which he lives."*

---

* *The British parliament's insistence on its right to levy taxes on the North American colonies, and its intermittent efforts to exercise the right, were leading causes of the American Revolution. Parliament formally renounced the right by an act of 1778. — PR*

† *Lord North (1732–1792), British prime minister during the American War of Independence.*

NEW BRUNSWICK

Amos Botsford: Some may say they are proud of New Brunswick, and I would not underrate her, but I confess I would be prouder of her did she form part of the united colonies. I, as a New Brunswicker, going to Nova Scotia and seeing there her varied resources, viewing from the Citadel at Halifax her beautiful harbour, would prefer to feel it was a portion of my country; going to Newfoundland or Prince Edward Island, I should like to regard them, not as an alien, but as a citizen; but when I go to Canada, then it is that those yearnings for nationality are quickened and strengthened. When I look upon her magnificent mountains, her vast lakes, her wondrous Niagara; when I stand upon the Citadel of Quebec and gaze upon the blue mountains of the Saguenay, or when my eyes linger upon the Plains of Abraham, where Wolfe fell in the last and final struggle for British supremacy on the continent; and when sailing on her magnificent rivers, or speeding on her railroads, I witness her commercial greatness and realize her vast resources, then I cannot fail to have deep interest excited, and a strong desire to participate more closely in their benefits. No person, unless they examine for themselves, can have any idea of her vast resources and public works.

— *Legislative Council, April 4, 1866*

James Gray Stevens: [Canada] is a country that will draw the weaker provinces towards it and give strength to them. The geographical lines of distinction between the provinces will be swept away, and we shall be amalgamated as one people. We shall all be bound together, so that if you touch the smallest member of the body, the heart will feel the throb and send forth all its power to protect it. We look with ardent hope for the establishment of this glorious empire, whose greatness shall be measured only by comparison and who in a few short years shall rival the parent stem from which it sprung.

— *House of Assembly, June 18, 1866*

John Mercer Johnson: Every effort should be made to make us forget our provincial identity, so we would be one people from Sarnia to Newfoundland. [If] we go into it we must not talk of Canada as a foreign country, but be one people under one general government.

— *House of Assembly, July 2, 1866*

RED RIVER

William Cummings: [The convention is considering a proposal that military force in the colony should be supplied by natives — that is, inhabitants of the colony.] Who are "natives of the country"? Does it include all born in the country — Indians, half-breeds, and everyone else?

Louis Riel: I am a native of the country and I would say that it means the people now in the country, without any distinction.

Thomas Bunn: Not including the Indians?

Riel: We do not know that they were born here. (Laughter.)

Bunn: I have seen some so young in the middle of winter that I think they must have been born here. (Laughter.)

Riel: [There is no need for foreign troops who might be prejudicial to one section of the local population.] In asking our rights at any time, we might unreasonably or unfairly be put down by foreign troops. Here would be the good of native troops. With a governor among us representing Canada, having immense influence, and at the outset feeling disposed perhaps to lean towards Canadians, would it not be well that we should have a local force?

Judge John Black: [He quotes from the British North America Act to illustrate the queen's prerogative as commander of military forces.] The great object of all government is, undoubtedly, due protection of life and property. On what is that protection principally founded? On the naval and military power. Why, then, should we put ourselves forward as a community who wish to be deprived of this great advantage? . . . You may perhaps say you are afraid of the government under which you propose to place yourselves doing something against you; but you are looking forward to responsible government, and no government of that character would persist in any course which was plainly opposed to the general interests and wishes of the community* . . .

I have sufficient confidence in Canada to be led to the convic-

---

What community? This entire debate is occurring in the context of the inhabitants' fear of being swamped by an influx of outsiders, mainly

LOUIS RIEL
(1844–1885),
convicted traitor,
martyr, and symbol of
western alienation.
Though possibly illegal,
Riel's provisional
government of 1869–70
was a justifiable means
of defending the
community in the face
of pending annexation
to Canada.
Unfortunately, the
"execution" of Thomas
Scott earned Riel the
enmity of Protestant
Ontario. Though
amnestied, he was
expelled from the House
of Commons when
elected in 1873 and
sought safety in
the United States. On
returning to Canada
in 1884 to aid his
people settled on the
Saskatchewan River,
he led a futile uprising
and was hanged, despite
his suspected insanity
and the jury's
recommendation
of mercy.

tion that the intentions are just towards this country, and that in assuming the government of it she will virtually be giving you a guarantee for the promotion of your interests. Canada has already said enough to give you reasonable ground for the strongest assurance that your rights as British subjects will be duly respected, and for my own part I see no reason why Canada should not be invited to take up the government as soon as possible, and so put an end to this period of distraction and trouble which weighs so heavily upon every mind and is inflicting injury upon every interest in the country. (Cheers.)

Riel: [The convention now turns to the following clause in Red River's list of terms of admission: "That treaties be concluded between the dominion and the several Indian tribes of the country."] Had the Indians the whole claim to the country? Here we ask the Canadian government to settle with the Indian; and I would ask for the consideration of the convention. Are Indians the only parties in the country who have to be settled with for land claims? If so, all right. But if . . . the half-breeds would have to be dealt with, then the article as it stood was too general. I have heard of half-breeds having maintained a position of superiority and conquest against the incursions of Indians in some parts of the country. If so, this might possibly be considered to establish the rights of the half-breeds as against the Indians. But I merely suggest this for consideration. The article, I presume, refers to a settlement with the Indians of the whole territory, and, let me ask, is not that too liberal?

George Flett: For my part, I am a half-breed, but far be it for me to press any land claim I might have as against the poor Indian of the country. (Hear, hear.) We have taken the position, and ask the rights, of civilized men. As to the poor Indian, let him by all means have all he can get. He needs it, and if our assistance will aid him in getting it let us cheerfully give it. (Cheers.)

James Ross: As a half-breed of this country, I am naturally very anxious to get all rights that properly belong to half-breeds. I can easily understand that we can secure a certain kind of right by placing ourselves on the same footing as Indians. But in that case,

Canadians. Given the propensity of responsible government to empower majorities, Black's professed faith in it seems either naive or sinister. — PR

we must decide on giving up our rights as civilized men. The fact is, we must take one side or the other. We must either be Indians and claim the privileges of Indians — certain reserves of land and annual compensation of blankets, powder, and tobacco (laughter) — or else we must take the position of civilized men and claim rights accordingly. We cannot expect to enjoy the rights and privileges of both the Indian and the white man. Considering the progress we have made, and the position we occupy, we must claim the rights and privileges which civilized men in other countries claim.

Pierre Thibert: The rights put forward by half-breeds need not necessarily be mixed up with those of Indians. It is quite possible that the two classes of rights can be separate and concurrent. My own idea is that reserves of land should be given the half-breeds for their rights.

Riel: The half-breeds have certain rights which they claim by conquest. They are not to be confounded with Indian rights. Great Britain herself holds most of her possessions by rights of conquest.
— *Convention at Fort Garry, English and French*
Delegates in Council, February 1, 1870

"We must seek to preserve the existence of our own people. We must not by our own act allow ourselves to be swamped."

Riel: [At this point the convention is considering a proposal for adult male franchise, with a one-year residency requirement.] I would call attention to the fact that under this article we decide on the rights both of foreigners and natives. Of course, whatever our decision is, some parties will have fault to find. As a principle of action, we must seek to do what is right and, at the same time, have a special regard to the interests of the people of this country. We must seek to preserve the existence of our own people. We must not by our own act allow ourselves to be swamped . . . In this connection, all outsiders are to be looked upon as strangers* — not merely Americans, but Canadians, English, Irish, and Scotch. All are strangers in the sense that they are outsiders, that they do not appreciate the circumstances in which we live, and

---

* *Riel poignantly expresses the sense of peril felt by members of this tiny and very distinct society, threatened with a swamping influx of outsiders because of the high-handed transfer of their homeland to Canada. Unlike the other colonial settlements, the Red River Colony had not been allowed to vote on the question of joining Canada.* — PR

are not likely to enter fully into our views and feelings. Though in a sense British subjects, we must look on all coming in from abroad as foreigners . . .

> — *Convention at Fort Garry, English and French*
> *Delegates in Council, February 3, 1870*

BRITISH COLUMBIA

Henry Crease: If we watch the progress of events, they all point to the same end, to the growth of a new universal sentiment of nationality in British America. It is clear that events all gravitate in that direction.

Amor De Cosmos: In the direction of Confederation or nationality?

Crease: I say sir, that the current of events points to Confederation and ultimately to nationality.

J.S. Helmcken:* It is absurd to suppose that the same laws, whether civil, commercial, or industrial, will be found equally advantageous to all parts of this great continent. It manifestly cannot be so; the conditions are different. We know what is best for ourselves and are able to legislate to effect that. We have no wish to pay Canada to do our legislation.

No union between this colony and Canada can permanently exist unless it be to the material and pecuniary advantage of this colony to remain in the union. The sum of the interests of the inhabitants is the interest of the colony. The people of this colony have, generally speaking, no love for Canada; they care, as a rule, little or nothing about the creation of another empire, kingdom, or republic; they have but little sentimentality, and care little about the distinctions between the form of government of Canada and the United States. Therefore, no union on account of love need be looked for. The only bond of union outside of force looked for — and force the dominion has not — will be the

---

* Helmcken was one of the three delegates whom Governor Musgrave appointed to negotiate terms of union with Canada. In view of the force and lucidity of these remarks, one can see why the terms they secured were so favourable to British Columbia (or at least to British Columbians of European stock). — PR

material advantage of the country and the pecuniary benefit of the inhabitants.

Love for Canada has to be acquired by the prosperity of the country and [by] our children.

— *Legislative Council, March 9, 1870*

Joseph Trutch: I believe, sir, that many of the objections which have been raised to Confederation have arisen from prejudiced feelings. I have no reason to be prejudiced against or partial to Canada. I believe that Canadians as a people are not better than others and no worse. I have no ties in Canada, no particular reason for entertaining any feeling of affection for Canada; and if I did not believe that the advance which we make will be met in a becoming spirit (hear, hear), then I should be of [the] opinion that Confederation would be nothing more than an union on paper, one not beneficial to this colony or to Canada. There are statesmen there, sir, who know that it would be useless to try to beat us down on terms, for what would be the use of Confederation if it afterwards turned out that this colony would be injured, rather than benefited by it?

Henry Holbrook: The Indians, also, should be secured the same protection that they have under our own government. They are now content with us, and with the way in which the laws are administered, and it is quite possible that they may hereafter be a source of great trouble, if they are not considered as well as white men . . .

— *Legislative Council, March 10, 1870*

"I am not disposed to regret the occurrence of the difficulty in the Red River, for it will teach the Canadian government, and all governments, that though you may buy and sell territories, you cannot transfer the human beings therein, like so many serfs and chattels, to a fresh allegiance with impunity; that the consent of the people must be first obtained; and that though the soil may be sold, the soul is free."

E.G. Alston: I am not disposed to regret the occurrence of the difficulty in the Red River, for it will teach the Canadian government, and all governments, that though you may buy and sell territories, you cannot transfer the human beings therein, like so many serfs and chattels, to a fresh allegiance with impunity; that the consent of the people must be first obtained; and that though the soil may be sold, the soul is free.

— *Legislative Council, March 11, 1870*

Thomas Humphreys: As this stands, it throws the whole power into the hands of the Canadians. The lieutenant governor will be a Canadian and will name Canadians. We ought to know by whom these appointments are to be made.

John Robson: It is a great pity that these sectional differences should be allowed to prevail; we ought to consider ourselves British Columbians. The governor general, with the consent of his council, appoints the lieutenant governor, and the lieutenant governor, with the advice of his cabinet, recommends the senators.

Helmcken: No, no.

Robson: Yes, it is so; he recommends to the governor general, who appoints. It is a great pity to raise these disputes about Englishmen and Canadians.

Humphreys: It is all very well to talk that way. I maintain that the Englishmen sitting at this table have said less as to nationality than the Canadians. We want to be governed by British Columbians.
— *Legislative Council, March 18, 1870*

Helmcken: We had better drop these nationalities.

Holbrook: I have very great pleasure in bringing this resolution forward with reference to the Indian tribe . . .

Crease: I ask the indulgence of the honourable member whilst I interpose a few words. On a former occasion a very evil impression was introduced in the Indian mind on the occasion of Sir James Douglas'* retirement. I ask the honourable gentleman to be cautious, for Indians get information of what is going on.

Holbrook: My motion is to ask for protection for them under the change of government. The Indians number four to one white man, and they ought to be considered. They should receive protection.

Crease: These are the words that do harm. I would ask the hon-

---

* Douglas (1803–1877), governor of Vancouver Island and first governor of British Columbia, showed scrupulous respect for Indian customs, rights, and needs. His successors' ignorance and indifference abandoned British policy towards the indigenous population into the hands of Joseph Trutch, whose attitude was quite different. Douglas's retirement in 1864 coincided with the murder of a road-building party and a European settler by some Chilcotin Indians near the head of Bute Inlet. — PR

ourable magisterial member for New Westminster [Holbrook] to consider.

Holbrook: I say they shall be protected. I speak of Indians of my own neighbourhood on the Lower Fraser.

Robson: I rise to a point of privilege. I think that the warning of the honourable attorney general (Crease) is necessary. This is the sort of discussion which does harm.

De Cosmos: Don't report it.

Holbrook: I do not view it in that way. I say that the Indians of the Lower Fraser are intelligent, good settlers. I ask that they receive the same protection under Confederation as now.

Humphreys: I would ask what protection they have now?

Holbrook: They have protection in being allowed to occupy land, and they enjoy equally with white people the protection of the law, and I ask the house to keep them in the same position.

Crease: If the Indian had not better protectors than the honourable magistrate from New Westminster, I should not envy them their protection. The honourable gentleman must have forgotten the directions of the imperial government to His Excellency, the governor, in Lord Granville's* dispatch.

Robson: The honourable Mr. Holbrook has told you that he speaks on behalf of 40,000 Indians. I speak in the name of 65,000.† I am inclined to think we should not pass this matter over entirely; we ought to point out our desire that the Indians should be cared for. Now, the Canadian Indian policy has been characterized as good, even by American statesmen. Our own policy is not worth the name. I consider it to be a blot on the government. I will, therefore, propose as an amendment the following: "That the Indian policy of Canada shall be extended to this colony

---

*Granville George Leveson-Gore, 2nd Earl Granville (1815–1891), colonial secretary, 1868–70. — PR

† Just as Holbrook grossly overestimates the Indian population, so Robson grossly overestimates the entire population. — PR

WHAT THEY SAID ABOUT IDENTITY

immediately upon its admission into the dominion, and that the necessary agencies and appliances for an efficient administration of Indian affairs may be at once established." The Canadian government occupies the position of guardians to Indians. They are treated as minors.* There is a perfect network of Indian agents in Canada, and through them the Indians are made presents of agricultural implements, seeds, and stock. Now, if we let it go forth to the Indians that their interests are being considered, and that this will be greatly to their advantage, I say, by making the Indians feel all this, there will be less danger of exciting any unpleasant feeling among them. We should set the Indian mind at rest and let them feel that Confederation will be a greater boon to them than to the white population.

Robert Carrall: We have the full assurance[†] in Lord Granville's dispatch[‡] that the Indians must be protected. I do think the honourable gentlemen are only heaping up resolutions trusting to overload the whole system. The honourable member for New Westminster has affirmed how good the Canadian system is. The goodness of that system is in itself sufficient to render the resolution needless. I shall, therefore, vote against it and the amendment.

Holbrook: I must vote against the amendment.

Humphreys: I disapprove of what both the honourable members stated. These gentlemen know nothing of the question. I will

---

*Although an ardent defender of constitutional liberty and equality when the subject is responsible government, Robson does not think Indians should be regarded in law as equal to white people. It is appropriate to treat Indians as "minors" — that is, as children. They should be given presents, and may be lied to. Holbrook, in contrast, argues that Indians should enjoy equally with white people the protection of the law. — JA

† As we know, the British and Canadian governments protected the Indians of British Columbia as effectively as responsible government protected the Métis of Manitoba. — PR

‡ A dispatch to Governor Musgrave, with instructions to publish it on his arrival in British Columbia, which announced the imminent transfer of Rupert's Land to Canada and the British government's desire that British Columbia should join the dominion, with which she would now share a border. The dispatch was instrumental in persuading the majority of the colonial élite to accept such a union, to which most of them had previously been indifferent. — PR

"Take away the Indians from New Westminster, Lillooet, Lytton, Clinton, and these towns would be nowhere. I say the Indians are not treated fairly by us, and all they want is fair dealing from the white population."

show you why. Take away the Indians from New Westminster, Lillooet, Lytton, Clinton, and these towns would be nowhere. I say the Indians are not treated fairly by us, and all they want is fair dealing from the white population. At Lillooet I was told there were upwards of 16,000; and $17,000 [worth of] gold dust was purchased from Indians. Take away this trade and the towns must sink. I say, send them out to reservations and you destroy trade; and if the Indians are driven out, we had all best go too.

Robson: The honourable member for Lillooet [Humphreys] says that the Canadian policy will ruin the country and the Indians. I say, then, to be consistent, he must move an amendment that it shall not apply. To say that the Canadian policy will ruin the country shows simply ignorance.

Francis Barnard: I am convinced that the honourable attorney general [Crease] is right.

Alston: I must support the honourable member for New Westminster [Robson]. I say there is no Indian policy here, and I am sure that the Canadian policy is good.

Robson: I was induced to put an amendment because there is a resolution; otherwise, I would not have interfered.

Crease: My esteemed colleague, the honourable registrar general [Alston], says we have no Indian policy. I say our policy has been, let the Indians alone.

Alston: No, no!

Barnard: The reason I ask for the withdrawal of the resolution is that we cannot keep back from the Indians anything that happens here, and it will have a bad effect.

Crease: As these words may go forth, I wish to state on behalf of the government that the care of the Indians will be the first care of the imperial government and the local government.

Humphreys: I do not apprehend any danger from any discussion* in this house.

There are two lines of argument in this debate and it is difficult to say

Alston: I suggest the withdrawal of the resolution.

Carrall: I say that the Canadian policy has caused them to grow and prosper. I am at a loss to understand why honourable members should be afraid to trust to it.

Helmcken: The honourable member for Cariboo seems to find it difficult to understand my position. I think it right to endeavour to get the best terms we can and to point out difficulties. It is the duty of every man to do so. I am perfectly willing to sit here and make the best terms possible. When [the delegates] come back from Canada, it will be time enough for me to decide whether or not I shall support Confederation. I am now anti-confederate, but I may become a confederate if the terms are good. I say if the Indians are to be stuck on reservations, there will be a disturbance. I think, sir, that it will be well that there should be some opposition.

Robson: I wish to state I will withdraw my amendment if the honourable member will withdraw his motion.

Holbrook: I cannot do so* consistently with my duty.
— *Legislative Council, March 25, 1870*

NEWFOUNDLAND

J.O. Fraser: From all the information he had yet gathered upon the matter, he apprehended we were in no way warranted in

---

which is more fascinating. There is the equality debate (Should Indians be treated as the equals of non-Indians?), and there is the attempt to cover it up. To keep discussions in a parliamentary legislature secret runs counter to every principle of parliamentary government. Even in a quasi-representative legislature like British Columbia's (where appointed members are in the majority), open debate must be the rule. Secrecy is allowed in cabinet meetings and in party caucuses, but not in the House of Commons. Without this requirement for open debate we cannot be sure that political élites are not conniving behind our backs to pass laws benefiting themselves at our expense. And it is obviously just such connivance that Robson and company are endorsing. The bad conscience of members on this issue of open debate is very apparent. — JA
* *The amendment was withdrawn. Mr. Holbrook's resolution was lost by a vote of 20 to 1.*

fearing the disposition of the other colonies, and he was sorry that so absurd an idea prevailed as that "we are to be sold to the Canadians." If this consideration can be consummated, he firmly believed it would rebound greatly to the benefit of Newfoundland and that, instead of being regarded as enemies, we would be received as friends and brothers by the other provinces; our sympathies and interests are in many respects identical. That identity was not the result of our position, but the result of the blood that flows in our veins, our national antecedents and traditional, and the common sentiment of unity that animates a people flowing from a common stock.

— *Legislative Council, February 14, 1865*

"[Some object that] the peculiarities of our circumstances and the want of identity of interest with the other provinces, and our different pursuits, render [Confederation] inapplicable to us . . . To his mind the variety of pursuits formed the strongest reason why communities should confederate, because this caused the exchange of productions and supplying their mutual necessities; the interests of all were conceived by the association."

Ambrose Shea: [Some object that] the peculiarities of our circumstances and the want of identity of interest with the other provinces, and our different pursuits, render [Confederation] inapplicable to us. It appeared to him that, logically, to carry out the views of those who so object, that tailors and shoemakers, and all other trades, should each form distinct and separate communities apart from those whose pursuits were different. To his mind the variety of pursuits formed the strongest reason why communities should confederate, because this caused the exchange of productions and supplying their mutual necessities; the interests of all were conceived by the association.

[W]hen we look to other confederations, do we find no differences in their pursuits? What can be more diverse than the trades and avocations of the people of the different parts of the United States? . . . John Stuart Mill,* one of the profoundest thinkers of the day, in speaking of the conditions necessary for the beneficial confederation of states, says "the strongest of all is identity of political antecedents; the possession of a national history, and consequent community of recollections; collective pride and humiliation, pleasure and regret, connected with the same incidents in the past." Have we not these essentials in strict accord

---

* *The quotation is from chapter 16 of his* Considerations on Representative Government. *Oddly enough, that chapter discusses the ingredients of "nationality." It is chapter 17 which discusses the necessary conditions for federation on the American or Swiss model. I suspect that the slip reflects the intensity of Shea's desire, evident in other excerpts of his speeches printed here, to submerge his identity as a Newfoundlander in a larger British North American identity. — PR*

with those provinces with whom we propose to confederate, and when we consider the experience on which such views are founded, how small is the weight that should attach to objections that are thus so strikingly rebutted.

— House of Assembly, February 21, 1865

William Whiteway: He believed that considerable advantage to this colony would result from the free intercommunication which would be brought about between the several provinces now separated, and to a certain extent antagonistic. Free intercourse with our neighbours would tend to elevate our minds from those narrow and selfish views which invariably prevail with men living in an isolated condition. If it were calculated to do no more than to raise our thoughts above and draw them away from our present sectarian differences, and give us something to think about outside of ourselves and our petty disputes, it would be a benefit, and promote social happiness.

— House of Assembly, February 28, 1865

PRINCE EDWARD ISLAND

Joseph Arsenault: Some honourable members had spoken as if entering Confederation would be selling our country. He did not see it in that light. He viewed it as an alliance, and that with people like ourselves. Those here who claimed to be descendants of natives of Scotland, Ireland, England, or France, going to Canada would meet with the same class of people, (hear) the same customs, institutions, and laws as were here. He viewed it in the light of the alliance of a young gentleman to a lady. If the one was suited for the other, it would be an advantage to both. But one important condition was, it must be mutual, otherwise it would be an injury, if not the ruin of them both; and such were the conditions required before we should think of joining with the dominion. Were we united with the Canadas, we would still have the management of all our local affairs, but if the union was effected against the will of the people the alliance would not be happy, consequently he would be sorry to give a vote that would mar the happiness of the country.

— House of Assembly, March 10, 1868

"He believed that considerable advantage to this colony would result from the free intercommunication which would be brought about between the several provinces now separated, and to a certain extent antagonistic. Free intercourse with our neighbours would tend to elevate our minds from those narrow and selfish views which invariably prevail with men living in an isolated condition."

PART FOUR

WHAT THEY SAID ABOUT THE NEW NATIONALITY

Casting the Quebec Resolutions in legal language at the London Conference, 1866.

Chapter Nine

FEDERAL
UNION

*Issued "under the authority
and supervision" of "several
Government Departments,"
the* New Official Atlas of
the Dominion of Canada *included maps of
Newfoundland in addition
to the maps of the seven
provinces of the federation.
Among the special features of
the atlas were the statistical
tables, the compilations of
"General Information
specially written up by
competent authorities in
each Province," and the
"emigration and steamship
chart," showing the principal
routes by steamship from
Great Britain, and their
connection by rail with
the Pacific coast.*

O N THE EVE OF CONFEDERATION there are plans afoot for two smaller unions. It wouldn't be right to call them trial runs. "Near things" might be better, for they nearly come about.

The first is the legislative union of the Maritime provinces. In 1864, Nova Scotia, New Brunswick, and Prince Edward Island are on the brink of merging their separate identities to form one province with a single parliament. (A legislative union resembles a unitary state; there is only one constitutional level of government.) The second is the federal union of the Canadas. (A federal union has two levels of government, each with constitutional powers.) In strict terms of law at this time, the Canadian provinces are Canada West and Canada East, but in daily speech they retain the old names: Upper and Lower Canada. Thrown together in a legislative union in 1840, Upper Canada (soon to become Ontario) and Lower Canada (Quebec) are now casting around for ways to loosen the ties and to secure their separate identities. In short, the British North American imagination is buzzing with ideas about union: three provinces? Two? Federal union, legislative union?

Mix, match, add rhetoric, and the result is the formula that comes out of the Quebec Conference: federal union of the Canadas, the Maritime provinces, and Newfoundland.

Canadian Confederation is one of the world's most successful and longest-lasting federal systems. This is not to say that there haven't been problems. And how Canadians love to dwell on those problems: the quarrels between the levels of government, the threats, the crises! Not to mention the disputes in the courts and in the classroom about what the Fathers intended in the first

place. More scholarly ink has been spilt on the issue of the federal division of legislative powers than on any other aspect of Confederation. Yet, surprisingly, scholars have seldom turned to the legislative debates to find out just what was said.

NOVA SCOTIA

Getting around at the Charlottetown Conference of 1864!

James Johnston: My scheme originally was for union of the whole of the British American provinces. It seems, however, there are such difficulties in the way of this greater union as to render it impracticable for the present. I look at the union of the lower provinces*as a step towards the larger one. I have never favoured a union of the provinces by way of federation, for it did not appear to tend to the great object we had in view. What we want is to produce a real unity — make the parts that are now separate a homogeneous whole — give them a oneness of existence and of purpose.

— *House of Assembly, March 28, 1864*

Charles Tupper: I need not tell the house that a great deal of discussion has taken place in times past as to whether a legislative or federal union would be the best mode by which these provinces could be united, and I believe that I will be able to show this house that whilst a legislative union was really not practically before us — for there were difficulties lying in its path such as to render its adoption impossible — yet the union which was devised by the Quebec Conference possessed all the advantages of both† without the disadvantages that attended each separately. No person who is acquainted with the character of legislative union but knows, when it is proposed for a country with the area and extent of territory that British America possesses, its realization is attended with great difficulties, if not with insuperable obstacles. No person who is acquainted with what has taken place in the imperial parliament but knows that great as that country has become under a legislative union, yet the difficulties con-

---

* *Johnston is describing the proposed union of the Maritime provinces, which was to have been discussed at the Charlottetown Conference of September 1864. — PR*

† *Advocates of Confederation commonly tried to assure those who disliked the idea of federal union that the Quebec scheme secured all the advantages of legislative union as well. — PR*

nected with the union are such as at this moment to be occupying the attention of the foremost statesmen of Great Britain.

The difficulties in the way of a legislative union are that the legislature has not only to be occupied with the discussion of the great and leading questions which touch the vital interests of every section of the country, but to give its attention largely to matters of merely local concern. At present, the [British] parliament is obliged to take up and consider from five to six hundred local bills. When we consider that this body of six hundred men — the most influential and important assemblage of statesmen in the world, are called upon to give their attention upon some five hundred bills, which are not of general but of purely local concern, you can imagine the difficulty of carrying on the legislation of such a country. It is not strange that under such circumstances the parliament is obliged to sit eight out of twelve months in order to accomplish the legislation required at their hands.

If a legislative union were devised for British North America, the people occupying the different sections would not have the guarantee that they have under the scheme devised that matters of a local character would occupy the attention of the local legislatures, whilst those of a general nature would be entrusted to the general legislature. Therefore the scheme that was devised gave centralization and consolidation and unity that it was absolutely indispensable should be given. On the other hand, instead of having copied the defects of the federal constitution — instead of having the inherent weakness that must always attend a system where the local legislatures only impart certain powers to the government of the country — quite a different course was pursued,* and it was decided to define the questions that should be reserved for local legislatures, and those great subjects that should be entrusted to the general parliament. Therefore, whilst

---

* In considering the division of legislative power, the Quebec Conference rejected the American model, which specified the powers of the general legislature and left everything else to the local ones. They did so because they thought it made the federal government constitutionally inferior to the individual states. Tupper here states in part what they did instead: i.e., specify the powers of both the general and the local legislatures. One can see from no. 29 of the conference resolutions that they also gave the general legislature the power to legislate for the peace, welfare, and good government of the federated provinces. For this reason, some spoke of the arrangement as a reversal of the American model, though in fact it was a compromise. — PR

the unity and consolidation connected with legislative union was obtained on the one hand, due care and attention to local matters interesting to each province were provided for by the preservation of local parliaments, and these powers were so arranged as to prevent any conflict or struggle which might lead to any difficulty between the several sections . . .

It was proposed . . . that all the questions of leading general importance should be entrusted to the general government . . . To the local governments were reserved powers of an important character, though of a local interest, which could be exercised without any interference whatever with the unity and strength of the central government . . . The local governments would not interfere with the powers of the general government, or weaken its strength and unity of action, but would be able to deal with such questions as touch the local interests of the country — the construction of roads and bridges, public works, civil jurisdiction, etc. . . .

Was our representation in the Commons the only guarantee that our rights would not be trampled upon? It is ample security; but I am ready to show the house the most extravagant demand that could enter into the mind of any man was conceded in the scheme of government for these provinces. I need not tell this house of the potent influence that is exercised in legislation by the Legislative Council. We have seen several striking examples of questions on which three-fourths of this body concurred, and yet this house did not succeed in attaining its object because it did not meet with the concurrence of the upper branch. It requires two to make a bargain and pass a law. I ask you, then, if you wish for a guarantee that the security of the people of the Maritime provinces will never be ignored, could you have a stronger one than that 600,000 people in these Maritime provinces should have obtained, under such a constitution, the same representation in the upper branch as was given to Upper Canada with 1,400,000 and to Lower Canada with 1,100,000? This we have for all time to come, although Upper Canada may increase to millions of people. Then I would ask the intelligent people of this country if the parties who devised the constitution did not give us all the security that our rights and interests could demand.

— *House of Assembly, April 10, 1865*

John Bourinot: [The scheme] provides for a federal union of these provinces. I have no hesitation in saying that if the conference had devised a legislative union, it would have been

preferable. Everyone knows what the local legislatures will be under this scheme — very insignificant bodies. Another portion of the scheme provides that the lieutenant governors shall be selected by the governor general at Ottawa. What class of men shall we, then, have for our local governors? These very men who formed the convention. But how would they be looked upon? The position of lieutenant governor would become a mockery in the estimation of the public. I can understand the principle that induced the British government to elevate Mr. Hincks* to a colonial governorship, and should like to see it extended to Mr. [Joseph] Howe, who has far higher claims than the former to such a position; but anyone must see that the people would never approve of any public man being made governor in his own colony.

It has never yet been fully explained why we have been given local legislatures in this scheme. It might be satisfactory to the Lower Canadians, but it would never do for these other provinces. The municipal system that is in full operation in Canada West, or the very system of county sessions that exists here now, might have done the work assigned to the local legislatures. If the Lower Canadians would not agree to legislative union, an arrangement might have been made so as to give them the control of those matters in which they felt especial interest without interfering with the rest of the provinces. I am glad, however, that some gentlemen who formed part of the conference had some respect for that section of Canada which has been so trampled upon by the western Canadians for years past. It is known to many that Upper Canada has long been endeavouring to deprive Lower Canada of many of those institutions and rights which they value — the very principle upon which the union was formed[†] it has been attempted to destroy. Just in that way would the Upper Canadians, in case of a confederation, endeavour to override the interests and rights of these Maritime provinces . . .

— *House of Assembly, April 17, 1865*

---

* *Sir Francis Hincks (1807–1885) played a leading part in the struggle for responsible government in Canada and was premier from 1851 to 1854. From 1856 to 1869 he was governor, first of Barbados and the Windward Islands and then of British Guiana. He was Canadian minister of finance, 1869–73.*
† *Bourinot alludes to the sectional basis of parliamentary representation. Maritime critics of the Quebec scheme tended to favour that idea, since it would give them more seats in the general legislature than representation by population. By* western, *Bourinot means Upper as opposed to Lower Canadians. — PR*

"Talent and energy will assert their proper positions in the general legislature as it does here and everywhere under free institutions. Nova Scotia may be a small province, but her men will be able to hold their own, I trust, in the united parliament. "

William Henry: We propose only to transfer certain powers to a legislative body comprising a fair representation of our own, chosen on the principle of population. It is not a confederation in the strict term of the word. It is a legislative union to a large extent. The people will elect their representatives as they do now, and each county will have its member in the general parliament. Objection has been taken to the principle of representation based on population, but what else can you have? We could not expect to have as large a representation as Canada, nor could Prince Edward Island ask as many representatives as Nova Scotia or New Brunswick, and if the numbers were not to be equal, I ask these gentlemen upon what principle would they be regulated except on that of population? . . .

We are told that this is not a legislative union, because all the subjects that come before a legislature are not embraced in it. If they are not embraced in it, Nova Scotia has not therefore much cause for complaint. Education, roads and bridges, control of our jurisprudence, and other subjects in which we take the deepest interest are left to our own control. Then we have the same amount per head for our local government that they have in Canada, and if we manage to spend more money in proportion to our population than she does, it is only right we should pay for it. We go into that union on the same terms. Every man, woman, and child will owe the same debt — receive the same amount from the general exchequer — as each man, woman, and child in Canada, and we shall have our full share of all the expenditures by the general government for important public objects.

Talent and energy will assert their proper positions in the general legislature as it does here and everywhere under free institutions. Nova Scotia may be a small province, but her men will be able to hold their own, I trust, in the united parliament. The nineteen men she will select to represent her will, I have no doubt, be able to protect her interests . . .

Party government must prevail in the new parliament. There must, as in all countries under responsible government, be a government and an opposition, and Nova Scotia will exercise with her nineteen members a sufficient influence. There is no party, however strong, that can afford to neglect the legitimate local interests of any one of their supporters. This government came into power some years ago, with a majority such as was never seen before in Nova Scotia, and who can allege that the local interests of any section were neglected? It is true that no govern-

ment can satisfy the demands of all their followers — nor can they in adopting a general line of policy satisfy their friends; but I am now referring to the local interests that are to be represented . . . I am free to say that the gentlemen from Nova Scotia will get their fair share of everything that they require, for there is no party at Ottawa that could refuse it to them with impunity. We all know that the Irish party, comparatively few in number, to a large extent, controlled public matters for years in the British parliament.*

— House of Assembly, April 16, 1866

John Tobin: [The Quebec Resolutions] were submitted to the imperial government, and Mr. Cardwell [the British colonial secretary] only takes exception to two of the resolutions — with respect to the constitution of the Legislative Council† and the pardoning power‡ granted to the lieutenant governors. After having been examined by the statesmen and press of England, as well as

---

* The Irish nationalists under Daniel O'Connell and later under Charles Parnell did, on a number of occasions in the nineteenth century, control the balance of power at Westminster. Their usual strength was about eighty seats. — IG

† Cardwell, the colonial secretary, criticized the proposal for a fixed number of members, divided proportionately according to region. In the federal scheme, of course, this was an essential counterbalance to representation by population in the House of Commons. Cardwell's objection was met by giving the governor general discretion to appoint six extra members, three from Ontario and Quebec and three from the Maritime provinces. — PR

‡ This was an incident of the royal prerogative, and some doubted whether an officer not directly appointed by the British government could constitutionally exercise it. Because of Cardwell's objection, the London Conference of 1866 transferred the power to the governor general. The question was important because the constitutional status of the lieutenant governors bore on that of the provinces. If the queen was not directly represented in the provincial governments, then they must be subordinate to that of the dominion. The British government and the Supreme Court of Canada both took this position. On becoming premier of Ontario in 1872, Oliver Mowat set out to establish that the lieutenant governor did directly represent the queen, and that the provinces, therefore, were in essence constitutionally equal to the dominion. In the end he succeeded, establishing in the process the lieutenant governor's right to exercise the prerogative of pardon so far as offences against provincial law were concerned. — PR

McGee's book on federations was published in both English and French. The French edition does not include the appendix on the New Zealand Constitution.

of North America, and approved by such eminent authorities on both continents, I think these resolutions must be entitled to much respect; and therefore I cannot go to the length that some people do in respect to this scheme. Although delegates may be appointed by the provinces to discuss the question of colonial union in England, the resolutions must form the platform — the basis of that discussion.

William Ross: [It has been said] that this house will remain. But take away from us the power of self-government, and you take away what we most dearly cherish. The Quebec scheme is largely copied from the constitution of New Zealand,* and it is singular that the constitution of that country was published by Mr. McGee about the time that our delegates were giving away Nova Scotia to meet Canadian necessities. In New Zealand there are nine different provinces, each having its own distinct local government, and there they complain that they are expensive, without any benefits arising from the expenditure. In that country they are strongly advocating separation, and the whole province of Auckland is unanimous in agitating a separation from the southern Island. The confederation works injuriously to the interests of the people, and we are about adopting what they are most anxious to reject. The governor of New Zealand is called

---

As the only British territory with a federal constitution, New Zealand was an important precedent. The New Zealand constitution of 1852, an act of the British parliament, divided the colony into six provinces (not nine, as Ross is reported as saying) with representative and responsible institutions. But the Quebec Resolutions cannot be called a "copy." The Quebec formula guarantees both federal powers and provincial powers; the provinces are to be secure in their areas of legislative competence. New Zealand, in contrast, guaranteed only the federal powers. There was a list of subjects on which the provinces were not to legislate, but no corresponding restriction on the general government. In Notes on Federal Governments, Past and Present *(1865), Thomas D'Arcy McGee published the New Zealand Act in full, describing it as the outstanding example of a federation with strength at the centre.* Notes *ambitiously surveys ancient and modern associations of states to preach the moral that loose confederations are less stable, allow less liberty, and contribute less to the arts and commerce. It finds proof of New Zealand's superior formula in the colony's thriving economy. In 1876 the New Zealand Constitutional Act was rescinded. New Zealand is now governed in the fashion of Great Britain by an "unwritten" constitution. — JA*

the superintendent,* and is elected by the people; but here our local governor, selected by the government at Ottawa, would be some creature that had claims on the political party in power and who would not have popularity enough to get a seat at Ottawa. Such will be the men who will be the future governors of these colonies. The House of Assembly is bad enough now, but then it will be worse; they will be like the case of a certain house from which the moneychangers were driven.†

If we are to have British institutions, why do we not follow their pattern? When Scotland was united to England, the local parliament was abolished, and such was the case in Ireland. If we are to have union, let it be a legislative one. There is something grand in the idea of one government, one legislature — but in retaining the local legislature, we will have the expense without any corresponding benefit — the shadow without the substance — a nest of corruption for persons who will not be able to obtain seats at Ottawa.

— House of Assembly, April 17, 1866

NEW BRUNSWICK

The New Brunswick legislative building.

Robert Thomson: By adopting this scheme we surrender our independence and become dependent upon Canada, for this federal government will have the veto power upon our legislation. The 51st section of the scheme says: "Any Bill passed by the General Parliament shall be subject to disallowance by Her Majesty within two years, as in the case of bills passed by the Legislatures of the said Provinces hitherto; in like manner any Bill passed by a local Legislature shall be subject to disallowance by the Governor General within one year after the passing thereof." Here is a written constitution with certain rights given and accorded to the local legislatures, and certain rights are given to the general government. Suppose there is a conflict between the two governments, where is the appeal? In the United States they have an appeal to the judges of the land; but here the general

---

During the drafting of the BNA Act in 1867, British officials did their best to reduce the status of the provinces as established by the Quebec and London resolutions. One method was by calling the provincial head of government superintendent *instead of* lieutenant governor. *The colonial delegates rejected the change. — PR*

† *Matthew 21:12. — IG*

government has an arbitrary veto* and we have to submit. I think this is a very serious defect in the constitution.

— *House of Assembly, June 1, 1865*

Abner McClellan: Another objection taken was, the bills framed by the local legislatures would be liable to be disallowed by the general government. I do not see the point of this objection, as our local bills may now be disallowed by a power farther off, and whereas in the general government we should have representatives to explain and support them, in England we have none at all.

— *House of Assembly, June 2, 1865*

John McMillan: It has been said that under Confederation we should dwindle down to a mere municipality, yet this session only two measures have come before us — the Treasury Note Bill and the Post Office Bill — that would not be discussed in the local legislature. But, it is asked, who would come here as a representative under Confederation? I reply that our young men of intellect and power would come here to obtain a political education, to fit them for positions in the general government, and for a governorship of the colonies. It is a high and grand principle of ambition implanted in the human heart and [will] . . . animate our young men to raise themselves to positions of rank and power.

— *House of Assembly, June 5, 1865*

William Gilbert: [Honourable colleagues] talked about checks in the upper house to the principle of representation by population. But what check could there be unless it came from the people themselves? Would [they] say that fifteen representatives for New Brunswick in the lower house in the general confederated parliament would be sufficient if the proportion of representation for the lower provinces remained as it was under the scheme? Would anyone say that it would be a sufficient safeguard to the province if the lower house sought to override its rights to have that

---

* Thomson succinctly states the reason the federal power of disallowance was so controversial: it was discretionary and not subject to judicial appeal. Of course, the analogous imperial power was subject to strict constitutional constraints as an interference with colonial self-government, and Oliver Mowat later asserted that the Quebec Conference had understood that the dominion's veto power would be subject to similar constraints. See A.-A. Dorion's discussion in this chapter for an astute, though ultimately unjustified, criticism of that arrangement. — PR

increased representation in the upper branch? (Here the honourable member referred, in illustration of his argument that the upper house could not check encroachment, by pointing to the British House of Lords — the most powerful and peculiarly privileged political body in the world — to show that even that august body was unable to check the popular principle. He gave as an instance the passage of the first Reform Bill in England,* when in the face of the resolution of the majority of the House of Lords to oppose it, they, with the Iron Duke at the head, had been forced to give way to the determination of the people that the bill should pass.) If his honourable colleague said he would agree to representation by population, if neutralized by some check in the upper branch, he was, knowing as he must, how powerless any check there would be to the popular principle, in fact as thoroughgoing and as strong a unionist as George Brown himself.

— *House of Assembly, March 27, 1866*

Albert J. Smith: Delegates . . . have probably taken the idea [for representation by population] from the plan adopted by the constitution of the United States. There they have representation by population in the House of Representatives. But in the Senate it is provided that every state alike send two senators. And it must be remembered that the Senate of the United States has executive as well as legislative functions; it has power even to veto many of the acts of the president. What he does must have their approval and consent. They have a check on the House of Representatives. But under the provisions of this scheme, the people's house will be the all-important and all-powerful branch, for they will be able even to overturn the executive of the country. It is not so in the United States. While the framers of this scheme have copied this provision from the United States, have they given us the same checks as are provided there? Not at all. There every state, large and small, sends one [sic] representative to the Senate.

Thus Canada is not only to have the great majority in the lower house, but in the Legislative Council she is to be represented by forty-eight members,† whilst all the lower provinces

---

Passed in 1832, it provided for only a modest extension of the franchise. It was vehemently opposed by Wellington — "the Iron Duke" — and other peers.
†*Smith's monolithic conception of United Canada is remarkable, given that the Quebec scheme had originated in an agreement to federalize that province. — PR*

SIR SAMUEL LEONARD
TILLEY
(1818–1896), Loyalist
and druggist. Tilley
entered politics to
promote the prohibition
of alcohol. In 1854 he
became provincial
secretary in New
Brunswick's first
responsible cabinet.
Excepting a year in
1856–57, he retained the
office (which included
the Finance portfolio)
until defeated over
Confederation in 1865;
from 1861 he was also
premier. In 1866 he
regained the premiership
and proceeded to carry
the province into
Confederation. Though
a Reformer, he served in
John A. Macdonald's
federal cabinets from
1867 to 1873 and 1878
to 1885, and as minister
of finance he designed
and implemented the
National Policy of
industrial tariff
protection. He was
lieutenant governor of
New Brunswick in
1873–78 and 1885–93.

will only have twenty-four . . . It may be asked why we should
have an equal number with them in the second branch? I say
because they have full power and control in the lower house . . .
In the United States the senators are elected by the people,* and
not for life, but one-third of their numbers every two years. But
here they acknowledge no sway from the people, and with all this
Canada is to have a two-thirds majority in that house . . .

Now how are differences and controversies on this subject to
be settled? Have they a superior court to which the matter can be
carried as in the United States, where differences between states
and the general government can be carried and settled? No, there
is nothing of the kind provided. Is it not important that there
should be some tribunal where disputes of this nature may be
settled; and I ask the attorney general to look into the matter and
provide for some means of appeal. But even then there is the
other power they possess of vetoing any action of the local legislatures. Should we submit that Canada should have the power to
abrogate and nullify all or any of our legislation, with no power
to which to appeal? They have also left us the power of managing
our own private or local affairs, but the question may be raised
what is private and local, and then who is to determine?

S.L. Tilley: The honourable member [Smith] stated that it was
probable our local legislature would be left without any powers,
and dwindle down so low that its action would be a mere farce.
Now, whatever may be the opinion of the honourable member
with regard to this legislature, or of Mr. Brown† in reference to
the local government of Upper Canada, I believe that our constitution will remain just as it is. It is a fact that out of the whole

---

*Smith is mistaken: until 1913, U.S. senators were elected by their state
legislature. — PR*

†*At the Quebec Conference, Brown is reported to have urged that the local
legislatures should consist of a single chamber elected for a fixed term of three
years. The executive officers would be elected by the legislature from outside
its ranks, and would have the right to speak in the legislature but not to
vote. He justified his proposal by emphasizing the "insignificance" of the
powers that the Charlottetown Conference proposed to assign to the local governments. Historians have identified this expression of Brown's views with
those of his party, in order to brand the Ontario Reformers' defence of
provincial rights within Confederation as a volte-face; but to the extent that
his views on this occasion represented a repudiation of the Reformers' normal*

number of bills passed by this legislature in 1864, all but seven would have come before us in Confederation, and all but three during the last session. No, the work to be performed will not dwindle down to insignificance.

— House of Assembly, June 27, 1866

Tilley: He [Smith] says we have not a sufficient number of representatives in the upper branch of the legislature. There might be some concessions made to us in this. When the arrangement was made, and representation by population was conceded, it was considered that there was a great protection given to the Maritime provinces, for New Brunswick was to have one representative for every 25,000 of her population, Lower Canada one to every 50,000, and Upper Canada one to every 75,000 . . . In every case the interests of the Maritime provinces are nearly identical, and there is scarcely an important question that can come up in which Lower Canada would not be with us . . . Again there is a protection in the fact that the number of representatives in the upper branch cannot be increased by the crown.

Francis Hibbard: Presuming the constitution is made, will there never be a means of amending it?

Smith: The American constitution has a provision for amendment.*

Hibbard: Perhaps the delegates will see that a provision for that is inserted in ours.

— House of Assembly, June 28, 1866

C.N. Skinner: He would, if he could, secure some modification to the provision for representation by population. He heard that this could not be done, but still he would claim it as a right and a benefit to all the colonies. The Quebec scheme was started at the time of war in the United States, before [Ulysses S.] Grant had taken Richmond or [William] Sherman had made his grand march through Georgia to the ocean, when they thought that the

---

concern for Upper Canadian autonomy, there is no reason to suppose that he was speaking for anyone but himself. — PR

* Neither the Quebec scheme nor the BNA Act made any provision for amending the Canadian Constitution. The omission caused lasting uncertainty as to the proper procedure.

republic was in the throes of dissolution, and consequently it was the negation of all that was found in the American Constitution. There the states have the power, and that power they wield for the general good. But in the Quebec scheme the general government take all the power and dribble it out to the separate states. This was a feature of the scheme he had always been opposed to. If the delegates had intended to have formed a separate nationality, he could have forgiven them for this, but they did not, neither did the people desire a new flag or the power to make war, to coin money, or any other functions performed by an independent power. All they wanted was to form a union for the purposes of commerce and defence. If the provinces had been going into a legislative union they would not have needed a scheme, the common law would have sufficed as the basis, but in a federal union it was necessary that the constitution should be a written one, and it requires the greatest care and deliberation in the preparation of its provisions.

"If New Brunswick or Nova Scotia were to pass a law which they found to be required and it was afterwards declared unconstitutional by the general government, it would cause a great deal of discontent. The whole might be obviated by placing the matter in the judiciary, for the reverence of our people for the bench is deep and constant."

Then the central government had a veto power over all the acts of the provinces. If New Brunswick or Nova Scotia were to pass a law which they found to be required and it was afterwards declared unconstitutional by the general government, it would cause a great deal of discontent. The whole might be obviated by placing the matter in the judiciary, for the reverence of our people for the bench is deep and constant . . . Yes, if the veto power were in the hands of the judges, the people would bow to their decisions, but they would not if left with politicians.

Then he did not see any check by which the constitution was secured to us provided the other provinces wished to alter it. The constitution of the United States provided that it could not be altered without an appeal and vote of three-fourths of the states. He thought if this were done we should be much safer. Then if they could alter the general constitution, why may they not after a time obtain the power to alter the local constitution? If these things were not secured, he would have it done.

— *House of Assembly, June 29, 1866*

Charles Fisher: The model of our constitution has been the British parliament. The head of our government is to be the queen's representative. We only apply the principle of the American Constitution as far as they work out some of the principles we have adopted as incident to our position . . . I think the constitution provides checks in the upper branch. This branch is

entirely distinct from the American Senate. The Senate, together with the people, can make treaties, and they require no further action from the legislative body, but a treaty made by the government of Great Britain is a powerless instrument unless enacted by the parliament . . . In the United States Senate each state has an equal representation; he objects to the scheme because it does not make this provision . . .

In the United States all power is in the people, and they confer a certain portion of that power upon the government of the different states, another portion to the federal government, and another portion they keep themselves.* There is no analogy between their government and ours; they require a court of appeal as necessary to their condition. Our parliament is all-powerful, all the power that is not conferred upon the local legislature is given to the general government. The tendency of this arrangement is to a legislative union. It will arise out of this in the future, and be the final result.

— *House of Assembly, June 30, 1866*

"In regard to the establishment of a court for the determination of questions and disputes that may arise between the federal and local governments as to the meaning of the act of union, I am opposed to having the judiciary or fourth branch to override the other three. The power of the judges in the United States is different from the power of the judges in our country."

John Mercer Johnson: In regard to the establishment of a court for the determination of questions and disputes that may arise between the federal and local governments as to the meaning of the act of union, I am opposed to having the judiciary or fourth branch to override the other three. The power of the judges in the United States is different from the power of the judges in our country. There they have the power to say to nine-tenths of the legislature, you have no right to pass that law, and therefore prevent the legislature of the country from legislating for the advantage of the country. It is not necessary in our case, because we stand in a very different position from what they do in the United States. When the United States legislatures pass laws which conflict with each other, it may be necessary to have a court of appeal; but we have the imperial parliament behind us, and this makes the distinction between us.

Suppose the general government passed a law that infringed upon the rights of the local legislatures; that must receive royal sanction before it can become law, and we can bring the matter before the imperial parliament and get redress.

— *House of Assembly, July 2, 1866*

---

* Fisher's understanding of the U.S. Constitution is more exact than that expressed by his colleague John Mercer Johnson in chapter 6. — PR

"But under responsible government, all experience goes to prove that, however paradoxical it may appear, minorities in the legislature are more to be feared than majorities, as small minorities frequently turn the scale."

Edward Chandler: [Another] objection that I notice is the constitution of the Legislative Council, which elicited a great deal of discussion, but was ultimately agreed to quite unanimously . . . If Canada increases as she has in the past, our representation will become as three to one compared with hers, for the number of members in the upper house is fixed for all time to come and cannot be altered. Now, I ask, what greater protection could be afforded in the construction of the Legislative Council than has been provided? The upper house will represent the colonies, and supposing the possibility of any measure passing the lower branch or of the whole Confederation, the safeguard is provided and the Legislative Council would stop the measure.

But under responsible government, all experience goes to prove that, however paradoxical it may appear, minorities in the legislature are more to be feared than majorities, as small minorities frequently turn the scale, and therefore we have less danger to apprehend in this union. In Canada there always has been and always will be two parties. Now, it will be evidently the policy of each of these parties to seek the countenance and assistance of the lower colonies, who, on questions involving the fate of the general government, as well as in minor matters, would really control the vote; and if they should combine against us, it would only drive us into combination, and our comparative weakness would tend to ensure our success, because we should immediately enlist the sympathies of one party or the other, as well as cement and secure the sympathies of the several lower provinces in action for the assistance of each other and their united interests . . .

It will be said that in Congress there are two representatives from each state, and the same system should be adopted in the federal Legislative Council, but those who make such remarks forget the difference in the constitutions of the two houses; they forget that there the system of executive responsibility that obtains here is unknown, and that the president has, for the time being, a supreme power. The Senate of the United States has not only legislative but as well executive powers, and can at any time adjourn its legislative session and go into secret executive session. Its assent is required to all treaties, and to make peace or declare war; it confirms the appointment of judges and ambassadors, and all other general appointments; it has the power of impeachment, and is therefore a great court of justice, so that having such vast powers it is unlike any body under our constitution.

We have, I think, in the constitution of the Legislative Council,

provided all the guards and recognized all the local rights that can be reasonably asked for, and New Brunswick certainly stands in a better position than any of her sister colonies. While Nova Scotia has 100,000 more inhabitants than New Brunswick, the representation in the council is the same, because the basis of the council is not population but territorial . . .

— *Legislative Council, April 4, 1866*

CANADA

John A. Macdonald: There were only three modes . . . that were at all suggested by which the deadlock in our affairs,* the anarchy we dreaded, and the evils which retarded our prosperity could be met or averted. One was the dissolution of the union between Upper and Lower Canada, leaving them as they were before the union of 1841. I believe that that proposition by itself had no supporters. It was felt by everyone that, although it was a course which would do away with the sectional difficulties which existed — it would remove the pressure on the part of the people of Upper Canada for the representation based on population, and the jealousy of the people of Lower Canada lest their institutions should be attacked and prejudiced by that principle in our representation — yet it was felt by every thinking man in the province that it would be a retrograde step, which would throw back the country to nearly the same position as it occupied before the union. It would lower the credit enjoyed by United Canada, it would be the breaking up of a connection which had existed for nearly a quarter of a century, and, under which, although it had not been completely successful and had not allayed altogether the local jealousies that had their root in circumstances which arose before the union, [still] our province, as a whole, had nevertheless prospered and increased. It was felt that a dissolution of the union would have destroyed all the credit that we had gained by being a united province and would have left us two weak and ineffective governments, instead of one powerful and united people. (Hear, hear.)

The next mode suggested was the granting of representation by population. Now, we all know the manner in which that ques-

---

* *Macdonald refers to the polarization of Canadian politics by the issue of representation by population, the situation that persuaded him and Cartier to agree to George Brown's proposal to federalize United Canada.* — PR

tion was and is regarded by Lower Canada; that while in Upper Canada the desire and cry for it was daily augmenting, the resistance to it in Lower Canada was proportionably increasing in strength. Still, if some such means of relieving us from the sectional jealousies which existed between the two Canadas, if some such solution of the difficulties as Confederation had not been found, the representation by population must eventually have been carried; no matter though it might have been felt in Lower Canada, as being a breach of the treaty of union,* no matter how much it might have been felt by the Lower Canadians that it would sacrifice their local interests, it is certain that in the progress of events representation by population would have been carried; and, had it been carried — I speak here my own individual sentiments — I do not think it would have been for the interest of Upper Canada. For though Upper Canada would have felt that it had received what it claimed as a right, and had suc-

*What treaty? The sectional basis of parliamentary representation was established by the British statute of 1840 that united Upper and Lower Canada — a statute passed without any consultation with French Canadians and without their concurrence. In 1856 another British statute enabled the Canadian legislature to institute representation by population. By treaty, Macdonald must mean that, in the eyes of French Canadians, sectional equality was so fundamental to the Canadian Constitution that they would have perceived the legislature's use of its legal power to alter it as a breach of trust amounting to what the philosopher John Locke termed a dissolution of government.

Macdonald's recognition and implicit acceptance of this idea places him in a tradition of Canadian constitutional thought dating at least from the 1820s to the present day. In the 1820s both Lower Canadian Patriotes and Upper Canadian Reformers had seen the Constitutional Act of 1791 (the British statute that constituted the two colonies) as being in effect a treaty between their respective peoples and the imperial power, and on that basis they had denied that the British Parliament had the right to alter the act without the consent of the people affected. After Confederation, this idea of the necessity of consent to constitutional change would find expression in the compact theory of Confederation, which insisted that the consent of all the provinces was a prerequisite for any amendment of the British North America Act, or at least any that diminished provincial powers. On the basis of this theory the patriation of the Canadian Constitution in 1982 against the wishes of the government of Quebec has been characterized as a Lockean dissolution of government. — PR

ceed[ed] in establishing its right, yet it would have left the lower province with a sullen feeling of injury and injustice. The Lower Canadians would not have worked cheerfully under such a change of system, but would have ceased to be what they are now — a nationality,* with representatives in parliament, governed by general principles, and divided according to their political opinions — and would have been in great danger of becoming a faction, forgetful of national obligations, and only actuated by a desire to defend their own sectional interests, their own laws, and their own institutions. (Hear, hear.)

The third and only means of solution for our difficulties was the junction of the provinces either in a federal or a legislative union. Now, as regards the comparative advantages of a legislative and a federal union, I have never hesitated to state my own opinions. I have again and again stated in the house that, if practicable, I thought a legislative union would be preferable. (Hear, hear.) I have always contended that if we could agree to have one government and one parliament, legislating for the whole of these peoples, it would be the best, the cheapest, the most vigorous, and the strongest system of government we could adopt. (Hear, hear.) But, on looking at the subject in the conference . . . we found that such a system was impracticable. In the first place, it would not meet the assent of the people of Lower Canada because they felt that in their peculiar position — being in a minority, with a different language, nationality, and religion from the majority — in case of a junction with the other provinces, their institutions and their laws might be assailed, and their ancestral associations, on which they prided themselves, attacked and prejudiced; it was found that any proposition which involved the absorption of the individuality of Lower Canada . . . would not be received with favour by her people. We found, too, that though their people speak the same language and enjoy the same system of law as the people of Upper Canada, a system founded

---

Lower (i.e., French) Canadians are a nationality because (as Macdonald explains below) the treaty of union underpins a federal system, under which they are effectively self-governing. Under representation by population they would "cease to be a nationality" because their reduction to minority status within a purely unitary system would destroy the conditions that make them self-governing. Rather than being divided into political parties according to their principles, they would become a faction: a political bloc with sectional loyalties that transcend their commitment to the polity. — PR

on the common law of England, there was as great a disinclination on the part of the various Maritime provinces to lose their
individuality, as separate political organizations, as we observed
in the case of Lower Canada herself. (Hear, hear.) Therefore, we
were forced to the conclusion that we must either abandon the
idea of union altogether or devise a system of union in which
the separate provincial organizations would be in some degree
preserved.

We, in Canada, already know something of the advantages
and disadvantages of a federal union. Although we have nomi-
nally a legislative union in Canada — although we sit in one
parliament, supposed constitutionally to represent the people
without regard to sections or localities, yet we know, as a matter
of fact, that since the union in 1841 we have had a federal union;
that in matters affecting Upper Canada solely, members from
that section claimed and generally exercised the right of exclusive
legislation, while members from Lower Canada legislated in matters affecting only their own section. We have had a federal union
in fact,* though a legislative union in name . . .

The conference having come to the conclusion that a legislative union, pure and simple, was impracticable, our next attempt
was to form a government upon federal principles, which would
give to the general government the strength of a legislative and
administrative union, while at the same time it preserved that liberty of action for the different sections which is allowed by a
federal union. And I am strong in the belief that we have hit upon
the happy medium in those resolutions, and that we have formed

---

* Listening to Macdonald, you might wonder why it had been found necessary
to federalize what was already a federal union in fact. One reason was that
United Canada was not in fact a legislative union in name only, and that on
several occasions Lower Canadian votes had imposed on Upper Canada institutions and policies that offended Upper Canadian public opinion: most
notoriously, publicly funded Roman Catholic schools. Throughout his speech,
Macdonald resolutely ignores this Upper Canadian grievance, though it was
largely to blame for the political deadlock that had moved Cartier, Brown,
and himself to pursue Confederation. He ignores Upper Canadians' interest
in preserving their distinct society; he ignores the option of federalizing
United Canada rather than pursuing a broader Confederation; he ignores
the existence of a standpoint from which the French-Canadian minority
appears as an alien oppressor, imposing unwelcome policies on Upper Canada
in alliance with his own party. — PR

"It is the fashion now to enlarge on the defects of the constitution of the United States, but I am not one of those who look upon it as a failure. I think and believe that it is one of the most skilful works which human intelligence ever created; is one of the most perfect organizations that ever governed a free people. To say that it has some defects is but to say that it is not the work of Omniscience, but of human intellects."

a scheme of government which unites the advantages of both, giving us the strength of a legislative union and the sectional freedom of a federal union, with protection to local interests.

In doing so we had the advantage of the experience of the United States. It is the fashion now to enlarge on the defects of the constitution of the United States, but I am not one of those who look upon it as a failure. (Hear, hear.) I think and believe that it is one of the most skilful works which human intelligence ever created; is one of the most perfect organizations that ever governed a free people. To say that it has some defects is but to say that it is not the work of Omniscience, but of human intellects. We are happily situated in having had the opportunity of watching its operation, seeing its working from its infancy till now. It was in the main formed on the model of the constitution of Great Britain, adapted to the circumstances of a new country, and was perhaps the only practicable system that could have been adopted under the circumstances existing at the time of its formation. We can now take advantage of the experience of the last seventy-eight years, during which that constitution has existed, and I am strongly of the belief that we have, in a great measure, avoided in this system which we propose for the adoption of the people of Canada the defects which time and events have shown to exist in the American Constitution.

In the first place, by a resolution which meets with the universal approval of the people of this country, we have provided that for all time to come, so far as we can legislate for the future, we shall have as the head of the executive power the sovereign of Great Britain. (Hear, hear.) No one can look into futurity and say what will be the destiny of this country. Changes come over nations and peoples in the course of ages. But, so far as we can legislate, we provide that, for all time to come, the sovereign of Great Britain shall be the sovereign of British North America. By adhering to the monarchical principle, we avoid one defect inherent in the constitution of the United States. By the election of the president by a majority and for a short period, he never is the sovereign and chief of the nation. He is never looked up to by the whole people as the head and front of the nation. He is at best but the successful leader of a party. This defect is all the greater on account of the practice of re-election. During his first term of office, he is employed in taking steps to secure his own re-election, and for his party a continuance of power. We avoid this by adhering to the monarchical principle — the sovereign

whom you respect and love. I believe that it is of the utmost importance to have that principle recognized, so that we shall have a sovereign who is placed above the region of party — to whom all parties look up — who is not elevated by the action of one party nor depressed by the action of another, who is the common head and sovereign of all. (Hear, hear and cheers.)

In the constitution we propose to continue the system of responsible government, which has existed in this province since 1841 and which has long obtained in the mother country. This is a feature of our constitution as we have it now, and as we shall have it in the federation, in which, I think, we avoid one of the great defects in the constitution of the United States. There the president, during his term of office, is in a great measure a despot, a one-man power, with the command of the naval and military forces — with an immense amount of patronage as head of the executive, and with the veto power as a branch of the legislature, perfectly uncontrolled by responsible advisers, his cabinet being departmental officers merely, whom he is not obliged by the constitution to consult with, unless he chooses to do so. With us, the sovereign, or in this country the representative of the sovereign, can act only on the advice of his ministers, those ministers being responsible to the people through parliament.

Prior to the formation of the American union, as we all know, the different states which entered into it were separate colonies. They had no connection with each other further than that of having a common sovereign, just as with us at present. Their constitutions and their laws were different. They might and did legislate against each other, and when they revolted against the mother country they acted as separate sovereignties, and carried on the war by a kind of treaty of alliance against the common enemy. Ever since the union was formed the difficulty of what is called "State Rights" has existed, and this had much to do in bringing on the present unhappy war in the United States. They commenced, in fact, at the wrong end. They declared by their constitution that each state was a sovereignty in itself, and that all the powers incident to a sovereignty belonged to each state, except those powers which, by the constitution, were conferred upon the general government and Congress. Here we have adopted a different system. We have strengthened the general government. We have given the general legislature all the great subjects of legislation. We have conferred on them, not only specifically and in detail, all the powers which are incident to sov-

"We have given the general legislature all the great subjects of legislation. We have conferred on them, not only specifically and in detail, all the powers which are incident to sovereignty, but we have expressly declared that all subjects of general interest not distinctly and exclusively conferred upon the local governments and local legislatures shall be conferred upon the general government and legislature."

ereignty,* but we have expressly declared that all subjects of general interest not distinctly and exclusively conferred upon the local governments and local legislatures† shall be conferred upon the general government and legislature. We have thus avoided that great source of weakness which has been the cause of the disruption of the United States. We have avoided all conflict of jurisdiction and authority, and if this constitution is carried out, as it will be in full detail in the imperial act to be passed if the colonies adopt the scheme, we will have in fact, as I said before, all the advantages of legislative union under one administration, with at the same time the guarantees for local institutions and for local laws, which are insisted upon by so many in the provinces now, I hope, to be united . . .

[A]ny honourable member on examining the list of different subjects which are to be assigned to the general and local legislatures, respectively, will see that all the great questions which affect the general interests of the confederacy as a whole are confided to the federal parliament,‡ while the local interests and local laws of each section are preserved intact and entrusted to the care of the local bodies . . . Besides all the powers that are given in the 37th and last item of this portion of the constitution, [it] confers on the general legislature the general mass of sovereign legislation, the power to legislate on "all matters of a general character, not specially and exclusively reserved for the local governments and legislatures." This is precisely the provision which is wanting in the constitution of the United States.§ It is here that we find the

---

These would include the power to legislate on the regulation of trade and commerce, military and naval defence, navigation and shipping, currency and coinage, and naturalization and aliens — all functions traditionally belonging to the crown.

† *An accurate paraphrase of the final subsection of resolution no. 29.*

‡ *The confederal system that is the British North America Act of 1867 addresses the distinction between general (national) and particular (local) interests by a strict constitutional division of powers between levels of government. Modern politicians have evaded the wisdom of that division by offering — indeed, by bribing the provinces into — shared-cost social, economic, and taxation programs that have had the effect of centralizing and unifying levels of government originally intended by our founders to remain constitutionally distinct and separate. — WDG*

§ *Macdonald sees the weakness of the American Constitution not in its failure to assign to Congress the residuary power as a whole, but in its failure to*

weakness of the American system — the point where the American constitution breaks down. (Hear, hear.) It is in itself a wise and necessary provision. We thereby strengthen the central parliament and make the Confederation one people and one government, instead of five peoples and five governments, with merely a point of authority connecting us to a limited and insufficient extent.

With respect to the local governments, it is provided that each shall be governed by a chief executive officer, who shall be nominated by the general government. As this is to be one united province, with the local governments and legislatures subordinate to the general government and legislature, it is obvious that the chief executive officer in each of the provinces must be subordinate as well. The general government assumes towards the local government precisely the same position as the imperial government holds with respect to each of the colonies now: so that as the lieutenant governor of each of the different provinces is now appointed directly by the queen, and is directly responsible, and reports directly to her, so will the executives of the local governments hereafter be subordinate to the representative of the queen, and be responsible and report to him . . .

There are numerous subjects which belong, of right, both to the local and the general parliaments. In all these cases it is provided, in order to prevent a conflict of authority, that where there is concurrent jurisdiction in the general and local parliaments, the same rule should apply as now applies in cases where there is concurrent jurisdiction in the imperial and in the provincial parliaments, and that when the legislation of the one is averse to or contradictory of the legislation of the other, in all such cases the action of the general parliament must overrule, ex-necessitate,* the action of the local legislature. (Hear, hear.)

— *Legislative Assembly, February 6, 1865*

---

assign a general power to legislate, where the national interest demands it, on matters falling outside its specified jurisdiction. He forcefully articulates the delegates' reasons for giving the federal legislature such power. — PR

* This refers to no. 45 of the Quebec Resolutions, which is expressed in section 95 of the BNA Act. Centralist scholars cited this so-called federal paramountcy provision as evidence of the founders' intention to create a dominant central government. As Macdonald notes here, however, such a rule is a necessary incident of concurrent legislative power. There is no point in having a general legislature, however wide or narrow its powers, if the local legislatures can overrule it at will. — PR

> *"Some parties . . . pretended that it was impossible to carry out federation, on account of the differences of races and religions. Those who took this view of the question were in error. It was just the reverse. It was precisely on account of the variety of races, local interests, etc., that the federation system ought to be resorted to and would be found to work well."*

George-Étienne Cartier: He was well aware that some members of the house, and a number of people in Upper Canada, in Lower Canada, and in the lower provinces, were of the opinion that a legislative union ought to have taken place instead of a federal union. He would say, however, at the outset, that it was impossible to have one government to deal with all the private and local interests of the several sections of the several provinces forming the combined whole. (Hear, hear.) The next question to be considered, therefore, by those who had set to work to discover a solution of the difficulties under which we had laboured was: What was the best and most practicable mode of bringing the provinces together so that particular rights and interests should be properly guarded and protected? No other scheme presented itself but the federation system, and that was the project which now recommended itself to the parliament of Canada. Some parties . . . pretended that it was impossible to carry out federation, on account of the differences of races and religions. Those who took this view of the question were in error. It was just the reverse. It was precisely on account of the variety of races, local interests, etc., that the federation system ought to be resorted to and would be found to work well. (Hear, hear.)

George Brown: I cannot help feeling that the struggle of half a lifetime* for constitutional reform — the agitations in the country and the fierce contests in this chamber — the strife and the discord and the abuse of many years — are all compensated

---

* *Brown was forty-five years old, which suggests that he is looking back to 1843, when he arrived in Canada and became engaged in the struggle for responsible government. To Brown and his supporters, that struggle had not ended with the coming of responsible government to United Canada in 1848 because that event had left Upper Canada under the heel of Lower Canada. From this standpoint, Brown sees Confederation as the realization of the federal solution he had persuaded the Reform Party to adopt in 1859: the establishment of separate governments for Upper and Lower Canada, and the assignment of matters of common concern to "some joint authority," in which for legislative purposes the two peoples could be represented according to population. But Macdonald and Cartier have presented Confederation as the realization of the policy of British North American union which their government had adopted in 1858. In short, we see here a struggle for priority between champions of the rival policies, even as they protest that the Quebec scheme combines the best features of both. — PR*

Toronto Liberals cheer
Globe *editor and publisher*
George Brown at his offices
at 23 King St. West.

by the great scheme of reform which is now in your hands. (Cheers.) The attorney general for Upper Canada [Macdonald], as well as the attorney general for Lower Canada [Cartier], in addressing the house last night, were anxious to have it understood that this scheme for uniting British America under one government is something different from "representation by population" — is something different from "joint authority" — but is in fact the very scheme of the government of which they were members in 1858 . . . For myself, sir, I care not who gets the credit of this scheme — I believe it contains the best features of all the suggestions that have been made in the last ten years for the settlement of our troubles. The whole feeling in my mind now is one of joy and thankfulness that there were found men of position and influence in Canada who, at a moment of serious crisis, had nerve and patriotism enough to cast aside political partisanship, to banish personal considerations, and unite for the accomplishment of a measure so fraught with advantage to their common country. (Cheers.) . . . But seven short months have passed away since the coalition government was formed, yet already are we submitting a scheme well weighed and matured, for the erection of a future empire, a scheme which has been received at home and abroad with almost universal approval . . .

The constitutional system of Canada cannot remain as it is now. (Loud cries of hear, hear.) Something must be done. We cannot stand still. We cannot go back to chronic, sectional hostility and discord — to a state of perpetual ministerial crises. The events of the last eight months cannot be obliterated; the solemn admissions of men of all parties cannot be erased. The claims of Upper Canada for justice must be met, and met now. I say, then, that everyone who raises his voice in hostility to this measure is bound to keep before him, when he speaks, all the perilous consequences of its rejection . . .

The very essence of our compact is that the union shall be federal and not legislative. Our Lower Canada friends have agreed to give us representation by population in the lower house, on the express condition that they shall have equality in the upper house. On no other condition could we have advanced a step; and, for my part, I am quite willing that they should have it. In maintaining the existing sectional boundaries and handing over the control of local matters to local bodies, we recognize, to a certain extent, a diversity of interests; and it was quite natural that the protection for those interests, by equality in the upper

chamber, should be demanded by the less numerous provinces. Honourable gentlemen may say* that it will erect a barrier in the upper house against the just influence that Upper Canada will exercise, by her numbers, in the lower house over the general legislation of the country. That may be true, to a certain extent, but honourable gentlemen will bear in mind that that barrier, be it more or less, will not affect money bills. (Hear, hear.)

Hitherto we have been paying a vast proportion of the taxes, with little or no control over the expenditure. But, under this plan, by our just influence in the lower chamber, we shall hold the purse strings. If, from this concession of equality in the upper chamber, we are restrained from forcing through measures which our friends of Lower Canada may consider injurious to their interests, we shall, at any rate, have power, which we never had before, to prevent them from forcing through whatever we may deem unjust to us . . .

For myself, sir, I unhesitatingly say that the complete justice which this measure secures to the people of Upper Canada in the vital matter of parliamentary representation alone renders all the blemishes averred against it utterly contemptible in the balance. (Continued cheers.) But, Mr. Speaker, the second feature of this scheme as a remedial measure is that it removes, to a large extent, the injustice of which Upper Canada has complained in financial matters. We in Upper Canada have complained that though we paid into the public treasury more than three-fourths of the whole revenue, we had less control over the system of taxation and the expenditure of the public monies than the people of Lower Canada. Well, sir, the scheme in your hand remedies that. The absurd line of separation between the provinces is swept away for general matters; we are to have seventeen additional members in the house that holds the purse; and the taxpayers of

---

* In these debates the party leaders in particular are trying to convince the legislature and the electorate to accept a compromise. Macdonald needs to cajole English-Canadian conservatives who dislike the very idea of federal union as unstable, if not republican. Brown is trying, without alienating that group, to reassure his own supporters that the Quebec scheme is not just a legislative union with federal trimmings. Cartier needs to allay similar fears among French Canadians, whom he is asking to accept representation by population in the federal House of Commons. In each of the other colonies, confederates face similar tasks of justification. This means that one can't take at face value what either they or their opponents say about the proposal. — PR

the country, wherever they reside, will have their just share of influence over revenue and expenditure. (Hear, hear.)

We have also complained that immense sums of public money have been systematically taken from the public chest for local purposes of Lower Canada, in which the people of Upper Canada had no interest whatever, though compelled to contribute three-fourths of the cash. Well, sir, this scheme remedies that. All local matters are to be banished from the general legislature; local governments are to have control over local affairs, and if our friends in Lower Canada choose to be extravagant, they will have to bear the burden of it themselves. (Hear, hear.) . . .

But, Mr. Speaker, there is another great evil in our existing system that this scheme remedies: it secures to the people of each province full control over the administration of their own internal affairs. We in Upper Canada have complained that the minority of our representatives, the party defeated at the polls of Upper Canada, have been, year after year, kept in office by Lower Canada votes, and that all the local patronage of our section has been dispensed by those who did not possess the confidence of the people. Well, sir, this scheme remedies that. The local patronage will be under local control, and the wishes of the majority in each section will be carried out in all local matters. (Hear, hear.)

We have complained that the land system was not according to the views of our western people; that free lands for actual settlers was the right policy for us — that the price of a piece of land squeezed out of an immigrant was no consideration in comparison with the settlement among us of a hardy and industrious family; and that the colonization road system was far from satisfactory. Well, sir, this scheme remedies that. Each province is to have control over its own crown lands, crown timber, and crown minerals — and will be free to take such steps for developing them as each deems best. (Hear, hear.)

We have complained that local works of various kinds — roads, bridges and landing piers, court houses, gaols, and other structures — have been erected in an inequitable and improvident manner. Well, sir, this scheme remedies that; all local works are to be constructed by the localities and defrayed from local funds. And so on through the whole extensive details of internal local administration will this reform extend . . .

But, Mr. Speaker, I am further in favour of this scheme because it will bring to an end the sectional discord between

"The questions that used to excite the most hostile feelings among us have been taken away from the general legislature and placed under the control of the local bodies. No man need hereafter be debarred from success in public life because his views, however popular in his own section, are unpopular in the other — for he will not have to deal with sectional questions; and the temptation to the government of the day to make capital out of local prejudices will be greatly lessened, if not altogether at an end."

Upper and Lower Canada. It sweeps away the boundary line between the provinces so far as regards matters common to the whole people — it places all on an equal level — and the members of the federal legislature will meet at last as citizens of a common country. The questions that used to excite the most hostile feelings among us have been taken away from the general legislature and placed under the control of the local bodies. No man need hereafter be debarred from success in public life because his views, however popular in his own section, are unpopular in the other — for he will not have to deal with sectional questions; and the temptation to the government of the day to make capital out of local prejudices will be greatly lessened, if not altogether at an end . . . a most happy day will it be for Canada when this bill goes into effect, and all these subjects of discord are swept from the discussion of our legislature. (Hear.)

We had either to take a federal union or drop the negotiation. Not only were our friends from Lower Canada against it, but so were most of the delegates from the Maritime provinces. There was but one choice open to us — federal union or nothing. But in truth the scheme now before us has all the advantages of a legislative union and a federal one as well. We have thrown over on the localities all the questions which experience has shown lead directly to local jealousy and discord, and we have retained in the hands of the general government all the powers necessary to secure a strong and efficient administration of public affairs. (Hear, hear.) By placing the appointment of the judges in the hands of the general government, and the establishment of a central court of appeal, we have secured uniformity of justice over the whole land. (Hear, hear.) By vesting the appointment of the lieutenant governors in the general government, and giving a veto for all local measures, we have secured that no injustice shall be done without appeal* in local legislation. (Hear, hear.) For all dealings with the imperial government and foreign countries, we

---

*Brown justifies the machinery of federal interference in local affairs as a means of protecting minorities against the power of local majorities. In the Canadian debates, the only minority whose situation arouses much concern is the anglophones of Lower Canada. Later efforts to activate the machinery in defence of Roman Catholic and francophone minorities in other provinces proved uniformly unsuccessful, since even constitutionally sanctioned intervention was widely condemned (by French as well as English Canadians) as an offence against the principle of provincial autonomy. — PR

have clothed the general government with the most ample powers. And, finally, all matters of trade and commerce, banking and currency, and all questions common to the whole people we have vested fully and unrestrictedly in the general government. The measure, in fact, shuns the faults of the federal and legislative systems and adopts the best parts of both, and I am well persuaded it will work efficiently and satisfactorily. (Hear, hear.)

— *Legislative Assembly, February 8, 1865*

"What is so conducive to the prosperity of a country as well-protected rights of property and vested interests? This feature was deeply ingrained in the British mind, and in that of the United States also."

John Sanborn: It was said that the civil laws of Lower Canada were now consolidated into a code, and this would enhance our credit; and if based on sound principles and rendered permanent, it would undoubtedly do so, for what is so conducive to the prosperity of a country as well-protected rights of property and vested interests?* This feature was deeply ingrained in the British mind, and in that of the United States also, insomuch that the American Constitution provides that no law could be passed which affects the rights of property. This was exemplified in the celebrated Dartmouth College case, in which Webster so distinguished himself, when the endowment was maintained and perpetuated. But to what power were the rights of property committed in these resolutions? When the minister of finance appealed to moneyed men abroad for a loan, could he say the constitution had provided guarantees against injurious changes, when it was known that the laws relating to property were left open to the caprice of the local governments? Where was the security of the great religious societies of Montreal, if a sentiment hostile to monopolies were carried to extremes in the local parliament?

E.-P. Taché: The general legislature had power to disallow such acts.

---

* *Here the issue is that of protecting the rights of another sort of minority: the wealthy. The wish to protect these citizens against local majorities provided a major impulse to the formation of the American union. In the Dartmouth College case of 1819, the U.S. Supreme Court decided that the federal constitution precluded a state legislature from amending a corporate charter granted by its predecessor. (Daniel Webster argued as counsel for this result.) Sanborn worries that, by assigning property and civil rights to the local legislatures, the Quebec scheme subjects them to the whim of local majorities. The ensuing exchange over the propriety and efficacy of disallowance as a remedy foreshadows later controversies. Note the divergent*

James Currie: This would be an interference with local rights.

John Ross: It would preserve local rights.

John Sanborn: It was a wise power and commended itself to all; it was, however, not an ordinary power to be commonly resorted to, but an extreme power, and one almost revolutionary. It was a power somewhat similar to that which existed in the second branch of the legislature to stop the supplies, but in its very nature not one often to be exercised; and it could not be frequently exercised without destroying the very foundations of society, and occasioning evils of the greatest magnitude . . .

— *Legislative Council, February 9, 1865*

L.-A. Olivier: As much power should have been entrusted to the local governments, and as little as is consistent with the functions it will have to discharge to the central government, and my reason for entertaining this opinion is that the supreme government, with its power of the purse and its control of the armies, will always be more disposed to stretch its prerogatives and to trench upon the domain of the local governments than to narrow down and retain [*sic*] its authority . . . As it is now, if the scheme goes into operation, the local governments will be in danger of being crushed (*écrasés*) by the general government . . .

I hear it said that Confederation, as it is proposed, will be a federal union — but it seems to me that it will be rather a legislative union, at least as far as regards the most important interests of Lower Canada. The 29th section of the scheme submitted to us says: "The Federal Parliament shall have the power of making laws for the peace, the well-being, and the good government of the Confederate provinces, and in particular in respect of the following matters." The powers of the federal government will be in reality unlimited. The fact of the enumeration of these thirty-seven heads does not in the least restrain the power of the federal government from legislating on everything. The exceptions are few . . .

I shall also inquire whether the federal government will not

---

usage of the term local rights. *To Currie, an Upper Canadian reformer, it signifies the rights of the autonomous local community vis-à-vis the federal government; to Ross, a Lower Canadian Conservative, it signifies those of individuals vis-à-vis local governments. Note also Sanborn's sage remarks on the practical limitations of the federal veto power.* — PR

have the right to enact that religious corporations shall no longer exist in the country, or that they shall not be allowed to hold real property, except what is absolutely necessary for their lodging accommodation. According to the resolutions which have been submitted to us, the federal government would certainly have this right . . . The 43rd resolution defines the powers of the local governments, and article 15 of that resolution declares that they make laws respecting "property and civil rights, excepting those portions thereof assigned to the General Parliament." That article reserves to the local legislatures nothing relative to religious corporations,* and the federal government would have full power to decree that those corporations shall not hold immovable property . . .

The same might be said of most of the institutions to which Lower Canada is attached. I am therefore right in saying that, so far as those things which Lower Canada most holds to are concerned, Confederation is in fact a legislative union, because upon the federal government is conferred the right of legislating upon those subjects which Lower Canada holds most dear . . .

I have already stated that the plan submitted for our approval is exceedingly complex and that it is not easy to foresee the difficulties that will arise between the local governments and the federal government. It may, perhaps, be asserted that these difficulties cannot be very serious, inasmuch as the local governments will not possess any large powers; but if it is designed to make them real governments, and not mere municipalities, they may be opposed to the central government on a host of questions.

Take, for instance, the question of the fisheries. Article 17, of the 29th resolution, gives to the federal parliament the power of legislating on the "sea coast and inland fisheries." Under the 8th article of the 43rd resolution, the local legislatures will also have the right of the legislating on the "sea coast and inland fisheries." . . . And if the laws they make are in opposition the one to the other, what will be the result? And this may well happen, for we

---

* *Olivier's remarks exemplify French Canadians' fears that the proposed Confederation will imperil their national integrity. Note that, just as Sanborn apprehends danger to the property rights of religious corporations from the local legislative power, so Olivier fears such danger from the federal legislative power. The discrepancy underlines the need for caution in taking contemporary comments on the scheme as objective and accurate evidence of its nature and intent.* — PR

know that in the Gulf, for instance, there are fisheries which are of the highest importance for the people of Lower Canada, as well as for the people of the adjoining colonies, of which the latter have taken possession, and sought to exclude our people from them. Now, if the local government of Lower Canada made laws to protect its subjects and insure to them the right to these fisheries, would it not be in the power of the federal government to interfere and prevent it? And if this were to happen, would it not give rise to endless antipathies and struggles between the two governments? Lower Canada would not suffer such an interference without feeling it very strongly; and what I have just said with reference to the fisheries might also occur with reference to a large number of questions. And it is quite evident that if the local government, acting in the interests of a province, were arrested in its action by the federal government, the people would take sides with their local government and become disaffected towards the central government.

— *Legislative Council, February 13, 1865*

"The first point to which I directed my attention was to ascertain what guarantees Lower Canada would find in Confederation for its laws, its religion, and its autonomy. I find the guarantee of all these things in that article of the scheme which gives to Lower Canada the local government of its affairs and the control of all matters relating to its institutions, to its laws, to its religion, its manufactures and its autonomy."

N.-F. Belleau: The first point to which I directed my attention was to ascertain what guarantees Lower Canada would find in Confederation for its laws, its religion, and its autonomy. I find the guarantee of all these things in that article of the scheme which gives to Lower Canada the local government of its affairs and the control of all matters relating to its institutions, to its laws, to its religion, its manufactures and its autonomy. Are you not all prepared, honourable gentlemen, and you especially members from Lower Canada, to make some few sacrifices in order to have the control of all those things to which I have just referred, and which are all to be within the jurisdiction of the local governments[?] . . . For my part that we shall have the control of our local affairs in Lower Canada, under the Confederation, is a sufficient inducement to vote in favour of the scheme now submitted to us, even although it offered us no other advantage . . .

The honourable member [Olivier] also contends that the local governments ought to have larger powers . . . and that the federal government ought to have fewer powers. To hear him, one cannot help thinking that the experience of history is entirely lost on certain individuals. He must have been aware, however, that it is in reference to the rights of particular states that civil war now exists in the United States; nevertheless, he would implant in this country the same germ of discord. He would have more power

below and less authority above. For my part, I say the very contrary, if we wish to have a strong government capable of enforcing respect for its authority when it shall be necessary to enforce it . . .

Let us never lose sight of the fact that our national representatives will always see that Lower Canada shall have in the federal government one, or perhaps two, representatives — the number is not of importance. What is of importance is the fact that such one, or such two members, should represent in her Executive Council the national representation, which will be composed of sixty-five members, in the federal legislature . . . I insist somewhat at length upon this point, because the operation of the principle of responsible government in the federal legislature is lost sight of. I beg to call the attention of Lower Canada members to this. Suppose it were proposed to adopt a law in the federal legislature calculated to injure Lower Canada, our sixty-five representatives in the House of Commons discuss the law, and decide that they must oppose it; they at once communicate with the members of the government representing Lower Canada and inform them that they cannot accept the measure, and that if it be passed they will coalesce with the minority, which always exists under responsible government, and that they will overthrow the ministry. Such is the weight of our influence in the federal government; and if this were not lost sight of, there would be no grounds for fear. The influence of Lower Canada will enable her to make and unmake governments at pleasure, when her interests shall be at stake or threatened.

— *Legislative Council, February 14, 1865*

Philip Moore: The question of the veto power was very ably discussed, at one time, in the United States Congress, and that discussion led to a qualification of the veto power in the constitution of the United States, so that now any bill passed by both houses may be vetoed by the president within ten days thereafter, by assigning reasons for doing so. Both houses may then, however, again take up the measure, and if they pass it by a two-third vote it becomes the law of the land, independent of the president's will. Now, I would have the veto power applied in a similar way in our new constitution. Exercising it in an arbitrary manner, as the federal power is privileged to do, it must, from the very nature of things, create dissatisfaction and difficulty between the two governments.

— *Legislative Council, February 16, 1865*

A.-A. Dorion: The Confederation I advocated was a real confederation,* giving the largest powers to the local governments, and
merely a delegated authority to the general government — in that
respect differing *in toto* from the one now proposed which gives
all the powers to the central government and reserves for the
local governments the smallest possible amount of freedom of
action. There is nothing besides in what I have ever written or
said that can be interpreted as favouring a confederation of all the
provinces. This I always opposed . . .

Now, sir, when I look into the provisions of this scheme, I find
another most objectionable one. It is that which gives the general
government control over all the acts of the local legislatures.
What difficulties may not arise under this system? Now, knowing
that the general government will be party in its character, may it
not for party purposes reject laws passed by the local legislatures
and demanded by a majority of the people of that locality? This
power conferred upon the general government has been compared to the veto power that exists in England† in respect to our
legislation; but we know that the statesmen of England are not
actuated by the local feelings and prejudices, and do not partake
of the local jealousies that prevail in the colonies. The local governments have therefore confidence in them and respect for their
decisions; and generally, when a law adopted by a colonial legislature is sent to them, if it does not clash with the policy of the
empire at large, it is not disallowed, and more especially of late it
has been the policy of the imperial government to do whatever
the colonies desire in this respect, when their wishes are constitutionally expressed . . .

But how different will be the result in this case, when the gen-

---

* *The idea of solving United Canada's constitutional problems by federalizing the union had originated with Dorion in 1856. Much of his speech is
devoted to reconciling his advocacy of such a federation with his opposition to
the Quebec scheme.* — PR

† *Dorion's remark confirms Oliver Mowat's later claim that the Quebec
Conference had adopted the federal veto on the understanding that it would be
subject to the same constitutional constraints as the imperial power to disallow
colonial legislation. But Dorion goes on to predict that party-political exigencies will thwart that intention. In the long run, though, the expectations
of the Quebec Conference were fulfilled. The veto power has not been used
since 1943. Nowadays the federal government will not veto legislation
enacted to promote a province's secession.* — PR

"We may find parties so hotly opposed to each other in the local legislatures that the whole power of the minority may be brought to bear upon their friends who have a majority in the general legislature, for the purpose of preventing the passage of some law objectionable to them, but desired by the majority of their own section. What will be the result of such a state of things but bitterness of feeling, strong political acrimony, and dangerous agitation?"

eral government exercises the veto power over the acts of local legislatures. Do you not see that it is quite possible for a majority in a local government to be opposed to the general government; and in such a case the minority would call upon the general government to disallow the laws enacted by the majority? The men who shall compose the general government will be dependent for their support upon their political friends in the local legislatures, and it may so happen that, in order to secure this support, or in order to serve their own purposes or that of their supporters, they will veto laws which the majority of a local legislature find necessary and good. (Hear, hear.) We know how high party feeling runs sometimes upon local matters even of trivial importance, and we may find parties so hotly opposed to each other in the local legislatures that the whole power of the minority may be brought to bear upon their friends who have a majority in the general legislature, for the purpose of preventing the passage of some law objectionable to them, but desired by the majority of their own section. What will be the result of such a state of things but bitterness of feeling, strong political acrimony, and dangerous agitation? (Hear, hear.)

— *Legislative Assembly, February 16, 1865*

J.-O. Beaubien: He tells us that as Lower Canada is to have 65 representatives in the general legislature out of 194, these 65 members from Lower Canada will always be able to preserve their rights by taking sides with the opposition to turn out the government. Does the honourable member really suppose that all the members from Lower Canada would make common cause on any question? Does he not know that there will always be a minority among them of different origin and religion who will probably take part with the government or with the majority? . . . Do we not know that the difficulties which gave rise to the plan of Confederation were produced by the coalition of an Upper Canada minority with the Lower Canada majority? And what happened to Upper Canada might very well happen to Lower Canada.

— *Legislative Assembly, March 2, 1865*

Taché: Some honourable gentlemen have told us that this was not a federal union . . . One gentleman who took this view read the 29th section [*sic*], in order to show that the general government, if it chose, could repeal any of the local acts of the different local legislatures — that the general government, for instance,

could do away with our religious or benevolent corporations, or deprive them of their property. I think the honourable gentleman must have been rather short-sighted when he read the 29th resolution, for he omitted a very important part of it . . . I have no doubt my honourable friend acted in good faith; but being rather short-sighted, he did not read the whole clause; otherwise he must have arrived at a different conclusion. The 29th section says: "The general parliament shall have power to make laws for the peace, welfare, and good government of the federated provinces (saving the sovereignty of England), and especially laws respecting the following subjects." Then follows a list of all the subjects committed to the general government. But the resolution does not finish there. There is something that comes after all that, and it is this: "And generally respecting all matters of a general character, not specially and exclusively reserved for the local governments and legislatures." Now I would ask honourable gentlemen if an act incorporating a religious body or benevolent society here in Lower Canada is a subject of a general character: Is it not a subject purely local? (Hear, hear.) Take, for instance, the Sisters of Charity. Could the general government, under this clause, interfere with the privileges of those ladies? I say they could not . . . I think it is quite evident from a reading of the resolution that, if Confederation takes place, the general government will have no power to interfere with such matters. (Hear, hear.)

— *Legislative Council, February 20, 1865*

H.-L. Langevin: The honourable member for Hochelaga [A.-A. Dorion] speaks of the English as though they were our natural enemies. For my part, I do not think they are; moreover, the question before us is not the formation of a local government only. We are considering the establishment of a confederacy — with a central parliament and local parliaments. The central or federal parliament will have control of all measures of a general character, as provided by the Quebec Conference; but all matters of local interest, all that relates to the affairs and rights of the different sections of the confederacy, will be reserved for the control of the local parliaments . . .

As regards the seventeen additional members which Upper Canada will have in the federal parliament, I am not alarmed at their presence any more than at that of the members from the lower provinces because, in parliament, there will be no questions

"We are considering the establishment of a confederacy — with a central parliament and local parliaments. The central or federal parliament will have control of all measures of a general character, as provided by the Quebec Conference; but all matters of local interest, all that relates to the affairs and rights of the different sections of the confederacy, will be reserved for the control of the local parliaments . . ."

of race, nationality, religion, or locality, as this legislature will only be charged with the great general questions which will interest alike the whole confederacy and not one locality only. Our position then is excellent, and all those who frankly give expression to their opinions must admit that the representatives of Lower Canada at the Quebec Conference have carefully guarded her interests . . .

Under Confederation there will no longer be domination of one race over another, and if one section should be desirous of committing an act of injustice against another section, all the others would unite together to prevent it. But suppose that an unjust measure was passed in the House of Commons of the federal legislature, it would be stopped in the Legislative Council; for there we shall be represented equally with the other sections, and that is a guarantee that our interests will be amply protected . . .

The honourable member [Dorion] has taken occasion to find fault with the clause of the resolutions which provides that the lieutenant governors shall be appointed by the central government and sees in it great danger, especially to Lower Canada. Mr. Speaker, I should very much like to know what protection the population of the different provinces derive from the fact that the governors of the British North American provinces are sent out to us from England. Under the existing system, our governor is responsible neither to the people nor to the house; he depends entirely upon the English government, to which he is responsible. Under the system proposed, the lieutenant governors will be appointed by the central government, to which they will necessarily be responsible for their actions. And in that government we shall have more than one vote; we shall be represented in it by our ministers, who will be there to cause every encroachment or arbitrary act which the lieutenant governor may allow himself to commit to be condemned. If the central government should refuse to do us this justice . . . we should have our sixty-five representatives to protest and to vote at need against a government which should dare to act in such a way. In that respect we should have much better guarantees than at present . . . as the people will have a voice in these appointments, [and] from the fact that we shall have our responsible ministers in the central government who will be sustained and supported by the members from our section . . .

— *Legislative Assembly, February 21, 1865*

*"The great advantage
which I see in the
scheme is this, that the
powers granted to the
local governments are
strictly defined and
circumscribed . . . There
can, therefore, be no
difficulty under the
scheme between the
various sections — no
clashing of authority
between the local and
central governments in
this case, as there has
been in the case of the
Americans."*

John Rose: The great advantage which I see in the scheme is this, that the powers granted to the local governments are strictly defined and circumscribed, and that the residuum of power lies in the central government.* You have, in addition to that, the local governors named by the central authority — an admirable provision which establishes the connection of authority between the central power and the different localities; you have vested in it also the great questions of the customs, the currency, banking, trade and navigation, commerce, the appointment of the judges, and the administration of the laws, and all those great and large questions which interest the entire community, and with which the general government ought to be entrusted. There can, therefore, be no difficulty under the scheme between the various sections — no clashing of authority between the local and central governments in this case, as there has been in the case of the Americans. The powers of the local governments are distinctly and strictly defined, and you can have no assertion of sovereignty on the part of the local governments, as in the United States, and of powers inconsistent with the rights and security of the whole community. (Hear, hear.)

Then, the other point which commends itself so strongly to my mind is this, that there is a veto power on the part of the general government over all the legislation of the local parliament. That was a fundamental element which the wisest statesmen[†] engaged in the framing of the American Constitution saw, that if it was not engrafted in it, must necessarily lead to the destruction of the constitution . . . This power having been given to the central government, it is to my mind, in conjunction with the power of naming the local governors, the appointment and payment of the judiciary, one of the best features of the scheme, without which it would certainly, in my opinion, have been open to very serious objection. (Hear, hear.)

— Legislative Assembly, February 22, 1865

---

* *This speech is one of only two such declarations in the Canadian debates. (The other is that of Aquila Walsh.) As a leading spokesman for the anglophones of Lower Canada, Rose's main task was reassure that group that the Quebec scheme protected their interests as a minority within Lower Canada. Hence his approving emphasis on the apparatus of central control over the local governments. His perception of the residuary power can be understood as a blend of loose language and hyperbole, with perhaps a tinge of wishful thinking. — PR*

† *James Madison in particular advocated empowering Congress (not the executive) to veto state legislation.*

"Where there are two great parties in a nation — as there have been with us — it is quite clear that, when they agree to effect a settlement of the constitutional difficulties which have separated them, this can only be accomplished by mutual compromise to a greater or less extent. And the true question to be determined in this discussion, and by the vote at the close of this debate, is this — whether this is a fair compromise or not."

Alexander Mackenzie: Some honourable gentlemen have asserted, and truly asserted, that this measure is not as perfect as it might have been — and that it is not as complete as some of us might have desired it to be . . . But, where there are two great parties in a nation — as there have been with us — it is quite clear that, when they agree to effect a settlement of the constitutional difficulties which have separated them, this can only be accomplished by mutual compromise to a greater or less extent. And the true question to be determined in this discussion, and by the vote at the close of this debate, is this — whether this is a fair compromise or not. I am prepared to say it is perhaps as fair as could reasonably be expected, and I have therefore no hesitation in giving it all the support in my power. (Hear, hear.) In its main features it is the very scheme which was proposed by the Toronto convention* — only carried to a greater extent than the convention thought advisable or possible at the time. The speeches which were delivered at that convention, as well as the resolutions which were passed, showed clearly that it was the opinion of the delegates there present that a Confederation of the whole provinces would be desirable, if it were possible to attain it as speedily as they expected they could obtain a federation of the two provinces of Canada . . .

Personally, I have always been in favour of a legislative union where it can be advantageously worked. If it could be adapted to our circumstances in these colonies, I would at this moment be in favour of a legislative union as the best system of government. I believe that is the general opinion of the people in the west. But it is the duty of every public man to shape his course . . . according to the circumstances which may prevail locally. And it is quite clear that, if the legislative union could not be worked well with Upper and Lower Canada, it would work still worse with the other provinces brought in. There remained, therefore, in my opinion, no other alternative than to adopt the federal principle, or to dissolve entirely the connection which exists between Upper and Lower Canada at the present moment; and

---

A reference to the Reform Party convention of 1859, which approved the federalization of United Canada. Like George Brown, Mackenzie asserts that the Quebec scheme is consistent with the policy then adopted. The convention had responded warmly to the idea of a broader British North American union, but had adopted the policy of federalizing United Canada as being more immediately practicable. — PR

that I would look upon as one of the greatest calamities which could befall us. Even if this scheme were more objectionable than it is . . . I would without hesitation accept Confederation rather than dissolution. (Hear, hear.) . . .

It is reasonable and just to insert a provision in the scheme that will put it out of the power of any party to act unjustly. If the power that the central authority is to have — of vetoing the doings of the local legislature — is used, it will be ample, I think, to prevent anything of that kind. But the veto itself is objected to . . . Well, sir, under the British Constitution, in all British colonies, and in Great Britain itself, there is a certain elasticity to be presumed. Everything is not provided for, because a great deal is trusted to the common sense of the people. I think it is quite fair and safe to assert that there is not the slightest danger that the federal parliament will perpetrate any injustice upon the local legislatures, because it would cause such a reaction as to compass the destruction of the power thus exercised. The veto power is necessary in order that the general government may have a control over the proceedings of the local legislatures to a certain extent. The want of this power was the great source of weakness in the United States. So long as each state considered itself sovereign, whose acts and laws could not be called in question, it was quite clear that the central authority was destitute of power to compel obedience to general laws. If each province were able to enact such laws as it pleased, everybody would be at the mercy of the local legislatures, and the general legislature would become of little importance. It is contended that the power of the general legislature should be held in check by a veto power . . . resident in the local legislatures, respecting the application of general laws to their jurisdiction. All power, they say, comes from the people*
and ascends through them to their representatives, and through the representatives to the crown. But it would never do to set the local above the general government. The central parliament and government must, of necessity, exercise the supreme power, and the local governments will have the exercise of power corresponding to the duties they have to perform. The system is a new and untried one, and may not work so harmoniously as we now

> *"Under the British Constitution, in all British colonies, and in Great Britain itself, there is a certain elasticity to be presumed. Everything is not provided for, because a great deal is trusted to the common sense of the people."*

---

* *This was no new idea in European political thought; it could be traced back at least to the sixteenth century — for example, to the Scottish Calvinist writer George Buchanan. It received its most powerful expression in John Locke's* Second Treatise of Government *(1690). — IG*

anticipate, but there will always be power in the British parliament and our own to remedy any defects that may be discovered after the system is in operation.

Alexander Morris: I believe it will be found that all the conditions are combined in the scheme now before us that are considered necessary for the formation on a permanent basis of a federative union. I hold in my hand a book of some note on *Representative Government*, by John Stuart Mill, and I find that he lays down three conditions as applicable to the union of independent states, and which, by parity of reasoning, are applicable to provinces which seek to have a closer alliance with each other, and also, thereby, a closer alliance with the mother country. The conditions he lays down are, first:

> That there should be a sufficient amount of mutual sympathy among the populations.

And he states that the sympathies which they should have in common should be:

> Those of race, language, religion, and, above all, of political institutions, as conducing most to a feeling of identity of political interest.

Luther Holton: Hear, hear.

Morris: We possess that strong tie of mutual sympathy in a high degree. We have the same systems of government, and the same political institutions. We are part of the same great empire, and that is the real tie which will bind us together in future time. The second condition laid down is:

> That the separate states be not so powerful as to be able to rely for protection against foreign encroachment on their individual strength.

That is a condition which applies most forcibly in our case. (Hear, hear.) The third condition is:

> That there be not a very marked inequality of strength among the several contracting states.

A.-A. Dorion: Hear, hear.

Morris: Allow me to proceed with the extract:

> They cannot, indeed, be exactly equal in resources; in all fed-
> erations there will be a gradation of power among the
> members; some will be more populous, rich, and civilized
> than others. There is a wide difference in wealth between
> New York and Rhode Island.

Just as there is between Canada and Prince Edward Island. I trust I
have satisfied my honourable friend from Hochelaga (Honourable
Mr. Dorion) that Mr. Mill's views* are entirely applicable to our
position. (Hear, hear.) . . .

I believe the scheme will be found in fact and in practice — by
its combination of the better features of the American system with
those of the British Constitution — to have very great practical
advantages. I shall read an extract from an article in the London
Times, written in 1858, bearing on this subject, and which brings
very clearly into view the distinction between the system which
has been proposed for our adoption and which has been adopted
in the United States. The great weakness of the American system
has lain in the fact that the several states, on entering the union,
claimed independent jurisdiction; that they demitted to the central government certain powers, and that they claimed equal and
sovereign powers with regard to everything not so delegated and
demitted. The weaknesses and difficulties of that system have
been avoided in the project now before us, and we have the central power with defined and sovereign powers, and the local
parliaments with their defined and delegated powers,† but subor-
dinated to the central power. The article says:

> It is quite clear that the Federal Constitution of the United
> States of America forms a precedent which cannot possibly be

---

* *The reference is to chapter 17 of* Representative Government *(1861).*

† *This is a very clear example of an intelligent and well-informed man completely misconceiving the proposed division of legislative power. There was in
fact no constitutional difference between the powers assigned to the general
and the local legislatures. As Joseph Cauchon points out below, both sets of
powers represented an identical devolution of authority by the British parliament.* — PR

followed in its principles or details by the united colonies, so long as they remain part of the dominions of the Imperial Crown. The principle of the American Federation is, that each is a sovereign state, which consents to delegate to a central authority a portion of its sovereign power, leaving the remainder which is not so delegated absolute and intact in its own hands. This is not the position of the colonies, each of which, instead of being an isolated sovereign state, is an integral part of the British Empire. They cannot delegate their sovereign authority to a central government, because they do not possess the sovereign authority to delegate. The only alternative as it seems to us would be to adopt a course exactly the contrary of that which the United States adopted, and instead of taking for their motto *E Pluribus Unum*, to invert it by saying *In Uno Plura* . . . The first steps towards a Federation of the American Colonies would thus be to form them all into one state, to give that state a completely organized government, and then to delegate to each of the colonies out of which that great state is formed, such powers of local government as may be thought necessary, reserving to the Central Government all such powers as are not expressly delegated. The Government of New Zealand forms a precedent well worthy the attention of those who are undertaking this arduous negotiation.

And I cannot doubt that the framers of this constitution have studied the precedent as well of the proposed constitution of Australia, as that of the constitution of New Zealand which has been in use for ten years past.

— *Legislative Assembly, February 23, 1865*

M.C. Cameron: Union with the United States, I hope, will never take place. (Hear, hear.) Still I cannot help believing that this is the tendency of the measure; for when we have a legislature in each province, with powers coordinate with those of the federal legislature — or if not possessing coordinate powers, having the same right at least to legislate upon some subjects as the general legislature — there are certain to arise disagreements between the local and the general legislature which will lead the people to demand changes that may destroy our connection with

M.C. Cameron's campaign broadsheet for the Canadian election of 1863: "My Principles are the same as when last I solicited your suffrages — a Conservative, I have been and will continue to be the advocate of fair and equal justice to all classes of the people, without reference to party, color, race or religion."

the mother country. The federal character of the United States government has been referred to to prove that it has increased the prosperity of the people living under it; but in point of fact the great and relentless war that is now raging there . . . is the strongest comment upon the working of the federal principle — the strongest argument against its application to these provinces. (Hear, hear.) The French element in Lower Canada will be separated from us in its local legislature and become less united with us than it is now; and therefore there is likely to be disagreement between us. Still more likely is there to be disagreement when the people of Upper Canada find that this scheme will not relieve them of the burdens cast upon them, but, on the contrary, will subject them to a legislature that will have the power of imposing direct taxation in addition to the burdens imposed by the general government. When they find that this power is exercised, and they are called upon to contribute as much as before to the general government, while taxed to maintain a separate local legislature . . . they will look to the other side of the line for union . . .

The 33rd subsection* gives to the general government the power of "rendering uniform all or any of the laws relative to property and civil rights in Upper Canada, Nova Scotia, New Brunswick, Newfoundland and Prince Edward Island, and rendering uniform the procedure of all or any of the courts in these provinces; but any statute for this purpose shall have no force or authority in any province until sanctioned by the legislature

---

* Cameron refers to no. 29 of the Quebec Resolutions, which defines the power of the general legislature. (It is reproduced in section 94 of the BNA Act.) Pursuant to the Quebec and London resolutions, subsection 92(13) of the act assigned to the provinces the power to legislate on property and civil rights. It has been suggested that section 94 was a "fast-track" provision, designed to permit the common-law provinces to assimilate their laws without activating the machinery of constitutional amendment. Its terms reflected two assumptions: (1) that amendment of the constitution, at least in matters affecting the federal-provincial relationship, would require the unanimous agreement of the provinces, and (2) that French Canadians valued their civil law so highly as a badge of nationality that the government of Lower Canada (Quebec) might be loath to consent to changes in subsection 92(13) even if they did not affect Lower Canada. — PR

thereof." So that, in reality, no such law will be binding until it has the sanction of the local legislature of the province particularly affected thereby.

Such being the guarded terms of the resolution, why is it not made applicable to Lower Canada as well as to the other provinces? . . . I can easily understand the feeling of the French people and can admire it — that they do not want to have anything forced upon them whether they will or not. But that they will not allow you to contemplate even the possibility of any change taking place for the general weal, and with their own consent, in their laws . . . I do not understand. And having feelings of this kind, and manifesting them so strongly as they do in this document, it appears to me that in going into this union we do not go into it with the proper elements. We go into it with elements of strife and dissension, rather than of union and strength. (Hear, hear.) That is to be regretted; for if a change is to be made affecting the destinies of the people of this country, it is lamentable that we do not find patriotism enough among the representatives of the people to be willing to give and take . . .

— *Legislative Assembly, February 24, 1865*

"If a change is to be made affecting the destinies of the people of this country, it is lamentable that we do not find patriotism enough among the representatives of the people to be willing to give and take."

Christopher Dunkin: Look now . . . at the Legislative Council under the proposed Confederation: What is it? There is a sort of attempt to prevent its numbers from resting on a population basis; and this is about the only principle I can find in it. (Hear, hear.) It would seem to have been thought that as the [lower] branch of the legislature was to be shared between the provinces in the ratio of their population, there must be some other rule followed for the upper chamber. So we are to have twenty-four for Upper Canada, twenty-four for Lower Canada, twenty-four for the three lower provinces, and four for Newfoundland . . . and these legislative councillors, thus limited in number, are to hold their seats for life . . . As vacancies occur, they are to be filled as we are now told — and this is the strangest thing of all — not by the provincial legislatures, nor by any authority or under any avowed influence of the local kind, but possibly by the general government. And forsooth, this is called the federal feature of our system! (Hear, hear.) . . .

I have to ask honourable gentlemen opposite how they are going to organize their cabinet for these provinces, according to this so-called federal scheme? (Hear, hear.) I think I may defy them to show that the cabinet can be formed on any other prin-

ciple than that of a representation of the several provinces in that cabinet. It is admitted that the provinces are not really represented to any federal intent in the Legislative Council. The cabinet here must discharge all that kind of function, which in the United States is performed, in the federal sense, by the Senate. And precisely as in the United States, wherever a federal check is needed, the Senate has to do federal duty as an integral part of the executive government, so here . . . we must seek such substitute for it as we may, in a federal composition of the Executive Council; that is to say, by making it distinctly representative of the provinces. Well, I must say that this sort of thing is utterly variant from, and inconsistent with, British practice and principle; with the constitutional system which makes the whole cabinet responsible for every act of government. The British cabinet is no cabinet of sections, but a unit . . .

Great Britain has not, in any true sense of the term, federated herself with any of her colonies. She just retains a nominal supremacy over them.

John Scoble: It is a real supremacy.

Dunkin: No, it is only nominal as regards its exercise. It is not real in the sense of amounting to a substantial, practical exercise of power over the colonies. For these nearly five and twenty years past, I can call to mind no legislative act of ours disallowed by the home government.

An Honourable Member: Yes, there was one — Mr. Hincks' Currency Act.

Dunkin: Well, I believe that was. But in that case we got our own way in effect directly afterwards. I am referring more particularly, of course, to what may be called the conduct of our own domestic affairs. There is no mistake but we have had given to us by Great Britain a control practically unlimited over our own affairs; she lets us do what we like, while professing to retain a perfect nominal supremacy over us. She appoints our governor general, but when he comes here, he does what we want, not what she may want. She can, if she likes, disallow all our statutes; but for all practical purposes she never does. She may, if she chooses, alter or repeal the charter of our liberties which she granted to us, but she never thinks of doing such a thing, and we know she will not.

Well, here in this proposed constitution — looking to the relations which are to subsist between the federation and the provinces — in lieu of a real federation, such as subsists between the United States and the different states, we find an attempt to adopt to a considerable extent the British system* of a stated supremacy, not meant to be in fact the half of what it passes for in theory. But, however such a system may work as between Great Britain and her colonies, it by no means follows that it admits of extension to this case. If the vaguely stated powers of our so-called federation are to be merely nominal, they will be insufficient; if not nominal, they will be excessive. Either way, the United States' idea of an attempted precise statement of the powers meant to be given and used is the true one . . .

What are the relations to be established between our general and local governments? We are told to take for granted that no clashing of interest or feeling need be feared; that the federal union offered us in name will be a legislative union in reality. Yet, whoever dislikes the notion of a legislative union is assured it will be nothing of the sort. Now, sir, I do not believe you can have all the advantages of these two systems combined in one. (Hear, hear.) A legislative union is one thing; a federal union is another. The same system cannot be both at once. You cannot devise a system that shall have all the advantages of the one and of the other; but it is quite possible that you may devise one that will combine the chief disadvantages of both, and that is, I fear, pretty much what this system does. (Hear, hear.) . . .

To be sure there is the grand power of disallowance by the federal government, which we are told, in one and the same breath, is to be possessed by it, but never exercised.

Cartier: The presumption is, it will be exercised in case of unjust or unwise legislation.

Dunkin: The honourable gentleman's presumption reminds me of one, perhaps as conclusive, but which Dickens tells us failed to

---

* Dunkin recognizes that the Quebec Conference, in basing its federal scheme on the constitution of the British Empire, meant to subject the general government's legal powers to the constitutional constraints that governed Britain's dealings with her self-governing colonies. That is, the provinces were to enjoy the same autonomy (within their allotted jurisdiction) as they had hitherto. — PR

satisfy his Mr. Bumble. That henpecked beadle is said to have said, on hearing of the legal presumption that a man's wife acts under his control: "If the law presumes anything of the sort, the law's a fool* — a natural fool!" (Laughter.) If this permission of disallowance rests upon a presumption that the legislation of our provinces is going to be unjust or unwise, it may be needed; but under that idea, one might have done better either not to allow, or else to restrict within narrower limits, such legislation.

— *Legislative Assembly, February 27, 1865*

"[Christopher Dunkin] denounced this scheme because it is so very different from and, in his opinion, inferior to the United States Constitution. Well, sir, I accept of it because of its British and monarchical features."

Hope Mackenzie: He [Dunkin] denounced this scheme because it is so very different from and, in his opinion, inferior to the United States Constitution. Well, sir, I accept of it because of its British and monarchical features . . . I look upon it as a scheme more national than federal in its character — as looking more to a national union of the people than a union of sections, and it is chiefly because of this feature of it that it commends itself to my judgement. (Hear, hear.) . . . I stand as an advocate of national unity, and I would not accede to the principle of state sovereignty in this Confederation, the provinces delegating certain powers to the general government and reserving the residuum of power to themselves. (Hear, hear.) . . .

I would remind the house of the early ruin that threatened the United States under their first constitution, which was an embodiment of this vicious principle, and how clearly the great men of the first year of the republic foresaw the ruin it threatened to bring upon them. Washington . . . was incessant in his correspondence with the leading patriots of the day to obtain their opinions upon a new constitution, and Madison replies as follows:

> Conceiving that an independence of the states is totally irreconcilable with their aggregate sovereignty, and that a consolidation of the whole into one simple republic would be as inexpedient as it is unattainable, I have sought for some middle ground which may at once support a due supremacy of the national authority, and not exclude the local authorities wherein they can be subordinately useful.

Mr. Jay's convictions in favour of central supreme authority are

---

* *The reference is to* Oliver Twist. *In actual fact, Mr. Bumble's language is somewhat cruder. — PR*

equally strong. He says: "What powers should be granted to the Government so constituted, is a question which deserves much thought." I think the more the better, "the states retaining only so much as may be necessary for domestic purposes." Hamilton* . . . equally anxious with his co-patriots to save his country from the anarchy and ruin that he saw approaching as the inevitable result of a partitioned sovereignty, thus addressed the head of the republic:

> All Federal Governments are weak and distracted. In order to avoid the evils incident to that form, the Government ratif of the American Union must be a national representative system. But no such system can be successful in the actual situation of this country, unless it is endorsed with all the principles and means of influence and power which are the proper supports of government. It must, therefore, be made completely sovereign, and state power, as a separate legislative power, must be annihilated.

. . . I think, sir, it becomes us in framing a constitution for these provinces to profit, not only by the early but by the later experience of our neighbours — to enquire how far they succeeded in eradicating the evil from their new constitution, and to what extent their present troubles are chargeable to what is left in their system of the dangerous principle referred to. Let us profit by the wisdom of the framers of the American Constitution, and by the experiences of that country under it — not to copy their work, but to help us when framing a constitution for ourselves to steer clear of the evils that they have felt. Believing that the Quebec Conference has done so and has presented to us the framework of a constitution, the leading features of which are in unison with the constitutional principles of the British monarchy, and consistent with that allegiance which we all owe and cheerfully yield to the throne of Britain, I cheerfully endorse the scheme. (Hear, hear.) . . .

A.-A. Dorion: I find that the powers assigned to the general parliament enable it to legislate on all subjects whatsoever. It is an error to imagine that these powers are defined and limited by the

---

James Madison, John Jay, and Alexander Hamilton were authors of The Federalist, *a set of eighty-five papers published in New York City newspapers in 1787–88 over the pen-name Publius, which advocated ratification of the federal constitution adopted at Philadelphia in September 1787.*

29th clause of the resolutions. Were it desirous of legislating on subjects placed under the jurisdiction of the local legislatures, there is not a word in these resolutions which can be construed to prevent it, and if the local legislatures complain, parliament may turn away and refuse to hear their complaints because all the sovereignty is vested in the general government, and there is no authority to define its functions and attributes and those of the local governments . . . What authority have you constituted which can come forward and say to the federal parliament — "You shall not do such and such a thing, you shall not legislate upon such and such a subject, because these matters are reserved to the local governments"? There will be no such authority, and consequently it will have sovereign power, and can do all that it pleases, and may encroach upon all the rights and attributes of the local governments whenever it may think proper. We shall be — I speak as a Lower Canadian — we shall be at its mercy, because it may exercise the right of veto on all the legislation of the local parliaments, and there again we shall have no remedy. In case of difference between the federal power and the local governments, what authority will intervene for its settlement?

Cartier: It will be the imperial government.

Dorion: In effect there will be no other authority than that of the imperial government, and we know too well the value assigned to the complaints of Lower Canada by the imperial government.

Cartier: The delegates understood the matter better than that. Neither the imperial government nor the general government will interfere, but the courts of justice will decide all questions in relation to which there may be differences between the two powers . . . Should the general legislature pass a law beyond the limits of its functions, it will be null and void *pleno jure*.

Dorion: Yes, I understand that, and it is doubtless to decide questions of this kind that it is proposed to establish federal courts.

Cartier: No, no! They will be established solely to apply and adjudicate upon the federal laws.

Dorion: . . . If the differences between the federal and the local parliaments are not to be submitted to the decision of a supreme federal court, I do not see who can possibly decide them. (Hear,

"There will be no absolute sovereign power, each legislature having its distinct and independent attributes, not proceeding from one or the other by delegation, either from above or below. The federal parliament will have legislative sovereign power in all questions submitted to its control in the constitution. So also the local legislatures will be sovereign in all matters which are specifically assigned to them."

hear.) We are told that the Federal Court of Appeals will not be charged with the decision of matters in dispute between the legislatures, but they will only have to give final judgments in cases decided by the local inferior courts. Well, for my part I cannot approve of the creation of this court. The great inconveniences of it to us Lower Canadians may easily be seen. Thus, when a cause shall have been argued and decided in all our courts, we shall still have to go before a Federal Court of Appeal* composed of judges of all the provinces, and in which we shall probably have only one judge, who may be selected out of the English population. And this is the protection afforded to us . . .

Joseph Cauchon: The honourable member for Hochelaga [Dorion] talked to us of conflicts between the federal parliament and the local houses, and of the sovereign power of the central government over the legislatures of the provinces. But what, then, is this sovereign power over the attributes of the provincial legislatures? . . . There will be no absolute sovereign power,† each legislature having its distinct and independent attributes, not proceeding from one or the other by delegation, either from above or below. The federal parliament will have legislative sovereign power in all questions submitted to its control in the constitution. So also the local legislatures will be sovereign in all matters which are specifically assigned to them.

— *Legislative Assembly, March 6, 1865*

Aquila Walsh: In the scheme submitted to us, I am happy to observe that the principal and supreme power is placed in the hands of the general government, and that the powers deputed to the local governments are of a limited character.

— *Legislative Assembly, March 8, 1865*

D. Ford Jones: Notwithstanding some honourable gentlemen have praised the federal system in the States as worthy of imitation, still I think our proposed system much to be preferred. It differs in this — the United States federal system was formed

---

* *Dorion anticipates later complaints about the incompetence of common-law judges on the Supreme Court of Canada to construe Quebec's civil code.* — PR
† *Cauchon points out that the Quebec scheme is one of coordinate sovereignty, since the federal and the provincial legislatures will receive formally identical distributions of power from the British parliament.* — PR

from a number of sovereign states, with sovereign powers, delegating to a central power just as much or as little of their power as they chose . . . Our case is exactly the reverse. Instead of the central government receiving its power from the different provinces, it gives to those provinces just as much or as little as it chooses. Hear what the 45th resolution says — "In regard to all subjects in which jurisdiction belongs to both the general and local legislatures, the laws of the General Parliament shall control and supersede those made by the local legislatures, and the latter shall be void so far as inconsistent with the former." This places the whole control in the hands of the general government, making the union as nearly legislative as the circumstances of the various provinces would admit. So much is this the case that the honourable member for Hochelaga [Dorion] fears that it would eventually result in a legislative union — a result to my mind devoutly to be desired. (Hear, hear.)

— Legislative Assembly, March 9, 1865

John A. Macdonald: The other day the honourable gentleman [Luther Holton] paused to say . . . that in taking the course I have done on this question — that of advocating a federal instead of a legislative union — I violated all the principles of my former life having a bearing on this subject. Mr. Speaker, it is quite true that after a careful examination of the constitution of the United States, in connection with its practical working, and the civil war which has grown out of it, I saw many weaknesses in connection with the federal system, as operated in that country, and I was desirous as any man could be in taking part in the conference relating to union between the provinces of British North America, that as much [of] the legislative form of government as possible, and as few of the weaknesses which experience had shown to exist in the American Constitution, should be incorporated in ours. I do not like to refer to any remarks of mine in times past; but as this charge has been brought against me, I will read, by permission of the house, a passage from a speech of mine, in relation to representation by population. And I might here say that it is the only speech I ever delivered in my life which I have ever taken any particular trouble to revise . . . I said:

The only feasible scheme which presented itself to his (my) mind, as a remedy for the evils complained of, was a confederation of all the provinces. (Hear, hear.) But in speaking of a

confederation he must not be understood as alluding to it in the sense of the one on the other side of the line. For that had not been successful. But then he did not say so from any feeling of satisfaction at such a result. Far from him be any such idea. He heartily agreed with the junior member for Montreal (Honourable Mr. McGee) in every word of regret which he had expressed at the unhappy and lamentable state of things which they now witnessed in the States, for he remembered that they were of the same blood as ourselves. He still looked hopefully to the future of the United States. He believed there was a vigour, a vitality, in the Anglo-Saxon character and the Anglo-Saxon institutions of the United States, that would carry them through this great convulsion, as they had carried through our mother country in days of old. (Loud cheers from both sides of the house.) He hoped with that honourable gentleman (Honourable Mr. McGee) that if they were to be severed in two — as severed in two he believed they would be — two great, two noble, two free nations would exist in place of one. (Hear, hear.) But while he thus sympathized with them, he must say, let it be a warning to ourselves that we do not split on the same rock which they had done. The fatal error which they had committed — and it was, perhaps, unavoidable from the state of the colonies at the time of the revolution — was in making each state a distinct sovereignty, and giving to each a distinct sovereign power, except in those instances where they were specially reserved by the constitution and conferred upon the general government. The true principle of a confederation lay in giving to the general government all the principles and powers of sovereignty, and that the subordinate or individual states should have no powers but those expressly bestowed upon them. We should thus have a powerful central government, a powerful central legislature, and a decentralized system of minor legislatures for local purposes.

These, sir, were the opinions I uttered in a speech delivered in 1861; and I say that the constitution which this house, by a majority of three to one, has carried out as far as I am concerned is, in spirit and letter, that which I then pointed out* . . .

Macdonald's claim that the Quebec scheme conforms to his stated preference of 1861 deserves the same credence as the Reformers' claim that it conforms

Holton: I think I owe the honourable attorney general west [Macdonald] a word of explanation. I was not so fortunate as to be in parliament in 1861, and I have never happened to read the speech from which he quoted . . . It now appears that in his speech of 1861 he shows that at that time he contemplated the possibility of a modified sort of federation — a federation very different, however, from the joint authority of the honourable member for South Oxford [George Brown], who argues that this is the very measure of the convention of 1859.

Brown: It is on the same basis.

Holton: It is the same basis; but in the one, the federal authority has the preponderance — in the other the local authority.

Brown: This includes the best features of both systems.
— *Legislative Assembly, March 13, 1865*

BRITISH COLUMBIA

W.T. Drake: The idea of consolidating the British possessions on this continent is an idea which is likely to carry people away. The idea of assisting to found a large and wide-spreading country might be dazzling to some. But if we are to be turned over to Canada with no change in our form of government, no alteration in the management of our political affairs, where is the advantage of any change? The officials will be chosen by the dominion government instead of the crown; we should be transferred from the rule of statesmen at Downing Street to that of politicians at Ottawa . . . All our political rights will be taken away, the whole of the legislation will pass out of our hands into that of the dominion at Ottawa; those laws upon which we shall be entitled to pass an opinion will be much of the same nature as those upon which a municipality or vestry may vote, but which are beneath the dignity of a colony. All power of raising taxes, except . . . for provincial purposes, shall be subject to the provisions of the Organic Act, which we have no power to change. Any terms

---

to their party platform of 1859. Luther Holton goes on to point out the incompatibility of the two claims, and Brown responds by repeating the position that both he and Macdonald took in their opening speeches: the scheme is an inspired compromise. — PR

which we can impose must be subject to the provisions of the "British North America Act."

My position, therefore, is correct when I say that our power will not exceed that of a municipality. We are told that we are not fit for representative institutions or responsible government. Then we shall go into the dominion as a crown colony — bound hand and foot . . . Moreover, sir, I would ask if we be confederated upon these terms, what guarantee has the colony that the terms will be carried out? We all know that when compacts are made between a large and a small power, the larger can break the treaty with impunity when an emergency arises . . . The benefits of the larger provinces of Canada will always take precedence of those of British Columbia, whose representatives will be in a small minority. And I would never consent to Confederation on any terms without an imperial guarantee that the terms would be observed and kept. History tells us that in a compact between a larger and smaller country, the smaller must go to the wall.

— Legislative Council, March 9, 1870

"The benefits of the larger provinces of Canada will always take precedence of those of British Columbia . . . History tells us that in a compact between a larger and smaller country, the smaller must go to the wall."

Henry Holbrook: I shall be glad to see inserted in the terms a clause empowering our local government to make her own tariff, so as to protect our farming interests, in a similar manner as, under the imperial government, the Isle of Man and the Channel Islands* have rights reserved . . .

T.L. Wood: It cannot be denied that the idea of Confederation and general alliance between the British colonies in North America is a very captivating idea. The existence of a homogeneous nation tending to act as a counterpoise to the great republic to the south of us is a great political idea, but it is an idea most dangerous and difficult to carry out. When I voted in 1867 for Confederation on fair and equitable terms, I had in my mind Confederation in the general acceptation of the word as understood by all political writers and by the world in general — a union of free and self-governed states, united by a federal compact for purposes of offence and defence, of peace and war; and

---

* *The Channel Islands are all that remain of Britain's once-extensive possessions in France. With lieutenant governors representing the queen in both Jersey and Guernsey, the islands have their own assemblies, legal systems, and currency. The Isle of Man is another possession of the British crown, with wide independent powers exercised by a two-chamber assembly. — IG*

for the purposes of maintaining and preserving uniformity in laws and institutions which affect the social and commercial relations of life; such laws and institutions as criminal law and practice, the general administration of justice, and the laws regulating commerce and navigation. Such a Confederation I then believed to be possible. I am foolish enough to believe it still; but Confederation as understood by Canadian and imperial statesmen — Confederation as effected by the Organic Act of 1867 — is not confederation at all. I would, indeed, throw the word confederation to the winds, since by confederation is obviously meant union, incorporation, and absorption. The Organic Act of 1867 provides for the entire transfer of all effective legislative power and control to Ottawa, as the seat of the dominion government, where, owing to the much greater wealth and population of Canada, the influence and authority of Canada bear all before it.

It is a principle too obvious for proof or dissertation that confederation in its proper sense can only thrive where the states bound together by the federal compact are not only free but where they are nearly equal. Excess of power in any one state is fatal to the interests of the rest. No, sir, the word confederation has no application to the intended movement. Lord Granville, in his dispatch, no longer calls it by such a term. Union and incorporation are spoken of . . . and the movement really is one of incorporation, absorption, and annihilation . . .

Amor De Cosmos: There is no reason that we should not have our interests protected.

J.S. Helmcken: The Organic Act says so.

De Cosmos: The Organic Act says no such thing . . . The government of Canada is based on the popular will; and that is the highest guarantee that we shall be treated fairly by the dominion. I have never heard of Scotland being injured because she had a smaller representation in parliament than England.

Wood: Yes, yes. Two revolutions* followed immediately upon union.

---

* The Jacobite risings of 1708 and 1715 were at least as much a protest against the Hanoverian succession as an attempt to overthrow the union

De Cosmos: Yes, but that doesn't affect my proposition. A little bloodletting,* however, does no harm occasionally. I would not object to a little revolution now and again in British Columbia after Confederation, if we were treated unfairly; for I am one of those who believe that political hatreds attest the vitality of a state. The honourable and learned member for Victoria says that all power will be taken by Confederation. Why, sir, the honourable gentleman cannot have read the Organic Act. For he will find the exclusive powers of the dominion and the provinces clearly set forth in it . . . If the dominion refuse to keep the terms and repudiate their part of the bargain, we can appeal to the imperial government to release us.

Wood: Let us have it in black and white.

De Cosmos: Why, let the [Organic] Act be repealed and down go the terms. The sovereign power is in the parliament of England. It made the act, and if it is violated without redress, it can repeal it, and the power of Canada ceases . . . And with reference to the local constitution, it may be necessary for us to know whether our governors cannot be elected as in the United States, instead of being appointed on the English principle; and whether we may not acquire the right to pass local laws over the veto of the governor, by a two-thirds vote of the legislature . . .

— *Legislative Council, March 10, 1870*

NEWFOUNDLAND

Ambrose Shea: [The Quebec Conference] proposes a constitution based as nearly as circumstances would permit on the principles of the British Constitution, and which, while of the federal character, avoids the prominent causes of weakness and failure which the working of the American system has disclosed . . . To [the] general government and legislature will be confided the larger powers now possessed by the several local governments, conferring on it the amount of authority necessary for the due

---

between England and Scotland. With rising prosperity, the union became secure after the 1740s. — IG

* *This heedless statement echoes the Jeffersonian and Lockean view that revolutions from time to time are good for the political health of a country. Not so good, however, for those whose blood is let. — IG*

conservation and protection of the interests of the several communities whose guardianship it would assume. There was not in this arrangement, as had been represented for unworthy purposes, and to raise a cry amongst the unlettered and unwary, any selling of the interests of one colony to another, but a proposal is made by which the several colonies, on principles of honourable and equitable partnership, agree to concede a certain portion of the powers they severally possess to a central authority in which they are fairly represented, and where the aggregate of these powers may be used with greatly increased efficacy for common purposes of public advantage.

The local government would be retained, with smaller powers, having under its control the expenditure of 80,000 pounds sterling per annum and the management of peculiarly local affairs. The roads, public institutions, and other kindred matters would be in the hands of the local legislature; but the operations of the general government would be entirely independent of the action of the local bodies. The modifications of the present local governmental machinery are left to the several bodies themselves, to determine according to the peculiar circumstances of each colony; but the necessity of reducing them, in one shape or another, to meet the altered condition of affairs and lessen the expenses would not be a matter of question.

— *House of Assembly, February 2, 1865*

"The provinces were not entering on this scheme with the idea that they would be so many distinct antagonisms, requiring each to guard themselves against the encroaching spirit of the rest; but on the contrary, they propose to come together for purposes of mutual co-operation."

Ambrose Shea: Can we rationally suppose that the Confederation would be governed by men so deficient in statesmanship as to legislate in disregard of the circumstances and feelings of the people their measures would affect? It requires but little reflection to satisfy a thinking mind of the groundless nature of such apprehensions and of the ample guarantees we have against the imposition of heavy taxation. The provinces were not entering on this scheme with the idea that they would be so many distinct antagonisms, requiring each to guard themselves against the encroaching spirit of the rest; but on the contrary, they propose to come together for purposes of mutual co-operation which all stand in need of, and which can only be secured by a course of action in which the just rights of all are respected and upheld. The common interests of the lower provinces at least are acknowledged by all who speak on this subject, and their views on the question of taxation would necessarily be identical. If Canadian statesmen had the wish, will anyone assert that they

would have the power to press taxation against the combined resistance of the lower provinces? Experience gives us no warrant for assuming that an attempt could be made so hostile to the spirit and genius of representative combinations,* but such strange argument[s] had been used in relation to this question that even such remote and almost impossible contingencies it became necessary to examine and rebut.

He had shown the utter futility of such legislation if it were enacted, but in the case he had imagined the weight of public opinion throughout the confederacy would come to the support of those against whom oppression was directed and the influence would be such as no government would be able to resist. But he would go further and suppose that were such a measure accomplished, we should still have the security that lies in an appeal to the imperial government to whom all the legislation of the Confederation must be sent for approval.

— *House of Assembly, February 21, 1865*

PRINCE EDWARD ISLAND

J.H. Gray: I would remark upon . . . our share in the representation in the general parliament and the complaints of the objectors that we have too few members. When the revolted provinces ordained and established their constitution, it was provided that representatives from any state might be sent to parliament in the proportion of one member to every thirty thousand of the population. The state of Delaware, large and influential, as well as that of Rhode Island, somewhat similar in extent to this colony, did not think it against the interests of their people to enter their union with one member each; this island is invited to enter the proposed Confederation with five.

We are also told that our four members in the [Legislative] Council will be no protection to our interests and that the custom obtaining in the United States is far better. Now let us take this view of the question and follow the United States system. Vancouver, Columbia, Red River, Upper Canada, New Brunswick, Nova Scotia, Newfoundland, and Prince Edward Island each sends two members to the upper chamber. If a question arose affecting our sectional rights, interests, and privileges,

---

Shea affirms that the deliberative nature of representative institutions favours compromise rather than the tyranny of the majority. — PR

do we imagine that our two members could carry the point against the other sixteen? But I would ask has a case ever occurred in which such injustice was attempted or even hinted at, as the opponents of Confederation are so grievously afraid of? At the time of the revolution, the white population of the whole thirteen states was less than that of Canada at this time. The population of Canada is now considerably more than thirty times that of this island, and if we are to follow the plan of the United States to mete out even-handed justice, we must first portion out Canada into thirteen sections, approximating to what the United States were at the time of union, not what they now are.

But, I would ask, is it necessary that we should go into this Confederation with our hearts and minds filled with suspicions? Is it a foregone conclusion with us that all the other provinces will unite to do injustice to one particular section of their common country? Yet we have all these dark surmisings, and much more freely enunciated by all parties who oppose the Confederation. "Where will the interests of Upper Canada be," cries Mr. Cameron,* "when the other provinces hold a majority of thirty against her in the lower, and fifty-two in the upper chamber?" Then M. Dorion cries out for poor Lower Canada. Then comes New Brunswick, Nova Scotia, and Prince Edward Island. Let us say, "away with such unworthy suspicions, they should not be held by liberal and enlightened men." As I said before, such a case has never occurred in the history of nations, and is it not monstrous doctrine to pretend that it could ever occur with us in this age of reason?

— *House of Assembly, March 25, 1865*

Frederick Brecken: With respect to the political part of the report I think we have reason to complain. The principle of representation by population is sought to be enforced on too sweeping a scale; but as this principle is a *sine qua non* with the people of Upper Canada, and is, I believe, at the bottom and root of the Confederation scheme, we might expect to see it applied to the lower house; but I see no reason why the constitution of the

---

As British North Americans debated the Quebec scheme, they were heard in each others' colonies as well as their own. Here Gray paraphrases a passage of M.C. Cameron's speech of February 24 in which Cameron quotes from a speech given by Leonard Tilley of New Brunswick the previous November. — PR

upper house should not have been assimilated to that of the Senate of the United States; but I do not attach much importance to this, as I believe the more representatives we have, the more our difficulties would increase. We have no men of fortune amongst us; at any rate, none foolish enough to engage in politics. Honourable members from distant parts of the island, from the North Cape and East Point, can spare a few weeks during the winter months to attend to their legislative duties, but it would be found a very different matter to be obliged to leave home and business, and that, too, very likely in the winter season, for three of four months in the year to attend the general legislature at Ottawa. The public men of this island cannot afford to do so, even if willing. The sacrifice of interest which a seat in the confederate assembly would entail would be greater than our public men could afford; and if to remedy this they are adequately paid, then their constituents would begin to suspect that their personal interests might outweigh their regard for the interests of the colony. I doubt much whether men of stake, and really interested in the welfare of the country, could be found willing to offer themselves. Indeed, so far as our representation is concerned, it might as well be wiped out of the report altogether.

There is another objection to the new constitution, as it applies to this island. What, I would ask, looking at the wide range of subjects reserved for the general government, will there be left to engage the attention of our local legislature? As it is, with the management of all our affairs, the subjects that most frequently engage our attention are not of a very broad or elevating character. If from the subjects to be assigned to our local legislature we withdraw education and the management of our highways, matters which, when once properly provided for, do not admit of being tinkered at every session, what will be left for us to do?

We might have a party for bringing in a measure that all pigs should wear rings in their noses, but on such a question it would be difficult to keep together either a government or an opposition, unless they were to differ as to the description of the metal the rings should be made of; but to be serious, I believe if we went into Confederation we would find our local government a nuisance too cumbersome and expensive for the work assigned it and, before long, would be petitioning to have it done away with, and to have municipal institutions instead. This very building with its empty walls and untenanted offices would stand a

> *"We are told that by going into the union we will rise from being a small and obscure colony to be part of a great country. This may, in some degree, be true; but, practically, we are called upon to yield up to a very great extent the control and management of our public affairs, a great privilege, which once parted with is not easily regained."*

frowning remonstrance against the policy of the honourable colonial secretary [W.H. Pope] and his union friends; he would take fright at the sight of its decaying walls.

We are told that by going into the union we will rise from being a small and obscure colony to be part of a great country. This may, in some degree, be true; but, practically, we are called upon to yield up to a very great extent the control and management of our public affairs, a great privilege, which once parted with is not easily regained.

George Howlan: The subject which the people of this island are now called upon to consider is the report of a delegation not authorized by this house, and one by which the constitution of this colony is to be wrested from us. In considering the question of Confederation, we ought to view it not as it would affect us at present, but as it would probably operate upon the interests of this colony in all time to come.

The principle of representation by population in the lower house is borrowed from the American system; yet the Quebec Conference did not follow out the same model with respect to the constitution of the upper branch. In the neighbouring republic, each state has the privilege of sending two representatives to the Senate, no matter now small its population. New York with its population of 3,097,894 has only the same number of senators in Congress as the state of Rhode Island with its population of 147,545. The difference between the population of these two States is as 20 to 1, greater fully than it is between that of Upper Canada and this island; yet while this report allows Upper Canada twenty-four members in the Legislative Council of the Confederation, this colony is only allotted five. Instead of all the provinces being allowed the same number of members each in the upper house, according to the principle of the United States' Constitution, each of the Canadas is to have as many councillors as all the lower provinces put together. Then again, the members of this body are to be appointed for life, a system which would undoubtedly bring about a deadlock, the very state of affairs in Canada which Confederation is intended to remedy . . .

Representation by population might be very well for Canada herself, but in a general union of the colonies it would operate injuriously for the Maritime provinces, as they could not expect to protect their interests when they would have to contend with 100 of a clear majority over their own representation . . .

It is well enough for those to go into Confederation who have not been able to manage their own affairs, but for us to do so in the prosperous state of our revenue would be but committing political suicide. Some of the delegates, however, inform us that we may obtain £250,000 to buy proprietary lands.* There is nothing in the report to this effect; all that I see promised is interest for a certain sum. If the honourable member for St. Peters were in the general legislature, and to rise to ask for a grant of £200,000 to purchase proprietors' lands, could he have the face to point to a certain paragraph of the report and say I claim this sum as a constitutional right? (Laughter.) But, it might be said, he would have four other members to aid him in urging our rights. Our delegates, did they wish to ensure our rights, had a much better opportunity to gain this point at a conference of a few individuals than in a house of 194 members. Their first object ought to have been to get a settlement of our land question — the only question which is a grievance in the colony — and then they might have come with some show of reason and asked us to go into Confederation. But they ask us to give up our constitution — for what? Simply the glory of belonging to a country with four millions of people? (Hear, hear.) I believe our people prefer representation in the imperial parliament to union with Canada, for though they might scarcely have one member in the British House of Commons, they would at least feel that their liberties were in the hands of people that could be trusted.

— *House of Assembly, March 28, 1865*

> *"They ask us to give up our constitution — for what? Simply the glory of belonging to a country with four millions of people? I believe our people prefer representation in the imperial parliament to union with Canada."*

George Coles: Again with respect to our local legislatures under the Confederation scheme, what would it amount to? We would be a laughingstock to the world. The city council would be a king to such a legislature. In this house scarcely anything would be left us to do, but to legislate about dog taxes and the running at large of swine. Some honourable members have referred to the great advantage of this colony being allowed to retain its local legislature. Probably they intend to remove to Canada themselves and care little about what they leave behind them.

— *House of Assembly, March 31, 1865*

---

* To some islanders, the chief or only point of entering Confederation was to obtain help in solving the land question. They were unable to secure this goal at the Quebec Conference, but the London Conference of 1866–67 did pass a resolution committing the dominion government to such a course. — PR

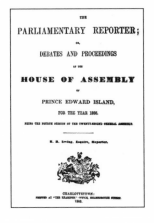

T.H. Haviland: The cry raised by our anti-confederates in general was that, by Confederation, we would be deprived at once of all the consideration and advantages of a resident and independent government; and for the prospect and benefits of free trade and extended commerce which were held out to lure us into the connection, all we would realize would be increase of taxation burdens and duties, wholly ruinous to our prosperity, and that altogether for the relief and benefit of Canada. The only advantages it was, most unjustly and ungenerously, said by anti-confederates which would result to Prince Edward Island from her being included in the contemplated Confederation would be experienced by a few of her politicians who, for the rewards of venality, had agreed to barter away their own honour and the rights and liberties of their country. By those who thus, perversely, and, he might say dishonestly, argued, it was most carefully kept out of sight that, according to the proposed scheme of Confederation, there would be no degradation of any of the provincial legislatures and governments. These, on the contrary, would be preserved intact; and each province would retain the entire control and management of its own local and internal affairs. It was true, indeed, that the general government would, undoubtedly, and of necessity, exercise supervision of the individual states; but the power of the federal government to interfere with the exclusively internal affairs of any of the confederated provinces would be of the most limited and inconsiderable character.

In all the arguments brought to bear against Confederation, it was also very carefully kept out of view that its accomplishment, upon terms fair and just to every section of it — and upon no other terms did he wish, or had he ever desired, to see it established — would not only be the means of happily extinguishing those little waspish political feuds and jealousies which had so long acted as a drag upon our progress and been a disgrace to us as a people, but would also, by putting the impost duties and other sources of public revenue upon a uniform basis, under the control of the federal government, put an end to the anomaly of separate customs establishments, and the conflicting and perplexing commercial regulations which existed, and which had almost of necessity arisen out of the disunited state of these provinces.

Again, the recognition of another benefit which would result from a union of these provinces had been carefully eschewed by our island anti-confederates: he meant identity of laws and uniformity in the modes of their administration. The existence

within territories of the same nation — territories lying near to one another, alike in climate, natural productions, and the social condition of their inhabitants — the existence, he said, within such territories of a multiplicity of laws, each having a distinct local application upon almost every question of human rights; and of a plurality of courts — each peculiarly constituted and having its peculiar rules of practice — administering those laws hampered the ordinary administration of justice, tended to the promotion of crime, and seriously inconvenienced commercial intercourse between the various parts of these territories. The desirability of the contemplated Confederation was, in his opinion, greatly heightened by the certain prospect which it afforded of the removal of these grievous anomalies by means of judicious and remedial action on that score by the federal legislature.

— *House of Assembly, May 8, 1866*

Chapter Ten

MINORITIES AND MINORITY RIGHTS

⟢⟐⟣

T HE TERM "MINORITY RIGHTS" is often used to describe
and justify multicultural programs to encourage and
strengthen diversity in public life. The speakers in our debates
use it in an older sense, one not entirely forgotten today, but not
easy to reconcile with the idea of programs to enhance diversity.
They belong to the school of thought that believes cultural and
religious differences are a potential source of antagonisms threatening civil peace.

Memories of the terrible religious wars of seventeenth-century
Europe are at work. From communal traditions and from their
study of history, the legislators conclude that passionate antagonism towards peoples of another nationality or religion is always a
human possibility. In Prince Edward Island, W.H. Pope deplores
religious partisanship. Newfoundland's Daniel Prowse wrings his
hands over that "bane to our community," "sectarian and political
differences." Speakers in Canada and Nova Scotia nervously congratulate themselves on the lack of antagonism among religions
and among "races."

But although they may not wish to *encourage* diversity, the legislators adamantly believe it should be *tolerated*. Some of them
describe it as ineradicable. Many of them are religious men who
wish to see the particular institutions they cherish continue, and
understand very well that they in turn must respect the religion
and traditions of others. Hence the repeated praise for religious
liberty in these debates.

In short, in the matter of religion, culture, and politics, they
are adherents of John Locke's doctrine of the separation of church
and state in the *Letter Concerning Toleration* (1690). To put an end

to religious wars, Locke banishes religion and religious distinctions from the political sphere. Politics is to concern itself with the people's legal rights and material welfare, not their hopes and fears for the life hereafter. Moreover — the other side of the coin — the state is not to interfere with religious teachings and practices as long as they do not transgress the law.

The core of Locke's teaching is clear. But questions remain on the periphery. Does his formula allow public funding for religious schools? Does it allow policies to inculcate loyalty to the larger nation? These crucial issues surface especially in the Canadian debates.

NOVA SCOTIA

"[The Canadians] would find in the Maritime provinces . . . a united people . . . a country in which civil and religious liberty is enjoyed by all, and in which I am happy to know there exists no hostility between different races or religions."

Charles Tupper: The house will see that if the subject of a union with Canada were even in contemplation, no wiser step could take place than the union of the Maritime provinces in the first instance. Hostile as I believe the sentiment of Canada is at the present time to a union with the Maritime provinces, the day is not far distant when it will be for the interest of both to unite, and Canada will, I have no doubt, seek in that union the solution of those difficulties that are now found insuperable in the government of the country. These provinces, I am proud to know, would present a sufficient area, population, and resources to exercise no small amount of influence in the scale between the two sections in which Canada is divided. They would find in the Maritime provinces that which they seek for in vain in their own country — that is, a united people — divided by no sectional antagonism and embarrassed by no separate system of jurisprudence. They would find a country in which civil and religious liberty is enjoyed by all, and in which I am happy to know there exists no hostility between different races or religions. We would present a country to their view that might be united on a common bond of union with Canada — a union which is essential to the solution of the difficulties that now divide the two great sections of that province. This union when required will be, as I have said, more easy of accomplishment when these Maritime provinces are united than at present.

— *House of Assembly, March 28, 1864*

John Tobin: I would . . . prefer a legislative union of the provinces, but I feel that it is impracticable, in view of the fact

that it is opposed by Lower Canada, with its large French population and peculiar laws and institutions which they have retained since the time of [James] Wolfe. Their prejudices must be respected, and therefore I believe, from my conversation with gentlemen of influence in Lower Canada, that we cannot have a legislative union at present, though I do not know what may be in the womb of time. The first course that is to be pursued to adopt is a federal union, as propounded in the Quebec scheme.

— *House of Assembly, April 17, 1866*

NEW BRUNSWICK

John McMillan: The honourable president of the council has referred to the differences in race and creed of the people of Canada. I will quote on this subject an extract from one of the most eloquent men on this continent, Mr. D'A. McGee: "I venture, in the first place, to observe that there seems to be a good deal of exaggeration on the subject of race, occasionally introduced both on the one side and the other in this section of our country. This theory of race is sometimes carried to an anti-Christian and unphilosophical excess. Whose words are those — 'God hath made of one blood all the nations that dwell on the face of the earth'?"* This is the right view to take of this question. Look at the attitude of the mother country; there they are composed of all peoples, and yet they go on quietly and harmoniously.

— *House of Assembly, June 5, 1865*

William Needham: [An] objection to this scheme is that two languages are to be used. One-half of the members will get up and jabber in French, and not one of our members will understand what they are saying. The courts of law are conducted in French too. In Lower Canada one lawyer talks to the jury in French and another in English. This is a system with which we want nothing to do.

— *House of Assembly, April 3, 1866*

Bliss Botsford: History shows us that great difficulties always arise from the dividing of the people into distinctive classes, and this has been clearly illustrated in Upper and Lower Canada. These distinctions of race and language are, I see, to be perpetu-

---

* *The words are St. Paul's before the Council of the Areopagus in Athens. See Acts 17:26.*

ated . . . And not only is the difference of race to be perpetuated, but they provide also for the continuance of two languages in the federal government and federal courts. I believe they should have decided that the language of the country should be either one or the other, and when you, sir, as one of the judges of the Court of Appeals, shall be called on to decide on some difficulties which may arise . . . you will be addressed by some of the lawyers in the polite language of France, whilst others will quote authorities in England . . . Instead of these differences of race and language being abolished or confined to the places where they have previously existed, we find that this class distinction is to be propagated and engrafted upon provinces where it has never been before. This has been the cause of the trouble between Upper and Lower Canada, and serious difficulties must arise from it here.

— *House of Assembly, June 29, 1866*

PRINCE EDWARD ISLAND

W. H. Pope: How would such reunion affect this island? It must be plain to every gentleman of this committee that the legislation of this island cannot be of a nature calculated to develop its resources and to promote its prosperity, so long as the inhabitants are divided into two parties, the one violently antagonistic to the other; so long as the chief object of one party is to hold office, and of the other to obtain office. I readily admit, Mr. Chairman, that, in my opinion, we have party legislation in the worst form, and that neither of the parties into which we are divided is free from the influence of party spirit. Party animosities are violent, in all communities, in proportion to their size. Our community is a very limited one, and the differences which divided us partake of a religious character. Thirty-five thousand of our inhabitants are arrayed in bitter antagonism to the remaining 45,000. We have 35,000 Roman Catholics, the majority of them Irish, of the extreme ultramontane stamp, and we have 45,000 Protestants, the majority of whom are Scotch Presbyterians, many the sons of Convenanters,* who will never submit to the rule by Roman Catholics. If this island were united with the neighbouring provinces,† our

---

* *In 1638, during their struggle with Charles I, the leaders of Scotland drew up a National Covenant under which the people pledged to defend the Presbyterian faith.*

† *This sentence refers not to Confederation but to the proposed legislative*

Protestant population would have less cause to dread popish supremacy than they have at present, religious animosities would be weakened, and great good would be the consequence.

"The enlarged field of subjects of political discussion would elevate the minds of the people and extinguish the narrow feelings which at present embitter the parties into which we are . . . divided."

Benjamin Davies: My own opinion is that a union is only a question of time — that it must occur sooner or later. Situated as we are at present, we are powerless at the Colonial Office on the most important subject of the land question, and it cannot be doubted that we would occupy a more influential position if we formed a part of a great united province. The enlarged field of subjects of political discussion would elevate the minds of the people and extinguish the narrow feelings which at present embitter the parties into which we are, and have been, divided.

— *House of Assembly, April 18, 1864*

NEWFOUNDLAND

F.B.T. Carter: [W]e ought all to regard the public good, and not private and personal considerations. [A] beneficial result of Confederation would be that the acerbity of feeling which had marked our political contests would be done away with. For a long time past there had been a constant struggle for power between the two religious parties* into which our population is divided, and election after election was sought to be carried in certain districts by means which we all deprecated. With Confederation, the effort would be to return to the federal House of Commons the ablest men, and those who possessed the greatest share of public confidence, irrespective of creed. Did honourable gentlemen wish to see election riots again? Confederation would bring larger questions to occupy the attention of politicians. There were parties in this community who traded on their piety, and when they wanted a relative provided for, they claimed an appointment for him, not on account of his fitness, but said, "It is

---

union of the Maritime provinces which was on the table in 1864. One would not necessarily hope for similar effects from a federal union, which would leave the local government in being — though, as we see below, Newfoundlanders did express such hopes about Confederation a year later. — PR

* The population was divided fairly evenly between Roman Catholics, mainly of Irish origin, and Protestants, mainly of English stock. After the establishment of representative government in 1832, this ethno-religious division found expression in an often violent political rivalry.

our right as a religious community." Was that the way to promote the efficiency of the public service?

— *House of Assembly, February 2, 1865*

Daniel Prowse: I consider that if Confederation will only put an end to the sectarian and political differences which are such a bane to our community; if it will only put down the small fry of newspapers and petty politicians who help to fan the flames of religious strife, and who fatten like political vultures upon our local sectarian difference; if Confederation will only do this, as I trust, in time, that it will, I, for one, will hail it as the greatest boon that could ever be conferred upon this colony.

— *House of Assembly, February 6, 1865*

Robert Pinsent: We are told that Confederation will relieve us from political turmoil and sectarian strife, that under its benign sway the contending passions of the people will be appeased, that the voice of faction will be hushed. We would all hail the day when such a happy state of things should come to pass. Where but in the improved morality of the people, and in the happier tone of the public mind, was the hope to be found of that halcyon time? Our local constitution, that gave rise to those local differences, would, under confederacy, still exist, though in a moderated form. We would continue to have periodical elections for the local legislature, with their attendant differences and troubles; and in addition to that we would have elections for the general parliament.

— *Legislative Council, February 14, 1865*

Hugh Hoyles: He would briefly refer to the objections urged against the proposed Confederation. It had been objected that, in going into the union, we were giving up our independence — our right to independent legislation. Every savage entering society gave up a portion of his independence, but did he lose by the change? True, if we went into Confederation, we would give up a portion of our present control of our affairs. But he did think that we would be well quit of it. What was the history of this colony since we had a local legislature? It was not one on which we could look with satisfaction.

Why, since 1832 we were violently agitated, every four years, with party strife, aggravated by the rancour of religious differences; and our representatives came together excited by the

---

"If Confederation will only put an end to the sectarian and political differences which are such a bane to our community; if it will only put down the small fry of newspapers and petty politicians who help to fan the flames of religious strife, and who fatten like political vultures upon our local sectarian difference; if Confederation will only do this . . . I, for one, will hail it as the greatest boon that could ever be conferred upon this colony."

bitterest feelings towards each other. And after they met, the object of one party in that house was to hold on to office, and of the other to turn them out; and, in the nearly equal division of the parties which prevailed, it was found that neither the one party nor the other could do much for the promotion of the public good. If the strife of parties should have a narrower scope and have less bitterness, as the objects contended for would have less importance, from the concession of power to be made to the general government, would it not be a great benefit to the community? On the other hand, if we gave up some power which we at present held, would we not have an equivalent in the share we should receive in the general government?

— *House of Assembly, February 14, 1865*

George Hogsett: They say that religious feeling is broken down in Canada, and that that was the result of Confederation. He (Mr. Hogsett) denied that such was the case; the same elements that influenced the legislatures in the dominion, whilst separately constituted, existed today and would ever continue to exist, whilst differences of faith, differences of interest, and differences of races exist.

— *House of Assembly, February 23, 1869*

CANADA

E.-P. Taché: Lower Canada had constantly refused the demand of Upper Canada for representation according to population, and for the good reason that, as the union between them was legislative, a preponderance to one of the sections would have placed the other at its mercy. It would not be so in a federal union, for all questions of a general nature would be reserved for the general government, and those of a local character to the local governments, who would have the power to manage their domestic affairs as they deemed best.

If a federal union were obtained, it would be tantamount to a separation of the provinces, and Lower Canada would thereby preserve its autonomy together with all the institutions it held dear, and over which they could exercise the watchfulness and surveillance necessary to preserve them unimpaired. But there might be a portion of the inhabitants of Lower Canada who might at a first glance have greater reason to complain than the French Roman Catholics, and these were the English Protestants. And

SIR ÉTIENNE-PASCHAL
TACHÉ
(1795–1865), doctor.
"The last cannon which
is shot on this continent
in defence of Great
Britain will be fired by
the hand of a French
Canadian." Taché fought
for Britain and his
homeland in the War
of 1812, then became a
leader of his profession
and a leading Patriote.
He sympathized with
the rebels of 1837,
but did not take up
arms. He was an MPP,
1841–46, and a
legislative councillor,
1848–65. He served in
every ministry, Liberal
and Conservative,
until 1857. He was
co-premier, 1855–57,
and in March 1864 he
returned to government
as leader of the Great
Coalition formed to
pursue federal union
and Confederation.

why? Because they were a minority; but he thought that if they took the trouble fully to consider the subject, they would be reassured and satisfied with the scheme. First a great event had taken place; the law of Lower Canada had been consolidated,* and the English-speaking people residing in that section had got reconciled to it; in fact they were well satisfied therewith. In this respect, then, they were secure. But they might say that the majority in the local legislature might hereafter be unjust to them, but he thought that, on looking at the past, their fears might be allayed.

Before the union of the provinces, when the large majority of members in the legislature were French, the English inhabitants had never found cause of complaint against them. In no instance had injustice been attempted. The difficulty was that the minority wanted to rule and wanted to possess the whole power of the state in their hands. That the people of Lower Canada always acted towards the English with liberality was best exemplified by facts. Before the union, while the constituencies were almost exclusively French, English Protestant gentlemen were frequently returned to parliament, and he had now opposite to him an honourable member who had for twenty years represented an entirely French and Roman Catholic county. He doubted if in the course of those twenty years that honourable member had ever been asked whether he were Scotch or Protestant. They took the man for his sterling worth . . .

Much has been said on the war of the races, but that war was extinguished on the day the British government granted Canada responsible government, by which all its inhabitants without distinction of race or creed were placed on a footing of equality.† (Hear, hear.) . . . This life was one of compromise. Not only was forbearance needed in public life, but in domestic life. If one

---

Lower Canadian anglophones — especially the business class — had long resented the French customary law that prevailed in the province on account of the obstacles it presented to commercial enterprise. The abolition of the Lower Canadian legislature by the union of 1840, and the rise of a commercially minded francophone bourgeoisie, facilitated a blending of French-Canadian social and English commercial values. The process culminated in the codification of the civil law between 1859 and 1866. (Note also Sanborn's passing reference in chapter 9.) — PR

† Legally speaking, French and English Canadians had always been equal, but it was responsible government which had opened the doors of political

member in a family insists on having all his own way, there will be trouble, and so through all possible relations of humanity. He believed the French Canadians would do all in their power to render justice to their fellow-subjects of English origin, and it should not be forgotten that if the former were a majority in Lower Canada, the English would be in a majority in the general government, and that no act of real injustice could take place, even if there were a disposition to perpetrate it, without its being reversed there.

— Legislative Council, February 3, 1865

George-Étienne Cartier: We could easily understand how a feeling against the federation project was raised in the minds of a few of the British residents of Lower Canada by fears of such difficulties as those which occurred in the days of Mr. Papineau,* relative to the passing of laws relating to commercial matters. (Hear, hear.) These difficulties had been of a very inconvenient nature, Mr. Papineau not being a commercial man and not understanding the importance of these measures. He considered Mr. Papineau was right in the struggle he maintained against the oligarchy at that time in power; but he had never approved of the course he took with reference to commercial matters and in opposition to measures for the improvement of the country. But this precedent could not be urged as an objection to federation, inasmuch as it would be for the general government to deal with our commercial matters. There could be no reason for well-grounded fear that the minority could be made to suffer by means of any laws affecting the rights of property. If any such enactments were passed, they would fall upon the whole community. But even supposing such a thing did occur, there was a remedy provided under the proposed constitution.†

— Legislative Assembly, February 7, 1865

---

power to French Canadians. Note, by the way, how Taché's remark excludes Indians from the ranks of Canadian humanity. — PR

* Before the rebellion, the francophone majority under the leadership of Louis-Joseph Papineau had espoused an agrarian ideology which was hostile to commercial values and interests. Its stranglehold on the Lower Canadian House of Assembly had presented an insuperable barrier to legislation in the interests of commerce. — PR

† An allusion to the power of the federal government to disallow provincial legislation.

George Brown: But I am told that to this general principle of placing all local matters under local control, an exception has been made in regard to the common schools. (Hear, hear.) The clause complained of is as follows:

> 6. Education: saving the rights and privileges which the Protestant or Catholic minority in both Canadas may possess as to their denominational schools at the time when the union goes into operation.*

Now, I need hardly remind the house that I have always opposed and continue to oppose the system of sectarian education, so far as the public chest is concerned. I have never had any hesitation on that point. I have never been able to see why all the people of the province, to whatever sect they may belong, should not send their children to the same common schools to receive the ordinary branches of instruction. I regard the parent and the pastor as the best religious instructors — and so long as the religious faith of the children is uninterfered with, and ample opportunity afforded to the clergy to give religious instruction to the children of their flocks, I cannot conceive any sound objection to mixed schools. But while in the conference and elsewhere I have always maintained this view, and always given my vote against sectarian public schools, I am bound to admit, as I have always admitted, that the sectarian system, carried to the limited extent it has yet been in Upper Canada, and confined as it chiefly is to cities and towns, has not been a very great practical injury. The real cause of alarm was that the admission of the sectarian principle was there, and that at any moment it might be extended to such a degree as to split up our school system altogether. There are but a hundred separate schools in Upper Canada, out of some four thousand, and all Roman Catholic.

But if the Roman Catholics are entitled to separate schools and to go on extending their operations, so are the members of the Church of England, the Presbyterians, the Methodists, and all other sects. No candid Roman Catholic will deny this for a moment; and there lay the great danger to our educational fabric, that the separate system might gradually extend itself until the whole country was studded with nurseries of sectarianism, most

---

* *This clause is subsection 6 of resolution 43, which itemized the powers of the local legislatures.*

hurtful to the best interests of the province, and entailing an enormous expense to sustain the hosts of teachers that so prodigal a system of public instruction must inevitably entail. Now it is known to every honourable member of this house that an act was passed in 1863, as a final settlement of this sectarian controversy. I was not in Quebec at the time, but if I had been here [in the legislature] I would have voted against that bill . . . It had, however, this good feature, that it was accepted by the Roman Catholic authorities and carried through parliament as a final compromise of the question in Upper Canada. When, therefore, it was proposed that a provision should be inserted in the Confederation scheme to bind that compact of 1863 and declare it a final settlement, so that we should not be compelled, as we have been since 1849, to stand constantly to our arms, awaiting fresh attacks upon our common school system, the proposition seemed to me one that was not rashly to be rejected. (Hear, hear.) . . .

But it was urged that though this arrangement might perhaps be fair as regards Upper Canada, it was not so as regards Lower Canada, for there were matters of which the British population have long complained, and some amendments to the existing School Act were required to secure them equal justice. Well, when this point was raised, gentlemen of all parties in Lower Canada at once expressed themselves prepared to treat it in a frank and conciliatory manner, with a view to removing any injustice that might be shown to exist; and on this understanding the educational clause was adopted by the conference.

— *Legislative Assembly, February 8, 1865*

John Sanborn: He would fail in his duty if he did not touch upon . . . the situation in which the English of Lower Canada would be placed. The honourable premier [Taché] had remarked at some length upon the disposition to toleration and the indulgent spirit evinced by his people in past times, and he (Sanborn) was not prepared to detract from this. He would freely and fully concede the point. He had always lived in the midst of a mixed population, and his division was more French than English, and it would ill become him to cast reflections on their liberality and desire for fair play or justice to others. But this was the time, when treating of important arrangements for the future, to lay aside all unnecessary delicacy, and by our action to lay down the guarantees for the perpetuation of these kind feelings and this spirit of toleration so long existing, and which he devoutly hoped would never cease.

"It would . . . be a grievous mistake to overlook the safeguards and rules necessary to perpetuate kindly feelings and to prevent the disposition to aggression which existed more or less in all minds. That principle — the love of power — was found in every human heart, none were exempt from it, and the history of the world showed that no people had ever risen superior to it. "

No greater calamity could befall the English, or, in fact, both races, than the introduction of religious discord among the races of Lower Canada. (Hear, hear.)

It would, however, be a grievous mistake to overlook the safeguards and rules necessary to perpetuate kindly feelings and to prevent the disposition to aggression which existed more or less in all minds. That principle — the love of power — was found in every human heart, none were exempt from it, and the history of the world showed that no people had ever risen superior to it. The honourable premier had recognized this truth in the remarks he had made in regard of the difficulties between Upper and Lower Canada. The French Canadians had persistently refused the demands of Upper Canada for representation by population because of the terror they felt that, if granted, their institutions would be in danger; and he had told the French members in the house that under the new constitution their rights were so effectually guarded that their autonomy was fully secured — the safeguards thereof being put in their own hands. But, at the same time, the English, who were a fourth of the population, and who, by habit and tradition, had their own views of public policy, were left entirely without guarantee other than the good feelings and tolerant spirit of the French. Was this safe? The only safeguard they were to have was in regard of education, but in regard of the rights of property* they were to be left to the legislature.

— *Legislative Council, February 9, 1865*

L.-A. Olivier: I have no objection, whatever, to grant to the Protestants of Lower Canada, for all future time, the rights they now enjoy, or any other rights and guarantees which may be deemed reasonable and equitable, but I cannot vote to adopt the resolutions until I am informed whether the Roman Catholics of the west[†] are to be dealt with in the same manner . . .

— *Legislative Council, February 13, 1865*

N.-F. Belleau: The honourable member for Wellington (Honourable Mr. Sanborn) laid great stress on the danger which might be incurred by the Protestant minority in the local legislation of Lower Canada. He fears that they might not be sufficiently

---

* This passage immediately precedes Sanborn's remarks on that subject in chapter 9. — PR

† He means Upper Canada, not the prairies and British Columbia.

protected by the Catholic majority in respect of their religion, their schools, and possibly their property. I am astonished to hear such language from the lips of a man who, like myself, represents a division more than one-half of the population of which is French Canadian and Catholic, for that fact is in itself a proof of the liberality of our fellow-countrymen. I heard that remark with pain; but I can tell him that the Protestant minority of Lower Canada have nothing to fear from the Catholic majority of that province; their religion is guaranteed by treaty, and the schools and the rights which may be connected with them are to be settled by legislation to take place hereafter . . .

But even granting that the Protestants were wronged by the local legislature of Lower Canada, could they not avail themselves of the protection of the federal legislature? And would not the federal government exercise strict surveillance over the action of the local legislatures in these matters? Why should it be sought to give existence to imaginary fears in Lower Canada? I say imaginary, because the liberality of the inhabitants of Lower Canada — a liberality of which they gave proof long, long ago, by enacting the emancipation of the Jews* before any other nation in the world had dreamed of such a measure — is well known. No; far from wishing to oppress other nationalities, all that the French Canadians ask is to live at peace with all the world . . .

The honourable member for Lanaudière (Honourable Mr. Olivier) . . . stated that the minorities in Upper and Lower Canada wished to know the fate reserved for them before voting for Confederation. If he had reflected a little, he would have learned that the fate of the minorities will be defined by the law, that their religion is guaranteed by treaties, and that they will be protected by the vigilance of the federal government, which will

> *"The liberality of the inhabitants of Lower Canada — a liberality of which they gave proof long, long ago, by enacting the emancipation of the Jews . . . is well known."*

By an act of 1832, the Lower Canadian legislature removed all legal impediments to Jewish participation in politics. Belleau's claim to world priority is quite unfounded, and even as regards British North America is misleading. Lower Canada was in fact the only North American colony where Jews were expressly barred from election to the legislature. This discrimination was done by resolution of the House of Assembly in 1809. Elsewhere, except Upper Canada, such impediments resulted from measures against Roman Catholics, which either expressly limited certain political privileges to Protestants or made them dependent on affirmations of Protestant belief. Upper Canada, having no such restrictions, never needed to enact a measure like the Lower Canadian act of 1832. — PR

never permit the minority of one portion of the Confederation to be oppressed by the majority.

— *Legislative Council, February 14, 1865*

A.-A. Dorion: It is evident . . . that it is intended eventually to form a legislative union of all the provinces. The local governments, in addition to the general government, will be found so burdensome that a majority of the people will appeal to the imperial government for the formation of a legislative union. (Hear, hear.) I may well ask if there is any member from Lower Canada, of French extraction, who is ready to vote for a legislative union . . . The honourable member for Sherbrooke [Alexander Galt] stated at the dinner to the delegates given at Toronto, after endorsing everything that had been said by the honourable president of the council:

> We may hope that, at no far distant day, we may become willing to enter into a legislative union instead of a federal union, as now proposed. We would all have desired a legislative union and to see the power concentrated in the central government as it exists in England, spreading the aegis of its protection over all the institutions of the land, but we found it was impossible to do that at first. We found that there were difficulties in the way which could not be overcome.

Honourable members from Lower Canada are made aware that the delegates all desired a legislative union, but it could not be accomplished at once. This Confederation is the first necessary step towards it. The British government is ready to grant a federal union at once, and when that is accomplished the French element will be completely overwhelmed by the majority of British representatives. What then would prevent the federal government from passing a set of resolutions in a similar way to those we are called upon to pass, without submitting them to the people, calling upon the imperial government to set aside the federal form of government and give a legislative union instead of it? (Hear, hear.) Perhaps the people of Upper Canada think a legislative union a most desirable thing. I can tell those gentlemen that the people of Lower Canada are attached to their institutions in a manner that defies any attempt to change them in that way. They will not change their religious institutions, their laws, and their language for any consideration whatever . . .

I know there is an apprehension among the British population in Lower Canada that, with even the small power that the local government will possess, their rights will not be respected. How, then, can it be expected that the French population can anticipate any more favourable result from the general government, when it is to possess such enormous powers over the destinies of their section of the country? Experience shows that majorities are always aggressive, and it cannot well be otherwise in this instance. It therefore need not be wondered at that the people of Lower Canada, of British origin, are ready to make use of every means to prevent their being placed at the mercy of a preponderating population of a different origin. I agree with them in thinking that they ought to take nothing on trust in this matter of entering upon a new state of political existence, and neither ought we of French origin to do so, in relation to the general government, however happy our relations to each other may be at present.

Thomas D'Arcy McGee: That is a glorious doctrine to instill into society. (Hear, hear.)

Dorion: Well, it is the doctrine generally acted upon, and correctly so. When my honourable friend makes a contract with a friend and neighbour to be filled even a few months in the future, does he not have it put in legal form, in black and white? Of course he does. And when we are making arrangements calculated to last for all time to come, is it not vastly more important that the same safe and equitable principle should be recognized? (Hear, hear.) The honourable gentleman recognized it himself* in the most marked manner, by placing in the resolutions guarantees respecting the educational institutions of the two sections of Canada.

— *Legislative Assembly, February 16, 1865*

John Rose: I believe that the rights of both minorities — the French minority in the general legislature and the English-speaking minority in the local legislature of Lower Canada — are properly guarded . . . With reference to this subject, I think that I, and those with whom I have acted — the English-speaking members from Lower Canada — may in some degree congratulate ourselves at having brought about a state of feeling between

"I believe that the rights of both minorities — the French minority in the general legislature and the English-speaking minority in the local legislature of Lower Canada — are properly guarded."

---

* *McGee had insisted on the proviso which George Brown quoted above. — PR*

"There has been, ever since the time of the union . . . a cordial understanding and friendly feeling between the two nationalities which has produced the happiest results. Belonging to different races and professing a different faith, we live near each other; we come in contact and mix with each other, and we respect each other; we do not trench upon the rights of each other; we have not had those party and religious differences which two races, speaking different languages and holding different religious beliefs, might be supposed to have had."

the two races in this section of the province which has produced some good effect. (Hear, hear.) There has been, ever since the time of the union . . . a cordial understanding and friendly feeling between the two nationalities which has produced the happiest results. Belonging to different races and professing a different faith, we live near each other; we come in contact and mix with each other, and we respect each other; we do not trench upon the rights of each other; we have not had those party and religious differences which two races, speaking different languages and holding different religious beliefs, might be supposed to have had . . . But if, instead of this mutual confidence; if, instead of the English-speaking minority placing trust in the French majority in the local legislature, and the French minority placing the same trust in the English majority in the general legislature, no such feeling existed, how could this scheme of Confederation be made to work successfully? (Hear, hear.) . . . And I think I may fairly appeal to the president of the council [Brown] that if, during the ten years in which he has agitated the question of representation by population, we the English in Lower Canada had listened to his appeals . . . where, I ask him, would have been our union today? Would not a feeling of distrust have been established between the French and English races in the community that would have rendered even the fair consideration of it utterly impracticable? (Hear, hear.) Would the French have in that case been ready now to trust themselves in the general legislature, or the English in the local legislature of Lower Canada? No; and I pray God that this mutual confidence between two races which have so high and noble a work to do on this continent, who are menaced by a common danger, and actuated by a common interest, may continue for all time to come!

The apprehension . . . which has been expressed to me by gentlemen in my own constituency is this, that with respect to the local legislature, it will be competent for the French majority in Lower Canada to blot out the English-speaking minority from any share in the representation, and so to apportion the electoral districts that no English-speaking member can be returned to the legislature. That is an apprehension upon which I would be very glad to have an expression of opinion by my honourable friend the attorney general east [Cartier]. As I read the resolutions, if the local legislature exercised its powers in any such unjust manner, it would be competent for the general government to veto its action . . .

Cartier: There is not the least doubt that if the local legislature of Lower Canada should apportion the electoral districts in such a way as to do injustice to the English-speaking population, the general government will have the right to veto any law it might pass to this effect . . .

Luther Holton: Would you advise it?

Cartier: Yes, I would recommend it myself in case of injustice. (Hear, hear.) . . .

Rose: What I wish to do now is point out the objections I have heard on the part even of some of my own friends to this scheme — objections which . . . are grounded on an undefined dread of evil rather than on anything that they actually now see obnoxious in the scheme itself. These fears, I have said, are vague and unde-fined, and difficult therefore to combat. If I go among one class and ask them what they fear, I am told — "Oh, you are going to hand us over to the tender mercies of the French; the English influence will be entirely annihilated; they will have no power in the community; and all the advantages we have gained during the past twenty-five years by our union with the people of our own race in Upper Canada will be entirely lost." I can but answer — "What are you afraid of? . . . You have, in conjunction with a majority of your own race, power in the general legislature to appoint the local governors, administer justice and name the judges, to control the militia and all other means of defence, and to make laws respecting the post office, trade, commerce, naviga-tion; and you have all the great and important interests that centre in the community I represent — all matters that affect the minority in Lower Canada — within your control in the federal legislature . . ." "Well," I am answered, "all that may be true enough; but we shall not get a single appointment. The adminis-tration of local affairs in Lower Canada will be entirely in the hands of the French majority, and they will control all the patronage." You say to them again — "Is it the exercise of patronage you are afraid of? Is not the appointment of the judges, the patronage of the post office, the customs, the excise, the board of works, and all the other important branches of the administration in the hands of the federal government? What is there, then, but a few municipal officers to be appointed by the local legislatures? And for the sake of this petty patronage, are

you going to imperil the success of a scheme that is fraught with such important consequences to all the provinces of British North America . . . ?"

Well, these questions I have put, and these explanations I have made, but some still seemed to entertain an undefined dread that they could not realize to themselves — a dread which to a great extent appears to be shared by my honourable friend opposite (Honourable Mr. Dorion) in regard to the general legislature. Well, if we look to the history of the past twenty-five years and see how we have acted towards each other, I think neither party will have any cause for apprehension* . . .

John Sandfield Macdonald: The government ought to address themselves at once to the question, whether they are to make the same provision for the Catholics of Upper Canada as for the Protestants of Lower Canada . . . Depend upon it, when the time comes for the Protestants of Lower Canada to ask what they assert to be their rights, they will be expected to stand up also for the Catholics of Upper Canada and deal out to them the same justice which they expect the Catholics of Lower Canada to extend to them.

— *Legislative Assembly, February 22, 1865*

"[The] feeling of nationality has been our sole difficulty in working our present political system. But I do not believe for one moment that it would be possible or perhaps desirable to extinguish that strong feeling of nationality. Break down that feeling and all patriotism will be broken down with it."

Alexander Mackenzie: I believe that that feeling of nationality has been our sole difficulty in working our present political system. But I do not believe for one moment that it would be possible or perhaps desirable to extinguish that strong feeling of nationality. Break down that feeling and all patriotism will be broken down with it. (Hear, hear.) I do not think it would be fair, or kind, or honourable, to attempt to do so. When Britain conquered the country, she accepted the responsibility of governing a foreign people in accordance with their feelings, so far as consistent with British policy. That feeling of nationality obtains so strongly in all countries that, where attempts have been made, as in Austria, to break it down, they have signally failed. When such an attempt failed, though made by a despotic government, with a powerful army at its command, how could we expect it to succeed in a free country? In Austria, at this moment, eighteen

---

* *Rose is expressing the fears of his fellow Lower Canadian anglophones so that Cartier, speaking for French Canadians and for the government, can affirm that they are groundless.* — PR

different nationalities are represented in the national councils; and notwithstanding all its military power and *prestige*, Austria has been compelled to accord local parliaments or assemblies to every one of those eighteen nationalities. (Hear, hear.) I have felt, therefore, that it would be utterly impracticable to obtain representation by population so long as the French people believed, as I came to find they did believe, that this concession to us would involve destruction to them as a separate people.

Holton: That is what they fear will be the result of the scheme now proposed.

Mackenzie: No; I have yet to learn that they have any such fear. The attorney general east (Honourable Mr. Cartier), in his speech a few evenings ago, adverted to the position taken by the French inhabitants of Lower Canada at the time of the French Revolution and claimed credit for them because they remained loyal to the British crown, when all the other North American colonies threw off the British sway. The honourable gentleman's claim was perfectly just. But I believe that they were actuated by another feeling beyond the feeling of loyalty* — that they felt their only safeguard as a distinct people, the only way to preserve their nationality, was to remain attached to Great Britain. Their existence for twenty years as a French colony under British rule was not perhaps sufficient to give that attachment which they have now to the British government. But it was perfectly clear to them that, if they entered the American union, they would be absorbed and lost, just as the French colony of Louisiana has since been. (Hear, hear.)

— Legislative Assembly, February 23, 1865

Christopher Dunkin: Under [this scheme] Lower Canada has all sorts of special exceptions† made, as the phrase runs, in her favour. The Legislative Council is to be named in a peculiar manner, so far as its members from Lower Canada are concerned.

---

* Mackenzie hints astutely at the contingent nature of French-Canadian loyalty in 1775. He does not presume to suggest that it persists ninety years later — but why mention it at all? — PR

† Nowadays some Canadians look to such asymmetries as the salvation of Canadian federalism. Of course, a look at the Quebec Resolutions will show that such special arrangements were not limited to Lower Canada. — PR

The other provinces may have their laws made uniform, but an exception in this respect is made for Lower Canada, and as if to make it apparent that Lower Canada is never to be like the rest of the Confederation, it is carefully provided that the general parliament may make uniform the laws of the other provinces only — that is to say, provided those provinces consent to it, but by inference it cannot extend this uniformity to Lower Canada, not even if she should wish it. Supposing, even, that the other provinces were to desire to adopt our Lower Canadian system, according to the letter of this constitution, one would say they cannot do it. They may become uniform among themselves, but Lower Canada, even though her people were to wish it, must not be uniform with them . . . Thus, in one way and another, Lower Canada is to be placed on a separate and distinct footing from the other provinces, so that her interests and institutions may not be meddled with.

"I say this system, as a whole, and these peculiarities and exceptions in regard to Lower Canada are adopted with a special view to remedy our Canadian difficulties of race and creed. But, sir, this is no way at all of avoiding or lessening trouble from this cause."

I say this system, as a whole, and these peculiarities and exceptions in regard to Lower Canada are adopted with a special view to remedy our Canadian difficulties of race and creed. But, sir, this is no way at all of avoiding or lessening trouble from this cause. It is idle to pretend that by this system collision is going to be prevented. Under the legislative union of the Canadas, even worked as it has been, the tendency of the minorities in Upper and Lower Canada, respectively, has been towards the maintenance of the union, towards the avoidance of all intemperate language and prejudiced feelings, towards the pulling down of the feuds that before divided them and the respective majorities. And the result has been that while just before the union the feud between the races in Lower Canada was at its highest and bitterest point, it has since then all but disappeared* . . . Indeed, there has been a more tolerant state of feeling in both camps than in any other community so divided as to race and creed that I know of.

But the moment you tell Lower Canada that the large-sounding

---

* From Dunkin's Lower Canadian perspective, the union period was indeed one of striking harmony compared with that preceding the rebellion. He rightly gives credit to the constitution of 1840, which discouraged French Canadian militancy by destroying its institutional bastion, the Lower Canadian legislature. He ignores, however, the alienating effects of the union on Upper Canadians, many of whom saw it as depriving their province of the fruits of responsible government. — PR

powers of your general government are going to be handed over to a British-American majority, decidedly not of the race and faith of her majority, that moment you wake up the old jealousies and hostility in their strongest form. By the very provisions you talk of for the protection of the non-French and non-Catholic interests, you unfortunately countenance the idea that the French are going to be more unfair than I believe they wish to be. For that matter, what else can they well be? They will find themselves a minority in the general legislature, and their power in the general government will depend upon their power in their own province and over their provincial delegations in the federal parliament. They will thus be compelled to be practically aggressive to secure and retain that power. They may not, perhaps, wish to be; they may not, perhaps, be aggressive in the worst sense of the term . . . but whether they are or not, there will certainly be in this system the very strongest tendencies to make them practically aggressive upon the rights of the minority in language and faith, and at the same time to make the minority most suspicious and resentful of aggression. The same sort of alienation, as between the two faiths, will be going on in Upper Canada . . .

Thank God, Mr. Speaker, I do not need, as I stand here, to defend myself from any charge of bigotry as against any sect or party. There was a time in Canada when it was most difficult for any person who spoke my tongue to stand up and say that the French Canadians ought not to be politically exterminated from the face of the earth. I stood out steadfastly against that doctrine then. I remember well the painful events of that sad time. I foresee but too distinctly the fearful probability there is of that time coming again through the adoption of these resolutions. And I do not shrink from the danger of being misunderstood or misrepresented, when I now stand up here and warn the country of this danger. If trouble of this sort ever arises, it is one that will extend very rapidly over the entire confederacy. In all parts of it, in every province, there are minorities that will be acted upon by that kind of thing. In the lower provinces, and in Newfoundland, things are but too ripe for the outburst of hostilities of this description. Talk, indeed, in such a state of things, of your founding here by this means "a new nationality" — of your creating such a thing — of your whole people here rallying round its new government at Ottawa. Mr. Speaker, is such a thing possible?

We have a large class whose national feelings turn towards London, whose very heart is there; another large class whose

"We have a large class whose national feelings turn towards London, whose very heart is there; another large class whose sympathies centre here at Quebec, or in a sentimental way may have some reference to Paris; another large class whose memories are of the Emerald Isle; and yet another whose comparisons are rather with Washington. But have we any class of people who are attached, or whose feelings are going to be directed with any earnestness, to the city of Ottawa, the centre of the new nationality that is to be created?"

sympathies centre here at Quebec, or in a sentimental way may have some reference to Paris; another large class whose memories are of the Emerald Isle; and yet another whose comparisons are rather with Washington. But have we any class of people who are attached, or whose feelings are going to be directed with any earnestness, to the city of Ottawa, the centre of the new nationality that is to be created? In the times to come, when men shall begin to feel strongly on those questions that appeal to national preferences, prejudices, and passions, all talk of your new nationality will sound but strangely. Some other older nationality will then be found to hold the first place in most people's hearts. (Hear, hear.)

— Legislative Assembly, February 27, 1865

J.-O. Beaubien: When France abandoned this country and England took possession of it, from that moment French immigration entirely ceased and gave way to immigration of persons of foreign origin — of British origin. From that period the English population increased from day to day in this country, and at the present time the French Canadians are in a minority in united Canada. Under these circumstances, I am of opinion that it would be at once an act of imprudence and one characterized by a lack of generosity* on our parts to wish to prevent the majority of the population of the country from displaying greater aspirations for our common country, and from desiring its advancement and more rapid progress in an onward direction, at the same time drawing closer the bonds which unite us to the mother country. I have reflected on these matters, and although I am not disposed to submit to injustice to my country or my countrymen, yet I am ready to enter into a compromise with persons of other origins . . . Today our position is an excellent one; we are strong as a party, we have statesmen at the head of the affairs of our country who are devoted to its interest . . . and united together by the ties of interest and friendship; and above all, we have ever had confidence in those who prepared the project of a constitution now submitted for our consideration; it is evident, then, that a more favourable opportunity could not possibly be found for effecting constitutional changes than the present circumstances afford . . .

---

* *With exquisite lucidity, Beaubien maps out the true course of national survival under the circumstances created by France's abandonment of his people, a history that has obliged them to share their homeland with foreigners. — PR*

The Conservative Party has always opposed representation by population under the present union because, under this union, we are face to face with the population of a country of which the products are different from ours, and of which the interests are not always identical with ours . . . This cause of dissension has always existed, and always will exist in Upper Canada, not because it is necessary to the support of such or such a party, but because it is the result of a provision of the constitution, and because the interests of Upper Canada are not the same as ours. And if we do not effect a settlement of this question now, these dissensions will, ere long, be renewed and the difficulties increased. Here is an opportunity of removing these difficulties by uniting ourselves with the lower provinces; and I think Lower Canada would do well not to lose the opportunity. Under Confederation, the political parties into which the provinces will be divided will find it necessary to form alliances, and our alliance will be courted by all, so that we shall in reality hold the balance of power . . . I have always remarked that material interests are of great weight in the formation of parties, and the conduct of the French Canadians, with relation to their religious institutions, never inspired any uneasiness or distrust in our fellow-countrymen of a different origin from ours when they found it in their interest to form an alliance with us; and I am certain we shall find, under like circumstances, the same disposition among the inhabitants of the lower provinces.

— *Legislative Assembly, March 2, 1865*

Joseph Perrault: Formerly France possessed all this part of the continent. The settlers of that period, the farmers, fishermen, hunters, and trappers travelled over the whole extent of those immense possessions which were known by the name of New France. At the moment what remains to her of a territory that was equal in extent to Europe itself? A wretched little island* at the entrance of the Gulf, a foothold for her fisheries, and a few acres of beach on the coast of Newfoundland. When we consider that fact, when we see French power completely destroyed on this continent, are we not justified in looking closely into the project of constitution now submitted to us, which has for its object, I repeat, simply to complete the destruction of the influence of the French race on this continent? Has not the past taught us to

---

* *Two islands in fact: France was left with both St. Pierre and Miquelon.*

dread the future? Yes, Mr. Speaker, the policy of England has ever been aggressive, and its object has always been to annihilate us as a people.* And this scheme of Confederation is but the continued application of that policy on this continent; its real object is nothing but the annihilation of French influence in Canada . . .

We know how long Scotland and Ireland resisted the encroachments of England.† The struggle was protracted and obstinate. But these two nations were compelled to succumb to political encroachment, under the pressure of the powerful assimilating tendencies of the English nation. But let us see what means England used to attain her ends. Impartial history tells us, as it will tell of the means employed today to annihilate our race on this continent. History records, in letters of gold, the names of those who have bravely struggled for the lives and liberties of nations, but it also holds up to execration the memory of those who barter those liberties and those rights for titles, honour, power, or gold. We now enjoy responsible government, dearly earned by a century of heroic struggles, and before yielding an inch of the ground we have conquered, we should see what we are likely to gain by the proposed constitutional changes . . .

If we study the history of our struggles since the cession of Canada, we shall find that our public men were always attached to the crown of England up to the time when they were compelled by the arbitrary and unjust conduct of the imperial government to have recourse to arms to obtain respect for our political rights and our liberties; and it was thus in 1837 that we gained responsible government. (Hear, hear.) But in order to hold up to view the spirit of aggression and encroachment which has always characterized the English population in America, I shall give a historical sketch of the struggles through which we had to pass, in the course of a century, to attain at last our present constitution, which it is my wish to preserve, but which our ministers wish to destroy in order to substitute for it the scheme of Confederation. This historical sketch will demonstrate to us that

---

* *The union of Ireland with England was imposed by England in 1800. However, the union of England and Scotland in 1707, though opposed by some Scots, was negotiated by treaty between the two nations.* — IG
† *Perrault's speech, much longer than any other in the Canadian debates except Dunkin's, consisted largely of an anti-English diatribe based on François-Xavier Garneau's* Histoire du Canada, *a pioneering account of his people's struggle for survival before and after the Conquest.* — PR

we owe no gratitude to England for those political reforms which were obtained for us only through the unyielding patriotism of our great men, who, with intelligence, energy, and perseverance, valiantly strove for the constant defence of our rights. We shall also see that, if they obtained the system of government and the political liberty for which they struggled, it was because we had for our neighbours the states of the American union, and that side by side with the evil was its remedy. We shall see that whenever England stood in need of us to defend her power, she made concessions to us; but that when the danger was once over, colonial fanaticism always attempted to withdraw those concessions and to destroy the influence and liberties of the French race . . .

— *Legislative Assembly, March 3, 1865*

Édouard Rémillard: I listened with pain to the language used by the honourable member for Richelieu [Perrault]. Should what he said in French be repeated by someone in English, I should greatly fear that it would give rise to prejudice against us among the English members. (Hear, hear.) Last year he said to the members from Upper Canada, "The French Canadians are learning the use of arms, and if you insist upon having representation based upon population they will be turned against you"; and this year he says that one Lower Canadian can stand against ten Upper Canadians. He considers himself fortunate in being under the protection of the English flag, and yet his whole speech was one insult to the English government. (Hear, hear.) Does he forget, then, that the French Canadians are in a minority? He talked a great deal about the great men who saved our nationality; but if those men had made use of such language as the honourable member has done, they would not have obtained that which they did obtain. (Hear, hear.) Our nationality would long since have passed away . . . Fortunately his speech was not understood by the English members of this house, and consequently it could produce no effect upon them; and those who did understand him, moreover, are aware that he spoke for himself alone, and that he does not represent the opinions of the French-Canadian members or of the French-Canadian people.

"We desire that Canada should be a united people, ignoring sectionalism, and basing our institutions on one broad principle of Canadian nationality, which shall blend all races, and in time obliterate all accidental distinctions of language, religion, or origin."

James O'Halloran: The reason why so large a portion of the people of Lower Canada of French origin will not consent to a legislative union is the very reason that makes it desirable to the English-speaking population of Lower Canada . . . We desire that

Canada should be a united people, ignoring sectionalism, and basing our institutions on one broad principle of Canadian nationality, which shall blend all races, and in time obliterate all accidental distinctions of language, religion, or origin. Our French-Canadian fellow-subjects will not consent to this. If they will not hear our arguments, let them listen to their own. If federalism is necessary for the protection of their rights, it is necessary in a tenfold degree for the protection of the rights of the English-speaking minority. They tell us we may rely upon their well-known liberality and toleration. We cannot consent to hold our liberties by mere sufferance, when we are entitled to hold them by right. It would be unworthy of us to submit to such humiliation . . .

The English-speaking population of Lower Canada . . . consume more than one-half of the dutiable goods that are brought into this country, and pay one-half of the taxes; and yet the money which they would pay into the public chest would be distributed by a majority over whom they had no control — a majority who would not in any manner sympathize with them; and their taxes would be applied to objects which they might not deem desirable — which they might, perhaps, consider detrimental to their interests. And they would be completely without remedy, should this proposed constitution unfortunately be imposed upon them. (Hear, hear.) It is painful to me to be compelled to refer to these matters. It is not with pleasure that I bring before the house the antagonism which would inevitably arise between the two nationalities should they be brought together into one legislature, with such a vast disproportion between their means of taking their own part. We are told, and told very truly . . . that hitherto the two races in Lower Canada have lived in peace. But it would be impossible that they could any longer live in peace; it would be impossible that with such a disparity of numbers, and with such antagonistic interests, they should not come into conflict. It would be a constant warfare . . . You are not bringing peace, but a sword. (Hear, hear.)

— *Legislative Assembly, March 8, 1865*

Joseph Dufresne: We French Canadians, a minority in the country, cannot dictate to the majority. (Hear, hear.) I shall not endeavour to excite popular prejudices, as the honourable member for Richelieu [Perrault] has done. I do not desire to be too severe with the honourable member, or to condemn him too strongly;

for his mode of treating this question may be simply the result of some peculiarity of mental organization;* I merely wish to show that his views as to the dangers of the future are not a whit more sound than the views upon which he must have acted during the past. He has exhausted the library of parliament in order to show, in black and white, that the people of England are the greatest oppressors upon the face of the earth — (hear, hear, and laughter) — in order to demonstrate a fact which is not true, for he has cited to us nothing beyond the mere views of certain historians,† whose opinions only go for what they are worth. (Hear, hear.)

"What good can result from . . . ransacking history in order to hold up a single page, the record of an evil deed? What was the condition of public manners among the nations at the period of the events . . . connected with Acadia?"

It is not my purpose to undertake the defence of a people who have no need of me to defend them, nor to avenge the insults offered them by the honourable member; but I must say that I repudiate all he has said against the English people and against England; against the institutions and government of that country, and against her system of colonial administration. (Hear, hear.) What good can result from thus ransacking history in order to hold up a single page, the record of an evil deed? What was the condition of public manners among the nations at the period of the events he has spoken of, connected with Acadia?‡ Why bring up that matter now? What good can it do? Does the honourable member desire to provoke the prejudices of a sensitive and powerful nation against us? Does he want to bring about the ruin of this country? The honourable member, in his youth and inexperience, has rendered us a very questionable service. (Hear, hear.) He rakes up an event which occurred one hundred years ago and taunts a conquering nation with her mode of dealing with the vanquished! Surely this is a strange way of serving his fellow-countrymen — of labouring to promote their welfare and interests!

— *Legislative Assembly, March 10, 1865*

---

* This is the "parliamentary" way of calling someone crazy.
† The mid-nineteenth century was the heyday of belief in the possibility of historical objectivity, a belief epitomized by the aspiration of the German historian Leopold von Ranke (1795–1886) to record the past "as it actually was." Dufresne's awareness of the subjectivity of the exercise stands in refreshing contrast to Perrault's naive appeal to "impartial history." — PR
‡ With similar historical sophistication, Dufresne chides Perrault for judging the Acadian deportation according to modern standards of conduct. — PR

The convention at Charlottetown, Prince Edward Island, of delegates from the legislatures of Canada, New Brunswick, Nova Scotia, and Prince Edward Island; photographed on September 1, 1864.

PART FIVE

HOW TO MAKE
A CONSTITUTION

Confederation Chamber, formerly the Legislative Council room, in the Provincial Building, Charlottetown, with the table and chairs used at the conference of 1864.

Chapter Eleven

CONSULTING THE PEOPLE IN CONSTITUTION MAKING

<hr>

W HO SHOULD HAVE THE FINAL WORD on Confederation, the people or the legislators? Are the provinces required to call elections or to poll public opinion in a referendum? Or will it be enough to pass resolutions in the provincial parliaments and assemblies?

The Nova Scotians go at these questions hammer and tongs. Many argue that direct appeal to the people is not necessary because the British principle of parliamentary sovereignty gives legislators all necessary power to approve constitutional amendments. In the British form of government, parliamentary sovereignty is valued as a vital guarantee of political freedom and individual rights, an aspect of the rule of law. It is the principle that protects us against arbitrary decisions by the party in power. We cannot be forced to obey a government's decisions or a bureaucrat's preferences — and certainly cannot be forced to pay taxes — unless those decisions, preferences, and taxes are given the form of law and are duly authorized by a majority of our representatives in parliament. So highly prized is this principle that the vote in parliament is deemed necessary and sufficient for both ordinary law and constitutional law. It is the time-honoured British procedure for constitution making. And for many Nova Scotians, that's all that needs to be said. End of argument.

For others it's the beginning. Can parliamentary sovereignty really give parliaments the right to make a new country? It's one

thing to insist that our representatives approve ordinary statutes and the day-to-day business of government. It's quite another, surely, to say that they can tear up constitutions and make new ones. Confederation would dissolve ("destroy," according to some speakers) the provincial constitutions and make them anew on a different footing, with reduced legislative powers. It would create a new, federal level of government. It would indeed make a new country, giving the people a new identity and new nationality. On such a profound issue, surely the people themselves should speak.

The debate is passionate and at times highly theoretical. Yet it is not difficult to follow. The underlying issues are familiar to Canadians today from the debates of the late 1980s and early 1990s on the Meech Lake and Charlottetown constitutional accords.

In the Atlantic region, only Nova Scotia goes into Confederation without consulting the people in a general election. With the parliment nearing the end of its term, Tupper's government finally amasses the necessary majority and passes the union resolution. In Prince Edward Island, in contrast, there appears to be little opposition to the idea of consultation. In New Brunswick, controversy on the issue of consultation is pre-empted by the fact that a general election is held shortly before the legislature meets to discuss it. And in Newfoundland the confedertes concede the necessity of consultation, and go down to defeat in the election of 1869.

British Columbia holds an election — at the urging of the British government — but not Red River. In the Red River settlement neither the people nor their representatives in the constituent assemblies are allowed the power of the final word.

The special case of Canada is the subject of chapter 12.

NOVA SCOTIA

"[He] would . . . like to know whether the government were prepared to state if Confederation was to take place without consulting the house or without being referred to the people of this country."

William Annand: [He] would . . . like to know whether the government were prepared to state if Confederation was to take place without consulting the house or without being referred to the people of this country . . . It was a matter of very serious import to the people of this province when they learned from such authority that their rights and privileges were to be swept away* without their being consulted.

— *House of Assembly, March 7, 1866*

* *This is ideological warfare. "Consent," "deliberation," and "rights and priv-*

Charles Tupper: No gentleman who was here in the first session of the house (1864) would dare to say that it is unconstitutional for the parliament to change the constitution. They recorded a resolution* by unanimous consent on the journals of this legislature which authorized the change of our constitution without any reference of the people whatever.

There is not a man who does not know that this proposition [for maritime union] was for a more extreme change in the constitution of this country than the one now proposed. The Quebec scheme proposes to leave to Nova Scotia her own government and parliament as far as local questions are concerned, and to have a general parliament with general powers in reference to matters common to all the provinces; but the resolution of 1864 was to surrender the entire constitution of the country, and take away the seat of government in all probability from Nova Scotia and place it in New Brunswick, or wherever it might be agreed upon. It provided that scheme of legislative union should go into operation and become law — not when it had received the sanction of the people — but the consent of the provincial legislatures, and Her Majesty's approval . . .

Annand: [It has been] said that both sides of this house were represented at the Quebec convention. I think differently. The Liberal and Conservative sides were represented, but not the two great parties which on this great question divide the people of this country. My desire is, in the event of a new convention, not

---

ileges of the people" versus "the rights of this house" are the key rhetorical weapons used all through the Nova Scotia debates. In defence of tradition, constitutional precedent, filtration of common opinion, and the distinctions of merit and leadership, Tupper and others argue for the rights of parliamentarians to speak as experts for and in the best interests of the people. Annand, whatever may be the strategic element, is the opposing voice of the rising democratic ethos. He takes the view that even if "a majority of this house" wanted to join Confederation but did not seek the consent of the people, it would be a worthless venture. At the time this must have been a most radical statement. The people? He wanted the legislature to "defer to their prejudices" (meaning their inclinations). That meant a sharp retreat from the specific purpose of a traditional legislature to filter hasty opinion of all kinds through deliberation by the well-informed. — WDG

* The resolution authorized delegates to the Charlottetown Conference of 1864 to agree to legislative union of the Maritime provinces.

to see this house represented as to its political proclivities, but in respect to the position of the question of Confederation in this province. Will the ablest statesmen of British North America say that this question is not now better understood than when they met at Quebec? Will they say that their ability is so great that they were able in the midst of exhaustive festivities to have a perfect constitution for these provinces? They might give themselves that credit, but the people of this country do not.

This question should not be dealt with hastily. There is no necessity why this scheme should be forced upon the people; if it is to come, let it come quietly; let the public mind be educated up to it; but if you do not wish to make this country a second Ireland, to bring these provinces into inextricable troubles, do not force union upon them. I believe that the people might be educated to accept a scheme of union if it was just. I believe, influenced by a desire to meet the wishes of the British government, they are ready to make large sacrifices; but to force the measure upon them without their consent would be a grave and fatal mistake. It would be fatal to the success of that union which gentlemen are so anxious to bring about. We know how the Irish union was accomplished,* but I trust no such influences will prevail in this country.

I can suppose a majority of this house prepared to accept union, but unless they have the people behind them, any measure they might pass would not be worth the paper on which it was written. You must carry with you the sentiment of the people. Even if you are entirely wrong on the question, you should defer to their prejudices and give them time to consider the subject calmly and deliberately, but not to force it upon them at all hazards.

— *House of Assembly, April 5, 1866*

Tupper: The time to ascertain whether a question is constitutional or not — to obtain a dispassionate opinion from the public mind in the country — is not when it is a subject of excitement and controversy. You must go back and study the pages of the history of our country to ascertain if you can find upon the record what are the real and deliberate utterances of public men on both sides of politics. I am prepared to go back and turn up the page of Nova Scotia's history and give to the house the statements of

> *"I can suppose a majority of this house prepared to accept union, but unless they have the people behind them, any measure they might pass would not be worth the paper on which it was written. You must carry with you the sentiment of the people."*

---

* Much arm twisting and bribery were employed to induce the Irish parliament to accept the union and vote itself out of existence. — IG

SIR CHARLES TUPPER
(1821–1915),
a doctor and enthusiast
for both Maritime and
British North American
union. As Conservative
prime minister of Nova
Scotia (1864–67), he
did his utmost to take
the province into
Confederation despite
strong public opposition.
He succeeded because
his party possessed a big
parliamentary majority
and did not have to face
the electors while
Confederation was in
process. In 1866 he won
parliamentary approval
to send delegates to the
London Conference by
pretending that they
would demand, and
could achieve, serious
changes in the Quebec
agreement.

A centralist who
preferred legislative to
federal union, Tupper
was prime minister of
Canada for ten weeks
in 1896.

public men of all shades of politics that will be clear and conclusive on the subject. The house will recollect that many years ago the Honourable Mr. [James William] Johnston, when sitting on the opposition benches, proposed a resolution providing for a union of British North America. That resolution became the subject of calm and dispassionate discussion, as it should always obtain at the hands of the legislature. Two of the ablest men who have ever figured in the affairs of the country were sitting on the government side. I refer to Mr. [Joseph] Howe and Mr. [William] Young. These gentlemen discussed the question in all its aspects, and it was never questioned whether the parliament had the power of dealing with the constitution . . . His Grace the Duke of Newcastle gave his opinion [agreeing with Howe]. To this may be added the . . . opinion of the present colonial minister . . .

So, you have the three prominent men of the day [Howe, Johnston, and Young] committing themselves in the most unequivocal manner to the declaration that under the constitution of the country, the mode of dealing with this question was a convention of public men, and that the scheme should have effect given to it by the people's representatives assembled in parliament . . .

So, at a time when the question was calmly debated and when there was no excitement, you have these distinct utterances of all these able statesmen, both British and colonial, that the parliament of the country has power to change the constitution of the country, and that that is the proper mode of dealing with such a subject.

Therefore I say that the legislature is justified in taking such action upon the vital and important question as in their deliberative opinion is calculated to promote the best interests of the province and of British North America. It will thus be seen that the issue that has been raised by parties for purposes of their own — who wish to overthrow the existing administration and come into power themselves — is swept away like chaff before the wind, neither constitutional principle nor precedent being found to support their views.

After having brought the opinions of all these eminent public men to prove the proper and constitutional mode of dealing with the subject — after having shown that in the whole history of Great Britain and of the United States no parallel can be found for the appeal to the people* which has been proposed — I think

---

* Tupper invokes the then well-known historical fact that the American constitution was only narrowly ratified by the new states and was created by

the opponents of union are not in a situation to challenge the right of this house in the exercise of its legitimate functions to pursue such a course as the interests of our common country demands. They cannot find one example of a question like this being referred to the people at the polls, either in Great Britain or the United States. There is one, but it is not one which they are likely to adduce for adoption by a British assembly. It is the occasion on which the people of France were driven at the point of the bayonet to the polls,* to sustain a perfect despotism† in the country, to part with every vestige of liberty that freemen value.

Adams Archibald: We have been told, and I am astonished to hear . . . that we are proceeding to strike down the principles of responsibility which have given free government to the people of this country. Now, what is stamped on the very forefront of the Quebec scheme? That the general government shall be conducted on the principles of responsibility to the entire people, just as our own now is at this moment, so that the principles of

---

individuals who had no special authority or leave of the people to invent a new constitution. Many have since described that process as a second American revolution, or counter-revolution. The first revolution of 1776 was in the name of liberty. The constitutional revolution of 1787 was in the name of strong government. Indeed, the deepest ambition of its chief architect, James Madison, was to curtail the burgeoning democratic spirit that had so unsettled the states between 1776 and 1787. His famous Federalist Paper No. 10, *certainly widely read at the time, stated the common traditionalist position that democracies "have ever been spectacles of turbulence and contention," and have been "as short in their lives as they have been violent in their deaths." — WDG*

* Both Napoleon and Napoleon III established their authority by a mixture of repression and rigged plebiscites. — PR

† Tupper reminds the house that there is no necessary connection between democracy and liberty. Until this century, students of law and government were commonly taught to appreciate the historical lesson of the "cycle of constitutions." In Book VI of The Rise of the Roman Empire, *Polybius called the phenomenon "anacyclosis," and meant by it that political systems tend to rotate in a cycle from abuses of monarchy or dictatorship, to the oppressions of aristocracy, to the licentiousness of democracy, and back to monarchy or dictatorship again. The experience of the French voters driven by bayonet to vote, followed in lock-step cyclical fashion by the Terror, then Napoleon, was but the most recent historical example. — WDG*

the federal government are precisely those which we possess in this country.

Our legislature is left to be moulded as we choose; our local administration, unless we wish otherwise, will be the same as at present, so that every principle of responsibility to the people is retained as it is now. In the local administration the responsibility lies to this people; in the general administration, to the people of the entire group. The old altars remain — the worshippers have still the same faith; but in the metropolitan cathedral, or to borrow a figure from the Presbyterian Church, in the National Assembly, will be those who have the care of all the churches. Therefore, while we leave intact the government of the country, all we do is to have these matters, which are of common and general concern, transferred to the general legislature.

We are told that the time for changing institutions is the time of peace and prosperity, that the only time for union is when we can calmly and deliberately consider all the arguments and objections. Such a doctrine falsifies the entire current of history. When was ever a union effected between independent communities with jealousies and rivalries which independence begets, except under the presence of the most urgent necessities? What gave birth to the union over our border? Was the proposition submitted to the different states in time of peace? Not so. The union, such as it was at first, was cemented only under the pressure of war with the mother country. If the people of the states had waited for union till that pressure had ceased to exist, they would have been destroyed piecemeal and would have had no union at all. From 1774 till the time of peace, the government had been carried on under a Congress which arose at the promptings of necessity and assumed a centralized power, but when peace came the centralization ended, the states pulled apart, prejudice and passion deluded them, and it was not until ruin stared them in the face that they were again forced to unite with closer bands and in a more solid union.* The same has been the case with the other unions of the world. All the other unions of independent states

---

*Archibald refers to the fact that after 1776, as new American state governments were hastily erected, the ageless lessons of unchecked rule began. In that same year Thomas Paine's famous pamphlet Common Sense (with some estimates of up to 500,000 copies sold!) ridiculed the ancient idea of mixed government and checks and balances on the uses of power, urging the American people to throw out all impediments to the expression of their will.

WILLIAM ANNAND
(1808–1887), farmer,
journalist, and publisher.
Annand rose to political
prominence as the
devoted lieutenant of the
reformer Joseph Howe,
whose newspaper,
the *Novascotian*, he
bought in 1843. His
apparently unscrupulous
business practices while
provincial finance
minister contributed to
the large Conservative
election victory of 1863.
After first opposing
Confederation, he
modified his stance in
1865 to demand a new
constitutional conference
and a better deal for his
province. In 1866–67 he
and Howe lobbied in
London against Nova
Scotia's inclusion, and
as premier, 1867–74,
he campaigned for her
secession, breaking with
Howe when the latter
came to terms with John
A. Macdonald.

that have had any permanence are those which have been
cemented under the pressure of urgent necessities.

— *House of Assembly, April 10, 1866*

Annand: [Even if] there should be a majority in the house in
favour of a transfer of our privileges to a government to be organized six or eight hundred miles off, yet the gentlemen who
oppose the bargain will go down honoured to posterity . . . There
had been discussions in past years in reference to union, and
there had been diversities of opinion, some being in favour of
legislative and some in favour of a federal union; but I challenge
any gentleman to show me that, beyond the mere expression of
abstract opinion in favour of union, any resolution was ever proposed. The country was then peaceful, contented, and prosperous;
no one here thought of changing our constitution for the sake of
connection with Canada. Some of us entertained views favourable
to a union of the Maritime provinces, but no one dreamed of
giving up our present institutions and accepting a subordinate
status in another country.

I then ask, how does this question of Confederation arise? By
what necessity has it been produced? Does it arise from the
necessities of the people or the legislature of Nova Scotia? Why,
sir, we all know that but for the necessities of Canada, as admitted
by the provincial secretary [Tupper] himself and by his colleague
in the delegation, that question would never have been pressed
upon our attention. Am I to understand, as was said elsewhere,

---

*They did. By 1786 the upper houses in nearly all the new states either had
become a mirror of the lower house or were dissolved outright. Legislators,
often elected annually, had become powerless to deviate from the views of
their electors. Nine of thirteen states created their own navies and seized
ships of other states as they enforced tariffs against each other or disputed
boundaries. Seven states printed their own unfunded paper money. With
unchecked will the people quickly passed laws for the confiscation without due
process of the private property of Loyalists, and for the cancellation or postponement of personal and corporate debts. Some state legislatures were even
administering justice. The Vermont legislature, for example, managed to
block about 90 per cent of all court actions. Alexander Hamilton, one of the
authors of* The Federalist Papers, *described the states of that time as
"wretched nurseries of unceasing discord." The American founders reacted
to this democratic chaos swiftly, and the lesson was obviously not lost on
Canada's founders. — WDG*

that owing to the Canadian necessities — owing to the fact that the government of Canada had come to a deadlock, there being three changes of administration in three years and parliamentary government having become impossible, therefore it was that the people of Canada to rid themselves of their difficulties, financial and political, cast their eyes upon these provinces as affording a means of escape?

We all know what took place in 1864. A resolution passed authorizing the appointment of delegates to confer on the question of a maritime union; those delegates proceeded to Charlottetown, and there they were met by Canadian speculators in politics, by whom they were spirited away to Quebec, and were seduced from their allegiance to this country and from the mission with which we charged them. In October, after a fortnight's debate at Quebec, and amidst exhaustive festivities, they passed resolutions favourable to a union of the provinces of British America. These gentlemen have said that this delegation was authorized by the ministers of the crown and by the governor general, but it had no authority from us. The debate at Quebec was conducted in secret, all its deliberations were carried on with closed doors, and there is good reason to believe that but for the accidental publication of those resolutions the scheme might have been passed at last session.

But we are told also that the queen (God bless Her Majesty) is in favour of the scheme. Under our constitution the queen can do no wrong;* she is not responsible for a word contained in the speech with which parliament is opened, but her ministers are charged with that responsibility. The queen, we may imagine, has something else to think about than the affairs of British North America in her household and the exercise of domestic virtues. I attach no importance therefore to that argument, and gentlemen opposing must be weak indeed for argument when they bring Her Majesty's name into the debate. Her name should not be mentioned here.

We are told that the governor, the hero of Kars,† is in favour

---

*A constitutional axiom which expresses the essence of responsible government: that the monarch's ministers are responsible for the acts of her (or his) government. Annand points out that it is both constitutionally improper and logically absurd to invoke Queen Victoria's supposed support for Confederation. — PR

† Sir William Fenwick Williams (1800–1883), commander-in-chief British

of it. I do not desire to say anything disrespectful of that highly respectable and able general — I respect him as a warrior who stood true to the colours of his country and faithfully served his sovereign — but I would undertake to find in the backwoods of Musquodoboit men who understand the bearing of the questions and the necessities of the province as well as he.

(Upon interruption being caused by disturbance in the galleries, they were cleared at the insistence of Mr. Stewart Campbell, but were subsequently reopened.)

The names of the general and of the admiral* have also been introduced into the debate to give weight and authority to the scheme of Confederation. These are the proper judges in time of war — we are ready to follow them into the field and to fight under their flag upon the sea — but it is highly indecorous to bring the names of these functionaries here and, least of all, should the clergy be so prominently referred to within these walls . . . [If] it be true, as has been represented, that all this combination is on the side of the government, I ask how is it that the great body of the people are arrayed against them . . . The provincial secretary [Tupper] may quote these distinguished names and refer to these organs of popular opinion, but how is it that he does not at this moment open a single constituency in the country? There have been three elections since the scheme was propounded, and at every one of these the government has been "routed horse, foot and artillery." What do I care for the opinions to which he has referred, when I know he dare not open a single constituency and that the greatest misfortune that could befall him would be a vacancy in any of the seats? I therefore hurl back the allusions he has made.

My mind can carry me back to the time when we were struggling for responsible government.† We asked Her Majesty's

---

forces in North America 1859–65, lieutenant governor of Nova Scotia 1865–67. A Nova Scotian by birth, and putative illegitimate member of the British royal family, he was celebrated for his stalwart defence of the Turkish town of Kars during the Crimean War. — PR

* *General Sir Charles Hastings Doyle (1804–1883), commander of British forces in the Atlantic area; administrator and lieutenant governor of New Brunswick, 1866–67; lieutenant governor of Nova Scotia, 1867–73. Admiral Sir James Hope (1808–1881), commander-in-chief North America and the West Indies, 1863–67. — PR*

† *This rather vague allusion may refer to the opposition that General Sir*

ministers for the concession and we had them against us, we had against us the press of England, Her Majesty's representative, and the general here, but we were right, we pressed for the rights and privileges of a free people and achieved the system that we now enjoy. Therefore away with the arguments drawn from the opinions of the admiral, and general, and governor. Their feeling is to obey the imperial authorities, and their opinions may be expected to be moulded by their government.

The provincial secretary gave us an argument the other day on the subject of an appeal to the people. He said it was our constitutional right to deal with the question. We may have the abstract right to do so,* but I put it to them, one and all, when we were elected three years ago, if members had told their constituents that they would, if elected, destroy the constitution of the country, how many of them would have been here? The trust reposed in them was for a very different purpose — it was that they should transact the public business according to the well-understood wishes of their constituents.

— *House of Assembly, April 13, 1866*

> "If members had told their constituents that they would, if elected, destroy the constitution of the country, how many of them would have been here?"

John Locke: When the lieutenant governor ventures to carry out any scheme of union in opposition to the wishes of the people, he identifies himself improperly with a party. This house is elected to legislate according to the well-understood wishes of the people, and this particular scheme, changing the constitution, it was never empowered to carry out. In adopting the scheme we do not carry out those wishes, and if the people had the opportunity of expressing their views they would return such a majority that twelve members would not be found† to support the scheme.

Taking the . . . view . . . that annexation to the United States will follow annexation to Canada, it will be seen that we are doing a positive injury to Great Britain by confederating, because the

---

Colin Campbell (1776–1847), governor of Nova Scotia, 1834–40, presented to the movement for responsible government led by Joseph Howe. — PR

* *Those who assert the legislature's right to act without consulting the people justify their position by an appeal to constitutional precedent. Annand and Locke deny the power of mere constitutionality to legitimize legislative action in this matter contrary to the will of the people. — PR*

† *In fact, in September 1867, when simultaneous elections were held to the provincial legislature and the Canadian House of Commons, confederates won only one federal and two provincial seats. — PR*

moment she loses her colonies, England must become a second-
or third-rate power . . . As loyal men, we should stand by our
country in this emergency. It is not certain that New Brunswick
will fall in with the scheme. A telegram informs us that a majority
of the assembly will move for the recall of the governor, and that
will postpone Confederation for some time. It seems to me that
the government are too hot and too hasty in this matter. Give us
time to consider the question. I do not ask them to dissolve and
go to the country, but I think we should have the chance of one
year more to see if the people will be indoctrinated into favouring
the measure. Not that I expect them to willingly favour such a
union, for I want none. We are prosperous and happy as we are.

I ask the house not to agree to the proposed delegation, for
we very well know that the delegates will come back with the
Quebec scheme,* Mr. Cardwell [the colonial secretary] having
taken a decided stand in its favour. I therefore call upon the government to stay their hand and to give the country time to
consider what is the best course to pursue. But if this new scheme
to send a delegation to England to settle terms of union there
should be carried in this house, I would demand as a right of the
people of this province that, after terms being agreed upon by the
British government and the delegates, it should be referred back
to this people for their sanction. If any other course is pursued,
you trifle with the liberties and privileges of a free people in bartering them away without giving them a voice in the matter, and
the consequences, be what they may, will rest upon the men who
have so acted.

> *"If this new scheme to send a delegation to England to settle terms of union there should be carried in this house, I would demand as a right of the people of this province that, after terms being agreed upon by the British government and the delegates, it should be referred back to this people for their sanction. If any other course is pursued, you trifle with the liberties and privileges of a free people."*

Hiram Blanchard: It was suggested by Mr. Annand that the
people be called on to vote on the question of Confederation
alone, but I cannot think that he seriously proposed that we
should do what no British country ever did before — resort to a
"plebiscite" on this question.

Stewart Campbell: It has been done in Nova Scotia.

> *"I cannot think that [Mr. Annand] seriously proposed that we should do what no British country ever did before — resort to a 'plebiscite' on this question."*

---

* The issue before the legislature in 1866 is whether to send delegates to the
London Conference, which was to revise the Quebec agreement before its
enactment by the British parliament. Confederates try to disarm opposition
by presenting the proposed conference as an opportunity for fundamental
renegotiation, but Locke is rightly dubious. — PR

Blanchard: This reference is to the vote taken upon the municipal corporations' bill, but this was simply as to the adoption in each county of a purely local measure; but did anyone ever hear of a question of colonial policy being so submitted? That precedent is no parallel to this case, and I challenge gentlemen who take that side of the question to lay their hands upon any case in which a question of this kind was sent in that way to the people. If such a mode is un-British, uncertain, and unreliable, how are we to adopt it? What are we to depend on for the decision? We recently took away from a large portion of the people the electoral franchise.* Are we to send this question to the electors, or to the whole people, and under what regulations? We have heard a good deal about appeals to the people, and I would like to look back at the history of this country to show, as I believe I can, that such an appeal is not desirable or necessary.

William Henry: . . . When responsible government was conceded to us, the principle of total independence did not accompany it. We may pass an act here, but it must be ratified by the home government. We are dependent and should, where necessary, modify our views and measures to some extent when imperial and intercolonial interests are at stake. Whilst we are a dependency, we have the protection of the mother country and she can at the same time ask from us the yielding of certain rights as British subjects, for the benefit of the whole empire. We are asked to . . .

Thomas Killam: To sell us.

Henry: The honourable member says to sell us; I would tell him that he would not ask a great deal to sell us to the United States tomorrow. (Cheers in the galleries.) I contend whenever overpowering interests of the empire demand it, the imperial government may fairly ask us to modify and amend our constitution, and that the representatives of the people can constitutionally consider and pass upon the subject.

Let us then look calmly at the position we occupy. We are told that this matter should be submitted to the people. I would ask these gentlemen to give us examples where such a course has been pursued . . . I can understand why, if a resolution was moved

---

In 1854 Nova Scotia had introduced universal manhood suffrage, but in 1863 the province reverted to a property-based franchise.

for annexation to the United States, some gentlemen would not see anything improper in it, but when we move one, under the authority of the British government, with the view of joining the sister colonies, in order to give us strength and security, they prate about the constitutionality of the proceeding. Suppose the British parliament in the interests of the empire should pass an act for the consolidation of those provinces, could the constitutional right of doing so be impugned?* The British government have not intimated a desire to pursue that course, but no person can deny its right to adopt that course. All, however, that they have done is to manifest their desire that we should manage the affair in our own way, and to give us their opinion that it is for our own advantage that we should unite without delay.

When gentlemen attempt to introduce a novel doctrine in this legislature, they should adduce some argument derived from the practice of other countries in support of their position. Can they show us an instance of a question, after it has passed the legislature, having been sent to the people? When a government introduces, but fails to carry, a measure, they can go to the country and test the public opinion. When a measure is proposed by a government and passed, the constitutional doctrine prevails that the gentlemen within these walls represent the feelings of their constituents. That must be the constitutional test,† other-

---

*Most definitely! As far back as 1823, Upper Canadian Reformers and Lower Canadian patriotes had denied both the legal and the constitutional right of the British government to reunite those two provinces without their consent. William Baldwin had based his opposition on the idea that a constitution, as a corpus of fundamental law, must by definition be subject to the control of those whose lives it regulates. He argued that the British parliament could not enact the union bill without the consent of the communities affected, "for if so, we had no constitution at all, the provincial legislature would have no rights and privileges, nor the people any security." Henry's argument here, and his earlier contention that a colony had no constitutional right to set up its own particular interest against the general interest of the British Empire, are propositions to which Sir John Beverley Robinson, the Upper Canadian Tory, would have subscribed in the days before responsible government, but I am not sure that any Canadian would have paid them even lip service in the 1860s: see, for instance, the conservative Christopher Dunkin's idea of the constitutional relationship between self-governing colonies and the mother country in chapter 9. — PR

† Henry invokes a ground-rules argument that a simple constitutional test of

wise every measure of importance should be submitted to the people after its passage through the legislature. We are told that the people are opposed to this scheme, but that has to be proved. The people are hardly yet aware of the exact nature of the resolution, and therefore cannot be said to be opposed to it. Some persons have objected to the Quebec scheme; some have favoured a legislative union; others are in favour of a modification of the former measure. Various opinions prevail, but nearly all wish union of some shape or other. I hold that it is perfectly constitutional to pass this resolution, that we have an undoubted right to do so. Gentlemen will remember that it is only a short time since that the legislature of Jamaica passed an act to destroy their own constitution.* Did these anti-confederate gentlemen come forward and declare that to be unconstitutional? Not at all.

— *House of Assembly, April 16, 1866*

> *"I am a free man. I claim the rights and attributes of a free man, speaking in the presence of a British free assembly. I have the right to criticize the judgement they have formed and an equal right to give expression to my own."*

Campbell: I am a free man. I claim the rights and attributes of a free man, speaking in the presence of a British free assembly. I have the right to criticize the judgement they have formed and an equal right to give expression to my own. Therefore when this list of authorities is paraded before us, I cannot but feel that it is an empty parade — it is worth nothing in my estimation — it does not weigh a tittle in the scale. I feel, sir, and I claim the right to express the sentiment, that those individuals, eminent though they be, are not more capable of forming an opinion upon this subject than myself, and I might add that my judgement is

---

representation in the house determines the validity of laws, for failing this the locus of the law-making initiative would shift from the house to the people, and the legislature would lose all legitimacy. The ground-rules argument works well until challenged by the accusation (Campbell, below) that, to make an "irrevocable change" in the constitutional framework of rights without the authority of the governed changes the whole game and therefore the ground rules with it, thus neutralizing the argument. — WDG

* Inspired by the emancipation of slaves in the United States, Jamaican blacks staged the so-called Morante Bay rebellion in 1865. The rebellion was brutally suppressed, and in its wake the frightened, white-dominated Jamaica Assembly abdicated its powers into the hands of the crown. By an order-in-council of 1866 the last remnants of the representative system in Jamaica were swept away and replaced by crown colony government: a striking example of how differently Britain treated her white and her coloured colonies. — IG

formed under the influence of a responsibility which does not attach to them. In saying this I mean no disrespect to any of them, and I feel well assured that none of them would charge me with any design of disrespect. I therefore think that the allusions to which I have referred were unjust and reprehensible attempts to influence this assembly.

What is the measure that we are now called upon to sanction? Twist it or turn it as you please, it is no less than a decided change in our constitution; and how has the scheme effecting that change been brought here? Have the people of this country at any time suggested the expedience of the proposal to the government or the legislature? No. This house was elected entirely independent of that question — it was not before the people when we were elected. Had the case been otherwise, we should not perhaps have seen the faces of some gentlemen who are sitting here today.

[The decision to discuss British North American union at Charlottetown] was a fatal step — a step subversive of the powers of the legislature, and injurious to the feelings and interests of the people of this country. That was the step which has caused so much agitation, so many heartburnings, if not worse, throughout this country. Had they come back here and told the people of this province that they failed in their original mission, and that no union of the Maritime provinces could be effected, they would at least have afforded the people an opportunity of saying how far they were disposed to go into the larger question. They did not do this, but they took upon themselves the whole responsibility of concocting the scheme called the Quebec scheme.

Many gentlemen have hitherto spoken of the scheme then arranged, but I have been surprised that, long as it has been before us, scarcely one syllable has been uttered in this debate in reference to it. It has been praised abroad as a great and magnificent scheme, but what is its position now? "But yesterday it might have stood against the world, now none so poor to do it reverence,"* and it is here, or not here just as men may choose. We have heard something about petitions presented to this house against Confederation, we have yet heard nothing of petitions in

---

*But yesterday the word of Caesar might / Have stood against the world; now lies he there, / And none so poor to do him reverence." Julius Caesar, Act 3, Scene 2. Campbell is deriding the government's pretence that the terms of Confederation can be substantially renegotiated at the proposed London Conference. — PR

its favour. And now we are asked to deliberately ignore the expressed sentiments of this people: we are told that these petitions are to be disregarded and that no notice is to be taken of the rights of the electors. We are reminded of the action of the British parliament in dealing with the reform question, and we are told that that measure involved an important change in the constitution of the country, and no one ever contended that parliament was incompetent to deal with it without reference to the people; but will anyone tell me that the question was not before the people of Great Britain before the last general election? That is the answer which I give to those who assert that this legislature has the right to deal with an irrevocable change in the constitution, and refer to the action of the British parliament in justification of the step.

But some gentlemen argue that on this question, of all questions, the people should not be appealed to, because the people would decide on other issues and not on this.* From whom does this statement come? Does it not come from those who ought to use language more respectful — language precisely the reverse — from the administration which the breath of the people has created? It comes from gentlemen who hold their offices by virtue of the popular voice, and yet the inhabitants of this country are to be told that they are incapable of pronouncing a judgement on this particular question; that other subjects would be introduced, and that no decision could be obtained upon this particular subject. Have the people lost all discernment and discrimination that this, the most important question that ever agitated the public mind, is one upon which no reliable opinion could be formed and expressed?

Sir, I think very differently of the people; I believe they would appreciate the magnitude of the proposition, and while they would be disposed to condemn much of the public conduct of the administration their intelligent discernment would lead them to sink all other considerations and all other questions of policy, in order that upon this they might pronounce the decision of their minds and hearts. It will be perceived that I am for submitting

---

* Campbell is proposing that the government call an election on Confederation. The question is whether voters can be persuaded to focus on the single issue of Confederation, setting aside party loyalty and particular political complaints. He takes up the idea of a referendum in the next paragraph when he speaks of "another mode of testing [the people's] opinions."

this question to the people. Sir, I hold that in a matter which concerns their interests for all time to come, it is our duty to them. But taking the argument of the other side, and supposing that the people are not as intelligent as I assert they are,* there is another mode of testing their opinions, and that is by submitting to them the question of Confederation, pure and simple. We are told that this is not a British practice — that there is no precedent for this; but I reply that we have on our statute book a precedent . . .

The provisions of the municipal corporation bill require that it should be submitted for every man to vote upon, favourably or otherwise, and I therefore maintain that we have an illustrious precedent for the course that we suggest. But if there were no precedent, I might properly introduce here what was improperly introduced the other day by the attorney general, a reference to the law of necessity — I would say, here is a case the like of which has never occurred, and for which there can be no precedent. Here is an unparalleled case, and therefore we are justified in establishing a precedent. We can find no precedent for the attempt to subvert and destroy the constitution of the country, and hence I think that in this special emergency we are not merely at liberty, but are abundantly and imperatively called upon to take that course which will best meet the necessities of the case and promote the interests of the people. It lies not upon us who oppose this measure, but upon those who insist on its passage, to prove the necessity, uncalled for by the people, for taking away the institutions of the country.

Sir, I was astonished when I was told yesterday that in addition to all the arguments that could be adduced in favour of Confederation, the circumstance that all the lawyers and trained politicians were in favour of it should be a reason for the adoption of the scheme without any appeal to them. Sir, I protest

> *"Here is a case the like of which has never occurred, and for which there can be no precedent. Here is an unparalleled case, and therefore we are justified in establishing a precedent. We can find no precedent for the attempt to subvert and destroy the constitution of the country, and hence I think that in this special emergency we are not merely at liberty, but are abundantly and imperatively called upon to take that course which will best meet the necessities of the case and promote the interests of the people."*

---

* This is one of the few explicit mentions of the problem of the intelligence of the people in all the debates. But it was a concern of every mind occupied with the meaning of democracy. If we accept what seems inescapable — that a small number are always brighter and more capable than others — then how can we approve a system that by weight of sheer numbers transfers rule to the less bright? Campbell takes the utilitarian view that, as government is for the good of all the people, then on a measure that threatens to alter all government irrevocably, their intelligence must be tested by asking their consent. What is exposed here is the eternal conflict between "experts" and the "people." — WDG

Consulting the People

"Sir, it is not for lawyers or for trained politicians that we are to act in this place. This is the people's house; their interests must be the polar-star of every man's action here."

against such a doctrine, and the people will protest against it . . . [S]ir, it is not for lawyers or for trained politicians that we are to act in this place. This is the people's house; their interests must be the polar-star of every man's action here, and this measure is to affect those interests for weal or for woe forever.* If we have a ministry that is not agreeable to our wishes and that does not promote the interests of the country, we may bear with it for a while, knowing that the time will come when the people will assert their rights and substitute better men, but in reference to this measure only pass it now and it will be passed forever — the doom of Nova Scotia will then be sealed.

Charles Hamilton: I shall now turn your attention to another feature in this question. Let me suppose that there is an individual desperately sick. The physician attending him feels hardly able to grapple with the disease alone and calls in assistance. The physicians then hold a consultation, but they may disagree. How are they to settle the difficulty? They will consult the best authorities on the question and the men who have written and given the results of their experience, and the issue is that the weight of authority carries the day. The same thing may be said in respect to a court of law. The judges consult the authorities and bring to bear all the examples relating to the case, and decide accordingly. I do not wish to draw any invidious comparisons between individuals, but I would ask who have advocated Confederation in Nova Scotia.† We find on the list the late R.J. Uniacke, the present judge in equity, Mr. Howe, the chief justice, the provincial secre-

---

* It is a mark of political freedom in liberal democracies that ordinary statutes are not enacted to last "forever." A party or group of interests that loses in the legislature can pick itself up, dust itself off, and start all over again with a fresh appeal to the next parliament. Not so with constitutional amendments, especially constitutional change on the scale of Confederation. Every speaker in this debate is aware of the distinction between constitutional law (the law for making law) and ordinary legislation, but few put it so aptly as Campbell. To Campbell it seems obvious that the irrevocable character of Confederation necessitates the appeal to the people. We will see later in these debates that others, just as conscious that Confederation will "seal" their "doom," draw the opposite conclusion. — JA

† Uniacke, a long-time attorney general of Nova Scotia, was well known as an advocate of the idea. James William Johnston (1792–1873), judge-in-

tary, Mr Archibald, Honourable Mr. Henry, Honourable Mr. McCully, Honourable Mr. Ritchie, and others I need not now name. Here is an array of men who have occupied a very prominent position in Nova Scotia; every one of these gentlemen have expressed themselves in favour of union, and no better authorities can be cited than they. Mr. [Joseph] Howe said, years ago, it was the dream of his boyhood and the purpose of his political life, but I am told that it was only a theory with him — theory generally precedes practice; now is the time to put that theory into practice — never was there a more auspicious period to do so than now. When I say that the most eminent men in this province have supported, and are supporting Confederation, I need hardly add that the same thing may be said of the other provinces . . . If you can produce an array of talent* against Confederation like what I have given as supporting it, I would like to hear of it.

James McDonald: There is one argument which has been used by the opponents of the scheme which requires consideration. I admit that, if it be true, it is a fundamental argument, for it lies at the very basis of the question we are discussing. It is one which should therefore be fully and satisfactorily answered before we

---

equity and sometime attorney general, and William Young (1799–1887), chief justice of Nova Scotia, made speeches from the bench in its support. Tupper (provincial secretary), Archibald (MPP, leader of the Liberal Party), Henry (attorney general), and Jonathan McCully (1809–1877, member of the Legislative Council) all represented Nova Scotia at the Quebec Conference. John William Ritchie (1808–90) was government leader in the Legislative Council. Joseph Howe had also favoured British North American union at one time, though he was a leading opponent of the Quebec scheme. — PR

* Hamilton argues for seeking experts on both sides of the question. Latent in his call for "an array of talent" is the suggestion that the people may have interests, but do not necessarily know them because they are not sufficiently intelligent, or, to be more charitable, not well informed. In other words, perhaps their interests, which may be inarticulate or unconscious, must be interpreted and decided on their behalf. In America, Madison (in Federalist No. 10) had articulated this preference for talent in government by calling for a republican system that would "refine and enlarge the public views by passing them through the medium of a chosen body of citizens." These citizens were to be "representatives whose enlightened views and virtuous sentiments render them superior to local prejudices and to schemes of injustice." — WDG

ask the people of Nova Scotia to accept this measure at our hands. That argument, if I understand it aright, and as it has been advanced by all the speakers on the opposite side, and more particularly by the only lawyer who is supporting the opposition, is this: that we are not in a position constitutionally to pass on the measure in this legislature; that this house, in its legislative capacity, is not competent to decide upon this important measure, affecting as we all admit it does, to a large degree, the rights and interests of the people, without a reference to them at the polls. If this be true, we are attempting to discuss a question with which we have no right to deal — we are assuming a power and authority which the constitution does not invest us with — and we would be guilty of one of the highest crimes of which public men can stand convicted before the people who have entrusted their rights to their hands. If, however, as I contend, we have a right to pass upon this question under the constitution handed down to us from the earliest days of constitutional authority, then the question assumes a different aspect, and we have only then to consider whether it is not for their benefit and welfare* that the people should seek by this union to become an integral part of what in a short time must be one of the commanding nationalities of the world.

I must say that I was astonished not only to hear a lawyer but other members of this legislature who, from their position, ought to be somewhat versed in constitutional knowledge — for I need not tell you it does not require a legal mind to understand the general principles of constitutional law upon which the rights and interests of this parliament are based — attempt to delude this

---

* Of note is the manner in which McDonald argues forcefully for both sides of the question even as he explains his preference. Namely, that in what concerns the people, a government under the British model has the constitutional right and duty to legislate "for their benefit and welfare," which he knows is a model pointedly distinct from the more radical American notion of commitment to government by the people. At issue throughout is the fact that all representative systems exercise a right of substitute judgement, whereby a few decide for all. This was seen to be the sole device that made modern democracy possible as a form of rule over extended territories with large populations, it being received opinion since the influence of Montesquieu and de Tocqueville that direct democracy can only work for small concentrated populations. The background to the ideological battle in these debates is the understanding that, to give up the device of representation, of the right to govern for the people, was to threaten the chief virtue of the entire system. — WDG

house with the style of argument resorted to by the honourable member for Halifax [Annand] and the honourable member for Guysborough [Stewart Campbell] in dealing with this important branch of the subject . . .

In propounding an argument radically striking at what I consider one of the highest privileges of this legislature, he [Campbell] ought to have given us the result of his reading, and have shown this house and country at least one instance in the whole constitutional history of England where the right of parliament to deal with a question like this was denied. I challenge the honourable member, and any gentleman in this house who assumes the same views, to show me in the whole constitutional history of England down to the present time a single case in which it was contended that the parliament of England, or of any colony enjoying the blessing of the British Constitution, were not absolutely and constitutionally authorized in their legislative capacity to discuss and finally decide upon any measure* which in their opinion touched the rights and interests of the people they represented. I shall not occupy any time in debating a question which is as plain as the sun at noonday.

But I feel it important that the people of this country should be rightly informed on the question, and see how baseless are the assertions of those who contend that the representatives of this house — that the legislature of this country, for some reasons — have been arrogating to themselves a power which is not delegated to them by the constitution and are bartering away most unjustifiably (to quote the honourable member for Yarmouth) the rights and liberties of the province. In order that the people and the country may be satisfied on this point I will read one or two authorities of very high standing — which are recognized in England as of the highest weight in matters of constitutional law and practice. May† in his word on the privileges of parliament says:

> *"I challenge the honourable member, and any gentleman in this house who assumes the same views, to show me in the whole constitutional history of England down to the present time a single case in which it was contended that the parliament of England, or of any colony enjoying the blessing of the British Constitution, were not absolutely and constitutionally authorized in their legislative capacity to discuss and finally decide upon any measure which in their opinion touched the rights and interests of the people they represented."*

---

*McDonald and others who opposed submitting the Confederation scheme to a popular referendum were constitutionally correct. There was at the time no precedent in British constitutional practice for referendums. Since the sixteenth century the doctrine of parliamentary omnicompetence — meaning that there is nothing, constitutionally speaking, that parliament cannot do — had been generally accepted. — IG

† Sir Thomas Erskine May, Baron Farnborough (1815–1886), wrote A Practical Treatise on the Laws, Privileges, Proceedings, and Usage

The legislative authority of Parliament extends over the United Kingdom and all its Colonies and foreign possessions, and there are no limits to the power of making laws for the whole empire than those which are incident to all sovereign authority — the willingness of the people to obey, or their power to resist. Unlike the Legislatures of many other countries it is bound by no fundamental charter or constitution; but has itself the *sole constitutional right of establishing and altering the laws and Government of the empire*. [Emphasis in original.]

In addition to this, I shall quote the opinion of one of the highest authorities on all such matters — from a book which is not only of the highest authority but is familiar to every man of ordinary reading and information. Sir W. Blackstone,* treating of the power of parliament and quoting from Coke, says:

The power and jurisdiction of Parliament, says Sir Edward Coke, is so transcendent and absolute that it cannot be con-

---

Proceedings, and Usage of Parliament *(1844). It became the standard British guide to parliamentary practice. McDonald quotes the opening paragraph of chapter 2, "Power and Jurisdiction of Parliament."*
* *Sir William Blackstone (1723–1780) was the leading jurist of his day. His* Commentaries on the Laws of England *(4 vols., 1765–69) went through many editions and became the standard guide to the common law in both the British Empire and the United States. Sir Edward Coke (1552–1634), Lord Chief Justice of England, 1613–16, the most eminent English judge of his day, was dismissed from the bench by King James I for upholding the supremacy of the common law against the monarch's prerogative powers. As an MP in the 1620s, he upheld the liberties of parliament. He was the chief mover behind the Petition of Right of 1628, a protest by parliament against Charles I's alleged abuse of his powers.*
McDonald here uses the doctrine of parliamentary sovereignty to justify the legislature in committing Nova Scotia to Confederation without consulting the people, but the doctrine had a wider significance in the history of Canada and the British Empire. Eighteenth-century British constitutionalists, among whom Blackstone was pre-eminent, construed Coke's account of the authority of parliament to mean that the king-in-parliament at Westminster was supreme throughout the empire. It was on this basis that parliament asserted in the 1760s its right to tax the American colonies, thereby precipitating the revolution. Colonial jurists put a different construction on Coke's doctrine, understanding it as an assertion of the king's

fined, either from cause or persons within any bounds . . . [Parliament] *can change and create afresh even the constitution of the kingdom and of parliament themselves . . .* It can in short, do anything that is not naturally impossible. [Emphasis in original.]

Archibald McLelan: I do not consider it necessary to weary the house with a discussion of the arguments against the measure because I believe that we have not the right to change, in the manner proposed by this resolution, our constitution. It is not in our commissions. The supporters of the resolution argue on the extent of our powers; but I look more to our right to do so,* without first consulting those whom we represent. If I understand responsible government, it means that we either have the sanction of the people to carry a measure, or that we shall decide upon questions in such a way as we feel will meet their approval — that we must ever keep in view a going back to the people to

"If I understand responsible government, it means that we either have the sanction of the people to carry a measure, or that we shall decide upon questions in such a way as we feel will meet their approval — that we must ever keep in view a going back to the people to have our acts approved or condemned."

sovereignty in conjunction with his various parliaments throughout the empire. Seen in this light, Westminster's sovereignty was confined to the United Kingdom, and both American and Irish Whigs denied that it extended to their countries. This same interpretation of Coke's doctrine underlay the assertion of colonial sovereignty, and the associated demand for responsible government by William and Robert Baldwin and like-minded Upper Canadian Reformers, in the 1820s.

As quoted here, May reiterates Blackstone's version of the doctrine. In later editions, May inserted an acknowledgement that colonial responsible government had impinged somewhat on parliament's authority. — PR

* Like Annand and Locke, McLelan distinguishes between constitutionality and legitimacy. Constitutional precedent may give the legislature the power to commit the province to Confederation, but only popular sanction, given in a general election or by referendum, can convey the right to do so. Is this position inconsistent with the principles of responsible government? The Nova Scotian anti-confederates argue that the authority of the legislature as against the people extends only to ordinary legislation, not to fundamental constitutional reform, and Joseph Howe, the province's leading theorist of colonial responsible government, is of their number. Not only that, but William Baldwin, a leading Upper Canadian theorist, had taken the same position on the Union Bill of 1822. He had denied not only the British parliament's right to amend the provincial constitution without the colonists' consent but also the right of the provincial legislature to give such consent without a specific popular mandate, given in a general election. — PR

have our acts approved or condemned. The charter of our rights is not found in any one dispatch from the Colonial Office, but runs through a number, granting one concession after another, all tending to this one point — that the people shall be consulted, and to them we are responsible for our action here. Under this resolution before us, public opinion cannot have its legitimate influence. It is not proposed that the action of members is ever to be passed upon by the people. Neither can it be said that because the question of union has been for some years agitated that we were empowered at the last general election to pass it. The resolution of this house in 1864, on which the honourable provincial secretary lays such great stress, speaks of the obstacles to union and of the desirability of having "the question set at rest." From the action of the delegates appointed under the resolution it was supposed to be "set at rest" as impracticable, and therefore was not a question before the people at the last general election, and to pass it now and put it forever beyond their reach would be unconstitutional and unjust.

The supporters of this resolution claim Lord Durham as one of the early promoters of a union of the colonies. I refer them to his views on this point, as given in his report to the British government. He says: "But the state of the Lower Provinces, though it justifies the proposal of an union, would not, I think, render it *gracious or even just* on the part of the Parliament to carry it into effect without *referring it for the ample deliberation and consent of those Colonies.*" Strongly as Lord Durham advocated a legislative union of these colonies, he tells us it would not be just to adopt it without the approval of the people.* But I find that even the politicians of Canada admit that it should be referred to the people, if there be any doubt as to the opinions which they held. Mr. Cameron,† in the Canadian assembly, after approving of the

---

*McLelan quotes from the "General Review and Recommendations" of Durham's Report. It is likely, however, that legislative approval without prior reference to the electorate would have met the criterion of popular sanction as Durham conceived it. — PR

† John Hillyard Cameron, a leading Upper Canadian Conservative, voted to approve the Quebec agreement, but then moved a resolution calling for the British government to refrain from final action until the scheme had been referred to the people at a general election. It is remarkable that both J.H. Cameron and his seconder, M.C. Cameron (who opposed Confederation), were of the High Tory wing of the Upper Canadian Conservatives. — PR

scheme, proposed a reference to the people, arguing that if they gave their approval the union would be more permanent.

You are proposing to pass a resolution upon which no man voting for it will go back to the people for the ratification of his act . . . [If] you can obtain a majority to favour it, then you may hope for it to be enduring. It is one of the principles inherent in the minds of all claiming British origin to accept and obey the opinions of the majority. I do not believe, however, that a majority can be found to assent to a proposition which would sweep away our constitution and even blot out the name of Nova Scotia from the map of the world.

William Blackwood: I always believed in responsible government and the principle upon which that sort of government rests — that the people shall be ruled according to their well-understood wishes. A member who knows the views of his constituents on this question should be prepared to give his vote like a man; but a member not knowing those views, or knowing that a majority of those whom he represents are against the measure, is in duty bound to vote against the resolution which will take away their privileges without appeal. I feel it to be my duty to refrain from giving away the rights of the people without affording them an opportunity of expressing their opinions and judging for themselves. If the great intelligence possessed by the people of this country were brought to bear on this house tonight, it would be seen that they would not part with their rights without a struggle. Union may be a good thing, but I should like to be sure that we are going to gain some substantial advantages by it.

I find in the speeches of those who advocate the scheme a great deal of mere theory. Looking at the matter as a surrender of some of our privileges, I think it behooves us to examine well before passing the resolution. I have yet expressed no opinion on the principle of union, but I will now say to the house and to the country that I will assent to no scheme until the people have passed upon it. By the division tonight we may establish what will be called a union, but will that be a union of the people?* Give me a union of heart, and thought, and action — a union that will strengthen the arm and nerve the heart upon every occasion. The people, I maintain, are able to judge of the question for them-

---

* *Blackwood anticipates the argument that Confederation was a union of governments, not of peoples.* — PR

selves, and if they choose union I will gladly assent, but if they reject the scheme, away goes the proposition. It may be said that this legislature constitutes the united wisdom of the country; and, while I admit that a large amount of intelligence is to be seen around these benches, I feel that, in the locality which I represent, there are men from whom I should like to hear.

James Fraser: I will tell the house candidly that my opposition to the resolution before us is not due to any hostile feelings in reference to the principle of union. I do not think it necessary that petitions should come from my constituents to inform me of their wishes, because, living as I do among them, I must be aware of their views, and unless a very great change has taken place since I left them I know that they are not prepared to adopt the proposition of union at present. At this time last year a scheme of Confederation was before the people, and they had an opportunity of examining and judging it. They did examine it, and a majority of them became opposed to it — not because a great deal of pains and talent had not been taken with the measure; because now that we are about to form a new delegation, I do not think that we can send gentlemen of more talent and more knowledge of the business they have to perform than those who went before.

"The spirit of liberty will make itself heard wherever it exists. Let us take care of our rights, for political expediency in limiting a people's freedom is a dangerous principle and will never satisfy a free people."

William Lawrence: There can be no great love of union where the parties to be joined have not the slightest desire to associate with each other. Right or wrong, beneficial or otherwise, it is impossible to persuade the mass of the people that the system which gives to them an equal voice in the government of the country is not the best. How many of the present members would be here if they said to the people, in 1863, that they were going to change the constitution of the country?

A mere politician, thrown up by the dark and turbid waters of party, actuated by self-interest, can have no lasting influence over a question of this sort. This is no party question; it passes beyond all such considerations, and such feelings should be far from every mind. Gentlemen mistake the feeling of the people of this country if they hope to excite their admiration or secure their confidence by displaying such newborn zeal in forcing Confederation on the people. The spirit of liberty will make itself heard wherever it exists. Let us take care of our rights, for political expediency in limiting a people's freedom is a dangerous principle and will never satisfy a free people. I believe one of our great objects, at

the present time, should be to foster a spirit of peace and harmony amongst our own people, and harmony can only be maintained by a patriotic, wise, and noble use of power. The people in every part of this country must feel that their rights are protected. So far from lending ourselves to any scheme which would threaten the safety or prosperity of our country, we should not hesitate to plant ourselves in opposition even to our political associates when they seek to promote it.

We are a free people, prosperous beyond doubt, advancing cautiously in wealth, under the protection of our good old flag, the only banner which floats over a limited monarchy and a free people. Under the British Constitution we have far more freedom than any other country on the face of the earth. We have sprung from a nation in whose veins the blood of freedom circulates, and who carry everywhere the deepest attachment to their sovereign. It is the spirit of that constitution which unites and invigorates every part of the empire, down to the lowest member, but to pass Confederation, without asking the voice of the people, will only be sowing the seed of dissatisfaction and contention among a very large portion of our population. A representative of the people is bound by the highest moral obligations to respect their wishes and obey their will, when their sober judgement has been ascertained . . .

Now I deplore the intolerant spirit which I see every day manifested around these benches; it is utterly inconsistent with the true spirit of freedom. The foundation of free constitutional government is the voice of a majority of the people, and so long as it deserves the name and wins the affection of the people it can never be in any great danger. Now if a question of right arises between the constituent and the representative body, by what authority shall it be decided? If you leave it to the judges, they will tell you that the law of parliament is above them. What then remains but to leave it to the people to decide themselves?

[In] regard to Confederation, I say frankly that whenever a majority of the people speak in favour of union, let them have it; but I will not consent to a change of the constitution without their consent. If the representatives are unfaithful to their trust and abuse their powers by disposing of the birthright of the people, then responsible government is not worthy of the name. We have no right to surrender the liberties and privileges which we were appointed to guard. The multitude, even though they know very little of political science, can form a good practical judgement

"We have no right to surrender the liberties and privileges which we were appointed to guard."

upon government in general and even a better one than those in office, who cannot see their own defects and errors . . .

The principle which lies at the foundation of our constitution is that which declares the people to be the source of political power. A constitution written on paper is not a safe one; a constitution to be safe must be written on the hearts of the people. The powerful temptation to betray our trust, held out by the government, to surrender up our own convictions, ought to be resisted; a steady adherence to truth, whether in favour or out of favour, must mark the course of every man who will not lose his own respect. I do not despise popularity, I respect it. But it is that popularity which follows, not that which is sought after; and if there be one quality which a representative of our country ought to cultivate at the present time above all others, it is independence. Not a defiance of the well-understood wishes of the people; his course should be a manly and steady adherence to principle, through good report and evil report; a stout defiance of what he considers right through sunshine and through storm . . . Our liberty, once taken away, may never return.

Thomas Coffin: I regret that I am obliged to address the house at this late hour of the night; but as we are denied the privilege of another day's debate, and as the death-knell of my country is sounding, I do not wish to give a silent vote. The subject before the house is one of too great magnitude to be passed over lightly; it is a question of greater magnitude than any that has hitherto been before the legislature. It is one calculated to sweep away our constitution, the dearest rights of Nova Scotians as free men; it is one, sir, calculated to raise the ire of every one of Nova Scotia's sons; it is one that cannot be passed without ignoring the rights of the electors of Nova Scotia.

Sir, I regret exceedingly that a resolution was passed in this house in 1864, authorizing a delegation to consult as to the propriety of a union of the Maritime provinces, for out of that has grown the delegation to Quebec, and there with closed doors a consultation was held which ended in bartering away this fine province, the people, and the constitution to Canadian rule. There we have been sold, there we have been valued, there the rights dear to us of governing ourselves, and of being in ourselves a free, independent, and contented people, were given up. And when it is known through the length and breadth of the land that this resolution has been passed, then it is that the indignation of

"The principle which lies at the foundation of our constitution is that which declares the people to be the source of political power."

the people will be aroused to an extent perhaps that will be calculated to weaken the strong feelings of attachment to their rulers that had hitherto existed.

— *House of Assembly, April 17, 1866*

Killam: These delegates were to go and see if they could agree on some measure that would suit the members of this legislature better than the Quebec scheme.* There has never been any measure of union submitted to this house for its deliberation . . . We are hereafter to be bound by a paper constitution which has never been submitted to us for our consideration . . . If this bill is passed, we are deprived of the power of hereafter legislating for ourselves. We shall certainly have a voice in the general parliament, but that the people don't want at all. Nothing can reconcile the people to the manner in which this measure is being forced upon them. They might have submitted to an act of union, if the British parliament and people had declared that it was positively necessary for imperial purposes, but that has not been the case. It appears by the papers that Her Majesty's ministers have all the time been under the delusion that, in promoting the measure, they are pleasing the people of Nova Scotia — a delusion created and fostered by the delegates.

It is not difficult to understand the motives that have prompted the delegates to take the course they have. These politicians wish to put themselves out of the power of the people — to obtain place and emolument without the wishes of the people being at all consulted. The public men of New Brunswick dissolved the legislature when they returned from Quebec, and the people returned a large majority opposed to union with Canada. Another election subsequently took place, and the people, for some reason or other, reversed the verdict they had given previously. So the people of New Brunswick have been appealed to twice on this question, whilst the people of Nova Scotia have not been consulted even once. The course pursued by these gentlemen is, as far as I know, unprecedented in the history of legislation. Even Napoleon did better than they have done.

I look upon this act of parliament, if it is passed, as destroying the colonial system.† If British colonies anywhere find that their

---

It is now 1867, and the delegates to the London Conference have returned. The BNA Act had in fact become law on February 29, but evidently the news has not yet reached Nova Scotia.

† Killam's statement encapsulates several ideas: (1) The constitution of the

rights and privileges can be transferred at any time to another country against their wishes — to some other people with whom they can have no sympathy — they will feel that their security and prosperity rest upon a very insecure basis.

Tupper: It was stated that if the British government had only proper information on this question — if that dark cloud which prevented them from seeing the real facts of the case was only blown away they would sustain the views of gentlemen opposite. Well, all that had been done; I hold in my hand the statement of the colonial secretary, the Earl of Carnarvon, who submitted this question with great ability to the House of Lords. But first let me ask when these gentlemen were advocating responsible government in this country, what did they tell us they were going to give us? The institutions of republican America? No. *The despotism of France?* No. They said that they intended giving us responsible government, the British system of government, so that the people of this country might be governed in precisely the same manner that the people of the British Islands are governed. Who are the best interpreters of the British system? When gentlemen raise an issue upon constitutional practice, they should sustain their course by reference to the authorities of that country from which we take our system.

In fact, we have the opinion of the statesmen and press of all parties in England in support of the principle — that our legislature has the authority of legislating on all matters touching the constitution for this country, save where it conflicts with imperial interests. I confess I feel mortified when we enjoy the great principles of responsible government — when these principles had been worked out so as to reflect the highest credit upon all parties — when Nova Scotia has advanced to that position of intelligence that she could be entrusted with the management of her own affairs; I felt mortified, I say, to see the very men who had laid claims to having given us this constitutional system

British Empire is based on the principle of respect for the integrity of the colonial communities. (2) The law is the source of our security as individuals and the framework upon which we build our lives. Even ordinary laws should not be altered casually, and only by due process. (3) The constitution, as the fundamental law of the community, which regulates the process by which ordinary laws are made, must by definition be subject to the control of those whose lives it regulates. — PR

"No man, sir, in the history of constitutional legislation ever heard of so unstatesmanlike a course as a government dissolving the parliament in which they had a clear, undoubted majority to carry a measure which they believed would promote the general prosperity of the country."

going to the foot of the throne and attempting to prove, as far as all the evidence they could gather would prove, that this province was unfit for the government she enjoys — that we were in that condition of corruption and ignorance that the parliament of the country could not be trusted to discharge those legislative duties which had been entrusted to them under our constitutional system.

The honourable member for Yarmouth [Killam] asked why we did not submit the question to the people as they did in New Brunswick. No man, sir, in the history of constitutional legislation ever heard of so unstatesmanlike a course as a government dissolving the parliament in which they had a clear, undoubted majority to carry a measure which they believed would promote the general prosperity of the country . . . They have not in the whole range of constitutional government a single precedent in favour of the course they have chosen to pursue.

The intelligent sentiment of the people of this country is in favour of union . . . I know enough of appeals to the people to be aware that it is quite possible for the public sentiment to be in favour of a measure, and yet for this measure to be unsuccessful when put to the people. I believe a public man is bound in the advocacy of public measures to study as far as possible what is required to promote the public good, and to go as far as he can in his public legislation as the public sentiment will sustain him. I believe that the intelligent sentiment of the country is in favour of this union, but then the mode by which it might be defeated would be this: whilst the opponents of the measure in the ranks of the Conservative Party would withdraw their confidence and support from the government, gentlemen who oppose the measure, but prefer another party in this province, would combine with the former, for the purpose of defeating the men in power. How could I have any doubt as to the intelligent sentiment of this country? Long ago it was acknowledged as a question removed from party — one which public men, irrespective of party considerations, should unite in promoting.

I do not deny that there has been a large and formidable opposition to this measure, but I believe when the people look at it without reference to other public questions or any considerations of a party character, when it is no longer *sub judice* but becomes the law of the land, the constitution of the country for weal or woe, all classes will combine to sustain it, and the opponents of union themselves will feel that there is but one course to

pursue if they wish to lay claim to the character of statesmen and patriots — and that is to work out our new institutions in a manner that will be most conducive to the interests of the province at large. (Cheers.)

" I deny the right of any body of delegates, however appointed, to make laws for us. My idea of responsible government is that the administration shall be carried on according to the well-understood wishes of the people, and I hold that the gentlemen who crossed the sea as delegates knew that the people were opposed to any such change as they proposed to make; that they were arbitrarily seeking to change the constitution contrary to the well-known sentiments of the people."

Annand: The provincial secretary [Tupper] spent nearly an hour in enlarging upon the rights and powers of parliament. No one disputes the power of parliament. What we were discussing is not the power, but the sound and wise exercise of that power by a body elected for very different purposes — elected to carry on the business of the country under the existing constitution. We are told by high authority that parliament can do anything but make a man a woman,* and while we may admit that it might be right on the part of the imperial parliament to override the constitution of colony were a great state necessity to arise we have no right under the limited powers which we possess to transfer to a body of men assembled on the other side of the water our legislative functions.

This measure is not the result of the action of the parliament of the country; the Quebec scheme and the bill before the imperial parliament have never been before us. And I deny the right of any body of delegates, however appointed, to make laws for us. My idea of responsible government is that the administration shall be carried on according to the well-understood wishes of the people, and I hold that the gentlemen who crossed the sea as delegates knew that the people were opposed to any such change as they proposed to make; that they were arbitrarily seeking to change the constitution contrary to the well-known sentiments of the people.

McDonald: But what is the duty of the people in the present

---

* *Attributed to Henry Herbert, 2nd earl of Pembroke (c. 1534–1601). This doctrine was formulated in the sixteenth century by the political theorist Sir Thomas Smith and the theologian Richard Hooker, and reiterated with great force in the early seventeenth century by the jurist and MP Sir Edward Coke. It was summed up in the eighteenth century by the constitutional historian Sir William Blackstone, who wrote, "[parliament] can change and create afresh even the constitution of the kingdom and of parliament . . . It can in short do everything that is not naturally impossible . . . [W]hat the parliament doth no authority upon earth can undo."* Commentaries on the Laws of England, *1st ed. (1765). — IG*

crisis? What will the loyal Scotchmen, Irishmen, and Englishmen of this country do? Are they ready to take the extreme step urged by the honourable member for East Halifax [Annand] to become rebels and traitors because Mr. Annand is a disappointed partisan? I ask the intelligent people of this country to do this — to act as honourable, sensible men should do on every question — to consider it calmly and on its merits. I do not ask them to take the views of the politicians of Canada, of New Brunswick, or of Nova Scotia; but I ask them, and it is fair to ask them, to take the views of the parliament and people of England, the body of men who, for centuries, have ruled the destinies of the world — who have worked out the free institutions of England in a manner that attracts the admiration of other nations. I ask the people of this country if, with the unanimous opinions of such a body in favour of union, they are ready to attach any value to the sentiments of the honourable gentlemen opposite.

— House of Assembly, March 18, 1867

"I have been reading a nobler page than Blackstone ever wrote — a page which bears the impress and imprint of God himself: I mean 'the human face divine.'"

McLelan: I would . . . refer to the taunt made by the financial secretary [James McDonald]. He said we had brought a case here without a precedent to support us, although we had a whole year to obtain such precedents if they existed. I tell him that I have had an abundance of authorities for the position I have taken — authority which I have not sought in the musty pages of Blackstone* . . . I have been reading a nobler page than Blackstone ever wrote — a page which bears the impress and imprint of God himself: I mean "the human face divine." I have

---

* In this impassioned speech, McLelan repeats what had become everyday assumptions since the onset of the Romantic movement in the late eighteenth century. Before this time the Classical and Christian model of society had held sway in art, literature, and philosophy, and Christ in morality. Far from having a "human face divine," man was prone to excess, depravity, and error. However, the newly popular Romantic conceits, so evident here in McLelan's words, turned this model upside down. Rousseau, for example, had praised the "noble savage" and argued that man is not sinful, but naturally innocent and pure. Wordsworth and Keats praised the divine insight and poetry of the common man. Robust, uneducated Highlanders were heroes in Sir Walter Scott's widely read historical novels, and James Fenimore Cooper had made the simple frontiersman and the American Indian famous for natural fortitude and wisdom. Susanna Moodie's Roughing It in the Bush *(1852) is a Canadian example of this prevalent trend. Romantic glorifica-*

read the authority which sustains us every day in the year in the faces of my fellow countrymen. Our authority is the look of intelligence on their countenances; I see that in their faces which declares that they have the souls and the reasoning and reflecting powers to enable them to decide on a question affecting them and their posterity as this does.

These men till the soil, engage in commerce and fisheries; they have, by their labours and enterprise, given us, under the blessing of Providence, all our prosperity, and I take them as my authority. Fifty thousand of these men are devoting their time and means to learn defence; ready to lay down their lives to protect their country, their homes, and their altars. They have during the year paid into the treasury through the customs, excise, and other departments nearly two millions of dollars of their hard earnings, and I say the men who thus in their persons and property are to be affected by this measure are my authority for saying that they should be allowed to decide the question. It is not only to the copies of this authority that are already abroad that I can refer, but every reprint preparing for circulation confirms that authority. These men are training children; they have sons who will be either taught principles and instilled with feelings that will lead them to rally round the old flag of England or will lead them beneath a foreign standard to attempt, perhaps, the humiliation of England. When I see that, I feel that my authority for maintaining the rights of the people is strong and conclusive, and should be recognized as such by this legislature.

In order to meet the sophistry and destroy the cobwebs which some gentlemen learned in the law are disposed to weave about the question, it is not necessary to labour the argument. I care not how many precedents from old Blackstone are brought — I care not if they bring old Blackstone from the grave — there is a principle of common sense that would trample them all under foot and proclaim that this right belongs to the people. The very term "responsible government" tells us that the people should decide the question . . . I can scarcely restrain my feeling within reasonable bounds when I see the determination of gentlemen opposite to ignore the feelings and rights of the people on this question. Responsible to whom? Pass the bill and your responsi-

Anti-Confederation election banner from Nova Scotia. It hangs proudly in the Nova Scotia public archives to this day.

tion of the common man became the underlying theme of the modern democratic spirit. This was the mood that enabled McLelan to see "the imprint of God himself" in the faces of the people. — WDG

bility is at an end. Our system of government implies that you have either had the sanction of the people or intend to return to them for ratification. This bill does not contemplate that you should do that, for the very act destroys the constitution, and is contrary to the term — responsible government. The gentlemen who have spoken on the other side affect to treat lightly the opinion of the people, but who gave us all our positions? Who sent us here but the people? It is but a few years since they and all of us were portions of the people, and now, forsooth, because they are placed in power beyond the control of their constituents, they presume to ignore the rights of those who sent them here and to destroy the hand that lifted them to positions of honour. I can scarcely restrain my feeling within reasonable bounds when I see the determination of gentlemen opposite to ignore the feelings and rights of the people on this question.

The provincial secretary tells us that the man would be an idiot who would dissolve parliament as long as he could command a majority. If that doctrine were carried out, it would be found one of the most tyrannical and monstrous that could be uttered: men have lost their heads for putting in practice doctrines less obnoxious. Does he mean that so long as a man can by any means, however corrupt, command a majority in parliament, he may do what he pleases* with the people and their property? No such doctrine can be maintained: there must be some limit, and the men whom the people have sent here to transact their business, and to go back to them with an account of their stewardship, should consider that this question affects the people and their posterity, and they should not assume the unnecessary responsibility of passing it without their instructions, lest, when the evils of this union are realized, they live to be perpetually reproached for their action — live to be told that, members of parliament though they were, they had no more right to force this measure upon their countrymen than they will have to enter heaven with so great a crime against the manhood of Nova Scotia unrepented of.

Archibald: My honourable friend [McLelan] has delivered to us a most impassioned harangue. Not content with giving us his views in the most emphatic manner — not content with

---

* *A succinct statement of the view that due process cannot justify unjust legislation.* — PR

announcing that no good will come in this world to those of confederate faith — he goes on further, and in his closing sentences shuts us out from any hopes of happiness in the world to come. (Laughter.) Is it any wonder that I should feel a little embarrassed in rising to speak after being thus formally excluded from everlasting bliss? (Renewed laughter.) How are we to ascertain what is, or what is not, constitutional? Is it not by examining practice and precedents of that august assembly on which our own is modelled? Is it not by consulting those writers on constitutional history who expound and develop the principles of which these precedents and practices are the illustrations?

Let my honourable friend address our reason or our judgement — let him quote authority or precedent. Let him give the opinions of lawyers, of historians, of philosophers, or of statesmen, and I listen to him with deference. But when he talks of measuring the length and breadth of the faces of his neighbours, and asks us to accept that as an argument, can he wonder that I consider such reasoning as bordering on farce? The idea of a legislature having no power to decide except upon questions that have been sent to the polls for the opinion of the people is entirely un-English. A doctrine to that extent has never been propounded even in the republican institutions of our neighbours, but so far as there is any foundation at all for such a doctrine, it is republican and American as opposed to British and constitutional principles.

——◆——

"It is . . . tyrannical, wrong, and unjust in the extreme . . . to refuse the people the ordinary right of passing on a measure that is to affect them and their children forever. What is the end and object of government but the happiness and welfare of the people?"

——◆——

Campbell: It is . . . tyrannical, wrong, and unjust in the extreme . . . to refuse the people the ordinary right of passing on a measure that is to affect them and their children forever. What is the end and object of government but the happiness and welfare of the people? Governments are not institutions created for the purpose of hampering a few officials, but to enlarge the interests and promote the prosperity of the country in entire subordination to the well-understood wishes* of the people.

— *House of Assembly, March 19, 1867*

---

* *This formula, used so often in Nova Scotia, seems to have originated in a message from Lord Sydenham (1799–1841) to the legislature of Upper Canada in 1840. Sydenham summarized his instructions as governor general as being that the country should henceforth be governed "in accordance with the well-understood wishes and interests of the people." He meant the*

NEWFOUNDLAND

Henry Renouf: He did say that this house had no power to come to a decision on the matter. We should give no opinion on it this session. It was a new question to the house; and he did trust that no attempt would be made to bind this colony until the people had time to give expression to their opinions on the subject.

Thomas Glen: [Mr. Glen wished to know whether it was the intention of the government to force the matter through the house this session.]

Hugh Hoyles: The government never forced any matter through the house. They were always satisfied with submitting their views to the house and accepting the decision of honourable members upon them.

Glen: Was he to understand that the resolutions to be submitted by the government would, as regards this colony, affirm the report of the conference?

Hoyles: Certainly. Such would be the effect of the resolutions, if concurred in by the house.

Glen: The constitution was granted, not to the House of Assembly, but to the people of Newfoundland, and he (Mr. Glen) considered the people were entitled to be consulted before we came to a decision on the subject.

"It had been urged by some honourable members, in thoughtless ignorance of the nature of the discussion, that the [Quebec] conference should not have been held with closed doors."

Hoyles: The question would be submitted to the house, and it would be for honourable members to decide what course would be adopted. The government were prepared to acquiesce in the decision of the house.

— *House of Assembly, January 27, 1865*

Ambrose Shea: It had been urged by some honourable members, in thoughtless ignorance of the nature of the discussion, that the [Quebec] conference should not have been held with closed doors.

phrase to signify something less than responsible government, but it quickly became identified with that system. See also its use by T.L. Wood (British Columbia) in chapter 2 and William Ross (Nova Scotia) in chapter 5. — PR

He (Mr. Shea) regretted that secrecy was a necessary condition of the deliberations of that conference, for it would have been well had it been possible that the whole public of British North America were present, to be witnesses of the great ability displayed by the prominent statesmen of the sister provinces, their grasp of mind, and the singleness of purpose which animated their course, with the deep sense of responsibility felt by all who took part in these proceedings of high historic interest and grave importance. The spectacle would have done good for the people whose interests were at stake, and have frowned down the narrow-minded and ignorant views we now see exhibited in certain quarters of that work, and the men who were its promoters.

— *House of Assembly, February 2, 1865*

"We were here to deliberate, and not as mere delegates. As to what was the duty of members to their constituents, he would quote the opinion of Burke, whose opinions on constitutional questions were admitted by all parties to be entitled to the greatest weight."

E.D. Shea: Let the constituents, by all means, be consulted, but before we call on them for their opinions, let honourable members express their own and let the country give the final verdict upon them. He thought that was the right course and that anything short of it would be a shirking of the question. We were here to deliberate, and not as mere delegates. As to what was the duty of members to their constituents, he would quote the opinion of Burke, whose opinions on constitutional questions were admitted by all parties to be entitled to the greatest weight. (Here the honourable member quoted from a speech by Burke to his constituents at Bristol, as follows):

It ought to be the happiness and glory of a representative to live in the strictest union, the closest correspondence, and the most unreserved communication with his constituents. Their wishes ought to have great weight with him; their opinions high respect; their business unremitted attention. It is his duty to sacrifice his repose, his pleasure, his satisfactions, to theirs — and, above all, ever and in all cases, to prefer their interest to his own.

But his unbiased opinion, his mature judgement, his enlightened conscience, he ought not to sacrifice to you, to any man, or to any set of men living. These he does not derive from your pleasure — no, nor from the law and the Constitution. They are a trust from Providence, for the abuse of which he is deeply answerable. Your representative owes you, not his industry only, but his judgement; and he betrays, instead of serving you, if he sacrifices it to your opinion.

> *"It was our duty as representatives to give our constituents the benefit of our judgement; and they would afterwards exercise their judgement upon their representatives, and reject us, if they were not satisfied with our conduct."*

It was our duty as representatives* to give our constituents the benefit of our judgement; and they would afterwards exercise their judgement upon their representatives, and reject us, if they were not satisfied with our conduct. The question was prejudged by some honourable members, and it was our duty to express our deliberate opinion upon it, after that cool and calm consideration which its importance to the country, to its people, and to those who would come after us imperatively demanded. Let no honourable member shrink from the responsibility of his position. Let all speak out in the face of the country, and let the constituencies afterwards say† whether they will accept or reject the terms of the proposed Confederation.

— *House of Assembly, February 6, 1865*

Ambrose Shea: If there had been a general concurrence of opinion on the question in the house and throughout the country, and if the neighbouring colonies had proceeded with it, it would have been perfectly legitimate to dispose of the matter this session. But in the divided state of public opinion, such a course was never thought of . . . The honourable member [Stephen March] has made a misstatement which he (Mr. Shea) would not allow to pass uncontradicted. Who authorized him to say that if he (Mr. Shea) had his way, the measure would be passed this session?

---

* E.D. Shea is one of the few to see the seriousness of the conflict of principle between the duty of a representative to render his judgement — arguably a principle that still underlies the institution of parliamentary democracy — and the opposing principle which is gaining strength again today of taking instruction from electors. He argues that under the first principle, unhappy electors have the final remedy of dismissing their representatives at the polls, but sees that the two systems cannot be mixed without a stalemate of authority. The representative may act either as a leader giving his informed opinion or as a mouthpiece for the opinions of electors, whether they are informed or not, but he cannot easily do both at once, for under the first system he may either express or oppose their will, but under the second he is himself deprived of will. — WDG

† Note that while Shea upholds the legislator's independence vis-à-vis his constituency, he asserts that it is for the electors, not the legislature, to commit the colony to Confederation. Below, his brother Ambrose argues that the legislature could have done so if there had been no serious opposition, but not under the circumstances. — PR

Stephen March: Yourself. You said you would dispose of it, and if your constituents did not like it, they might reject you at the hustings.

Ambrose Shea: The honourable member did not understand the question. He (Mr. Shea) felt the responsibility of the question too much to do anything of the kind. From the very first he said it was too serious a question to be disposed of without due consideration and that he did not desire that it should be carried by a narrow majority. What he said was that these were his opinions on the question, and if his constituents did not like these opinions they must choose a representative whose opinions they approved, not that he would carry it without consulting them. He (Mr. Shea) would state his opinions when he went before them, fairly and openly, and would submit himself to their vote; but his opinions were his own.

— House of Assembly, February 13, 1865

Daniel Prowse: He regretted the position in which honourable members opposite were placing themselves on this question of union. In their hearts they were favourable to it, but out of deference to the prejudices of ignorance they were going to use it as a party question. Confederation, in this country, never ought to be a party question. It involves the interests of the whole country too deeply and too seriously to be treated in that way.

— House of Assembly, February 4, 1869

PRINCE EDWARD ISLAND

W.H. Pope: Mr. Chairman, the question under discussion is one of great importance to our people, and it is proper that they should be fully consulted, that the matter should be fully discussed and, notwithstanding my individual opinions, I shall not be prepared to vote for a union until after they shall have been consulted and the question discussed among them.

— House of Assembly, April 18, 1864

John Longworth: Our proper course is to make the matter an open question and thereby allow all parties the opportunity of discussing the subject freely and of recording their opinion upon it according to their unbiased judgement. I, for one, am determined to do no act to prejudice the constitutional right of the

"I conceive it to be our duty to return to the people intact the rights and the constitution with which we were entrusted, and which we were bound to uphold when we were elected to this house."

people to decide on this great question, as I conceive it to be our duty to return to the people intact the rights and the constitution with which we were entrusted, and which we were bound to uphold when we were elected to this house.

George Coles: I contend that it was the duty of the government to declare their principles and then appeal to the people at once, and not to wait until the house was in session some time before they agreed upon the policy — then perhaps only to put off the question. It was the duty of the government, instead of acting as they have done, to have aimed at leading public opinion and then taken the case to the polls.

J.H. Gray: This is a matter calculated to affect the interests and welfare of every subject in British America irrespective of party, race, or faith; and, consequently, to divest it as much as possible from a party question, three members of the government, three members of the opposition, and one independent member of this house were appointed to proceed to Quebec as delegates. This delegation was nominated on precisely the same grounds as the first was appointed.* When the request came from Canada for the colony to send delegates to confer on the question of a union of the whole of the provinces, surely it was not necessary to call the legislature together to consider the propriety of acceding to the request. If this were the case, of what use would the executive be? It would, indeed, be a do-nothing government. There was no occasion to seek new powers from the legislature; the two delegations were for precisely the same purpose, only the latter was to consider the subject on a grander scale. The one scheme was for united provinces comparatively unimportant, the other was for consolidating the same provinces into a Confederation which would form a state as large as the entire continent of Europe.

But, sir, I have recently learned that there are three great commandments for politicians — of which I was entirely ignorant when I entered political life. The first of these is for the politician to take good care of himself and his pocket; the second is to crush his enemy; and the third is to attend to the good of the country. And,

---

* *Gray maintains that, having obtained legislative authority to appoint delegates to consider Maritime union, the government needed no further authority to nominate delegates to consider Confederation, which was essentially the same issue. — PR*

sir, I fear that the third is sometimes wholly forgotten in the zeal to carry out the other two. (Applause.) Acting on these rules, therefore, it is fair game for the honourable leader of the opposition to endeavour to trip up the government on any pretence whatever.

At Quebec I expressed the opinion that this was a question for the people to decide; when I returned here, however, I found the statement had gone forth — like many more which were untrue — that this question was to be carried without an appeal to the people. I immediately wrote a letter to the different newspapers in the colony stating some of my views of the subject and assuring the people that the measure could not be sanctioned without an appeal to them . . . I understand it is the intention of the government of Nova Scotia to submit the report of the delegates to the House of Assembly, and if but a majority of that body were in favour of the scheme, that then there would be an appeal to the people.

Coles: Honourable members may say that this is not a government question; but I am determined to make it one, so that if it be taken to the polls, the people may have the matter fairly before them. Some may be disposed to say that the terms are not very favourable to this colony; but they have confidence that the gentlemen at Ottawa will do what is fair. Now, I am of opinion that the people of this island would not be satisfied to leave the matter in this way. To have honourable members acting like loose fish on such a question is dangerous.

George Sinclair: Our legislative constitution will be a mere farce if the government are allowed to do as they please irrespective of the formally expressed opinions of this house. If it is the privilege and the duty of this house to criticize and pass judgement upon the acts of the government, what is the use of calling us together after our rights have been taken from us by the government? The honourable member for Belfast (Honourable Colonel Gray) took credit to himself for the composition of the island delegation — that it embraced men of opposite opinions, gentlemen selected from each of the political parties in the legislature. That affords to my mind a very strong argument in favour of cautious deliberation, for there is always cause to fear that the prospect of honours and emoluments may be held out to induce unanimity of sentiment between parties* who were previously opposed to each other.

---

* *Oh, how difficult it is to make a constitution! Sinclair points to one of the*

Longworth: Mr. Chairman, if the honourable member is of opinion that all the leading men of British North America have united to sell the rights of the people, he should show that the arguments they have made use of are unsound.

Sinclair: I said that the people should view the proceedings with caution.

Longworth: The inference to be drawn from the honourable member's remarks is as I have stated, and the very argument he uses shows the propriety of putting the question before the people. If it were introduced here as a government measure, that very fact would have a tendency to influence the opinions of some on a matter which should be divested of all party views and spirit.

Nicholas Conroy: Mr. Chairman, if party feeling has not been sunk on this question in this house, it has been pretty well laid aside in the country. At Tignish, a part of the district which I have the honour to represent, where the people are very much divided in their political opinions, my colleague and I lately attended a meeting at which everyone appeared to be opposed to the proposed union. I never saw a time when newspapers were so much sought after, and the speeches delivered at public meetings so generally read.

— *House of Assembly, March 1, 1865*

W.H. Pope: The resolutions passed by the conference were not, in any particular, in accordance with the views of the representatives of each province and colony. Taken together, they embodied

---

major problems. Constitution-making seems to call for co-operation among political parties. The constitution should not be the creation of any one party because, among other things, it describes the rules of party competition. Government and opposition should co-operate in the constitutional process to lend legitimacy and to ensure that everything possible is done to avoid bias. For exactly this reason the provincial delegations to the Charlottetown and Quebec conferences included both government and opposition leaders. But note what Sinclair is saying. When you allow government and opposition to cosy up together, watch out! They'll scratch each others' backs and forget the people entirely. The whole point of responsible government is to ensure that parties do not *co-operate to their mutual advantage, but compete with each other for the voters' approval and to secure the people's advantage. — JA*

a constitution which, as I considered, received the unanimous support of the members of the conference. Gentlemen with whom I was associated in the delegation representing this island have, I am aware, since their return to the island, denounced that which in Canada they approved. It is not my intention, Mr. Speaker, on the present occasion to call in question the right of these gentlemen to change their views, nor shall I charge them with inconsistency. I do not feel myself at liberty to allude to the course pursued by honourable gentlemen at the conference, nor to quote from their speeches delivered there. There is one very strong reason why the expressions of members, while at the conference, should not be quoted. It is this. It was understood that the deliberations should be considered private. There is no record to which to appeal in the event of the correctness of statements attributed to honourable members being called in question.

It has been objected that the deliberations of the conference were conducted with closed doors. The reasons for such an arrangement are obvious. The admission of the public would to some extent have prevented that free and full discussion which was so desirable, while the daily publication of the expressions of members would have prevented unanimous conclusions.

— *House of Assembly, March 24, 1865*

"It has been objected that the deliberations of the [Quebec] conference were conducted with closed doors. The reasons for such an arrangement are obvious. The admission of the public would to some extent have prevented that free and full discussion which was so desirable."

Sinclair: A subject of such importance as this should have been before us for years and canvassed fully by the press and the people ere it was submitted to the house in the form which it assumes in the report under discussion. It has not originated with the people and almost the first clause which it contains deprives them of a right, as it provides places for at least seventy-seven councillors* in a general parliament of the colonies where they will be independent of the people and independent of the crown. What authority had the delegates to go to Canada and thus sign away our rights? They may say that they were invited by the governor general.† I say the governor general has no power to interfere with the constitutional liberties of the people of this colony. The people or their representatives alone should take up this question.

— *House of Assembly, March 29, 1865*

* *Seventy-six, actually: see resolutions 8 and 9. — PR*
† *The sovereign's representative in Lower Canada before 1841, and the province of Canada subsequently, held the title of governor general of British North America, which is why his counterparts in the other colonies held the*

Edward Whelan: We know that a great change of opinion has taken place in all the other colonies. Has it not been the case in Canada? And in New Brunswick, where the government came in with a large majority a little more than twelve months ago, has not a change taken place there? In all the other colonies public opinion has been undergoing a change in reference to this question. It has changed in the Nova Scotia legislature, inasmuch as last winter Dr. Tupper could not venture to ask the house to pass a resolution in favour of Confederation, and this year it has been carried by a majority of thirty-one to nineteen. Does not this show that there is a change in public sentiment? That it is progressing with the progress of intelligence all over the continent? Does it not show that public men have a right to exercise the privilege at times of correcting their ideas?

"Who, pray, in his senses would suppose that a written constitution could be framed that would be acceptable to all the people concerned in it?"

I scorn the man — I say it without disrespect to any gentleman in this house or community — I scorn the man who says he is incapable of changing his mind on important public questions. I change mine from time to time, if it is in conformity with the progress of the age in which I live. And I do not think I bring any discredit upon myself by doing so . . . I was there [at the Quebec Conference] as a delegate, and though I objected to some of the details, yet I felt myself in that position that I could not refuse to accept it as a compromise. The delegates from all the provinces had complaints to make about it; and who, pray, in his senses would suppose that a written constitution could be framed that would be acceptable to all the people concerned in it? Could it be possible that a constitution, affecting the rights of nearly four millions of people, would be so framed that no fault could be found with it? When it came up that the constitution was to be framed on the principles of representation by population, I had to yield to the majority.

I bow to the public opinion of this country in reference to all public questions. When I returned from Canada, in 1864, I called meetings and told my constituents the opinion I entertained, and which I will probably entertain as long as I live; but I told them

---

title of lieutenant governor. However, the governor general had never exercised political authority outside the colony in which he resided, and under responsible government any attempt to do so would have been unthinkable. Sinclair refers to the fact that the Canadian government had invited delegates from the other colonies to the Quebec Conference in the name of the governor general. — PR

that I would not seek to force it upon them. This is the proper course for a representative of the people to take. I conceive that a spirited man, like the honourable the leader of the government, may sometimes seek to control public opinion, but let him take this advice: the better way is to follow public opinion while he seeks to control it.*

T.H. Haviland: [M]en of every party and of the most conflicting political opinions were brought together in the [Quebec] conference, for the purpose of considering whether measures could not be devised for the greater security of our free institutions, for the consolidation of British power in these provinces, and for the more thorough establishment and perpetuation therein of the ennobling and invigorating principles of the British Constitution.

— *House of Assembly, May 8, 1866*

> *"Every representative of the people should be strictly a miniature of his constituency."*

Kenneth Henderson: I am not aware that the fact of my being a member of the Executive Council precludes me from exercising my right as a member of this house, and I do [say] that, in view of responsible government which we enjoy, every representative of the people should be strictly a miniature of his constituency,† and

---

* Whelan is the first to propose a practical middle ground in what is essentially an irresolvable conflict in the theory of political power. He suggests that both sides are wrong: power lies neither with the people nor the representative, but in a practical relationship between them in which the opinion of the people must ultimately carry the day, even as it is guided. The ship of state is under sail, not steam. It is blown about by the wind of public opinion, but may be steered close to the course by its leaders if they use the wind well. — WDG

† Here we have a concise statement of the delegate view, that the representative is to behave as a mouthpiece for his electors and must vote as instructed, or resign. The modern Reform Party of Canada purports to be a "bottom-up" party operating on a similar principle of delegation, and its members of parliament are required to vote with party policy or with the party caucus unless a majority of constituents "have instructed him or her to vote otherwise." On issues of conscience they are required to "vote in accordance with the expressed will of their constituents," even if, as a member of parliament, they morally disagree. This idea is in profound conflict with the traditional notion of representative parliamentary democracy in the Western world. Taken to its logical conclusion, it seeks to implant a direct democratic ideal that repudiates filtration, deliberation, and policy by compromise, and yet wishes to do this via a representative system that rests on those very assumptions. — WDG

that the present construction of the executive is an anomaly — that it and the principles of responsible government do not harmonize. But in mitigation of that I would state that when one of that number, a member of the House of Assembly, accepted a certain official appointment and appealed to his constituents after declaring that he was a "red-hot unionist," with that fact before them, his constituency returned him, and I understand from public prints that he had given a pledge that so far as their interests were concerned, his particular views on Confederation should be kept in abeyance . . . I hold that the only consistent representative of the people is he who acts like his honour at the opposite end of the table (Mr. McDonald) who, if he holds opinions favourable to Confederation, has locked them up and advocates the views of the people. That is the duty of every representative. If his views undergo a change, and he hold opinions antagonistic to those of his constituents, it is either his duty to convince them that they are wrong or, failing to do that, to retire and let the people return another who will represent them.

— *Legislative Council, May 10, 1866*

William McNeill: One hundred years ago his [McNeill's] grandfather came to this country and, in common with others, had to encounter many hardships, such as clearing their farms, opening up new roads, and contending with wild beasts and land agents. The country had since prospered, and that entirely by the industry of the people. We had no resources for the construction of our public works. The other provinces derived a revenue from their public lands, and it appeared to him hard that a resort to any unfair means should be thought of to force us into a connection with dislike. It was not but one hundred years since we were separated from Nova Scotia. Since then we had managed our own affairs as well, if not better, than our neighbours, and if Canada had studied her own interests she would have seen that it was no use to be proposing new terms. To accept of any terms would be to give up our independence. We elected our men for four years and could replace them with others, if they did not do right, but once into Confederation, what power would we then have to alter the government?

It had been laid down that parliament could not destroy itself, and this was admitted by good authority and laid down by some of the best minds in England. He did not think Nova Scotia was fairly dealt with, and with her example before us he believed this

island would never return men to the legislature who would destroy our parliament.

Alexander Laird: The peace of the dominion, he feared, was nearly at an end. This very day a paper had been put into his hand, containing a series of resolutions proposed in the Ontario legislature by no less a person than Mr. [Edward] Blake, complaining that the solemn compact entered into between the provinces had been broken and the British American Act violated by the dominion parliament giving to Nova Scotia nearly $2,000,000 more than was specified in that act.*

Then, again, the North-West Territory had been purchased, at a cost of £300,000 sterling. What right, he asked, had the people of the several provinces to pay this money for lands which should be the property of the settlers in that country? It was no wonder that the half-breeds of Red River had rebelled against being literally sold, no wonder that the Honourable Joseph Howe[†] should caution them to look after their own rights and inhabitants of the territory. Now was the time for them to see to their lands, and not be like this colony, oppressed by a system which nothing short of a miracle could relieve us from.[‡]

— *House of Assembly, March 8, 1870*

George-Étienne Cartier leading the captive settlement of Red River into Confederation; detail from J.W. Bengough's Caricature History of Canadian Politics.

After the Nova Scotia legislature had committed the province to Confederation in 1866, Joseph Howe led a campaign to extricate it from that commitment. After successive British governments (there were three in the years 1866–68) had declined to release Nova Scotia from Confederation, Howe made the best of it by extracting better financial terms for the province from the government of Canada. Led by Edward Blake (1833–1912), the Liberal opposition in parliament and the Ontario legislature challenged the federal government's right to make such an arrangement without the consent of all the provinces. The controversy thus saw the first articulation of the compact theory of Confederation, which envisaged Confederation as an interprovincial compact amendable only with the consent of all the participants. — PR

† After concluding this financial agreement with Ottawa, Howe entered the federal cabinet. Later in 1869, as secretary of state for the provinces, he visited the Red River Colony ahead of William McDougall, the newly appointed lieutenant governor. The Liberals later tried to blame him for the Métis's refusal to allow McDougall to enter the territory. — PR

‡ A reference to the large absentee landowners. — PR

NEW BRUNSWICK

James Boyd: We would like to hear what the delegation, appointed for the purpose of considering the practicability of effecting a legislative union of the Maritime provinces, have done? We have got no report of their doings. The people did not care about having their money squandered away without having something to show for it. Why is not this report brought before us at once? That delegation was sent the 9th of April last, to perform certain duties, which duties they did not discharge. They then went to Canada and allowed the Canadians to haul the wool over their eyes, by giving balls and parties, until, I believe, they got nearly crazy and allowed themselves to be bought and sold for eighty cents a head.* But when the question was left to the people, they said, No! we don't want your Confederation scheme, you only want to aggrandize yourselves at the expense of the people of this province.

— House of Assembly, April 29, 1865

Robert Hazen: Who, I ask, gave the delegates their power? What power has the crown to appoint delegates to confer about the disposal of our rights or a change in our political organization? Who has the power and who should appoint such delegates? Most certainly the people. But did the people give those delegates any power? Not so. I have a very high respect for some of the delegates, my friend Mr. Chandler, for instance, but what right had he to speak for me at the Quebec Conference? I say he had none! I say that those gentlemen at Quebec had no power from the people of this province to act for them, and so they have declared at the elections.

— Legislative Council, May 17, 1865

Charles Connell: With reference to Confederation, it was a great mistake that the matter had not been brought before the legislature and discussed . . . If that had been the case, the people would not have been misled the way they have been on this question of Confederation and would have arrived at a different result,† for I believe a large majority of the country are in favour of Confederation.

— House of Assembly, May 25, 1865

---

* A reference to no. 64 of the Quebec Resolutions, which was enacted as section 118 of the BNA Act.

† He refers to the recent general election, which installed the anti-confederate

SIR ALBERT JAMES SMITH (1822–1883), lawyer, businessman, and Loyalist insider who opposed the establishment. An independent-minded and radical member of Liberal governments under Charles Fisher and Leonard Tilley, in 1865 Smith split the party over Confederation. When a general election made him premier, he was backed by a hotchpotch majority of Liberals and Conservatives, some favouring legislative union and others no union. It quietly disintegrated, and after a year he was forced to resign. In 1867 he commenced a successful career in federal politics, including service in Alexander Mackenzie's cabinet from 1873 to 1878.

John Cudlip: [This] is a question affecting our whole political existence — affecting the constitution of our country. It is a question upon which every person in the country has a right to express his opinion, and the people of the country have done so and expressed an opinion, and I think it now becomes the duty of their representatives to send a delegation to England to protect their rights. The delegation which was appointed to confer on a union of the Maritime provinces took upon themselves other duties which the legislature had not assigned to them, and to avoid falling into the same error we wish this delegation* to be appointed by the representatives of the people. It is not right that after the people of this country have expressed their opinion at the polls against Confederation, that this agitation should be kept up directly or indirectly as has been done.

— *House of Assembly, May 30, 1865*

John Costigan: It has been stated . . . that the more the people became acquainted with this Confederation scheme, the better they would like it. Now, if the government really thought it was a good scheme, they should not have been afraid of having it discussed. Whatever the intention of the government may have been, the facts show they did not want the people to become acquainted with the scheme. If that had not been the case they could have brought it up before the house, and then referred it to the country at the general election; people then could have . . . the . . . information which they would have gained by the question being debated on the floor of the house. This would have put the matter in a fair light; but I believe the government did not have confidence enough in it themselves to bring it before the house, for they did not think they could carry it through.

Albert J. Smith: They say the public are not sufficiently enlightened. Some gentlemen say that they will spend two years

---

government led by Albert Smith. If the government had referred the Quebec scheme to the legislature beforehand, he avers, the electorate would have been more fully informed and would have decided differently. — PR

* The Smith government has moved the appointment of a delegation to discuss maritime union. Cudlip differentiates between the proposed delegation and that sent to Charlottetown in 1864 without legislative sanction, one that had shirked its appointed task and discussed Confederation instead. — PR

enlightening the public mind. Do you think there is nothing but pure patriotism and love of country in this? It is an arrogance which no man ought to assume; to state that the people are steeped in ignorance, only one or two being able to grasp the mighty scheme of Confederation, and it is necessary for them to go forth and enlighten the people.

— *House of Assembly, June 1, 1865*

George Hill: I do not think it right that we should burden ourselves with debt and deprive ourselves of all power to regulate our own affairs for the sake of giving twenty-five men* a larger field in which to exhibit themselves . . . The proper method† would have been to have submitted the question to a direct vote of the people, apart from all political considerations or the popularity of this or that candidate.

Andrew Wetmore: The action of those delegates [to the Charlottetown Conference] was a direct violation of responsible government, for it was their business and duty to attend to what the people sent them to look after and the consideration was not given that should have been given to the voice of the people of this province. They treated those resolutions with the greatest contempt, and in direct violation of them they go to Canada at great expense to the people of this province and there mature a scheme to destroy and sacrifice the country in which they live.

— *House of Assembly, June 3, 1865*

> *"The only way in which the constitution of a free, intelligent, and independent people can be changed at all is by revolution or the consent of the people."*

William Gilbert: Although it is the imperial policy to unite these colonies, yet they will not unite us unless by our own consent because the only way in which the constitution of a free, intelligent, and independent people can be changed at all is by revolution or the consent of the people . . .

It might be proper and correct in questions affecting the domestic policy of the province, affecting our public works or any other great leading interest connected with our own local affairs, that when an honourable member of this house has conscientiously changed his opinion from those he was pledged to observe

---

* *The fifteen MPs and ten senators allotted to New Brunswick by the Quebec Resolutions. — PR*

† *The government should have submitted the Quebec agreement to the people in a referendum, not a general election. — PR*

"This Confederation strikes at the whole constitution of the country, strikes at the constitution of this house, and, if carried, no subsequent house could alter or repeal what we might do."

at the hustings, to vote in this house according to his changed opinions and in opposition to his pledges, because a member of this house represents not only a local constituency but also the whole people, and because at the next election his successor, should he be not returned, could repeal the effect of his vote, and a succeeding house could undo what a previous house had done. Such cases have often happened in England and in the colonies.

This Confederation strikes at the whole constitution* of the country, strikes at the constitution of this house, and, if carried, no subsequent house could alter or repeal what we might do. No subsequent house could retrace the steps which we had taken. Like the fall of a tree, a subsequent house would be lifeless. The act had been committed; therefore, sir, no member could justify himself before his country, however much his opinions might have changed in reference to the desirability of a union, to vote for it in this house when he is pledged to his constituents to vote against it.

— *House of Assembly, March 26, 1866*

William Needham: I dissent from the opinion . . . that this is an imperial question† which they have a right to legislate upon. I say they have not, and I want them to hear it on the other side of the water. After they gave us a constitution, no power on earth can legislate it away without our consent, and it is a wrong doctrine to propound on the floors of this free assembly. She can only legislate for her own imperial interest, and when she comes to interfere with our independent rights it is an act of usurpation and tyranny that free men never will submit to. A voice once went from this great North American continent when tyranny was exercised by the British ministry at home over a then free people, and we see the results. When they sought to tax the North American colonies without giving them representation in

---

* In the year since the 1865 election, the tide of public and legislative opinion has turned strongly in favour of Confederation. Gilbert explains why it is legitimate for elected legislators to change their vote on ordinary matters without consulting their constituencies, but not on this issue. — PR

† Like Killam of Nova Scotia, Needham denies the right of the British parliament to impose Confederation on his colony against the will of the people. Like Upper Canadian Reformers in the 1820s, he sees the grant of representative institutions to a colony as an irrevocable surrender of sovereignty by the imperial government. — PR

the British parliament, the people rose as one man and wrested, by rebellion, or, as it is now termed, by revolution, one of the brightest jewels from the crown of Great Britain. Let Mr. Cardwell beware, for the spirit of those men is here and the power is here. Let him beware how he attempts to infringe upon our constitutional rights, for we would be unworthy of the name of being the descendants of the Anglo-Saxons were we to submit to such infringement of our rights.

— House of Assembly, April 2, 1866

Timothy Anglin: It is said that you, the people of New Brunswick, must abandon everything — sacrifice your independence, throw away your property, and place yourselves completely under the control of Canada, because Mr. Cardwell says you ought to do so. That would be an unreasonable, slavish loyalty. We say we object to the scheme, more particularly to the principle of representation by population; but we are told that the people of Upper Canada have fought for that for twenty-five years and they will never give it up. Some people say they object to the federal principle; but the people of Lower Canada say they can only be protected by that and they never will consent to any other scheme. All our objections go for nothing; we must consent to anything Upper or Lower Canada may demand. They may refuse to consent to this or that, but if we refuse to accept any of the terms which they choose to give us we are denounced as being disloyal.

— House of Assembly, April 7, 1866

Smith: I ask every honourable member here if it was not the duty of the government to give some information of what they intended to do? Is it enough to state that the delegates will endeavour to obtain better terms if they can? Who will be the delegates that are to be clothed with this tremendous power to settle and determine for the people of this country what their constitution shall be for all time to come? Where, in the history of a free country, can you find such powers have been given to any individuals to determine a scheme of union so important and so tremendous in its consequences as this must be to the people of this country, without any reference to the legislature or people? Is it not right that any scheme of union which may be agreed upon in England should be submitted to the house again for their approval?

I may be entirely in error and my judgement may be erroneous, but it does seem to me to be but reasonable that the people of this country should have some voice in the matter, because it has not been said that the people of the country have affirmed the Quebec scheme. I believe a large portion of the country are opposed to the scheme in many of its provisions and features. They have affirmed the principle of union without reference to the Quebec scheme.* If then delegates go home to England and act in conjunction with delegates from the other provinces, is it not right that the people of this province, who are so seriously to be affected by it, should have some voice as to whether the scheme they had agreed upon was good or bad? Should they not have a right to pass judgement upon it?

— *House of Assembly, June 26, 1866*

John Mercer Johnson: The legislature when they meet are the people, and they have not only the power to deal with subjects that were before the people when they were elected, but they have power to deal with all questions that may occur during their existence. They are the people for all legislative purposes, and they have the power to change the constitution when they think the country requires it. The imperial parliament has dethroned and elected sovereigns† without appealing to the people.

— *House of Assembly, July 2, 1866*

"The legislature when they meet are the people, and they have not only the power to deal with subjects that were before the people when they were elected, but they have power to deal with all questions that may occur during their existence. They are the people for all legislative purposes."

BRITISH COLUMBIA

J.S. Helmcken: When certain terms have been agreed upon between the government of this colony and the dominion parliament, they will come back to the people for ratification. It remains then for the people to organize, so as to be ready at the proper time to give their verdict, for the responsibilities will ultimately rest with the people, and it is for them to say whether they will have Confederation or not.

---

* A general election has returned Leonard Tilley to power. Smith recognizes this result as a vote for Confederation, but not necessarily for the Quebec scheme. — PR

† In 1688 parliament dethroned James II; in 1714 it offered the throne to George I. Johnson's invocation of those ancient acts in this instance illustrates the conservative force of historical precedent. — PR

"It appears that the governor wishes to have a popular vote upon the question of Confederation. I say then, let there be an extended suffrage given, so that the voice of the people may be heard in this house."

David Ring: It appears that the governor wishes to have a popular vote upon the question of Confederation. I say then, let there be an extended suffrage given, so that the voice of the people may be heard in this house. I hope that the people will have the opportunity of expressing their opinion, aye or no, whether they will have Confederation. The people should not be bound by what occurs in a council constituted as this is. The proper way to find out the opinion of the country is for the governor to give us the enlarged representation promised. Let the question come before the people in a fair way.

— *Legislative Council, March 9, 1870*

Joseph Trutch: [In] its first introduction into this council, this measure must necessarily be a government measure. The constitution of this house renders it imperative that the initiatory steps should be taken by the government, although the final acceptance of the terms will properly rest with the people. His Excellency has told us that the ultimate acceptance or rejection of the terms of union with Canada, after they have been submitted to the dominion government, shall be left to the popular voice of this country.

Henry Holbrook: As regards myself, I shall abide by such decision, whatever it may be, as I consider the people themselves are the best judges as to whether they will benefit, or otherwise, by becoming part and parcel of the Dominion of Canada. Let it go to the people and settlers of the colony, and by their verdict let it be decided.

T.L. Wood: Can we doubt that the vote will be in favour of Confederation? The people of this country will sell themselves for the consideration of the present, and posterity will hereafter ask indignantly what right had we to shackle them and to deprive them of rights which cannot be sold. We shall reap the benefit, and those that come after us will reap the disadvantages and humiliation. It is not in the power of the present generation to dispose of the birthright of its descendants. Liberty and self-government are inalienable rights. The original view of the matter still remains, and when once the material benefits are enjoyed or forgotten, and the consciousness of disadvantage is apparent, reaction will set in; a party of repudiators and repealers will arise, who with great show of justice will clamorously

demand the reversal of an organic change, founded on political error and wrong.

Although our masters at Ottawa may be ever so amiable and ever so pure, the moment we feel the yoke we shall repent; it is not in the nature of Englishmen to submit to tyranny of any description, and dissent, such as our posterity will express, will be on only too sound grounds.

— Legislative Council, March 10, 1870

Ring: I deny that it is the desire of the people to have Confederation, but, I say, let the people have an opportunity of expressing their opinions in this house. Let the disenfranchised districts have first restored them the rights of which they have been defrauded. But let the franchise be restored,* then let the general question of Confederation come before an enlarged representation; and I say that Confederation should be put alone, aye or no. "Shall we have Confederation?" and not upon what terms shall we have it. The proper course is to dissolve the house, issue new writs, and let the people say whether they want Confederation; and after they have said yes, then descend into the particulars of it.

The honourable member for Victoria District [Amor De Cosmos] puts it as if the voice of the people has been heard. I ask how? Through newspapers? Conventions? Speeches? I say this is not the proper way. Let the people speak in this house, through a full body of representatives of their own choosing.

— Legislative Council, March 11, 1870

Henry Crease: Honourable members must remember that these resolutions will be submitted to the people . . . and our common object must be to make these terms acceptable to the people. They will have to pass upon them in the last resort, and to say we will or we will not have them.

— Legislative Council, March 18, 1870

---

* The British government wished British Columbia's annexation to Canada to be initiated by the colony's Legislative Council after a general election to be held on the issue. Americans could vote under the existing franchise, but, fearing that they would oppose Confederation, Governor Musgrave had proposed to the British government that aliens be disenfranchised. — PR

RED RIVER

Thomas Bunn: He thought that there were good reasons why the meeting should not be an open one, and he begged to move that the meeting sit with closed doors.*

Judge John Black: The accommodation was too limited to allow of a public meeting, and the proceedings would be fully made known by the secretaries.

W.B. O'Donoghue: [He] wished to have the doors open because on the last occasion, when they were shut, considerable dissatisfaction was expressed.

Black: [He] thought that the list [of rights] might be curtailed in some points and very materially extended in others. Let us look at what has been done in the other provinces. The settling of lists of rights formed the subject of long, difficult, and delicate deliberation, not only in Canada but England, as far as the provinces in Confederation were concerned. It may therefore be very difficult to define all the minutiae of the rights belonging to this country. It may, however, appear to the convention that it would be sufficient if [Commissioner Donald] Smith gave pretty distinct assurances respecting what may be called the main lines — if he can assure us all those things which justice and reason seem to demand. What I apprehend our French friends peculiarly desire is assurances respecting the cardinal points — the great princi-

---

The Fort Garry convention, where most of the Red River speeches are given, is unique among the representative assemblies debating Confederation. Indeed, it is unique in Canadian history. It is not a legislative assembly or parliament, but a true constitutional convention, a "constituent assembly" — a representative body established solely for the purpose of drafting a constitution. It conducts none of the ordinary business of government in the colony. The convention was authorized by a mass meeting of settlers who gathered in the freezing open air on January 19 and 20, 1870; it then met behind the closed doors of the Fort Garry Court House for fifteen days. There were forty delegates to the convention, twenty elected by the inhabitants of the French parishes, and twenty by the English parishes. The most important order of business was to draw up a list of conditions on which Red River would enter Confederation. This list of conditions, revised several times, is called a "bill of rights." — JA

ples of a full representation in the direction of the affairs of the country, for instance, and other important points.

Donald Gunn: I have seen the bill of rights, and was here [at a convention of the previous November, organized by Riel] when it was discussed. At the meeting at which it was adopted I was present, but my constituents had given me no power to vote for such a bill. They merely sent me there to watch the proceedings and report to them what was going on. We English delegates believed our rights would be granted to us. But still we met our French friends here, although, as I have said, neither Mr. [James] Ross nor myself took any active part in the discussion — believing that we had at that time no authority to transact business.

— *Convention at Fort Garry, English and French*
Delegates in Council, January 26, 1870

Louis Riel: [After days of consultations] we have shown ourselves to the world to be capable of discussing, creditably, matters of the utmost political consequence. If differences have occurred, they have been only such as would naturally arise between men of intellect and reason in discussing important matters. (Cheers.)

— *Convention at Fort Garry, English and French*
Delegates in Council, February 3, 1870

Riel [to Commissioner Donald Smith]: Is your commission such as to enable you to guarantee us even a single article of the list of rights?

Donald Smith: I believe that the nature of my commission is such that I can give assurances — full assurances — so far as any such guarantee can be given, that the government of the dominion would so place the right guaranteed before parliament that it would be granted. This would be done in some instances
. . .

Riel: In some instances!

Smith: As to all the rights, in the form in which they have been handed me, I certainly cannot answer.

Riel: So you cannot guarantee us even a single article in the list?

Smith: The [dominion] government will certainly bring the

matter before parliament, but it is the parliament which must finally decide.*

Riel: You are embarrassed. I see you are a gentleman and do not wish to press you. I see that the Canadian government has not given you all the confidence which they ought to have put in your hands. At the same time we will hear your opinion, although we are satisfied you cannot grant us, nor guarantee us, anything by the nature of your commission.

          — *Convention at Fort Garry, English and French*
             Delegates in Council, February 7, 1870

Riel: I assume that some of the English delegates are a good deal hampered and bound, and in that possibility have possibly deceived us. You may be bound by certain pledges [from the electorate], but I do not see how you can let these stand in the way of union.

I know you are bound by your people; but why did you not say so when we were organizing the committee? What was the use of appointing the committee, if you could not act? . . . Let us give public notice of what you think and have said today, and get an expression of public opinion. If it is your duty to go back, go; and if you do not come again, why your people can stay as they are. As for us, we will work as we have done — we will do, not our work alone, but your work — without distinction.

If you do not come back, we will look upon what has been done as nothing at all. We will make out a new bill of rights, form a provisional government,† and try to make it obeyed. On my life I will say so. If the prejudices of your people are to prevail, they may do so, but it will be in my blood.

John Fraser: I do not know that we have received from our

---

* Smith means the parliament of Canada. Without a syllable of consultation with its people, the Red River Colony has been annexed to Canada along with the rest of the North-West Territory. The elected delegates of the people may deliberate earnestly on the proper ordering of their country, but ultimately its constitution will be written in Ottawa. — PR

† In its role as constituent assembly, by definition a body with the authority to make and unmake governments, the Fort Garry Convention created a "provisional government," with Riel as its president. The deliberative committee of this provisional government consisted of twelve English and twelve French delegates, and called itself the "Legislative Assembly of Rupert's Land."

Métis resistance fighter.

people the necessary powers to sanction us in setting to work to form a government. Such a thing as our forming a provisional government never came into their heads when they sent us . . . They did not give us carte blanche — to do as we liked. We must have time for reflection and consulting our constituents.

Riel (walking the chamber and soliloquizing): My goodness. I like better to fight than work this way.

> — *Convention at Fort Garry, English and French Delegates in Council, February 9, 1870*

Bunn: [Gives notice of motion] "That the Government of England, the Canadian Government, and the Hudson's Bay Company have ignored our rights as British subjects, when they entered into arrangements on the subject of the transfer of the government of the North West to the Dominion of Canada without consulting the wishes of the people of the North-West Territory."

> — *Rupert's Land, Legislative Assembly [of the provisional government], March 15, 1870*

Bunn: [He insists] that the motion read "our rights as British subjects," and not "le droits des gens"* and "the rights of men" as it did currently.

Riel: The French phrase used in the original motion is very expressive and alludes to our rights as men† — a people — a nation. In that capacity we have been ignored . . .

---

* What is going on here is not quite clear. "Le droit des gens" is generally translated as "the law of nations," not as "the rights of men." The relationship between the law of nations and the rights of the Métis would be more obvious if Riel did not admit to being a British subject. The Swiss jurist Emmerich de Vattel (1714–1767) writes in his Le Droit des Gens *(1758) that "When several independent families are settled in a country they have the free ownership of sovereignty over the whole, since they do not form a political society. No one may lay claim to sovereignty over that country, for this would be to subject those families against their will, and no man has the right to rule over persons born free unless they submit voluntarily to him" (Book II, section 97). However, unless Riel ascribed his British status to something other than Britain's sovereignty over his birthplace, Vattel's statement seems inapplicable to the Métis. — PR*

† Much is hidden in these few lines. The debate centres on what is perhaps

Alfred Scott: [He suggests "our rights as a people" instead of "as British subjects."]

Bunn: I object to the alteration. It is only as British subjects that we have any right to complain of the transfer [from the Hudson's Bay Company to Canada]. If we were the subjects of any other power, we would not have a word to say in the matter.

Scott: I still think the words "British subjects" not only unnecessary, but that they take away from the real essence of the motion.

Riel: We have, of course, our rights as a people and, standing on these general rights, we say we have been ignored and we complain. But, these rights being granted to us, we feel sure we are always British subjects. In effect there seems little difference between the two wordings proposed.

Bunn: There is not very much difference. But for the purpose of being concise, I prefer to leave my motion as it stands. I grant

---

the central constitutional distinction of modern history — namely, the question whether "rights" are real concrete claims and protections against particular governments or abstract universal rights of all men regardless of place or history. Bunn almost alone speaks for what is now recognized as the more English view, and Riel and others for the more French view. The difference between the two conceptions is especially poignant for Canada. At the time of this debate, educated people familiar with European and English history were aware that this very distinction had inflamed the French National Assembly in 1789. After studying various American constitutions and bills of rights, the French deputies, in framing their Declaration of the Rights of Man and of the Citizen, *expressly decided to take what they thought was a higher road and to legislate rights "for all times and all nations."*

Edmund Burke reacted by just as hotly inflaming the hearts of the English against the revolutionist preference for what he called "metaphysical rights" and accurately predicted the Terror as their outcome. For it was the fateful combination of the Declaration's *abstract terminology with Rousseau's mystical idea of the "general will" that made it dangerous, simply because particular meanings are inevitably attached to abstract terms by representatives and then presented as the "will of the people" whether the people perceive it as such or not. Bunn smells this incipient danger and seeks to avoid it by insisting in effect that the rights of subjects have meaning only if they are exercisable through legal precedent against an actual power. — WDG*

the principle advocated by the president [Riel], that every people have rights, but from whom must they claim them? Suppose in accordance with that general principle we say we have rights, from whom must we claim them? From the crown of England, undoubtedly, as British subjects.

O'Donoghue: [Governments and the Hudson's Bay Company] have entirely ignored our rights as a people.

Riel: The people, of course, had the right to be consulted. There is only the right of conquest against it.

Curtis Bird: [The use of "British subject"] does not alter our rights as a people in any way, but rather strengthens them. Suppose we were aliens, manifestly it would not lie in our mouth to complain of the transference to Canada. But as British subjects, and as such only, have we a right to complain.

Riel: After all, there is here in some respects distinction without a difference. We complain not because we are British subjects merely, but because we are men. We complain as a people — as men — for if we were not men we would not be British subjects.

O'Donoghue: Unquestionably, it is our business, as a people, to say that we cannot be bartered away as an article of commerce . . . [O]ur people were deprived of a right common to all men — and of course they felt aggrieved. (Cheers.) The honourable member for Mapleton (Mr. Bunn) would have us affirm that it was only because we were British subjects we had a right to be consulted. Now, I would go further, and hold with the honourable the president [Riel] that, as men, we cannot be trafficked in — bartered away at the pleasure of any government. We are free men and as such have rights altogether apart from those we acquire by being British subjects. (Cheers.)

> — *Rupert's Land, Legislative Assembly*
> *[of the provisional government], March 16, 1870*

"I grant the principle . . . that every people have rights, but from whom must they claim them? Suppose in accordance with that general principle we say we have rights, from whom must we claim them? From the crown of England, undoubtedly, as British subjects."

"We are free men and as such have rights altogether apart from those we acquire by being British subjects."

Chapter Twelve

DIRECT DEMOCRACY:
PRO AND CON

 (decorative divider)

A MONG THE PROVINCES ENJOYING responsible parliamentary institutions, two go into Confederation without
an election: Nova Scotia and Canada. Not surprisingly, these are
the two with the liveliest debates on constitution making.

A notable feature of the Nova Scotia debate is that the arguments divide neatly into two categories. As we saw in chapter 11,
the Nova Scotia confederates, almost without exception, believe a
parliamentary vote on union suffices, while the anti-confederates,
to a man, insist that the people must also be consulted, in a referendum or an election.

At first reading the Canadian debate seems to fall into the
same pattern. Many speakers, including John A. Macdonald,
argue for Confederation and against direct popular participation.
Others oppose Confederation and support direct participation.
But a closer look suggests a different picture. What are we to
make of J.H. Cameron, who votes for the parliamentary resolution to unite the colonies, but then moves an amendment calling
on the British government to refrain from action until the people
of the province have had their say? Cameron is not alone. A
number of Canadian speakers support both Confederation and
direct popular participation.

In Canada the issue of consultation refuses to go away. It rises,
clear and passionate, above the arguments for and against
Confederation. At its heart is a difference of opinion about "the
people." Those who favour direct popular appeal incline to the
idea that the people form a collectivity. The hope is that a referendum or single-issue election will reveal the uncomplicated will
of this collectivity. In contrast, those who argue for the suffi-

ciency of the parliamentary vote are more likely to think a population is characterized by competing, not easily reconcilable, views and interests. They conclude that direct democracy too easily translates into clout for particular classes and interests — the "squeaky wheels." The so-called authoritative voice of the people may turn out to be nothing more than the voice of the strongest groups. On this argument it is better to make constitutions in parliaments where the demands of particular groups can be challenged and where traditions of formal deliberation give "sober second thought" a chance.

Which offers the superior guarantee of the people's rights: direct democracy or unfettered parliamentary deliberation? The jury is still out. Arguments for direct democracy remain at the centre of Canadian politics, still lively, still promising, still troublesome.

CANADA

"[The] government . . . presented the scheme as a whole, and would exert all the influence they could bring to bear in the way of argument to induce the house to adopt the scheme without alteration, and for the simple reason that the scheme was not one framed by the government of Canada, or by the government of Nova Scotia, but was in the nature of a treaty settled between the different colonies."

John A. Macdonald: [The] government . . . presented the scheme as a whole, and would exert all the influence they could bring to bear in the way of argument to induce the house to adopt the scheme without alteration, and for the simple reason that the scheme was not one framed by the government of Canada, or by the government of Nova Scotia, but was in the nature of a treaty settled between the different colonies, each clause of which had been fully discussed, and which had been agreed to by a system of mutual compromise. Of course it was competent to the house to vote against the address as a whole, or to adopt amendments to it, but if they did so, it would then be for the government to consider whether they would press the scheme further on the attention of the house . . .

[He] had no hesitation in expressing his belief that, if the scheme was not now adopted in all its principal details, as presented to the house, we could not expect to get it passed this century. It had been only in consequence of a very happy concurrence of circumstances, which might not easily arise again, that the different provinces had been enabled to arrive at the conclusion now presented, and he should exceedingly regret in the interests of Canada and of the future of British North America if anything should delay beyond this year the completion and conclusion of this great scheme.

The resolutions on their face bore evidence of compromise; perhaps not one of the delegates from any of the provinces would have propounded this scheme as a whole, but being impressed

with the conviction that it was highly desirable with a view to the maintenance of British power on this continent that there should be Confederation and a junction of all the provinces, the consideration of the details was entered upon in a spirit of compromise. Not one member of the Canadian government had his own views carried out in all details, and it was the same with the other delegates. But after a full discussion of sixteen days, and after the various details had been voted on, the resolutions as a whole were agreed to by a unanimous vote; every one of the delegates, whatever his view to any of the details, being satisfied to adopt the whole scheme as adopted by a majority for each individual resolution, and to press it upon his own legislature as the only practicable scheme that could be carried; such being the case, he trusted the government would have the support of a very large majority of the house in carrying the scheme just as it stood, members sacrificing their individual opinions as to particular details, if satisfied with the government that the scheme as a whole was for the benefit and prosperity of the people of Canada.

"[Was] the intention of the government to carry this measure into force without submitting it to the people?"

John Sandfield Macdonald: By what authority [had] the government . . . undertaken to negotiate a treaty? . . . All forms of the house should be strictly observed, so that there should be no infringement upon the rights of the minority.

Thomas Ferguson: [Was] the intention of the government to carry this measure into force without submitting it to the people?

John A. Macdonald: If this measure received the support of the house,* there would be no necessity of going to the people. If, however, the measure were defeated, it would be for the government to consider whether there should not be an appeal to the country. (Hear, hear, and laughter.)

Macdonald exposes much of the motivation — and perhaps some falseness — behind the whole debate by suggesting that when the government has the confidence of the house, it is deemed also to have the support of the people, and therefore stands behind the theory of political representation. But if not, it may switch to the opposing theory and seek the people's direct support in order to pass a bill and circumvent the house. This attitude raises the problem of sincerity: How much of the anti-representation and pro-democracy argument in these debates was sincere and philosophically grounded rather than merely pragmatic? It was likely a mixture of both. — WDG

[The] representatives of the various colonial governments, after this treaty* had been made, agreed to go home and press upon the legislatures of their respective provinces this measure as a whole, and to present in all the colonial legislatures addresses identical in their nature to Her Majesty, asking her to pass an act based upon these resolutions, such address being an expression of the deliberate opinion of the colonies. It would then become the duty of the imperial government and legislature to act as they pleased in the matter.

— *Legislative Assembly, February 3, 1865*

George Brown: Mr. Speaker, I am told that this federation scheme may be all very right — it may be just and the very thing the country needs — but this government had no authority from parliament† to negotiate it. The honourable member for Cornwall (Honourable John S. Macdonald) particularly pressed this objection . . .

Luther Holton: It is quite true.

George-Étienne Cartier: No, the reverse is true.

Brown: I am astonished to hear such a statement repeated. No one knows better than the honourable member for Chateauguay [Holton] and the honourable member for Cornwall that in the ministerial explanations brought down to this house, at the time of the formation of this government, it was distinctly declared that the government was formed for the special purpose of maturing a scheme of federal union, and that it would take means, during the recess, for opening negotiations with the Maritime provinces, to bring about such a union.

---

* Canadian and British statesmen involved in the founding of the Dominion of Canada often referred to both the Quebec agreement and the BNA Act as an intercolonial treaty. Later generations took such allusions as evidence of the validity of the compact theory of Confederation. Anxious to discredit that theory, twentieth-century centralists hypothesized that the term had not been meant literally, but as a device to persuade first the Canadian legislature and then the British parliament to accept the package presented to them and so forbear from trying to amend it in detail. — PR
† The provincial legislature.

Holton: But not to conclude them.

Brown: What we have done is entirely subject to the approval of parliament. The honourable member for Cornwall is the very last man who should have raised such an objection, for he attended a caucus of the Liberal members of the assembly, heard the whole plans of the government explained, precisely as they have been carried out, and he was the very person who moved that I should go into the government to give them effect. (Hear, hear.)

Christopher Dunkin: And I heard something more said — that nothing should be done which did not leave the house perfectly free.

Brown: I can assure my honourable friend that, as far as that goes, he never was more free in his life than now. (Laughter.) We do not pretend to say that anything we have done binds this house — any member may object if he pleases — but I do say we received the approval of the house for opening negotiations, and it is a miserable pretence to say anything to the contrary. (Hear, hear.) We did no more than has been done by every government, under the British system, that ever existed. We have but made a compact, subject to the approval of parliament. So far as this government is concerned, we are firmly committed to the scheme; but so far as the members of the legislature are concerned, they are as free as air; but I am confident that this house will almost unanimously accept it, and not with changes and amendments, but as a whole — as the very best compromise arrangement that can be obtained.

Holton: We have not the treaty-making power.*

Holton refers to the legal sovereignty which constitutes an independent nation. Lacking such sovereignty, the colonies could not conclude a treaty with a sovereign power unless the British government acted for them. This argument was used in the 1930s to discredit the compact theory of Confederation, but it is quite irrelevant, since Confederation did not involve a treaty with a foreign power. When contemporaries called the Quebec agreement a treaty, they were speaking metaphorically; but the metaphor derived force from the autonomy enjoyed by self-governing colonies within the British Empire. — PR

Brown: The honourable gentleman is entirely wrong when he says we had no power to make this compact with the Maritime provinces. We had full power, express instructions to enter into it.

Holton: Did the parliament of England give you that power?

Brown: No; the honourable gentleman ought to know that the treaty-making power is in the crown — the crown authorized us specially to make this compact, and it has heartily approved of what we did. (Hear, hear.) But, Mr. Speaker, I am told that the people of Canada have not considered this scheme, and that we ought not to pass it without appealing to the electors for their approval. Now, sir, a statement more incorrect than this, or more injurious to the people of Canada, could not be made. They not only have considered this scheme — for fifteen years they have been earnestly considering it — but they perfectly comprehend it. (Hear, hear.) If ever a question was thoroughly debated in any country, the whole subject of constitutional change has been in Canada. There is not a light in which it could be placed that has not been thoroughly canvassed . . . *

Never, I venture to assert, was any great measure so thoroughly understood, and so cordially endorsed by the people of Canada, as this measure now under consideration. (Hear, hear.) The British government approves of it — the Legislative Council approves of it — this house almost unanimously approves of it — the press of all parties approves of it — and though the scheme has already been directly submitted to fifty out of the one hundred constituencies into which Canada is divided,† only four candidates ventured to appear at the hustings in opposition to it — all of them in Lower Canada — and but two of them were elected. (Cheers.) And yet, sir, we are to be told that we are stealing a march upon the country; that it is not understood by the people; and that we must dissolve the house upon it, at a vast cost to the exchequer, and at the risk of allowing political partisanship to dash the fruit from our hands at the very moment we are about to grasp it! (Hear, hear.) Sir, I have no fears whatever of

> *"I am told that the people of Canada have not considered this scheme . . . Now, sir, a statement more incorrect than this, or more injurious to the people of Canada, could not be made. They not only have considered this scheme — for fifteen years they have been earnestly considering it — but they perfectly comprehend it."*

---

* *Brown here reviews an assortment of proposals for Canadian union and British North American union dating back to the 1830s.*

† *This statement is puzzling, since Canada was divided into 130 constituencies for the purpose of representation in the Legislative Assembly alone, and there were also constituencies for elections to the Legislative Council. — PR*

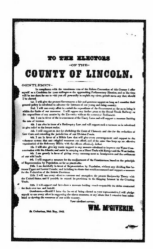

In this campaign broadsheet for the Canadian election of 1863, Reform candidate William McGiverin says nothing about proposals to federate the Canadian provinces or about Confederation. He does promise to "give the present Government a fair and generous support so long as I consider their general policy is calculated to advance the interests of our young and rising country."

an appeal to the people. I cannot pretend to speak as to the popular feeling in Lower Canada, but I think I thoroughly understand the popular mind of the western province, and I hesitate not to say that there are not five gentlemen in this chamber (if so many) who could go before their constituents in Upper Canada in opposition to this scheme, with the slightest chance of being returned. (Hear, hear.)

It is because I thoroughly comprehend the feelings of the people upon it that I urge the adoption of this measure at the earliest possible moment. The most gross injustice is to be rectified by it; the taxpayer is to be clothed with his rightful influence by it; new commercial relations are to be opened up by it; a new impulse to the industrial pursuits of the country will be given by it — and I for one would feel myself false to the cause I have so long sustained, and false to the best interests of my constituents, if I permitted one hour unnecessarily to pass without bringing it to a final issue. (Cheers.) It was only by the concurrence of most propitious circumstances that the wonderful progress this movement has made could have been accomplished. Most peculiar were the circumstances that enabled such a coalition to be formed as that now existing for the settlement of this question — and who shall say at what hour it may not be rent asunder? And yet, who will venture to affirm that if party spirit in all its fierceness were once more to be let loose amongst us, there would be the slightest hope that this great question could be approached with that candour and harmony necessary to its satisfactory solution? (Hear, hear.)

Then, sir, at the very moment we resolved to deal with this question of constitutional change, the Maritime provinces were about to assemble in joint conference to consider whether they ought not to form a union among themselves — and the way was thus most propitiously opened up for the consideration of a union of all British America. The civil war, too, in the neighbouring republic; the possibility of war between Great Britain and the United States; the threatened repeal of the Reciprocity Treaty; the threatened abolition of the American bonding system for goods in transitu to and from these provinces; the unsettled position of the Hudson's Bay Company; and the changed feeling of England as to the relations of great colonies to the parent state — all combine at this moment to arrest earnest attention to the gravity of the situation, and unite us all in one vigorous effort to meet the emergency like men. (Hear, hear.)

The interests to be affected by this scheme of union are very large and varied — the pressure of circumstances upon all the colonies is so serious at this moment that if we cannot now banish partisanship and sectionalism and petty objections, and look at the matter on its broad intrinsic merits, what hope is there of our ever being able to do so? An appeal to the people of Canada on this measure simply means postponement of the question for a year — and who can tell how changed ere then may be the circumstances surrounding us? Sir, the man who strives for the postponement of this measure on any ground is doing what he can to kill it almost as effectually as if he voted against it. (Hear, hear.)

Let there be no mistake as to the manner in which the government presents this measure to the house. We do not present it as free from fault, but we do present it as a measure so advantageous to the people of Canada that all the blemishes, real or imaginary, averred against it sink into utter insignificance in presence of its merits. (Hear, hear.) We present it, not in the precise shape we in Canada would desire it, but as in the best shape the five colonies to be united could agree upon it. We present it in the form in which the five governments have severally adopted it — in the form the imperial government has endorsed it — and in the form in which we believe all the legislatures of the provinces will accept it. (Hear, hear.) We ask the house to pass it in the exact form in which we have presented it, for we know not how alterations may affect its safety in other places, and the process of alteration once commenced in four different legislatures — Who can tell where that would end? Every member of this house is free as air to criticize it if he so wills, and amend it if he is able — but we warn him of the danger of amendment and throw on him all the responsibility of the consequences. (Hear, hear.) We feel confident of carrying this scheme as it stands — but we cannot tell what we can do if it be amended. (Hear, hear.)

Let not honourable gentlemen approach this measure as a sharp critic deals with an abstract question, striving to point out blemishes and display his ingenuity; but let us approach it as men having but one consideration before us — the establishment of the future peace and prosperity of our country. (Hear, hear.) Let us look at it in the light of a few months back — in the light of the evils and injustice to which it applies a remedy — in the light of the years of discord and strife we have spent in seeking for that remedy — in the light with which the people of Canada would regard this measure were it to be lost, and all the evils of past

years to be brought back upon us again. (Hear, hear.) Let honourable gentlemen look at the question in this view — and what one of them will take the responsibility of casting his vote against the measure?

Sir, the future destiny of these great provinces may be affected by the decision we are about to give to an extent which at this moment we may be unable to estimate — but assuredly the welfare for many years of four millions of people hangs on our decision. (Hear, hear.) Shall we then rise equal to the occasion? Shall we approach this discussion without partisanship, and free from every personal feeling but the earnest resolution to discharge conscientiously the duty which an overruling providence has placed upon us? Sir, it may be that some among us will live to see the day when, as the result of this measure, a great and powerful people may have grown up in these lands, when the boundless forests all around us shall have given way to smiling fields and thriving towns, and when one united government, under the British flag, shall extend from shore to shore. But who would desire to see that day if he could not recall with satisfaction the part he took in this discussion? Mr. Speaker, I have done. I leave the subject to the conscientious judgement of the house, in the confident expectation and belief that the decision it will render will be worthy of the parliament of Canada. (The honourable gentleman resumed his seat amid loud and continued applause.)

— *Legislative Assembly, February 8, 1865*

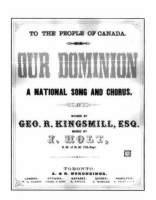

Ontario prepares to celebrate Confederation Day with a "national song and chorus."

Thomas D'Arcy McGee: Everything we did was done in form and with propriety, and the result of our proceedings is the document [the Quebec Resolutions] that has been submitted to the imperial government as well as to this house and which we speak of here as a treaty. And that there may be no doubt about our position in regard to that document we say, question it you may, reject it you may, or accept it you may, but alter it you may not. (Hear, hear.) It is beyond your power, or our power, to alter it. There is not a sentence — aye, or even a word — you can alter without desiring to throw out the document. Alter it, and we know at once what you mean — you thereby declare yourselves anti-unionists. (Hear, hear.) On this point, I repeat after all my honourable friends who have already spoken, for one party to alter a treaty is, of course, to destroy it.

If we reject it now, is there any human probability that we shall ever see again so propitious a set of circumstances to bring

about the same results? How they came about we all know. (Hear, hear.) The strange and fortunate events that have occurred in Canada, the extraordinary concessions made by the leaders of the governments below — Dr. Tupper, the Nova Scotian premier, for instance, admitting to his confidence, and bringing with him here as his co-representatives, Honourable Messrs. Archibald and McCully, two of his most determined political opponents — Can we ever expect, if we reject this scheme, that the same or similar things will occur again to favour it? Can we expect to see the leader of the Upper Canadian Conservative Party and the leader of the Upper Canadian Liberals sitting side by side again, if this project fails to work out, in a spirit of mutual compromise and concession, the problem of our constitutional difficulties? No, sir, it is too much to expect.

Miracles would cease to be miracles if they were events of everyday occurrence; the very nature of wonders requires that they should be rare; and this is a miraculous and wonderful circumstance, that men at the head of the governments in five separate provinces, and men at the head of the parties opposing them, all agreed at the same time to sink party differences for the good of all, and did not shrink, at the risk of having their motives misunderstood, from associating together for the purpose of bringing about this result. (Cheers.)

— *Legislative Assembly, February 9, 1865*

"This is a miraculous and wonderful circumstance, that men at the head of the governments in five separate provinces, and men at the head of the parties opposing them, all agreed at the same time to sink party differences for the good of all, and did not shrink, at the risk of having their motives misunderstood, from associating together for the purpose of bringing about this result."

James Aikins: With regard to the [Quebec scheme] I think that a very great deal depends upon the resolutions themselves. If we are to have framed a new constitution upon them as a basis, all of them, in my opinion, should be thoroughly canvassed and examined; and this house as well as the other branch of the legislature ought not to be prevented by the government of the day from expressing its opinions with regard to their merits. (Hear.) It is said by many honourable gentlemen that the people are in favour of this scheme. I think the people are in favour of a scheme of Confederation, but I think it depends altogether upon the details of that scheme whether they will give it their approval or not.

I think . . . that we who are placed here to conserve and protect the interests of the public should be extremely careful and analyze these resolutions thoroughly, and ascertain as nearly as possible what their effect is likely to be, before we take the responsibility of voting for them. I have no hesitation in declaring that there never was a period in the history of Canada when the people suf-

fered more than they do at present. (Hear, hear.) When we find that property has depreciated in value within the last five years, 20, 30, 40, aye and even 60 per cent; when we find that the crops of the country have been steadily decreasing in quantity and value within that period; when we find that the people are dissatisfied with the manner in which the country has been governed during the last eight or ten years; when we find all this, we may believe that they are prepared to accept almost any change that promises a relief from their present difficulties. But we were placed here to conserve their interests, to look after their welfare, and should not hastily adopt any scheme, proposed by any government — whether all of one party stripe or not — without fully examining it and weighing the results likely to flow from it. (Hear, hear.)

— *Legislative Council, February 10, 1865*

Benjamin Seymour: In the United States, no change of constitution can be effected without the consent of two-thirds of both branches of the legislature, and that must afterwards be sanctioned by three-fourths of the state governments . . . Then what are the constitutions of the state governments? I have here a clause taken from the constitution of one of the states (Connecticut), which provides that:

> Whenever a majority of the House of Representatives shall deem it necessary to alter or amend this constitution, they may propose such alterations and amendments, which proposed amendments shall be continued to the next General Assembly, and be published with the laws which may have been passed at the same session, and if two-thirds of each house, at the next session of said Assembly, shall approve the amendments proposed, by yeas and nays, said amendments shall, by the Secretary, be transmitted to the town clerk in each town in this state, whose duty it shall be to present the same to the inhabitants thereof, for their consideration, at a town meeting legally warned and held for that purpose; and if it shall appear in a manner provided by law, that a majority of the electors present at such meetings shall have approved such amendments, the same shall be valid, to all intents and purposes, as part of this constitution.

That is the way one of the oldest states guards the rights and liberties of its people . . . Now, honourable gentlemen, I have shown

that this scheme has no precedent, even on the other side of the line. Among all the wild republican theories of our neighbours,* they have never proposed to change the constitution in this manner — never changed it, at all events, without the consent of the people, obtained in some form or other . . .

In England no important change in the laws is ever carried without being discussed in parliament, session after session, followed by an appeal to the people upon it. Even so unimportant a change — or what would, in comparison with this scheme, be here regarded as so unimportant a change — as the extension of the franchise has been discussed in parliament for years, and submitted to the people before passing into law . . . Here you propose to change the constitution — to change the whole fabric of society — in fact to revolutionize society, without asking the consent of the people, and without the possibility — at any rate, the reasonable possibility — of this important change ever being reconsidered. Does not this important subject affect every freeholder in the country as much as it affects us, and are there not thousands of people in the country who have as great an interest in it as the members of the Executive Council of Canada? And yet, forsooth, these gentlemen prepare a scheme, bring it down to this house, and tell the representatives of the people that they are not at liberty to ascertain the wishes of the people respecting it, nor to alter it in any manner, but that they must take it as it is. Still we are told, notwithstanding all this, that this is freedom, and that we are a free people.

"You propose to change the constitution — to change the whole fabric of society — in fact to revolutionize society, without asking the consent of the people, and without the possibility — at any rate, the reasonable possibility — of this important change ever being reconsidered."

---

* *We sense that Seymour is very angry. And rightly so. It is one of the ironies of political history that even in countries said to be most free, constitutions are generally handed down to the people, and not made by them. This was so for the Athenians and Romans, even though each rested on a public belief that legitimacy comes from consent of the people. The American and Canadian constitutions were both created by élite action with consent engineered after the fact. Seymour was correct that before him was a plan "to revolutionize society." Arguably, this method for making constitutions is very Canadian: our Charter of Rights and Freedoms of 1982 was specifically created to subordinate the sovereignty of parliament to an abstract code of rights open to interpretation only by unelected judges, yet this profoundly revolutionary change to Canada's historical constitution was never submitted to the people for approval. The failed Meech Lake and Charlottetown accords followed similar élite methods of construction. — WDG*

Alexander Campbell: You are at liberty either to accept or reject it. (Hear, hear.)

Seymour: Well, that is all very well, but we are told we must accept the scheme as it is; and all the influence that the government can use — which I fear will be successfully used — (hear, hear) — will be employed to carry it through without the people having an opportunity of saying yea or nay upon it. We are told it is not British to permit this — even to pass a short act allowing the people to vote upon it; but if this is not British, neither is the proposition itself. (Hear, hear.) I entreat honourable members not to pass a measure of this importance without delaying it some little time, at all events, for the purpose of obtaining an expression of public opinion upon it. The people who are to be governed by it, who are for all time to come to live under this constitution, certainly have a right to be consulted before it is consummated.

David Christie: My honourable friend from the Home Division (James Aikins), in speaking of this conference [the Quebec Conference] the other day, said he would have preferred if it had been a party matter, and he took the ground that if it had, it would have been better for the country.

Aikins: I beg the honourable gentleman's pardon. What I said was that I regretted very much that the measure had not been taken up and discussed as a party measure. For although I was of opinion that it could not be carried as a party measure, if it had been so taken up it would have been more thoroughly scrutinized and discussed before the people.*

Christie: I think the explanation of my honourable friend quite bears out what I stated, that he thought it should be made a party measure.

Aikins: I thought the country would be the gainer if it were.

Christie: In what way?

Aikins laments that the formation of a coalition to pursue Confederation has had the effect of stifling public deliberation on this most important topic. — PR

Aikins: By the fuller discussion we would have.

Christie: The honourable gentleman, I see, has not changed the ground which he took the other day, and which is precisely as I stated it. He thinks it would have been to the public advantage if this question had been taken up and discussed by a party. In this, in my judgement, he is entirely wrong; and I say he can find no instance of a constitution having been revised by a party.

James Currie: Well, I submit an instance — the amendment to the United States Constitution, prohibiting slavery, which was passed last month, and which was proposed by a party.

"It is not desirable that any constitution should be the work of a party; in so important an undertaking, all party spirit should be laid aside. Why? Because men of all parties are alike interested in the formation of a constitution, and because in the construction of such an instrument, the collective wisdom of the leading men of all parties is needed. Besides, a constitution so framed will be more likely . . . to live in the hearts and affections of the people."

Christie: A number of the representatives in the federal Congress who voted for it were Democrats, and without their concurrence and support it could not have been carried. Besides, that was only an amendment, not a revision of the constitution. The constitution of the United States was not the work of a party. The revision of the constitution of the State of New York, in 1846, was not the work of a party. It is not desirable that any constitution should be the work of a party; in so important an undertaking, all party spirit should be laid aside. (Hear, hear.) Why? Because men of all parties are alike interested in the formation of a constitution, and because in the construction of such an instrument, the collective wisdom of the leading men of all parties is needed. Besides, a constitution so framed will be more likely, as my honourable friend from Wellington [John S. Sanborn] has so well said, to live in the hearts and affections of the people . . . In order that I may not misrepresent the position taken by the honourable gentleman, let me quote his language, as reported in the newspapers. He held:

> That the elective members had received a sacred trust to exercise; that they were sent here by their constituencies to represent them, and to do that only. Under these circumstances, how could they conceive they had the power to vote away the rights of their electors? That was not their *mandat*, and if they did, they would be doing that which they had no authority to do; they would be doing that which they could not do without going beyond the authority confided to them.

Now it must be frankly admitted that if the honourable gen-

tleman's position be correct, then his objection would be fatal to any elected member giving his concurrence to the scheme of the conference.

But honourable gentlemen, let us inquire what is the position of a representative. Two elements enter into the idea of representation — namely, power and duty. A representative derives the former from his constituents acting by their majority, under the constitution. From what source does he derive the latter? Obviously not from his constituents, because even the majority are not agreed on all points connected with the discharge of his duty. My honourable friend (Honourable Mr. Sanborn) has spoken of the position of a representative as being that of a trustee. I shall quote from a very able work on the British commonwealth,* in which that position is, to my mind, very fully and very satisfactorily proved to be incorrect. Cox says:

> From whom does [the representative] derive the duty of expressing this or that opinion in parliament? . . . The very majority who voted for him are rarely, perhaps never, all agreed on any one point on which their opinions have been compared with his. Some of them differ from him on some points, some on others, but they all voted for him, from personal consideration, or because of their agreement with him on those points which they respectively deemed most important. In the minority, also, are probably some electors who assent to some, and dissent from others of his opinions. The essential conditions of a valid trust to express particular opinions in parliament are then wanting. The persons nominating him to his office, do not concur as to the opinions which he is to express.†

The only other possible limitation might exist in the constitution. I shall look then at the instrument from which we derive

---

*The term later came to be applied to the British Empire, but Cox applies it to Britain herself as an expression of his belief that the proper end of politics is not class warfare but the harmonizing of diverse interests — hence his insistence on the MP's duty to represent all interests in his constituency, not just those of his supporters. — PR

† Christie is quoting from Homersham Cox's The British Commonwealth: or a Commentary on the Institutions and Principles of British Government (London: Longman, Brown, Green and Longmans, 1854),

our powers as legislative councillors, and shall quote from the imperial act of 1854, intituled "An Act to empower the legislature of Canada to alter the constitution of the Legislative Council, and for other purposes." The first section is as follows:

> It shall be lawful for the legislature of Canada, by any act or acts to be for that purpose passed, to alter the manner of composing the Legislative Council of the said province . . .

Then in the third section it is provided:

> That it shall be lawful for the legislature of Canada, from time to time, to vary and repeal all or any of the provisions of the act or acts altering the constitution of the said Legislative Council.

These are the powers given us by our constitution. (Hear, hear.) They are of the most ample character. We were elected, pursuant to an act passed in consequence of the exercise of these powers. And, coming from the people, the members of this house were put in possession of these powers the moment they were elected. None of them at their elections pledged themselves not to exercise the powers granted by the constitution. They were not asked by their constituents to do so. How then, by voting for this or any other measure altering the constitution of the Legislative Council, can they be said to betray the trust reposed in them by their constituents?

My honourable friend from Wellington admits that under the constitution we have the power to alter the constitution of this house in so far as it relates to Canada, but he says we are not authorized to extend our action to the other provinces, in a scheme of federal union. That is begging the question. I answer

---

145–46. The quotation is taken from chapter 13, where Cox follows Blackstone in arguing that every MP is expected to serve for the whole country, and therefore cannot be regarded as a delegate whose function is merely to register the views and interests of his constituents. Grounding his study in the philosophies of Aristotle, Locke, Blackstone, and Mill, Cox proposes that the supreme purpose of government is to promote morality. When this is done, the effect will be to increase national wealth. He views the existing British Constitution as the embodiment of "the Christian doctrines of peace and goodwill" (xxi). — IG

his objection that any change affecting the elective principle is a breach of trust.

Besides, we do not propose to enact a system of government embracing all British North America. We have not the power to do so. We merely propose to address Her Majesty* on the subject. The imperial parliament alone has that power; but if we have power without a breach of trust to alter the constitution of the Legislative Council of Canada (and my honourable friend admits this), then certainly we cannot be guilty of a breach of trust in suggesting a change embraced in a constitution for the various provinces.

This scheme, like all other constitutional compacts, is a compromise between the conflicting opinions of its framers; and on the whole, it is a fair compromise. This feature is not peculiar to our plan of Confederation. My honourable friend will find in *The Federalist*,† and from the correspondence of the able men who framed the "Articles of Confederation," that compromise and concessions of opinion were submitted to. But out of them all grew the wonderful fabric of the American Constitution . . .

I have to apologize for having detained the house so long —

A specious argument, since it was a foregone conclusion that the British parliament would act on such a request. Christie's attempt to justify the proposed course by citing the legislature's statutory power to amend its own organization is equally disingenuous. Sanborn and Vidal point out the flaws in his reasoning below. — PR

† On October 27, 1787, readers of the New York Independent Journal were treated to the Federalist No. 1, the first of eighty-five such articles written by Madison, Hamilton, and Jay, that Thomas Jefferson subsequently described as the best commentary on the principles of government ever written (see James Madison, Alexander Hamilton, and John Jay, The Federalist Papers [London: Penguin Books, 1987]). They were published in an effort to persuade the people of New York State to ratify the constitution of the United States, which had been drafted that very summer in Philadelphia and which is now the oldest written constitution in history. The "great national discussion" over the Constitution had divided Americans bitterly, and it was ratified in most states by very narrow margins. But it soon became a symbol to the world and to Americans themselves of a good republican constitution.

Canadian criticisms of the American Constitution were mainly on two grounds: it did not include the monarchic principle, which alone transcends the divisiveness of political parties; and it granted all residual powers to the states, that is, the right to do anything not specifically assigned by the

(cries of "no, no," "go on") — but, before sitting down, I must refer to the amendment of which my honourable friend from Niagara Division [James Currie] has given notice. It is as follows:

> That upon a matter of such great importance as the proposed Confederation of this and certain other British colonies, this house is unwilling to assume the responsibility of assenting to a measure involving so many important considerations, without a further manifestation of the public will than has yet been declared.

My honourable friend . . . does not tell us whether he intends to propose that public opinion shall be tested by an appeal to the people in the way of a dissolution of the Legislative Assembly, or by submitting the scheme in its integrity to a popular vote. If we recommend the former course, we should place ourselves in rather a strange position. If we advised His Excellency to dissolve the House of Assembly, while we sat quietly by to see what was going on, it would be in effect saying, "We have scruples as to whether public opinion has, or has not, endorsed these proposed constitutional changes; but, if your Excellency will be so kind as to dissolve the House of Assembly, those scruples will be resolved by a general election." (Hear, hear, and laughter.) I think that would be an extraordinary course for this house to take — and a course which I think would not be considered by the country at large a very becoming one. (Hear, hear.)

If the other plan be what my honourable friend intends by his

---

Constitution to the central government. In the Canadian view, it was this granting of excess power to the states that helped engender the U.S. Civil War. So the Canadian founders ensured that residual powers in Canada would belong to the central government.

Notwithstanding these defects, the American Constitution garnered enormous worldwide admiration for the manner in which it consolidated so much political wisdom by forcefully, and yet subtly, separating, checking, and balancing the powers of government in order to make abuses difficult.

The Canadian federalists took a page from the American book of that name in that they fought to preserve centralism, a strict division of powers between provinces and central government, a mixture of the monarchic, aristocratic, and democratic principles, and argued, just as had James Madison, that such a system best protected all the people, and not just a majority of them. — WDG

notice, then I say it is a process of ascertaining the popular sanction entirely unknown to the British Constitution. It is a process unknown even to our friends on the other side of the line, except in those cases where the general or state constitution expressly provides for it.

[The] process of submitting any statute to the popular vote, in order to give it the force of law, is unheard of in British constitutional practice. (Hear, hear.)

John Sanborn: [Though] I concede to my honourable friend from Erie Division (Mr. Christie) every credit for great candour and soundness of judgement, still I must say that, when he enters into the province of law, he is travelling a little, as we say in the profession, out of the record — and that anyone who is familiar with the doctrine of trusts could not fail to see the falseness of his reasoning in that particular. As regards a trust, of course, the person who has a mandate given to him must act according to his discretion under the circumstances. But then he must do so within the trust that is given him, and not beyond the trust.

Christie: Of course.

Sanborn: [The] act empowering the legislature of Canada to change the constitution of the Legislative Council . . . cannot properly be invoked as giving authority with reference to bringing in other provinces to form a new confederacy.

Christie: But my honourable friend will observe that we are not legislating now — that we are merely passing an address.

Sanborn: We must feel that, according to the rules of law, we are asked here to go beyond the duties which our electors sent us into this house to discharge. I contend that neither any act on our own statute book, nor any imperial act, authorizes us to assume that they elected us to come here to demolish the whole fabric of our constitution and to seek to form another and entirely different political system, embracing a number of other provinces, so that our identity is entirely swamped and lost.

— *Legislative Council, February 15, 1865*

"Neither any act on our own statute book, nor any imperial act, authorizes us to assume that [our electors sent us] here to demolish the whole fabric of our constitution and to seek to form another and entirely different political system, embracing a number of other provinces, so that our identity is entirely swamped and lost."

Currie: I think we should pause before adopting these [Quebec] resolutions. I think we want some more information before we

adopt them. Before we vote away our local constitutions — before we vote away in fact our whole constitution — we should know something of what we are going to get in place of what we are giving away.

Honourable gentlemen may perhaps argue that there is no necessity for this question going to the people — no necessity for further time being allowed to the people of Upper Canada or of Canada generally to consider this matter. Why, honourable gentlemen, has it not been stated by every honourable member who has taken the floor to address the house on this question that it is the most important question ever submitted to this or any other British colonial legislature? And yet many of those honourable members are unwilling that the people of this country should have any further time to consider this important matter — although, by the laws of our land, no municipality has a right to enact or pass a by-law creating a little petty debt, not to be paid off within a year, without submitting it first to the vote of the people. (Hear.)

Honourable gentlemen assign as a reason why the matter should not be submitted to the people that we have had a number of elections to this house since it was known that the scheme of Confederation was under the consideration of the government, and that these elections went favourably to the scheme. I would ask, honourable gentlemen, how many elections have we had in Upper Canada since the scheme was printed and laid before the people? I would like to see the honourable gentleman stand up who had been elected to come here to vote upon this scheme since it was submitted to the people. It is true we have had one election in Upper Canada since that time . . . the election in South Ontario, a constituency until recently represented by one of the honourable gentlemen who entered the ministry which brings this scheme before us — our present esteemed vice-chancellor of Upper Canada, Honourable Mr. Mowat.* What did the candidates say at that election? Both of them, as stated by my

---

* *Oliver Mowat (1820–1903), premier of Ontario, 1872–96, minister of justice, 1896–97, lieutenant governor of Ontario, 1897–1903. He took part in the Quebec Conference as a Canadian cabinet minister, but resigned his office immediately thereafter to become a chancery judge. He and John A. Macdonald between them drafted most of the resolutions presented to the conference. His role at Quebec and acumen as a constitutional lawyer gave authority to his later advocacy of provincial rights as premier. — PR*

Tilley   Brown   Cartier   McGee   Macdonald   Tupper   Mowat   McDougall   Galt

CONFEDERATION LEADERS

C.W. JEFFERYS
BASED ON PHOTOGRAPHS BY NOTMAN ETC.

A watercolour in black and white by C.W. Jefferys of prominent leaders at the Quebec Conference of 1864.

honourable friend, in asking the suffrages of the people, had to promise that, if elected to parliament, they would vote for a submission of this scheme to the people. (Hear, hear.) And that is the last election we have had in Upper Canada.

Honourable gentlemen, it is quite true that the resolutions have gone through the length and breadth of the land; but where has there been that discussion in Canada to which resolutions of so much importance are entitled — except in Lower Canada, where I am told that fifteen counties have repudiated the resolutions when they were submitted to public meetings? . . .

Did the basis on which the government was formed authorize them to enter into this compact? The basis on which the government was formed speaks for itself. The measure they promised the people of Upper Canada was simply a measure to settle the existing difficulties between Upper and Lower Canada. They were to form Upper and Lower Canada into a federation upon such a basis as would hereafter allow the other provinces, if agreeable, and if they could agree as to terms, to also enter the federation. These are the bases on which the present government was formed,* and these are the bases on which the members of that government went to the country and asked for the support of their constituents.

"Well," honourable gentlemen say, "they have brought down a larger scheme." Yes, but who asked them to bring down that scheme? It is said that it makes no difference which scheme was laid before the house; but I contend that it makes all the difference, for if these resolutions had reference simply to Upper and Lower Canada, they would be susceptible of amendment by this house. In such a case, honourable gentlemen would not have come down as we now see them, shaking their resolutions in the face of the members of the legislature and saying, "Here is a treaty which you must accept in its entirety or not at all." They would not be warning us

---

* *Currie asserts that the government's policy as announced in June 1864 gave priority to federalizing United Canada. In fact, Brown and Cartier could not have brought John A. Macdonald into the fold without agreeing to pursue a broader British North American union, with Canadian federation as a fallback position. At first, however, Brown justified the coalition to his doubting supporters as a means to achieving the Reform program of 1859 (representation by population and Canadian federation), and did not start puffing* confederation *(as opposed to* federation*) until the Charlottetown Conference approached. — PR*

at our peril to alter a word or erase a line on pain of being branded as disunionists, or perhaps something worse than that.

Walter Dickson: I would take this opportunity of saying that I do not think the observation made by an honourable gentleman [David Christie], to the effect that it would be in bad taste for this house to suggest a dissolution of the other branch of the legislature, should have any influence . . . We argue for delay, and we are perfectly willing you should delay the measure until after the next general election. But, if the government think that delay will be so dangerous to the measure, there is a constitutional remedy open to them, which, of course, it would not be proper for me to refer to in a more pointed manner. I do not argue for a week or a month's delay. I think there ought to be a much longer time allowed. I think the question ought to be submitted to the people of this country for their approval.

I do not want the thing to be gone about in a peddling kind of style, one honourable gentleman running here and another there, and endeavouring in that way to learn the views of his constituents. If we cannot have the usual constitutional mode of arriving at the true views, opinions, and impressions of the people in relation to the scheme, I do not want any delay at all. I do not want the opinion of the people taken, unless it can be done in such a manner as will give us something upon which we can depend. If an honourable gentleman consults the electors in one portion of his constituency and they are opposed to the scheme, while those of another section of the same constituency are in favour of it, he is no better off than when he began. Nor do I believe in taking a vote of the constituencies, "yea or nay," on the measure, in the manner in which the people have to vote with reference to stopping the supply of intoxicating drink under the Temperance Act. (Laughter.) I go for the whole British constitutional mode, or nothing. I have no idea of wishing to see honourable gentlemen going round among their constituents, knocking at every door, and asking: Do you go Confederation? (Laughter.)

Campbell: My honourable friend [Walter Dickson] says, "If there is to be delay, let it be a substantial delay; let it be such a delay as will ensure a dissolution of parliament; such a delay as will enable the people to speak in that manner, and in that manner only, that is known to the British Constitution." I can respect that sentiment . . . But, honourable gentlemen, contrast

that view with the idea suggested by the honourable gentleman [James Currie] . . . What does the honourable gentleman say? He says, give us twenty days or a month.

Currie: I said that was the least time I would ask.

> *"If you adopt the British constitutional way, then there will have to be a dissolution of parliament; but if you adopt the American system, the people will be called upon to vote 'yea or nay' on the scheme as it stands."*

Campbell: What could be done with twenty days or a month's delay? The honourable gentleman knows very well that it is not possible, and that under no system of government could such a plan, as his mind has suggested, by any possibility be sanctioned by the legislature. Would the people of New York State, or any of the states of the union, sanction a proceeding of that kind? On the contrary, they would adopt the course at once of having the scheme submitted to a direct vote of the people.

If you adopt the British constitutional way, then there will have to be a dissolution of parliament; but if you adopt the American system, the people will be called upon to vote "yea or nay" on the scheme as it stands. Let it be expressed in one way or the other, fairly and constitutionally, in accordance with our system of government . . . I am sorry that my honourable friend [Dickson] who spoke last should have felt himself called upon to adopt a scheme so entirely contrary to what I know are his views as to what is correct and proper, according to those constitutional and British views which he entertains.

Dickson: I have always held that a general election was the proper constitutional mode of learning the people's views, and I distinctly stated that I did not care to have a short delay.

Currie: All I suggested was that the government might at least give twenty days or a month, if they would grant no more.

Campbell: My honourable friend [Dickson] is charged with the duty of representing his constituency on the floor of this house, and it is to be supposed that he is well capable of representing them in point of intellect and good judgement when he is called upon to say whether or not he believes the scheme, as a whole, to be a desirable one for the country. (Hear, hear.) But he seems to ignore all that. He does not seem willing to pronounce his judgement upon this scheme. He will not say that it is so objectionable that he will vote against it on the merits of the case. If he is unable to come to a decision, he ought to resign his position and

give place to someone who can come to a decision. But look at the position of a man who says, in effect, "I have no opinion of my own; if the people whom I represent are favourable to the scheme, I have not a word to say; I will vote for it to please them, though I disapprove of it."

Gentlemen, let him give his constituency the benefit of his best judgement and consider whether, reflecting upon the fact that there are five different provinces to be consulted, and constituencies upon constituencies to be canvassed, that which he desires can be ascertained in any better way than by this house, considering itself a fair representation of the sentiment of Canada, coming to an immediate decision.

It is painful to me that any honourable gentleman, who professes a desire to advance the union, should yet shelter himself, in opposing it, under an objection to some of the details. Does my honourable friend seriously propose to submit to the country all those various details?* Can he imagine that he could get an intelligent expression from any part of the country on those details? All he could get would be a general opinion in favour of Confederation, and we are all satisfied that he would have that. I believe there are but two or three honourable members in this house who are really opposed to Confederation. Take ten thousand people from the country, and you will find nine thousand of every ten in favour of Confederation.

Well, gentlemen, it being granted that we are all in favour of union, how are the details to be settled? Is it possible that the nearly four millions of people who compose the provinces to be affected by the union should meet together *en masse* and settle those details? It is not possible, and those who argue that the scheme should originate with the people know very well that it is not possible. Well, then could the parliaments of all these provinces assemble together and agree upon a scheme of Confederation? Look at the difficulties that we have to encounter on every point of the details in carrying the scheme through this house . . . There is no other practicable way than that delegates should meet together as they have done and frame resolutions on the subject, upon which the act constituting the union could be founded.

My honourable friend [Currie] contemplates delay until there

> *"Well, gentlemen, it being granted that we are all in favour of union, how are the details to be settled? Is it possible that the nearly four millions of people who compose the provinces to be affected by the union should meet together* en masse *and settle those details? It is not possible, and those who argue that the scheme should originate with the people know very well that it is not possible."*

---

* Campbell here makes the best argument against consulting the electorate.
— PR

shall be an expression of the people taken through a dissolution of parliament. Well now, how can a dissolution of parliament be brought about in a constitutional manner?* Suppose this scheme to receive the support of an immense majority of the lower house, as it plainly does, and also of a large majority in this house, how, I would ask, under our system of government, can a dissolution be brought about? A dissolution is unknown to the British Constitution, as carried out in this province, except when a measure, originated by the government, does not receive the support of parliament. Receiving the support of more than two-thirds of the representatives of the people, as the present government does, how is it possible that parliament could be dissolved to suit the views of a small minority? That is asking quite too much, even if it were possible to grant it. (Hear, hear.) What, therefore, do honourable gentlemen ask when they ask that the scheme be submitted to the people? They ask us as a government to leave that which we consider the safe, sound British constitutional mode of procedure and resort to the American system of obtaining assent to constitutional alterations, by taking the votes, yea and nay, of the individual members of the whole community.

Is it possible that any honourable member of this house desires that the people should have the opportunity of saying yea or nay to each clause of these resolutions? What conclusion then can we arrive at, but that those who oppose the passage of the scheme through this house, by moving and supporting amendments to it, are desirous of defeating it, and make those amendments for that purpose? (Hear, hear.)

A. Vidal: The honourable gentleman [Christie] made the remark that we were not altering the constitution, but that the question before us was one simply for an address to the crown. Now, strictly speaking, this statement is correct; but I ask honourable gentlemen if it is fair or candid to endeavour to lead the house to believe that this motion, which is undoubtedly for an address, is not in effect for a change in the constitution? Are we not plainly told that no imperial legislation will take place on this subject unless such an address as this receives the assent of the Canadian

---

Perhaps by the assembly, as the house affected, asking the governor general to do it. It might be a novelty, but Campbell's argument — that what has never been done can never be done — would preclude all constitutional innovation. — PR

legislature? I hold, therefore, that the motion before us, though it be for an address to Her Majesty, is in effect a measure, which has for its object a change of the constitution.

How singular are the different views which are taken of our position and powers according to the manner in which we may vote upon this question! In one breath we are told that we are the representatives of the people and we have a perfect right to vote upon it as we may see fit; and in a few minutes afterwards, we are informed that if we do not vote upon it in a certain manner, we do not represent the people. I cannot possibly reconcile the two statements.

— *Legislative Council, February 17, 1865*

"Some of the speakers, imbued with democratic-republican ideas, have gone so far as to deny one of the most essential and fundamental principles of the British Constitution — that is to say, that the parliament may change the constitution without special appeals to the electoral body, and without recourse to popular conventions. It is evident that they wish to lead us towards a social republic."

Joseph Cauchon: Some of the speakers, imbued with democratic-republican ideas, have gone so far as to deny one of the most essential and fundamental principles of the British Constitution — that is to say, that the parliament may change the constitution without special appeals to the electoral body, and without recourse to popular conventions. It is evident that they wish to lead us towards a social republic, government, and legislation in full force. The Roman armies in the days of the decadence of the empire made and unmade emperors; but it never occurred to them to make laws and administer affairs of state. This had to be reserved to our republicans, who are against Confederation because they desire annexation to the United States, and who raise all kinds of obstacles in order to attain their end. (Hear, hear.)

Here there are useless debates provoked in order to kill time; there, petitions covered with false signatures or names obtained under false pretences; and the forlorn hope of democracy, who in the streets threaten with riots and gibbets all who wish for the union of the provinces, and thereby, in its time, constitutional monarchy and parliamentary government. (Hear, hear.) But for those who, like myself, move in another circle of ideas, who have other aspirations, and who are unwilling to accept on any condition their share of a debt of three thousand millions, and an annual burden of five hundred millions of dollars; for those the theory and practice of English constitutional law alone possess attractions. (Hear, hear.)

It is therefore in the parliamentary history of Great Britain, and not in that of American institutions, that I shall seek a rule of conduct to guide me under the circumstances. In 1717 the British

soil was invaded by the Pretender.* The Tories, who were not in power, but who wanted to rise to it precisely like the honourable members in opposition whom I see before me, exclaimed, like them, that the church and religion of the country were in danger. Observe well the similarity. These Tories wished to elevate a Catholic prince to the throne. (Laughter.) The Whigs, who held the government, and who saw in the approaching election the certainty of the downfall of the reigning dynasty, determined to prolong the existence of the parliament for four years more without an appeal to the people. Their adversaries exclaimed, as do ours today, about violation of the constitution, and accused them of evading, by violent means, an appeal to the people, to maintain themselves in power.

Setting aside . . . extraordinary circumstances which demanded extraordinary remedies, we assert that parliament in its integrity has power to alter the constitution and even the succession to the throne.† As to us, we do not propose to go so far; we simply ask the imperial parliament to give us a new constitution, and even that parliament will only with our consent make use of that power which it has a right to exercise without our con-

---

*The reference is to the abortive Jacobite rising in 1715 against the new Hanoverian dynasty of George I. The Pretender was James Stuart, son of James II, who had been driven off the throne in 1688 on account of his Catholicism. A number of Tories supported the treasonous attempt to bring back the Stuarts, and thereby condemned themselves to many years in the political wilderness. — IG

The invasion, actually in December 1715, was aimed at placing the son of the deposed James II on the throne. This son, James, became known as the Old Pretender, to distinguish him from his son Charles, the Young Pretender, who made his own bid for the throne thirty years later. The rising of 1715 was quickly suppressed and the government exploited it by carrying the Septennial Act of 1716, which required a general election to be held every seven years as opposed to the triennial elections that had been instituted by an act of 1694. Like James Johnston of Nova Scotia, Cauchon here invokes rather antiquated precedents to justify his reluctance to refer the issue of Confederation to the electorate. James O'Halloran cogently criticizes his position below. — PR

† The English parliment did so in 1689 when it recognized William III and Mary II as joint monarchs and adopted the Bill of Rights, which sharply curtailed the powers of monarchy. This was the so-called Glorious Revolution that John Locke, William Blackstone, and Edmond Burke so greatly admired. — IG

Confederation Day: Parade of the 13th Hussars in Toronto. The picture shows the cover of a military dance, "The Welcome Galop," composed in the regiment's honour. The 13th Hussars are famous as the "Noble Six Hundred" who, in the words of Tennyson, "rode into the valley of death" at Balaclava in the Crimean War.

⭆•⭇

"Our constitution is constructed upon the model of the British Constitution, and . . . members do not and cannot receive an imperative order from their electors. Each representative, although elected by one particular county, represents the whole country, and his legislative responsibility extends to the whole of it."

⭆•⭇

sent. (Hear, hear.) Let it be observed, Mr. Speaker, that I am only considering now the question of power and right; the question of what is fit and expedient is quite another matter. We might do well or we might do ill by taking this course, but as we act in our capacity of representatives of the people, it is for us to decide whether it is expedient or advantageous that an appeal should be had to the people under the circumstances . . .

In closing, Mr. Speaker, I may be allowed to say to the house that in a debate of such a solemn character, and when such great destinies as regards the future of the whole of British North America are at stake within these walls, let us have the courage to rise superior to passions, hatreds, personal enmities, and a miserable spirit of party,* in order to allow our minds to soar more freely in the larger sphere of generous sentiments, and of great and noble national aspirations. We possess all that we want — all the necessary elements of greatness and prosperity to found an empire in America. Let us boldly set to work, sheltered by the flag and protected by the powerful aegis of the empire which leads us on to undertake the task. (Prolonged applause.) †

— *Legislative Assembly, March 2, 1865*

Cauchon: Our constitution is constructed upon the model of the British Constitution, and . . . members do not and cannot receive an imperative order from their electors. Each representative, although elected by one particular county, represents the whole country, and his legislative responsibility extends to the whole of it. If, there, I am convinced that any legislative measure presented by the government or by a member of this house is of a nature to save Lower Canada, I must vote for that measure, even though my constituents are opposed to it. My electors might punish me afterwards, but they could not impose upon me duties which I

---

*Here is a ringing declaration of the principle of unity that underlies all modern liberal democratic rule, a statement to be engraved over the doors of every parliament. — WDG

† The debate of March 2 is marked by a stunning number of references to constitutional authorities. The speakers attempt to anchor the constitutional changes they are effecting firmly within the British tradition of constitutional monarchy, while painting the opponents of the scheme as apologists for violent, anarchic republicanism of the sort found in the United States, France, and ancient Rome. Revolutionary republicanism, they hold, always begins with appeals to human rights, but invariably ends in bloodshed and tyranny. — IG

consider to be entirely beyond their jurisdiction and to relate to the very constitution of the country. (Hear, hear.)

— *Legislative Assembly, March 6, 1865*

"You, sir, and I were sent here to make laws, not legislatures. We were sent here to work out the constitution of this country — not to undermine and destroy it."

James O'Halloran: [I]f I had any hesitation in pronouncing on the merits of this scheme, I might have taken a preliminary exception to the jurisdiction of this house to pass this measure. You, sir, and I were sent here to make laws, not legislatures. (Hear, hear.) We were sent here to work out the constitution of this country* — not to undermine and destroy it. There is not an elector from Gaspé to Sarnia, however humble he may be, who has not just as much right to pronounce upon this question as you and I have. Therefore, if it were my wish to shirk this question, which it is not, I could justify myself by saying it was no part of my mandate, or of the compact between me and those who sent me here. When we assume the power to deal with this question, to change the whole system of government, to effect a revolution, peaceful though it be, without reference to the will of the people of this country, we arrogate to ourselves a right never conferred upon us, and our act is a usurpation.†

We are not living today in a time of revolution or of great emergency; but, even if our circumstances were different, I doubt very much if any of the precedents that have been referred to, as having occurred many years ago and in troublous times, could again be practised or adopted, even in England, from which country we draw all our precedents. The precedents which have been invoked in approval of the course that has been adopted by the government prove too much. If they form a justification for the course we are pursuing, then you might prove by the same means that this house had the power to perpetuate its existence beyond the limit fixed for the termination of the present parliament or vote ourselves members for life. We might just as well constitute ourselves life members of the federal legislature of the proposed confederacy as to take the action that is contemplated.

---

* *He probably means "work" (i.e., operate) the existing constitution rather than "work out" a new one. After all, the house had been elected in 1863, before the prospect of a new constitution arose. — PR*

† *This is the most concise summary of the claim that the act of representation in a liberal democracy, regardless of how well supported by the law and custom of a people, breaks the underlying trust inherent in the principle of representation itself if used to radically alter the terms of the initial trust. — WDG*

I know that it is represented as very important that the measure should be carried into immediate operation; but that is a matter of mere expediency and has nothing to do with constitutional principles. (Hear, hear.) The Irish union has been triumphantly referred to as a precedent for this measure. To my mind it is a most unfortunate one and little deserving of our imitation. Let me show you how this matter has been regarded by one whose authority will not be disputed. I read from May's *Constitutional History of England*,* page 505 of the 2nd volume. Speaking of the union of Ireland with England, he says:

> A great end was compassed by means the most base and shameless. Grattan, Lord Charlemont, Ponsonby, Plunkett, and a few patriots continued to protest against the sale of the liberties and free constitution of Ireland. Their eloquence and public virtue command the respect of posterity; but the wretched history of their country denies them its sympathy.

This, sir, is the judgement of the impartial English historian upon the means by which this great national crime[†] was consummated, and it is the just encomium on the noble few whose patriotic efforts failed to prevent it. I read it, in anticipation, as the future history of the wrong now about to be perpetrated on the people of this country; and while it implies, on the one hand, in no doubtful terms, the well-merited praise of the small band who stand here tonight for the rights of the people, in opposition to this scheme, it pronounces, on the other, the just condemnation of those who trample on those rights and who

---

* *Thomas Erskine May,* The Constitutional History of England since the Accession of George Third, 1760–1860, *2 vols. (Boston: Crosby & Nichols, 1863). What O'Halloran omits to mention is that a few pages later, May gives a very upbeat opinion on the consequences of the union: "Freedom, equality, and honor have been the fruits of the union and Ireland has exchanged an enslaved nationality for a glorious incorporation with the first empire of the world." — IG*

† *The union of Ireland with Britain was imposed by the British government in 1800 and involved the extinction of the parliament of Ireland. It was hardly analogous with the proposed union of the British North American provinces, since the latter was not being imposed by Britain. Moreover, under Confederation, the colonial assemblies would continue to exercise important powers as provincial legislatures. — IG*

*"Of the press . . .
I must say that the
moment they were
relieved from the
necessity of supporting
party manoeuvres —
the moment a subject
of sufficient
importance was
submitted for
consideration — they
seem to have risen at
once to the level of the
subject and to have
abandoned all those
unhappy and rancorous
personalities which, in
times past, were too
apt to disfigure
their pages."*

forget, in the pride of their brief authority, who it was that raised them to the positions they occupy, not that they might coerce, but carry out the will of the people, the only rightful source of all political power. (Cheers.)

— *Legislative Assembly, March 8, 1865*

Richard Cartwright: Ever since this project has been fairly before us, a very marked improvement has taken place in the whole tone and temper of public discussion. Of the press, in particular, I must say that the moment they were relieved from the necessity of supporting party manoeuvres — the moment a subject of sufficient importance was submitted for consideration — they seem to have risen at once to the level of the subject and to have abandoned all those unhappy and rancorous personalities which, in times past, were too apt to disfigure their pages.

Sir, I believe the people of Canada have learned a lesson which they will not easily forget. I believe that henceforward it will not be found so easy to array citizen against citizen, race against race, as it has been heretofore. I believe our people have discovered that men who rise to be the heads of great parties are not of necessity villains and scoundrels — that both sides may have great political principles to maintain — that the words Reformer and Revolutionist, Conservative and Corruptionist, are not absolutely convertible terms, and that men who have given up the best part of their lives, and sacrificed too often the best part of their fortunes in the service of their country, have had some better and higher reasons than mere love of jobbery and intrigue for doing so. To me, sir, this appears a matter of great moment. It is only too notorious how much of the misery and misfortune which has befallen the United States is to be traced to the systematic degradation of the public men.

It is well for us that the matter is still in our own power. It is well for us that we have still the choice whether we will have statesmen or stump orators* to rule over us — whether this house shall maintain its honourable position as the representatives of a free people, or whether it shall sink into a mere mob of delegates,

*"It is well for us that
the matter is still in our
own power. It is well for
us that we have still the
choice whether we will
have statesmen or stump
orators to rule over us
— whether this house
shall maintain its
honourable position as
the representatives of a
free people, or whether
it shall sink into a mere
mob of delegates, the
nominees of caucuses
and of wire-pullers."*

---

* Can Cartwright really be saying that speakers in parliament ("statesmen") are superior in intelligence and character to speakers in the arena of public debate ("stump orators")? Surely not; he knew of course that everyone in parliament had to win his seat by stumping the country. Moreover, he clearly believes public discussion of political affairs is crucial. Unless informed by debate

the nominees of caucuses and of wire-pullers.* It is still in our power to decide whether we shall secure a fair share of the best talent we possess to carry on the affairs of the country, or whether we will ostracize from our councils every man of superior ability, education, or intelligence.

J.-B.-E. Dorion: I do not mean to repeat what has been said during the debate; but before proceeding, I may be allowed to draw a contrast between our manner of acting and that of our neighbours in the United States when constitutional changes are in question. In the United States — that country which people take so much pains to represent as the hotbed of all political, social, moral, and physical horrors — they do not play with the written constitutions of the several states any more than with that of the American union.

There, whenever a constitution is to be amended, generally, it requires a vote of two-thirds of each of the two houses. If it is the constitution of the United States which is to be amended, the

---

among the populace at large and by a free press, parliament's decisions will be less satisfactory. Nevertheless, parliament must have the final word. Why? Although Cartwright doesn't fill out the argument, let me suggest how it goes. Stump oratory is appropriate in its place — on the hustings — where it mobilizes and canvasses popular opinion. But once in parliament, stump orators must begin to act like statesmen. The formal rules of parliamentary debate encourage legislators to take the jumble of noisy, particular opinions that surface in an election and make of them a statesmanlike program in the public interest. All will go well as long as the press and public don't try to usurp parliament's role, and parliamentarians don't resort to shouting matches as if they were still on the campaign trail. Cartwright's is the best argument so far against the appeal to the people. But see J.-B.-E. Dorion's response. — JA

* Cartwright expresses the fear that delegation leads to sectionalism and factions, to hundreds of particular interests warring with each other, resulting in no common good. Today, when democracy has become so universally and uncritically idealized, we forget that this was not the case in 1867. For example, Prime Minister Disraeli in his speech introducing the 1867 Reform Bill assured his fellow members of parliament: "It will never be the fate of this country to live under a democracy." Britain's Fraser's Magazine *summed up this common feeling in an 1832 article on democracy when it opined that about democracy, "we read one convincing tale, the despotism of the many occasioning the misery of all, and terminated by the absolute power of the few. It is repeated from Athens to Bogota." — WDG*

measure must also be sanctioned by a majority in each of the legislatures of the several states. If the amendment relates to a local constitution, besides a two-thirds vote of the two houses, the amendment must be ratified by a convention of delegates from the different parties in the state, selected specially for the occasion. The United States are now occupied with the consideration of an amendment of their constitution, the object of which is the abolition of slavery. The amendment has been adopted by the Congress and by the Senate of the American union, and must be ratified by a majority of the local legislatures before it forms a part of the constitution. It will even be necessary to take into the account the states which are now in rebellion. We see at once the guarantees they are provided with, that no radical change shall be adopted without the consent of the people, who are allowed sufficient time to weigh all the considerations which may operate in favour of any projected change. This is the method of proceeding among our sagacious neighbours in matters of importance; and, as a thing of course, they have established a political status which leaves far behind it all that human wisdom had previously devised to secure the peace and prosperity of the nations of the New World.

But in our dear Canada, with all the English precedents of which so much account is made, we do not require such precautions. It is quite enough that men should have been found guilty of misapplication of the public money, that they shall have abused each other as political robbers for ten years, to bring about a coalition of the combatants, to make them hug each other till all feeling of personal dignity is lost and all regard for principle is forgotten. It is enough, I say, that we have a scandalous union — a state of political profligacy — like that perpetrated in 1864, to believe in our right to do what we please. (Hear, hear.)

With a majority of thirty or forty votes, we hesitate at nothing. The constitution, which hampers the curvetings and prancings of our leading chiefs too much, and rather curbs their personal ambition — which circumscribes in short the range of their speculative operations — is found to be inconvenient. It is assailed with relentless blows; it is to be thrown down without asking the leave of those most concerned; and in its place is to be set up a new order of things under which there is to be no more regard for political principles than for the rights and wants of the people. A simple parliamentary majority of one will be sufficient with us to overthrow the entire political order of things, and we have no appeal from so important a decision, save an appeal to an authority three

> *"The constitution, which hampers the curvetings and prancings of our leading chiefs too much, and rather curbs their personal ambition — which circumscribes in short the range of their speculative operations — is found to be inconvenient. It is assailed with relentless blows; it is to be thrown down without asking the leave of those most concerned; and in its place is to be set up a new order of things under which there is to be no more regard for political principles than for the rights and wants of the people."*

thousand miles off, which may add something to the scheme to make it less acceptable to us than it already is. (Hear, hear.) The people may hereafter condemn their representatives, but the mischief will be done! This is all the consolation we shall have. Is not the contrast between our stupid method of doing things, and the prudent rational proceeding of our neighbours, a very striking one? And truly they are our superiors in all political respects.

Paul Denis: I must say conscientiously what I think of the extraordinary speech which [J.-B.-E. Dorion] has just delivered. The honourable members of the opposition have, since the commencement of this debate, held one course — they have constantly appealed to the prejudices of a class* who, for the protection of their interests, uniformly depend on those who represent them here, and who, in order to make sure of their allegiance and perpetuate it, work secretly and in the dark to obtain the signatures of unsuspecting parties to petitions which they send round the country and use afterwards to ensnare the confidence of members of this house. (Hear, hear.) Fortunately, they have hitherto had but little success in their undertakings and have made but small progress in their attempts to injure us. These gentlemen make a loud outcry against the resolutions introduced by the government; but if they are as bad as they say they are, why do they not themselves prepare some remedy for the troubles and difficulties of the country, instead of limiting their exertions to cries and reproaches? But no. It is always the same thing with them. "Great cry, and little wool."

The opposition have always had but one object in view, and that was not the good of the country but the attainment of power. This has been the aim of all their actions . . . Their intention is to frighten the people . . . by enlisting prejudices of all kinds against the measure now under discussion — trying by every petty subterfuge and shabby artifice to bring back the honourable member for Hochelaga (Mr. A.-A. Dorion) to power.

— *Legislative Assembly, March 9, 1865*

---

* This member concisely pinpoints the complaint of the government and the irony in the position of the opposition: a representative who has been elected specifically to protect the interests of a large class of less capable people who are dependent on his expertise for their welfare argues against himself when he appeals to them for leadership. — WDG

J.H. Cameron: Why is Canada to be treated upon an entirely different rule from that which has been adopted in the other provinces?* The legislature of New Brunswick was dissolved in order that the people might be appealed to on this question. The honourable attorney general of Newfoundland has declared that it is the intention of the government of that colony to appeal to the people upon it, and that nothing will be done until their opinion is obtained. (Hear, hear.) In Nova Scotia, too, the government do not, as I understand, make it a government question. It is not to be put in that position, and if a difficulty arises in having it adopted by the legislature the government of Nova Scotia are prepared to dissolve their legislature too. I do not say anything about Prince Edward Island — its acceptance or rejection of the scheme would be of very small account. But their legislature will, no doubt, also be dissolved, in order that the people may have an opportunity of expressing their opinions upon it, if their House of Assembly is found hostile — a step which, no, doubt, our government would have taken if this house had shown itself hostile to the measure. Because this house is not hostile, and because ministers found themselves strong enough to carry it by a large majority, they declared they would take the course they have adopted, although in the other provinces the case has been put on an entirely different footing. (Hear, hear.)

Now, sir, let us consider why we should be placed in the same position in which the legislatures and people of the lower provinces are placed. We hear it stated on all sides of this house that the whole country is in favour of this measure. If so, why should there be any hesitation about asking the country to confirm by an election that which is so clearly advantageous and which is so sure to be carried? . . . We are arranging to adopt an entirely new state of governmental existence and are proposing to

---

* On March 10 the Legislative Assembly approved the Quebec Resolutions by a vote of 91 to 33. Now John A. Macdonald has moved that a committee be appointed to draft an address to the queen based on the resolutions, and Cameron is moving an amendment to prevent the British parliament from acting on the resolutions until a general election has been held in Canada.

Cameron makes much of the fact that the other colonial governments have handled the Quebec Resolutions differently, but of course the other governments either disliked the scheme or faced far stronger opposition in prosecuting it — all going to show that it was primarily a Canadian enterprise, undertaken for Canadian purposes. — PR

embrace a large area of country under this new form of government. We are claiming for it, and desire that it shall have its best and safest foundation in the hearts of the people. And, sir, will you not find it stronger in the hearts and more deeply rooted in the estimation of the people if you appeal to them and obtain their sanction to it and their support in carrying it out? (Hear, hear.)

In proposing that it shall have the sanction of the people, I do not contemplate the absurdity, unknown to our form of government, of asking them for a direct yea or nay upon it. No such thing as that has ever been entertained in my mind. I propose to have it done in a constitutional manner. My whole political history would have shown any man acquainted with it that there could have been no such democratic idea harboured by me as to go without the walls of the constitution in order to do an act which could be better done within it . . .

An appeal has been made to history, and it has been said that appeals to the people on questions of this kind are unknown under the British Constitution. The cases of the union between England and Scotland, of the union between Great Britain and Ireland, and of the union of the Canadas themselves have been referred to; and it has been asked if in any of those cases an appeal was made to the people, and an answer given in the negative. I am not prepared to accept that answer as altogether correct in point of fact. In the first of those cases, where resistance was perhaps the greatest, an appeal was made to the people . . .*

It has been said that [an appeal to the people]† takes away, in point of fact, from the legislature the power which the legislature has, by denying the right of the legislature to make any such change. I do not say anything against the power of the legislature. The legislature has, within the limits that are assigned to it, all the rights which its charter gives it . . . It is clear that we have not the same power as the imperial parliament — other-

> *"My whole political history would have shown any man acquainted with it that there could have been no such democratic idea harboured by me as to go without the walls of the constitution in order to do an act which could be better done within it."*

> *"I do not say anything against the power of the legislature . . . But the question is: Is it wise to give these resolutions the force of law? Is it proper to do so? Is it the most just course to take towards the people of this country, to declare that in a matter of this importance we will legislate for them, to the extent of introducing an entire change of the constitution?"*

Cameron goes on to explain, among other things, that the Scottish parliament which voted for union in 1707 had been summoned specifically to consider that matter, as had the one before it.

†*Although Cameron favours an appeal to the people for such fundamental matters, he clearly understands the ever-present threat to the entire theory of representation. Namely, once we openly acknowledge that direct control over policy lies by right with the people rather than with their representatives, the legitimacy of parliament is undermined and the whole system can be halted on any matter, however trivial. — WDG*

wise we should not be obliged to that body for its sanction of these resolutions. And there are limitations of the power of the imperial parliament itself, to which we also are subject. We cannot make any act of ours permanent, any more than we can make ourselves permanent, because another parliament has the right to repeal what we have done. We cannot of ourselves enact this measure into a law . . . But the question is: Is it wise to give these resolutions the force of law? Is it proper to do so? Is it the most just course to take towards the people of this country, to declare that in a matter of this importance we will legislate for them, to the extent of introducing an entire change of the constitution?

" I do not see why the taking of a direct vote — yea and nay — would be an unconstitutional proceeding."

M.C. Cameron: [At] this enlightened day, when the people interfere and have a right to interfere in the management of their own affairs, no such change as this should take place without their having a voice in it. I do not feel . . . that it is absolutely necessary that a dissolution of this house should take place for the purpose of obtaining an expression of the popular will. I do not see why the taking of a direct vote — yea and nay — would be an unconstitutional proceeding. (Hear, hear.) We find that in those bodies which the people are empowered to create, and which are as much representative bodies as we are, the township and county councils — whenever a debt is to be created over a certain amount, affecting the communities over which those councils exercise control — the question must first be left to the people to pronounce upon it before it can become law . . . If you force this scheme upon the people without asking for their consent, and if they wake from the apathy which they feel now, to find that they are saddled with burdens which they never contemplated, you make them opponents of the union, and worse opponents than if you asked them now whether they approved of it or not; and so you will have a dissatisfied people labouring under burdens which I fear will eventually create serious discontent throughout the length and breadth of the land. (Hear, hear.) And there is this additional reason for referring the question to the people, now that the other provinces have rejected the scheme, and I presume their governments will not dare to press it forward in opposition to the wishes of the people.

Brown: [We] have already adopted an address praying Her Majesty to pass an imperial statute giving effect to the resolutions of the Quebec Conference; and the honourable member for Peel

[J.H. Cameron] now asks that we shall pass a second address praying that the said imperial act shall be subject to the approval, and shall not be law until it obtains the approval, of their high mightynesses the 130 gentlemen who may happen to sit in the House of Assembly of the next Canadian parliament. (Hear, hear.) He would have us approach the throne saying: "May it please Your Majesty — here is the constitution which has been adopted by the governments of the five British American provinces; we declare to you that this is the new constitution we want for British America; we pray Your Majesty to give effect to it; we pray that the imperial parliament may pass an act enforcing this new constitution on all these provinces, and that Your Majesty will assent to it. But at the same time we ask Your Majesty to do this only on one condition, namely, that the legislature of Canada — not the present one, but the next legislature that may be chosen — shall have the opportunity of criticising and dissecting the work of the imperial parliament, and of kicking Your Majesty's bill out of the chamber on the first day it meets." (Hear, hear, and great laughter.) . . .

John A. Macdonald: Well, my honourable friend from Peel [J.H. Cameron] submitted that the appeal [to the people] should be made in one way, the constitutional way, and that was the way my honourable friend from North Ontario [M.C. Cameron] did not like. How could my honourable friend suppose that a vote like that could be taken in a country whose constitution is modelled on the constitution of England? By what contrivance known to our constitution could we take such a vote? There is none such. There is no means, no system, by which we could make an appeal of that kind* and in order to do it we should have to subvert the principles of the British Constitution. The honourable

---

*In this masterful speech Macdonald summarizes powerfully the central claims of the representative system as a critique of direct democracy. There is no legal precedent and no system of appeal to the people. Such an appeal would be a fundamental alteration of British constitutional principle, a repudiation of the duty to represent Her Majesty as well as the people, and would defeat the theory of power that legitimizes the whole system in the first place. Like other defenders of the government's role, he associates democracy with a tyranny whenever the passions of the people, who by definition cannot express "calm and deliberate judgements," are exploited. He is clever to argue that the threefold compound constitutional system actually protects the people — what Leatham (below) described as "the rights and property of the meanest

*"Sir, a reference to
the people — a direct
reference to the people
— of a question of this
kind may be the means
by which a despot, an
absolute monarch, may
get that popular
confirmation and
approval which he
desires for the laws
necessary to support
a continuation of his
usurpation . . . [I]n
every free country
where there is a
constitution at all,
the vote must be taken
by the constituted
authorities, the
representatives of the
people, and not become
a mere form and cover
to tyranny, but a
measure which accords
with the calm and
deliberate judgements
of the people, as
expressed through
their representatives."*

gentleman knows there is no means of doing it. We might, indeed, pass a law declaring that the people shall vote yes or no on this question; but such a law would in itself be a change in our constitution, and I would like to see any man representing Her Majesty in this country give his sanction to a measure of that kind, which would be a subversion of the first principles of British constitutional government. Sir, we in this house are representatives of the people, and not mere delegates; and to pass such a law would be robbing ourselves of the character of representatives . . .

Sir, a reference to the people — a direct reference to the people — of a question of this kind may be the means by which a despot, an absolute monarch, may get that popular confirmation and approval which he desires for the laws necessary to support a continuation of his usurpation. It may be the means by which a despot, at the point of the bayonet, may ask the people to vote yea or nay on the measure he proposes; but in every free country where there is a constitution at all, the vote must be taken by the constituted authorities, the representatives of the people, and not become a mere form and cover to tyranny,* but a measure which accords with the calm and deliberate judgements of the people, as expressed through their representatives. (Hear, hear.) . . .

---

subject in the realm" — better than pure democracy. In other words, Canada's mixed system is a higher form of democracy than the one proposed by the democrats themselves. — WDG

*Macdonald is not saying merely that referendums are inappropriate because they are not in line with British tradition. He makes the far stronger claim that referendums lead to tyranny and are especially dangerous in "a question of this kind," that is, in constitution making. We must take this argument seriously.

It makes several claims. First, parliament represents everyone; a vote in parliament speaks for the "calm and deliberate judgements of the people." Thus no further appeal to the people is necessary. Second, the rules of parliamentary debate offer the best formula for rising above bias. Parliament's formal process of deliberation and decision making keeps tempers cool and militates against statements of prejudice. In short, parliament should have the last word in constitution making because it is the authoritative body that represents all, and it is committed to respect for all in constitutional law.

He rejects constitution making by referendum because it makes a party or faction sovereign. I suggested above that Cartwright rejects the appeal to the people because he thinks it will result in a jumble of competitive and biased demands. Macdonald's view is a little different. He is afraid that one faction

Now what is the opinion entertained upon this subject in England? I was exceedingly pleased to read lately the report of a speech delivered to his constituents, at Huddersfield, by Mr. Leatham, a member of the imperial parliament. He is, I believe, a brother-in-law of Mr. John Bright and belongs to the advanced liberal school of English politicians, known as the Manchester School;* and although educated in the political doctrines of that school he yet had the courage to get up before the people of Huddersfield, as radical a constituency as any in all England, and spoke in strong language against the Permissive Bill, a temperance measure . . . because he held that it was unconstitutional to hand over to the people the power of voting directly upon a law before it came into effect. Allow me to read to the house the language employed by Mr. Leatham† . . . It is not long, and it seems to me exceedingly instructive. *The Times*, in an article on the speech, says:

> Mr. Leatham's argument on this subject is well worthy of attention, not only for its bearing on the question of compulsory temperance, but from the much wider range of subjects to which it is applicable. "It is," he says, "the essence of representative government that the electing class, which is analogous to the class paying rates, shall possess no direct legislative power; and the principle of parliamentary representation is

---

or perhaps one person ("the despot") will rise triumphant out of the jumble of demands, a faction or person that claims to speak for everyone but in fact represents at best the majority of the moment. Thus in Macdonald's mind the choice is between constitution making by a faction and constitution making by a body representing all. To allow a faction to make the constitution is to condone the constitutional subordination of some to others. Such subordination in law is tyranny.

Is Macdonald's the better argument? It is not an insubstantial one. It does not of course originate with him, as he would admit; it has its source in the constitutional historians and authorities cited so often in this debate. — JA

* *Bright (1811–1889) was the Quaker pacifist MP from Manchester and Birmingham. He was a leader of the Manchester School, a political grouping which favoured free trade and laissez-faire principles. In conformity with this libertarian philosophy, he also opposed the privileges of the Established Church of England, and legislation limiting the hours of adult workers in the textile factories. In 1866 he favoured extending the vote to all adult male householders, but he was never a true democrat. — IG*

† *William Henry Leatham, MP (1815–1889).*

that not even the representative principle shall alone legislate. We have taken the precaution to protect the rights and property of Englishmen by the prerogatives of the crown, the privileges of the lords, and the authority of a representative assembly. All these constitute the threefold and invaluable shelter which we have raised over the rights and property of the meanest subject in the realm. But here is a proposition which, with naked and revolutionary simplicity, proposes to intrust the property and maintenance of the rights of a large class of persons to diminutive, homogeneous, democratic, and irresponsible parliaments set up all over the country, in place of a central, responsible, compound, and constitutional one. It seems to me that this strikes at the root of a constitutional and representative system."

"Why, sir, for what do we come to this house, if it is not because we are supposed to be convinced by argument, if it is not that we are to sit down together and compare notes and discuss the questions that may come before us, and to be convinced according to the force of the reasons that may be advanced for or against them?"

These, sir, are the words used by an advanced reformer, a member of one of the most advanced schools of politicians in England. They are words of wisdom and ought to rest with weight on the mind of every admirer of representative institutions who does not wish to see those institutions degraded in this country and representation become mere delegation. (Hear, hear.) Why, sir, for what do we come to this house, if it is not because we are supposed to be convinced by argument, if it is not that we are to sit down together and compare notes and discuss the questions that may come before us, and to be convinced according to the force of the reasons that may be advanced for or against them? And if we are honest, conscientious men, we change our opinions as we become convinced that that which we held before was wrong and the opposite right. But if the other doctrine obtains, that we are not representatives but delegates, we might as well meet here and pass measures without any discussion whatever, every man voting according to the instructions of the commission which he holds in his pocket from his constituents. (Hear, hear.) . . . The small paragraph I have read from Mr. Leatham's speech contains very shortly the wisdom of ages, and I might appeal, if further testimony were required, to all the great men who have acted on the political stage of England. Mr. Pitt scouted at the idea;* and it was never countenanced by any of the great public men of England . . .

---

* *William Pitt the Younger, who was prime minister of Britain for most of the last two decades of the eighteenth century, campaigned vigorously but*

My honourable friend [J.H. Cameron] refers us to the language of the Constitutional Act* to show how limited our constitution is; but by that act we are empowered, in the widest language that could be employed, to make laws for the peace, welfare, and good government of the people of Canada. There could be no larger powers conferred upon us, and although it is quite true that our political existence is only statutory . . . yet this is equally true — that we stand, with regard to the people of Canada, precisely in the same position as the House of Commons in England stands with regard to the people of England. (Hear, hear.) And no man who values representative government would consent to sit here under a less extensive commission — no man will get up and disclaim the possession of such powers. But my honourable friend says we can only pass resolutions and cannot change our constitution except by addressing the sovereign, praying her to give them effect through the imperial parliament; and he argues from this that we ought to go to the people and have a new parliament to do it. A new parliament can, however, do nothing more than we can do.†

Sir, I believe in my conscience that this house, more than any house since 1841, represents truly and faithfully the people of Canada. If the members of this house do not represent the country — all its interests, classes, and communities — it never has been represented. (Hear, hear.) If we represent the people of Canada, then, in the words of the Constitutional Act, we are here

> *"Sir, I believe in my conscience that this house, more than any house since 1841, represents truly and faithfully the people of Canada. If the members of this house do not represent the country — all its interests, classes, and communities — it never has been represented. If we represent the people of Canada, then, in the words of the Constitutional Act, we are here to pass laws for the peace, welfare, and good government of the country . . . If we do not represent the people of Canada, we have no right to be here. But if we do represent them . . . we have a right to go to the foot of the throne and declare that we believe it to be for the peace, welfare, and good government of the people of Canada to form of these provinces one empire, presenting an unbroken and undaunted front to every foe."*

unsuccessfully for reforms that would have made parliament more representative of the people. In frustration he once exclaimed, "This House is not the representative of the people of Great Britain; it is the representative of nominal boroughs, of ruined and exterminated towns, of noble families, of wealthy individuals, of foreign potentates." (Quoted in Theodore F.T. Plucknett, Taswell-Langmead's English Constitutional History, 11th ed. [London: Sweet & Maxwell 1960], 564.) — IG

* He means the Union Act of 1840.

† Can Macdonald mean this seriously? His entire argument against holding a general election is specious because — like everyone on his side of the question — he simply chants the mantra of constitutional precedent, ignoring the argument for treating Confederation as a special case. But he can hardly have supposed that his opponents thought a general election necessary in order to augment the constitutional powers of the legislature as distinct from investing it with the moral authority of a mandate to act in the matter. — PR

to pass laws for the peace, welfare, and good government of the country . . . If we do not represent the people of Canada, we have no right to be here. But if we do represent them . . . we have a right to go to the foot of the throne and declare that we believe it to be for the peace, welfare, and good government of the people of Canada to form of these provinces one empire, presenting an unbroken and undaunted front to every foe; and if we do not think we have this right, we are unworthy of the commission we have received from the people of Canada. (Hear, hear, and cheers.)

— *Legislative Assembly, March 13, 1865*

THE QUEBEC RESOLUTIONS

Report of resolutions adopted at a conference of delegates from the provinces of Canada, Nova Scotia, and New Brunswick, and the colonies of Newfoundland and Prince Edward Island, held at the city of Quebec, October 10, 1864, as the basis of a proposed confederation of those provinces and colonies.

1. The best interests and present and future prosperity of British North America will be promoted by a federal union under the crown of Great Britain, provided such union can be effected on principles just to the several provinces.

2. In the federation of British North American provinces, the system of government best adapted under existing circumstances to protect the diversified interests of the several provinces and secure efficiency, harmony, and permanency in the working of the union would be a general government charged with matters of common interest to the whole country, and local governments for each of the Canadas and for the provinces of Nova Scotia, New Brunswick, and Prince Edward Island, charged with the control of local matters in their respective sections. Provision being made for the admission into the union on equitable terms of Newfoundland, the North-West Territory, British Columbia, and Vancouver.

3. In framing a constitution for the general government, the conference, with a view to the perpetuation of our connection with the mother country and to the promotion of the best interests of the people of these provinces, desire[s] to follow the model of the British Constitution, so far as our circumstances will permit.

4. The executive authority or government shall be vested in the sovereign of the United Kingdom of Great Britain and Ireland, and be administered according to the well-understood principles of the British Constitution by the sovereign personally or by the representative of the sovereign duly authorized.

5. The sovereign or representative of the sovereign shall be commander-in-chief of the land and naval militia forces.

6. There shall be a general legislature or parliament for the federated provinces, composed of a Legislative Council and a House of Commons.

7. For the purpose of forming the Legislative Council, the federated provinces shall be considered as consisting of three divisions: 1st, Upper Canada; 2nd, Lower Canada; 3rd, Nova Scotia, New Brunswick, and Prince Edward Island, each division with an equal representation in the Legislative Council.

8. Upper Canada shall be represented in the Legislative Council by twenty-four members, Lower Canada by twenty-four members, and the three Maritime provinces by twenty-four Members, of which Nova Scotia shall have ten, New Brunswick ten, and Prince Edward Island four members.

9. The colony of Newfoundland shall be entitled to enter the proposed union, with a representation in the Legislative Council of four members.

10. The North-West Territory, British Columbia, and Vancouver shall be admitted into the union on such terms and conditions as the parliament of the federated provinces shall deem equitable, and as shall receive the assent of Her Majesty; and in the case of the province of British Columbia or Vancouver, as shall be agreed to by the legislature of such province.

11. The members of the Legislative Council shall be appointed by the crown under the great seal of the general government and shall hold office during life; if any legislative councillor shall, for two consecutive sessions of parliament, fail to give his attendance in the said council, his seat shall thereby become vacant.

12. The members of the Legislative Council shall be British subjects by birth or naturalization, of the full age of thirty years, shall possess a continuous real property qualification of four thousand dollars over and above all incumbrances, and shall be and continue worth that sum over and above their debts and liabilities, but in the case of Newfoundland and Prince Edward Island, the property may be either real or personal.

13. If any question shall arise as to the qualification of a legislative councillor, the same shall be determined by the council.

14. The first selection of the members of the Legislative Council shall be made, except as regards Prince Edward Island, from the Legislative Councils of the various provinces, so far as a sufficient number be found qualified and willing to serve; such members shall be appointed by the crown at the recommendation of the general executive government, upon the nomination of the respective local governments, and in such nomination

due regard shall be had to the claims of the members of the Legislative Council of the opposition in each province, so that all political parties may as nearly as possible be fairly represented.

15. The Speaker of the Legislative Council (unless otherwise provided by parliament) shall be appointed by the crown from among the members of the Legislative Council, and shall hold office during pleasure, and shall only be entitled to a casting vote on an equality of votes.

16. Each of the twenty-four legislative councillors representing Lower Canada in the Legislative Council of the general legislature shall be appointed to represent one of the twenty-four electoral divisions mentioned in schedule A of chapter first of the Consolidated Statutes of Canada, and such councillor shall reside, or possess his qualification, in the division he is appointed to represent.

17. The basis of representation in the House of Commons shall be population, as determined by the official census every ten years; and the number of members at first shall be 194, distributed as follows:

Upper Canada	82
Lower Canada	65
Nova Scotia	19
New Brunswick	15
Newfoundland	8
and Prince Edward Island	5

18. Until the official census of 1871 has been made up, there shall be no change in the number of representatives from the several sections.

19. Immediately after the completion of the census of 1871, and immediately after every decennial census thereafter, the representation from each section in the House of Commons shall be readjusted on the basis of population.

20. For the purpose of such readjustments, Lower Canada shall always be assigned sixty-five members, and each of the

other sections shall at each readjustment receive, for the ten years then next succeeding, the number of members to which it will be entitled on the same ratio of representation to population as Lower Canada will enjoy according to the census last taken by having sixty-five members.

21. No reduction shall be made in the number of members returned by any section, unless its population shall have decreased, relatively to the population of the whole union, to the extent of five per centum.

22. In computing at each decennial period the number of members to which each section is entitled, no fractional parts shall be considered, unless when exceeding one half the number entitling to a member, in which case a member shall be given for each such fractional part.

23. The legislature of each province shall divide such province into the proper number of constituencies and define the boundaries of each of them.

24. The local legislature of each province may from time to time alter the electoral districts for the purposes of representation in the House of Commons and distribute the representatives to which the province is entitled in any manner such legislature may think fit.

25. The number of members may at any time be increased by the general parliament, regard being had to the proportionate rights then existing.

26. Until provisions are made by the general parliament, all the laws which, at the date of the proclamation constituting the union, are in force in the provinces, respectively, relating to the qualification and disqualification of any person to be elected or to sit or vote as a member of the Assembly in the said provinces, respectively, and relating to the qualification or disqualification of voters and to the oaths to be taken by voters, and to returning officers and their powers and duties, and

relating to the proceedings at elections and to the period during which such elections may be continued, and relating to the trial of controverted elections and the proceedings incident thereto, and relating to the vacating of seats of members and to the issuing and execution of new writs in case of any seat being vacated otherwise than by a dissolution, shall respectively apply to elections of members to serve in the House of Commons, for places situate in those provinces respectively.

27. Every House of Commons shall continue for five years from the day of the return of the writs choosing the same, and no longer, subject, nevertheless, to be sooner prorogued or dissolved by the governor.

28. There shall be a session of the general parliament once at least in every year, so that a period of twelve calendar months shall not intervene between the last sitting of the general parliament in one session and the first sitting thereof in the next session.

29. The general parliament shall have power to make laws for the peace, welfare, and good government of the federated provinces (saving the sovereignty of England), and especially laws respecting the following subjects:

    1. The public debt and property.
    2. The regulation of trade and commerce.
    3. The imposition or regulation of duties of customs on imports and exports, except on exports of timber, logs, masts, spars, deals and sawn lumber, and of coal and other minerals.
    4. The imposition or regulation of excise duties.
    5. The raising of money by all or any other modes or systems of taxation.
    6. The borrowing of money on the public credit.
    7. Postal service.
    8. Lines of steam or other ships, railways, canals, and other works, connecting any two or more of the provinces

together or extending beyond the limits of any province.

9. Lines of steamships between the federated provinces and other countries.

10. Telegraphic communication and the incorporation of telegraph companies.

11. All such works as shall, although lying wholly within any province, be specially declared by the acts authorizing them to be for the general advantage.

12. The census.

13. Militia — military and naval service, and defence.

14. Beacons, buoys, and lighthouses.

15. Navigation and shipping.

16. Quarantine.

17. Sea coast and inland fisheries.

18. Ferries between any province and a foreign country, or between any two provinces.

19. Currency and coinage.

20. Banking, incorporation of banks, and the issue of paper money.

21. Savings banks.

22. Weights and measures.

23. Bills of exchange and promissory notes.

24. Interest.

25. Legal tender.

26. Bankruptcy and insolvency.

27. Patents of invention and discovery.

28. Copy rights.

29. Indians and lands reserved for the Indians.

30. Naturalization and aliens.

31. Marriage and divorce.

32. The criminal law, excepting the constitution of courts of criminal jurisdiction, but including the procedure in criminal matters.

33. Rendering uniform all or any of the laws relative to property and civil rights in Upper Canada, Nova Scotia, New Brunswick, Newfoundland, and Prince Edward Island, and rendering uniform the procedure of all or any of the courts in these provinces; but any

statute for this purpose shall have no force or authority in any province until sanctioned by the legislature thereof.

34. The establishment of a general court of appeal for the federated provinces.

35. Immigration.

36. Agriculture.

37. And generally respecting all matters of a general character, not specially and exclusively reserved for the local governments and legislatures.

30. The general government and parliament shall have all powers necessary or proper for performing the obligations of the federated provinces, as part of the British Empire, to foreign countries, arising under treaties between Great Britain and such countries.

31. The general parliament may also, from time to time, establish additional courts, and the general government may appoint judges and officers thereof, when the same shall appear necessary or for the public advantage, in order to the due execution of the laws of parliament.

32. All courts, judges, and officers of the several provinces shall aid, assist, and obey the general government in the exercise of its rights and powers, and for such purposes shall be held to be courts, judges, and officers of the general government.

33. The general government shall appoint and pay the judges of the superior courts in each province, and of the county courts in Upper Canada, and parliament shall fix their salaries.

34. Until the consolidation of the laws of Upper Canada, New Brunswick, Nova Scotia, Newfoundland, and Prince Edward Island, the judges of these provinces appointed by the general government shall be selected from their respective bars.

35. The judges of the courts of Lower Canada shall be selected from the bar of Lower Canada.

36. The judges of the court of admiralty now

receiving salaries shall be paid by the general government.

37. The judges of the superior courts shall hold their offices during good behaviour, and shall be removable only on the address of both houses of parliament.

38. For each of the provinces there shall be an executive officer, styled the lieutenant governor, who shall be appointed by the governor general in council, under the great seal of the federated provinces, during pleasure: such pleasure not to be exercised before the expiration of the first five years, except for cause: such cause to be communicated in writing to the lieutenant governor immediately after the exercise of the pleasure as aforesaid, and also by message to both houses of parliament, within the first week of the first session afterwards.

39. The lieutenant governor of each province shall be paid by the general government.

40. In undertaking to pay the salaries of the lieutenant governors, the conference does not desire to prejudice the claim of Prince Edward Island upon the imperial government for the amount now paid for the salary of the lieutenant governor thereof.

41. The local government and legislature of each province shall be constructed in such manner as the existing legislature of such province shall provide.

42. The local legislatures shall have power to alter or amend their constitution from time to time.

43. The local legislatures shall have power to make laws respecting the following subjects:

    1. Direct taxation, and in New Brunswick the imposition of duties on the export of timber, logs, masts, spars, deals, and sawn lumber; and in Nova Scotia of coals and other minerals.

    2. Borrowing money on the credit of the province.

    3. The establishment and tenure of local offices, and the appointment and payment of local officers.

    4. Agriculture.

    5. Immigration.

    6. Education; saving the rights and privileges which the Protestant or Catholic minority in both Canadas may possess as to their denominational schools at the time when the union goes into operation.

    7. The sale and management of public lands, excepting lands belonging to the general government.

    8. Sea coast and inland fisheries.

    9. The establishment, maintenance, and management of penitentiaries, and of public and reformatory prisons.

    10. The establishment, maintenance, and management of hospitals, asylums, charities, and eleemosynary institutions.

    11. Municipal institutions.

    12. Shop, saloon, tavern, auctioneer, and other licences.

    13. Local works.

    14. The incorporation of private or local companies, except such as relate to matters assigned to the general parliament.

    15. Property and civil rights, excepting those portions thereof assigned to the general parliament.

    16. Inflicting punishment by fine, penalties, imprisonment, or otherwise for the breach of laws passed in relation to any subject within their jurisdiction.

    17. The administration of justice, including the constitution, maintenance and organization of the courts, both of civil and criminal jurisdiction, and including also the procedure in civil matters.

    18. And generally all matters of a private or local nature, not assigned to the general parliament.

44. The power of respiting, reprieving, and pardoning prisoners convicted of crimes,

and of commuting and remitting of sentences in whole or in part, which belongs of right to the crown, shall be administered by the lieutenant governor of each province in council, subject to any instructions he may from time to time receive from the general government, and subject to any provisions that may be made in this behalf by the general parliament.

45. In regard to all subjects over which jurisdiction belongs to both the general and local legislatures, the laws of the general parliament shall control and supersede those made by the local legislature, and the latter shall be void so far as they are repugnant to or inconsistent with the former.

46. Both the English and French languages may be employed in the general parliament and in its proceedings, and in the local legislature of Lower Canada, and also in the federal courts and in the courts of Lower Canada.

47. No lands or property belonging to the general or local governments shall be liable to taxation.

48. All bills for appropriating any part of the public revenue, or for imposing any new tax or impost, shall originate in the House of Commons or House of Assembly, as the case may be.

49. The House of Commons or House of Assembly shall not originate or pass any vote, resolution, address, or bill for the appropriation of any part of the public revenue, or of any tax or impost to any purpose, not first recommended by message of the governor general, or the lieutenant governor, as the case may be, during the session in which such vote, resolution, address, or bill is passed.

50. Any bill of the general parliament may be reserved in the usual manner for Her Majesty's assent, and any bill of the local legislatures may in like manner be reserved for the consideration of the governor general.

51. Any bill passed by the general parliament shall be subject to disallowance by Her Majesty within two years, as in the case of bills passed by the legislatures of the said provinces hitherto, and in like manner any bill passed by a local legislature shall be subject to disallowance by the governor general within one year after the passing thereof.

52. The seat of government of the federated provinces shall be Ottawa, subject to the royal prerogative.

53. Subject to any future action of the respective local governments, the seat of the local government in Upper Canada shall be Toronto; of Lower Canada, Quebec; and the seats of the local governments in the other provinces shall be as at present.

54. All stocks, cash, bankers' balances, and securities for money belonging to each province, at the time of the union, except as hereinafter mentioned, shall belong to the general government.

55. The following public works and property of each province shall belong to the general government, to wit:
    1. Canals.
    2. Public harbours.
    3. Lighthouses and piers.
    4. Steamboats, dredges, and public vessels.
    5. River and lake improvements.
    6. Railway and railway stocks, mortgages and other debts due by railway companies.
    7. Military roads.
    8. Custom houses, post offices, and other public buildings, except such as may be set aside by the general government for the use of the local legislatures and governments.
    9. Property transferred by the imperial government and known as ordnance property.
    10. Armouries, drill sheds, military clothing, and munitions of war.
    11. Land set apart for public purposes.

56. All lands, mines, minerals, and royalties vested in Her Majesty in the provinces of Upper Canada, Lower Canada, Nova Scotia, New Brunswick, and Prince Edward Island, for the use of such provinces, shall belong to the local government of the territory in which the same are so situate; subject to any trusts that may exist in respect to any of such lands or to any interest of other persons in respect of the same.

57. All sums due from purchasers or lessees of such lands, mines, or minerals at the time of the union shall also belong to the local governments.

58. All assets connected with such portions of the public debt of any province as are assumed by the local governments shall also belong to those governments respectively.

59. The several provinces shall retain all other public property therein, subject to the right of the general government to assume any lands or public property required for fortifications or the defence of the country.

60. The general government shall assume all the debts and liabilities of each province.

61. The debt of Canada not specially assumed by Upper and Lower Canada, respectively, shall not exceed at the time of the union $62,500,000. Nova Scotia shall enter the union with a debt not exceeding $8,000,000. And New Brunswick, with a debt not exceeding $7,000,000.

62. In case Nova Scotia or New Brunswick do not incur liabilities beyond those for which their governments are now bound and which shall make their debts at the date of union less than $8,000,000 and $7,000,000, respectively, they shall be entitled to interest at 5 per cent on the amount not so incurred, in like manner as is hereinafter provided for Newfoundland and Prince Edward Island: the foregoing resolution being in no respect intended to limit the powers given to the respective governments of those provinces by legislative authority, but only to limit the maximum amount of charge

to be assumed by the general government; provided always that the powers so conferred by the respective legislatures shall be exercised within five years from this date or the same shall then lapse.

63. Newfoundland and Prince Edward Island, not having incurred debts equal to those of the other provinces, shall be entitled to receive, by half-yearly payments in advance from the general government, the interest at 5 per cent on the difference between the actual amount of their respective debts at the time of the union, and the average amount of indebtedness per head of the population of Canada, Nova Scotia, and New Brunswick.

64. In consideration of the transfer to the general parliament of the powers of taxation, an annual grant in aid of each province shall be made, equal to 80 cents per head of the population as established by the census of 1861, the population of Newfoundland being estimated at 130,000. Such aid shall be in full settlement of all future demands upon the general government for local purposes and shall be paid half-yearly in advance to each province.

65. The position of New Brunswick being such as to entail large immediate charges upon her local revenues, it is agreed that for the period of ten years from the time when the union takes effect, an additional allowance of $63,000 per annum shall be made to that province. But that so long as the liability of that province remains under $7,000,000, a deduction equal to the interest on such deficiency shall be made from the $63,000.

66. In consideration of the surrender to the general government by Newfoundland of all its rights in mines and minerals, and of all the ungranted and unoccupied lands of the crown, it is agreed that the sum of $150,000 shall each year be paid to that province by semi-annual payments; provided that that

colony shall retain the right of opening, constructing, and controlling roads and bridges through any of the said lands, subject to any laws which the general parliament may pass in respect of the same.

67. All engagements that may, before the union, be entered into with the imperial government for the defence of the country shall be assumed by the general government.

68. The general government shall secure, without delay, the completion of the intercolonial railway from Rivière-du-Loup through New Brunswick to Truro, in Nova Scotia.

69. The communications with the North-Western Territory, and the improvements required for the development of the trade of the Great West with the seaboard, are regarded by this conference as subjects of the highest importance to the federated provinces, and shall be prosecuted at the earliest possible period that the state of the finances will permit.

70. The sanction of the imperial and local parliaments shall be sought for the union of the provinces, on the principles adopted by the conference.

71. That Her Majesty the Queen be solicited to determine the rank and name of the federated provinces.

72. The proceedings of the conference shall be authenticated by the signatures of the delegates, and submitted by each delegation to its own government, and the chairman is authorized to submit a copy to the governor general for transmission to the secretary of state for the colonies.

THE
LEGISLATORS

NEWFOUNDLAND

LEGISLATIVE COUNCIL
CLIFT, James Shannon
FRASER, J.O.
MORRIS, Edward
TESSIER, Peter

HOUSE OF ASSEMBLY
CARTER, Frederick Bowker Terrington
CASEY, John
GLEN, Thomas
HAYWOOD, John
HOGSETT, George James
HOYLES, Hugh
KAVANAGH, John
KENT, John
LITTLE, Joseph Ignatius
MARCH, Stephen
PARSONS, Robert John
PINSENT, Robert John (earlier, member
     of Legislative Council)
PROWSE, Daniel Woodley
RENDELL, Stephen
RENOUF, Henry
SHEA, Ambrose
SHEA, Edward Dalton
TALBOT, Thomas
WHITEWAY, William Vallance

PRINCE EDWARD ISLAND

LEGISLATIVE COUNCIL
ANDERSON, Alexander
BEER, George
HENDERSON, Kenneth
LORD, William W.
McDONALD, Andrew Archibald
McLAREN, James
PALMER, Edward

HOUSE OF ASSEMBLY
ARSENAULT, Joseph A.
BRECKEN, Frederick
COLES, George
CONROY, Nicholas
DAVIES, Benjamin
DUNCAN, James
GRAY, John Hamilton
HAVILAND, Thomas Heath
HENSLEY, Joseph
HOWLAN, George William
KELLY, Francis
LAIRD, Alexander
LONGWORTH, John
McAULEY, Roderick
McEACHEN, John
McLEAN, James
McNEILL, William S.

POPE, James Colledge
POPE, William Henry
SINCLAIR, George
WHELAN, Edward

NOVA SCOTIA

HOUSE OF ASSEMBLY
ANNAND, William
ARCHIBALD, Adams G.
BLACKWOOD, William
BLANCHARD, Hiram
BOURINOT, John
CAMPBELL, Stewart
COFFIN, Thomas
FRASER, James
HAMILTON, Charles Cottnam
HENRY, William A.
JOHNSTON, James William
KAULBACH, Henry Adolphus Newman
KILLAM, Thomas
LAWRENCE, William Dawson
LeVESCONTE, Isaac
LOCKE, John
LONGLEY, Avard
McDONALD, James
McLELAN, Archibald Woodbury
MILLER, William
ROSS, William
SHANNON, Samuel Leonard
TOBIN, John
TOWNSEND, William H.
TUPPER, Charles

NEW BRUNSWICK

LEGISLATIVE COUNCIL
BOTSFORD, Amos E.
CHANDLER, Edward B.
HAZEN, Robert L.
MITCHELL, Peter
ROBINSON, John James

HOUSE OF ASSEMBLY
ANGLIN, Timothy W.
BEVERIDGE, Benjamin
BOTSFORD, Bliss
BOYD, James
CAIE, W.S.
CONNELL, Charles
COSTIGAN, John
CUDLIP, John W.
FISHER, Charles
GILBERT, William James
GILLMOR, Arthur Hill
HATHEWAY, George L.
HIBBARD, Francis
HILL, George Frederic
JOHNSON, John Mercer
KERR, George
LEWIS, John
McCLELLAN, Abner Reid
McMILLAN, John
NEEDHAM, William
SKINNER, C.N.
SMITH, Albert J.
STEVENS, James Gray
THOMSON, Robert
TILLEY, Samuel Leonard
WETMORE, Andrew

CANADA

LEGISLATIVE COUNCIL
AIKINS, James C.
ARMAND, Joseph F.
BELLEAU, N.-F.
BUREAU, J.-O.
CAMPBELL, Alexander
CHRISTIE, David
CURRIE, James G.
DICKSON, Walter H.
McCRAE, Walter
MOORE, Philip H.
OLIVIER, Louis-Auguste

REESOR, David
ROSS, John
RYAN, Thomas
SANBORN, John S.
SEYMOUR, Benjamin
TACHÉ, Etienne-Paschal
VIDAL, A.

LEGISLATIVE ASSEMBLY

BEAUBIEN, J.-O. (later, member
    of the Legislative Council)
BLANCHET, Joseph G.
BROWN, George
CAMERON, J.H.
CAMERON, M.C.
CARTIER, George-Étienne
CARTWRIGHT, Richard J.
CAUCHON, Joseph
DENIS, Paul
DORION, Antoine-Aimé
DORION, J.-B.-E.
DUFRESNE, Joseph
DUNKIN, Christopher
FERGUSON, Thomas
HAULTAIN, Frederick W.
HOLTON, Luther H.
JOLY, Henri
JONES, D. Ford
LANGEVIN, H.-L.
MACDONALD, John A.
MACDONALD, John Sandfield
McGEE, Thomas D'Arcy
McGIVERIN, W.
MACKENZIE, Alexander
MACKENZIE, Hope
MORRIS, Alexander
O'HALLORAN, James
PERRAULT, Joseph
RANKIN, Arthur M.
RÉMILLARD, Édouard
ROSE, John
SCOBLE, John

WALLBRIDGE, T.C.
WALSH, Aquila

RED RIVER

LEGISLATIVE ASSEMBLY AND CONVENTION AT FORT GARRY

BIRD, Curtis
BLACK, Judge John
BUNN, Thomas
CUMMINGS, William
FLETT, George
FRASER, John
GUNN, Donald
O'DONOGHUE, W.B.
RIEL, Louis
ROSS, James
SCOTT, Alfred H.
SMITH, Donald A.
THIBERT, Pierre

BRITISH COLUMBIA

LEGISLATIVE COUNCIL

ALSTON, E.G.
BARNARD, Francis J.
CARRALL, Robert W.W.
CREASE, Henry P.P.
DE COSMOS, Amor
DRAKE, W.T.
HELMCKEN, John Sebastian
HOLBROOK, Henry
HUMPHREYS, Thomas B.
RING, David B.
ROBSON, John
TRUTCH, Joseph W.
WALKEM, G.A.
WOOD, T.L.

Appendix C

AFTERWORD
ON BOOKS

A COUNTRY'S HISTORIOGRAPHY, the historians' interpretation of events, is often as fascinating — and illuminating — as the bare story of the happenings. Canada is no exception. Unfortunately, valuable books and sources on Canadian history may be available only in university libraries and public archives. Canadians have been careless about making classic texts available. Any major Canadian bookseller can find you the *Federalist Papers*, the famous collection of essays on the American founding by James Madison, Alexander Hamilton, and John Jay. You ask in vain for comparable Canadian material. Though the Canadian founding offers nothing quite like the *Federalist Papers*, it has its own essential documents, and they have long been out of print.

This difficulty holds even for relatively recent productions, such as G.P. Browne's *Documents on the Confederation of British North America*, Carleton Library (Toronto: McClelland & Stewart, 1969), and Peter B. Waite's *The Confederation Debates in the Province of Canada, 1865*, Carleton Library (Toronto: McClelland & Stewart, 1963). Both were editions of nineteenth-century publications. Browne's book reprinted the compilation by John A. Macdonald's long-time secretary, Sir Joseph Pope, of the proceedings at the Charlottetown, Quebec, and London conferences, together with British Colonial Office correspondence and drafts of the British North America Act. Waite's was a selection from the verbatim report of the debates in the Canadian legislature. Both would be perfect companions for *Canada's Founding Debates* — if only readers could still find them.

Comprehensive accounts of Confederation fall into categories corresponding with phases in our country's history. In the late

nineteenth and early twentieth centuries, Canada's growing importance in the British Empire and its pioneering role in the establishment of colonial self-government encouraged scholars to describe Canadian history in terms of "the struggle for responsible government" and the "achievement of federation." A good example is W.P.M. Kennedy, *The Constitution of Canada* (London: Oxford University Press, 1922). One could do worse than begin one's research here. As an essay in legal history, *The Constitution of Canada* fairly swings along. It offers a clear exposition of constitutional principles and a good overview of events. The bibliographic notes are invaluable. But Kennedy is long out of print. Moreover, his emphasis on constitutional development was all but forgotten until the 1990s.

The First World War nurtured an assertive nationalism in historical writing which played down the glories of British constitutional liberty in favour of an emphasis on the limits imposed by Canada's status as a British dominion. This attitude persisted even after 1931, when the Statute of Westminster formally established Canada as a fully independent state. The Great Depression promoted demands that the federal government be accorded power to deal with economic and social difficulties, and anti-colonial sentiment came to focus on the reluctance of the imperial Privy Council, still (until 1949) Canada's final court of appeal, to meet these demands by abandoning its traditional respect for the autonomy of the provinces. In brief, the growing sense of Canadian nationhood and the economic travails of the 1930s fostered an approach to Confederation which emphasized the founders' nation-building purpose as well as their economic and political motives. A classic example of this approach was Donald Creighton's *British North America at Confederation* (Ottawa: King's Printer, 1939), written for the Royal Commission on Dominion-Provincial Relations (Rowell-Sirois Commission).

In the centennial decade of the 1960s, nationalist and centralist orthodoxy found expression in three major works on Confederation: Peter B. Waite, *The Life and Times of Confederation* (Toronto: University of Toronto Press, 1962), Donald Creighton, *The Road to Confederation* (Toronto: Macmillan, 1964), and W.L. Morton, *The Critical Years: The Union of British North America* (Toronto: McClelland & Stewart, 1964). After these books, however, Canadian historians stopped writing about Confederation. Three major accounts in as many years was perhaps enough to

be going on with, especially when supplemented by biographies of the founders: Donald Creighton on John A. Macdonald (published in two volumes in 1952 and 1955, and reissued by the University of Toronto Press in 1998), J.M.S. Careless, *Brown; of the Globe* (Toronto: Macmillan 1959–63), and Andrée Desilets, *Hector-Louis Langevin* (Quebec: Les Presses de l'Université Laval, 1969). Nevertheless, three decades were to pass before the next comprehensive study of the founding appeared: Christopher Moore's *1867: How the Fathers Made a Deal* (Toronto: McClelland & Stewart, 1998).

This long silence reflects more than temporary exhaustion of the subject. The 1960s witnessed an upheaval in social studies, the consequences of which we are still living with today. Canadian historians all but abandoned political and constitutional history in favour of the "new social history." Political scientists turned from the study of political institutions and law to political sociology and culture. Though perhaps fruitful in many respects, this revolution had unfortunate consequences. An entire generation lost sight of Canada's constitutional history — the very generation that would be faced in the 1970s and 1980s with the task of radically revising and reimagining Canadian democracy and rights. The ossified centennial orthodoxy proved inadequate to the task. The decision of the Supreme Court in 1981 that patriation of the constitution could proceed without the consent of Quebec rested on a very shaky understanding of Canada's founding and constitutional development. A decade later, in the debate on the Charlottetown constitutional accord, our ignorance of Canadian history was strikingly apparent. Almost no one in that debate referred to historical principles. Almost no one, whether for or against the accord, had anything good to say of Canada's present constitution and form of government.

Christopher Moore's *1867* was written in the shadow of these failures. It sets out to understand the recent constitution-making debacles by comparing them with the astounding success of the 1860s: the "deal" under which we still, in large part, live. Moore's volume reflects the beginnings of a new historical approach to Confederation and to Canadian constitutional history from 1867. This new approach is marked by a concern for some long-forgotten themes, such as the importance of responsible government, and by a willingness to take the British American politicians of the mid-nineteenth century seriously as political thinkers. Leading examples of this revisionism include Robert C.

Vipond, *Liberty and Community: Canadian Federalism and the Failure of the Constitution* (Albany, NY: SUNY Press, 1991); Janet Ajzenstat and Peter J. Smith, eds., *Canada's Origins: Liberal, Tory, or Republican?* (Ottawa: Carleton University Press, 1995); and Paul Romney, *Getting It Wrong: How Canadians Forgot Their Past and Imperilled Confederation* (Toronto: University of Toronto Press, 1999). Vipond and Romney set out a new, historically informed understanding of Canadian federalism and of the role of the courts in interpreting it. Ajzenstat and Smith show that parliamentary liberalism, including responsible government, and populist republicanism were the influential ideologies in pre-Confederation Canada.

The centennial account of Confederation was unsatisfactory because it divorced federalism from responsible government. It ignored what responsible government meant to the founders as an expression both of individual political rights and of collective rights to provincial autonomy. Thus it neglected the founders' concern for general civil rights and the rights of political minorities, leaving us with the familiar image of the Fathers of Confederation as "practical" men who were neither equipped nor inclined to reflect on theories of government and popular rights. Moreover, it saw in the founders' often-quoted intention to create a more centralized union than the United States only a formula for central dominance.

Of course, it is well known that John A. Macdonald wanted the most highly centralized union he could get. But it is a mistake to think of the authors of Confederation, as the centennial account tended to do, as though they were just clones of Macdonald. Macdonald did not get his own way in everything, by any means. Parts 3 and 4 of *Canada's Founding Debates* document the concern of many British American legislators to preserve their provinces' autonomy, and the solemn assurances of leading confederates that the new constitution would meet this concern. From this point of view, the British North America Act is best understood as a compromise that balances federal and provincial powers.

Where Macdonald did conspicuously get his way was in the endorsement of constitutional principles, at both the federal and the provincial levels, to preserve the rights of individuals against the demands of temporary majorities. Parts 1 and 5 of this book document the concerns of legislators in this regard. Macdonald was also successful in the creation of a political entity capable of

extension across the continent to the Pacific Ocean. That purpose is celebrated in Part 2.

Readers of *Canada's Founding Debates* will find Moore's *1867* helpful as a guide to Confederation because it recounts developments year by year, and even day by day, in the legislatures of the Province of Canada and the Maritime colonies. However, it needs supplementing as regards the colonies that stood aloof in 1867 and those that joined between 1870 and 1873. For a blow-by-blow description of events in these places, readers might turn to the following: for British Columbia, Derek Pethick, "The Confederation Debate of 1870," in W. George Shelton, ed., *British Columbia and Confederation* (Victoria: University of Victoria, 1967); for Newfoundland, James Hiller, "Confederation Defeated: The Newfoundland Election of 1869," in James Hiller and Peter Neary, eds., *Newfoundland in the Nineteenth and Twentieth Centuries* (Toronto: University of Toronto Press, 1980); and for Red River, W.L. Morton, *Manitoba: The Birth of a Province* (Altona, Man.: Manitoba Record Society, 1965). Also useful are Kenneth G. Pryke, *Nova Scotia and Confederation* (Toronto: University of Toronto Press, 1979), and Phillip Buckner, "The Maritimes and Confederation: A Reassessment," *Canadian Historical Review* (1990), and the replies to Buckner in the same issue. Buckner helpfully argues that historians have underestimated the degree of support for Confederation in the Maritimes.

Is Confederation still relevant? Is it still worth studying?

Many things have changed in this country since Confederation, including the expansion of the franchise, the development of new political parties and extra-parliamentary organizations in all parties, the proliferation of political interest groups, staggering advances in material wealth, and — perhaps most significant — the growth of the regulatory and welfare state. The Charter of Rights and Freedoms (1982), "executive federalism" (government by First Ministers' conferences), and the phenomenon of "globalization" (especially the use of international organizations and tribunals to determine domestic politics) are but three of the developments that severely modify the parliamentary and federal formula devised by the founders. And yet!

How are we to understand and evaluate these changes if we lose sight of our origins? Juggling liberty and community, protecting minorities: these are still Canadian objectives. In a free country there will always be debate about means and policies.

Political wrangling never ceases, thank goodness. But if we forget the original constitution in the British North America Act, with its formula for parliamentary government, guarantees for political and national minorities, and a balance of federal and provincial powers, we will truly have lost our bearings.

PICTURE
CREDITS

McMaster University

First page, *Legislative Debates*, Nova Scotia, 1866 (our page 7)

First page, *The Newfoundlander*, March 2, 1865 (p. 8)

First page, *Legislative Debates*, New Brunswick, 1867 (p. 20)

First page, *Legislative Debates*, Canada, 1865 (p. 78)

Cover, Thomas D'Arcy McGee, *Notes sur les gouvernements fédéraux* (JC 355M2414) (p. 268)

Metropolitan Toronto Reference Library

Canadian Confederation Medal (T16623) (p. 3)

Cover, British North America Act, 1867 (*Maclean's*, October 1982) (p. 13)

Portrait, J.A. Macdonald (T31118) (p. 71)

Portrait, George-Étienne Cartier (S-7557) (p. 72)

J.S. Helmcken and Robert Carrall at Niagara Falls (owned by the Provincial Archives of British Columbia) (D-10 7061) (p. 76)

Queen Victoria's Proclamation (S-556) (p. 85)

Portrait, George Coles (Fathers of Confederation series, *Toronto Star*: Artist: Irma Coucill) (p. 100)

Waiting, engraving of dogs, from William Cosmo Monkhouse, *The Works of Sir Edwin Landseer* (759.2 L12.6) (p. 110)

Portrait, George Brown (T15166) (p. 114)

Advertisement for the Great Western (p. 164)

"The Fenians Are Coming" (broadside) (p. 174)

"The Ideal John Bull," from Sir Max Beerbohm (cartoonist), *The Second Childhood of John Bull* (London: Stephen Swift, 1901) (741 B24.7) (p. 225)

New Official Atlas (p. 261)

Man in a skiff at the Charlotte Conference (S-9875) (p. 262)

Toronto Liberals Cheer George Brown (S-7791) (p. 286)

Election broadside, M.C. Cameron (p. 305)

Confederation Chamber, Charlottetown (p. 356)

Election broadside, Wm. McGiverin (p. 426)

"Our Dominion" (Canadian Series of Jackdaws, 971.04 HS96) (p. 428)

"The Welcome Galop" (Canadian Series of Jackdaws, 971.04 HS96) (p. 448)

National Archives of Canada

Portrait, Louis Riel (C 18082) (p. 248)

The Fathers of Confederation in London. Confederation Life Collection. Artist: J.D. Kelly (p. 260)

Portrait, Frederick Carter (C 6186) (p. 220)

Portrait, Samuel Leonard Tilley (PA 12632) (p. 272)

Portrait, Étienne-Paschal Taché (PA 74100)
(p. 334)
The Convention at Charlottetown, 1864
(C 733) (p. 354)

National Gallery of Canada
Otto R. Jacobi, *Old Parliament Buildings,
Ottawa* (no. 9990) (p. 119)

National Library of Canada
Great Fenian Scare (C 48516) (p. 174)

New Brunswick, Provincial Archives
The Ferry to Charlottetown (P5-146) (p. 242)
New Brunswick Legislature (P5-396) (p. 269)
First page, *Legislative Debates*, New Brunswick,
(March 1866) (P110-774) (p. 329)

Nova Scotia, Public Archives
Portrait, William Annand (p. 364)
Anti-Confederation banner (N 4149) (p. 391)

Ontario Archives
Portrait, A.-A.Dorion (acc. 3964, S. 3002)
(p. 17)
Portrait, Ambrose Shea (S 619) (p. 152)
Colonial Building, Newfoundland (acc. 2189,
S 2619) (p. 152)
Portrait, A.J. Smith (S. 222) (p. 407)
Confederation Leaders at Quebec. Artist:
C.W. Jefferys (RG 2, 344-0-0-1, AO 4390)
(p. 440)

**Prince Edward Island, Public Archives
and Records**
First page, *Legislative Debates*, Prince Edward
Island, 1865
Photographer: Barbara Morgan (p. 159)

First page, *Legislative Debates*, Prince Edward
Island, 1866
Photographer: Barbara Morgan (p. 325)

**Thomas Fisher Rare Book Library,
University of Toronto**
First page, *Legislative Council Debates*, British
Columbia (Gov. Doc. B.C. [Colony] L)
(p. 23)

York University, Saywell Collection
Portrait, Charles Tupper (1607) (p. 361)

Books
J.W. Bengough, *Caricature History of Canadian
Politics* (Toronto: Grip Printing and
Publishing, 1886): The Crusading
Campaigner (p. 134); Joseph Howe
(p. 175); "Uncle Sam Kicked Out"
(p. 183); Uncle Sam (p. 192); Britannica
(p. 204); Miss Canada (p. 213); George-
Étienne Cartier (p. 230); Cartier leading
Red River into Confederation (p. 405)

Colin Davies, *Louis Riel and the New Nation*
(Agincourt: Book Society of Canada,
1980): Métis resistance fighter (p. 417)

Lena Newman, *The John A. Macdonald Album*
(Montreal: Tundra Books, 1974), cartoon
drawings by Bengough: cartoon, John A.
Macdonald (p. 313); cartoon, "Mirth"
(John A. Macdonald) (p. 477)

W. George Shelton, ed., *British Columbia and
Confederation* (Victoria, BC: University of
Victoria, 1967): portraits of John Robson
(p. 30) and Joseph Trutch (p. 194)

INDEX

absentee landowners, 405n
agriculture, 137–38, 137n
Aikins, James C., on direct democracy, 429–30,
    432–33
Alston, E.G.
  on responsible government, 52–53
  on what a Canadian is, 251, 255–56
ambition, 94–95
  of politicians, 123–24, 125, 126, 128–29,
    149–50, 158, 162, 270
  prosperity and individual ambition (*see under
    individual legislators*)
  See also career opportunities
amendment of constitutions
  amendment of BNA Act, 278n
  British provisions, 431
  colonial constitutions before Confederation,
    386–87, 386–87n
  difference from ordinary legislation, 375, 375n
  lack of amending provision in Quebec
    Resolutions or BNA Act, 273, 273n
  legislative competence, 378–80, 434–35, 438,
    441, 446
  provincial constitutions after Confederation,
    24n, 28
  U.S. provisions for amendment, 430–31,
    452–53
America. *See* United States
American Declaration of Independence, 155n
American Revolution, 134, 158, 184, 187, 237,
    241, 245, 245n, 410
Anderson, Alexander, on responsible government,
    62
Anglin, Timothy W., on making a constitution,
    410
anglophones in Lower Canada, 289n, 333–334,
    334n, 337, 338–39, 341–44, 352
Annand, William
  on being British or Canadian, 209

biography, 364
on equality of representation, 106–8
on making a constitution, 358, 359–60, 364–67,
    389
on parliamentary government, 95
on prosperity and individual ambition, 125–26
annexation
  to Canada, 367–68, 413n
  to the U.S., 99n, 169, 176, 178–79, 187,
    188–89, 192–93, 194, 196, 199, 201, 367,
    446
    Confederation to protect against, 140–41,
      170–71, 174, 175, 177, 180–81, 182–83,
      189–91, 192n, 195, 197, 211–12
    Victoria petitioners for, 215n
Archibald, Adams G.
  on being British or American, 171–72
  on being British or Canadian, 214
  on making a constitution, 362–64, 392–93
  on prosperity and individual ambition, 124
  on what a Canadian is, 236–37
Archibald, Samuel, 238n
aristocracy, 18, 18n
  earned privilege ("natural aristocracy") in
    British North America, 17, 17n
  in Great Britain, 49–50, 50n, 51, 81, 94, 98
  importance of, to a self-governing community,
    41n
Aristotle, 41n
Armand, Joseph F., on parliamentary
    government, 91–92
Arsenault, Joseph A., on what a Canadian is, 258
Atlas of the Dominion of Canada, 261
Australia, 304
autonomy. *See* self-government

Bacon, Lord, 139
Bagehot, Walter, 67n
balance of power, 276, 349

Baldwin, Robert, 86, 86n, 215n
Baldwin, William, 370, 380n
Barnard, Francis J.
  on prosperity and individual ambition, 142–43
  on responsible government, 45–47
  on what a Canadian is, 255
Beaubien, J.-O.
  on federal union, 296
  on minorities and minority rights, 348–49
Beer, George, on prosperity and individual
    ambition, 161–62
Belleau, N.-F.
  on federal union, 293–94
  on minorities and minority rights, 338–40
Berryer, Pierre, 91
Beveridge, Benjamin, on prosperity and
    individual ambition, 130
bicameral system. See House of Commons;
    Senate
Bill of Rights (Britain), 447n
Bird, Curtis, on making a constitution, 419
Black, Judge John
  on equality of representation, 118
  on making a constitution, 414–15
  on responsible government, 66–68
  on what a Canadian is, 247–48
Blackstone, William, 67n, 379–80, 379n, 389n,
    391
Blackwood, William, on making a constitution,
    382–83
Blake, Edward, 405, 405n
Blanchard, Hiram, on making a constitution, 368,
    369
Blanchet, Joseph G., on parliamentary
    government, 94–95
BNA Act. See British North America Act, 1867
Botsford, Amos E.
  on being British or Canadian, 202–3
  on constitutional liberty, 20
  on responsible government, 74–75
  on what a Canadian is, 246
Botsford, Bliss, on minorities and minority rights,
    329–30
Bourinot, John
  on being British or Canadian, 208–9
  on equality of representation, 107
  on federal union, 264–65
  on prosperity and individual ambition, 127
Boyd, James
  on equality of representation, 112
  on making a constitution, 406
Brecken, Frederick
  on being British or American, 198–99
  on being British or Canadian, 223–25
  on federal union, 321–33
  on responsible government, 63–64
Britain
  constitution. See British Constitution
  and Canadian nationalism, 173, 173n

British Columbia
  concern with intercontinental railway, 143,
    143n
  isolation of, 170, 215, 217
  lack of responsible government, 23–24, 23–24n
  Legislative Council, 23n, 27n
British Constitution, 90, 91, 145, 154, 167, 178,
    179, 191, 206, 231, 281, 448, 448n
  appointed upper house, 78
  checks among branches, 19, 96 (see also checks
    and balances)
  developed by experience, 20
  and minority rights, 19–20
  modified to suit circumstances, 68
  praised, 384
  principles preserved in BNA Act, 59–60
  Quebec scheme accords with, 178, 310, 318
British Empire, 201, 203, 206, 207, 211, 212,
    219, 223
  assertion of colonial sovereignty, 380n
  Britain's attitude to the colonies, 426
  Britain's power over colonies considered
    nominal, 307–8, 308n
  colonies are important to strength of Britain,
    367–68
  constitution of, 386–87n
  dependence of colonies, 369, 370, 370n
    continues after Confederation, 236
  government (see imperial government)
  imperial statute gives effect to Quebec
    Resolutions, 457
  "laws of nature," 227, 227n
  loyalty to Britain (See loyalty)
  sovereignty of British monarch, 379–80n
British government, 340
  grant by Britain of representative government a
    surrender of sovereignty, 409–10, 409n
  power over Canada, 318
  See also imperial government
British heritage distinguishes colonies from U.S.,
    168
British institutions, 180, 185, 197
British liberty, vs. American equality, 18n, 19
British North America Act, 1867, 237n, 269n,
    305n, 317
  amendment of, 278n
  central authority, 60
  provinces may amend constitutions, 24n, 28
  section 26, 87n
British parliament, 302
  Irish nationalists in, 267, 267n
British subjects, 248
  Red River settlers claim rights as, 417–18,
    417–18n
Brown, George, 103, 109
  biography, 114
  on constitutional liberty, 14–16
  on direct democracy, 423–28, 457–58
  on equality of representation, 114–15

Brown, George (*continued*)
  on federal union, 285–90, 315
  on parliamentary government, 83–88
  on prosperity and individual ambition, 133–37
  on separate schools, 336–37
Buchanan, George, 301n
Bunn, Thomas
  on making a constitution, 414, 417–19
  on what a Canadian is, 247
Burke, Edmund, 27n, 33n, 395, 418n
Bute, Lord, 47–48n

cabinet
  executive control of expenditure, 71, 71n
  must maintain support in Commons, 22, 30, 48, 48n, 75, 79
  organization of federal cabinet to represent provinces, 306–7
Cameron, J.H., 420
  on direct democracy, 455–57
Cameron, John Hillyard, 381n
Cameron, M.C.
  on direct democracy, 457
  on federal union, 304–6
Campbell, Alexander
  on being British or Canadian, 208
  on direct democracy, 432, 442–45
  on parliamentary government, 88
Campbell, Stewart
  on being British or Canadian, 213–14
  on making a constitution, 368, 371–75, 393
  on what a Canadian is, 243
Canada East. *See* Lower Canada
Canadian Confederation Medal (1867), 3
Canadian identity, 229. *See also* identity; *See also* under *individual legislators*
Canadian nationality. *See* nationality
Canadian Pacific Railway, 143n
Cardwell, Edward, 223n, 267, 267n, 368, 410
career opportunities, 159, 160
Carnarvon, Earl of, 387
Carrall, Robert W.W.
  on being British or American, 195–96
  on responsible government, 27–28, 36–38
  on what a Canadian is, 254, 256
Carter, Frederick Bowker Terrington
  on being British or Canadian, 220–21
  biography, 220
  on minorities and minority rights, 331–32
  on responsible government, 59–60
Cartier, George-Etienne, 176n
  on being British or American, 182–85
  biography, 72
  on direct democracy, 423
  on equality of representation, 113–14
  on federal union, 284, 308, 311
  on minorities and minority rights, 335, 343
  on prosperity and individual ambition, 133
  on responsible government, 71–72

  on what a Canadian is, 229–31
Cartwright, Richard J.
  on constitutional liberty, 18–20
  on direct democracy, 451–52
Casey, John
  on prosperity and individual ambition, 143
  on responsible government, 55–56
Cauchon, Joseph, 303n
  on direct democracy, 446–49
  on federal union, 312
central authority, concession of some powers to interpretation of Confederation, 319
  states' rights issue in the U.S., 282, 293, 301, 303, 304, 309–10, 313, 314, 437n
central government
  must be above provincial governments, 301, 309–11, 314
  necessity of, 60
  powers of (*see* federal government, powers)
  smaller provinces must be protected from larger, 225
  in the U.S., 179
    opinions of framers of the U.S. Constitution, 309–10
  See also federal government
central provinces, 123
centralism, 437
centralization
  of B.C. government in Victoria, 38, 43
  of Canadian government (*see* central government; federal government)
  Mill's thoughts, 53n
Chandler, Edward B.
  on equality of representation, 113
  on federal union, 276–77
  on prosperity and individual ambition, 131–32
Channel Islands, 316, 316n
Charlottetown Conference (1864), 262, 365, 408
Charter of Rights and Freedoms (1982)
  human rights, 155n
  to be interpreted by judges, 431n
checks and balances
  in the American system, 180n, 437n
  on betrayal of public interest by politicians, 123
  in British Constitution, 19, 96, 190n
  and mixed government, 190n, 458–59n, 461
  under responsible government, 180n
  Senate a check on Commons, 77, 79–80, 84, 92–93, 96, 190n, 270–71, 274, 276, 298
  on a territorial governor, 65n, 66, 66–67n, 68–69, 68n, 69
children. *See* posterity
Christie, David
  on being British or American, 191
  on direct democracy, 432–38
church, separation from state, 229, 327–28
citizenship. *See* vote
civil code of Canada East, 290, 305n, 312n, 334n, 346

civil rights, provinces assigned legislative power on, 305–6, 305n

civil war
Confederation avoids threat of, 14, 34
in the U.S., 14, 48–49n, 102, 157n, 170, 171, 179, 179n, 181, 182, 185, 186–87, 197, 220, 282, 293, 305, 314, 426, 437n

classes
educated, 40, 44
labouring, 15, 32, 40, 44, 51
lack of hereditary aristocracy, 17, 17n
middle, 51
See also aristocracy

Clift, James Shannon, on prosperity and individual ambition, 147

Coffin, Thomas, on making a constitution, 385–86

Coke, Sir Edward, 379n, 389n

Coles, George
on being British or Canadian, 224–27
biography, 100
on federal union, 324
on making a constitution, 398, 399
on parliamentary government, 99–101
on prosperity and individual ambition, 160–61
on responsible government, 63

Colonial Building, Newfoundland, 152

colonial governments
competence to decide on Confederation questioned, 377–80
England supports competence of, 387–88
responsibility to British officials, 23

Colonial Office, 158, 158n, 162n, 171, 221, 222

colonial secretary, 240, 387

colonial sovereignty, 380n

colonies
B.C. protests loss of independence, 217
common heritage and interests
an argument for Confederation, 257, 258
lacking between Maritimes and Canada, 243
dependence continues after Confederation, 232, 232–33n
"double subservience" concern from Newfoundland, 58, 98
right to change own constitutions questioned, 369–70, 370–71n

Common Sense (Paine), 363n

communication among colonies
B.C. has poor exchange with Ottawa, 217
would improve after Confederation, 258

community of interests among provinces, 257, 258

compact theory of Confederation, 278n, 405n, 423n. See also states' rights issue in U.S.

competition of political parties, 123–24
benefits voters, 400n

compromise
limits discussion, 432–33
needed for provincial approval of Quebec

Resolutions, 399, 399–400n, 400, 421–22, 433, 436
political necessity of, 114–15n
Quebec scheme as, 300, 429

Confederation
abstract idea of union, 162
arguments of opponents
control of revenue and taxes by centre, 109–10, 109n, 224–25, 224n, 227, 237–39, 237n
distance separating colonies, 213, 216, 217
domination of smaller provinces by larger, 24–26, 32, 52, 55, 74, 141
"double subservience" to Ottawa and England, 58, 98
expenses, 138
loss of freedom and power, 101, 161, 224–28, 322–23, 324
no rise in status of provinces, 232, 232–33n
separation from Britain as result, 226–27
tax increases predicted, 55–56, 62, 128, 130, 138–39, 141, 151, 157, 161, 217
a threat to liberties, 144–46, 144n
U.S. invasion would not be stopped, 202
arguments of supporters
combined resources for future prosperity, 126, 127, 131–33, 140, 149
controversies reduced, 124–25, 124n, 289
emigration from Canada to the U.S. halted, 177
improved communication among provinces, 258
increased resistance against U.S. takeover, 170–71, 174, 175, 177, 178, 180–83, 189–91, 192n, 194–98, 199, 211–12
increased trade, 132, 134, 136–37
shared mutual interests, 194, 257, 258, 302, 348–49
special interests of French Canadians protected, 235
strengthening of weaker provinces, 246
uniformity of laws, 325–26
B.C. not ready in 1870, 52, 194, 315–18
Brown supports Quebec scheme, 285–90, 425–26
building the structure of a country, 133
concerns of smaller provinces (See Confederation, arguments of opponents)
election on the issue, 373–74, 373n, 388, 397, 413, 425, 439, 441, 442–43, 445
only Nova Scotia and province of Canada hold no election, 420
idea arises from political deadlock in the Canadas, 280n, 365
and immigration, 135–36
Macdonald sees as only feasible scheme, 313–14
Mill on necessary conditions of, 257
New Brunswick, public opinion, 97n
Newfoundland perspective, 55-62

Confederation (*continued*)
  not a party issue, 400n, 448
  P.E.I. perspectives, 162-63
  perception of advantages necessary for support,
    250–51
  principle of, 194
  and prosperity, 142, 145, 148
  Red River not consulted on issue, 249n, 251,
    416n, 417–19
  referendum on, 110, 373n, 374, 378n, 408n,
    420, 459–60n
  and responsible government, 23–24, 28, 36,
    55n, 67–68, 380n, 387–88, 389, 391–92
  supported by English government and press,
    387, 390
  a union of governments, not peoples, 382, 382n
Confederation Chamber at Charlottetown, 356
Connell, Charles, on making a constitution, 406
Conroy, Nicholas, on making a constitution, 400
conservatism, 16
  natural conservatism of people, 33, 35, 35n
Conservative parties in colonies, 17
  support responsible government, 23
constitution
  of Australia, 304
  of Britain. (*see* British Constitution)
  of the British Empire, 386–87n
  of colonies, 57, 224, 226
    changing, 375n, 435, 443, 445–46, 449, 452,
      457
    competence of colonial legislatures to
      change, 378–80, 438, 441
    would be changed by Confederation, 372,
      374, 386–87, 386–87n
  constitutional change in the U.S. and England,
    430–31
  emotional support necessary, 231
  federal (1867), 203–4, 231, 281–84 (*see also*
    British North America Act, 1867)
  making a constitution (*see under individual*
    legislators)
  of New Zealand, 268–69, 268n, 304
  Newfoundland, 59–60
  proposed federal, 198
  provincial, post-1867
    amendment of provincial constitutions under
      BNA Act, 24n, 28
    See also provincial governments
  subject to control of the people, 370n, 387n
  of the U.S. (*see* United States, constitution)
Constitutional Act of 1791, 278n
constitutional amendments. *See* amendment of
  constitutions
constitutional convention at Fort Garry, 414–19,
  414n
constitutional law, 377–80
constitutional liberty. *See under individual legislators*
constitutionality, distinguished from legitimacy,
  380n

Cooper, James Fenimore, 390n
coordinate powers, 303n, 304, 312, 312n
Costigan, John
  on equality of representation, 111–12
  on making a constitution, 407
courts, 135, 274
  appeal court, 289
  for disputes between governments (Supreme
    Court), 272, 275, 311, 312, 312n
  power over legislature
    in Canada, 431n
    in the U.S., 275
  two languages to be used in, 330
  See also judges; judicial review
Cox, Homersham, 434–35n
Crease, Henry P.P.
  on being British or American, 193–94
  on being British or Canadian, 215
  on constitutional liberty, 13–14
  on making a constitution, 413
  on responsible government, 28, 31
  on what a Canadian is, 250, 252–53, 255
Cudlip, John W., on making a constitution, 407
cultural diversity, 14, 15, 72, 155, 184, 327
culture, Canadian, vulnerability to influence of
  U.S., 168–69, 168–69n
Cummings, William
  on equality of representation, 118
  on what a Canadian is, 247
Cunard, Samuel, 222
Curran, John Philpot, 126n
currency, 221
  uniformity of, 224
Currie, James G.
  on being British or American, 181–82
  on direct democracy, 433, 438–39, 441–43
  on federal union, 291

Dartmouth College case, 290, 290n
Davies, Benjamin
  on being British or American, 197–98
  on minorities and minority rights, 331
deadlock between upper and lower house, 95, 99,
  227
  less likely with appointed Senate, 82–88, 84n,
    87n
decentralization, 314. *See also* compact theory of
  Confederation; provincial governments;
  states' rights issue in the United States
Declaration of the Rights of Man and of the Citizen,
  418n
De Cosmos, Amor
  on being British or Canadian, 217
  on federal union, 317, 318
  on responsible government, 36, 36n
  on what a Canadian is, 250, 252
defence, 236, 243
  against the U.S., 59, 171–73, 177, 183, 197,
    219

delegated powers
  by central to provincial governments,
    misunderstandings, 312–13
  not delegated from provinces in Canadian
    system, 304
  to central government from states in the U.S.,
    304
deliberation, political, or direct democracy, 421,
  422n, 456–57, 456n, 458n
demagogy, 91
democracy, 17–18, 91, 377n
  demagogues, 91
  direct (*see* direct democracy)
  elected Senate (*see* Senate, elective)
  excess of, in the U.S. after 1776, 363–64n
  and the intelligence of the people, 374n
  no necessary connection with liberty, 362n
  no permanent office for legislators, 82, 82n
  problems of elected president in the U.S.,
    71–72, 71–72n
  and qualifications to vote, 44, 44n, 49 (*see also*
    vote)
  referring Confederation to the people, 359–60,
    359n (*see also* public opinion)
  representative (*see* representative government)
  and Romantic views on innocence and nobility
    of common man, 390–91n
  "tyranny" of, 18n, 43–44, 52, 72n, 452n, 458n,
    459, 459–60n
  in the U.S., 185, 430, 431
Denis, Paul, on direct democracy, 454
dependence of colonies, 232, 232–33n, 369, 370,
    370n
despotism, allusion to dominance by central
    government, 101
Dickson, Walter H., on direct democracy, 442–43
direct democracy, 377n
  constitutional change in the U.S. involves the
    people directly, 430, 431
  opposing theory to political representation,
    421, 422n, 456–57, 456n, 458n, 459
  popular participation in Confederation decision
    (*see* public opinion)
  See also under individual legislators
disallowance
  federal veto of provincial legislation
    central government strengthened, 299,
      309–10
    colonies fear loss of independence, 269–70,
      270n, 272, 274
    conflicts feared, 295–96
    necessary to avoid "provincial rights" issues,
      301
    power could be used in case of unjust laws,
      342–43
    practical limitations of, 291, 291n, 296–97,
      308
  imperial veto of colonial legislation, 158n, 222,
    222n, 295, 295n, 307

veto power of monarch or U.S. president (*see*
    veto)
dissolution of parliament, 388, 443, 445
  in New Brunswick, 455
diversity
  cultural, 14, 15, 72, 155, 184, 327
  of ethnic groups, 229, 230–31, 285, 329–30,
    331n, 341–42
  of language, 329–30
  of local interests, 285
  of nationalities, 114, 230–31, 230–31n, 235
  of religion, 230–31, 327, 329, 330–31, 331n,
    332, 333
division of legislative powers, 286–97, 299, 333
doctors, 150
Dorion, Antoine-Aimé
  biography, 17
  on constitutional liberty, 17–18
  on federal union, 295–96, 303, 310–12
  on minorities and minority rights, 340–41
Dorion, J.-B.-E.
  on being British or American, 192–93
  on direct democracy, 452–54
"double subservience," 58, 98
Douglas, James, 252, 252n
Doyle, Sir Charles Hastings, 366
Drake, W.T.
  on federal union, 315–16
  on responsible government, 42–44
due process, cannot justify unjust legislation, 392n
Dufresne, Joseph, on minorities and minority
    rights, 352–53
Duncan, James, on prosperity and individual
    ambition, 159–60
Dunkin, Christopher
  on direct democracy, 424
  on federal union, 306–9
  on minorities and minority rights, 345–48
  on prosperity and individual ambition, 140–41
  on what a Canadian is, 235–36
Durham, Lord, 104–105, 104n, 108, 124n, 128n,
    240, 381

Eastern Townships, 233
education, 151, 154, 336–37
  promoted by Confederation, 145, 146
  sectarian schools (*see* separate schools)
  See also schools
election on Confederation, 388, 397, 413, 420,
    425, 439, 441, 442–43, 445, 455, 455n
emigration to the United States, 177, 192
employment, 192
  Newfoundland considers Confederation and,
    145–47, 152–53
England
  policy towards colonies, 183
  union with Ireland, 153–54, 153–54n, 244
  union with Scotland, 102n, 107–8, 130n, 146,
    244

equality
American, vs. British liberty, 18n, 19
of Native Indians, 251, 252–56, 252n,
254–56n
in religion, 154
of representation (*see under individual legislators*)
European emigration, 133
executive control of expenditure, 71, 71n
executive council. *See* Senate

Family Compact, 89, 89n
Federal Court of Appeals, 312
federal government
powers, 263, 289–90, 291–93, 291n, 295, 297,
299, 303, 312, 318–19
delegation of powers to provincial
governments, 312–13
disallowance of provincial legislation (*see*
disallowance)
military power, 247–48, 247–48n
no constitutional difference from provincial
powers, 303n, 304
residuary power, 299, 299n
seen as unlimited in Quebec Resolutions,
310–11
presumed superior to provinces, 309–10
of the U.S., 235, 236, 309–10 (*see also* states'
rights issue in the United States)
federal parliament, 283
federal union, 261, 262n, 264, 285, 300, 304, 333
of the British Empire as a whole, 236
of British North America, 236, 437n
conditions for (Mill), 302–3
experience of United Canada, 280, 280n
first step before legislative union, 340
proposed in Quebec scheme, 279, 280–81
relations between federal and provincial
governments, 308–9, 308n
See also coordinate powers; delegated powers;
disallowance; *See also under individual
legislators*
federalism
centralization (*see* central government; central
parliament; central provinces;
centralization; federal government)
concerns of smaller provinces, 128, 129–30
decentralization (*see* provincial governments)
in New Zealand, 268–69, 268n, 304
not safeguard of provinces' individuality, 216n,
217
in the U.S., 235, 236
The Federalist Papers, 436n
federalization of United Canada (approved by
Reform Party, 1859), 300n
Fenians, 173–74, 174n, 210
Ferguson, Thomas, on direct democracy, 422
Fisher, Charles
on being British or Canadian, 203
on federal union, 274–75

fisheries
Atlantic, 147
federal powers a potential source of discord,
292–93
Flett, George, on what a Canadian is, 248
Fort Garry constitutional convention, 65–69,
65n, 414–19, 414n
founding fathers of the U.S. government. *See*
Hamilton, Alexander; Jay, John; Jefferson,
Thomas; Madison, James
franchise for electors. *See* vote
Fraser, James (Nova Scotia), on making a
constitution, 383
Fraser, J.O. (Newfoundland), on what a Canadian
is, 256–57
Fraser, John (Red River), on making a
constitution, 417
free trade
among colonies, 224
among the provinces, 127, 127n, 135, 138, 153
barriers to trade outside Canada increased after
Confederation, 128n
freedom, 168
Confederation without election limits freedom,
383–84, 385, 431, 431n
of conscience, 229
of religion, 64, 154, 327, 328
See also liberty
French Canadians, 15, 87n
accomplishments, 233–34
and British Canadians, two races in Canada,
184–85, 231n, 233
disagreement more likely with provincial
legislature, 305
important in all five colonies, 232
loyalty to Britain during American Revolution,
184–85, 345
and nationality, 138–39, 233–34, 233n, 235,
344–45
political power secured by responsible
government, 73, 73n
protection of special interests through
Confederation, 235
responsible government opens doors to
politicians, 334–35n
Taché expresses feelings of, 333–35
See also Lower Canada
future of British North America, 168, 169. *See
also* posterity

Gilbert, William James
on being British or American, 177–78
on federal union, 270–71
on making a constitution, 408–9
Gillmor, Arthur Hill
on being British or American, 178
on parliamentary government, 96
Glen, Thomas
on making a constitution, 394

Glen, Thomas (*continued*)
  on prosperity and individual ambition, 147
"Glorious Revolution" (1688–89), 48n, 101n,
  231n, 447n
Goods and Services Tax (GST), 87n
government, purpose of, 174–75n
governor general, 87n, 101, 112, 201, 204, 204n,
  220n, 252, 265, 267, 269
  advised by executive council or cabinet, 22
  follows wishes of colonial governments, 307,
    308, 308n
  institution of, in the colonies, 18
  and invitations to Quebec Conference, 401,
    401–2n
governor, territorial
  role discussed at Red River, 65–69
  veto of, 66, 66–67n, 68–69, 68n
Granville, Lord, 26, 26n, 253, 253n, 317
Gray, John Hamilton
  on being British or Canadian, 222–23
  on federal union, 320–21
  on making a constitution, 398–99
Gunn, Donald, on making a constitution, 415

Halliburton, Sir Brenton, 238n
Hamilton, Alexander, 124n, 310, 310n, 364n,
  436n
Hamilton, Charles Cottnam
  on equality of representation, 111
  on making a constitution, 375–76
Hatheway, George L., on being British or
  American, 177
Haultain, Colonel Frederick W., on prosperity
  and individual ambition, 140, 141
Haviland, Thomas Heath
  on being British or American, 198
  on being British or Canadian, 228
  on federal union, 325–26
  on making a constitution, 403
  on parliamentary government, 101–2
Haywood, John, on prosperity and individual
  ambition, 150–51
Hazen, Robert L., on making a constitution, 406
head of state. *See* governor general; monarchy
Helmcken, John Sebastian
  on being British or American, 194
  on being British or Canadian, 217
  on federal union, 317
  on making a constitution, 411
  on prosperity and individual ambition, 141,
    142
  on responsible government, 45
  on what a Canadian is, 250–52, 256
Henderson, Kenneth
  on making a constitution, 403–4
  on prosperity and individual ambition, 161
Henry, William A.
  on being British or Canadian, 210–12
  on federal union, 266–67

on making a constitution, 369–71
  on what a Canadian is, 242–43
Hensley, Joseph, on being British or Canadian,
  223
Hibbard, Francis
  on federal union, 273
  on prosperity and individual ambition, 133
Hill, George Frederic
  on being British or Canadian, 202
  on making a constitution, 408
  on prosperity and individual ambition, 129
Hincks, Francis, 265, 265n
Hobbes, Thomas, 227n
Hogsett, George James
  on being British or Canadian, 221
  on minorities and minority rights, 333
  on parliamentary government, 97–98
  on responsible government, 57–58, 61
Holbrook, Henry
  on being British or American, 195
  on federal union, 316
  on making a constitution, 412
  on prosperity and individual ambition, 142
  on what a Canadian is, 251, 252, 253, 254, 256
Holton, Luther H., 315n
  on direct democracy, 423–25
  on federal union, 302, 315
  on minorities and minority rights, 343, 345
  on prosperity and individual ambition, 136
Hope, Sir James, 366
House of Assembly. *See* House of Commons
House of Commons
  in Britain, 106
  cabinet responsible to, 22, 30, 48n, 79
  influence of voters on, 26
  open debate, 252, 253, 255, 256n
  representation by population, 70–71, 241–42
House of Lords in Britain, 80–81, 80–81n, 100,
  100n, 271, 271n
Howe, Joseph, 175, 175n, 265, 376n, 380n, 405,
  405n
Howlan, George William, on federal union,
  323–24
Hoyles, Hugh
  on making a constitution, 394
  on minorities and minority rights, 332–33
  on prosperity and individual ambition, 149–50,
    155–56
human nature, innocence and virtue extolled in
  Romantic view, 390–91n
human rights, 154–55n
Humphreys, Thomas B.
  on responsible government, 29, 44–45
  on what a Canadian is, 251–55

identity
  colonies fear loss of in union, 24–26, 25n,
    161–62, 163, 164, 242
  and political institutions, 167

immigration, 139, 198, 348
  Confederation and, 135–36, 142
  and voting qualifications, 117
impeachment, of U.S. president, 276
"imperial federalists," 202n
imperial government, 318
  approves laws of Confederation, 320
  decides disputes between federal and provincial
    governments, 311
imperial sovereignty, vs. responsible government,
    23
independence
  and colonial dependence, 232, 232–33n
  of colonies, 159, 167, 200, 242
    federalism not safeguard of political
      individuality, 216n, 217
    and the creation of a nation, 230n
    of new nation from Britain, 204–5, 204n, 207,
      208–9
    objections in Nova Scotia to dependence on
      Canada, 237–39
    of provinces, 224, 332
    of the U.S. from Britain, 235
individual freedom or community good, 200
institutions, 167
  British, 168, 169, 170–71
  of new nation, 170
Inter-Colonial Railway, 130, 130n, 188
intercolonial treaty, 421, 423n
Ireland, forced union with England (1800),
    153–54, 153–54n, 244, 450, 450n
Isle of Man, 316, 316n
isolation
  of British Columbia, 170, 215, 217
  of colonies, 258
  of New Brunswick, 132
  of Newfoundland, 153, 155–56

Jacobite rising (1715), 447, 447n
Jamaica, 371, 371n
Jay, John, 309–10, 310n, 436n
Jefferson, Thomas, 436n
Jews, 339, 339n
Johnson, John Mercer
  on being British or American, 179–89
  on federal union, 275
  on making a constitution, 411
  on responsible government, 75
  on what a Canadian is, 246
Johnson, President Andrew, 64, 64n
Johnston, James William, 375–76n
  on being British or American, 168–69
  on federal union, 262
Joly, Henri
  on prosperity and individual ambition, 138–39
  on what a Canadian is, 233–34
Jones, D. Ford, on federal union, 312–13
judges
  appointment of, 143, 160, 289

superior to legislatures under Charter of Rights
    and Freedoms, 431n
under parliament at time of Confederation, 384
See also courts
judicial review (constitutional)
  interpretation of Charter of Rights and
    Freedoms, 431n
  not provided for in Quebec resolutions, 311,
    312, 312n
  in U.S., 275

Kaulbach, Henry Adolphus Newman
  on being British or American, 175
  on what a Canadian is, 243
Kavanagh, John, on responsible government, 57
Kelly, Francis, on responsible government, 62
Kent, John, on prosperity and individual
    ambition, 144, 156–57
Killam, Thomas
  on being British or Canadian, 212–13
  on making a constitution, 369, 386–87

La Fontaine, Jean de, 138–39, 138n
Laird, Alexander
  on making a constitution, 405
  on prosperity and individual ambition, 163
land question, 324n, 331
land settlement policy, 136
land system, 288
Landseer, Edwin, 110
Langevin, H.-L.
  on federal union, 297–98
  on what a Canadian is, 235
languages
  loss of language feared by French Canadians, 193
  two official languages, 329, 330
law
  constitutional amendments (see amendment of
    constitutions)
  constitutional law, 377–80, 387n
  of nature, 227, 227n
  rule of, 16–17, 16n, 19
    necessary for liberty, 229
Lawrence, William Dawson
  on making a constitution, 383–85
  on prosperity and individual ambition, 126–27
laws, 151
  B.C. desires to make its own, 250
  code of civil law in Lower Canada, 290, 305n,
    312n, 334n, 346
  Confederation would bring uniformity to,
    325–26
lawyers, 60, 143, 150, 179, 377
legislative assembly. See House of Commons
legislative competence to change constitution,
    378–80, 438, 441
Legislative Council
  appointed, 88–89, 90
  in British Columbia, 23n, 27n, 50

Legislative Council (*continued*)
  dominion (*see* Senate)
  elective, 77, 78
    elective Senate (*see* Senate)
    Newfoundland, 63
    Prince Edward Island, 77
    Province of Canada, 77, 78, 89, 96
  patronage, 89
  See also Senate
legislative union, 261, 262–63, 262n, 264–65,
    266, 269, 285, 351
  opposed by Lower Canada, 279, 329
  of provinces, anticipated as eventually
    following federal union, 340
  same system cannot be both federal and
    legislative, 308
  in United Canada, 280, 280n
legislators
  list of legislators quoted in this book, 473–75
  powers and responsibilities (*see* representative
    government)
  See also individual legislators
legislature
  division of power between federal and
    provincial, 263–64, 263n (*see also* federal
    government; provincial governments)
LeVesconte, Isaac, on what a Canadian is, 237–39
Lewis, John, on prosperity and individual
    ambition, 130
liberal democracy, 190n, 448n
Liberal parties in colonies support responsible
    government, 23
liberalism, 17, 200
liberty, 127n, 170–71, 180
  British liberty vs. American equality, 18n, 19
  Confederation a threat to provincial, 144, 144n
  constitutional (*see under individual legislators*)
  inalienable right to, 412
  meaning of for speakers, 229
  no necessary connection with democracy, 362n
  and poverty, 154–55
  religious, 327, 328
  respect for law also needed, 16–17
  and rights of oppressed communities, 16n
  See also freedom; self-government
lieutenant governors, 22, 28n, 95, 97, 112, 168,
    201, 251, 252, 265, 367, 401–2n
  appointed by federal government, 289, 298
  powers of, 318
    pardoning power, 267–68, 267n
  responsibility of officials to, 53–54
"life, liberty, and property," 200
life, liberty, and the pursuit of happiness, 191
Little, Joseph Ignatius, on parliamentary
    government, 98–99
local interests, 180
local legislatures, 176, 201, 263, 265, 266
  powers of, 272–73
  See also provincial governments

local politicians, 146
Locke, John, 16n, 35n, 154–55n, 278n, 301n,
    327–28
  on being British or American, 175–76
  on the impermanence of office in liberal
    democracies, 82n
  on making a constitution, 367–68
  on private property, 92n
  on what a Canadian is, 242
Locke, John (Nova Scotian legislator), 175–76
London Conference (1866), 87n, 267, 368n, 386,
    386n
Longley, Avard, on prosperity and individual
    ambition, 125
Longworth, John, on making a constitution,
    397–98, 400
Lord, William W., on responsible government, 65
Louisiana, 135, 192–93, 233
  absorption into the U.S., 345
Lower Canada
  anglophones in, 289n, 333–34, 334n, 337,
    338–39, 341–44
  code of civil law, 290, 305n, 312n, 334n, 346
  establishment of provincial legislature will
    increase disagreement, 305
  guarantees for laws, religion, and autonomy in
    Quebec scheme, 293
  as a nationality, 233–34, 233n, 235, 279, 279n,
    344–45
  opposes legislative union, 279, 329
  opposes representation by population, 113–15,
    278, 279n, 286, 287n, 333, 338, 349
  representatives in the House of Commons, 296
  special exceptions made in Quebec Resolutions,
    345–46
lower house. *See* House of Commons
Loyalists, 175–76, 197
loyalty
  to Britain, 18–19, 18n, 168–69, 170–71,
    175–76, 180, 195–97, 201, 202, 203, 204–5,
    213–14, 215, 228
    of French Canadians during American
      Revolution, 242, 345
  to the individual colonies/provinces (*see*
    Confederation, arguments of opponents;
    self-government)
  to the new dominion, 174–75

Macdonald, John A., 420, 439n
  on being British or Canadian, 203–7
  biography, 313
  on direct democracy, 421–23, 458–63
  on federal union, 277–84, 313–14
  on parliamentary government, 78–83
  on the representative system, 458–63, 458–59n
  on responsible government, 70–71
Macdonald, John Sandfield
  on direct democracy, 422
  on minorities and minority rights, 344

Mackenzie, Alexander
  on federal union, 300–302
  on minorities and minority rights, 344–45
  on parliamentary government, 93–94
Mackenzie, Hope, on federal union, 309–10
Madison, James, 124n, 309, 310n, 376n, 436n, 437n
majority decisions, 19. *See also* democracy
Manchester School, 460, 460n
mandate, 433, 438, 449, 462n
Manitoba. *See* Red River settlement
March, Stephen
  on being British or Canadian, 219
  on making a constitution, 397
maritime element of national greatness, 183–84
Maritime union, 112, 124, 221, 222, 261, 262, 262n, 328, 330–31, 330–31n, 359, 365, 398n, 426
  delegates discuss Confederation instead, 406, 407
markets. *See* trade
May, Sir Thomas Erskine, 378–79, 378n, 380n, 450, 450n
McAulay, Roderick, on prosperity and individual ambition, 158
McClellan, Abner Reid
  on federal union, 270
  on prosperity and individual ambition, 128–29
McCrae, Walter
  on being British or American, 190–91
  and parliamentary government, 89–90
McCully, Jonathan, 376n
McDonald, Andrew Archibald, on responsible government, 64–65
McDonald, James, on making a constitution, 376–80, 389–90
McDougall, William, 405n
McEachen, John, on being British or Canadian, 225–26
McGee, Thomas D'Arcy, 176n, 268n
  on being British or American, 185–90
  on being British or Canadian, 207–8
  on constitutional liberty, 16–17
  on direct democracy, 428–29
  on minorities and minority rights, 341
  on what a Canadian is, 232
McGiverin, William, 426
  on prosperity and individual ambition, 139
McLaren, James, on prosperity and individual ambition, 162–63
McLean, James, on parliamentary government, 101
McLelan, Archibald Woodbury
  on being British or American, 172–73
  on equality of representation, 108–10
  on making a constitution, 380–82, 390–92
  on what a Canadian is, 243–45
McMillan, John
  on equality of representation, 112

on federal union, 270
on minorities and minority rights, 329
on prosperity and individual ambition, 127
McNeill, William S.
  on making a constitution, 404–5
  on prosperity and individual ambition, 163–64
merit theory of political representation, 107n
Métis, 21, 34–35, 116–17, 247, 248–49. *See also* Red River settlement
Mill, John Stuart, 42–43, 42–43n, 52, 52–53n, 107n, 151, 257, 257n
  on conditions for a federal union, 302
  on distinction between "nationality" and "federal representative government," 230n
  on the upper house, 93
Miller, William, 129n
  on what a Canadian is, 242
Milton, John, 126n
minority rights, 19–20, 21, 206
  of anglophones in Lower Canada, 289n, 333–34, 334n, 337, 338–39, 341–44, 352
  and British Constitution, 19–20
  of French Canadians, 340, 341–42, 345–47, 348
    Perrault distrusts English majority, 349–51
    Perrault's views repudiated, 351, 352–53
  Jews, 339, 339n
  Native Indians, 251, 252–56, 252n, 254–56n
  protection of, under British principles, 39, 198
  and representation by population, 115n
  vulnerability of, where aristocracy lacking, 41n, 49n
  and the wealthy, 290n
  See also under individual legislators
Mitchell, Peter
  on being British or American, 178–79
  on parliamentary government, 96
  on prosperity and individual ambition, 132–33
mixed government, 17n, 59, 68, 68n, 70, 220
  monarchic, aristocratic, and democratic elements check one another, 190n, 458–59n, 461
  three parts correspond to Christian image of human, 83n
monarchical principle, 185, 240, 241
monarchy, 17–18, 19, 60–61, 101, 204, 220n, 448n
  above the people, but below God, 54n
  head of executive power in Canada, 220, 220n, 281–82
  ministers, not monarch, are responsible to people, 72n, 365, 365n
  powers of, 67n
    appointment of additional Canadian senators (to 1982), 87n
    appointment of British peers, 101
    curtailed by British Bill of Rights, 447n
    veto of monarch (or governor), 66, 66–67n, 68–69, 68n, 180
  representing and uniting the people, 39, 39n, 72n

monarchy (*continued*)
  responsibility of officials to, 53–54
money. *See* currency
money bills, 71, 109n, 287
Monroe Doctrine, 189, 189n, 194, 197
Montalembert, Charles, 91, 91–92n
Montesquieu, Charles, 17n
Moodie, Susanna, 390n
Moore, Philip H.
  on federal union, 294
  on what a Canadian is, 232–33
Morris, Alexander, on federal union, 302–4
Morris, Edward, on prosperity and individual
    ambition, 147–48
Mowat, Oliver, 267n, 270n, 295, 439n
Mulroney, Brian, 87n
municipal government, 36
Musgrave, Anthony, 26n, 27n, 28, 29, 31, 37,
    250n, 254n

nationality, 217, 229–30, 230n, 232, 279n
  of colonies or provinces, 161–63, 237–39, 245,
    246, 252
  of French Canadians, 138-39, 233–34, 233n,
    235, 344–45
  of the new dominion, 173n, 243, 246, 250, 257,
    257n, 347–48
  will take time to develop, 250, 251
Native Indians, 116, 247, 248–49
  protection of rights, 251, 252–56, 252n,
    254–56n
  treaties with, 248
"natives," Red River discusses term, 247
natural rights, 180, 390–92, 390–91n
Needham, William
  on being British or Canadian, 201–2
  on making a constitution, 409–10
  on minorities and minority rights, 329
  on prosperity and individual ambition, 131
New Zealand, 304
  constitution, 268–69, 268n
Newfoundland, responsible government in,
    57–58
ninety-two resolutions, 86
North-West Territories, 136, 139, 139–40n, 149,
    405
  purchased by Canada, 254n, 416n
  See also Red River settlement

O'Donoghue, W.B.
  on making a constitution, 414, 419
  on responsible government, 66, 68
O'Halloran, James
  on direct democracy, 449–51
  on minorities and minority rights, 351–52
Olivier, Louis-Auguste
  on federal union, 291–93
  on minorities and minority rights, 338
  on parliamentary government, 90–91

  on prosperity and individual ambition, 137–38
"one person, one vote," 107n, 115n
open debate in Commons, 252, 253, 255, 256n
opinion of the people, 393, 394
opposition parties, 57, 69–70n, 454
Orange order, 176n

Palmer, Edward
  on prosperity and individual ambition, 163
  on responsible government, 62
Papineau, Louis-Joseph, 335, 335n
parliamentary government, 190n, 206n
  changing the constitution, 378–80, 438, 446, 447
  deadlock between upper and lower house,
    80–88, 84n, 87n
  in federation, 178n
  powers of parliament, 389, 389n
  praised in debates, 22
  upper house (*see* Legislative Council; Senate)
  See also responsible government; *See also under*
    individual legislators
parliamentary sovereignty, 357–58, 379n
party government, 266
  opposition parties, 399
patronage, 89, 152–53, 331–32
  in provincial governments, 288
  in the U.S. system, 282
Perrault, Joseph
  on minorities and minority rights, 349–51
  on responsible government, 72–73
petitions, 446
  against Confederation (in Nova Scotia), 372–73
Pinsent, Robert John
  on minorities and minority rights, 332
  on parliamentary government, 97
  on prosperity and individual ambition, 148–49,
    153–54
  on responsible government, 58–59
Pitt, William, the Younger, 461–62n
Plato, 44n
plebiscite, 368–69
"plural" voting, 107n
political executive. *See* cabinet
political liberty, 90. *See also* democracy; liberty
political parties, 56–57, 75, 276, 300, 330, 333
  competition among, benefits public, 123–24,
    400n
  compromise for Confederation, 300, 399–400n,
    421–22, 429, 433, 436
  Confederation necessitates a rise above party
    spirit, 448
  opposition parties, 57, 69–70n, 266
  patriotism comes before party claims, 126
politicians. *See* ambition, of politicians
Pope, William Henry
  on being British or American, 196–97
  on being British or Canadian, 221–22
  on making a constitution, 397, 400–401
  on minorities and minority rights, 330–31

population, 147
  forecasts for new nation, 132, 149
  size at Confederation, 205
population growth, 214, 276
population size and dispersion, and responsible
    government, 27, 29, 30, 37–44, 41n, 46, 51,
    53, 74–75
populist tyranny, 190n, 206n. *See also* tyranny
posterity, 168, 412, 413
  arrangements for, 337–38
  awareness of importance of decision for future,
    428
  Confederation will affect, 323, 392, 393
poverty, 116, 116–17n, 117, 147, 157
  and liberty, 154–55
power
  retention by ruler, 53
  to the people, or to a ruler, 53–54, 54n (*see also*
    democracy)
president, of the United States
  impeachment of, 276
  veto powers of, 68n, 180, 180n, 282, 294
the press
  commended for high level of discussion, 451
  as educators for reform, 54
  as exponent of public opinion, 54–55
  freedom of, 64
  as troublemakers, 39
Prince Edward Island
  responsible government in, 53, 62–65, 74
  subordination to central government feared,
    101, 161, 224–28, 322–23, 324
professions, 150
property, provinces assigned power to legislate
    on, 305–6, 305n
property qualification, 116–18
property rights
  of English in Lower Canada, 335, 338
  hereditary or earned, 91–92, 92n
  of religious corporations, 290, 292, 292n,
    296–97
prosperity
  of emigrants to the U.S., 192
  and individual ambititon (*see under individual
    legislators*)
  of Prince Edward Island before Confederation,
    163
provincial governments, 241, 284
  control matters causing local dissension, 289
  form of, 125–26
  powers of, 269–70, 269n, 288, 291, 292, 295,
    299, 303, 319, 325
    no constitutional difference from federal
      powers, 303n
provincial rights
  amendment of constitutions under BNA Act,
    24n, 28
  responsible government necessary before
    Confederation, 32–35, 32n, 35n

provisional government at Red River (1870),
    416–17, 416n
Prowse, Daniel Woodley
  on being British or Canadian, 218
  on making a constitution, 397
  on prosperity and individual ambition, 151–52
  on responsible government, 56
public debt, 210n
public opinion, 215n, 216, 439
  changing, on Confederation, 402, 409n
  consultation on Confederation (argued against),
    437–38, 444
  Maritime provinces appeal to, 455
  may need guidance, 403
  and popular vote on Confederation, 412
  of Red River settlers, 416
  should be consulted before decision made,
    367–68, 373–75, 382–85, 390–94, 397–98,
    399, 420, 432, 449, 453–54, 457
public works, 152, 288

Quebec Conference (1864), 136, 144–45, 178,
    197, 219, 406
  Confederation scheme viewed favourably by
    Britain, 223–24, 225
  desire to retain connection to Britain, 204–5,
    208
  division of legislative power, 263–64, 263n
  scheme produced for federal union (*see* Quebec
    Resolutions)
  secrecy of deliberations, 394–95, 401
  votes on upper house, 99–101
Quebec Resolutions, 60, 103, 105, 123, 130n,
    156, 180, 198, 210, 261, 305n, 372
  adoption by provinces argued, 438–39
  allocation of seats in federal House of
    Commons, 151n
  analysis of details urged, 429–30
  appointment of additional senators, 87n
  Brown and McGee urge adoption by legislature
    of Canada, 425–29
  defended by Brown, 285–90
  division of new nation into regions, 77–78
  powers of general government, 274
  result of compromise, 429
  scheme as a whole carried by unanimous vote,
    422
  text of resolutions, 465–72
  warnings against amendment of scheme, 427,
    428

railway
  B.C.'s argument for intercontinental railway,
    143, 143n
  Inter-Colonial Railway, 130, 130n, 132
  St. Lawrence and Atlantic Railway, 209–10n
Rankin, Arthur M., on responsible government,
    73–74
ratification, 411

rebellion
   of 1837 in province of Canada, 41, 41n, 46,
      46n, 63, 72, 73–74
   possible if responsible government denied, 35,
      45
   Red River, 405, 416–17, 416n
Reciprocity Treaty, 136–37, 136–37n, 181, 186,
   426
Red River settlement, 39, 104, 248
   annexed to Canada without consultation, 249n,
      251, 358, 416n, 417–19
   bill of rights, 414–15, 414n, 416
   Fort Garry convention, 414–19, 414n
   from idea of territory to idea of province, 65n,
      69
   not permitted to vote on Confederation, 358
   Riel's provincial government of 1869–70, 248,
      251, 405, 416–17, 416n
Reesor, David, on parliamentary government, 88,
   89
referendum on Confederation, 373n, 374, 378n,
   408n, 420, 459–60n
Reform Bill (Britain), 80–81, 81n, 100n, 108,
   271, 271n
reform parties in colonies, support responsible
   government, 23, 90, 90n
Reform Party of Canada (twentieth century), 27n,
   403n
reform, preferred to revolution, 20
regional concerns. *See* Confederation, arguments
   of opponents
regional divisions under Quebec Resolutions,
   77–78
regional economic conditions, 123
regional representation, in Senate, 77–78, 80,
   87n, 97–99, 103, 264, 267n, 271–73,
   276–77, 286–87, 306
religion, freedom of, 64, 154, 327, 328
religious corporations in Quebec, 290, 292, 292n,
   296–97
religious differences, 327, 329, 330–31, 331n,
   332, 333
Rémillard, Édouard, on minorities and minority
   rights, 351
Rendell, Stephen, on responsible government,
   60–61
Renouf, Henry
   on equality of representation, 118
   on making a constitution, 394
   on prosperity and individual ambition, 152–53
   on responsible government, 60, 61–62
representation, 449n
   equality for Upper and Lower Canada after
      union, 113–14 (*see also under individual
      legislators*)
   in federal legislation for Prince Edward Island,
      160, 160n
   "no taxation without representation," 409–10
representation by population, 70–71, 104–9,

   104n, 242, 270–71, 277–79, 277n, 313–14,
      321, 410
   concession to Upper Canada in return for
      regional representation in Senate, 286, 287
   defended by Tupper, 104–6
   in the House of Commons, 87n, 103, 266,
      267n, 323
   merit theory ("property and classes, as well as
      numbers"), 107n
   "one man, one vote," 107n
   opposed by Lower Canada, 113–15, 278, 279n,
      286, 287n, 333, 338, 349
   "plural" voting, 107n
   population growth of centre feared, 111
   preferred to representation by region, 113
representative government
   candidates for election, 322
   a few decide for all, 377n
   included in speakers' concept of liberty, 229
   laws passed by elected representatives are valid,
      370–71, 370–71n
   legislators have power to deal with all
      questions, 411
   Mill's opinions discussed, 52, 52–53n
   qualifications to vote, 44, 44n, 49
   readiness for, 37n, 51–52
   representative must follow voters' directions,
      367, 403–4, 403n
   representative must trust own judgement,
      196–97, 395–96, 396n, 443–44, 454, 454n,
      462–63
   representative should heed public opinion but
      may also guide it, 403, 403n
   representative a trustee, 434, 435, 438
   representatives chosen for talents, 374n,
      375–76, 376n
   representative's judgement or voters' directions,
      27n, 396n, 461
   responsible government a form of, 23, 34, 41n
   See also under Macdonald, John A.
republic, 95, 169
republicanism, 19, 169, 180n, 448n
republicans, 446
reservations for Native Indians, 256
residual powers, 299, 299n, 436–37n
resources of nation after Confederation, 126,
   127, 140, 149
responsible government, 155, 215n, 219, 282
   attainment by Province of Canada, 90n
   balance of power in the legislature, 276
   cabinet responsible to Commons, 22, 30, 48,
      48n, 75, 79
   comes to United Canada in 1848, 285n
   common belief of French and English
      Canadians, 15n
   and Confederation, 23–24, 28, 36, 55n, 67–68,
      380n, 387–88, 389, 391–92
   as a form of representative government, 23, 34,
      41n, 48

responsible government (*continued*)
form in the U.S., 53
lack of, 36–37, 43–44,
history in Britain, 47–48n, 48
important for Lower Canada, 294
lacking in B.C., 23–24, 23–24n
ministers, not monarch, are responsible, 72n, 365, 365n
necessary before Confederation, 32–35, 32n, 35n
in Newfoundland, 57–58, 59, 61–62
and population (size, dispersion, character), 27, 29, 30, 37–44, 41n, 46, 51, 53, 74–75
in Prince Edward Island, 53, 62–65
in the provinces, 236
Red River lacks, and doesn't ask for, 23, 65n
secures liberties, 144–45
two aspects of, 22
vs. imperial sovereignty, 23
See also parliamentary government; *See also under individual legislators*
revenues, provinces resent loss of control to central government, 109–10, 109n, 224–25, 224n, 227, 237–39, 237n
revolution, 317–18, 317n, 318n
American (*see* American Revolution)
British forefathers preferred reform to, 20
English Revolution of 1641, 47n
French Revolution, 48n
"Glorious Revolution" of 1688–89, 48n, 101n, 231n, 447n
necessary for political improvement, 29
right of, 16n, 35n
threatened if people's demands not met, 81
Riel, Louis
biography, 248
on constitutional liberty, 21
on equality of representation, 115–16
on making a constitution, 415–19
on responsible government, 65–66, 69–70
on what a Canadian is, 247–50
rights
to choose Confederation, 380n
concrete claims or abstract universal rights, 417–19, 417–18n
direct democracy or parliamentary deliberation, 421
guaranteed by colonial constitutions, 98
individual vs. collective, 19, 200
of man, 191, 417–19, 417–18n
of minorities, 19–20, 21
natural, 180, 390–92, 390–91n
of the people, consultation on Confederation, 358–59, 358–59n, 397–98, 399
promoted by Confederation, 157, 235
property (*see* property rights)
of provinces (*see* provincial rights)
of Red River settlers, 414–19, 417–18n
of smaller provinces, 319–20

Ring, David B.
on being British or Canadian, 217
on making a constitution, 412, 413
Ritchie, John William, 376n
Robinson, John James, on responsible government, 74
Robson, John
on being British or Canadian, 217
biography, 30
on prosperity and individual ambition, 141–43
on responsible government, 23–24, 30–35, 36n, 53–55
on what a Canadian is, 252–56
Romantic glorification of the common man, 390–91n
Rose, John
on federal union, 299
on minorities and minority rights, 341–44
Ross, James
on equality of representation, 116–17
on responsible government, 65n, 68–69
on what a Canadian is, 248–49, 252
Ross, John, on federal union, 291
Ross, William
on federal union, 268–69
on prosperity and individual ambition, 126
Rousseau, Jean Jacques, 37n, 48n, 54n, 390n, 418
royal prerogative, 267
rule of law, 357
Rupert's Land, transfer to Canada, 254n, 416n
Russell, Earl, 108, 108n
Ryan, Thomas, on parliamentary government, 92–93

St. Lawrence and Atlantic Railway, 209–10n
Sanborn, John S.
on direct democracy, 438
on federal union, 290–91
on minorities and minority rights, 337–38
on what a Canadian is, 231
schools, 117–18, 135, 336–37
Scoble, John, on federal union, 307
Scotland
representation in British parliament, 107–8, 146
union with England (1707), 102n, 130n, 456n
Scott, Alfred H.
on equality of representation, 117–18
on making a constitution, 418
Scott, Sir Walter, 390n
Second Reform Act of 1867 (Britain), 116n
sectional basis of parliamentary representation, 265n, 278
self-government
in British colonies, 200, 244–45
and disallowance, 270n
fitness for, 31–33, 31n, 35, 50
impossible within Confederation, 24–26, 25n, 150–51

self-government (*continued*)
  inalienable right to, 412
  included in speakers' concept of liberty, 229
  and the independence of colonies, 161–64
  not lost by joining the dominion, 57, 63–64
  self-preservation as "first law of nature," 227, 227n
  valued by provinces, 268
  See also Confederation; representative government; responsible government
self-reliance, 47
Senate
  appointed, 60, 77, 78, 79, 83n, 89, 93
    Macdonald and Brown see less chance of deadlock, 82–88, 84n, 87n
  appointments
    of additional senators, 87, 87n, 95, 100, 306
    by leaders of lower house, 85–86n
    for life, 306, 323
    limited term of, 87–88
    partisan, 79–80
  check on House of Commons, 77, 79–80, 84, 92–93, 96, 270–71, 274, 276, 298
  elective, 77, 78–79, 78–79n, 95
    Brown's opposition to, 83–88, 84n
    candidates for election, 85
    principle defeated at Quebec Conference, 99–100
    U.S. system, 85–86n
  elective franchise for senators, 89
  independent body, 80, 88, 89
  initiation of laws by, 84n
  members from same class as Commons, 81–82
  money bills, 84
  partisanship, 79–80, 84
  of provinces, 252
  regional representation, 77–78, 80, 87n, 97–99, 103, 264, 267n, 271–73, 276–77, 286–87, 306
  secondary in importance to the lower chamber, 94
  of the U.S., 85–86n, 94, 98, 271, 272, 274–75, 276, 307
    equal representation for small and large states, 320, 321, 323
  See also Legislative Council
separate schools, 336–37, 338, 339, 341. *See also under* Brown, George
separation of church and state, 229, 327–28
Sewell, Jonathan, 239, 239n
Seymour, Benjamin, on direct democracy, 430–32
Shannon, Samuel Leonard
  on being British or American, 169, 176–77
  on what a Canadian is, 239–42
Shea, Ambrose
  on being British or Canadian, 219
  biography, 145
  on federal union, 318–20
  on making a constitution, 394–97

on prosperity and individual ambition, 144–46, 156–57
  on responsible government, 56–57
  on what a Canadian is, 257–58
Shea, Edward Dalton
  on making a constitution, 395–96
  on prosperity and individual ambition, 147
  on responsible government, 57
Sinclair, George
  on being British or Canadian, 227–28
  on making a constitution, 399–401
  on prosperity and individual ambition, 159
Skinner, C.N., on federal union, 273–74
slavery, 163, 170, 191
  U.S. constitution amended to prohibit, 433, 453
Smith, Adam, 124n
Smith, Albert James, 406–7n
  biography, 407
  on federal union, 271–73
  on making a constitution, 407–11
  on prosperity and individual ambition, 129–30
Smith, Donald, no power to guarantee Riel's Bill of Rights, 21, 414, 415–16, 416n
sovereignty
  of provinces
    bearing of states' rights issue on, 274, 316–17
    not required for intercolonial treaty, 424n
    See also compact theory of Confederation
  of states in the U.S., 179, 179n, 274, 314 (*see also* states' rights issue in the United States)
Spencer, Herbert, 48–49, 49n
state of nature, 390–91n
states' rights issue in the United States
  as a cause of civil war, 179, 179n, 282, 293, 436–37n
  and provincial sovereignty, 274, 316–17
  state sovereignty causes central government weakness, 301, 303, 304, 309–10, 312–13, 314
  See also compact theory of Confederation
Stevens, James Gray
  on constitutional liberty, 20
  on parliamentary government, 96–97
  on what a Canadian is, 246
supremacy
  of British government, 318
  of federal government, misunderstandings over, 312–13
  of federal laws, 309–10
  of federal or provincial governments, 315
  of imperial government, 311
  Supreme Court necessary to decide differences, 311, 312, 312n
Sydenham, Lord, 393–94n

Taché, Étienne-Paschal
  on being British or American, 180–82
  biography, 334
  on federal union, 290, 296–97

Taché, Étienne-Paschal (*continued*)
  on minorities and minority rights, 333–35
  on what a Canadian is, 233
Talbot, Thomas, on prosperity and individual
    ambition, 144, 146–47, 154–55
tariffs, 127–28n, 224
taxation, "no taxation without representation,"
    409–10
taxes
  British taxes on colonies a cause of American
    Revolution, 245
  increase predicted under Confederation, 55–56,
    62, 128, 130, 138–39, 141, 151, 157, 161,
    217
  on knowledge, 163n
  on land and income in Britain, 94
  in United Canada, 287
taxing power
  colonies set own taxes (pre-Confederation),
    227, 237–38, 237n
  held by both central and provincial
    governments under Quebec scheme,
    224–25, 224n, 305
  retention by established classes, 49, 52
territory. *See* North-West Territories; Red River
    settlement
Tessier, Peter, on being British or Canadian,
    218–19
Thibert, Pierre, on what a Canadian is, 249
Thomson, Robert
  on being British or Canadian, 201–2
  on federal union, 269–70
  on prosperity and individual ambition, 128, 130
three estates (monarch, senate, commons), 59, 68,
    68n, 70, 83n, 220
Tilley, Samuel Leonard
  biography, 272
  defeated in election on Confederation (1865),
    97n
  on federal union, 272–73
Tobin, John
  on federal union, 267–68
  on minorities and minority rights, 328–29
toryism, 17
Townsend, William H., on being British or
    Canadian, 209–10
trade, 130–32, 187
  increased, argument for Confederation, 132,
    134, 136–37
  threatened repeal of Reciprocity Treaty,
    136–37, 136–37n, 181, 186, 426
Trudeau, Pierre, 144n
Trutch, Joseph William
  attitude towards Native Indians, 252n
  on being British or American, 194–95
  on being British or Canadian, 215
  biography, 194
  on making a constitution, 412
  on responsible government, 24, 38–41

on what a Canadian is, 251
Tupper, Charles
  on being British or American, 170–71, 173–75
  on being British or Canadian, 208, 209
  biography, 361
  disagrees with appeal to the people, 360–62,
    361–62n
  on equality of representation, 104–6
  on federal union, 262–64
  on making a constitution, 359–62, 387–89
  on minorities and minority rights, 328
  on prosperity and individual ambition, 124–25
tyranny
  of democracy, 18n, 43–44, 52, 72n, 190n, 206n,
    319–20, 320n
  of hereditary rulers, 18n
  of stronger provinces over weaker, 413
  See also Confederation

unemployment, problem in Newfoundland,
    145–47, 152–53
Uniacke, Richard John, 238n, 375, 375n
union
  annexation of colonies by the U.S. (*see under*
    United States)
  of the British North American colonies (*see*
    Confederation)
  federal (*see* federal union)
  forced union of Ireland with England (1800),
    153–54, 153–54n, 244, 450, 450n
  legislative (*see* legislative union)
  of Scotland and England (1707), 102n, 107–8,
    130n, 146, 456n
  of Upper and Lower Canada (1840), 72–73,
    125, 240, 240n, 278n, 346, 346n, 462n
  equal representation in legislature for both
    Canadas, 103, 104n, 105
  with the U.S., 164, 167
United States
  American equality vs. British liberty, 18n, 19
  American Revolution, 134, 158, 184, 187, 237,
    241, 245, 245n
  annexation of colonies, 99n, 169, 170, 175, 176,
    178–79, 180–82, 187, 188–90, 189n, 192–93,
    194, 195–96, 195n, 201, 210, 211, 213
  civil war, 14, 48–49n, 102, 157n, 170, 171, 179,
    179n, 181, 182, 185, 186–87, 197, 220,
    282, 293, 305, 314, 426, 437n
  constitution, 99, 155, 167, 178, 179, 179n,
    180n, 191, 198, 220, 235, 239, 271, 272,
    274, 275n, 281–84, 305, 433, 436-37n
  amended to prohibit slavery, 433, 453
  central government weakness in, 301, 303,
    304, 309–10, 312–13, 314
  criticisms of, 313, 314, 320–21, 436–37n
  oldest written constitution, 436n
  praise for, 436, 437n
  state power and states' rights issue (*see* states'
    rights issue in the United States)

United States, constitution (*continued*)
supreme authority of central government, 309–10
constitutional amendments, 452–53
deadlock between president and Congress, 64
defence against, 140–41, 167, 170–71, 174, 177, 190–91, 192n, 195, 197
differences from British colonies, 168
economic policies, 167
election of senators, 85–86n
held up as example of union promoting prosperity, 156, 157, 158
invasion of Canada during American Revolution, 184
lack of respect for executive, 71–72, 71–72n
Louisiana, 135, 192–93, 233, 345
military growth, 170, 186
preference for Confederation under Britain to annexation by the U.S., 170–71, 192n, 195, 196
passport system, 186
power of court over legislature, 275
president, 276, 281, 282
pro-American speech by Dorion, 192, 192n
procedure for constitutional change, 430–31
progress since American Revolution, 134, 203
responsible government in, 36–37, 43–44, 53
Senate, 85–86n, 94, 98, 271, 272, 275, 276, 307, 320, 321, 323
threat of invasion by, 174, 181, 190–91, 197, 202
threat of war with, 59, 95, 167, 177, 196, 201, 204, 205–6
trade with, 134, 187
repeal of Reciprocity Treaty, 136–37, 136–37n, 181, 186, 426
union with Canada, 164, 167
veto power of president, 68n, 180, 180n, 282, 294
vulnerability of culture to influence of, 168–69, 168–69n
"universal democracy," 190n
Upper Canada, and representation by population, 113–15
upper house. *See* Senate

Vattel, Emmerich de, 417n
veto
dominion veto of provincial legislation (*see* disallowance)
imperial veto of colonial legislation (*see* disallowance)
of monarch or governor in Britain or colonies, 66, 66–67n, 68–69, 68n, 180
of U.S. president, 68n, 180, 180n, 282, 294
of U.S. Senate, 271

Victoria, B.C., centralization of government in, 38, 43
Vidal, A., on direct democracy, 445–46
virtual representation, 107n
voice of the people, 66, 162, 368, 373, 384, 411
expressed through representatives, 413
See also public opinion
vote
broad franchise strengthens democratic element, 190n
and immigration, 117
"one man, one vote," 107n
"one person, one vote" and representation of minority populations, 115n
property qualification, 103, 104, 115–18, 369n
restricted under "merit theory," 107n
universal manhood suffrage, 63, 70–71, 70–71n, 91, 185, 369n
with residency requirement, 118, 249–50, 249n
"virtual representation," 107n
women's suffrage, 118

Walkem, G.A., on responsible government, 41–42
Wallbridge, T.C., on prosperity and individual ambition, 133
Walsh, Aquila, on federal union, 312
warfare
British colonists prepared for, 201, 205–6
threat of war with the U.S., 59, 95, 167, 177, 196
Webster, Daniel, 187, 187n
Wellington, Duke of, 186, 186n, 243, 243n, 271, 271n
Westminster. *See* British government; imperial government
Wetmore, Andrew
on making a constitution, 408
on prosperity and individual ambition, 129
Whelan, Edward
on being British or Canadian, 222
on making a constitution, 402–3
on prosperity and individual ambition, 158
Whiteway, William Vallance, on what a Canadian is, 258
Williams, Sir William Fenwick, 365–66, 365–66n
Wood, T.L.
on being British or Canadian, 215–17
on federal union, 316–18
on making a constitution, 412–13
on responsible government, 24–26, 47–52

Young, William, 376n